TESTIMONY THAT STICKS

Testimony That Sticks

THE ART OF COMMUNICATING PSYCHOLOGY AND NEUROPSYCHOLOGY TO JURIES

Karen Postal, PhD, ABPP-CN

OXFORD
UNIVERSITY PRESS

OXFORD
UNIVERSITY PRESS

Oxford University Press is a department of the University of Oxford. It furthers the University's objective of excellence in research, scholarship, and education by publishing worldwide. Oxford is a registered trade mark of Oxford University Press in the UK and certain other countries.

Published in the United States of America by Oxford University Press
198 Madison Avenue, New York, NY 10016, United States of America.

Library of Congress Cataloging-in-Publication Data
Names: Postal, Karen, author.
Title: Testimony that sticks : the art of communicating psychology and neuropsychology to juries / Karen Postal.
Description: New York, NY : Oxford University Press, [2019]
Identifiers: LCCN 2018033278 | ISBN 9780190467395
Subjects: LCSH: Forensic neuropsychology. | Jurors.
Classification: LCC RA1147.5 .P67 2019 | DDC 614/.15—dc23
LC record available at https://lccn.loc.gov/2018033278

To my mother, Susan Spangenberg. Thank you for the gift of unrelenting optimism that has fueled my best professional and other adventures.

To my sister, Anne Spangenberg, always my role model and my rock.

And to my children, Andrew, Robbie, and Carline Postal: becoming people who make me laugh and whom I admire. You are the best part of every day.

Contents

Acknowledgments

HEARTFELT THANKS TO the Forensic High Tea Gang, a group of friends and colleagues who share the joy of forensic practice and are an endless source of practical knowledge and uncommonly good advice: Nancy Hebben, Maggie Lanca, Robert Mendoza, and Cheryl Weinstein.

Thanks always to my editor, Joan Bossert, for her unwavering support and insight.

Contributors

William Barr, PhD, ABPP-CN
Director of Neuropsychology Division
Department of Neurology
NYU School of Medicine

The Honorable Judge Lynne Battaglia
Judge, Court of Appeals of Maryland (Retired)

Russell M. Bauer, PhD, ABPP-CN
Professor and Director, Doctoral Program in Clinical Psychology
Department of Clinical & Health Psychology
Gainesville, FL

Scott D. Bender, PhD, ABPP-CN
Associate Professor
University of Virginia School of Medicine

Yossef Ben-Porath, PhD, ABPP
Professor of Psychological Sciences
Kent State University

Erin D. Bigler, PhD, ABPP-CN
Professor of Psychology and Neuroscience
Department of Psychology
Founding Director
Magnetic Resonance Imaging (MRI) Research Facility
Brigham Young University
Provo, UT

Laurence M. Binder, PhD, ABPP-CN
Independent Practice
Beaverton, OR
Clinical Associate Professor of Neurology and Psychiatry
Oregon Health and Science University

Lynn Bennett Blackburn, PhD, ABPP-CN
Retired

The Honorable Jay Blitzman
First Justice, Middlesex Division of the Massachusetts Juvenile Court

Marcus Boccaccini, PhD
Professor
Psychology Department
Sam Houston State University

Nick Bogod, RPsych
Neuropsychology Service
Neurosciences Program
Vancouver General Hospital

Thomas J. Boll, PhD, ABPP-CN
Neuropsychology Institute

Kyle Boone, PhD, ABPP-CN
Clinical Professor
Department of Psychiatry
UCLA School of Medicine

The Honorable Heidi E. Brieger
Associate Justice, Massachusetts Superior Court

The Honorable Allison D. Burroughs
District of Massachusetts

David S. Bush, PhD, ABPP-CN, ABN
Independent Practice, Palm Beach Gardens, FL

Desiree Byrd, PhD, ABPP-CN
Board Certified in Clinical Neuropsychology
Assistant Professor of Neurology and Psychiatry
Icahn School of Medicine at Mount Sinai
New York, NY

Dominic Carone, PhD, ABPP-CN
Clinical Associate Professor
SUNY Upstate Medical University

Michael Chafetz, PhD, ABPP-CN
Algiers Neurobehavioral Resource, LLC
New Orleans, LA

Sara Cohbra, Esq.
Law Office of Sara Cohbra
California

Daniel Corrin, Esq.
Vancouver, BC

Darcy Cox, PsyD, RPsych, ABPP-CN
Independent practice
Vancouver, BC

Paul Craig, PhD, ABPP-CN
Independent Practice, Anchorage, AK
Clinical Professor
Department of Psychiatry & Behavioral Sciences
University of Washington School of Medicine (WWAMI Program)

Mark D. DeBofsky, Esq.
DeBofsky Sherman & Casciari P.C.
Chicago, IL

Robert L. Denney, PsyD, ABPP-CN, FP
Neuropsychological Associates of Southwest Missouri
Missouri Memory Center
Neurology Clinic
Citizens Memorial Healthcare
Bolivar, MO

Jacobus Donders, PhD, ABPP-CN
Chief Psychologist
Mary Free Bed Rehabilitation Hospital
Grand Rapids, MI

The Honorable John Fader
Chief Justice, Baltimore County Circuit Court, 3rd Judicial Circuit (retired)

Daryl Fujii, PhD, ABBP-CN
Veterans Affairs Pacific Island Health Care Services
Community Living Center
Honolulu, HI

Tannahill Glen, PsyD, ABPP-CN
Independent Practice
Jacksonville, FL

Paul Green, PhD
Independent Practice, Canada
President, Green's Publishing

Robin Hanks, ABPP-CN
Chief of Rehabilitation Psychology and Neuropsychology
Director of Training in Clinical Neuropsychology
Rehabilitation Institute of Michigan
Professor, Department of Physical Medicine and Rehabilitation
Project Director, Southeastern Michigan Traumatic Brain Injury System
Wayne State University School of Medicine

The Honorable Christina Harms
Retired
Director, Child and Family Psychological Evaluation Service ("CAFES")
Center of Excellence for Children, Families and the Law
William James College

David Hartman, PhD, MS, ABN, ABPP-CL
Medical and Forensic Neuropsychology
Chicago, IL

Nancy Hebben, PhD, ABPP-CN
Assistant Professor of Psychology (Part-time)
Department of Psychiatry
Harvard Medical School
Cambridge Health Alliance
Boston and Cambridge, MA

Robert Heilbronner, PhD, ABPP-CN
Chicago Neuropsychology Group
Northwestern University Feinberg School of Medicine

Tedd Judd, PhD, ABPP-CN
Cross-Cultural Specialist, Independent Practice
Bellingham, WA

Paul M. Kaufmann, JD, PhD, ABPP-CN
Chief Compliance Officer
University of Arizona

Robert Kinscherff, PhD, JD
Associate Vice President for Community Engagement
Office of the President
Associate Professor, Doctoral Clinical Psychology Program
William James College

John W. Kirk, PsyD, ABPP-CN
Kirk Neurobehavioral Health
Louisville, CO

Glenn Larrabee, PhD, ABPP-CN
Independent Practice, Sarasota, FL

Gregory P. Lee, PhD, ABPP-CN
Professor
Barrow Neurological Institute

W. Scott Liebert, Esq.
Law Offices of W. Scott Liebert
Wellesley, MA

David Lovejoy, PsyD, ABN
Senior Managing Partner
Northeast Neuropsychology, LLC
West Hartford, CT

Robb Mapou, PhD, ABPP-CN
Oceanside Neuropsychology
Rehoboth Beach, DE

Bernice A. Marcopulos, PhD, ABPP-CN
Professor
Department of Graduate Psychology
James Madison University
Associate Professor
Department of Psychiatry and Neurobehavioral Sciences
University of Virginia School of Medicine

Wendy B. Marlowe, PhD, ABPP-CN
Independent Practice
Seattle, WA

Michael McCrea, PhD, ABPP-CN
Professor and Eminent Scholar
Vice Chair of Research
Director of Brain Injury Research
Department of Neurosurgery
Medical College of Wisconsin

Lisa McDermott, LMHC
Mitigation Specialist
McDermott & Associates
Royal Palm Beach, FL

A. John McSweeny, JD, PhD, ABPP-CN
Professor Emeritus of Psychiatry, Psychology and Neurology
University of Toledo

Robert Mendoza, PsyD
Assistant Professor
Tufts University School of Medicine
President, Boston Forensic Associates
Boston, MA

Scott R. Millis, PhD, ABPP-CN
Professor
Department of Physical Medicine and Rehabilitation
Department of Emergency Medicine
Wayne State University School of Medicine

Wayne Miller, Esq.
Senior Partner
Miller & Tischler, PC
Farmington Hills, MI
Adjunct Professor of Law
Wayne State University School of Law

Nathaniel W. Nelson, PhD, ABPP-CN
Associate Professor
University of St. Thomas, Graduate School of Professional Psychology
Minneapolis, MN

Kate Nemens, Esq.
Supervising Attorney
Clubhouse Family Legal Support Project
Mental Health Legal Advisors Committee
Boston, MA

Kristie Nies, PhD, ABPP-CN
Ohio Health
Columbus, OH

Ira K. Packer, PhD, ABPP (Forensic)
Clinical Professor of Psychiatry
University of Massachusetts Medical School

Edward A. "Ted" Peck, PhD, ABPP-CN
Neuropsychological Services of Virginia
Richmond, VA

Shelley Peery, PhD
Independent Practice, San Francisco Neuropsychology, Inc.
San Francisco, CA

James Pier, PhD
Senior Managing Partner
Northeast Neuropsychology, LLC
Cheshire, CT

Neil H. Pliskin, PhD, ABPP-CN
Professor of Clinical Psychiatry & Neurology
University of Illinois College of Medicine
Chicago, IL

Brian Pomerantz, Esq.
The Law Offices of Brian Pomerantz
Los Angeles, CA
Carrboro, NC

Antonio Puente, PhD
2017President, American Psychological Association
Professor of Psychology
University of North Carolina Wilmington

Martin Rohling, PhD
Department of Psychology
University of South Alabama
Mobile, AL

David Schretlan, PhD, ABPP-CN
Associate Professor of Psychiatry and Behavioral Sciences
Associate Professor of Radiology
Johns Hopkins University

Robert A. Seegmiller, PhD, ABPP-CN
Director
Postdoctoral Fellowship in Clinical Neuropsychology
San Antonio Military Medical Center

Lisa Stanford, PhD, ABPP-CN
Division Director, Neurobehavior Health
Neuropsychology Clinical Training Director
Akron Children's Hospital

Tony Strickland, PhD
Associate Professor of Neurology
David Geffen School of Medicine at UCLA

Jerry Sweet, PhD, ABPP-CN
Vice Chair, Department of Psychiatry and Behavioral Sciences
Head, Psychology Division
Director, Neuropsychology Service
North Shore University Health System

Rodney A. Swenson, PhD, ABN
Clinical Professor of Psychiatry and Behavioral Science
University of North Dakota Medical School

Rodney Vanderploeg, PhD, ABPP-CN
Neuropsychology/Polytrauma Supervisory Psychologist
James A. Haley Veterans Hospital
Clinical Professor
Department of Psychiatry and Behavioral Neurosciences
University of South Florida
Tampa, FL

Cheryl S. Weinstein, PhD, ABPP-CN
Assistant Professor of Clinical Psychology
Beth Israel Deaconess Medical Center
Harvard Medical School

David J. Williamson, PhD, ABPP-CN, MBA[1]
Principal Medical Science Liaison
Janssen Scientific Affairs, LLC
Adjunct Associate Professor
Departments of Neurology and Psychiatry
University of South Alabama College of Medicine
Adjunct Associate Professor
Department of Psychiatry
Carolinas Healthcare System

Keith Owen Yeates, PhD, ABPP-CN
Professor and Ronald and Irene Ward Chair in Pediatric Brain Injury
University of Calgary

[1] The opinions expressed are solely the responsibility of Dr. Williamson and do not represent official positions or statements on the part of Janssen Scientific Affairs, LLC, the University of South Alabama, or Carolinas Healthcare System.

Prologue

HOW CAN WE effectively communicate complex, highly technical neuropsychological and psychological material that is outside of jurors' framework of understanding in a way that is engaging, compelling, and memorable?

Psychologists and neuropsychologists typically do not learn to provide clear, understandable testimony through formal instruction at the graduate or postdoctoral training levels. In fact, rather than offering instruction in communicating science to the general public in a direct, clear, and easily understandable manner, graduate school and the postdoctoral fellowship years might even be a time when we replace our normal vocabulary with jargon, and our everyday writing style with third-person, hard-to-access "research paper" prose. Our ability to communicate and connect with nonscientists may actually decline during our training process.

An important concept in this book is that complex ideas do not need to be "dumbed down" for members of the public to understand them. As psychologists and neuropsychologists we are accustomed to speaking and thinking in the particular language of our profession. The assumptions and jargon that we work with every day become invisible to us. When we communicate in the court system, we may lose track of the jargon we use and forget that others have never heard of our basic assumptions. Our messages might not be compelling to jurors because they lack merit, but because jurors cannot access them. This perspective leads directly to the idea that becoming an outstanding communicator on the stand is a learnable skill that requires us to actively create access for jurors to our messages.

Rather than focusing on testimony that "works" for plaintiffs or defense, the goal of *Testimony That Sticks* is to help neuropsychologists and neurobehavioral scientists engage in what Manfred Greiffenstein and Larry Cohen described as "productive testimony"[1] that transforms complex, highly technical information into understandable information juries can access and relate to. That is, the goal of learning how to be an outstanding communicator to juries is not "winning" but "helping the court understand."

So how can we learn to effectively testify in a way that is engaging, compelling, and memorable? This book is premised on the idea that most successful forensic clinicians have learned how to give productive testimony "on the job," hitting upon metaphors, analogies, and succinct summaries of concepts that are comprehensible and compelling to juries. These "pearls" that are productive in communicating complex concepts simply and effectively might be handed down from mentor to student, or shared among colleagues informally. Over the course of a 4-year qualitative research project I interviewed forensic psychologists and neuropsychologists and asked them to share their best strategies and techniques for creating access to our science for juries and other triers of fact. I also interviewed attorneys and judges to find out from their perspective what makes outstanding expert witnesses, particularly psychologist and neuropsychologist witnesses, and what they need from our profession to create more productive testimony.

As with the research project and subsequent book *Feedback That Sticks: The Art of Communicating Complex Neuropsychological Assessment Results*,[2] this book allows readers to be a "fly on the wall" as seasoned forensic neuropsychologists and psychologists communicate their assessment findings and methods directly to juries on a wide variety of neurological, psychiatric, and developmental conditions. Readers also have access to the thought bubbles of attorneys and judges as they watch expert testimony and weigh in on what works and what doesn't.

Similar to *Feedback That Sticks*, the interviews were "free range." I had a set of orienting questions, but the conversations were largely guided by the interests, opinions, areas of fascination, and perspectives of the judges, attorneys, psychologists, and neuropsychologists who participated. Much like a treasure hunt, interviews would turn a corner and reveal delightful surprises, such as Judge John Fader quoting Faulkner as he explained what made good expert testimony. Metaphors, stories, analogies, and pearls of wisdom about testifying were collected as they were offered, with much gratitude but no attempt at a systematic harvest. Consider this book a vivid complement to other more systematic volumes that describe the practice of expert mental health testimony. The interviews did not focus on how to conduct a forensic assessment; interviewees were specifically asked to focus on testimony, but when aspects of forensic assessment were highlighted as foundational for good testimony, those pearls were included as well.

To streamline the text, judges and attorneys are identified by the title "Judge" or "attorney" prior to their names. Psychologists and neuropsychologists are identified by their first and last names only. That is, if you don't see a designation otherwise, assume you are hearing from a forensic psychology or neuropsychology colleague.

The chapter structure is designed to lead readers through a process of re-thinking the way we have been traditionally taught to communicate as psychologists and neuropsychologists with each other and the general public. What does it mean to "sound like a doctor?" The first chapters focus on disrupting ingrained academic communication patterns, rethinking our relationship with the jury, and re-examining our social pragmatics and use of jargon on the stand and when interacting with attorneys through all stages of forensic work. With this groundwork, strategies for structuring direct examination are presented in Chapter 8. The next chapters present specific tools for direct examination, including creating access to the basic assumptions of our assessment techniques, engaging use of visuals, and specific analogies, metaphors and concise methods to explain specific psychological and neuropsychological disorders. With all of this in mind, cross examination is covered in Chapter 15, followed by a chapter presenting strategies for dealing with opinions (typically on cross) of other experts. Chapter 17: Testifying in a Diverse World follows, with perspectives on cultural/ linguistic/ gender and other relevant aspects of diversity that are present in infinite combinations amongst members of the jury, experts, judges and attorneys- and resonate with material presented in previous chapters. The book closes with chapters on preparation and managing anxiety, including clear, vivid strategies for report writing that challenge us to utilize accessible, engaging communication strategies at every stage of our forensic process.

This book will be helpful to students entering the world of forensic testimony. That said, just as the process of interviewing colleagues for *Feedback That Sticks* dramatically improved my own feedback skills, as I conducted the interviews for the *Testimony That Sticks* project, I found my own testimony on the stand transforming. To the experts I interviewed, and the midcareer experts already engaged in forensic practice whom I did not interview, here are more tools for all of our testifying toolkits so that we can be more productive on the stands with "Testimony That Sticks."

NOTES

1. Greiffenstein, M., & Cohen, L. (2005). Neuropsychology and the law: Principles of productive attorney–neuropsychologist relations. In G. L. Larrabee (Ed.), *Forensic neuropsychology: A scientific approach*. New York: Oxford University Press, pp. 29–91.
2. Postal, K., & Armstrong, K. (2013). *Feedback that sticks: The art of communicating complex neuropsychological assessment results.* New York: Oxford University Press.

TESTIMONY THAT STICKS

1 Disrupting Our Academic Communication Style

AS I TOOK MY seat at the Alan Alda Center for Communicating Science annual boot camp, I made eye contact with several of the 50 scientists who had traveled from all over the country to participate. I was clearly not the only one in the room who was terrified. In the service of learning to better communicate our corners of science to the general public, we had all signed up for a week of improv training.

Every one of us in that room—geneticists, physicists, physicians, and bench scientists—had grown up in the same academic tradition that tells us to communicate with jargon-filled, technical language, and to be so fearful of making an error that reading from slides verbatim at a conference appears to be a sane communication choice. Our years of scientific training had actually resulted in a net *loss* of our ability to communicate clearly and simply about the science we love.

The aha! moment came quickly. As we listened to 3-minute presentations of each other's work, we realized that none of us could understand each other. MDs, PhDs, and MD/PhDs in the room admitted that we actually felt stupid as we tried to decipher each other's impenetrable jargon and catch up with assumptions we had never heard of. In that moment, the convenient fantasy that members of the general public cannot understand our work because they aren't as "smart" or well educated as us was exploded. A *room full of smart people* couldn't understand each other's work because our academically based communication style is not accessible.

The Alan Alda Center staffers were anticipating this moment. They shared the statistic that 70% to 80% of scientists *attending their own field's academic conferences* report that they cannot fully understand presentations of other researchers.

We spent the next 5 days engaged in improv classes that helped us to create access to our messages through use of metaphors, analogies, and stories and to connect with our conversation partners so we communicated *with them* rather than *at them.* Interestingly, as improv exercises helped us learn to shift the focus of our communication from "me" to "you," the terror/stage fright most of us were experiencing at the beginning of the boot camp (and really through most of our professional careers when talking to others about our work) began to disappear. Rather than "Am I going to make a mistake?" or "How do I sound?" the focus shifted to "What does my conversation partner need from me?" and "How can I help him/her?"

A judge who agreed to be interviewed for the *Testimony That Sticks* project but preferred to remain anonymous expressed this concept in a compelling manner:

> *Stop thinking about yourself when you are on the stand. Start to think about the jurors. It is like the moment when you fall in love or have kids—you think about them first. Do that with the jury. Take yourself out of the equation.*

As we dive into the research collected in the *Testimony That Sticks* project, I want to share in this first chapter how principles of improv can help us disrupt the inaccessible academic communication style we all learned in graduate school. Shedding jargon, giving ourselves permission to allow emotion to creep back into our language, freeing up our body language, and using vivid, clear language allows us to create moments of genuine, productive communication with jurors and other triers of fact. At its heart, improv challenges us to be human, connect with others in ways that are meaningful to them, not take ourselves so seriously, and share the joy/fun we experience in the field we chose.

Many of the judges, attorneys, psychologists, and neuropsychologists I interviewed for the *Testimony That Sticks* project shared perspectives and strategies consistent with these improv principles. Throughout the chapter, I will take opportunities to map out how principles of improv connect with the specific strategies, perspectives, and verbatim pearls found in other chapters throughout the book.

YES, AND . . . TINA FEY'S RULES OF IMPROVISATION THAT WILL CHANGE YOUR LIFE

Our first handout at the boot camp was an excerpt from Tina Fey's brilliant book *Bossypants*[1] where she offers an entertaining overview of improv's foundational rules:

> *The first rule of improvisation is AGREE. Always agree and SAY YES. When you're improvising, this means you are required to agree with whatever your partner has created. So if we're improvising and I say, "Freeze, I have a gun," and you say, "That's not a gun. It's your finger. You're pointing your finger at me," our improvised scene has ground to a halt. But if I say, "Freeze, I have a gun!" and you say, "The gun I gave you for Christmas! You bastard!" then we have started a scene because you have AGREED that my finger is in fact a Christmas gun.*
>
> *Now obviously in life you're not always going to agree with everything everyone says. But the Rule of Agreement reminds you to "respect what your partner has created" and to at least start from an open-minded place. Start with a yes and see where that takes you.*

As an improviser, I always find it jarring when I meet someone in real life whose first answer is no. "No, we can't do that." "No, that's not in the budget." "No, I will not hold your hand for a dollar." What kind of way is that to live?

The second rule of improvisation is not only to say yes, but YES, AND. You are supposed to agree and then add something of your own. If I start a scene with "I can't believe it's so hot in here," and you just say, "Yeah . . ." we're kind of at a standstill. But if I say, "I can't believe it's so hot in here," and you say, "What did you expect? We're in hell." Or if I say, "I can't believe it's so hot in here," and you say, "Yes, this can't be good for the wax figures." Or if I say, "I can't believe it's so hot in here," and you say, "I told you we shouldn't have crawled into a dog's mouth," now we're getting somewhere.

To me, YES, AND means don't be afraid to contribute. It's your responsibility to contribute. Always make sure you're adding something to the discussion. Your initiations are worthwhile.

What does this have to do with testifying about psychology or neuropsychology? When we are asked questions on the stand like, "Doctor, isn't it true that all of us have OCD at some point or another?" an impulse might be to say some version of, "No, it's not that. It's this." Our response tells all who are listening that the attorney has asked a "stupid" question that exposed his ignorance about the DSM criteria for obsessive-compulsive disorder. So, we tell him, "No, you are wrong. Here is the right way to think about this." And we sound condescending as we offer a piece of arcane knowledge disconnected from what people in the room know about. We have emphasized the fact that the attorney asking the question has little knowledge of our field. Most importantly, we have lost the jury, who also had no idea about the "right" answer.

When we are asked, "Doctor, isn't it true that all of us have OCD at some point or another?" what if we used the "Yes, and . . ." technique? "That's a great question. Many of us have a tendency to be 'neat freaks.' But some people become so obsessed with the idea that they might get others sick if every surface isn't perfectly clean at all times that . . ." The practice of "Yes, and" has us begin with our listener. What has my communication partner brought to our interaction? What analogies, stories, and examples can I use that will be relevant to the person I am communicating with?

Staffers at the Alan Alda Center pointed out that when people listen to new information, particularly scientific information, they automatically think of the thing they know best—that is, they think of themselves. Any time we can humanize our message, connecting what we are saying to examples that are likely to resonate with people, we engage our listeners. I was struck by how many interviewees for the *Testimony That Sticks* project brought up the importance of using examples that jurors could relate to in their daily lives. Lisa McDermott, a mitigation specialist, notes that there is power in anecdotes that frame information in ways that are familiar to juries:

When you talk like an academic, it is sometimes hard for people to relate. I find juries connect more when experts use everyday examples. I had a client who had a very low IQ. I learned his family sent him out to get cereal for his 3-month-old son. He came back with a small box of Cheerios. For him that was baby cereal—because it came in a tiny box. That is a real-life example of poor adaptive functioning skills. Giving

> *examples makes it easier for a jury to relate to what "adaptive function" means, as opposed to just saying, "His adaptive function in the social domain was a score of . . ."*

Lisa Stanford takes this concept one step further, noting that instead of supplying real-world examples, she uses language that invites jurors to conjure up their own examples from their personal experience:

> *Your goal is to take the jury down that road between brain and behavior relationships. If you use real-world examples, for example conjuring up their own experience with coworkers, they are already making the leap between brain function and behavior without you having to make it for them. I would rather the jury conjure their own personal experience, because if it is mine, and they don't relate, then I don't have them. But if it is theirs, then they feel connected to me through their own experience.*
>
> *I might say to a jury, "If you are on the job with someone, what are the things you need them to be able to do? Sometimes we work with people and they can't do those things. [They get a picture in their mind.] This child has problems with [anger, memory] at school; you can imagine that that would make it really hard to function well on a job site."*

THROWING ENERGY BALLS

The improv exercise was simple. We stood about 20 feet away from a partner and lobbed an imaginary ball at them. Our partner caught the ball and threw it back. After several iterations, we began looking around. It was boring. An improv instructor who had paired with a scientist startled her partner by abruptly "throwing" the ball as hard as she could. Without missing a beat, the scientist staggered as he "caught it." The decorum of the room disappeared. Partners began "dropping" balls, "whiffing" throws, throwing aggressively, timidly, triumphantly. The game became engaging and fun.

When explaining a concept to the members of a jury, they are not responsible for how we "throw our balls"; we are. What kind of "energy" is our tone and body posture communicating? Has it been the same for the last 5 minutes? Are we speaking in a monotone? How about throwing out fresh energy by altering our volume or changing our posture? With traditional academic communication, words are clearly important. But tone of voice? Cadence? Rhythm? The idea that we can and should take responsibility for these nonverbal aspects of communications was startling.

The Alan Alda Center staffers pointed out that audience members' experience of a presenter "droning on" is a reflection not of the content of a talk but of the pattern of energy. The kind of energy we throw to our listeners can be as important as the content. As speakers, we can break a consistent pattern (like throwing a ball back and forth) so our listeners can hear the next sentence we speak with fresh ears. We can also think in advance about what our important points are and break our energy patterns just prior to those points.

Chapter 6, "Social Pragmatics of Testifying," explores this type of conversational energy as well as tone of voice, body posture, and facial expressions—the language behind the language of our testimony. The goal is not to create a false or misleading persona for a jury but rather to identify and eliminate the nonverbal barriers we put up as we talk to the general public about what we do that distract from our message and distance us from our true selves and from our audiences.

OWNING THE SPACE AROUND US

Picture the last conference presentation you attended. Was your colleague at a podium talking for an hour, or two, or three without ever moving? It is very likely. Another startling premise that improv instructors introduced was that we can take control of the physical space in which our communication takes place. Am I confining myself to a small, constrained bubble, taking up as little space as possible? Or am I free with my gestures and walking the room?

In one improv exercise we were asked to walk around a large room in random patterns without bumping into one another. None of us took up much space. We were then asked to start walking again, this time taking up maximum space. Our focus shifted to big steps, wide arm swings, and turning 360 degrees as we moved. I found myself having to force myself to take the bigger steps and feeling very uncomfortable as I increased my arm swing. Particularly as women, we are trained from an early age to move, sit, and talk in a "ladylike" fashion. "Ladylike" can be summarized as small, dainty, diminutive, soft, contained. Taking up a lot of space and even speaking with a voice to fill a room can feel like breaking a rule. The physical sensation after we stopped the exercise was striking. Like many participants in the room, I felt energized.

Judges, attorneys, and experts frequently shared how powerful it is when an expert (after asking permission from the judge) leaves the witness stand to speak to the jury members standing directly in front of them:

> *I want people to feel comfortable in the courtroom, so I pretty much allow most things unless I feel it's adversely impacting the jury, or the other side objects. At some point in a recent trial an expert asked to come down and show the jury something. He moved a flip chart with paper on it right in front of the jury and he ran a little tutorial. When you get out of the witness box and you are standing in front of the jury and just talking to them, it's very effective. You are teaching them something that they feel like they might need to know instead of trying to tell them what they should conclude. You own the space. Once an expert is off the witness stand and standing right in front of the jury, all of a sudden, instead of the lawyers running the show, the expert's in charge and looks authoritative just because he is running the presentation.*—Judge Allison Burroughs

----

> *I had an expert witness I used all the time when I was an attorney. I would ask him, "Can you explain to the jury?" And he'd say "Judge, can I step down?" "Go ahead," the judge would say to him. He would leave the witness box. Most judges will let you do that. And he would talk to them. He understood every single part of his business and you could see the jury nodding their heads, "yes."*—Judge John Fader

In her book *Presence: Bringing Your Boldest Self to Your Biggest Challenges*[2] Amy Cuddy asks, "What would happen if we adopt expansive postures even when we are feeling powerless?" Her research demonstrates that the way we carry ourselves can be a source of feelings of personal power, allowing us to feel more resilient, open, and confident. Initial findings suggesting that adopting stereotypically powerful postures produced feelings of power via a mediating variable of increased testosterone were not replicated, but the connection between adopting "power" postures and an increased emotional experience of power have been replicated.[3] Although adopting expansive poses and posture associated with power may feel artificial at first, she points out that many of us are unconsciously posing in powerless stances—more frequently than we realize—that produce feelings of anxiety and insecurity no more authentic to who we are than the feelings produced by more powerful stances.

One judge shared a fascinating piece of history about the phrase "witness stand" that underscores how important posture and body language are to the court system. Back in the day, witnesses stood while delivering testimony *specifically* so jurors had an opportunity to judge their body language, including posture:

> *The historical precedent to the witness stand is exactly what it sounds like. It was a wooden podium that the witness stood on to testify. The podium was encircled by a wood railing so the witness could hold himself up; the witness never sat down. This was to enable the jurors to "take the measure of the man." The jurors could tell whether the witness was nervous or lying based on his body language. Up in the dusty attic of my ancient courthouse are the original witness stands, which now we don't use. But, in some counties, police witnesses are still required to stand when testifying out of a nod to history but also out of respect for the jury's need to see them.*—Judge [Redacted]

In Chapter 6, "Social Pragmatics of Testifying," and Chapter 10, "Visuals," strategies for the use of body language and stepping out of the witness box are presented in detail.

ELICIT EMOTIONS

Another strategy to engage listeners championed by the Alan Alda Center is to evoke emotions and get personal. Ironically, this one might be hard for our profession. Many common practices in assessment distance psychologists and neuropsychologists from the humanity of what we do. In our reports, we use a distant tone, sometimes even referring to ourselves in the third person: "this examiner found . . ." Even when not using the third person to narrate, most psychologists and neuropsychologists leave out the "person" writing the text. It is rare to read "I saw" or "I conclude" in an assessment report. We speak in the language of standard scores and percentiles that literally transforms human behavior into numbers—and we often forget to translate the numbers back into human terms. During my interviews, many seasoned forensic experts shared that to be effective testifiers we have to undo that habit and bring the humanity and emotions back into our craft.

Easier said than done. Professionals tend to be afraid of emotions when speaking in public—when we think of becoming emotional we tend to think narrowly about crying. But there are a lot of other emotions to evoke: excitement, surprise, awe, concern, anger, and empathy. Why are emotions important? One of the answers is the concept of mirroring. When we see emotions in others we tend to mirror them. As speakers, we can embody the emotion we want jurors to experience.

Another reason to evoke emotions is that human beings are much more likely to pay attention to and remember information that is infused with emotions. Think of the well-replicated research on the ability to remember emotionally valent information. That is, when given material to remember, people recall emotionally charged information much more readily than emotionally neutral information.[4]

I am not suggesting that speakers "tack on" emotions to manipulate audiences. Rather, the idea is to stop forcing ourselves to artificially strip the emotional tone out of what we write about and how we speak. When we allow ourselves to express emotions that we are actually feeling, it invites our listeners to experience the emotions as well. After years of meticulously picking emotions out of our writing and presentations to achieve an "academic" scientific tone, expressing emotion can feel unnatural. The idea is not "adding emotion" to improve our connection with others; rather, the idea is taking off our "expert scientist suits" and allowing our natural emotions to emerge.

Bob Denney embraces sharing his excitement with juries:

> *My excitement over teaching comes out naturally for me. If anything, I have to rein it in a little bit if I am talking about something that I am excited about, and most of the time, I am excited about neuropsychology and testing and how we figure out what the answer is. Forensic work is like being a detective. And you can't always necessarily trust some of the things that you would want to rely on immediately. I get excited about the whole assessment method and explaining neuropathology and explaining why the test results mean what they mean and translating that into everyday common frames of reference. I hear from students that my excitement catches, and sometimes that excitement makes covering dry material more interesting.*

KNOW YOUR AUDIENCE

Alan Alda Center staffers recommended that scientists do legwork in order to know their audience prior to giving a talk. Arrive early to talk with audience members, poll the audience during the talk, read the conference program to find out what information the audience has already heard so we are not repetitive. That sound advice brought me back to my very early practicum training days, when I followed an organizational psychologist around as she gave talks to workers in large companies. We always got to the auditorium early and sat down next to audience members, asking them about themselves, their work, and their experiences. By the time the psychologist gave the talk, she was able to use examples that were meaningful and relevant to her audience—because she had taken the time to ask them.

During a conference presentation, we can arrive early and chat with audience members, or poll the audience at the beginning of our talk about who they are and what they are interested in finding out. During testimony, this is not possible. But attorneys will have detailed information about each jury member, from the questions they are asked prior to being seated and often from direct observations by the attorney and legal team during earlier phases of the trial. I have had attorneys show me a diagram of the jury box prior to my testimony and point out the professions, education, and perceived level of interest of each juror. Knowing who is on the jury helps us to *speak with* rather than *speak at* the people in the room.

> *My advice is "Speak to the jury." And when I say that, I mean not just looking at them, but really speaking* **to** *the jury. Everything I say is tailored to the jury's understanding. In my pretrial conference, I want to ask the attorneys to tell me everything they learned about the jury on voir dire. What are their educational backgrounds? What do they do for a living? What are their ages? That really helps me tailor my testimony. Because you want it to be useful. If I have a patient who is a 60-year-old farmer with a fifth-grade education, who I often see in my clinic here, I am not going to tailor all of my examples and analogies in the same way that I would for a 40-year-old guy from New York with a college education who works at the Mayo Clinic. You have to be able to tailor your explanations to the people who are listening to you, to make your feedback culturally, socially, cognitively, and personally relevant.*
>
> *Just recently I was testifying in a case where the defense attorneys were excited to have gotten a person on the jury who was a retired social worker and her grandson had a concussion and took 2 years to recover. They were all excited because he eventually recovered; their theory was the juror would know people do recover from concussion. I was like, "Oh my God! Now you want me to go out and testify that the plaintiff, who is 1 year out, is exaggerating his deficits?!"*
>
> *I spent a lot of time pondering that because I needed to find a way to explain postconcussive syndrome without making this woman hate me, making her think I thought her grandson must've been exaggerating since he had persistent symptoms. What I ended up doing was making sure that I was extremely conservative in describing things like attribution bias, effects of litigation, and diagnosis threat. Not only did I do my usual in avoiding pejorative terms, but I went way out of my way to make sure I was as gentle and as reasonable as possible.*—Tannahill Glen, PsyD, ABPP-CN

Chapter 5, "Relationship with the Jury," and Chapter 8, "Direct Examination," explore this concept in more depth.

"I AM" IMPROV

At the Alan Alda Center, in a 1-minute "I am" improv exercise, the goal was to find *other* things that connected participants besides being scientists. I laughed at myself every time I was surprised that "the MIT physicist" loved baking or "the geneticist" was a runner too. I had spent the first day or two of the boot camp thinking of many people solely in terms of their impressive scientific accomplishments and was surprised over and over to find out they were real, live human beings, with hobbies and everything! Humans feel good when we realize we have something in common. At first glance, an expert sitting in the witness box with a PhD in psychology may seem like an alien being to most jurors; we have nothing in common with that person. When jurors feel they have something in common with you as an expert, you are not just a generic scientist behind a podium but a person like them who is sharing information. When you share something about yourself that is personal, it helps your audience connect with you and therefore your message.

Chapter 4, "Establishing Credentials and Credibility," Chapter 2, "Setting the Truth on Fire," and Chapter 8, "Direct Examination," present specific strategies for sharing personal information.

ARE YOU PRESENT?

We stood in a circle and the first participant said "Zip!", making random eye contact with another person in the circle and throwing them an imaginary lightning bolt. "Zap!" The lightning bolt is caught and then thrown to a third member of the circle, "Zop!" The bolt is passed quickly through the circle, Zip, Zap, Zopping in a crazy pattern. Participants must be present and nimble to recognize and receive the eye contact and the bolt and accurately track whether the bolt is on Zip, Zap, or Zop. A variation of this game adds a "Boing": Members of the circle can hold up a shield to deflect the lightning, saying, "Boing!" while making eye contact with the participant who will receive the deflected trajectory. The sequence continues . . . Zip! Zap! Boing! Zop! Zip! Boing! Zap! . . .

Many improv exercises force participants to be highly focused, nimble, and attentive in the moment. Being present in the moment and nimble in our responses is critical for testifying, perhaps most so for cross examination. Are we really listening to the question we are being asked, or are we in our heads worrying about answers to complex questions about statistical minutiae that the attorney will never know to ask? Have we gotten swept up in the attorney's strategy of rapid-fire questioning "forcing" us to offer rapid-fire, unconsidered answers?

By being present and listening carefully to the questions we are actually asked, we can offer an answer that clearly and simply answers the question. Tom Boll asks,

> *Are you really, really, really, really listening to the question? Psychologists get so nervous they are not really listening to the question. They are so busy trying to figure out how they are going to answer that they are not really, really, really, really thinking about what the question is. What is that question really asking? I am going to answer what the question is really asking, or do I need to ask a question about it so I can answer?*

Attorney W. Scott Liebert agrees:

> *Listen to the question. As silly as that sounds, it's human nature in a setting where one's adrenaline is up—your heart will be racing—to forget to listen to the question. It is an anxious situation. Listen to the question and let the person asking finish the question. There is a human tendency to get the answer out, even before the question is out. There is a part of human nature where you want to please people. You want to have an answer and sound professional. If you understand the question, fine. But if the question is not clear, it is perfectly fine to say I am not sure if I understand what you are asking.*

This concept is further explored in Chapter 15, "Cross Examination," and Chapter 19, "Preparation for Court and Managing Anxiety on the Stand."

USE VIVID COMPARISONS

Vivid comparisons help listeners understand the meaning of the numbers we give them. Saying "It's really small" means different things to a nanotechnologist than it does to a geologist. "A thousand times smaller than the width of a human hair" is a vivid, meaningful way of describing small. The Alan Alda Center staff used the example of the computers that were used to help run the Voyager spacecraft in 1977. Here is the fact: The computer on the Voyager had 68 kilobytes of memory. So? Unless one knows a lot about computers, that's is not very exciting. Here is the fact in context: The smallest iPod Nano currently on the marketplace has 8 million kilobytes of memory. That comparison provides serious context.

Using vivid comparisons helps jurors understand important statistical concepts like effect sizes and base rates. Hearing that the difference between the plaintiff's verbal and nonverbal IQ indices is statistically significant sounds impressive until a vivid comparison is used: One in four people who have never had a head injury have a similar difference between their verbal and nonverbal abilities.

As another example, hearing that a study found a statistically significant difference between two groups of people sounds impressive to a juror until one learns about effect sizes. Grant Iverson's graph[5] comparing the effect size of thinking problems associated with concussion compared to the effect size of thinking problems associated with depression, benzodiazepine use, marijuana use, severe traumatic brain injury, and insufficient effort, among other metrics, was brought up again and again by seasoned forensic neuropsychologists. The power of this chart, which many interviewees report they enlarge for a courtroom visual, is that it provides a vivid, meaningful context to the abstract concept of effect size.

USE METAPHORS AND ANALOGIES

Many clinical phenomena can be vividly explained through the use of metaphor and analogies. When we compare an abstract concept to something that jurors have experience with, we are creating access to that abstract concept—an "aha!" moment. As psychologists and neuropsychologists, we can sit down and create metaphors and analogies to help us explain something; more commonly, we use metaphors and analogies we learned during training or ones we hear from other skilled clinicians.

Mind for metaphors

> *Some metaphors I come up with by the seat of my pants. Others I will sit and try to think of how to explain something, like how symptom validity tests work. Some metaphors really stick and I use them for years. Others I try them out and they don't really stick. I tend to think in metaphors—it is typically spontaneous.*
> —David Williamson, PhD, ABPP-CN

> *I am surprised when testifying and teaching how often an analogy will just pop into my head. Even when sitting on the witnes stand, it is not uncommon for*

an analogy to pop into my head. And I will use it. It helps really connect with jurors. That is really the essence of good testifying. Being able to translate scientific principles into common, lay language and understanding. And you can use analogies to do that. Those are absolutely golden. And juries will really appreciate it.—Robert L. Denney, PsyD, ABPP-CN, FP

David Hartman points out the importance of using metaphors where possible instead of test scores.

> *When an attorney asks:*
>
> *Q: How well did the person do on the tests?*
>
> *It is far better to answer the question with:*
>
> *A: "This is not a test issue. This is a person issue. This person is so badly damaged that they are a shell of a human being"*
>
> *Than:*
>
> *A: "He scored three standard deviations below the mean. That places him in the severe impairment category."*
> *When an expert turns a human tragedy into a discussion on statistics, you might as well give the jury an Ambien.*—David Hartman, PhD, ABPP-CL, ABN

Martin Rohling, PhD, uses metaphors from his own life experience:

> *A lot of what I do to try to communicate ideas is use metaphors people can relate to. I have been a lifelong sports fan and athlete, so I use a lot of sports metaphors. And before I became a neuropsychologist, I was trained as a mechanical engineer, so I use a lot of engineering examples. I try also to stay current with my metaphors. For example, if I give examples that include professional athletes who played in the '70s, people don't always understand those. I have to stay current.*

In the course of the interviews, I asked judges, attorneys, psychologists, and neuropsychologists to share the best metaphors and analogies they have used or heard during expert testimony. These lie at the heart of the *Testimony That Sticks* project and populate every chapter. As you hear these compelling metaphors and analogies, I hope you will be inspired to create your own. You will know if they're good; you will see the lightbulb shine through your listener's expression.

You will also have immediate feedback if they fall flat. Daryl Fujii warns that metaphors and analogies must be relatable to jurors. He shares a cautionary tale in which an expert used an analogy to the case of Phineas Gage to explain frontal lobe problems—and it fell flat:

> *The analogy or explanation an expert uses needs to be relatable on a cognitive level (not above the person's head) and also on an emotional level (this is where the culture, religion, rural/urban status, ethnicity, what have you, comes in). It also has to be accurate. As an example of an analogy that was not relatable or accurate, I was*

testifying in a capital murder case. The defendant had a TBI and then unfortunately very heinously raped and murdered a 12-year-old neighbor in a small town in the South. The trial was a circus. His defense team tried to plead impulse control. The expert used Phineas Gage as a way to explain the aftermath of his TBI. For the jury, it was clearly not effective. Using an 1800s example, with a metal pipe going through the head, was concretely different from the defendant's story of a closed head injury after being run over by a bus. The 1800s railroad spike was hard to relate to. The defense claimed he had a personality change and couldn't control his emotions. However, prior to the murder he was working and he would lose his temper, but it was not like an all-or-nothing thing. The example of Phineas Gage just wasn't relatable and it wasn't accurate. Not only did the analogy not make a connection, but I think it worked against the defendant.

RATHER THAN EXPLAIN WHAT YOU DO, EXPLAIN WHY IT IS INTERESTING

As scientists, we tend to focus on the details and methods of our work. We rarely focus on the "why." The Alan Alda Center staffers suggested that rather than explain what we do, we can focus on explaining why what we do is interesting. How can you, my listener, relate to what I do? This is the starting point of a conversation. When we make it interesting, our conversation partners will automatically have questions in their mind for us. Then we can share more details. One attorney asked during the credential phase of my direct testimony, "Doctor, what made you interested in neuropsychology?" I told the story of my first case during my internship, where a bright but very frustrated college student came to the clinic because he could not pass a math class despite hours of studying and tutoring. He was earning As in all classes but math. I described the puzzle of having all of his test results on a table in front of me, and my sense of satisfaction in discovering the solution to the problem by fitting together his history and test results. I also described how good I felt when the diagnosis, a learning disability, led to him getting the specific type of tutoring help he needed to graduate college. I told the jury that I still love the complex puzzle of combining the objective data with the psychological experience of patients, and my satisfaction in helping people. It was a very humanizing way of discussing my curriculum vitae—the jury learned something about me as a human rather than just hearing a laundry list of university degrees.

Chapter 4, "Establishing Credentials and Credibility," presents the idea of *person centered,* rather than just *method centered credibility* and shares multiple, engaging strategies for explaining who we are as professionals.

KNOW YOUR GOAL

What is our communication goal on the stand? Alan Alda Center staff recommended that scientists keep a specific goal in mind when communicating: "By the end of this presentation, I want to . . ." Keeping the goal focused on one or two things that we want people to take away from our communication allows us to be sharp and clear in our message and respects the reality of jurors' ability to process large amounts of information.

Focusing testimony on a few key points may help jurors and other triers of fact retain our testimony as they enter deliberations. Many interviewees discussed the importance of sticking to a few points. At the boot camp, we practiced starting with easy, basic examples and learned to say, "Here is a basic example, although it's actually more complicated. If you want I can go into more detail later."

Specific strategies for presenting the foundation on which our opinions are based in a streamlined, digestible manner and avoiding our habit of hanging out in the trees and forgetting to communicate about the forest are presented in Chapter 8, "Direct Examination." Chapter 15, "Cross Examination," includes a judge's recommendation that experts have a "ripcord answer" to fall back on during cross examination that contains critical elements of their core message.

GET TO THE "SO WHAT?"

Related to knowing our communication goal, improvisation instructors at the Alan Alda Center noted the importance of getting to the point early in our communication. When we read the newspaper, we look at the headlines first. When we are communicating to others, it is important to start with the "so what?" so people will be engaged enough to tune in for the details. Of course, as psychologists and neuropsychologists most of us have been trained to start with the details and then work up to our results; only at the very end of our reports, journal papers, or conference talks do we get into the diagnosis/conclusions and discussion about what it all means.

In Chapter 2, "Setting the Truth on Fire," and Chapter 8, "Direct Examination," many seasoned forensic clinicians share their preference for immediately orienting jury members by sharing the bottom-line conclusions and opinions with them as quickly as possible. Even in the context of sharing greater detail about the data and broader assessment, the practice of beginning with the "so what?" of the next set of details prior to jumping in will empower jurors to integrate the information as they hear it rather than to have to agree or disagree with your conclusions 10 minutes later.

Chapter 21, "Reports," describes strategies like the inverted pyramid that disrupt the traditional communication style that forces readers of forensic reports to wade through the details first and hear the "so what?" last.

IF IT MAKES YOU UNCOMFORTABLE . . .

None of these changes come easily. I was not the only one in the room at the improv boot camp looking over my shoulder, feeling as though I was breaking long-established rules. A ludicrous idea frequently popped into my mind during the week: "Am I really allowed to do this?" And a less ludicrous one: "Will I have the guts to do this in real life?"

Staff at the Alan Alda Center encouraged us with the maxim, "If it makes you feel uncomfortable, do it. It will help you grow." We were encouraged to pull out the tools we learned during the week and practice them when we found opportunities. In researching this book I came across Irving Younger, a charismatic trial attorney who toured the country in the 1970s and 1980s giving workshops to other attorneys about how win cases. He had a famous lecture called, "The 10 Commandments of Cross Examination."[6] At the end of the highly engaging lecture, where he laid out the rationale for following the commandments, he cautioned, "It takes 25 trials to be able to consistently use the commandments. If you stand up there and do what comes naturally, you will break the commandments. You must COMPEL yourself to practice differently." That advice is relevant for any of us who want to change our testifying behavior. We need to force ourselves to disrupt our comfortable but inaccessible habits of academic communication.

So let's dive in. Chapter 2, "Setting the Truth on Fire," sets a frame for testifying that is applicable to the topics covered in the remaining chapters, tackling the big existential questions of testimony. What is our purpose in the courtroom? What are the boundaries of our roles? How can we be most helpful to jurors and triers of fact?

NOTES

1. Fey, T. (2011). *Bossypants*. New York: Reagan Arthur Books.
2. Cuddy, A. (2015). *Presence: Bringing your boldest self to your biggest challenges.* New York: Little, Brown and Company.
3. Cuddy, A., Schultz, J., & Fosse, N. E. (2018). *P*-curving a more comprehensive body of research on postural feedback reveals clear evidential value for "power posing" effects: Reply to Simmons and Simonsohn (November 6, 2017). *Psychological Science, 29*(4), 656–666
4. LaBar, K. S., & Phelps, E. A. (1998). Arousal-mediated memory consolidation: Role of the medial temporal lobe in humans. *Psychological Science, 9*, 490–493.
5. Iverson, G. L. (2005). Outcome from mild traumatic brain injury. *Current Opinion in Psychiatry*, 18, 306.
6. Younger, I. (circa 1970) "The Ten Commandments of Cross Examination." Retrieved from https://www.youtube.com/watch?v=dBP2ifol-a8

2 Setting the Truth on Fire

GENERAL TESTIFYING STRATEGIES

WHEN ASKED WHAT makes a good expert witness, Judge John Fader quoted Faulkner:

> *It's like Faulkner said when he received the Nobel Prize. The writer has a great responsibility to tell the truth, but not just to tell the truth. The writer has a responsibility to tell it in a memorable way, to set it on fire. That is part of being in a courtroom. Some of your colleagues—they may be the smartest people on the face of the Earth, but they are so dry, while others are exuberant, they are full of life. A good expert witness sets the truth on fire for the jury.*

Judge Fader's perspective was echoed by many of the judges, attorneys, psychologists, and neuropsychologists interviewed for the *Testimony That Sticks* project and lies at the heart of this book. This chapter addresses general principles of expert testimony that apply whether we're testifying on direct or cross examination. Here we will tackle the big existential questions of our roles as experts: What is our purpose in the courtroom? What are the boundaries of our role? How can we be most helpful to juries and triers of fact? What are we doing when we are testifying well? How do we set the truth on fire?

OUR ROLES AS EXPERTS

Michael McCrea reminds us that jurors have the most challenging job in the courtroom:

> *Everyone's job in a court case is challenging, but I think you can make the argument that none is more challenging than a juror's job. Their job is tougher than the expert's*

job. They have to take the information they receive and integrate it into an overall impression in the case that then influences their decision. Then multiply that by the number of experts who appear in a case. Over a period of days they hear testimony from a number of fact witnesses and experts. And in a few hours they have to synthesize it into a decision.

Strong experts are not just communicating abstract information well, but also communicating information in a way that jurors can use to help inform them about the particular case. That is, strong experts frame their role as helping jurors to do their very difficult job. As Judge Allison Burroughs commented, "If you're a good expert, you aren't trying to convince the jurors that you are right. You are trying to give them enough information to make the right decision. You want to empower them as opposed to being the one with the power and the opinion."

Practically, though, what does empowering a jury with information mean? The word "empower" diverges from the common view of the expert as an active lecturer and the jury as a passive audience. Instead, it suggests active engagement on the part of both the expert and the jury.

ENGAGING JURIES

Judge Lynne Battaglia notes that expert witness testimony must be entertaining. Hearing a judge express that sentiment was startling at first. As academically trained professionals, we might joke around with our colleagues standing in the doorway of each other's office, but as the professional context becomes more formal, from our classrooms, to our consultation rooms, to a conference podium, and certainly to a courtroom, our instincts are to become ever more detailed and dry in our communication. Courtrooms are dry places. Aren't they?

> *Testimony must be entertaining. Not a song and a dance, but it has to be something that captures juries. That comes from having a really cogent presentation, and showing, not just telling or lecturing to, juries.*—Judge Lynne Battaglia

Robert Mendoza provides an analogy that narrows down the type of entertainment that is helpful in the courtroom, comparing good expert testimony to a *Frontline* documentary:

> *Jurors don't want to have somebody tell them what to think. They want to be informed and then come to their own conclusions. The perfect example is the PBS show* Frontline. *It's a wonderful mixture of content, a little bit of entertainment, and also a good pace. Giving the jury information about what they need to know can be done in many ways. Lecturing is not the answer. A great documentary is one that tells a story and provides content. Expert witness testimony is essentially a mini-documentary. We are there to educate, inform, and not lose the jurors' attention. In media terms, not losing attention means being entertaining.*

Many experts shared with me that they think of testifying as being similar to teaching. However, closer questioning revealed they were referring to a particular type of teaching: the type that is entertaining and succinct, involves storytelling, and empowers jurors to come to their own conclusions by connecting material to their own experiences.

STORYTELLING

Staff at the Alan Alda Center for Communicating Science shared a genius metaphor from the center's co-founder, Carl Sevina, about how to effectively communicate dry information: spray paint. He asks us to consider the ingredient list on the back of spray paint cans. What is the percentage of active ingredient? Usually about 10%; the rest is propellant. The point is that when communicating information, 10% is your message and 90% is the storytelling or narrative that makes it stick.

Stories engage listeners in an active imagining process, where we literally enter into the narrative at a neural level. NIH researcher Nuria AbdulSabur and her team, using fMRI and PET scanners, recorded what happens when humans hear stories. As opposed to listening to a set of facts, when we listen to stories, a lot more than the "language areas" of the brain are engaged. Stories activate areas that involve inference making, construction of situational models, and even motor areas in the brain.[1] As we listen to stories, we are *engaging* (connecting the story to our own experience) and *imagining* (literally constructing the experience in our minds). When we define "entertainment" the way that Judge Battaglia does, as capturing and engaging an audience, storytelling is an obvious choice.

But in a courtroom, more than one story is being told. Darcy Cox describes what is happening in courtrooms as "competitive storytelling":

> *I have a lawyer friend who frames trials as "competitive storytelling." He says, "I have my story. The other side has their story. We are going to try to tell our stories throughout the trial. The most compelling story wins."*

Later in this chapter we will look at the issues of the credibility of storytellers, hinging in part on their ability to stay firmly within their area of expertise and anchoring their narrative in data. For now, consider two storytellers. One drones on with information that the listeners have no access to: lists of tests, scores, areas of brain impairment, DSM diagnoses. The second weaves the data into a narrative, telling the story of the human being. Which narrative is more compelling?

Of course, in order to tell a compelling narrative, as experts we need to be able to understand, in our own minds, the story of the examinee, which is much larger than any cognitive or psychiatric diagnosis. David Hartman sees his challenge as a neuropsychology expert as taking numbers and turning them into a story, He notes that while most of our training focuses on brain-behavior patterns and methodology, that isn't enough when we wish to explain this information to nonprofessionals. We need to understand the whole human being so we can explain our findings in a way that has a force of narrative:

> *My job is to take a case from the raw numbers to a story, to a flow of narrative that takes the patient from whatever circumstances they were in prior to the accident or disease process and where they are now. In testimony, it is important for the neuropsychologist on the stand to tell the story of the patient. Some of that story will*

involve tests, but most of it should not. Most of it should be able to explain what this person is like as a human being. I saw someone a year ago who was working in a nursing home and was beaten very severely by an employee. The beating caused severe primary and secondary brain injuries, which did not resolve, and he eventually wound up in a nursing home. The attorney asked me to explain the injury in terms of the brain areas that were injured. I replied, "That's not the issue here. His brain has been so badly damaged that he has been reduced to a shell of a human being. He looks superficially as if he was human but there is nothing inside." If we can discuss our findings in terms of real, human consequences, we are doing our jobs. We are so clinically knowledgeable, but often we are willing to relegate ourselves to where a lot of psychiatry would love us to be, which is just test interpreters. We need to not buy into that. We need to be able to be eloquent clinicians on the stand, not just test interpreters.—David Hartman, PhD, ABPP-CL, ABN

Scott Millis also describes his testimony as storytelling:

I like to think of my direct testimony as a story. Is there a narrative that we can put to this? I am a quantitative person, but when it comes to structuring direct testimony, I switch into storytelling mode. How did this person come to be here today? I like to start with earlier history. I have found it helpful, particularly in mTBI cases where the main issue is not really head injury. Then I tell the story of attribution error. For example, after the injury, the person has begun to pay more attention to commonly occurring lapses in memory that in the past they would have just shrugged off. But since this injury they are paying more attention to those normal lapses. And they begin to think, "There is something wrong with my brain."

Many experts pointed out that when telling the story of the case, they do not use test scores:

I try to avoid relying only on test scores. Instead, I try to tell a story with a beginning, a middle, and an end that will make sense to the patient. I try to use findings from the evaluation without overwhelming them with T scores, percentiles, etc.— Christopher Grote, PhD, ABPP-CN

Of course, "telling a story" is sometimes a euphemism for telling a lie. Rodney Vanderploeg points out that two experts may be telling a similar narrative in terms of facts, but the narratives diverge regarding interpretation. Does competitive storytelling necessarily involve one false story? No. A plaintiff who was in a state of posttraumatic amnesia and thought he lost consciousness for all those hours is a good example:

I am telling the same narrative and providing an alternative understanding of what that narrative means. A good example of this is confusion and posttraumatic amnesia following a concussive event. If the plaintiff has no memory, they assume they are unconscious. Their belief about the severity of the injury is affected by the fact that they don't remember anything about it. How can you believe that you were conscious when you have no memory of it? Other observers at the scene—EMS, police officers—clearly document that the person is conscious: talking, walking, and doing other things. But the plaintiff's belief about the severity of the injury affects their experience. I am not saying that the person is lying; this is their perspective, and it is entirely reasonable for them to have it. The narrative that I tell as an expert is another way of understanding what is going on.

Paul Craig has a word of caution for experts who are tempted to tell a story that doesn't fit with good brain science and solid psychometric principles: "Importantly, the story should make sense in the context of the research and statistics, or I will be eaten alive during cross examination."

MORE THAN TESTS

Antithetical to the concept of the expert as storyteller is the expert who is test-bound. Many experts, judges, and attorneys cautioned against experts becoming mired down in their test data. Attorney Wayne Miller notes that his goal with his experts is to "try to make things more general so that a jury doesn't have to go off on some micro-minutia in a discipline that they can't possibly understand." Ironically, the same experts who put jurors to sleep with long recitations of inaccessible T scores, might not be test-bound at all in their clinical feedback sessions with their patients. We can all give ourselves permission to bring good clinical feedback skills to the witness stand.

Remember, we are clinical psychologists first

As neuropsychologists we are trained to use our data almost as the only tool for understanding patients. That's how a lot of junior neuropsychologists practice. Their inability to detach themselves from the test data creates a feedback loop of minutiae and complexity that juries don't resonate with. It is important to realize that we are clinical psychologists first, and neuropsychologists second. Our ability to look at someone's emotional life, their personality structure, their adaptation in their environments, really resonates with jurors. If you can get to the forest in your testimony and not get stuck in the trees, it creates a much more valid and rich picture about the questions that brought you to court.—anonymous

Anchoring testimony in common sense; describing 3D human beings

I read a lot of testimony from neuropsychologists. They often tend to describe numbers and test scores and assessment technology and procedures. It makes us sound like technicians and engineers. It bores and confuses people. Our testimony needs to describe a human being in a three-dimensional way. The testing is helpful in describing the person, but it is not an end in itself. That is a big problem with testimony and also reports. I am always a big believer in the importance of being a clinical psychologist first, or if not first, a clinical psychologist side by side with our specialized training in neuropsychology.—David S. Bush, PhD, ABPP-CN

When we are test-bound, the narrative about the human being in front of us is necessarily lifeless and one-dimensional. Similarly, when we focus on the individual as our only level of analysis, we miss rich contextual data that strengthens and animates the narrative. Neuropsychologists are often overly focused on the individual brain, but we know from family systems theory and community psychology that broader systems affect behavior. Our testimon can be much more engaging and resonant if we wrest our attention away from a specific focus on an individual's test scores and bring in the broader context of his or her life.

> *Explaining the data, but not being caught up in details and keeping to the larger picture, is an easier thing for other specialties. But the neuropsychologist, on the spectrum of people who testify, they seem to be the most susceptible to getting lost in the details of their data. Orthopedists aren't going to do it. Neurologists aren't going to do it. They talk about the person and the opinion. Because of the presence of the testing data, it's easier to get caught up in it. It's the old joke about the guy who loses his keys, and he is crawling under the lamppost. Someone asks him, "Where did you lose your keys?" And he says, "I lost them over there, but the light's a little better here." It's easier to look. I am comfortable in the light. I am comfortable with my data. I am comfortable with data and testing. But your job is to translate what your testing means for the real person, out in the real community.—Attorney, anonymous*

MORE THAN DIAGNOSES

Similar to the trap of being test- and score-bound is the trap of being diagnosis-bound. When an expert is focused on diagnostic categories, it's easy to lose sight of the narrative of the human being. While good clinicians focus on the person and not on the diagnosis, often experts feel their job is to describe the correct diagnostic category to juries, rather than focus on the impact of the disease process or mental health condition on the person's life. Rod Swenson will explain directly to jurors:

> *You will hear me talk about things that are complicated because the language we sometimes use is technical. But really, what matters about this injury is, "What is the impact on this person?" I saw a patient once who had multiple hemorrhagic contusions—hit by a car. When I walked into his hospital room, he was sitting on the side of the bed and said hello. I couldn't believe he was the right person. The most important thing is, "What is the impact of this injury on this particular person?"*

In describing the impact of a mental health problem on a person's life, experts may have to go beyond the specific criteria and language of the DSM-5 in order to connect the experience of the plaintiff or defendant to the experience of the jurors. Lisa McDermott, a mitigation specialist, points out that when experts share descriptions of behavior with juries rather than descriptions of diagnostic categories, juries can use the information to make better decisions:

> One expert I worked with referred to the father in the defendant's family as a "happy drunk." Jurors may relate to that one adjective. People will understand that this may

not be the guy who gets drunk and beats his wife; this may be the drunk who gets drunk and starts hugging everyone. You have defined him as alcohol-dependent based on your expertise. The "happy" part comes from the interviews that you read or descriptors used by the family. In context of a child's life, if I tell you his father was a happy drunk or I tell you his father was a mean drunk, it creates a very different impression. You envision very different experiences. That is just how the jury sees the history, too. Alcoholism does not describe a behavior; it describes a diagnosis. It is critical to bring in the other information to help frame the reference.

Here is what it might look like on direct testimony:

Q: As part of your evaluation, did you do any interviews? Did you talk to the defendant's mother?

A: Yes.

Q: Did she describe his father's behaviors?

A: Yes, the wife described him as a happy drunk. He was playful, affectionate, and danced with the children. They loved being awake when he came home. It was the most attention he ever paid to them. Most mornings he did not remember the night before, but they did.

EMPATHY: TELLING THE STORY OF THE HUMAN BEING AND BEING HUMAN WHILE TELLING IT

So much of what we do in the psychological or neuropsychological assessment process can distance us from the humanity of what we are doing: using checklists, true/false questions, and structured interviews to ask about painful experiences and symptoms; turning responses into numbers and percentiles; using third-person language in our reports to describe people. David Schretlen notes that while conducting an assessment it is important to get examinees to tell you how their symptoms feel, not just what their symptoms are: "We understand concepts. We empathize with feelings." Seeking this information produces testimony that is vivid and empathetic:

> *A:* When the voices started, he felt so frightened that he would hide in a closet. Now he has learned to distinguish real voices from hallucinations.

Shelley Peery notes that by bringing everyday experience to light either in the report or with the jury, you are humanizing the individual and humanizing the impact of his or her injury. Cheryl Weinstein agrees; she comments that whether you're an expert for the defendant or the plaintiff, it is very important to care about the person whom you have examined. That caring comes across to the jury.

Rodney Vanderploeg relates empathy in his practice to foundational psychotherapy training:

> *I genuinely feel empathetic to the people I see. I work primarily on the defense. Almost every person I see I wish I had seen them a year prior clinically, because they wouldn't*

be in the position they are in now. I trained in systems therapy and family therapy in grad school. In my era, we had to be in therapy, we had to do therapy. In internship, I had great psychoanalytically trained supervisors. The analytical and systems work helps me with empathy and understanding.

Lisa McDermott notes that experts sometimes focus on what happened to a child, but the defense team in a criminal case also needs its expert to explain how the child *felt* about what happened:

> *In some cases there are cultural issues that carry through generations. I had one client whose father was diagnosed with schizophrenia. The father stated he was a Babalu, a Santeria priest. He had delusions that were part of his schizophrenia, but people would pay to hear those delusions. When the father locked my client and his siblings in the house for 3 days, made them shave their heads, and slaughtered animals, it was no different than what his father did in the name of Santeria. But we needed to show that.*
>
> *In that case, we had an expert on Santeria. That testimony set up the scene, so by the time the psychological expert came on the stand, the jury would already know what Santeria is, what the religion is, the details of what is involved, and how the rituals were an accepted part of family life. The psychologist was there to talk about how this affected the child. The sacrifice was scary to the child, but his father's behavior was scarier. His father kept going to the window and threatening to jump because he felt like he could fly. The child was worried that if his father died, no one would come for the readings and he would not have anything to eat. That anxiety was more overwhelming to the child than the Santeria rituals. The fear of not having any food is what led him to seek to make money by any means available (here, joining a gang). That anxiety is important to contextualize. Jurors may not understand how anxiety can disrupt a child's life. An expert should talk to teachers, and find out if, as a child, the client would come to school anxious and unable to concentrate. Teachers might see symptoms of anxiety, but not realize that the anxious child is witnessing animal sacrifice or apparent recurrent suicide attempts by a parent. Through such collateral interviews and evaluation the expert has a better understanding of the event and a more compelling narrative.*

Similarly, attorney Sara Cohbra, who represents death-sentenced defendants in postconviction proceedings, notes that providing human details, not just diagnostic categories, allows jurors and other triers of fact to feel empathy:

> *Juries want to understand. If they feel like they are getting a lot of technical terminology, it is boring, hard to understand, and easy to dismiss. It is much more compelling to tie testimony closely to the human experience, to things that the jury and judge can identify with.*
>
> *What we want our experts to be able to do is to tie medical knowledge to the behavior our clients exhibit. In my practice, I do not want my experts simply to diagnose*

my client; I want my expert to describe my client's symptoms and behavior. Because many symptoms are present in many different psychiatric illnesses, and cognitive deficits arise from divergent sources, the diagnosis, or label, can be an unnecessary distraction. A diagnosis does not paint as thorough or helpful picture for the fact-finder as how the deficit impairs the client's ability to function.

There are some legal situations in which we have to have our experts diagnose the client, but those are few. Intellectual disability is one example, in my practice, because a client who proves he or she meets the diagnostic criteria for intellectual disability is ineligible for the death penalty. But for the most part I like my experts to stay away from diagnoses and instead describe symptom clusters and give specific examples of how the symptoms my client experienced affected his or her functioning.

Here is an example of how an expert can describe the clinical significance of a client's behavior: At the penalty phase of the trial the prosecutor has an opportunity to present aggravating factors about the client that are designed to persuade jurors to vote for death or for a judge to impose the death sentence. Many prosecutors think it is helpful to prove that the client has antisocial personality disorder, a diagnosis that is characterized solely by negative behaviors. In order to try to prove that the client suffered from antisocial personality disorder, district attorneys present information to demonstrate that the client had a conduct disorder as a child. They present information that the client was truant from school, or ran away from home, symptoms that are part of the conduct disorder diagnosis. We do an investigation into the client's background and present information about what was going on in the client's life at the time he was escaping home or not going to school. We want our expert to have information that explains this behavior in a mitigating way, so the expert can say, "Sure, he ran away from home, but he ran away because he was traumatized by his treatment at home: He was being neglected or beaten. He didn't go to school because he was mentally impaired, and the school didn't recognize that he was having so much difficulty in class. It was incredibly frustrating for him to go to school." What the prosecution is presenting as evidence to support a diagnosis of conduct disorder in fact is mitigating information that provides a compelling explanation for the client's behavior. It is humanizing and contextualizes those behaviors. It is much more compelling to tie the behaviors closely to experiences, feelings, and behavior that jurors or judges can identify with, so these fact-finders will understand: "If that happened to me, I would do that too." They may not identify with a cold DSM diagnosis, but they will identify with a kid who is beaten at home and therefore runs away.

COMMON SENSE

Tannahill Glen applies the "Jacki Watson smell test" to her testimony:

I have a "smell test" that I attribute to my mother. She is an 80-year-old crotchety woman. She always calls me when she reads something about neuropsychology in the news. And if it doesn't make common sense to her, if it doesn't pass her smell test, she will tell me, "What is all this nonsense about . . . ?!" I call it the Jacki Watson smell test. If she's not buying it, if it doesn't make sense to her, then I am not using it on the stand in front of a jury.

The issue of whether an opinion fits with common sense hinges in part on the expert's skill in using metaphors and analogies that translate concepts into "common" everyday phenomena that jurors are familiar with. Some experts may protest that their opinions are genuinely convoluted and therefore won't easily be understood, regardless of the language used to describe them. However, David Hartman notes that if you can't translate your opinion into common sense, maybe it *actually* doesn't make sense:

> *If you can't translate your opinion into some semblance of common sense, you really have to rethink what you are presenting. Because if it's that obscure, and that arcane, and that difficult, are you really dealing with what you think you are dealing with—some kind of "leading-edge disorder"? Or is your conclusion a belief masquerading as science? Science is supported by logic and peer review. Beliefs are not.*
>
> *Say you are dealing with someone who says that as a result of claimed Lyme disease they will never work again. That individual has had four normal Lyme titers and no evidence they have ever been bitten by a tick. You are now up on the stand struggling to explain why there is an insidious disorder based on invisible criteria. Perhaps the reason why you are having difficulty explaining it in a common-sense way is because it doesn't make any sense. You should not be promoting an argument based on faith, but describing a chain of inference based on objective data, logic, published science, differential diagnosis and common sense. Jurors want to understand "why." It is almost always the case that basic logic and common sense answers the "because."*

He notes that test results cannot be interpreted in isolation but must be interpreted in a larger common-sense context:

> *I had a complicated case where I asked the patient how he was doing. He said, "Terrible." I asked him why. He said it was all because of this particular psychological trauma. I asked him if his therapy was helping. He replied, "Oh, no. It's making me worse." I asked, "What do you think would get you better?" He became angry and said, "I decide when I get better! Nothing that anybody does for me is going to make me better! I decide. I take as much time as I want, and then when I decide that I am better, then I will consider going back to work!" This individual's performance and symptom validity tests were extremely exaggerated and implausible, but of course he was admitting to very extreme clinical symptoms that his treaters had credulously accepted at face value. The larger, common-sense pattern of exaggeration; severe, implausible symptom claims; no improvement; and the demand that no improvement is possible unless he says so is a pattern that most individuals would correctly label as self-serving and motivational. In my report, I explained that this is not someone who is making good use of therapy or benefiting from therapy. He has a very clear idea that he is not going to work until he decides it's time to work again.*

Dr. Harman will share interview details with jurors that will have much more common-sense impact than MMPI symptom validity scales:

> I often see people where the main issue is, can they return to work? One such individual claimed pain-related, nonspecific problems. They did general work, like cashier work. I took them through a series of questions in my exam, and then shared the sequence on direct.
>
> *Q: Do you feel that you can return to work?*
>
> *A: No, I have headaches.*
>
> *Q: How does that impair your ability to be a cashier?*
>
> *A: Oh, well, I couldn't do it for more than an hour without getting headaches.*
>
> *Q: What if you were able to break every hour, clear your head and go back?*
>
> *A: Oh, no, I couldn't do that.*
>
> *Q: Why not?*
>
> *A: Because my vision gets blurry after an hour and I couldn't focus.*
>
> *Q: OK, well, what if you alternated between being a cashier for an hour and then spent some of your time moving boxes or doing something that doesn't involve looking at small items?*
>
> *A: Oh, no, I couldn't do that.*
>
> *Q: Why not?*
>
> *A: Because I would have pain in my head and I couldn't lift boxes.*
>
> *Q: Well, OK, what would happen if you could take a break from your casher work every hour and at times you work on things that are not cashier, and at times you work with items, like boxes, but small ones that your company carries so the lifting would not be a problem?*
>
> *A: No, I couldn't do that.*
>
> *A: Why not? Because I just get tired easily.*
>
> *Q: What if you could alternate between your cashier job and a job with small boxes you take rest breaks, and when you are lifting the boxes they gave you a cart to sit in, so you would be able to sit down?*
>
> *A: Oh, no, I couldn't do that.*
>
> And it goes on and on, and every accommodation you suggest is met with another reason why they can't work. And when all other justifications run out, they finalize their objection with "I can't work because my doctor told me I can't work." It becomes clear that if the individual is ambulatory and otherwise functioning but endlessly rejects work accommodations, it is not a matter of "can" they return to work but "will" they return to work. I say to the judge or jury, "Let me explain to you what this individual said to me. (You have to have good short-term memory to do this!) No matter what you try to accommodate, this claimant will find a reason to reject the accommodation."

Judges commented during many of the interviews that juries are specifically instructed to rely on their common sense when they deliberate:

> *When I instruct the jury, I tell them—as do most judges—that they are to use their common sense. Then I borrow from this country music lyric that I love: "Nobody's asking you to outsmart your common sense." That is, you can accept or reject things that witnesses tell you whether or not they are experts. What that instruction does is empower people to trust themselves.*—Judge [Redacted]

BE SUCCINCT

Judge Allison Burroughs cautions, "I think most experts are on the stand way too long, way too long. You just don't need to be in the weeds on every single concept." Another judge, who preferred to keep her name redacted, told me that sometimes she watches an expert testify and knows by the look on his or her face that the witness is thinking, "Help! I'm talking and I can't shut up!":

> *This is bad. Jurors become confused when you as an expert overelaborate. You lose credibility. Cases are very scripted, and providing too much information loses the focus of the case.*

When communicating information, clear, concise language is almost always easier to understand and use. Judge Jay Blitzman uses the word "overselling" to describe experts who go beyond specific questions on direct or cross examination, adding more information:

> *With testimony, the best experts testify within the confines of their expertise and don't try to volunteer too much. They are more credible. They are harder to cross examine because they are not overselling. In other words, they are not volunteering information and not showing off in that fashion. They are addressing the actual questions and trying to deconstruct these concepts to make them intelligible to laypeople.*

The idea of overselling an argument reminded me of a radio interview with a political scientist who was explaining his large-scale research study. Each time the reporter asked the scientist a question, he enthusiastically answered her and then added several more points. He finally paused, somewhat bewildered by the amount he was talking, and joked, "I feel like a used car salesman, 'What do I have to do to get you into this argument?' "

Here are some additional takes on the issue of simplicity:

> *The "keep it simple and straightforward (KISS)" policy is a good one to consider. This includes responding to questions directly, honestly, and succinctly.*—Nat Nelson, PhD, ABPP-CN

Less is more. I tend not to drone on and on about concepts. I try to make them concise and organized, in language that everyone can put their arms around.—Michael McCrea, PhD, ABPP-CN

I use simple language about complex ideas.—Lisa Stanford, PhD, ABPP-CN

Oftentimes when we say less we communicate more. People can only assimilate so much information. I use simple, short, concrete examples.—David Schretlan, PhD, ABPP-CN

I keep everything I say in front of a jury to one, two, or three sentences. Very simple. You are talking about technical information. People will get lost in the weeds and bored out of their minds if you throw in too much information or jargon. This is ***really hard*** *to do for those of us who spend all day talking to colleagues about neuroscience. Even when you TRY not to use jargon, you inevitably do, so you have to run through your testimony a lot to get rid of these sneaky terms.*—Tannahill Glen, PsyD, ABPP-CN

Long, meandering testimony is not just hard to understand; it's annoying. Jerry Sweet points out that jurors are being taken from their jobs and families to hear the case and hence will find long, rambling testimony annoying:

One of the tensions I see when I go to court is between informing people and dealing with the fact that many of the jurors do not want to be there and no matter how short, the case may have already gone on way too long. A couple of years ago, I had a bad experience in court. I had been retained by the plaintiff for a very severe TBI case. It was going to trial for liability, and my testimony as to the damages should have been short and simple. I said to the attorney who was doing my direct, "We want me to be up there about 45 minutes; if we go longer than that, it will be a problem." Well, he got me up there and goofed around asking and re-asking the same kinds of questions. He kept me up there over an hour, and then there was cross examination. And then he re-directed for a long time after. As he was bringing in the next witness, I passed the attorney in the hallway and said, "You've lost the jury; they are half asleep! You have to go faster!" As experts, such matters are out of our hands.

The last thing you want to do is overload the triers of fact. You only want to talk about relevant issues. To the extent you are giving irrelevant information or extra information, you will lose the jury.—Yossef Ben-Porath, PhD, ABPP

Being succinct is closely associated with understanding the boundaries of our role in the courtroom. On direct, as discussed further in Chapter 8, "Direct Examination," the attorney will have a strategy to break the expert's testimony into smaller, digestible parts by asking questions. Rambling on will disrupt that rhythm. And on cross, as seen in Chapter 15, the dangers of rambling are legion.

Don't volunteer information

> *You don't volunteer information if they don't ask you. I might think, "Well, I would like to talk about that," but it is their responsibility to ask you.*—Jacobus Donders, PhD, ABPP-CN

Don't elaborate

> *Don't elaborate beyond the question you are asked. If you are going to elaborate, be very careful. Sometimes when you elaborate you get sloppy. If you say something in a sloppy way, sometimes it can be read back to you and misinterpreted in ways that you know that you didn't mean but it's hard to back out of because they can say that you said that. And you did. Clarifying questions—if an attorney asks a long, complex, five-page question, stop and clarify. Just say, "Look, sometimes it's hard for me to remember really long questions. Can you tell me the specific question?"*—David Williamson, PhD, ABPP-CN

With all of that said, there is a danger in oversimplifying. Attorney Kate Nemens cautions,

> *Expert clinicians should avoid jargon and speak plainly. However, it is possible to be so overly concerned with getting too complicated that experts can go a little too far in the other direction. In an attempt to try and communicate how they came to their conclusions in a simple way, they oversimplify it, and that can diminish the substance of their expertise, which is what we are coming to the expert for in the first place.*

Many cases have the type of complexity that resists simplification. Nancy Hebben describes a case where she recently wrote a 70-page report, the longest she has ever written:

> *The plaintiff's history was so jam-packed with medical records from decades of disabilities. He accumulated surgery after surgery and so many medical records.*
>
> *To the jury, it's impossible to go over that many records. I might summarize all of those records and say, "This is a man whose statement in his application for disability in 1989 was that he was completely disabled from any kind of work and he was getting worse."*

Specific strategies for communicating long, complicated information can be found in Chapter 8, "Direct Testimony," Chapter 11, "Visuals," and Chapter 20, Preparation for Court and Managing Anxiety on the Stand.

SCOPE OF TESTIMONY: WE ARE ONLY HERE TO TELL A PART OF THE STORY

This section discusses an important general principle of expert testimony: staying within our scope of practice. Experts are brought in to tell our corner of the story, but the attorney is responsible for the master narrative. The answer to the existential question "What are we doing here?" is "Only what we are trained to do; and within that training, only what the specifics of the case allow us to know and comment on."

Attorney Brian Pomerantz shares the following cautionary tale with the experts he works with:

> *I had a psychiatrist expert years ago. In the middle of a hearing, they asked him about a time period for which there were no records. He couldn't have an answer; there was no answer that as an expert he could give when they asked, "In 2005 what is going on?" The answer should have been, "In 2005 I can't tell you what's going on because there are no records, but I can tell you about all these other records . . ." That's the answer. Instead, this guy really wanted to help me. He really wanted to help my client. I think he liked my client. So, when they asked him about 2005 he opined on something for which he could not possibly have a decent basis for opining on: "Yes, he was bipolar in that period too."*
>
> *They said, "You can't possibly know that because you have no medical records for that period."*
>
> *He said, "Well, based on the other stuff . . ."*
>
> *They said, "You spent a long time talking about how he is manic at times and not manic at others. You are now claiming that you can say for a time period in which you have no records that he was manic?"*
>
> *When he did that, I did not sit there and smile. I was not thinking to myself, "It's really nice for him to help me out. I put my head in my hands and thought, 'I just lost the case.'" And I did. My client is in jail right now, and he will be for many more years.*
>
> *The expert stretched. And he stretched to help me. But don't help me. Don't help me like that! Don't try to help me. Don't stretch. If you testify to what you know, that will help me. Don't go beyond.*

Judge Allison Burroughs points out,

> *For an expert to say, "I don't know the answer to that" or "That is beyond my area of expertise" is very effective. It is credible. They rarely say it, though, because experts want to be hired again and they want somebody to be able to say to them, "Hey, you were super-helpful."*

Neil Pliskin warns that many attorneys pressure experts to step beyond their expertise:

> *You need to have complete conviction that everything you are saying is tied to the objective information in the data. As soon as you start responding to subtle pressure from the attorneys—"Well, can you add an addendum so you can say this? Do you think you can add this line into your report so it can help me?" I am very rigid about that. The test results are the test results.*

The motivation for experts to stretch beyond their scope of expertise during testimony may come from wanting to help an attorney, as Judge Burroughs points out, or help a client, as in attorney Pomerantz's cautionary tale. Some experts might step beyond their expertise due to an inflated ego (and may step beyond their expertise in their daily practice for the same reason) or because they are afraid they will look foolish if their answer is, "I don't know." An important thing to consider is that cross- examining attorneys, knowing experts can be easily discredited once they step beyond their scope of practice, will intentionally attempt to draw an expert "off sides" during cross. Keith Yeates points out, "There is nothing an attorney likes better than someone making definitive statements they can't defend or statements the other expert can demolish." Chapter 15, "Cross Examination," addresses this gambit in more detail.

Regardless of the motivation, Michael McCrea offers a useful strategy for identifying and course-correcting moments when he is likely to move beyond his expertise:

> *Everyone has some internal barometer that tells them when they are wandering off the fairway. That happens in public speaking, defending a dissertation, in many situations. It is a feeling that says, "I am going beyond my area of expertise. I better listen to my barometer and reset." That also relates to the type of cases you take on. I don't take cases that would be a stretch.*—Michael McCrea, PhD, ABPP-CN

One neuropsychologist expert describes a moment when he was testifying about a head injury and became drawn into a line of questioning that was outside his area of expertise (i.e., the issue of helmet protection):

> After offering my general impressions, the retaining attorney asked whether wearing helmets is highly preventative of sustaining TBI and if the claimant may have prevented having an injury had he worn a helmet. I responded that it was common knowledge that wearing helmets was preventative and that doing so probably would have limited the risk of sustaining a TBI. In retrospect, it may have been more advantageous to simply respond that the use of helmets was outside my area of practice and that I could not offer an opinion without resorting to speculation as to whether wearing a helmet would have in fact prevented a TBI in this case. The cross examination went something like this:
>
> *Q: Isn't it true you that you do not declare having expertise regarding helmets?*
>
> *A: That is true.*
>
> *Q: And isn't it true that you have no expertise regarding how they are manufactured?*

A: That is true.

Q: And isn't it true that you do not have expertise regarding whether one helmet is more effective than another?

A: That is also true.

Attorney W. Scott Liebert, who works with psychologists and others in his practice to reduce their malpractice risk and to help prepare them to testify, suggests that before taking a case, you should ask questions about testifying within your scope of practice:

> *Should you testify? What can you say? What is your role? What is the scope of your expertise? Did you engage in a thorough enough evaluation or work to come to opinions? What kind of questions would you ask yourself on cross? Do you have enough information to testify?*

Robert Kinscherff will refer out parts of a case to other psychologists who have greater expertise in a particular area of psychology practice than he does:

> *I don't give the Rorschach myself. There are people that do it better than I do. If I decide to use a battery that includes a Rorschach, I will ask a colleague who is a real testing maven to do it. I want someone who has done the "deep dive" into the Rorschach to explain it.*

Tom Boll also refers out portions of cases that he does not feel fall within his scope of practice:

> *Even though I am board-certified in clinical psychology and clinical neuropsychology, if there is a claim of PTSD, I will ask the attorney to get a PTSD expert on board. If you are testifying about PTSD, you need to be an expert in PTSD. The plaintiff may genuinely have PTSD but has had a licensed mental health counselor holding her hand for 3 months and she is not getting better. I don't treat, I don't write in the area. I know about it, but I am not the best. I want to do what I do best. I am the best here, but not there. If you want me on the team you will need to get players to cover every base.*

Many interviewees focused on the importance of saying "I don't know" when appropriate during testimony. Saying "I don't know" is a sign to others in the courtroom that you are not being drawn off sides:

> *It's important to say "I don't know." It is really necessary to represent the boundaries of our knowledge and expertise, to not overstate what we know or understand, or overstate the field. While we are good at a lot of things, we don't know the answer to every question. Triers of fact—juries and judges—respect when we say at times, "I don't know. It could be this, or it could be that." Acknowledging the limitations of our data and conceptual models is realistic and necessary at times, and it lends credibility to the opinions we are able to assert.*—David S. Bush, PhD, ABPP-CN

Experts don't use the phrase, "I haven't formed an opinion" enough. There is a lot of pressure to have an opinion about everything. Resist that pressure.—Manfred Greiffenstein, PhD, ABPP-CN

Don't step into waters where you don't belong. Don't be ashamed to say, "That is not my specialty" or "I don't know." Be honest with the limits of your knowledge.—David Schretlan, PhD, ABPP-CN

One of the best experts I have ever seen on the witness stand used to testify about a piece of equipment that got tampered with on a boat so that oil could be dumped overboard in the middle of the ocean instead of paying to be discharged at a port. He would say, "Look, I know this was obviously tampered with and this is why I think that." Then, when it came to the "who tampered with it," he would be honest about it. He would say, "A look at the logbooks show that these were the people on deck, so they are the likely people that could've done it." But he wouldn't say, "I think it was that guy or I know it was the defendant." He was willing to testify to his piece of it and let the rest of the evidence carry the rest of the day. Many experts feel like they have to get you over the finish line in their time on the stand, and that's not their job. Their job is to just give you the information that you need to put that piece of the puzzle in place.—Judge Allison Burroughs

An important variation of saying "I don't know" is helping juries, judges, and attorneys in the courtroom understand (where appropriate) that the reason you do not know is because the information is not knowable.

It is important to be very clear about what you know. "I know this," or "I don't know this," or "I know that no one knows this, because the literature isn't there." In testimony, an expert has to say sometimes not just "I don't know" but "I don't know and neither do you. And nobody is going to know."

When you have an examinee with an IQ in the low 70s, a history of multiple concussions, and polysubstance abuse, you don't know, and neither does any other expert, which factor affected which decision. It is important not to pretend that you can know on the stand.

Q: So, Dr. Williamson, did too many drugs cause Mr. Defendant to commit this crime?

A: This is a gentleman who has a lot of things going on that affect how he makes decisions. We know that folks who don't score high on IQ tests can be prone to being led around by others. And you probably know people in your life who are like that. He's also done a lot of drugs over time, and that's also bad for your thinking. Did the polysubstance abuse make it hard for him to make decisions and commit a crime? I can say it didn't help. Can I say polysubstance abuse made him commit the crime independent of his low IQ and other factors? That's impossible to say, because there is too much going on.—David Williamson, PhD, ABPP-CN

Yet another variation of "nobody can know" are questions that behavioral and neuroscience research just doesn't address. Robert Kinscherff tells the story of being a guardian ad litem in a case involving a 9-year-old child. One parent proposed that the transfer for visitation occur at one fast-food restaurant along the highway. The other parent proposed another one perhaps 5 miles on the highway closer to that parent's house:

> *They were arguing. The judge was getting frustrated. The judge turned to me and said, "What would you recommend?" I said, "The most important thing to do over time is to minimize the child's exposure to parental conflict. But I am afraid I have to tell you that there is nothing in behavioral science that allows me to choose between an Arby's and a McDonald's or the distance of 5 miles each way from either parent's home."*

Judge Christina Harms has similar advice:

> Some psychologists go farther than they have any basis for going in stating things like, "It is definitely my opinion that these children should spend Monday and Tuesday night with their mother." On cross examination they might rightly be confronted with:
>
> *Q: What course did you take in psychology graduate school, what book do you claim to rely upon, where is the source of your expert opinion that Monday and Tuesday is the right answer?*
>
> Psychology is rarely that precise, and the expert has got to be prepared to admit it. You are not being effective if you don't admit the limits of what you know. That's perfectly okay and in fact admirable. Don't feel that you have to be 100% certain, and don't take positions which, when you think about it, are more specific than in defensible. I think some psychologists think it makes them look weak to admit they don't know everything, but it frankly makes them look strong. On cross examination:
>
> *Q: Doctor, you say in your report that you would recommend that the children spend every other weekend with father, right?*
>
> *A: Right.*
>
> *Q: Well, would you be opposed to the children spending three out of four weekends with father?*
>
> It's never the right answer to say,
>
> *A:No, that's not what I recommended*
>
> Because then you get into
>
> *Q:Where's the science behind that?*
>
> The right answer is always the humble answer:
>
> *A: Well, that is not that far off from what I recommended and certainly that could work. I like my recommendation better, but yours is certainly not bad.*

Robert Kinscherff shares a cautionary tale about the risk of board action against your license if you offer an expert opinion that is not supported by behavioral science:

> *I recall a case where a psychologist was asked to give an opinion about the return of a child to a parent. The evidence was equivocal: Reasonable professionals could reasonably disagree whether the greater risk to the child was being placed back to a previously abusing parent or prolonged separation from a caregiver with whom the child might be unified. It was a close call. The parents ultimately filed a licensure action against the psychologist offering testimony, but the record clearly reflected the psychologist saying that there is no behavioral science under the circumstances before the Court to confidently answer the question of whether the greater risk was to return the child to care of the previously abusive parents, or to risk continued disruption of attachment in longer-term foster care should the child ultimately be returned to the parent. And the judge said, "I insist you give me a recommendation." And the psychologist said, "I have no basis in behavioral science to tell you which would be the greater risk for this child." And the judge said, "I am now ordering you to render an opinion." And the psychologist said, "I will offer you my personal opinion, Your Honor, but I am not offering the opinion as a psychologist because I have no basis on which to offer it as a psychologist." The psychologist then offered an opinion as an individual but not as a professional. The licensing board dismissed the complaint because the psychologist was responding to the insistence of the Court but had made it very clear that they were not offering a recommendation in their professional role. Had that psychologist bowed to the Court's pressure but not clarified that the response was not a professional opinion, who knows what the licensing board would have done?*

Ted Peck points out that one consequence of testifying beyond our expertise may be a Daubert or Frye hearing where a judge determines that we may not testify to a specific area or topic or limits our testimony:

> *You want to work within a professional comfort area so a motion to have a Daubert or Frye hearing does not lead to limiting your opinions or impeach your ability to offer your opinions. . . . Once your testimony is limited in one case, attorneys have access to that information, either through court records or through asking you at a deposition. That can haunt an expert through years of subsequent cases.*

An expert might forever after hear this question at the beginning of depositions or corss examination.

> *Q: Doctor, have you ever been barred from testifying about this in other courts?*

Recall that the attorney who hires the expert has the best interest of their client in mind, not the best interest of the expert. Should the attorney ask the expert to stretch and offer opinions beyond the expert's scope of practice or beyond the scientific literature, the outcome for that attorney's case may be that the expert's testimony gets barred or limited. That may represent just a bump in the road on that case for he attorney, but the implications for the expert's career from having his or her testimony restricted may be very long-lasting and damaging.

Jacobus Donders brings up the interesting issue of testifying about a medical test. Many of the variables neuropsychologists take into consideration in our clinical and forensic work involve the results of medical tests. For example, neuropsychologists regularly integrate brain scan findings, although we typically don't claim expertise in reading a scan as would a radiologist. We integrate the results of sleep studies without expertise in reading the EEGs and calculating the hypopnea index. While we should be clear about our area of expertise, it is also important not to be boxed out of testifying about the significance of medical information if we typically and appropriately use that information in the course of our practice. Dr. Donders offers advice for testifying about the results of a blood alcohol test without stepping beyond one's scope of practice:

> *Q: Doctor, are you saying you have an expertise in calculating blood alcohol levels?*
>
> *A: I am not a law maker, but I need to know what the law is. I need to know on the highway I can't go more than 65 mph. When I look at the medical record, and I see the blood alcohol level of .208. I do not need to know how that's measured. But I know how to interpret a .208 measurement. That means that you are stone cold drunk.*

IT'S NOT MY JOB TO TRY THE CASE

Closely related to the issue of testifying within our scope of practice is understanding what is clearly outside of our scope. Our role as an expert is not to try the case or win the case. This issue is in turn closely related to the next section, expert bias.

> *I always remind myself that it is the attorney's case, not mine. I will do what I can to covey the information. At the end of the day, the case is their responsibility.*—Yossef Ben-Porath, PhD, ABPP
>
> ------------
>
> *In my experience, neuropsychologists tend to overestimate the value of their testimony because they never hear all the evidence as presented to the jury.*—Paul Kaufmann, JD, PhD, ABPP-CN
>
> ------------
>
> I divorce myself from the emotions of the courtroom situation. My job is to answer the questions. My job is not to try the case. If the other side's attorney is smarter and asks the right questions—oh, well. I want to be known as someone who tells the truth. I don't want to be known as somebody who will sit there and try to work your case for you.
>
> Early in my career I had a patient who had a catastrophic frontal lobe injury after a car accident. There was a big bleed in the brain. When my students test patients in our clinic I tell them, "You are my eyes and ears. I want you to write down what you see. It doesn't matter how you write it." The defense's theory of the case was that the

patient was an alcoholic and that's why she had cognitive problems. They reviewed my clinic file and found a note from the student to me that they enlarged and brought into the courtroom. The note said, "Laughs inappropriately. Like a drunk."

Q: Dr. Pliskin, you said alcohol couldn't cause this. But look at what your student wrote. Can you read that out loud?

A: While she may have acted like she was a drunk, she was not drinking during the testing session; it was her condition that made her act like that.

Q: Doctor, that's a student who wrote that. What directions do you give your students?

A: I tell my students, because they are just learning about brain injury, I tell them just to write everything down that they see. That helps me to understand.

I don't say, "Yes, but!" If they try to pigeonhole me into saying "yes" or "no," I will say, "It can't be answered like that." I like to just answer with the fewest number of words possible.

It's the attorney's job to try the case, to know what the questions are that they should ask me. It's my job to answer the questions truthfully.—Neil Pliskin, PhD, ABPP

Recognizing that we're in the courtroom to share expertise, not win the case, allows us to be at peace when court circumstances overwhelm our opinions in a case.

Sometimes there is nothing you can do

Sometimes there is just nothing you can do to make things better in testimony. I testified as treating doctor on behalf of a man with severe frontal TBI in a wreck. The victim he hit also had severe TBI and was very sympathetic—beautiful, popular witness. I was put on the stand right between the victim's testimony and her mother's testimony . . . it's a wonder I wasn't burned at the stake. But I tried to convey to a very hostile courtroom the idea that the major personality change and behavioral alterations noted in the defendant were a direct result of the TBI as opposed to showing lack of remorse, and that typical incarceration would be dangerous for him. It fell on deaf ears.—Tannahill Glen, PsyD, ABPP-CN

WHEN EXPERTS LOSE OBJECTIVITY: BIAS

If experts intentionally or inadvertently take on a role of being responsible for winning a case, the likelihood of biased testimony increases. There is a vibrant literature on strategies to assess the presence of bias in one's assessments.[2] Whether the cause of the bias is narcissism, financial gain, social processes that foster alignment with attorneys, or misplaced and overzealous advocacy, credibility suffers when bias enters testimony.

One of my favorite judges once told me that when she is sitting in trial, her view is that the room is full of advocates. Everyone has a got a point of view of what's

supposed to happen. There are some who get paid for advocating a point of view; those are called lawyers. There are those that have a point of view who are not getting paid; they are called respondents or plaintiffs or defendants. When an expert witness begins to sound like they have an advocacy stance, sound like they have a dog in this fight, she just ignores their testimony, because she can't be confident that it is not spun or shaped by their personal points of view, those of the paid advocates, or dynamics with the parties in the case. Either way, she disregards them as just another advocate in a courtroom full of people who have a stake in a particular point of view. She wants to be educated by an expert witness, to follow the information relied upon and the expert opinions that rest upon that information. But she wants just that—she will make the case decisions.—Robert Kinscherff, PhD, JD

An interesting analogy is the need for psychotherapists to remain neutral lest they "disappear" in the interaction with a patient. If our role as experts is to help juries make good decisions, just like a psychotherapist who tells a patient what to do rather than helping the patient come to his or her own decision, we "disappear" in the jurors' decision-making process, becoming just one more player with an opinion. Are we helping juries decide by providing them with an engaging, fact-based narrative, or are we trying to decide for them?

One cannot tell who hired me

My ideal is to do an evaluation and write a report in which, other than the first line that says who hired me, you cannot tell who hired me.—Tedd Judd, PhD, ABPP-CN

The first principle is to state the facts. You are not there on a crusade or to win the case. You are there to help the jury or judge or magistrate make a decision. You have got to stay neutral. You have to stay objective. You have to make statements that are evidence-based. You can't go outside what our science allows. You swear to tell the truth, the whole truth, and nothing but the truth so help you God. That also means that you don't give a slightly different version depending on how well you like the person or how much they pay you. An overriding principle is, be factual and truthful.—Jacobus Donders, PhD, ABPP-CN

This is easy if you are being honest. Stick to your opinions and don't get caught up on one side or the other. Don't be worried about the outcome. Your job is to present your objective opinions.—Robert Heilbronner, PhD, ABPP-CN

Lawyers sometimes think that we are on their side. We hosted a symposium for psychologists and attorneys, where the psychologist speaker commented, "You know, we aren't on your side." And many of the attorneys were confused: "What do you mean? Of course you are on my side!"

I have seen experts sit at the attorney's table. This looks really bad. I have seen situations in which the attorney will come and talk to the expert in the courtroom in front of the jury, right before or during cross-examination of the opposing expert. This also looks bad.—Ira K. Packer, PhD, ABPP (Forensic)

Key difference between having a point of view and being an advocate?

Let's suppose I am doing a competence-to-stand-trial evaluation. Sometimes, any reasonable person would agree that the defendant is perfectly competent. At the other extreme, there would be a situation where everyone would agree the defendant is not competent—for example, a defendant who has a massive stroke following his arrest and is vegetative. The places where judges and juries need us the most are places where competence is a gray area. In a competence-to-stand-trial situation, the fundamental constitutional question is one of fairness. How "good"—capable as a defendant—do you have to be before it is fundamentally unfair to put you on trial because you have so little understanding of the nature of the proceedings and cannot communicate effectively with your attorney? At the extremes most people would agree: The incapacitated defendant following a stroke is not complicated; the entirely unimpaired defendant is not complicated. But for those with some degree of impairment, how capable a defendant has to be before legal proceedings are fair or unfair is simply not a clinical question. It is a social and moral question, and clinical training does not grant us special insight into "how fair is fair enough" to proceed in a legal case. We don't expect every defendant to be A⁺. In the old days, a D⁻ was a passing grade. If I look like I have a strong opinion about the competence or incompetence of a defendant when a reasonable person might reasonably disagree, then I as a judge or a jury might wonder whether I have taken a position that has led me to spin my information, shape it, or reflect my own personal—rather than professional—judgment about the adequacy of "fairness" in legal proceedings. We know this is a process. We are human beings; all of us develop thoughts and opinions about the people we work with and the circumstances in which we find ourselves professionally. My job is to be as clear as I can about what this defendant can and cannot do, and it is the job of the judge or jury to make a social and moral determination about how fair is fair enough.—Robert Kinscherff, PhD, JD

EXUBERANCE: WHAT EXPERTS LOVE ABOUT TESTIFYING

I began this chapter with Judge Fader's comments that some neuropsychologists are exuberant, setting the truth on fire. I want to end the chapter by sharing some of the many exuberant responses seasoned forensic experts gave me about why they love testifying: Why are we in the courtroom?

Of all things I do, I feel most comfortable on the stand. If you are comfortable with yourself and your knowledge of the field, bring it on! I own the limitations of my knowledge and my field.—Antonio E. Puente, PhD

I enjoy forensics. The cases can be more enjoyable than clinical cases for two reasons. First, forensic cases have higher stakes. We see many cases of mild cognitive problems secondary to a medical problem in clinical practice. We make a recommendation, but it won't make a lot of difference if you get one of these cases wrong or right. It makes a whole lot of difference if you get a forensic case wrong or right, particularly the criminal cases. The second thing I also really like examining—getting introspective about—is, "What is it that I can really say based on our science? What can we really say as neuropsychologists about real-life consequences and functioning?" This is where the rubber meets the road. It causes me to introspect about the state of our field.—Rus Bauer, PhD, ABPP-CN

Some people have personalities that fit well with forensic work. If you happen to have a personality where you enjoy adversarial argument or debating, it is really enjoyable. Forensic work is great training for thinking through what we do and being ready to defend our decision-making. It has distortions; the way attorneys think probabilistically is not the way we think. "More probable than not" is loose compared to how we think, but it makes you think rigorously about what you do.—Keith Yeates, PhD, ABPP-CN

I am too old to be doing this if I'm not having fun. And the really fun part of testifying for me is getting the opportunity to educate a group of people (i.e., the jury) about the relationship between human behavior and the brain.—Wendy Marlowe, PhD, ABPP-CN

NOTES

1. AbdulSabur, N., Xu, Y., Liu, S., Chow, H., Baxter, M., Carson, J., & Braun, A. (2014). Neural correlates and network connectivity underlying narrative production and comprehension: A combined fMRI and PET study. *Cortex, 57*, 107–127.
2. E.g., Sweet, J., & Moulthrop, M. (1999). Self-examination questions as a means of identifying bias in adversarial assessments. *Journal of Forensic Neuropsychology, 1*(1), 73–88.

3 Relationship with the Attorney

THE "TESTIFYING IS LIKE TEACHING" analogy breaks down quickly in an actual courtroom. When we teach, we are in control of the information exchange. We present information in our own classroom, in our preferred format, at our own pace, and include as many details as we see fit. When we testify, we are decidedly not in control of the information exchange. We bring our knowledge into a judge's courtroom. We wait until we are told to start testifying, often in a long line of other witnesses. We are asked a series of questions about our credentials to provide our opinion and, depending on our answers, may be limited in what we are allowed to say. Rather than sharing our opinion freestyle, we are then asked to share our opinions through a series of questions on direct testimony, and then through another series of questions on cross.

The point is that in our classrooms or consultation rooms, we orchestrate "what" and "how" information is shared. In the courtroom, others are in control of the process. The idea of walking into a courtroom without first establishing a clear, precise plan with the attorney who is orchestrating the information exchange should be a very unsettling proposition. Establishing a good working relationship with attorneys from the first contact through the trial sets up conditions where the information exchange is maximally productive. Chapters 8 and 15 address interactions with attorneys on direct and cross examination. This chapter is about establishing a clear, productive attorney–expert relationship that sets the stage for good testimony.

The benefit of establishing a good working relationship with attorneys is a two-way street. Ideally, attorneys educate neuropsychologists about the legal issue at hand, specific questions the expert will be asked to address, and the rules of testimony in the jurisdiction where the case is being heard. At the same time, neuropsychologists are educating attorneys about how we can contribute to cases. Together, a complex game plan for exchanging information during a trial is orchestrated.

EDUCATING ATTORNEYS ABOUT WHAT WE DO

Just like psychologists, attorneys have varied backgrounds and areas of expertise. Some may know mental health testing very well; others will not. Attorney W. Scott Liebert is an example of one who has a strong mental health background.

> *Prior to law school I had a graduate degree in elementary special education. I did a little bit of testing—I never administered tests once I was teaching, but I had familiarity with testing with kids. I worked in special education for 6 years and did some family counseling. After law school, I worked for the Department of Social Services for 5 years.* —W. Scott Liebert, Esq.

An expert working with Attorney Liebert will not have to take the time to share basic assumptions about testing theory. Other attorneys may be in the same boat as jurors—skilled in their own professions but not having access to our field's assumptions and jargon.

> *Remember that the attorney you are working with doesn't know neuropsychology like you do. When discussing the case with the person who engaged you, you need to use clear, understandable language without jargon.*—David Williamson, PhD, ABPP-CN

This concept is worth lingering on. We should immediately be disrupting traditional academic communication style in our interactions with attorneys, not waiting until we step on the witness stand. When we use clear, jargon-free, engaging communication with attorneys, we are giving them access to our knowledge as experts. We are also giving them a preview of how we are able to communicate the information in front of the trier of fact. If we can communicate a concept to them in a way that is engaging and makes good common sense, they will feel confident that we will be able to use those same skills in the courtroom.

> ***Explaining your opinions to attorneys is great practice for explaining to juries***
>
> *I worked on a case where the attorneys were new to Neuropsychology and had never tried a case with cognitive claims. I had to find a way to make my opinions understandable to the attorneys and that was great practice for making the opinions understandable to the jury.*—Desiree Byrd, PhD, ABPP-CN

William Barr notes that experts need to take the time to explain what we do with attorneys:

> *You have to sit down with attorneys, explain what you do, and explain why the other expert is not doing what you are doing. For example, the other expert is not well trained, they are giving tests that don't make sense, misinterpreting scores, and they are not giving performance validity tests. You need to spell out that discrepancy, whatever it is.*

Attorney Wayne Miller shares the value he places on experts who take the time to explain tests and interpretations in great detail:

> *Experts often don't tell us things the way that we need to know them. When an expert understands how lawyers think and is able to advise and guide in two disciplines at once, it's really valuable—like having two brains operating at once.*
>
> *I work with one expert where we might spend an entire day, over nine hours, together on the telephone going through the data piece by piece by piece. I don't understand it until he explains it to me. He will say, "Do you see how the other expert used this test to draw this conclusion? And do you see now how the data supporting the interpretation of the test is just wrong?" In one case this other side's expert had pulled out research to support a test interpretation and my expert was able to explain that the other expert just misused it completely. There is no way on God's green earth that jurors are ever going to be able to understand the misused data without some method of simplification or clear explanation—because I didn't even understand the test until he explained it to me. I didn't have access to the research until he showed it to me. In that situation, if that case had gone to trial, we were going to have a hell of a challenge in trying to explain to the jury why their expert misused the research, but based on my expert's information, I spent four hours in the deposition coming up with nugget after nugget that I would then have in hand to put together to make a cogent cross examination.*

David Hartman points out that attorneys may be used to dry, test-centered testimony by experts. Communicating with attorneys about alternative, human-centered styles of testimony allows attorneys and experts to craft a set of questions on direct testimony that elicits experts' opinions of the examinee as a person.

> *Many attorneys who have worked with neuropsychologists are probably more familiar with test-by-test testifying. Make sure that the attorney doing your direct examination is drawing you out on your opinion of the examinee as a person rather than the person as a series of test results.*—David Hartman, PhD, ABPP-CL, ABN

BEING STRAIGHTFORWARD WITH THE ATTORNEY WHO HIRED YOU

One of the most important things to realize as an expert, particularly in civil cases, is that attorneys want to win cases, but they are also running a business (or part of one). Their ability to make a living is predicated on managing risks in a case. "Managing risks" mean that they have clear, accurate information about the merits of a case. Experienced experts know that telling the attorney who hired them "straight-up" news that may not be favorable to their side's likelihood of winning provides crucial information as the attorney plans their financial strategy in a case. For example, if a neuropsychologist does not clearly disclose to the attorney the ramifications of failed performance validity tests or glosses over multiple factors other than a single, remote concussion that better account for a set of nonspecific symptoms of a plaintiff examinee in a concussion case, the attorney may proceed with the case assuming a strong set of facts from a psychological or neuropsychological perspective. The attorney may continue to put funds into the case such as hiring additional experts or creating expensive visuals for trial. When the case is lost, the attorney's financial losses are much greater than if they had decided, based on the expert's initial assessment, to either take a pass or minimize investment in the case.

When news isn't favorable, plaintiff attorneys have the luxury of saying, "Thank you very much for your assistance, Doctor; no need to write a report." Your involvement as an expert may end there. Many attorneys will ask another expert to give them a second opinion. One attorney who preferred to remain anonymous told me the story of one of his clients who had come to him complaining of terrible cognitive deficits after a mild head injury:

> *The first set of testing I got back was so positive: totally normal brain function. I didn't believe it. I sent her to someone else. That testing came back and said the same thing.*

Of course, some plaintiff attorneys will continue the process with a third, fourth, or fifth opinion until they get one that they feel furthers their goal in the case.

Defense attorneys don't typically have the luxury of a second opinion; once an evaluation of the plaintiff is conducted by their defense expert, it is generally discoverable. But they too will need clear information about the merits of a case, and the expert's straightforward communication will help them make decisions regarding settling or bring the case to trial.

I recall conducting an independent neuropsychological examination for a defense attorney with a lovely young college student who was hit by a drunk driver and sustained a severe traumatic brain injury. She was hemiparetic with multiple brain imaging findings and the expected accompanying neuropsychological deficits. I got the attorney on the phone and I said, "You know, the plaintiff neuropsychological expert was right on. She has [xyz] deficits; it is affecting her [abc]." The attorney says, "Well, I knew there would be deficits. Just don't let too many tear stains fall on your report." That attorney has hired me in subsequent cases. Honesty is valued, if not always enjoyed.

Attorney Brian Pomerantz tells the story of an expert he worked with on a case involving intellectual disability: "I didn't like his results, but I have called him ever since."

> *The psychologist told me, "I would really love to help you, but I can't. He has a lot wrong with him but he is not intellectually disabled. It would ruin my reputation if I said he was." That really upset me for that case, but do you know how many times I have called on that expert since? Because I know that if he says something is wrong, that's gold. I can trust him.*

That dog don't hunt

When an attorney calls and says, "I want to run something by you," that is fine with me. I don't want to waste anyone's time or money. When I think it is a noncredible issue, I will tell them. The Tennessee expression is "That dog don't hunt."—Kristie Nies, PhD, ABPP-CN

This is a terrible case for brain injury, but a wonderful case for everything else. Leave me out of it.

With litigants, I look at the whole case. Here's a guy who had an amputated leg. Girlfriend was killed in the accident. You have pictures that make it look like he was blown up. The attorney wants to focus on a mild TBI. All that's going to happen is you will have two fancy experts pissing and moaning about each other. In the end, he won't look like he had much of a brain injury, and the jury is going to wonder about everything else. Don't go there. Leave me out of this. This isn't a good case for brain injury, but it is a wonderful case for everything else. I turn away a modest number of patients on the review.—Tom Boll, PhD, ABPP-CN

Attorneys who are looking for straight answers will call me . . .

My opinion has become much more evidence-based with the ever-increasing body of peer-review research in neuropsychology. Consequently, I am more frequently called by defense attorneys at this point in my career. However, plaintiff attorneys who want straight answers to straight questions rather than someone who will serve an advocate for the plaintiff will also call me. —Paul L. Craig, PhD, ABPP-CN

Of course, there are some attorneys who are not happy hearing the straight truth.

If you don't aggravate at least one attorney, you aren't doing your job correctly

In one case, a large disability insurance company asked me to do an exam. I told the truth. The company comes back and says, "We think your bill was excessive for the work you did [I had never had anyone say that before or since] and therefore we are not going to pay you." I got my own attorney to get them to pay. The other side's attorney then called me as a witness. I ended up sitting there getting cross examined, uncomfortably, by the attorney who originally hired me. That, to me, is a badge of honor. I tell my students that if you don't aggravate at least one attorney when you are doing your work, then you are not doing it properly. Tell the truth. Someone is going to be unhappy. I want to be known as someone who tells the truth. —Neil Pliskin, PhD, ABPP-CN

Some experts I spoke with note that they have specific conversations with attorneys during the initial telephone call addressing the issue of "telling it like it is":

I will say to attorneys who call my office, "If you are looking for someone to further your agenda, use your words, or tell you what you want to hear, I am not the right person for you. If you want someone who will cleave to the data, and be honest and tell you whether or not you have a case, then I am your person. I am not a hired gun."—Lisa Stanford, PhD, ABPP-CN

Talk to retaining attorney about impartiality

Even before I take a case, I make a point of talking about impartiality, and ultimately telling the attorney that I will write about whatever I find. The expert has to be willing to go against the retaining attorney's interests if the findings do not support those interests. It does not matter if the attorney will never use you again. I have told plaintiff's attorneys that their clients are malingering. I have told defense attorneys that the findings are valid and indeed there is impairment. When a lawyer who has used me before comes back for another case, I make my independence clear and will tell them that again I am going to report whatever it is I find.—Mike Chafetz, PhD, ABPP-CN

DETERMINE YOUR ROLE IN THE CASE

In clinical practice, we are used to providing feedback and writing reports that address the whole person. An attorney who preferred to remain anonymous notes that the conversation he always needs to have with experts is: what is the specific legal issue in the case?

> *Experts want to go in their own direction. But in each case, there are discrete, specific issues that need to be addressed. It is so easy for an expert to do their own thing, and not address the legal question at hand. With the experts I work with, I like to say, "By the way, this is the real issue—you might as well focus on it." As an example, in a case that is all about whether the plaintiff can return to work at a bank, a very lucrative career, the neuropsychological expert might give a long report, but if that is the only question that I need the answer to, it is important that the answer is in there.*

Another way of framing the issue is, are you telling a narrative that your retaining attorney finds relevant? Darcy Cox points out that our role as experts is not to share abstract science, but to tell a story about the science that is relevant to the case:

> *You want to tell the story of the science as a whole, but specifically how it relates to the examinee. The best testimony is about how the science fits in with the specific facts in this particular case. I see a lot of people introduce our science broadly: "Here is Scientist X's work." But in each case the legal issues are different, and the legal issues are what the attorneys care about. They don't necessarily care about understanding our science as a whole. When I am working with an attorney, I want to hear as much as possible about what the legal issues are in the case so I can help them understand how our science applies in this specific situation.*

Tannahill Glen notes that there are often forces at work on cases that you know nothing about. Clear communication with the attorney who hires you is important to understand the larger context of the case.

> *There may be co-defendants, other judgments in other phases of the trial that you know nothing about. Speak at length with anyone who hired you.*

LEARN THE GROUND RULES OF COMMUNICATION IN THE JURISDICTION

In thinking about the two-way street of communication between attorneys and experts, one very important set of information experts need from attorneys is the ground rules for how the expert will function in the particular jurisdiction. Depending on the state, county, federal-versus-state jurisdiction, and many other variables, rules for how experts operate are different. The conversation with an attorney who hires you should always begin with asking for the basic ground rules. Discoverability of communication is a case in point.

Be careful what you communicate in writing to attorneys

> *I have learned to be very careful about how to communicate with attorneys via email since what one conveys could very well become discoverable in court.*—Nat Nelson, PhD, ABPP-CN

> *I have learned to be careful with all communication related to a case. I was a new user of a performance validity test and had some email communication with the author of the test. I learned the hard way to be careful about what I revealed to the attorneys. The author did not want the emails shared with the attorneys. I didn't want to lie and say I didn't have them. This could have been avoided. I took a metaphorical beating, but did not disclose the emails.*—Kristie Nies, PhD, ABPP-CN

Another important issue is limitations on the types of issues a psychologist is allowed to opine on in some states. For example, some states do not allow psychologists to offer opinions regarding medical causality (e.g. a concussion was caused by the motor vehicle accident in question). Careful wording, such as "the medical and other records are consistent with a concussion" or "not consistent with a concussion," is required to have an opinion admitted.

> *You don't go in and do salsa dancing at a rave. You have to know the rules/the steps of the dance. What are the parameters of what you can testify about; what do they need in terms of areas of content? Different state courts may have different procedural elements and restrictions. For example, a number of states, including Virginia where I practice, do not permit non-physicians to offer an opinion of your findings in terms of medical causality. If you are trying to offer an opinion you think is really important (e.g., you feel that the accident caused or not caused the injury), you may not be permitted to offer that opinion. Not only may you not be allowed to offer that opinion, but there may be a hearing outside of your presence that redlines certain statements in your report, not allowing you to make reference to certain opinions.*—Ted Peck, PhD, ABPP-CN

Forbidden words . . .

> In Virginia, you are frequently confronted with limitations on the use of certain words. In some Court jurisdictions, experts cannot use the word "malingering" in any way, shape, or form. If you are talking about failure of PVTs and you use the

term "malingering" in your report, your report might have severe limitations ordered by a judge, in a hearing in which you did not participate, in which the court reviewed the report and made a decision to redline or exclude certain statements made in said report. If I am asked to list which tests I have administered on the stand, I can't say the title "Test of Memory Malingering"; I have to use the acronym "TOMM" instead. On cross:

Q: Doctor, which performance validity test did you use?

A: I would be happy to answer that question, but I have been asked not to use certain terms.—Ted Peck, PhD, ABPP-CN

SHAPING OPINIONS

We are all recipients and manufacturers of various forms of "spin" or attempts to shape an opinion by framing an issue in a favorable way. As a child I always found that being the first one to "explain" a fight between my sisters and me to my mother led to me ending up in less trouble. Attorneys are ethically bound to advocate vigorously on behalf of their clients, and attempting to shape the opinions of experts is one way they do so. The shaping may be unconscious, as the story of the case is told to the expert from the perspective of the plaintiff or defendant. In other cases, the shaping may be more conscious as the attorney explicitly asks for changes in the expert's opinion that are more favorable to the case.

> *You have to be careful. Attorneys will try to shape your opinion. They are so subtle about it: "Now, I'm not trying to tell you what to say, but . . ."*—Keith Yeates, PhD, ABPP-CN

> *I try and not think too much of attorneys' expectations of me. I don't want to have their expectations bias me. I will talk to them in detail about the results, prognosis, and so forth. They will often want me to make it worse than it is or less worse than it is. They are constantly asking questions to shape or bias me into saying what they want me to say. Oftentimes I will get to a place where I say, "You know, the likelihood is going to be this, but I can't be exactly sure." And they always come back with, "Well, within a reasonable degree of medical certainty could you say . . ."*—Greg Lee, PhD, ABPP-CN

Attorney Brian Pomerantz notes that he specifically schedules time to speak with his experts just prior to conducting an assessment of his client and just after the assessment has been conducted, but prior to the opinion being formed. As he works on capital cases, with clients incarcerated at remote prisons, he uses the opportunity to drive experts to and from the remote sites to discuss the case:

> *A lot of these prisons are far away. They are built in the middle of nowhere. Sometimes you fly in and then have to drive hours to the prison. After one prison kicked us out at 2 p.m., my expert and I then had the whole afternoon before we went back the*

next day to do further evaluation. We had dinner at the hotel together. Right after an expert evaluates a defendant, that is valuable time. I always try to schedule time with my expert right after the evaluation. Let me drive you to the airport, let me have dinner with you, because I want to be able to hear your immediate impressions. And frankly, I want to be able to have my input before you fully form your opinions. Well, what about this? I have to spend time with you right after. I want to be able to dialogue with you and have my input.

A lot of time that dialogue goes in a different direction that I originally wanted. In one expert's case, I said, "Well, what about this?" And she said, "We don't have that. I know you want that, but we don't have that. It's depression." And I said, "But we can't win on depression." She said, "Yes, we can." And she was right. We had a 90-minute debate on the ride to the airport from the prison. As counsel, you sometimes need to give up your idea of what it is when an expert says, "It's not, and I can't give it to you credibly." You have to give it up. You may not want to give it up. In some cases, you may want to find another expert.

Darcy Cox notes that the shaping behavior goes both ways:

The attorney is telling the narrative from the minute he/she contacts you. Here is a summary of the case . . . Your interaction with an attorney becomes a negotiation about the story in the case.

In the best of situations, the dialogue between an attorney and expert becomes like Winnicott's idea of shared play, or the type of authentic shared communication that occurs in improv. The attorney holds up a story. The expert takes the story and says, "Yes, and . . ." The attorney tries that refined story out. Repeat.

GETTING "CROSSED" BY YOUR OWN ATTORNEY

Attorneys may forget, or "forget," important aspects of their expert's opinions and attempt to shape their opinions at trial. Darcy Cox tells the story of being essentially cross examined by the attorney who brought her to the case, on direct examination:

In this one case, a person was shot in the head. He and his buddies pulled out the bullet with a pair of pliers because he didn't want to go to the hospital. It turned out it was not a penetrating brain injury; it was probably not a brain injury at all. I was working with one of my favorite lawyers. I told him, "You have to understand, I cannot go on the stand and say this guy had a brain injury." Pretrial, he agreed not to bring up the brain injury. But on the stand, he tried to take me there unwillingly. On direct, I was actually being cross examined by my own retaining attorney. His gamble was that I would just roll over. It ended up working out well. It was a U.S. Federal court. The judge said to me, "Are you going anywhere with this?" And I said, "No, Your Honor, because there is nowhere to go." And the judge said, "OK, Counselor, move along."

Jerry Sweet tells a story of an attorney who was using him and his status as a psychologist as a vehicle for bringing in humiliating information likely to force a plaintiff to settle the case:

> *Sometimes within a case attorneys try to get you to collude with them. That is, an attorney may ask you not to express certain ideas or certain information as part of your opinion. Or the attorney may want you to say something you do not believe is accurate. I recall a case many years ago in which there was an allegation of injury associated with TBI. The defense attorney who had retained me said, midway through the case preparation, "Now, I understand that this woman has had an abortion. I am assuming that as a psychologist you are going to say something about that." He wanted to make that a big part of my opinion. The plaintiff was a staunch Catholic and was humiliated by the fact that she had an abortion. I said to the attorney that I didn't think it was at all relevant. I also told him that I was not going to bring it up and thought it would be wrong to do that. During the deposition, he asked me related questions. I made it clear on the record I thought the issue had no bearing on what was going on. This was the attorney who had retained me. A week or so goes by and I hear the case has settled. The plaintiff's attorney called me and was crying on the phone about why they settled. The other attorney had bullied both of them with this information about the abortion. It was shocking to me to hear that the attorney, knowing full well my opinion as a psychologist was quite different than his own, still intended to somehow make the plaintiff's abortion history part of the case. All I could say was that I was very sorry to hear of this and that I actually had told the retaining attorney that the abortion didn't matter.*—Jerry Sweet, PhD, ABPP-CN

PRETRIAL PREPARATION

Judges, attorneys, and experts were almost unanimous in stressing the importance of spending time in a pretrial conference.

> *The most important lesson is preparation. People worry about, "How will I do on the stand?" Preparation is everything. If you and the attorney who is asking the questions aren't on the same page, you won't understand the questions they are asking. For example, they will have narrow questions that they are looking for narrow answers to and broad questions where they are looking for broad answers. And you both should be clear about the way you plan to answer the questions so they are not surprised by your testimony on the stand.*—Ira K. Packer, PhD, ABPP (Forensic)

Without attorney prep, I spend too much time speaking

> *If I don't know where the attorney is going with the question, I tend to speak too much. Some attorneys do a lot of preparation. They let me know what questions they will be asking; others don't. If I don't know where they are going with a question, I might spend too much time heading in a direction that is not important for their strategy and I run the risk of looking like I am lecturing.*—Robert Mendoza, PsyD

I want to make sure I share a synopsis of the major issues in the case with the attorney in pretrial preparation. What are the issues I need to get across? I literally number them, in order of importance.—Scott Millis, PhD, ABPP-CN

I have worked with some very good attorneys who spent a lot of time with me in preparation for trial. They did not want me to be surprised. The goal of the hours of preparation was for me to be very clear about where they were going with the questions that they planned to ask, rather than them trying to shape my opinions.—Desiree Byrd, PhD, ABPP-CN

Because the perils of walking into a case without preparation for the expert are many, some experts ask about the attorney's practices around pretrial preparation before agreeing to take a case:

Being productive for a jury begins prior to the courtroom. It involves multiple conversations with a willing attorney about what direct and cross will be like. Some attorneys say just, "See you in court!" Others will come to your office for 6 hours. We will bang out what direct will look like, what cross will look like, how we might respond to cross. In those situations, I can get into a cadence with the attorney, what the conversation in the courtroom will look like.

It is prudent to ask the attorney right in the beginning—prior to any records review—about how they like to prepare experts for court. Get a sense of whether they will spend the necessary time. I recently had a case where the prep consisted of a half-hour phone consult. He asked if I had any visual aids for the jury and if I had an outline already done.

Attorney Brian Pomerantz insists that experts participate in pre-testimonial preparation because he wants to hear them think on their feet, hear their answers to questions, and, most importantly, hear what they think are better questions:

Prepping shouldn't just be experts saying, "Send me questions for direct." I refuse. I won't just send a set of questions. I want to hear your answers. I want to hear how you are on your feet, not after you have read it and thought about it for 10 minutes. One thing I love about working with seasoned experts, they say to me, "You are asking the wrong question; here is the question you want to ask." Because my expert is the expert. They know more than I will ever know about their area of expertise, by a thousandfold. You tell me what questions I need to ask to get the answer I need. Tell me how to frame it. I have no ego here. This isn't about me. The expert is a tool to help me win my case. I am happy when I win, not when my questions are used. If an expert wants to tell me 100% of the questions I need to ask to win my case, as far as I am concerned, I am a genius. Because I hired the right expert, I won.

Experts should be comfortable demanding that they are properly prepared. How many times have I prepared an expert and they tll me that the last time they went to trial they met the attorney 15 minutes prior. Experts should be comfortable saying, "Look, I am not coming unless you spend an hour with me to prepare me for testimony."- Attorney, anonymous

----

During the pretrial conference, many attorneys want a written treatise, what exactly you are going to say, so they can be 100% clear about how to elicit that story by them asking questions. Some attorneys don't make the time for those types of conferences, and testimony usually doesn't go well. They may have an idea on how they want to present things, but you don't know what that is. Having that become apparent on the stand is not a good thing.—Bernice Marcopulos, PhD, ABPP-CN

Attorney Brian Pomerantz notes that lack of pretrial preparation may constitute malpractice for both the attorney and expert:

You have to prepare your expert. If you are putting them on the stand, it is malpractice for both of you not to do a live run-through ahead of time. If I can't fly out, I can spend a long time on the phone. Or fly them out to where they will testify a day early.

SPECIFIC QUESTIONS TO ADDRESS DURING PRETRIAL PREPARATION

Given the importance of pretrial preparation, it makes sense for neuropsychology experts to go into those sessions with a specific agenda. Here is a set of questions compiled from advice of both seasoned experts and attorneys:

1. **What is the other side's argument, and how is this likely to come up on cross examination?**

   Experts should be asking the attorney to prepare them for the cross examination because the expert is not necessarily going to know what the other side's angle is going to be in the case. The attorney who is trying to put forward this expert does not do their job very well if they do not also say, "Look, this is opposing counsel's theory of the case in relation to your expertise. How would you answer this question? How would you answer that question?" If the attorney doesn't offer that information and prepare their expert, the expert should be asking, "What's the other side's argument?"—Kate Nemens, Esq.

2. **Here is my take on the relative weaknesses of my opinion. How should we address this on direct, and how do you think the opposing counsel will address this on cross?**

   In a conference with the attorney, I will want to bring up the cross-examining questions I have in my head: "If I am going after me, here's some of the ways I would do it." They know who the other attorney is—he might be really sharp. They are more aware of the context than I ever will be.—David Williamson, PhD, ABPP-CN

In my own practice, I will bring up possible cross-examination questions and suggest questions the attorney could ask me on redirect. For example, "The opposing attorney may bring up this study. If s/he does, ask me about this issue on redirect; I will explain the reason that particular study is not relevant/was flawed."

It is important to be clear about how perceived weaknesses in your own exam are handled on direct, so by the time you get to cross, the weaknesses are not a problem. You have already dealt with them on the direct. As an example, if you have a messy case, where you are convinced from external, collateral sources that the person you evaluated has impairment, but during the evaluation they suppress effort, you have to be able to explain to a jury on direct that poor effort on a neuropsychological evaluation does not necessarily mean there is not an underlying impairment. To expand on that ahead of time during direct is important as opposed to being confronted by it for the first time on cross examination.—Anonymous

3. **What is the composition of the jury?**

When I am testifying in courtrooms around the state of Alaska, I am testifying to people with highly variable levels of education and literacy. Likewise, Alaska Natives come from a very different cultural background than me. I like to ask the attorney who invited me to testify a few questions about the jury so I can better understand the people to whom I am presenting my testimony. I get a brief description of the jurors and their respective backgrounds. If there is an apparent "leader of the jury" I want to know about that person so I can be sure to establish and maintain rapport while testifying.—Paul L. Craig, PhD, ABPP-CN

I will ask about the composition of the jury. Attorneys spend a lot of energy picking juries. Sometimes they feel happy about the jury for a particular reason, or unhappy because of a particular reason. For instance, in a death penalty case defense attorneys who end up with a jury of conservative Republicans, they will assume the jury will not be sympathetic. Or in civil case, you hear, "I wanted mothers and grandmothers" for this case. It helps to know the composition of the jury before you sit down in front of the jury. They might tell you about what they have noticed about the jury. The elderly man in the corner is napping. The blue-haired lady will nod intently when you make eye contact with her. Attorneys can convey soft information about the composition of the jury that allows you to think about the way you will communicate with that jury. Geriatric? Gen-Xers? There are different cultural, political, age, "you name it" compositions, and to think about that ahead of time makes sense.—Anonymous

4. **Tell me about the judge.**

I will ask counsel in advance what they think of the judge and how to handle things. Some judges are more sympathetic than others. "What do you know about this judge and what strategies do you want me to use to handle it? Do you want me to offer more explanation or less? Is the judge going to get irritable if I talk too much?"—Nick Bogod, R.Psych

See Chapter 20, "Specific Testifying Situations," for a detailed discussion of issues to consider when testifying in front of a judge as opposed to a jury.

5. **Who is the other attorney? What is their style?**

Who is the opposing attorney? What is their style—polite, deferential, or argumentative? The attorneys may do a number of things in deposition to get a sense of how you will react on the stand. Have you had experience with this attorney? What are they like? If you have a fairly experienced attorney, civil, they have been up against an opposing attorney in the past. They will have insight into how that individual prepares their end of the case. Have seven or eight other neuropsychologists been hired? Is this an individual who hires a psychiatrist or neurologist to consult? Or do they handle the cross without other expert consultation?—Anonymous

----

I ask what the other attorney is like. Are they aggressive? Begin questions with, "you would agree with me that..."? That type of information is helpful for me as I prepare for cross examination.—Robert Heilbronner, PhD, ABPP-CN

6. **Who are the experts on the opposing side, and what are they expected to say?**

If other experts are testifying that may be disagreeing with your opinion, it is important to know that. How can we anticipate what the disagreement will be and head it off proactively? How do we address that? For example, a neurologist who diagnoses a post-concussive syndrome but uses no standardized testing, no SVTs, no premorbid activities, how can we disagree with the other opinions and explain why in a respectful manner?—Anonymous

7. **Are there any more records that I haven't seen?**

Records accrue in a case months after the expert's report has been finalized. Many attorneys will place experts on a distribution list, and as new records come in, the records are mailed to them as a matter of course. Scott Bender points out that it is wise to ask if there are any other records you haven't yet seen. If the attorney who retained you has received them in the mail, you may be asked about them on cross examination. Even if you didn't read them, they may ask why you didn't or imply that you should have.

8. **How should we introduce me as an expert?**

Chapter 4, "Establishing Credentials and Credibility," makes the argument in favor of clearly targeted questions designed to help jurors understand why an expert's opinion is relevant and credible. An important part of the pretrial conference is curating the list of questions so jurors are not subjected to hearing an expert's entire curriculum vitae.

9. **How do you want to communicate the narrative of the assessment? Are there other experts who will explain certain concepts before I go on the stand?**

In my own practice, as the attorney who brought me to the case and I discuss the flow of information, we will plan natural places in the narrative where I will stop talking and the attorney will ask another question. If there are other experts, we will discuss what information they will be presenting so I am not repeating information.

10. **How is the trial going so far?**

Depending on the timing, this type of question may be asked at a second pretrial conference, once the trial has started.

I ask the attorneys if there is anything I need to know, any new testimony that brought out information of which I was not aware, or if this judge really dislikes this kind of stuff. I say, "What do I need to know to be of assistance here?" This judge has an attention span of 5 seconds; the jury is already half asleep. I do like to know if possible about the juries. Who have they heard? Am I the first expert in my field to talk? I recall in one case there was unmistakable symptom magnification on the MMPI. Another expert tried to explain that away by saying the patient was tired or fatigued. I had already commented on VRIN and TRIN scores in writing. The hiring attorney had gotten the other expert to admit that it was not likely fatigue, so I did not have to belabor that.—Jacobus Donders, PhD, ABPP-CN

DEVIATING FROM THE PLAN

Of course, regardless of the number of hours spent on preparation, attorneys almost always deviate from the plan in a trial.

Preparing with attorneys prior to testifying is always desirable, and I always push for that. You may go through your testimony question by question: what you will be asked, what you will be saying, how it will be communicated. But nine times out of ten, the lawyers don't stay with those questions. I suspect it is because good trial lawyers think quickly, and they think quickly on their feet. If you are at a pretrial conference, and it is a relaxed situation without anxiety, I don't think they are necessarily at their best. Most do ask me, "How is the best way to lay this out?" I will tell them that a particular sequence will probably make most sense to the jurors. But once they are at trial, they think of something else, or in the context of what has been testified to so far at trial, I will say something and that will raise a question for them and they will follow up on that and break the original sequence of questions, in order to make sure the trier of fact understands my testimony.—Robert L. Denney, PsyD, ABPP-CN, FP

FINALLY,

As experts, we need to maintain perspective that to the attorney who brought us, we are one part of a complex case, and we do not always know what is at play in the larger context of the trial. For example, attorney Brian Pomerantz notes that he occasionally has to switch gears in mid-hearing and begin playing to the appeal:

> *I sometimes realize mid-hearing I am going to lose, and I begin playing to the court of appeal. I have to think ahead. When I am going to lose in the district court, sometimes in the middle of the hearing I know I am going to lose, so I start playing to the appellate court. That isn't something my experts need to worry about.*

It is important to keep in mind that we are guests in the courtroom, required to follow rules we may never have heard of, in an often fluid context we may not fully understand. Establishing and maintaining a strong working relationship with the attorney who does understand the rules and contexts of the courtroom is an important component of productive testimony.

In the next chapter, we enter the courtroom for the credentialing phase of direct testimony.

4 Establishing Credentials and Person Centered Credibility

THE COURT CALLS DR . . . .

After being sworn in and seated, the attorney begins the qualifying process, asking a series of questions about education, training, and experience. In most situations, this occurs in front of the jury. Who are you? What is a neuropsychologist or psychologist? What are your qualifications to be an expert in this particular case? Based on your specialized education, training, or practical experience in the subject matter laid out in the questioning process, the attorney will ask the court to admit you as an expert witness. How the credentialing is conducted and how you conduct yourself during the credentialing process is an opportunity to build credibility for the jurors or triers of fact. It is important to realize that an expert may be credentialed, but the credentialing process does not automatically translate to credibility in the eyes of the jurors.

PERSON CENTERED CREDIBILITY

Judge Lynne Battaglia points out an important difference in how scientists and courtrooms view credibility. She notes that judges and juries tend to think of credibility as hinging on the truthfulness and other personal qualities of the witness. In contrast, academics tend to think of credibility as hinging almost entirely on the soundness/ credibility of their research methods or assessment tools. This can be a startling realization for psychologists and neuropsychologists who are trained to think about credibility in terms of methods rather than the people explaining the methods. Viewing credibility as also "person centered" is a fundamental shift for many of us.

Neuropsychologists and psychologists seasoned in clinical work may have an intuitive understanding of person-centered credibility, generalizing years of experience establishing a personal connection as a first step in setting the stage for their patients to hear and accept their diagnoses and recommendations. Rod Swenson likens establishing credibility in the courtroom to the type of rapport clinicians attempt to establish with patients in their office:

> *It's like when I have a family in my office. I want them to know who I am, what I've done. I want them to know I was thorough. When they are in my office, they should feel like they are the only people I am thinking about. They need to develop a trust in me, because what I am telling them is changing their life. A jury is making a decision that can have an enormous impact on someone's life. You have to be confident, and they have to trust you.*

Just as earlier chapters make the argument for disrupting an academic communication style in our roles as expert witnesses, this chapter makes an argument for shedding a sole focus on an academic, "research-method" definition of credibility. As credibility is built during the expert's time on both direct and cross examination, this chapter will cover the general topic of credibility during all stages of testimony, including the credentialing phase. The discussion of credibility continues in and Chapter 5, "Relationship with the Jury," and Chapter 6, "Social Pragmatics of Testifying."

NOT JUST READING A CV

The credentialing phase could go like this:

> *Q: Doctor, is this your CV?*
> *A: Yes.*
> *Q: Doctor, where were you educated?*
> *A: I earned my undergraduate degree at the University of X and my PhD at the University of Y.*
> *Q: Did you complete an internship?*

I am bored writing this vignette so I stopped at the internship, but the expert in question would probably be asked to explain her postdoctoral fellowship and work sites from fellowship to the present before she is asked about her books and research publications. And the APA committees she chaired over the past 10 years. And the hospital committees she sits on. And the presentations she has given at national conferences.

I feel sorry for the hypothetical jury. They are bored and they are alienated. Here is the fundamental Catch-22 of the credentialing stage of testimony. To be admitted as an expert, a person has to have knowledge and experiences that members of the jury don't have. But people don't necessarily like or trust people who are too different from themselves. A long recitation of impressive education tells jurors that the expert is well educated, but jurors still don't know if the expert is credible. The entire country has been subjected for years to the CNN split screen-style argument among eminent experts who cite studies and statistics contradicting one another. When two or more experts all have impressive CVs, the decision about which expert's opinion is credible has to rest on other factors.

Lisa McDermott, a mitigation specialist, tells me how ineffective she suspects the typical credentialing process is:

> *The first part of any testimony is often a review of the expert's curriculum vitae to qualify her to testify. Lawyers often belabor this, boring the jurors or making the expert appear more like a "hired gun" than a subject-matter specialist.*

Robert Mendoza describes the problem this way:

> *After you've detailed this long CV of all of these expensive days of training, you are not going to sound like a guy someone would want to have a beer with. The first part of my testimony is an attempt to let jurors know that behind the CV is someone who could be their next-door neighbor. . . . By making eye contact with them, being deferential, not using technical terms, saying "thank you," "excuse me," and "would you please repeat something," I let them see that I am a person who values quality social interactions and not just somebody that has spent a ton of time in school.*

One way to reduce the alienating aspect of credentialing is to reduce the length of the process. Experts can work with attorneys to curate the set of questions the attorney will ask about their qualifications. What in this long academic education process and clinical career is relevant to this case? What information about my background will help you, the jurors, make a good decision about whether I have experience that is relevant to what you need to know to make your decision in this case? Glenn Larrabee comments, "When being credentialed, I don't want to put everything from my CV in there. I want to hit the highlights without being overwhelming."

Another benefit of working with attorneys to ensure that they are asking questions targeted to the most relevant aspects of your CV is that you will not have to "toot your own horn" later in testimony about research you've conducted, books you've written, or other professional activities that relate to your testimony; it's already out there.

> *I let other people ask me about my research. Some attorneys will ask during preparation, "Is there anything in your background that you think is relevant to this case?" And I will say, "Look at abstract #10." I want the relevant things that I have done and written about brought out during the credentialing process, so I don't have to stand up in court and say, "I've done all this. I've written all that." I don't want to share the information in a way that looks like I am tooting my own horn.*—Neil Pliskin, PhD, ABPP-CN

Throughout the chapter we will look at ways in which we can raise our credibility by disrupting inaccessible communication habits, being human, showing empathy, and not being arrogant. A word of caution, though: Keep it real. Judge Allison Burroughs points out that attempts to "fake" human qualities are transparent:

> Different experts come across as arrogant or unlikeable in different ways, and experts seem to come across as unlikeable way more than regular witnesses do. I am sure a lot of them are lovely people, but they often just come across as arrogant. One of the things that I've seen experts do is a contrived effort to look humble and self-effacing. It really doesn't come off very well.
>
> *Q: Dr. Expert, what did you do next in your career?*
>
> *A: Well, next I was lucky enough to be appointed a full professor at Harvard. And then I am humbled to say that I was able to do such and such . . .*
>
> You just want to roll yours eyes at them.

ELEMENTS OF PERSON-CENTERED CREDIBILITY

Someone you would trust in real life

Judge Christina Harms defines a credible witness as someone whom jurors or judges would feel comfortable consulting in their own personal life:

> *When a witness gets their back up or gets irritated or takes the bait during cross examination, it hurts their credibility. Ideally what you want to feel from a witness is a mature human being who seems grounded with a reasonable sense of self, someone who you'd feel comfortable consulting in your own personal life, because they are that capable, grounded, and centered. You want the expert to come across as somebody who you would admire professionally. You lose that, of course, if the expert has a short fuse or seems very full of themselves.*

Likability and warmth

Part of that comfort with an expert or professional arises from empathy and warmth. Nat Nelson points out:

> *Being oneself and conveying a spirit of sincerity toward others, regardless of the role in which one operates (e.g., clinician, expert, researcher), is an important part of effective practice. Advocating for objectivity in one's forensic role does not mean that one must surrender positive regard for the well-being of others. Relating to others with warmth, empathy, and respect is essential to building rapport irrespective of the evaluation setting.*
>
> ------------
>
> *No one cares what you know until they know that you care. Bringing in the personal side of what we do is so important. To be human is important. It's hard to make someone out as a hired gun if the jurors see you as a real person. I teach full time. In terms of getting students to pay attention to you, I know the content isn't the only*

important thing. It matters whether they like you. That determines whether they will listen to you.—Anonymous

This is an excellent point. What do we mean when we say we like someone? We feel the person is trustworthy, has something to say, is credible.

Don't forget that likability and warmth are important to people. They can't stop themselves from judging you on that, or at least coming to an opinion on you about that.—Marcus Boccaccini, PhD

Judge Burroughs provides a similar perspective:

> *When I was a prosecutor, I wanted an expert that I liked and trusted, because I don't love arrogant people and I don't like people that are slick. I wanted my question and answer of the witness to sound like a discussion that we might have over a cup of coffee. And I wanted a witness that could communicate with me conversationally, because that's my style in front of a jury.*

Show you are human

As we discussed in Chapter 1, it is easy to view highly credentialed scientific experts as monolithic, even within our own profession. Knowing a few human facts about someone shatters that reflexive tendency. We relax with the person: Of course it makes sense that they have kids and watch TV! Rus Bauer will invite attorneys to ask him a question or two about something personal in order to feel more human to jurors:

> *The attorney might ask additional questions about my background or where I am from. Rather than just a list of places I have worked. I like to say something personal about myself, like I am a Gators fan or I like to bike ride. I try to coach my attorneys to ask a question that might enable me to say something personal about myself. Younger attorneys who are going by the book might ask you to basically just read lines of your CV, so I ask attorneys to give me a lead-in.*

John Kirk also tries to make a personal connection, noting it makes you seem like a "real person":

> *"In addition to being a neuropsychologist., I am a father of two kids."*

Of course, balance is advisable. Kyle Boone offers a word of caution about bringing in aspects of her personal life: "I do not generally talk about my personal life. I worry that if that door is open, the opposing attorney might ask me anything about my personal life."

The use of humor is discussed further in Chapter 6, "Social Pragmatics of Testifying." Paul Craig comments that humor can be a way to be perceived as more human by the jury rather than as a disengaged scientist:

I like to use humor when I can. The best example I can think of from my experiences as an expert witness involved testifying at the request of plaintiff counsel in a significant TBI case—a well-documented brain injury with fairly good recovery but some persistent deficits, particularly nonverbal and visual spatial deficits. The defense started their cross. I always like to find a place to inject some appropriate humor to lighten up the mood a bit—humor that is not offensive or defensive. It lets the jury know I am human. This helps improve credibility and takes me out of the role of looking like an arrogant know-it-all expert and puts me in the role of a human being who is using common sense combined with scientific research to reach an expert opinion. The interaction with defense counsel progressed as follows:

Q: Dr. Craig, were you aware that this particular individual rode a snow machine down the Kuskokwim River 80 miles by himself during the winter after his injury?

A: I certainly hope that it was during the winter.

Even the defense counsel laughed along with the jurors and others in the courtroom.

Nancy Hebben agrees that occasionally using humor can be a positive: "In general, I want to come across as a person to the jury. I treat the situation with seriousness, but it's okay to smile and occasionally make a lighter comment."

Be confident

A judge who preferred to have her name redacted stressed the importance of confidence for establishing credibility:

> *Confidence is probably the most important part of courtroom demeanor. As a judge, I watch witnesses and can tell when an expert is confident. A confident witness projects that he or she knows the subject matter of the testimony. When you are not confident, it comes across. Some scientist experts are, by nature, self-questioning; their self-doubt is part of their DNA. It's part of their training; it's why they are scientists . . . But in the courtroom, questioning a conclusion or an idea has to be done in a way that doesn't project weakness, just thoughtfulness. In other words, the self-doubt that goes along with being a scientist has to be managed when the scientist is a witness.*

This point is worth emphasizing. Part of our drilled-in academic communication style is emphasizing doubts, uncertainty, and caveats about our work. When we talk about our doubts to colleagues, they understand that we are crossing our t's and dotting our i's, but we wouldn't be discussing the main finding in the first place unless we had significant confidence in the research. Members of the general public don't necessarily understand this assumption, however, so self-doubt must be contextualized: "The data overwhelmingly support this conclusion . . ."

Know the facts

Part of a confident, credible presentation is knowing the facts of the case cold. Attorney Sara Cohbra stresses that knowing the facts of the case is impressive to fact-finders:

> *Juries and judges are impressed when an expert has command of the facts of the case upon which the expert is basing her conclusions. It is important for the expert to know who described the client's behavior in a particular way, or which teacher observed problems with the client. Was it in elementary school or middle school when the client had the problem? Having a good command of the facts makes the fact-finder feels like the expert knows what she is talking about.*
>
> ------------
>
> *Credibility is about accuracy. When you make a misstep, someone can dwell on that. It is a wedge: "Well, you got this wrong. You got that wrong. Why should we think you are being careful or accurate?" Most folks, when they are back on their heels, it will get worse and worse. You will feel that way, you will be in trouble. Neuropsychologists should be comfortable with their data. Accurate. They should be comfortable that they haven't made mistakes. As a profession, neuropsychologists are more susceptible to this than other professions because they run a lot of numbers. There is a lot of testing. The probability of putting something in incorrectly is higher. The key is to make sure you accurately state the information you get, because credibility is so important.-Attorney, anonymous*

Chapter 15, "Cross Examination" discusses strategies for coping with errors in data or testimony.

Work harder

Closely related to whether we have an accurate, detailed command of the facts in the case is how hard we are willing to work. Credibility is enhanced when an expert is willing to put a substantial amount of time into a case.

> ***Be honest and competent and work hard***
>
> *I have three take-home points for testifying: Work hard; be honest; be competent. I try to work harder than the other expert. For example, in one case, I had gone in with my fellow to see a prisoner in jail. Both of us were with the prisoner one day from 9 a.m. to 3 p.m. and the next day from 9 a.m. to 1 p.m. The other expert had spent 2.5 hours with the prisoner, a seemingly inadequate amount of time for such a complex case. The other expert forgot there was a sign-in and sign-out sheet which later contradicted his trial testimony that he had been there for 6 hours. The sign-in and sign-out sheet was blown up at trial, at which time the expert had*

to admit he had not spent 6 hours there after all.— Christopher Grote, PhD, ABPP-CN

Attorney Sara Cohbra, who works with teams of attorneys in death penalty mitigation cases, makes the point that credibility arises from an extraordinarily thorough assessment. Her team provides resources for psychologists and neuropsychologists to engage in that type of highly detailed assessment:

> *The attorney's job is to help prepare experts to testify truthfully and credibly, and the first step is to give them resources to prepare an opinion that is defendable and reliable. In death penalty mitigation defense, we provide our experts with a lot of background materials. We gather records that precede and are contemporaneous to the time of the crime. The expert is evaluating the client now, in preparation for litigation, but the purpose of the evaluation is not only to understand current functioning (as an expert would do in evaluating someone for treatment) but also to understand the client's functioning in the past. We gather records to inform and support the expert's opinion. For example, we collect evidence including medical records, school records, and information from friends, teachers, and neighbors. We get statements from as many people as we can who can describe the client's behavior during relevant time periods. We need to do that so our experts feel confident coming to an opinion about functioning at a particular time, and having evidence to back up that opinion. Our expert must have this background information in order to offer a credible opinion that our client had organic deficits from childhood, or exhibited symptoms of mental disorder long before the crime.*
>
> *We also provide experts with the opportunity to meet with and evaluate clients on more than one occasion, over a period of time, so the expert has an opportunity to assess if the client's symptoms are waxing and waning or if the symptoms are more fixed. We want the expert to be able to say on the stand, "I saw the client one day, and when tested, he performed in this range. Then I tested him again 7 months later and the test results were consistent."*
>
> *Additionally, we often provide experts with the opportunity to talk to other people in addition to the client. For example, the client's siblings and parents may provide information that is helpful, and also may demonstrate similar behavioral or functional deficits that suggest a biological or genetic predisposition to the client's illness. The expert can gather richer information from a variety of sources than simply basing her opinion on what the client is telling her. In a criminal case, and particularly a death penalty case, the client is considered inherently unreliable, so additional information is necessary to corroborate what the client says. All of these parts of preparation lead to a comprehensive evaluation that in turn leads to credibility on the witness stand.*

Atelier versus Factory

The type of comprehensive assessment Attorney Cobhbra describes is in some ways the opposite of the brief, circumscribed psychological and neuropsychological assessments that our modern medical system increasingly demands. Rather than a factory, the highly credible expert's place of business can be thought of as a workshop or atelier. Each case is unique. The time required to carefully examine all of the records, sometimes dating years prior to the case, in hand and the time to conduct a thorough assessment, on multiple occasions if necessary, is expended; the expert is thoughtful about seeking additional data if needed and corroborating information in the unique context of the case. As most expert witnesses have clinical practices in medical settings where 24-hour turnaround times are necessary for patient care, engaging in forensic expert witness work demands that we consciously step into a workshop/atelier mode of assessment, and then step back out. Attorney Wayne Miller puts it this way: "Neuropsychology, for sure, there is science to it. But there is also an art and a craft. Like anything else, you really have to have a loving touch to what you do, a work ethic about what you do. And you have to sweat the details."

Come from a place of integrity

Paul Craig draws a clear connection between integrity and credibility:

> *If on cross I am asked a question that requires an answer that is not supportive of the case of the attorney who retained me, I will answer honestly rather than slipping into an advocacy role. I will not try to avoid the question or obscure the answer. I certainly will not give a deceptive or scientifically incorrect answer. When I answer hard questions transparently and honestly, it improves my credibility in the court. If I allow myself to slip into an advocacy role, that suggests I am slanted to one side or another, and my credibility declines accordingly.*

> ***Having a point of view vs. becoming an advocate***
>
> *As a judge, sometimes it is clear that the expert has not entertained any other possibility other than the one s/he is putting forward, and one feels like the expert has sold their soul. I had a case where the psychologist witness was just so convinced that this woman was a victim of battery, terrible battery, at the hands of a boyfriend, but the cross examination really made her look silly and quite firmly established that she had been bamboozled. Sure, the client was sympathetic. But experts need to ask yourselves, "Am I becoming blinded by my sympathy for the client, or my identification with the client? Am I becoming an advocate for the client?" Which you don't want to do. Rather, you just want to say, "I am here to talk to you about the science of what I know and what I've found out about this person, but I am not invested in the fight, I'm not." That's a really important thing, because conveying that you've lost your objectivity is a killer. There have been several cases that I can think of where I had clearly well-intentioned, clearly thoughtful, clearly pretty bright psychologists on the stand, but they had lost all objectivity and were just there to help their client persuade me of a given agenda and had clearly taken a role in the fight before me.*— Judge Christina Harms

Judge Battaglia stresses that in addition to lack of bias, integrity in expert witnesses is also about their genuine commitment and passion in a particular area of study. In her previous role as U.S. Attorney,

> *I used to have to get experts to defend the United States because we represent the National Institute of Health in any medical malpractice case. I was interested in finding a doctor who was truly interested in my case. (I would meet with them before I hired them and provide them with materials.) I wanted to know if they could convey that interest in a way that satisfied me that he or she was doing it not because they were being paid for it, or had an axe to grind, but really did believe that what was done in the case, or not done, was appropriate or not appropriate. I needed an expert whose opinion came from a place of integrity. When you are providing your services and you want to be convincing, it has to come from a place of integrity, not because you are trying to convince people. The larger point is to turn down cases where you do not feel convinced as an expert.*

See Chapter 2, "Setting the Truth on Fire," for further discussion of the issue of bias.

Relevant life experiences

Our credibility is enhanced when we share that we have had relevant life experiences. Twenty years of clinical work with people who have the same emotional or medical condition as the plaintiff/defendant is an example of this.

> *People talk about how jurors are sometimes averse to expert testimony. There are issues with jurors thinking that an expert is a hired gun—that is, she is just getting paid to say what the attorneys are asking her to say. We have to be careful to choose experts who have a pretty strong clinical background and who have done a lot of non-forensic work. These are the types of experts who see a much broader population and client base. They can talk about our client's functioning not just as compared to and in the context of people who have been accused of a crime, but more broadly as compared to and in the context of people out in the world who suffer from neurological problems or mental health problems.*—Sara Cohbra, Esq.

> *The jury needs to understand that you know what you are talking about. You do it all day, every day. For 30 years. What is your clinic like? I think it is a mistake when a neuropsychologist only does forensics; it shows. You need to establish that you see patients.*—Rod Swenson, PhD, ABN

> *Experts that are still involved with their field do better than experts that are professional experts. I also think the experts that are willing to testify on either side have more credibility with the jurors.*—Judge Allison Burroughs

This is not my primary job

Q: Dr. Hanks, do you do a lot of legal work?

A: This is not my primary job. This is very interesting to me, but the majority of what I do is take care of patients, train young neuropsychologists, and research. —Robin Hanks, PhD, ABPP-CN

I let jurors know I am a former social security disability examiner

I let jurors know that I am a former social security disability examiner. I use the model for disability determination. Is this person able to perform tasks that SSI looks at? Remember detailed or simple instructions, maintain pace, interact with the general public? Knowing that I have this background helps jurors know that I am experienced with these types of questions.—Lisa Stanford, Ph.D., ABPP-CN

Some particular life experiences, even if not directly related to the facts of a case, may raise credibility based on a universal respect for the activity. Rodney Vanderploeg highlights his work with military veterans for this reason:

I ask the attorney who has hired to ask me about what I do at the Veterans Administration. I work with vets and active-duty service members who have sustained severe TBI, traumatic amputation, and burns. That makes me knowledgeable, but it also makes me sympathetic to almost everyone. Almost every demographic appreciates military service and injury during military service.

And of course, people love sports.

Juries love sports. I have the lawyer in voir dire ask me questions about my work with the New York Jets.—William Barr, PhD, ABPP-CN

Robert Mendoza, likes to establish his credibility as a local resident:

I live in Boston. Sometimes, when I have used examples about statistics, I have invoked the names of local sports teams because in Boston, the Red Sox, Patriots, and Celtics inspire passions. It reminds jurors that you are a local guy. Same with street names. If I'm walking down Mass Ave., for example, I say, "Mass Ave." not "Massachusetts Avenue." It's Mass. Ave; I'm a local.

Be consistent

Testifying is not a zero-sum game. Your second career deposition may well include questions about your first. Your 50th deposition? "Doctor, isn't it true that in a 1989 deposition you said . . ."

It is important for attorneys to look at an expert's past reports filed with the court and the expert's testimony in prior cases. We want to know what the expert has

said prior to this case. We don't want to ask the expert to say something in our case that is completely contrary to what the expert has said before, because then the prosecution will attack the expert on these inconsistencies and the expert's credibility in our case will suffer. As an example, I worked on a case in which the expert for the defense had concluded that our client suffered from PTSD. The psychiatrist hired by the state did a lengthy videotaped interview with the client, but he didn't do what at the time was considered the gold standard PTSD interview. He did not use a structured interview or ask about the client's traumatic history. The state's psychiatrist came out of his interview and said, "No, this is not PTSD; it is antisocial personality disorder." On cross examination, he was asked, "How do you evaluate for PTSD?" The psychiatrist described what he had done on this particular case. The defense lawyer asked him, "You don't think it is important to do a structured interview? You don't think it is important to ask about the traumatic experiences?" When the psychiatrist said that these steps were not necessary, we were able to impeach his testimony and his conclusions with his own testimony from an earlier case, in which he said that these steps were indeed necessary.
—Sara Cohbra, Esq.

Chapter 15, "Cross Examination," will address strategies to cope with opinions that change over time, not because the expert is being inconsistent in testimony due to bias, but as bodies of research or evidence based medicine practices change.

Straightforwardness

Attorney Sara Cohbra makes the point that a straightforward response style is a credible response style:

We want experts to directly answer questions that they are asked. Being straightforward is really important to maintaining credibility with the jury. It is important for the expert not to be evasive when questions are asked, to answer questions directly, to acknowledge when the expert doesn't know something, and not to answer a question she can't answer. For example, if a prosecutor asks the expert on cross examination whether there is any literature on a particular subject and the expert doesn't know, she should say so rather than equivocating.

Charisma

Easy to say. Hard to have. I appreciate Attorney Sara Cohbra's useful operational definition:

Charisma is really important on the stand. People who are interesting and engaging are much more persuasive. It's hard to convey what charisma looks like, but I think experts should testify as Barack Obama speaks. President Obama comes across as colloquial but includes a great blend of informality and formality. He answers questions directly. He exudes empathy.

HOW TO LOSE CREDIBILITY

What are some third rails of credibility when testifying?

> ***Don't accept interviews in hallways***
>
> *You need to understand you are in the courtroom for a specific reason. If someone tries to interview you in the hallway, particularly with a high-profile case, you need to maintain a professional demeanor and not speak about the matter. Accepting an interview could be viewed as inappropriate, possibly defamatory in content, and destructive to your personal credibility.*—Ted Peck, PhD, ABPP-CN
>
> ------------
>
> Avoid exaggeration. An exaggerating expert loses credibility as quickly as an exaggerating examinee."—Laurence Binder, PhD, ABPP-CN
>
> ------------
>
> *We want to be careful that we are not asking our expert to go out on a limb. If our expert is uncomfortable saying something we don't want her to say it and not be able to stand firmly behind it. We lose when we ask the expert to express an opinion she does not firmly hold, or when we ask the expert to render an opinion about something for which there is inadequate support, especially when the expert has a lot of other well-supported and helpful things to say. If the expert loses credibility on one aspect of her testimony, she can lose credibility altogether.*—Sara Cohbra, Esq.

When I asked him about what hurts the credibility of an expert witness, Ira Packer immediately brought up the vocal inflection at the end of sentences:

> *If you are making a statement, the vocal inflection at the end of sentence goes down. If it goes up, it is a question. If your inflection is going up, the jury or judge will hear "I am not sure."*

This is known in the linguistic world as "upspeak." You know, the tendency to ask a question? At the end of each of your sentences?

I am bringing this up here largely to direct your attention to Chapter 6, "Social Pragmatics of Testifying." Nonverbal aspects of language are rich with mannerisms that help or hurt credibility.

TESTIFYING AS AN EARLY CAREER PERSON

We have literally all been there. But when an attorney on the opposing side catches wind there is a rookie on deck, sly smiles appear and it is open season. I recall being on a conference call with several attorneys on a legal team when one of them triumphantly declared, "Wait! Dr. Opposing Neurologist Expert's CV shows he had only graduated from his fellowship two months prior to seeing Mr. [Client]!" A relieved sigh echoed through the speakerphone. They clearly had ideas for his cross examination.

But there are benefits to being fresh out of training, like the fact that one's training is fresh. Many people as patients feel more comfortable with a (relatively) newly minted specialist than a graying Marcus Welby.

Testifying as an early career person

It's harder for an inexperienced person to testify. Establishing expertise is not just about years of experience. The new professional hasn't written. S/he doesn't have the years of experience with patients. I would feel very threatened as a new doctor getting on the stand trying to give an expert opinion. The young professional will be challenged. Less on what they say—they may be permitted to be an expert, but it doesn't mean their opinion will be found credible based on their experience.—Judge Lynne Battaglia

Everyone has to start somewhere

Everybody has to start somewhere. One of the worst times for any of our postdoctoral fellows is when the predictable question comes, because everybody knows our program uses postdoctoral fellows and we are very clear about that. So the question always comes,

Q: How many cases have you done before you did this one?

A: This is my first.

Q: How many times have you testified in court?

A: This is my first time.

I tell them to just stand up and square their shoulders. If the report is good, it's good, and every judge will be fine about it. The judge knows all of us tried our first case as attorneys and sat for the first time on a court case as a judge. The question is, "Is it good-quality work, and good testimony"? So just square your shoulders and say, "This is my first" and feel confident that your report is good and that the judge will know good when she sees it.—Judge Christina Harms

Ira Packer's runs the forensic psychology fellowship at the University of Massachusetts Medical Center and has a lot of experience training young forensic psychologists. He notes,

You need to convince yourself of your own credibility. The issue of credibility and presence on the stand is the same with a young professor. You come into a new teaching situation, your first year, you are young, the new person. How do you present yourself? It's important to say to yourself, "Look at how knowledgeable I am," "I am clear and articulate," "I am explaining things to you that you don't know." Of course, you are not saying those things out loud, but that increases your credibility.

Testifying while young

A lot of attorneys have been frank with me about things that I can't control: "You are really young." (I am actually older than I look.) I let the attorneys know they can ask me my age on the stand indirectly by asking what year I finished my training or graduated from college. At first I said to myself, "I am not going to stop dying my hair!" Then I did stop dying my hair and the issue went away completely. It appears that if you let yourself go gray, people will give what you say more weight.—Darcy Cox, PsyD, ABPP-CN

EXPLAINING WHO WE ARE

In a profession where most members of our own extended families are not clear what we actually do for a living, the credentialing of the neuropsychology expert must include an explanation to juries about who we are as a profession. The common fallback, "I practice the science of brain and behavior relationships," is abstract and may carry very little meaning for the typical juror. While the general public has a reasonable understanding of what a psychologist does, psychology experts may need to help jurors shift their understanding of "psychologist as psychotherapist" toward a professional with an assessment role. Pearls for explaining our testing procedures are in Chapter 8, "Direct Examination," and Chapter 9, "Explaining Assessment Methods and Tools." There are many clear, memorable explanations for our general roles. Which ones resonate will likely depend on the nature of your practice and your personality.

What is a neuropsychologist? In my own practice, I will say:

As a neuropsychologist, my job is to understand how people think. Neuropsychologists are trained as clinical psychologists first, and then we go through a 2-year postdoctoral fellowship to train us in diagnosing brain disorders like Alzheimer's disease, traumatic brain injury, and developmental disorders like autism and dyslexia. Part of my job is to determine if someone has a brain disorder—for example, if someone has normal age-related memory problems or is it Alzheimer's disease? The other part of what I do is determine the effects of a known brain disorder or injury on people's everyday thinking abilities. For example, how does the traumatic brain injury or stroke affect this person's ability to think and function?

And at times I will say,

Psychologists help people feel better. Neuropsychologists help people think better.

A neuropsychologist is an expert in the effects of real or suspected brain dysfunction and its impact on thinking skills, emotions, or behavior.—Robert Heilbronner, Ph.D., ABPP-CN

We evaluate memory, other mental abilities, and behavior in one of two types of people. One group is folks who have medically confirmed brain disease. And the question is, are there functional impairments like a stroke or brain tumor? The other group is persons who are experiencing symptoms that involve thinking or behavior. The point of the neuropsychological testing is trying to clarify a cause. Is it an early dementia that hasn't been picked up by brain imaging yet? Is the person complaining of memory problems because they are depressed? Or are they exaggerating their cognitive complaints to make money?—Manfred Greiffenstein, PhD, ABPP-CN

Neuropsychologists engage in objective and careful testing of various thinking skills.—Kyle *Boone, Ph.D., ABPP-CN*

I am a psychologist with a lot of extra training in how the brain works. I specialize in doing assessments on folks who either we know or suspect there is a brain condition. Like Alzheimer's disease, or strokes, or brain injury.—David Williamson, PhD, ABPP-CN

I had the occasion to take the deposition of Aaron Smith not too long before he passed, and he was asked, what is neuropsychology? Most of the time when you ask neuropsychologists this fundamental question, they say something like,

"It's the study of brain–behavior relationships." And no one really knows what that means. This is what Aaron said, and I thought it was brilliant. I've used it ever since.

Neuropsychology is like a thermometer. We know what normal is on a thermometer: 98.6. Neuropsychological testing helps us know whether a person is abnormal, because we know through a lot of studies what normal temperature is."—Wayne Miller, Esq.

Neuropsychologists are interested in brains and how they work. My particular area of interest is dementia. Clinical neuropsychology involves the application of that knowledge to real-world situations and people.—John McSweeny, JD, PhD, ABPP-CN

A neuropsychologist is someone who looks at the whole person: memory, attention, how they see things. Are they anxious, careful, and thoughtful? Did they get the questions right? Did they think they got it right? Do they get sad? I am looking at the whole person.—Cheryl Weinstein, PhD, ABPP-CN

I am a psychologist who has gotten additional training in the use of tests that help us understand people's thinking strengths and weaknesses.—Lynn Blackburn, Ph.D., ABPP-CN

I want the jury to be able to say to themselves, "Yeah, I remember Uncle So-and-So, or the guy down the street," or tie it to something they have personally experienced. [So I might say something like:]

I work with people that have problems with their brain that influences their behavior. For example, most of you have probably had a friend or family member who has had a stroke. Sometimes this causes problems talking or understanding what people are saying to you. This can be frustrating to the patient and his or her family. This is the kind of brain behavior problem that I am talking about. If you have ever seen someone who has suffered a severe traumatic injury to their head, you may notice things about how they behave that have to do with brain cells dying. That's the kind of thing I have been trained to assess and treat—Martin Rohling, PhD

Explaining teaching and forensic components of neuropsychology practice

In my practice, I train young people to do what I do. I am also called by attorneys and physicians who have questions about peoples' function and feel my area of expertise can be helpful to answer those questions. My area of expertise is relating something that may be wrong with the brain with changes in behavior that are of interest to law enforcement or the court system. In the case of personal injury, this person has claimed an injury to the brain and I am being asked to evaluate what that injury is so I can help the judge and jury understand what the person can and cannot do.—Rus Bauer, PhD, ABPP-CN

Dual training

I am a clinical psychologist, fully trained as a mental health professional, who went back to school to get additional training and experience in the brain and how it works. I wear two hats. I wear the hat of a fully trained mental health professional and the hat of a clinical neuroscientist. That's what makes neuropsychologists unique. We have that dual training. We know there are neurological conditions that present like they are mental health conditions and there are mental health conditions that present like they are neurologic.—Neil Pliskin, PhD, ABPP-CN

Understanding how people think is a small part of what MDs do, but for us it's a major focus

When an MD sees a patient for a clinical exam, behavior and thinking abilities are one small part of a much larger process that our physician colleagues evaluate in their patients, whereas neuropsychologists' specialty focus is on thinking abilities. We do evaluations of thinking and mood that are 4,6, 8 hours long. That really allows us to be specialists in these areas.—Neil Pliskin, PhD, ABPP-CN

I am a board-certified neuropsychologist. Basically, what it means is that I am a type of doctor who specializes in studying the relationship between how your brain functions and how you think, feel, and behave.—Dominic Carone, Ph.D., ABPP-CN

Neuropsychology is a branch of clinical psychology that is involved with evaluating people who have injuries or illnesses that affect how the brain works.—Anonymous

----

The difference between neuropsychology and rehab psychology

I am boarded in both rehabilitation psychology and neuropsychology. I will often get asked what the difference is.

The neuro part is talking about, is there something wrong with the brain as opposed to something else, and is it is of significance? And the rehab part is, now that we know there is something wrong how are we going to help fix this in your daily life? How can we help them do their job? Their schooling? Whatever they need to do.—Jacobus Donders, Ph.D., ABPP-CN

Q: What do you do as a neuropsychologist?

A: It's a cross between neurology and psychology. And what I do is look at how the brain affects behavior and your personality and emotions and thinking skills.—Tannahill Glen, PsyD, ABPP-CN

In this definition, you establish that physicians rely on neuropsychologists. First: what is that defines neuropsychology, and second: where do the patients come from.

Q: Are you licensed here in Illinois?

A: Yes, I am a licensed clinical psychologist.

Q: What is clinical psychology?

A: Clinical psychology is a specialty in which we evaluate and treat abnormal human behavior.

Q: What is clinical neuropsychology?

A: That is the subspecialty where we evaluate and treat abnormal human behavior that we know or suspect might be related to brain dysfunction.

Q: How do patients reach you?

A: Physicians such as neurologists who specialize in the nervous system and rehabilitation physicians who specialize in helping injured people get back into life again, or primary care physicians. They refer to us when either they know that something is wrong with the brain and they want to find out how that brain disorder affects the patient's everyday life, like handling finances, or driving, or living alone. Or they refer to us when they are not sure if a brain disorder is present. They want to know, is this a psychological condition, or a neurological condition that is affecting their memory, for example.—Jerry Sweet, PhD, ABPP-CN

How is it different from what a neurologist would do or what a psychiatrist would do? This question occurs to medical students, who ask, "What is it that you neuropsychologists do that is different from a neurological exam or a mental status exam?" Educating the jury about such differences might be helpful in a case in which the neuropsychologist has come to different conclusions than the neurologist or psychiatrist, or in explaining why both types of physicians commonly rely on a neuropsychologist to answer detailed clinical questions that involve real-life implications of impaired findings on our detailed testing.

Q: How is what you do different from what a neurologist would do?

A: The difference is how we measure. For example, in a neurologist's hands you might get a grip strength measurement by squeezing fingers. I, on the other hand, will pull out an instrument and put it in the patient's hand and I will get a numerical reading on how strong their grip is. We are using a measurement process that is more fine-tuned than what neurologists do. Our goal is to turn specific behaviors into numbers. A neurologist might give three to five words, then after a few minutes would come back to see if the words were still there in a person's memory. We give longer word lists and we use learning trials. That is, we provide more than one exposure. We would come back multiple times, to show over time how much they remember. Then finally we come back and ask, were these the words? So, we can look at the difference between recalling and recognizing. Then we would take that result and compare them to norms. So, we could take the patient's result and compare it to the expectation for someone of their age and education. It is a more precise and meaningful way to understand how a person's memory is functioning.—Jerry Sweet, PhD, ABPP-CN

A behavioral accountant

I have come to consider myself a behavioral accountant. Both accountants and neuropsychologists work with numerical spreadsheets. Financial accounting focuses on working with numbers that represent money, Neuropsychologists work with numbers that represent behavior. Financial accountants interpret their numbers in a variety of ways to create economic meaning, including economic predictions. Neuropsychologists engage in a kind of behavioral accounting in which we interpret numbers focused on real-life meaning in terms of diagnoses and everyday behavior, including behavioral predictions. Though the contents and goals are most often quite different, to me there are some strong parallels between financial accounting and what I've come to think of as a shorthand definition of clinical neuropsychology: behavioral accounting.—Jerry Sweet, PhD, ABPP-CN

We are on the borderland between psychology and neurology

We operate on the borderland of the psychological and the neurological. We pay more attention to medical or brain-related issues than your general psychologist. But we also pay more attention to psychological issues, culture, and society stuff than a typical

MD. We are the ones who are integrating all of that stuff.—William Barr, PhD, ABPP-CN

I evaluate how someone's brain is working, or not working.

Q: What is a neuropsychologist?

A: I evaluate how someone's brain is working, or not working.

Q: How do you do that?

A: A variety of tests have been developed that are known to measure certain areas of the brain. We know how people without neurological injuries and diseases perform on these tests. So when I see a patient, I give them these tests, and compare them to people of their same age and education to make it fair, and it tells me if there is an impairment and to what degree they are impaired. Then, within the context of the onset and course of symptoms, I determine if it all hangs together.—Kristie Nies, PhD, ABPP-CN

Neuro means brain. Psychology means the study of behaviors. Neuropsychology means the study of behaviors that relate to brain function. That's what I do.—Lisa Stanford, Ph.D., ABPP-CN

Inoculate on direct against the "You're not a neurologist" line of questioning

Q: Where do you get your patients?

A: Neurologists, primary care.

Q: Why do they send them to you?

A: Well, if their patients have a brain injury, neurologists and family doctors rely on me to tell them how their brain is functioning and how the injury impacts them.

Q: Do you mean a neurologist or neurosurgeon can't do that?

A: No. Neuropsychologists have to give specialized tests that look at how patients' behavior is impacted by the physical injury. They really rely on us to give them that information because they can't do that.—Rod Swenson, PhD, ABN

Q: What is a pediatric clinical neuropsychologist?

A: There is a strong relationship among our brain, how we think, and how we act. When you put those three things together and try to use one to inform the other, that is neuropsychology. Pediatric is the focus on children with medical issues, and child clinical is understanding how children think and learn and behave. We think about the brain in a lifespan perspective. I am trained to think across the lifespan, but

I focus on the early brain development and how things in our environment can have an impact on that.—Lisa Stanford, Ph.D., ABPP-CN

Explaining the role of a pediatric neuropsychologist in medical malpractice litigation

When you are watching your own children, you see them compared to other children, "Hey, they aren't doing this yet and other kids are, or they are doing this first." That's my job—to find out if a child is doing what they are supposed to be doing and if they are not doing what they are supposed to be doing. And what I do on a legal case is exactly the same as when I see a child in my clinical practice. My job is about seeing how well a child does in the face of an "injury" that makes it hard for them to do well. It's not about whether they deserve this (as in advocacy) or causation. It's about impact.—Lisa Stanford, Ph.D., ABPP-CN

What is a forensic psychologist?

I am a forensic psychologist. Psychology is a behavioral science which examines human behavior, thoughts, and emotion. A forensic psychologist is someone who relies upon behavioral science to try and understand a situation or individual, or address a specific legal question, based upon behavioral science and case-specific information that is sound enough to be used as evidence in a courtroom. There is a lot of information in a courtroom, but not all of it becomes evidence. So a forensic psychologist has to make sure that what they rely upon is sufficiently scientifically and clinically solid to be introduced as evidence because it is both reliable as behavioral science and forensically defensible.—Robert Kinscherff, PhD, JD

MAINTAINING CREDIBILITY

Preserving one's credibility as an expert witness is not a zero-sum game. Transcripts of testimony and trial narratives/opinions live on well after a case has ended. Missteps that seriously undermine an expert's credibility can be career-enders if they are brought up in subsequent trials.

Maintaining credibility is really critical because of the way the judges write up the narrative of the trial. Once a judge is critical of something, other attorneys will be able to look it up and be able to bring it up in other cases. It can be a career-ender. It is public record. "Didn't Judge Smith call you a liar?" 99% of the time judges don't do this; they say, "In this case I prefer Dr. X over Y, because they appeared to have a better command of the evidence in this case." I was aware of a neuropsychologist who got essentially turfed out because of a judge's comments.—Attorney, anonymous

Although hearings to limit an expert's testimony not conducted in front of a jury and Daubert hearings are not addressed specifically in this book, an important caution for experts is that having one's ability to testify excluded or limited in such hearings may be brought up in future cases as a means of impeaching the expert's qualifications. Because of this, many experts consider hiring their own attorney to consult with the attorney who brought them to the case in order to prepare for those types of hearings. Recall that the attorney who hires the expert is *not* the expert's attorney, and while an exclusion of testimony may represent a setback in their case, the exclusion may have long-lasting impacts on the career of the expert who has been limited.

FINALLY, AFTER THE CASE IS DONE

I will end the chapter with a story from Yossef Ben-Porath, who clearly did an excellent job establishing his credibility during a case:

> *A prosecutor who had hired me in a case sent me a manila envelope after the trial was over. Throughout the trial the defense attorney was drawing cartoons depicting his perception of how things were going in the case. The prosecutor sent me the ones in which I appeared. One depicts me standing next to a chart with an MMPI profile and pointing at it. The prosecutor says, "Tell me the significance of the MMPI" and I am saying, "Vote guilty." That was the defense attorney's interpretation. During the trial, the prosecutor made a big show of qualifying me. She asked me to send her books and articles I had written. She stacked them on the table and asked me about them one by one. She ended up with a big stack on her desk. One of the cartoons had two panels. The first has a hugely exaggerated stack, "Learned treatises written by Dr. Ben-Porath." In the other panel, the defense attorney is sitting at the other desk with a piece of paper that says "jail form" written by Dr. Smith (his expert).*

5 Relationship with the Jury

Jurors are thinking about justice and fairness when they are deliberating. I talk to juries after every trial. They are fully invested in the justice and fairness of their job. The courtroom belongs to the jury.—Judge [Redacted]

Because attorneys are asking the questions, expert witnesses might be lulled into the idea that our communication partner during testimony is the attorney who brought us to court on direct, or the opposing counsel who is questioning us on cross. But linguist Robin Lakoff, in her book *Talking Power: The Politics of Language*,[1] notes that this is a critical error:

> *To the observer, the discourse seems a dyad between lawyer and witness. But in terms of its function in a trial, both are in fact acting together as one participant, the speaker, with the jury as the hearer. Without this understanding, much about the examination procedure would be unintelligible: one partner telling the other, at great length, what the latter already knows.*

Even when we acknowledge that the "hearer" is the jury, because verbal communication during testimony typically moves in only one direction, from the witness to the jury, it is easy to assume that there is no direct relationship with the jury. The line of reasoning may look like this, "As an expert, I did an assessment and developed opinions, and I am going to simply download that information through a series of questions the attorney asks."

Disruption of the idea that a one-way flow of communication is a helpful way to testify begins with empathy for the difficult job jurors face and respect for their ability to do it.

> *We put 12 people in a room, a bunch of strangers who do not know each other, and we get them to come to an agreement on something really important. The judge that*

I clerked for told me that she thought juries were right something like 95% of the time. And I now think they are right even more than that. It's an amazing process. When you think about it from that perspective, the expert really should be thinking not about what they are saying but "What do these 12 people need? How can I help them?" And not be so invested in what the right decision is, but give them the tools to make the right decision themselves.—Judge Allison Burroughs

To ask the questions "What do the jurors need from me?" and "How can I share tools in a way that they can use them in order to do their job?" we have to accept the premise of a direct relationship between the expert and the jury.

The goal of this chapter is (1) to make the case that a productive relationship between the expert and the jury sets the stage for accessible, engaging direct testimony and (2) to develop a better awareness of our partners on the other side of the expert–jury relationship. Who are the jurors? How do we establish rapport? What is a productive tone? While this chapter introduces concepts and strategies, also see Chapter 6, "Social Pragmatics of Testifying," for additional "how-to's."

WHO IS LISTENING TO OUR MESSAGE?

Who are the people who need to access our knowledge of psychology and neuropsychology to make their decision? As experts, we do not have the opportunity to talk with the jurors to find out their back story, but the attorney who brought us to the case has had exactly that opportunity during jury selection. An important part of the pretrial conference is asking the attorney to give you a virtual introduction to each of the jurors. When the judge is the trier of fact, a similar virtual introduction prior to entering court is equally important. Many attorneys will create a map of the jury box and go through each juror's background with the expert. What education have they had access to? What do they do for a living? What are their life experiences that shape how they will process the information I am sharing? The answers to those questions, given that there are typically 12 people sitting in the jury box, is necessarily about diversity.

Say it in a few different ways: addressing diversity

One of the challenges when you are testifying is that you are speaking to a very diverse group of people who bring different sets of experiences, background, and education levels. Even if you try to communicate in a way that is easy to follow, it is hard to pitch it just right to all 12 people. One way to address this is to try to make your point more than once in different ways.—Yossef Ben-Porath, PhD, ABPP

Most juries are a cross-section of the local population. They are not necessarily college-educated. Recently, I asked the attorney to tell me about the jury. He said, to give you an idea of who is on the jury, the foreman's profession is baseball umpire. And he spelled it "empire." That told me two things. They were not highly educated people. There was at least one person who was a sports fanatic.—Jacobus Donders, PhD, ABPP-CN

In addition to understanding the diverse nature of jurors' educational and vocational backgrounds, it is important to understand that jury summonses arrive in the middle of complicated lives. The jurors listening to the case are currently experiencing the stressors all of us experience in our lives, like the demands of work, kids struggling in school, elderly parents who need care. They may be distracted by their own chronic pain or medical condition, worried about car payments, or tired due to trouble sleeping the night before. Some are experiencing extraordinary stressors. I once testified on a case that had to be delayed for an hour because a juror needed to be served with a domestic violence restraining order. He had a gun his girlfriend was concerned about.

It is also important to think about and understand the common experiences jurors bring to the courtroom arising from living in their particular region. In their entertaining book about the legal system, *Lawyers and Thieves*,[2] Roy Grutman and Bill Thomas point out that courthouses reflect the values and expectations of the surrounding community: "Justice is not democratic, it's local."

A jury where the jurors themselves might be disabled

> *In my region, everyone is pretty poor. They do not award large dollar amounts. It seems too high to them. Many are disabled, or living on $20,000 a year. So there are notoriously low settlements. Attorneys complain about it. You are talking to a jury where folks on a jury themselves might be disabled. They might think: I had a brain injury and I didn't get $200,000.*—Kristie Nies, PhD, ABPP-CN

Blue-collar jurors

> *I typically testify in a blue-collar community. The people work hard for their money and they don't want to give up money to people who don't have a legitimate injury.*—Robin Hanks, PhD, ABPP-CN

David Hartman recalled a murder case where the defense expert was going to explain neurologically why someone in their teenage years make impulsive decisions:

> *The trial took place in the rural Midwest, and the jurors were good solid farm people. These were folks who came right off the canvas of Grant Wood's American Gothic; very conservative, salt-of-the-earth people. They are taking this very seriously. The attorney who was representing the client asked the expert neuropsychologist:*
>
> *Q: Doctor, you are very well known in this area, are you not? And you know a lot about how the brain works?*
>
> *A: Yes, I do.*
>
> *Q: And how do you acquire your knowledge?*
>
> *A: I have spent many years studying the brains of aborted fetuses.*
>
> I was sitting in the back of the room and I looked at the jury after he said that; the jurors would probably have added this expert to the murder docket if they could have. They turned away from him in a non-subtle way and stopped listening to him. It is very important to understand the sensibilities of where you are and to whom you are talking.

ESTABLISHING RAPPORT

Establishing rapport in any setting involves making a human connection. The anxiety and formality of a courtroom situation may pull for us to wrap ourselves protectively in the expert role, stifling our ability to connect. Rod Swenson tells the compelling story of "Doctor Man" as a cautionary tale for experts:

> *There is a "school" at Harvard for attorneys who have lost a few cases and their confidence. They do a lot of mock trials. And the faculty will be talking to the attorneys attending the school, just having a regular conversation. And then the instructors say, "Why don't you present your case?" And the attorney's voice lowers, and he gets a very serious tone. He becomes "Lawyer Man." Would you talk like that to a person in real life? In a bar?*
>
> *You have to talk like you are real people. Good attorneys are very comfortable talking real. I see my job like that. You do not want to come across like Dr. Smarty Pants. You need to explain things to jurors simply, so they can understand. If you had that tone with a patient's family, they would say, "What an arrogant &^%." They would walk out mad, and they wouldn't have learned anything about their family member. Just like Lawyer Man or Lawyer Woman, you can't be "Doctor Man." You have to be a human being.*

Wearing the mantle of "expert" often looks like arrogance to others. And dropping an arrogant stance is a clear first step in establishing rapport. In discussing his operating principles for testifying, Manfred Greiffenstein stressed this point:

> *The first operating principle is "never look down on the jury." Never be condescending. Keep in mind many jurors do not have college degrees. and fine-tune your style to that.*

Robert Kinscherff cautions experts not to act like the smartest kid in class:

> *One of the tendencies of mental health professionals who testify is that we want to look really smart. We run the risk of annoying jurors because we are like the kid in high school who wants to be the smartest kid in the classroom. And that can play out in one of two ways: One is using a lot of jargon that jurors can't understand and the other is talking down to them as though they can't understand it. Jurors properly find both of those equally annoying and suspect that if the mental health professional can't break it down into comprehensible concepts, language, and logic, their testimony is suspect.*

This sentiment was echoed by several judges:

> *Some experts come across as real know-it-alls: "I am the smartest boy in my class and I am saying this is true, so it must be true." I don't think a lot of experts do a very good job of communicating information in an appealing way. It's better if experts just give their opinions in a normal way. Just answer the question. Jurors don't need to think that you're great. They hear your credentials. They know you are qualified and then*

they want to hear what you have to say in a regular way. Experts have to learn to talk to people. You could have the best education in the world. but you aren't the best trial expert if you cannot connect with real people.—Judge Allison Burroughs

----

So many people get wrapped up in being smart and communicating smartness to other people that they forget this simple fact: In order to sffectively communicate information, the listener has to understand it. Remember, you have an expertise, which is why you are testifying, but you are not smarter than everyone else in the courtroom.—Judge [Redacted]

I was particularly struck by Judge John Fader's admission that he would avoid hiring law clerks who were in the top 10% of their class for just that reason:

As a judge, when I hired a law clerk, I tried not to hire somebody that was in the top 10% of their class because a good deal of the time they had no idea what was going on. They sometimes couldn't see the forest for the trees. I'm in the people business; I am not in the paper business. I hired one law clerk who was in the top 10% of her class. She turned out great because she had practical experience. Laurie worked as a stewardess for People Airlines, and you have to be good to put up with that stuff on the weekend. She knew what she was doing. But you've got to be careful that you are surrounded by people who understand people.

Tannahill Glen notes that when in doubt, self-effacing comments are a good standby. She tells the cautionary tale of an expert whose rapport with the jury was damaged by a clever cross examination exposing his unwillingness to be self-effacing:

I read once that when Wayne Williams, the guy convicted of the child murders in Atlanta, was on trial, they had an expert that was testifying about how smart the defendant was. He was testifying about how Wayne Williams turned out to be very smart on his test. And the opposing side wanted to discredit this witness. They let him go on and on about how high the defendant's IQ was. Then they said, "Is he as smart as you, doctor?"

And the doctor was apparently caught off guard and haughtily said, "No, I don't ***think*** *so," in a voice that said, "As if!"*

You could see the jury recoil, apparently. They didn't like it at all. Being self-effacing and human is very important.

Many experts appreciate their own blue-collar or rural backgrounds as an important factor in allowing them to speak naturally and plainly to juries:

I don't come from a fancy-pants Ivy League background. I come from a working-class Detroit background. I can go back to that and use "plain speak" with juries.—William Barr, PhD, ABPP-CN

> *Part of connecting with juries is personality. I was raised on a farm. I never felt better or worse than anyone else. People are in the courtroom to do their jobs. I understand what people's jobs are. I bring that attitude to my testimony. Everyone else in the room is as good as I am. We are all just people.*—Lynn Blackburn, PhD, ABPP-CN

Attorney Brian Pomerantz has no problem taking a "one down" position to make a point when he is talking to a judge. He finds it much more effective than taking on the role of a know-it-all. He will say to the judge:

> *Maybe it's just me, but I can't understand the argument that the attorney is making. Perhaps they can explain it to me because I don't get it.*

An expert coming from a "smartest kid in the room" perspective but who uses simple terms to explain psychology and neuropsychology concepts will very likely come across to the jury as both arrogant *and* patronizing. The key is dropping the "smartest kid" perspective *and* using straightforward language. Neil Pliskin warns experts not to patronize:

> *It's important to avoid patronizing when using simple language. It's more a manner than anything else. I don't come across as "You ignorant savage! Let me dumb it down for you." Rather, I say, "Here's the way I understand it."*

ESTABLISHING TONE

Talk like you would to . . .

If the "smartest kid in class" tone is one we want to avoid, what tone is better? Judge Lynne Battaglia makes a compelling argument to talk like you would when you are enthusiastically describing what you do at a cocktail party:

> *Testimony should be very conversational. Jurors can't ask questions. But an expert always wants to have eye contact with the jury or the judge (whoever the trier of fact is) and provide a tone like dinner conversation, or cocktail conversation. You have a captive audience, to teach them about something that you have committed your life to. I don't think doctors think like this. If they did, they would share their enthusiasm.*

Coffee table with a group of guys

> *What is very important to me when I am testifying is to establish rapport with the jury, or good rapport with the judge, or arbitrators, if there is no jury. I establish rapport in the same way that I would around the coffee table with a group of friends. I engage the people I need to engage and make sure they appear to be following what I am saying. If somebody looks perplexed or distracted, I do what I can to re-engage that person or to explain in simpler terms the concept I am trying to communicate. I do whatever I can to maintain the focus and interest of the listener.*—Paul L. Craig, PhD, ABPP-CN

Get out of the grand rounds into the coffee shop

There is an academic "ivory tower" approach to teaching that is ineffective in a courtroom. People—and particularly jurors—don't like to be preached to or taught in a way that makes them feel patronized or "studentized." When you spend all your time writing and publishing articles, teaching, and working to get tenure, it might be hard to remember that the 14 jurors in the box may come from completely different backgrounds. If you can't put aside your academic communication style and find some other way of talking, your ideas don't get across.

I recently heard a case where a gastroenterologist testified. The issue concerned a small bowel perforation. The doctor had the standard blowup of the intestinal system. He went from top to bottom explaining how the intestinal system works. But it didn't come across as teaching. He spoke in everyday terms, the way he probably spoke to patients. I imagined that his patients love him because he said something like: Here's where the food comes in, this is where the enzymes meet the food, and here's the nine miles of tubing where this all happens and here is where it gets pooped out. It took him 25 minutes to explain it, but he really explained it to the jury in lay terms. If a juror thinks to himself, I would go to this doctor, or I would entrust my child to this doctor, then that witness has a huge credibility advantage.

On the other hand, there are doctors who are ineffective because they go out of their way to make the lawyer seem stupid. And they talk down to the jury. Or they might say sarcastic things that are better saved for grand rounds when they are teaching medical students. The best medical witnesses get out of the realm of the grand rounds and into a coffee shop.—Judge [Redacted]

Talk to the jury as if you are talking to your grandmother. Or great-grandmother. Respectful, but that is the level—so she will understand.—Cheryl Weinstein, PhD, ABPP-CN

When I worked as an attorney I represented a contractor in Baltimore County. He had a man working for him who I would use as an expert who worked himself up through every job in the construction business and was a vice president when I knew him. We never lost a case because I always said Mr. ____, can you explain to the jury . . . ? And he would talk to the jury like a bartender.

What do I mean "talked like a bartender"? He talked to them so that they can understand what is going on. You sit and you talk to the bartender about things and the bartender talks to you and there is communication back and forth. He was in a teaching role. He knew he was in a teaching role, but he had the experience and the common way of expressing to people what he was doing, why you can't weigh concrete under 40-degree weather, things of this sort. He could explain it all.—Judge John Fader

Like a feedback session . . .

Many experts I interviewed commented that talking to the jury is similar to doing a feedback session. They strive to hit a relaxed but informative tone, pitching information to multiple family stakeholders, with multiple perspectives and capabilities at once.

> *When I talk to a jury, I picture them sitting across a table from me, and I am trying to give them feedback on their child's function in a way that is meaningful to them, truthful, and incorporates the scientific data. So it is very easy for me to connect with a jury and have them see me as a person, and see how much I care about what I do. Whether I am working for the plaintiff or defense. I always turn toward them. I don't respond to the attorney. This is feedback to the jury.*—Lisa Stanford, Ph.D., ABPP-CN

> *I have a manner of speaking where I can communicate without dumbing things down. I think I got the experience giving feedback to families of people diagnosed with dementia, through trial and error, over a period of 20 years. All of those feedback sessions really honed my ability to talk about the brain very simply.*—Kristie Nies, PhD, ABPP-CN

> *With a jury trial, I try to frame it like I am doing feedback to a large family who has a brain-injured daughter or son or wife. I find that clinically, when I do that, you will have people in the room who understand what you are saying, and people in the room who can't understand why this is happening; you have people who say, "Yeah, he was always like that before!" You usually have every one of those dynamics represented in a jury. Some jurors are thinking, "This is all hokey—I can't see anything wrong with the plaintiff. How can they have a problem?" I try to use the same type of language that I do when I am giving feedback to a family. You don't get through to families very well if you are talking about "proactive interference on the California Verbal Learning Test." You have to find ways to explain. In essence that is what you are doing in a trial. You are explaining "How does this happen?" and "What is the impact?" to a diverse group of people.*—Rod Swenson, PhD, ABN

A few experts pointed out that their testimony is literally the only "feedback session" with the examinee they will ever do. Most experts do not give traditional feedback sessions in the context of forensic cases. As the first time the examinee hears the examiner explain the results of the independent psychological or neuropsychological evaluation occurs in open court, it is by definition an awkward way to share information with the examinee. Shelley Peery commented that sometimes as a fact or treating witness, she has had to share information about prognosis on the stand that she normally wouldn't in a therapeutic clinical context. She noted that that it increases your credibility as a human being if in that awkward moment of sharing your findings (which may contradict the plaintiff's or defendant's understanding of themselves) you remember that the person sitting is listening to this for the first time, and attempt to be gentle and sympathetic with the person.

I saw a patient with significant brain damage from an infectious process who was severely amnestic. My hopefulness for his recovery was what drove all of our treatment. But when I was asked to testify as a fact witness, I had to tell them that I actually didn't really want his wife to be present for my testimony because I would have to tell the facts. We definitely made progress with him to improve how he could stay at home by himself for much more time, but there was no way he was ever going to work again.

The patient himself agreed to step out, but the wife felt like it was her husband who she was taking care of and she needs to hear the truth. That just made it harder for me. And I think that made it a little bit more compelling for the jury because I sort of was talking to her. The jury understood that I was really hesitant about expressing this to her, so I was looking at her trying to be a little bit gentler but at the same time speak the truth. I was composed, but it was clear that I was choosing my words and trying to be frank yet gentle. Even if you are just hired as an expert and not a treater, you still know that this is going to impact the individual.

It's a bit challenging for me to sit here and testify in Mr. Jones's presence

To communicate to the jury that I am trying to be as respectful as possible, and as straight and honest as possible, I will sometimes say:

It's a bit challenging for me to sit here and speak about Mr. Jones in his presence in such a direct way. It is very important to me that he understands that it is my job to answer questions completely and honestly based on the scientific evidence and his test results. I realize that some of the things I may say may not be very pleasant for him to hear. I want to preface my testimony by acknowledging that it may be challenging for him to listen to my testimony. As I said before, it is my job to answer each question as directly and honestly as possible, even if it makes Mr. Jones or anybody else in the courtroom uncomfortable."—Paul L. Craig, PhD, ABPP-CN

Like a particular type of teaching . . .

The "testifying is like teaching" analogy was frequently brought up by experts. Interestingly, almost all had a very specific notion of a dynamic, interactive teacher. None aspired to testify like the Charlie Brown cartoon teacher, standing at the board and making incomprehensible "wonk wonk wonk wonk" sounds that almost mimic real language.

It helps to be a teacher. You get used to reading your audience, gauging whether they are listening, whether they are following you. Sometimes you have a sense that some concept hasn't registered with all of them I might try to say it another way.—Yossef Ben-Porath, PhD, APBB

You have to find a sweet spot, similar to presenting a scientific or clinically oriented lecture to a community group. These are people from the general population who are not steeped in neuroscience and medicine and certainly not in neuropsychology. My goal is to explain concisely and accurately very complex concepts in medicine and science in a way that is understandable and jurors can integrate into their overall perspective of the case.—Michael McCrea, PhD, ABPP-CN

In jury trials, most jurors are really paying attention. They want to know what you know. They are usually willing to meet you more than halfway. When on the stand, I see myself as a teacher to a really motivated group of students.—Darcy Cox, PsyD, ABPP-CN

For some, setting a teaching tone with expert testimony means the type of collaborative exploration also seen in psychotherapy.

Creating "aha!" moments

I see my role to educate the jury: about neuropsychology, about TBI. One of the things I have enjoyed most in my career is teaching seminars with interns and postdocs. I am doing exactly the same thing in court. I see no differences in teaching in either setting, postdocs or trial. My goal is not to give knowledge per se, but to help the audience develop an understanding, to really understand what the issues are. In a neuropsychology seminar or testimony, I can provide factual information, but those facts will not stick or connect unless I can provide some everyday examples. It is only when I provide some everyday examples that are related to my audience that they will get the "aha!" experience that they might get in good psychotherapy. I view good teaching and psychotherapy as very similar. I want my audience to get the "aha!" experience: "Okay, now I get it! Now I understand! I understand why the plaintiff thinks one thing and you think another."—Rodney Vanderploeg, PhD, ABPP-CN

Understanding where the jury is—and taking them one step beyond

When I did therapy, I saw my job as understanding where the patient is, and then taking them a small step beyond that to a new way of understanding or a new way of behaving and thinking about things. You can't do that unless you know where they are. That is what I see my role with the jury. That's why I like live testimony, so I can see whether they are dozing off or whether they are attentive. I can see when they are nodding. There is always one person on the jury who is a "nodder." If that person is nodding, I know that I am connecting their understanding of what is going on and moving it one step beyond.—Rodney Vanderploeg, PhD, ABPP-CN

Greg Lee, provides a great cautionary tale for testifying in a way that is too much like teaching in the driest sense of the word:

This was one of the worst experiences I've had in court.
The judge told me to shut up.

The attorney asked me to explain hemispheric asymmetry of cognitive functions, so I started a lecture. And the judge said, "I don't think we need to go into all this." I have no idea how I was explaining it; I'm sure it was kind of professorial and boring. Take-home message? Don't bore the judge. Or the jury.

His example reminds us that in the courtroom, your "students" don't have to be there in terms of attention. They can check out. There is no negative consequence for them, but the negative consequence for us is that our opinions are ignored. The real difference between being a teacher in a real classroom and adopting the role of one in the courtroom? If I give a boring lecture and they don't listen, they don't get a poor grade; I do.

Whatever tone one uses for courtroom testimony, Robert Mendoza makes a very good case for it to be a respectful one:

> *Although I feel competent, well trained, and experienced, when I am in the courtroom, I am a guest in someone's home. I am not an attorney, a judge, a jurist; hopefully I won't be a defendant! I am being asked to participate in a process in a house where they have their own rules about how you dress, how you talk, and when you talk. I am there for a specific purpose and there may be rules I am not accustomed to.*

INVITE THE JURY TO PARTICIPATE

Although in the relationship between the expert witness and the jury only the expert is speaking, expert witnesses have the ability to literally invite the jurors to actively engage with their testimony by posing questions and using examples that jurors can relate to and therefore actively imagine. Nancy Hebben advises, "It is important to include examples in your testimony that jurors can relate to their personal experience, so they can make their own judgment based on their experience." That is, the invitation to active engagement transforms one-way communication into a collaboration between expert and juror.

Ask jury to put themselves in the plaintiff's shoes

> I go back and forth between concepts I bring to the table and asking the jury to take part in what it might be like to be this patient. It causes them to think about what you are saying in terms of their experience, which is ultimately what a jury is supposed to do. "Disuse contributing to disability" is a good example. In many cases you will find deficits, but they are attributable to a year of disuse. In one case, I asked the jury,
>
> *Have any of you felt so bad about something that happened in your life that you didn't even want to get up in the morning? Has that happened to you even once? So, you can see that what looks on the surface to be a disability can actually be a mood issue."*—Rus Bauer, PhD, ABPP-CN

In his work on capital cases, Antonio Puente wants jurors to understand the level of grinding poverty that plaintiffs from Third World countries experience that does not exist in the United States. He notes,

> *It is important not to push an advocacy position. Rather, it's my job to engage the imaginations of jurors and provide unbiased information. I will say, "Imagine yourself in a situation where all of a sudden you were taken to Mexico. You had to figure out how to live . . ."*

David Williamson makes it a point to bring his testimony back to concrete experiences that jurors can relate to. In this example, he invites jurors to become active collaborators with his testimony by conjuring examples from their own childhood of what it is like socially for kids with a low IQ:

> *People who don't score high on IQ tests are often easily led around by others. You may have seen this growing up in your schools. Kids with low IQs might have been bullied or taken advantage of.*

Kristie Nies uses a Socratic method during her testimony to invite jurors to participate with her as she problem-solves to reach conclusions:

> *Let's think about this a minute . . . How did that happen? What would we need to know?*

Lisa McDermott points out that it is important to get in there and immediately connect your testimony about a diagnostic category with jurors' everyday knowledge. This immediate engagement allows jurors to be with you, step by step, as you explain a concept:

> *You can define something, like schizophrenia so that jurors know about the diagnosis and definition, but after providing that education, you need to personalize the information. This is particularly important for experts who are talking about commonplace diagnoses. For example, when defining ADHD, which may be familiar to a lot of jurors, it is important to give relatable descriptions of some of the behaviors that go with that diagnosis. This is far more credible than if you try to pull out statistics or studies, which are unfamiliar to most people.*

> *If you have ever been to jury duty, you will know. Jurors often recognize aspects of themselves in the case. It's a normal human phenomenon, and it's why the jury system works: We want a jury of peers, people who are able to relate their own life experience to a case. You can use that to your advantage in terms of clarifying some of the scientific information you have to relay.*
>
> *In one trial, a juror was a cat lady. I say that in the most affectionate way possible. She was an older single lady with lots of cats, and described that in her jury paperwork. One of the things I worked into my testimony was my grief response at losing my cat. On the stand I was taking about how my cat was really old and really grumpy and no one liked him anymore except for me. When he died it was devastating for me; it was like losing a family member. She appeared to empathize with that. I was saying, grieving is a normal part of loss—even when it's a cat.*—Tannahill Glen, PsyD, ABPP-CN

Of course, there are times when the personal experiences and background knowledge that jurors are invited to conjure may be inconsistent with the diagnostic categories and systems psychologists and neuropsychologists bring to the courtroom. Chapter 13, "Specific

Psychiatric and Neurological Disorders," discusses the importance of first connecting our descriptions of neuropsychiatric diagnostic categories like OCD, PTSD, or dementia to common everyday "vernacular" use of the terms, and then providing additional information jurors might not be aware of.

ESTABLISHING A VISUAL RELATIONSHIP WITH JURORS

While the literal conversation one is having on the stand is with the attorneys asking questions on direct and cross, most experts, attorneys, and judges highlight the importance of establishing a direct visual relationship with jurors when answering those questions. This fits with Robin Lakoff's description of the true communication partners being the expert and the jurors. After all, it is hard to have a conversation or a relationship with someone if you are not looking at them. As one judge noted,

> *Each juror should feel like you care about her. Jurors are predisposed to look up to you. In fact, they are also looking for help from you. If you make a practice of looking at each one of them, they feel cared for. Eye contact is a huge factor in gaining jurors' trust.*—Judge [Redacted]

Paul Craig outlines his strategy for establishing rapport with the jury, which begins with making eye contact:

> *First, look people in the eye, but not in a way that makes them uncomfortable. Second, look around the group throughout your testimony and make sure you have nonverbal communication with the jurors. As you are speaking with the jury, you need to be aware of nonverbal communication from them that tells you whether they are understanding what you are saying. Third, if the nonverbal communication tells you they are confused, like their facial expression suggests that one or more jurors are perplexed, restate your opinion using different words, with the intention of making your opinion as clear as you possibly can. If you have three or four people on the jury with whom you have established and maintained good communication, chances are you have them all.*

Speak to the jury

> *You do not provide testimony to the attorneys. You speak to the jury. Try to make eye contact with the jury.*—Rus Bauer, PhD, ABPP-CN
>
> ------------
>
> *As an expert witness, you need to speak directly to the jury. This means looking at the attorney as he/she asks a question and then looking to the jury to answer. It is important to listen to the jury as well. By reading their body posture and facial expressions, you know if you have explained something adequately.*—Nancy Hebben, PhD, ABPP-CN

Reading the room is important

> *Reading the room is important. Most juries can't ask the witnesses questions. The expert needs to get a sense of how engaged the jury is and try to tweak the manner and tone in which she is testifying if it seems that the jurors are not engaged. The jurors are more engaged when the expert is focused on the facts and describes how her clinical opinions are borne out by facts proven by multiple concrete sources. The defense attorney also should be tracking the reaction of the jury to the testimony and assisting the defense expert through appropriate questioning to be engaging and compelling.*—Sara Cohbra, Esq.

Participant and observer

> *It is important for neuropsychologists to be both a participant and an observer. This comes from the personality theorist Harry Stack Sullivan. You have to answer a question accurately, but you also have to pay attention to the way that you are coming across and the response from people that you are trying to communicate with. I like to pay attention to whether the jury looks glazed over to my responses, so I can make necessary adjustments in an effort to gain understanding. I always think of this role as what a good teacher tries to accomplish in the classroom.*—David S. Bush, PhD, ABPP-CN

In addition to using visual contact to directly engage with jurors and pick up nonverbal cues that can be used as signals that we need to explain information in alternate ways, or to stop being so long-winded, some experts use the nonverbal conversation between themselves and the jury to figure out which juror may be a leader, or influential with other jurors. Others had conflicting views, feeling that this was a distraction for experts.

Look for jurors who are with you

> *During direct examination, I spend a lot of time looking at the jury, particularly those members who appear to be engaged and attentive. Engaged jurors are influential with other jurors. On cross examination, most of my eye contact is with opposing counsel, except when I am going to make a major point, when I return to looking directly at the attentive jurors. This helps drive home my points.*—Glenn Larrabee, PhD, ABPP-CN

> *You want to develop a visual relationship with the jury. In most of my criminal cases I have been in the courtroom a couple of days already prior to testifying. That is because I am typically a prosecution expert, and therefore a rebuttal expert. I am going to rebut the defense's case. The court allows me to go in to observe testimony that I am going to rebut. By the time I testify, I have typically had a chance to observe the jury for a few days. I can see which jurors are responding, who is shaking their head. By the time I got up to testify, I know who I want to*

connect with. I want to connect with the more engaged jurors. If I convince them, they will be big advocates in the deliberation. Who is falling asleep? Some look not connected. What I am looking for is the juror on the edge of their seat, paying attention, responding nonverbally. I want to then make eye contact with them. Just like lecturing in a class. The ones who are looking at you, make eye contact. Other students will never look at you. It is almost self-selective. Whose eyes are there for me to engage with?—William Barr, PhD, ABPP-CN

The expert witness who talks to jurors is most effective. As a judge, I put no stock in some lawyers' advice to witnesses to find "alpha" and "beta" jurors and communicate with the jurors who you think are "leaders." The jurors you think are alphas turn out to be betas, and vice versa. You don't know. Make a practice of making eye contact with every juror. They all have an equal vote.—Judge [Redacted]

Don't try to distract yourself by trying to read the jury

I try to not be conscious of juror reactions because it can be distracting and is often misleading. Someone could be smiling at you and thinking, "What an asshole!" Some can look at you stone-faced but be thinking, "This guy is impressive." Don't distract yourself by trying to read the jury.—Manfred Greiffenstein, PhD, ABPP-CN

SLEEPY, INATTENTIVE JURORS

There is no communication to the expert clearer than one or more members of a jury nodding off. Experts ignore this communication at their peril. As Greg Lee, PhD, ABPP-CN, explains, "Don't bore the jury. When they start yawning, stop talking." Lynn Blackburn advises experts, "If you have to testify after lunch, the jury will be falling asleep. Talk louder. State the obvious if necessary: 'Maybe I am confusing people; I see some are drifting off!' "

This advice reminds us of the improv exercise I described in Chapter 1, where experts learn to throw "energy balls" at one another. Using the same vocal tone and cadence is inherently boring to any listener. As dynamic speakers, we can intentionally mix up our delivery, "throw different types of energy balls," to help engage our listeners.

Jurors may also look bored if they cannot access the expert's message. The expert who notices a bored juror may want to try using different analogies or metaphors in addition to using different vocal tones. This strategy needs to be used with caution, as creating longer testimony generally defeats the purpose of keeping jurors awake and engaged. Experts may want to try using a different analogy on the next question the attorney asks rather than augmenting their answer to the current question. See Chapter 2, "Setting the Truth on Fire," and Chapter 8, "Direct Examination," for strategies to create concise, brief testimony in the first place that is less likely to put jurors to sleep.

No matter how concise your testimony is, Lisa McDermott notes that in some trial contexts, juror fatigue is inevitable:

Capital trials are emotionally draining, by their nature. In addition, by the time of the penalty phase—when psycho-social experts testify—jurors have already sat through the guilt-innocence case. There is usually only about a week's break in between the two phases. Jurors are tired so it is important for the expert to be concise. When jurors are being asked to make life and death decisions, you want them to be attentive and willing to listen.

JURORS LITERALLY TAKING PART IN THE CONVERSATION

In some jurisdictions, jurors are permitted to ask questions of experts during the trial.

> *There are a lot of judges who have toyed with the idea of permitting jurors to ask questions that they review first. I have never done this because I think questioning witnesses at trial is the lawyer's job, and they have various strategic reasons for asking—or not asking—certain questions. Some judges think that juries want to get a certain piece of information, and if they don't get it by asking questions, they get very confused and frustrated.*—Judge [Redacted]

In situations where juries can ask questions, the questions are typically written down, vetted by the judge and the attorneys, and then read to the expert. Rod Swenson notes,

> *I look right at the jury, and I can immediately tell who asked the question because they are really attentive. I always say, "That's a great question." They are a little afraid that they have asked you a question. You need to make sure that you give it the importance that they did. It's a great experience, because you find that you forget to say things that are really important.*

The questions jurors submit function as immediate feedback for the expert about where there might have been a hole in your testimony.

> *In Arizona jurors can ask questions. They write their questions down and hand them to the judge. The judge determines which ones are asked. It gives insight into the thought process of the jurors. I didn't have a clue who asked which questions. In one case, the judge allowed three questions. Each was fairly technical. I recall thinking that they were technical and they didn't suggest a leaning one way or another. The questions reflected jurors trying to follow up and understand what I had said. I see no downside to it. But attorneys hate it because they lose control. As a witness, I can give an open-ended response.*—Yossef Ben-Porath, PhD, ABPP

POSTTRIAL FEEDBACK

Some experts and attorneys and many judges have the opportunity to speak with jurors after trials to hear from them how they experienced expert testimony. I was struck by the humbled tone that almost always arose when these conversations were discussed. I was also struck by how many experts, attorneys, and judges highly recommended that experts seize the opportunity to hear direct jury feedback if it ever is available.

Jury might remember three things you have said

If you are lucky, the jury will probably remember about three things you say. I have sat in focus groups after I have testified. The jurors will be asked, "What did you think of Dr. Swenson's testimony?" They will say, "Which one was he?" (this is after testifying for three hours). "Oh yeah, he was good." "Well, what did he say?" "Uh . . . he was good." If you get jurors to believe that you know what you are talking about and you are credible, and that the patient had [or didn't have] an injury, it's significant and then you have probably been very successful. We think jurors are hanging on every word we are saying, but it is really just a small snippet of what they are hearing over the course of a trial.—Rod Swenson, PhD, ABN

Jurors don't necessarily remember testimony of the experts

I was on one case where the jury gave a woman a large verdict. My findings instead had suggested that her brain function was intact. The defense attorney was allowed to call the jurors and ask them how they came to their conclusion. They were asked what they thought of me and other expert witnesses: "Who?" The fMRI witness? "Who?" What about the other experts? "We kind of remember them, but not really."—Christopher Grote, PhD, ABPP-CN

How observant jurors are

Here is an example of how observant jurors are. There was a very big case with many lawyers in the courtroom. It was an intellectual property case and I require local counsel to be in the courtroom, generally speaking. I don't have any control of out-of-town counsel. They may never appear in front of me again, but the local counsel are likely to be in front of me again, and I like them in the courtroom to make sure there is some accountability. During the trial they put a drive-in–sized movie screen in the courtroom. They did not want to just project on the jurors' individual screens; they wanted this big screen. The local counsel kind of sat halfway behind the screen. When I went back to talk to the jurors after the case, one of the first questions they ask was, "Who was that guy who was on his iPhone all day long behind that screen?" They see everything.—Judge Allison Burroughs

----

I like to ask jurors after trials to talk with me about their experience. When I ask specifically about how well they understood the expert's testimony, I have heard more good things than bad. Generally speaking, jurors are very appreciative of the experts' contributions. When the jurors don't like the experts, this is what I most commonly hear: "That expert talked too much." There is a zeal for explaining, but it is important that you edit your explanations. Don't repeat yourself and don't go on tangents. Jurors are already on information overload. Talking too much doesn't help. I also frequently hear: "That expert talked down to me."—Judge [Redacted]

I talk to juries after every trial. As a trial lawyer, I would have given my right arm to hear all the things I hear now. For example, it is incredible what juries see. Because they are watching and not speaking, they are like hawks: They do not miss a thing. Jurors have told me that they didn't like when one lawyer smirked at a witness's answer. They don't miss when someone cracks a joke or seems to be drinking too much water. They watch what people wear. They watch how people talk. They are offended by what they consider to be any disrespect to me—they take it personally. Juries are more aligned with judges than I ever realized. They believe that the judge is their champion and protector, so they disapprove of anybody who disrespects the judge. I always tell lawyers that because even when you don't agree with the judge you can't show it.

And the same goes for what experts think of lawyers. Experts can't say, "You are a complete and utter jerk" to an attorney with their body language because the juries pick it up. They want information that is untainted by emotion and side-taking. They just want raw data. They want raw information that they can use to make a decision. They don't want advocacy. Once they feel expert witnesses have taken a side, and are an advocate for a particular side, jurors are concerned that they have not told them the whole story, that they have only told them the stuff that helps their side.—Judge [Redacted]

FINALLY, JURY RESEARCH

While the focus of the Testimony That Sticks project is not on jury research, I had the good fortune to talk with Marcus Boccaccini, a jury researcher, and asked him for a 36,000-foot perspective on the field of jury research. To close this chapter, here is his explanation of how jury research is conducted, and a piece of advice for testifying that the research suggests.

Explaining models of jury research

There are two basic models for jury research: field studies and experimental situations. With real-world jury situations, or field studies, actual jurors are interviewed. They are in the process of making or have just made a decision in a real case. It is really difficult to get access to real-world juries. We can study people who are waiting for jury duty. In Texas, we were able to survey jurors at the end of civil commitment sexual predator trials and ask them about the factors that influenced their decision. It is great to be able to ask people who have just made a decision about someone's life. The drawback is that people often don't know why they made a decision. Separate research on human decision-making tells us that frequently people don't know why they make a decision. They might say it is x and y, but it is really b and c. Therefore, experimental jury studies are a real benefit: We can experimentally manipulate one or two variables. But of course, the drawback is that they are not real-world stakes. Put both types together, and they can show a more complete picture about what happens.

Jurors prefer testimony based on clinical judgment

Nothing is a truism, but in the realm of psychology testimony, there are several studies now that indicate that jurors prefer clinically based testimony to actuarial based. They want an expert to say, based on my years of experience, or my clinical judgment, this is what is happening. They don't want people to go into numbers and math and percentiles. That stands in contrast to what science tells us how we should go about making decisions.

There is a key conflict between science and practice as to what experts should do on the witness stand. Nobody has yet studied any sort of middle ground, one that shows you can get the best of clinical judgment and the best of science and you could put them together either better than or simply equal to the clinical judgment effect. I would like to hope that is what most people strive for. I would like to think there are very few experts who practice based on some purely statistical decision-making process. Even clinicians who use actuarial measures tend to report that they still use clinical judgment. I think that most practitioners actually use both. A goal for practitioners is to find a way to have their practice be science-based, and communicate it to jurors, but in a way that won't make them lose focus or stop paying attention because they don't understand the math.

NOTES

1. Lakoff, R. T. (1992). *Talking power: The politics of language.* New York: Basic Books, p. 91.
2. Grutman, R., & Thomas, B. (1990). *Lawyers and thieves.* New York: Simon and Schuster.

6 Social Pragmatics of Testifying

"RICKY, FIRST OF ALL, where did you learn to drive like that?!"

Will Ferrell, as rookie racecar driver Ricky Bobby in *Talladega Nights: The Ballad of Ricky Bobby*, puts his mouth near the television reporter's microphone, moves his lips—and no sound comes out.

"Can you speak up, Ricky?"

Ricky leans in with a soft voice, "The car . . . it handled real good . . ."

Ricky's hands begin to float up.

"I felt like I was on a spaceship . . . and, uh . . . I'm not sure what to do with my hands?"

"It would be real good just to hold them down by your side."

Ricky begins again, "Well, we were really happy with what was going on . . ."

As he speaks, both hands awkwardly drift up past the microphone in front of his face. The interviewer gently pushes his hands back down.

Social pragmatics is the language behind the words we speak. This language is visual (how we dress, our posture, hand gestures, and facial expressions) and it is auditory (the pitch, rate, and volume of our voice, and our vocal patterns). It is how we move when we approach the witness box, and it can change abruptly when cross examination begins.

Is social pragmatics important when we testify? Attorney Sara Cohbra notes that pragmatics "makes a really big difference. This is something that is really important but is hard to capture."

When Marcus Boccaccini talks about teaching his doctoral students about the importance of social pragmatics during testimony, he immediately brings up that scene in *Talladega Nights* when Will Ferrell's character, Ricky Bobby, has his first television interview. He points out that, just like Will Ferrell, whose boisterous, likable, relaxed character freezes in front of a camera, even seasoned clinicians often appear stiff and rigid when they testify. Recall from

Chapter 4, "Establishing Credentials and Credibility," that credibility is based in part upon warmth and likability. Thus, being awkward in a courtroom can be a barrier to building credibility with the jury.

In Chapter 5: "Relationship with the Jury," we heard Rod Swenson's cautionary tale of "Doctor Man." We often act like our idea about what an expert should sound like, unconsciously adopting a set of social pragmatics that result in us sounding pompous and arrogant, even when that set of social pragmatics doesn't fit with our own everyday personal and professional style. Adopting those types of speaking styles can create distance between ourselves and the jury.

This chapter will address the importance of social pragmatics during testimony. If we think of nonverbal language as a code, one of the purposes of this chapter is to identify which codes we are using to communicate the message behind our words. Are we using codes that reflect who we are, or are we unwittingly sending a message we don't want to send? The purpose of looking closely at the language behind our words is not to create a false or misleading persona for a jury. Really the opposite is true: The purpose is to identify and eliminate the nonverbal barriers we put up as we talk to juries (or in other situations in our professional lives) that distract from our message and distance us from our true selves and from others.

THE VERY LONG WALK TO THE WITNESS STAND

Social pragmatics are important factors in an expert's credibility even before testimony begins—and after the expert has been dismissed. Ira Packer notes,

> *From the moment I get to the courthouse, I am on. Because you don't know who the jurors are. They are walking in while you are walking in. They are in the elevator, they are in the bathroom; you just don't know who the people are. Anything you say or do can make an impression. Make sure you are professional from minute one. And make sure you stay professional to the last minute. Just because you are off the stand, you are not "off." If you stay in the courtroom afterwards, be very careful. If there is a jury, I don't stay in court. The jury is looking at you. Subtle movements may be interpreted—are you smirking, smiling? You just don't know how that looks. If you stay in the courtroom, you may seem to have a vested interest. You really need to convey the message, "I am here to share my expertise. I am not part of the legal team."*

A judge who prefers to remain anonymous also noted the importance of nonverbal communication before testimony even begins:

> *When you are called to the witness stand, it is your red-carpet moment. You walk up to the witness stand all the way through the courtroom. You get up in the chair. EVERYONE is looking at you. Ladies: no shoes you will trip in. Gentlemen, clothes that are comfortable and appropriate. The more comfortable physically that an expert is when testifying, the better she projects confidence.*

David Bush advises experts to take some time to organize their materials once they reach the stand:

> *Ted Blau would say that when he got to the stand, he would have two briefcases with all of his materials. Before he sat, he would take his time and lay his material out on the desk, unpack his briefcase. I stole that early on. I have always done that. It helps me breathe and relax. It also is an immediate behavioral statement that says, "I am in charge of my presentation here. I am going to be careful and organized in the way I approach my responsibility of testifying."*

Ted Peck notes that it is also important to pack up gracefully:

> *When you have finished your direct and cross, your attorney makes a motion, saying to the judge, "Your Honor, may Dr. Peck be excused?" At that point, the judge will say, "Yes, he is excused." The question is, how do you pack up your stuff neatly and professionally without making yourself look silly by dropping things? Try to be organized on the witness stand. When you are finished with a piece of paper, put it back in your chart, then you will be able to efficiently pack up. As quickly and professionally as I can I will load my stuff up and get out of Dodge City. If you are wearing comfortable shoes, don't slip out of the shoes while on the stand. Don't leave your glasses behind and have to come back into the courtroom. Where do you leave your coat? You should leave it right behind your retaining attorney. You want to be able to get it on the way out, but not so that you have to travel across the courtroom and interrupt the flow of the proceedings.*

THE LANGUAGE OF CLOTHING

Social science research tells us that what we choose to wear influences not only how others perceive and treat us[1] but also how we perceive ourselves.[2] Clothing is a powerful language that we use to communicate with others about our status, attitudes, and affiliations. The message our clothing conveys changes with the context of our setting and the set of assumptions of our "listeners." What message does wearing a suit send in an office where executives are wearing hoodies? What message does the hoodie send when walking into a courtroom of individuals dressed in traditional conservative suits? Do members of the jury share the basic assumptions that have led to hoodies being acceptable in high-tech business environments (e.g., ultra-casual dress suggests a brilliant person not thinking in traditional boxes), or do they interpret the clothing communication in a way that might be startling to the wearer (e.g., this person is making light of this situation, can't afford a suit, or doesn't know better)? Every time we get dressed in the morning we are establishing the first sentence in a dialogue we have with other humans. Their clothing, as well as their assumptions about our clothing, is the second sentence. Do our assumptions match? What are we saying to each other?

In addition to being a powerful communication channel, can clothing actually improve our performance on the stand? There is good reason to believe that the answer is "yes." In an intriguing set of studies, Michael Slepian and colleagues[3] found that wearing formal, high status clothing actually improves performance on tasks of abstract reasoning. Other studies have demonstrated that subjects wearing a white coat labeled as a high-status "lab coat" performed better on tasks of attention, while subjects wearing the same coat labeled as a "painter's coat" did not.[4] Kraus and Mendes[5] demonstrated that dressing in a business suit as opposed to sweats increases testosterone and improves performance in high-stakes, winner-take-all negotiating situations. These studies are striking in suggesting that dressing professionally not only influences our listener's perception of how competent we are but could actually improve our ability to reason and focus on the stand.

Robert Mendoza notes that while Silicon Valley may have evolved from the classic business suit, courtrooms in the United States generally have not:

> *Dress code in today's society is more relaxed than a generation ago, but you walk into any courtroom in the U.S. and they still want a coat and tie. They still want business attire. Being quirky is not acceptable. Not only will it not work, it's bad form.*

This sentiment was echoed by many judges, attorneys, and experts. One important point to consider is that when experts are told to wear "professional dress" or "business attire," no one is referring to the profession or business of psychology; they are referring instead to traditional office business dress. The long flowing skirts or Mr. Rogers sweaters that some in our profession favor are highly unlikely to be considered professional-looking outside of the tight-knit circle of our profession and our patients. Ted Peck cautions strongly against dressing this way:

> *Many novice psychologists don't have a good working understanding of what is socially acceptable attire. Males need to wear a tie. You need to wear a sport coat or suit. I have seen some witnesses wear Mr. Rogers–type sweaters with a tie. I don't think it works in court. You need to look like what is acceptable in that jurisdiction. For both women and men it is the same question of professional attire. There are some clothes that are not appropriate in court. You need to present yourself as a professional and in a way that is acceptable to the environment wherein you are working. The courtroom is where you are working that day.*

Tannahill Glen puts it this way:

> *The key to dressing is authenticity. If you can't present yourself authentically and still tailor your clothes to the situation, then it won't work. But like for any other situation in my life, when I'm going to court, I am going to dress appropriately.*
>
> *I recall in graduate school I'd bring my senior citizen mother to psychology conferences when they were in nice places, and she'd stare in amazement at the people who would show up: They couldn't dress themselves, they looked crazy, she said. You can't be taken seriously by patients if you don't look like you have sense enough to dress yourself. I don't know about you, but I want a doctor who can speak coherently and explain things. But also, they need to know how to button up their shirt. Or brush*

their hair. Or wear something that shows they've had contact with the outside world within the past 5 years. I look at it as presenting yourself professionally, but also in a way that is human and connects.

Dr. Glen also notes the importance of understanding regional variations in dress—that is, the language of clothing has dialects. Assumptions about what clothing means in one region of the country, or even county by county, can vary tremendously:

> *If you are in a big city, like Miami, then everyone is extremely well dressed. The women have their hair and nails done. It's different from city to city, but in Miami there is makeup, perfume, everything. If you come in looking like a dowdy frump, the people will look at you differently. But if you come in looking like everyone else in the room, including the jurors, then the chances of them accepting your opinion is greater. If you look like you don't have enough sense to dress yourself in the courtroom, then they will take that seriously. It's not a case of just "looking serious" but it's a matter of, do you have sense enough to dress for the occasion? It doesn't mean you have to wear all black. But if you are in Miami, you want to dress up. That's what everyone on the jury is expecting.*
>
> *If I am testifying in a small town in Florida where the majority of the people on the jury are wearing jeans, then I am going to dress down—like a pants suit, or more recently a shift dress with a cardigan, with beige shoes. Very simple things. Professional but not over the top. Take your cues from the jury.*
>
> *There was one case in south Georgia, a military town, there were a number of women on the jury. You'd think maybe you'd be dressing for a rural jury, but I figured it'd be more of an urban mix and I went in there with my usual high-heeled, pointy-toed shoes; I'm known for crazy shoes at work. The attorney who brought me there was delighted because the women on the jury were talking to me during the breaks trying to find out where I got my shoes. The defense attorney nearly had a kitten. The judge didn't seem to care.*

> *The clothes I choose when I go into court makes a difference. I am in a region of the country that is economically depressed. The jury will not be impressed by fancy clothes and excessive jewelry. I dress traditionally conservative, usually a skirt and jacket, not too flashy or trendy. I wouldn't wear bright red lipstick. That is my uniform for work anyway, and I wouldn't have to change that for a jury.*—Kristie Nies, PhD, ABPP-CN

> *It's important to dress professionally, not like a hippie or a grad student. Also, do not wear excessively expensive clothing or jewelry as some attorneys will try to use this to try and make this an issue of what you earn, not what you are there to offer as an expert.*—Nancy Hebben, PhD, ABPP-CN

> *You should look professional and conservative. Every year, I show the movie* My Cousin Vinnie *to prep my students for the Harvard Law mock trials. Vinnie shows up in an outlandish outfit and the judge yells at him.*—Ira K. Packer, PhD, ABPP (Forensic)

Attorney Mark DeBofsky offers some sound advice: "You do not want to put on anything that will call attention to yourself. You want the people who are listening to your testimony to focus on what you are saying, not on what you are wearing."

OUR BODIES IN SPACE

What do our posture, our hand gestures, our movement (or lack of movement) communicate to others? Our academic training places almost 100% of the focus on the content of our communication and almost none on how we position our bodies as we explain that content. Because we have not been in the habit of paying attention to our bodies in space as we talk about our science, watching a video of ourselves can be enlightening.

Posture

Just as the clothes we choose to wear influence how others perceive and treat us, the way we choose to carry our bodies in space influences others' perceptions of and reactions to us. As noted in Chapter 1, research suggests that adopting an open, expansive posture projects confidence to others and generates an internal feeling of confidence.[6]

As women, we may cross our legs and our arms while sitting, creating the smallest possible body volume. Our gestures may be small and contained. What are we communicating when we sit or move like this? Closed, protective body postures may project submission and lack of confidence.[7] In contrast, an open body posture with arms resting on the arms of the chair may convey higher status and confidence. Sitting slightly forward in the chair may signal engagement with the jury.

Just as women may want to avoid traditional "ladylike" postures that diminish confidence, men will want to avoid exaggerated postures that project arrogance. In a culture where "manspreading" (the habit of spreading one's legs wide open while sitting that one effectively takes up two seats) has become so common it has to be addressed with an advertising campaign on the New York subways,[8] experts may not be aware that their overly expanded posture on the stand is communicating privilege or overreach.

Just as many of us learned to do a body scan as a relaxation exercise by progressively relaxing each muscle group, an expert can go through a posture scan periodically while waiting for the next question during cross or direct examination. Am I curled in on myself protectively, or sitting up straight, in a relaxed, open posture? Am I sprawled unprofessionally? Am I appearing defensive with arms crossed over my chest—a different posture than the open one I had during direct? As with any change in social pragmatics, a change in habitual posture or body position best occurs over a period of months, as we practice being mindful of our bodies in space and consciously correct our posture.

Moving about the courtroom

In Chapter 10, "Visuals," a case is made for placing flipcharts or enlargements on easels in front of the jurors so experts have the chance to walk out of the witness box and speak directly to the jury. Leaving the witness box is always predicated on permission from the judge and can initially feel daunting to the expert. But what does that freedom of movement convey to jurors? Like a conference presenter who leaves the shelter of the lectern, walking down from the witness box can convey confidence and a willingness to leave the status of the raised witness box behind in order to share one's knowledge directly with jurors.

Facial expression and eye contact

While all of us may have eye contact and facial expressions that project warmth in our everyday interactions with people, just as Ricky Bobby in *Talladega Nights* loses his naturally engaging, warm personality in front of a camera, experts do in fact have to swim upstream against the chilling formality of the courtroom and their own nerves to consciously ensure that their natural warmth is expressed.

Lisa Stanford describes her use of body language, including eye contact and facial expression, to let jurors know that she is focused on them and that they are important to her:

> *I make very purposeful eye contact, a lot of warm facial expressions, smiling, leaning forward. I use a lot of nonverbal body language to let the jury know that they are the only thing I am thinking about now. And I want to make sure they understand what I am trying to tell them. That is all that matters to me in this moment. It's just us here. And I want to make it so the attorneys can't break that.*

David Williamson also emphasizes that he is conscious of projecting warmth when he is on the stand: "I don't want to come across as the cold, Vulcan neuropsychologist." Antonio Puente likewise allows the warmth he shares with his students and colleagues to stay with him when he is on the stand: "My manner on the stand is very folksy, down to earth; my goal is to engage people with human-to-human conversation using the best information possible. There is no place for arrogance when it comes to justice."

Presence

Warmth, confidence, direct eye contact, physically comfortable and open, grounded with a gravitas appropriate to the formality of the situation. This describes presence.

Just as a cross-examining attorney may try to draw experts off sides into stretching beyond their opinion, attoreys may try to draw experts off sides emotionally, shaking their presence, making them stumble into irritation, or, as in Ira Packer's cautionary tale, giggling:

> *Presence on the stand gets easier as you get older. I was a 27-year-old, early career psychologist 2 years into my job. This was a murder case that had a high media profile. At the time, many of the storekeepers in this city were Arab American, and the population was largely African American. Two African American kids went into*

a store and stole some stuff. As they were running out, the store owner pulls out a gun, shoots them in the back, saying, "I've had enough of this!" His legal team used an insanity defense. I did an evaluation and my opinion was that he did not meet criteria for the insanity defense. They then hired a psychiatrist from an Arabic state. The expert testified that the defendant was legally insane, as he had been "distracted from reality." I was thinking, "What the hell is this?" It was terrible testimony. I was the rebuttal witness. The expert was in his 50s and I was 27.

They had a great defense attorney who was very experienced and charismatic. "So! You are disagreeing with the eminent Dr. [opposing expert]?!"

I am looking at the audience and the district attorney starts smiling at this. One of my colleagues, unfortunately, was in the audience smiling at well. And I let out a little smirk at the description of the psychiatrist.

The attorney seized the moment, "Your Honor! My client is on trial for his life. This witness is laughing!" I know it's all for show, but nonetheless I am rattled.

The judge says, "All right, let's proceed. Repeat the question."

It is clear that the attorney's goal now is to get me to smile. "Once again. You have disagreed with the EMINENT . . ." And then he just stares at me for seconds before completing the question.

I am pinching myself, "You cannot smile . . . you cannot smile . . ."

At the end of the trial during closing arguments, the opposing attorney said, "Look, we have this eminent psychiatrist, and the prosecution is relying on this young, fresh-out-of-school whippersnapper."

The defendant got a hung jury. It should have been an open-and-shut case.

Physical gestures and "tells"

Scott Millis points out that if we focus on what our bodies are doing while we testify, we can identify "tells" of anxiety that we can use to make a course correction in the moment:

It is important to focus not just on content when testifying, but what your body is doing. When I am stressed I begin to breathe in a shallow manner. I think most people do. One of the things I force myself to do on cross is take a deep breath. It does two things. First, it forces me to breathe deeply and slowly. Second, that pause helps me to take control of the pace. If you think about it, the pause interferes with the attorney's ability to pressure you and badger you with rapid-fire questions. In taking the pause, and a physical breath, I take control of my testimony in a physical, nonverbal way.

A judge who preferred to have her name redacted also recommends that experts track their movements on the stand and warned against a "third rail" of physical movements in the courtroom:

> *NEVER let your hand touch any part of your body when you are on the witness stand—no touching of hair or clothes, no adjusting clothing, ties, scarves, blouses, belts, etc. Keep your body quiet so as not to distract from your words. Facial tics or hand movements are very distracting on the stand.*

While nonpurposeful hand movements are distracting, keeping one's hands folded during testimony may look unnatural. Comfortable, natural hand gestures to emphasize points are not only appropriate but, like an open posture, convey confidence. Lynn Blackburn comments, "We don't talk with our hands in our lap during real life. So, during testimony, I gesture, just as I would during a feedback session."

Greg Lee notes that he has never used visuals on the stand, such as enlarged charts or graphs. Rather, he explains impairment with hand gestures: "I have never used visuals. I will use my hands to explain relative impairment concepts. For example: 'We are expecting him to be here (right hand up) and here he is (left hand up)'."

VOICE

Expressed confidence is a form of communication that signals to our listeners the degree to which we are certain or uncertain about statements we make. The extent to which we signal confidence to others is affected in part by our own internal state (e.g., a "metacognitive" feeling of knowing our statement is true),[9] but it is also signaled by characteristics of our speech (e.g., rate and tone). While the literal content (the words we say) contributes to our listeners' perceptions of our confidence (e.g., "I am confident that . . ."), nonverbal cues have been found to be much more powerful.[10] Studies using evoked potentials suggests these judgments are made very rapidly.[11] Members of the jury can be expected to begin to process our expressed confidence within milliseconds.[12]

Rate of speech

There is mixed opinion in the literature about the effect of rapid speech on listeners' perceptions of expressed confidence. Some studies suggested that a slower rate of speech was associated with greater perception of confidence, while later studies suggest that moderate to faster speech is associated with confidence.[13] It is likely that there is a rate "sweet spot," with very slow speech suggesting hesitation, moderate to more rapid speech suggesting confidence, and very rapid speech suggesting anxious lack of confidence. Interestingly, there appear to be regional variations, where listeners have an ideal rate and speakers who vary from that rate may unwittingly project poor confidence.[14] Are you a Northeasterner testifying in the South? Your moderate rate of speech may seem lightning-fast to the jury.

When we are relaxed, confident, and in control our rate of speech is moderate. When we speak at a moderate rate, we are more likely to (1) be heard, (2) be perceived as credible, and (3) have time to formulate a clear, concise response.

One neuropsychologist who preferred to remain anonymous notes that he has a habit of speaking quickly in everyday life and makes a conscious effort to slow down in the courtroom.

I speak quickly. I try to monitor that. On the stand, I try to speak slowly. I overarticulate. Speaking slowly gives you time to think about the response.

I make a deliberate attempt to speak slowly. I have a tendency to talk fast, so much so that jurors will miss what I have to say. I also vary the cadence of my speech. It helps to keep the juries more in tune with what I am saying. Monotone delivery is very boring. By varying the cadence, I may stop midsentence, then begin to speak again. It helps me to control the pace, and emphasis. I will also vary the "energy" in the voice so it keeps them interested.—Scott Millis, PhD, ABPP-CN

A judge who preferred to remain anonymous also notes that a significant benefit of a slow cadence is that it gives jurors time to process often entirely new information that the expert is telling them.

Slow down when testifying so the jurors can absorb what you are saying, use the information in their brains, and make connections.

Upspeak and vocal fry

The phenomenon of vocal inflection rising at the end of a declaratory statement is known in linguistic circles as "upspeak." This style of speech is often associated with hesitancy, uncertainty, and lack of confidence. Tina Fey, in her book *Bossypants*,[15] asks us all to "speak in statements instead of apologetic questions. No one wants to go to a doctor who says, 'I'm going to be your surgeon? I'm here to talk to you about your procedure? I was first in my class at Johns Hopkins, so?' "

Another common vocal tic is known as "vocal fry" or "creak." This is when you lower your voice at the end of a word or phrase.

Both upspeak and vocal fry are common vocal styles of younger men and women, but women are often judged more harshly for using the style. In a fascinating National Public Radio "Fresh Air" episode, Terry Gross addressed the issue of gender in the social pragmatics of vocal tone, "From Upspeak to Vocal Fry: Are We 'Policing' Young Women's Voices?"[16] One of her guests, the journalist and Slate podcaster Jessica Grose, went to a vocal coach after being criticized for her upspeak and vocal fry by listeners who felt she sounded like their grandchildren: "In an effort to make my voice lower and more even, I will do 'vocal fry.' People find that irritating." Of course, she has also been criticized for having a voice that is too high. She points out that often advice to women about their vocal styles is like the maddening, unattainable advice about other aspects of women's workplace behavior, "Be aggressive but not too aggressive!"

After consulting with a vocal coach Grose noted, "I have started thinking of voice almost as the way I think about outfits. If I'm going for a job interview I'm going to wear a different outfit than when I'm out with my friends." She now consciously switches her vocal styles depending on her setting. (See Chapter 17, "Testifying in a Diverse World," for a discussion of the related concept, "code switching.")

Another guest on the show, Susan Sankin, a speech pathologist, stated,

When we present ourselves, the way we speak is our verbal image. Much the way people in the professional world typically don't go to work in sweats and a T-shirt, because they are more concerned about how they present themselves, a lot of the clients that come to see me are concerned about how they present themselves verbally. . . . Women are more criticized, but I see both men and women who want to change their voice. . . . They don't like the way they sound. They sound tentative to themselves. They sound unsure to themselves as well, and they feel that when they present themselves it sounds like they lack confidence, even though they are very capable, and they know that they have the capacity to sound better, more confident, more assured with some help. They just have developed a speech pattern that is a habit and they don't know how to break out of it. . . . If you are comfortable with your speech, that's great. If you are uncomfortable with your speech or feel it gets in the way of your professional goals, then change it.

Stanford linguist Penny Eckert, another guest on the radio show, did a study[17] where people over 40 view vocal fry as less authoritative. Younger people viewed fry and non-fry as equally authoritative. The take-home message from that study? You may want to assess the modal age of the jury before relaxing into your "weekend" vocal patterns.

Where am I going with all this? Ultimately, we all need to make the call of whether we're engaging in upspeak or fry. Is this vocal habit assisting my communication with jurors or is it communicating something that I don't intend?

Vocal tics

So, when many of us answer a question, we begin with a little verbal preface. Like I just did. Oliver James, in a *Guardian* essay,[18] describes "so" as a way of signaling that we are about to engage in a prepackaged explanation. It is the new "Look . . ." and rubs many the same (wrong) way. There is lore that says the use of "so" emerged from the hi-tech culture, where coders almost always felt no one could possibly understand them without lengthy pre-explanations. Speakers answering questions with "so" are letting us know that we will need to be briefed on the back story to be able to catch up to their actual answer. It often feels condescending.

"So" can also be a replacement for "um," "like," or "ah"—in other words, a meaningless (and distracting) filler. In my own practice, once alerted to this ubiquitous and potentially grating vocal habit, I became horrified at the frequency with which I was using it. In the office, I began to consciously break the habit, but it's insidious. During filming of a "day in the life" video for a legal case where an interviewer was asking me to explain various thinking problems a plaintiff was experiencing, I was relieved when the director had to reshoot an answer after someone walked through the set making noise. I had just caught myself starting that answer with "so"!

Attorney W. Scott Liebert notes that another vocal habit to avoid is the phrase, "to tell you the truth." Linguistically, this is a filler, a way of beginning a sentence. "These are common phrases we use when we are trying to gather our thoughts," he says, but in a courtroom, "the implication is everything that came before wasn't the truth."

While the literal content of some fillers like "to tell you the truth" clearly sends the wrong message, Ira Packer tells his trainees that it's okay to use "appropriate neutral fillers":

On the stand, you can pause prior to answering a question, but too long of a pause may seem awkward. You can say, "That's a good question." Or "In terms of his seizure history . . ." This buys you a little time.

The idea of identifying and eradicating vocal tics in the weeks prior to testimony is a far-fetched goal. It's more realistic to begin the process of self-assessment well before you need to go on the stand and practice culling vocal tics over a long period of time. Your patients, colleagues, students, and conference lecture attendees will thank you for your courageous linguistic self-reflection.

SOCIAL PRAGMATICS SPECIFIC TO CROSS

Because members of the jury typically do not have background knowledge that will allow them to know when an attorney asks a cross-examination question that is a direct, devastating hit to your opinion, or a completely out-of-left-field query that has nothing to do with the opinion at hand, jurors watch experts closely for changes in their body language or vocal pattern. Clear discomfort, abashment, or defensive anger coming from the witness may be the only sign to jurors that the expert's opinion has been effectively challenged.

This is why experts are warned not to "take the bait" or become emotionally upset on the stand. It signals to jurors that the question they were asked was a "hit" and thus a big deal. Holding your social pragmatics steady makes it hard for attorneys to appear to have damaged your opinion. Conversely, experts who appear to abruptly shrink in posture, change their tone of voice, speak more quickly, or lose eye contact with the jury may be sending nonverbal signals to the jury that they believe their opinion has been effectively devastated, even if in reality their nonverbal signals reflect anxiety over being asked *any* questions by the cross-examining attorney, astute or not.

Attorney Wayne Miller notes that the best witnesses are unflappable during cross examination:

In a particular case that was videotaped that I now use as a teaching example, I was extremely well prepared, and I thought I did a really good job against the opposing expert witness. As the trial was videotaped, I've used it as a teaching tool ever since. I have perpetually reviewed my cross-exam of the opposing expert witness. I have realized that I don't think I touched him. He did a tremendous job because he was unflappable. He refused to take the bait. It made him a very tough expert witness. Jurors are generally not equipped to handle things outside of the scope of their experience and I won't even be elitist about it. Who among us is able to handle things that are not familiar to us? They are looking to the emotional reaction of the expert to see whether they should be upset about the issue. As the defense expert showed no shame or guilt, the jurors never realized how badly he misused the data.

Nancy Hebben notes that when the cross-examination questions come out of left field, she consciously maintains the same social pragmatics she uses when on direct:

> *When the cross comes you want to maintain the same posture as during the direct. Maintain the same style of interaction with the jury. It's hard to not be nervous, particularly in the first days of testifying when you are new at it. There may be questions that set you off internally, but you have to not let it show.*

Rod Swenson describes keeping one's social pragmatics steady as "making it look easy":

> *You have to make it look easy. You can't be tense. You have to be confident but not arrogant and not argumentative. On cross exam, the attorney wants you to look arrogant, or that you are an advocate for the plaintiff. I look at cross-examining attorneys like a doubting family member. You aren't going to change his mind. But I go into cross knowing I am not going to change* **my** *mind! Even under cross you have to stay human, even when you are being attacked.*

An attorney who preferred to remain anonymous notes that just like presidential candidates, some experts can deflect criticism really well:

> *Some people can deflect criticism and others can't. You can see it in the presidential election. The jury immediately picks up on that. For example, some neuropsychologists who make a living as an expert can get defensive when confronted with that fact; others do not.*

Another important aspect of social pragmatics is eye contact. Cheryl Weinstein advises, "Speak to the jury, no matter what." By looking at the jury and focusing on them in cross, it reminds us that the point of our testimony is to clarify our assessments and our opinions for the jury. If an expert frames cross-examination questions as opportunities to make our opinions clearer, looking directly at the jurors focuses us on this goal. Of course, the cross-examining attorney's goal for the questions may be very different—to make experts look noncredible or to muddy the waters with questions that allow experts to discuss only small pieces of their assessment out of context. But if we look at the jury, it is easier to recall the real purpose of speaking on the stand: to clarify.

Resisting the physical response to threat

The advice to hold one's social pragmatics consistent between direct and cross is both important and difficult to carry out. Part of the natural shift in social pragmatics that one needs to avoid is generated from the unpleasant fact that the job of the attorney on direct is to ask you to share your wise and helpful opinions, while the job of the attorney on cross is to help the jury understand how incompetent and noncredible you are. That is, the key to following the advice is to resist a physical response to explicit or implicit threat.

What does that look like? In my own practice, as the courtroom makes the shift from direct testimony to cross examination, I replay in my mind how my body has felt as I have been sitting during direct examination: How I have been oriented in my chair? Which way have I been facing as I listen to and then answer questions? How often have I smiled and nodded as I listen to questions? What has my tone of voice, my rate of speech, and the length of my answers been? I then periodically check in during cross examination, doing a literal body scan, making sure that I stick to those same physical experiences. If anxiety due to the innate threat of cross examination has led me to stiffen up and change these nonverbals, I will consciously recalibrate.

Closely related is the benefits for one's own emotional state of consciously holding, or recalibrating to, a relaxed, open body posture, a calm vocal cadence, and a warm, friendly facial expression during cross examination. Many psychologists are familiar with the facial feedback hypothesis.[19]

As an undergraduate, my classmates and I replicated one of the better-known experiments that demonstrates the hypothesis by asking a random sample to hold a pen either with their teeth or with their lips while reading a Calvin and Hobbes comic strip. Sure enough, those holding a pen with their teeth (whose facial muscles were therefore posed in a smile) rated the comics as funnier than those holding the pen with their lips (whose facial muscles were therefore posed in a frown). The facial feedback hypothesis suggests that when we feel emotions, we respond with changes in facial expressions like smiles, but conversely, our emotional system also uses feedback from our muscles to understand what emotions we should be experiencing. When I am anxious I begin to breathe quickly. If I consciously slow my breaths, my emotional system will use the feedback that I am breathing slowly and deeply to understand that I am calm. Consciously arranging our muscles in a relaxed, open posture, keeping a warm facial expression and holding other social pragmatics steady from direct to cross not only sends signals to jurors that we are calm and confident, it sends the same message to our own limbic systems.

TRAINING SOCIAL PRAGMATICS

Trying to identify and change awkward or distancing social pragmatics we use during testimony is difficult. Marcus Boccaccini tells his students, "'Be expressive, use your hands while talking.' My students, trying to take my advice, will be talking and they recall, 'Oh! I'm supposed to move my hands!' and will suddenly pay attention to their hands. Which they didn't typically do. The result is these stiff and unnatural gestures." Dr. Boccaccini also comments on the risk of attempting to change social pragmatics, particularly when the change is new:

> *The research into nonverbals indicates that there is a risk of looking too rigid if you attempt to control your nonverbal behavior too carefully. Don't go up on the stand and be a big slouch. But at the same time, don't go up there and try to control your behavior. You will look uncomfortable. In our witness preparation research, we could find some effects for posture, but there was always a drawback: People who tried to change their posture often appeared more stiff and rigid.*

He notes that there should be a "confidence interval" around any change—that is, new changes will likely result in the witness looking uncomfortable. This argues strongly that experts should take steps well before testimony is scheduled to identify distracting social pragmatics that send unintended messages and gradually modify them over months, not days or weeks. But how can we identify the social pragmatics that should be changed?

Identifying changes

Ira Packer uses video social pragmatics training in his forensic postdoctoral program.

> *In our training program, we have a mock trial and we video it. We give advice to trainees prior to the trial: "Keep your voice loud and clear. Keep the same tone and cadence whether you are on direct or cross. Your body language should be still and comfortable. Don't fidget with your hands. Make sure to say yes or no, and not 'uh huh.' Do not nod. When you are feeling nervous, and you will, keep your head still, and keep your voice up. Especially when you are anxious. At times the attorney will get you to acknowledge that you may have misstated a fact, or had a minor error in your report. You need to remind yourself that this is not a fatal flaw. Acknowledge the point; it is never worth digging in if the attorney is correct. But even when you acknowledge, do it casually and calmly. Always keep your voice up. If you have a high, thin voice, bring down the register. If you know that your voice tone rises when you are nervous, consciously bring it down."*
>
> *When we review the mock trial video, we focus on social pragmatics. For example, are your hands quiet? If you use your hands expressively that is okay, but does it become distracting? We also review the voice. We pick up a lot of issues with the voice. It is common to not notice that your voice goes up a little when you are uncertain.*

Reviewing videotaped testimony gives us an outstanding opportunity to see and hear gestures, postures, vocal inflections, vocal tics, or other mannerisms that might not convey the message that we intend. Should you have the opportunity to attend a continuing education course in the format of a mock trial, ask a fellow attendee to record it for you.

Another more common opportunity to see yourself testify is a videotaped deposition or prerecorded testimony. Regarding the latter, occasionally experts who cannot attend a trial in person will have their testimony videotaped in advance. Typed deposition transcripts are not as helpful visually but can still be very useful to signal overuse of neutral or annoying vocal tics. Asking a colleague to videotape your next conference presentation, particularly the question-and-answer session, or having a videocamera set up as you teach a class is an excellent way to capture your speaking style, if not your testifying style.

Making changes

In Chapter 1, I described my experience at an Alan Alda Center for Communicating Science boot camp. On one of the last days of the week-long boot camp, we all went into the Stony Brook University School of Journalism's television studio and were interviewed about our research in a mock television segment. I am sure I was not alone in mentally rehearsing all of the new body posture, vocal inflection, and gestural changes I wanted to be sure to correctly execute while thinking on my feet about using vivid metaphors to communicate the specific content of what I planned to say. As you can imagine, when I reviewed my tape, I saw that I had made progress but had not been able to pull all of it together.

Changing social pragmatics is necessarily an exercise in mindfulness. And as with any mindfulness practice, the key is to engage in moments of awareness throughout your day and then nonjudgmentally shift your posture, gestures, vocal tone, or content. It's a process that takes months, and it can be done in your office, with colleagues, while teaching a class, or when giving a presentation. The goal is a gradual shift that eventually feels comfortable and natural.

FINALLY, HUMOR

Using humor is tricky in court. If a cross-examining attorney's goal is to escalate tension to draw an expert into responding in a noncredible, irritable, arrogant, angry way, use of humor can send a message that the expert is relaxed and not rattled. However, humor might also send a message that the expert is not taking the situation seriously or, even worse, is mocking the attorney.

We tend to be a dark profession, and therefore we don't know a lot about the positive effects and social uses of humor. There have been studies identifying humor as a common coping strategy for individuals exposed to secondhand trauma, such as police officers and social workers.[20] This suggests that, particularly during a trial involving violent crime or traumatic illness or injury, jurors may experience a moment of humor as helping them to cope with the trial content. Other studies suggest that laughter may lower stress hormones[21] and trigger the release of endogenous opioids.[22] In short, laughter relaxes us and makes us feel good.

In an engaging TED talk,[23] comedian Chris Bliss shares his theory of how humor helps people accept and understand information they would otherwise be closed to. He notes that fear and anxiety raise walls between people. Using humor releases endorphins and lowers the stress response, therefore lowering defenses. In his view, "The alchemy of laughter turns our walls into windows revealing a fresh and unexpected point of view."

Attorney Brian Pomerantz tells the story of one of his favorite experts on the stand effectively using humor during recross:

> The prosecution claimed my guy couldn't have all of these intellectual problems, because he is a Crip. They said that the Crips have a Crip school in prison where they teach you how to fake intellectual disability. I said to (my expert in the case),
>
> *Q: Is it possible that this guy went to a Crip school in prison to learn how to fake it?*
>
> *She said,*
>
> *A: I don't know; it's possible he went to the Crip school, but he wouldn't have passed.*
>
> This came up origially while sitting in her office during our prehearing preparation. Because she is witty, she made a joke. I said to her, "What do I need to ask you to get that exact answer again?" In the hearing, I used that question as the windup. She saw it coming. The judge lit up. He loved it. He ate it up. The state was making a big deal of this "Crips course" and she simply said, "He may have taken it, but he couldn't pass it. Because he can't learn. And here is why . . ."

Importantly, attorney Pomerantz clarified that the expert's use of the humorous rejoinder was planned in advance. During their pretrial preparation in her office, she initially made the witty joke, which also happened to be a great answer to the issue they knew would be raised by opposing counsel. Together, they decided it was appropriate.

Robert Heilbronner shares an anecdote about using humor during cross examination from one of his mentors, Bob Hart:

> Bob was on the stand as a treating witness. The plaintiff with a TBI was clearly severely impaired. The defense attorney comes on the stand and provides him with what the attorney assumes is a piece of information that will shatter his picture of the plaintiff as someone who is seriously impaired.
>
> *Q: Dr. Hart, would it surprise you to know that Ms. Smith plays poker with the other residents in her facility?*
>
> *A: Yeah, but how many games has she won?*

Ted Peck has a rule against using humor in court, because he feels the risks are greater than the payoff. He notes he violated his personal rule only once:

> If you are asked a really bad question you should never tell the court, "That's a really bad question." I was testifying in a complicated mold case with several witnesses. The case had been ongoing for over a week. I had been on the stand for 4 hours altogether and this was my third hour of cross examination. It was several years ago, when the CSI: Las Vegas show had the Gil Grissom character signing off. His character was going off the show and it received a great deal of TV publicity. The attorney made a mistake that I have been told attorneys should never make: asking the expert a question one doesn't know the answer to, and one where the expert can make some fun at your expense.
>
> *Q: Doctor, you have been testifying all afternoon. These juries today, they watch* CSI. *They know what evidence is. Did you collect any fingerprints? Did you collect any DNA? Where is your evidence to support your opinions?*
>
> Looking at the jury, I noticed that two jurors were asleep, so I changed the tone of my voice, raised my volume a little, changed my body posture, and exclaimed, "You're right!" At which point the two jurors woke up.
>
> *A: You're right! I don't collect DNA. I don't collect fingerprints. In my profession, we give tests of thinking and emotions and behavior, we give standardized, normed tests, and those tests produce test scores, and those scores, and how they are interpreted, are my evidence. And as Gil Grissom says on* CSI: Las Vegas, *we will let the evidence speak for itself!*
>
> The two jurors who had just woken up each raised their right hands in a "winner-type gesture" and said, "Yeah, Gil!" The cross-examining attorney didn't really know what to do next. He had to stop.
>
> The point is, you should be extremely wary of making a remark that expresses anything other than circumspect professionalism. You should venture out of that range with great hesitancy. There are some times, though, where you feel that what you're saying is an appropriate answer . . . Hopefully, the jury and Court will agree!

Lisa Stanford shares a story of gently pushing back at an attorney on cross who was giving her a very hard time about making a diagnosis without being an MD:

> *Q: Dr. Stanford, you are making a diagnosis when I think you shouldn't be.*
>
> *A: Why is that? Explain that to me.*
>
> *Q: Well, I will give you an example. My son comes up to me the other day and says, "Dad, you have two left feet." He is misdiagnosing me because I don't have two left feet. What do you think about that?*
>
> *A: Well, I think maybe you are just a bad dancer.*
>
> The whole courtroom was laughing. The judge was laughing. The attorney said, "No further questions."

Throughout the interviews experts, judges, and attorneys commented on the benefits and perils of using humor in the courtroom. The consensus emerged that if you're not sure, don't make a joke. Manfred Greiffenstein counseled, "Only one joke per trial. And choose that moment carefully." And Ira Packer cautions, "Very experienced experts can get away with more humor, but avoid humor if you are testifying while young. There can be some minor moments or levity; it's okay to go with the flow if there is a humorous moment in court, but don't try to be humorous."

NOTES

1. E.g., Reid, A., Lancuba, V., & Morrow, B. (1997). Clothing style and formation of first impressions. *Perceptual and Motor Skills, 84*(1), 237–238; Suedfeld, P., Bochner, S., & Metas, C. (1971). Petitioner's attire and petition signing by peace demonstrators: A field experiment. *Journal of Applied Social Psychology, 1*, 278–283.
2. E.g., Peluchette, J. V., Karl, K., & Rust, K. (2006). Dressing to impress: Beliefs and attitudes regarding workplace attire. *Journal of Business and Psychology, 21*(1), 45–63.
3. Slepian, M. L., Ferber, S. N., Gold, J. M., & Rutchick, A. M. (2015). The cognitive consequences of formal clothing. *Social Psychological and Personality Science, 6*(6), 661–668.
4. Adam, H., & Galinsky, A. D. (2012). Enclothed cognition. *Journal of Experimental Social Psychology, 48*(4), 918–925.
5. Kraus, M. W., & Mendes, W. B. (2014). Sartorial symbols of social class elicit class-consistent behavioral and physiological responses: A dyadic approach. *Journal of Experimental Psychology: General, 143*(6), 2330–2340.
6. Cuddy, A. (2015). *Presence: Bringing your boldest self to your biggest challenges.* New York: Little, Brown and Company.
7. Cuddy, A. (2015). *Presence: Bringing your boldest self to your biggest challenges.* New York: Little, Brown and Company.
8. Fitzsimmons, E. G. (2014, December 21). A scourge is spreading. M.T.A.'s cure? Dude, close your legs: "Manspreading" on New York subways is target of new M.T.A. campaign. *New York Times.* https://www.nytimes.com/2014/12/21/nyregion/MTA-targets-manspreading-on-new-york-city-subways.html?_r=0

9. Swerts, M. and Krahmer, E. (2005). Audiovisual prosody and feeling of knowing. *Journal of Memory and Language, 53, 81–94.*
10. Walker, Michael B. (1977). *Australian Journal of Psychology*, 29(1), pp. 45–57.
11. E.g., Jiang, X., & Pell, M. (2015). On how the brain decodes vocal cues about speaker confidence. *Cortex, 66*, 9–34.
12. E.g., Jiang, X., & Pell, M. (2015). On how the brain decodes vocal cues about speaker confidence. *Cortex, 66*, 9–34.
13. Apple, W., Streeter, L. A., & Krauss, R. M. (1979). Effects of pitch and speech rate on personal attributions. *Journal of Personality and Social Psychology, 37*(5), 715–727.
14. Street, R. L., Jr., & Brady, R. M. (1982), Speech rate acceptance ranges as a function of evaluative domain, listener speech rate, and communication context. *Communication Monographs, 49*(4), 290–308
15. Fey, T. (2011). *Bossypants*. New York: Reagan Arthur Books, p. 77.
16. NPR. (2015, July 23). From upspeak to vocal fry: are we "policing" young women's voices? *Fresh Air*. https://www.npr.org/2015/07/23/425608745/from-upspeak-to-vocal-fry-are-we-policing-young-womens-voices
17. Glass, I. (2015, January 23). If you don't have anything nice to say, SAY IT IN ALL CAPS. *This American Life*. https://www.thisamericanlife.org/radio-archives/episode/545/transcript
18. James, O. (2013, July 26). So, here's a carefully packaged sentence that shows me in my best light. *The Guardian*. https://www.theguardian.com/commentisfree/2013/jul/26/so-sentence-starter-artifice-manipulation
19. Strack, F., Martin, L., & Stepper, S. (1988). Inhibiting and facilitating conditions of the human smile: A nonobtrusive test of the facial feedback hypothesis. *Journal of Personality and Social Psychology, 54*, 768–777.
20. Craun, S., & Bourke, M. (2014). The use of humor to cope with secondary traumatic stress. *Journal of Child Sexual Abuse, 23*, 840–852.
21. Berk, L., Tan, S. A., Fry, W. F., Napier, B. J., Lee, J. W., Hubbard, R. W., . . . Eby, W.C. (1989). Neuroendocrine and stress hormone changes during mirthful laughter. *American Journal of Medical Science, 298*(6), 390–396.
22. Manninen, S., Tuominen, L., Dunbar, R. I., Karjalainen, T., Hirvonen, J., Arponen, E., . . . Nummenmaa, L. (2017). Social laughter triggers endogenous opioid release. *Journal of Neuroscience, 37*(25), 6125–6131.
23. Bliss, C. (2012). Comedy is translation [Video file]. https://www.ted.com/speakers/chris_bliss.

7 Jargon

One of the most difficult things as a trial attorney was getting doctors to understand that unless the hearer can understand what they are saying, everything else is lost.—Judge Lynne Battaglia

Chapter 6, "Social Pragmatics of Testifying," included a compelling piece of research demonstrating that people are more successful at high-stakes, winner-take-all negations when they are dressed in business suits as opposed to sweats. The actual title of the article was "Sartorial Symbols of Social Class Elicit Class-Consistent Behavioral and Physiological Responses: A Dyadic Approach." Even as a neuropsychologist with a doctoral degree I have difficulty decoding the article's title; I would never suspect it was a fascinating article about how power dressing makes us better negotiators. How would a bright engineer or an accountant on a jury be able to decode it? This is an object lesson in jargon "burying the lead. t." Similarly, when we use jargon during testimony, jurors cannot access our messages, no matter how important or compelling they are.

As discussed in previous chapters, one important component in disrupting the academic communication style is to identify and eliminate jargon from our vocabularies. I use the phrase "identify and eliminate" very specifically, because after years of using a particular piece of jargon, it can become invisible to us. I was shocked at some of the words that attorneys and judges pointed to when I asked them about unhelpful jargon psychologists and neuropsychologists use in court. This chapter first makes the case for eliminating jargon and then shines a light on (and offers replacement phrases for) many of these common terms.

THE ARGUMENT AGAINST JARGON

Judge Jay Blitzman describes an effective expert witness as one who makes the listener feel like a genius:

> *What makes a good expert witness? Someone who is able to demystify the jargon of a certain discipline. The commonality is using plain English to bring the concepts down into understandable bites so that laypeople like myself feel like a genius: "Oh! I understand that!" The listener feels like, "I can get it." Then you can have a conversation. The good experts have conversations. When you are lecturing at someone, it is very distancing; it's not a conversation.*

Judge Blitzman makes the important point that our use of plain English is the gateway into the conversational relationship with the jury. Are we using plain, regular, accessible, understandable language? If not, we literally cannot communicate *with* our listeners and will be left speaking *at* our listeners.

Attorney Mark DeBofsky notes that during direct examination, he will often have to interrupt the flow of testimony and ask, "Doctor, you and I might understand what you are talking about, but I am not sure that the judge and the jury will understand. Why don't you break this down?"

A good attorney will recognize when the expert has veered off into language that others in the court have no access to and will rehabilitate the testimony by asking for clarification. However, even if the expert then uses language that is clearer, his or her relationship with the jury has been damaged. Judge Battaglia notes that using jargon feels arrogant to listeners:

> *Medical witnesses are used to speaking to each other and so they use terms that are shortcuts. There is a certain arrogance in the use of the terminology, meaning it separates doctors from the rest of the population. Lawyers do it, too. It takes humility to be able to say, "This is what I am talking about. Broken down, this means 'x'" without feeling threatened by breaking it down into something simpler.*

This point is worth emphasizing. Jargon doesn't just create an access barrier to our messages; it makes people angry. Nancy Hebben notes that others often experience the use of jargon as experts' way of trying to demonstrate their intelligence: "It doesn't help the issue. It doesn't make you seem accessible. If I have to use a technical term, I just explain it."

Neil Pliskin rolls his eyes at experts who describe impulsive responding on the Stroop test as "the ability to suppress a preponent response":

> *You have to use language jurors can understand. You have to make it relevant. Use straight forward language people can understand while staying true to the information you need to impart. You don't want to come across as a big know-it-all or patronize people.*

Manfred Greiffenstein cautioned experts to be careful when they simplify their jargon. He explained that it's easy to be condescending when you simplify and it's hard to do it with respect:

> *Simplify the most complex terms. It's the same way I write my papers that I publish. That's what I was taught in graduate scool. Use the simplest language possible without being insulting.*

Paul Kaufmann makes an important point that even though we might lose some precision when we let go of some jargon, it's alright if the rephrase isn't 100% scientifically accurate:

> *When you translate jargon into regular language, some neuropsychologists might feel that the way you rephrased it may not be as scientifically accurate. It may not be fully scientifically accurate because it is less precise, but that is one purpose of being an effective expert: You take very complicated things and you are trying to assist the jury. Federal rule of testimony #702: You are there to assist the jury to make a decision. I keep that in the forefront of my mind.*

JARGON TO WATCH OUT FOR

Attorney DeBofsky tells the startling story of a case involving a spinal impairment where, 3 days into testimony, the judge said, "This may come off as a really stupid question, but what does the word *lumbar* mean?" This is an important cautionary tale. I was stunned when I heard it as I just assumed everyone knows what "lumbar" means. But common medical terms are often not familiar to even very highly educated individuals if their education is not in medicine or behavioral science. As experts who spend years using professional terms casually with colleagues, the fact that other outside the field do not know their meaning disappears. Here are some words to watch out for.

Endorse

I was taken aback when Judge Christina Harms told me that the word *endorse* is confusing for people. It had completely disappeared for me as sounding like jargon. She makes a strong argument:

> *The classic use in psychology of the word "endorse" is a real problem. The plaintiff "endorsed" feelings of depression, blah, blah, blah. For the rest of the world, "endorse" sounds like what athletes do with sneakers, like Nike. Or what you do with political candidates. I've endorsed Romney for president. It's a really bizarre verb to the legal world and, again, it makes everybody's head snap, so I've had to convince my postdoctoral fellows to stop using that word in forensic report writing.*

Cognitive

We use it so often as psychologists that it's easy to forget that most people don't know what *cognitive* means. Whether I'm on the stand or talking to my patients, my goal is to not use *cognitive*; I'll say *thinking abilities* instead. Manfred Greiffenstein noted that he would use *mental ability* instead of *cognitive*. Neil Pliskin substitutes the phrase *behavior and thinking abilities*.

Battery and Protocol

"His test battery was normal." Huh? Jurors will not be familiar with the word *battery* to describe a set of tests. They may picture a test given on a computer that is battery-operated, but more likely they just won't understand the sentence. "His test protocol was normal" is no better. Try "All of the scores on the tests he took during our day together were normal" or "the set of tests he took."

Gentleman

Lisa McDermott notes that common professional terminology can turn off jurors. When other psychologists hear a patient or defendant referred to as a "56-year-old gentleman" we understand that this is a longstanding convention and is not a value judgment on the part of the examiner. But jurors don't know about this convention:

> *You have to understand that if you are referring to the defendant in a death penalty case as a gentleman, you may have three jurors thinking in their minds, "This is not a gentleman." Terminology is important. "He is a 56-year-old gentleman" can be a loaded phrase to some. Using a client's name is also a way of humanizing the person.*

Independent

One attorney who preferred to remain anonymous notes that he is frequently frustrated when experts say, "He lives independently." In the medical field, we frequently use the phrase to mean simply that a person is not living in a group home or institution. In the legal world, however, a case might hinge on the accurate use the label "independent":

> *It is a significant issue for most of my clients: Can they live independently? I had a client the other day say she lives independently. Well, she lives independently, but her sister comes over every morning and helps. And her sister's husband makes all her meals. But they don't have any hired help, so she is independent! The term is not a medical term. You probably describe your grandmother as living independently, but she has maybe $10,000 worth of nursing services coming in a month. In my jurisdiction, it's all about me getting people the services they need. It's a relative term. My 92-year-old grandmother is independent. What I mean is, for her age and situation, as opposed to her cohort who are in care homes. It doesn't mean she doesn't need help.*

Impaired

Tom Boll, and many other experts I interviewed, take issue with the use of *impaired*, both because jurors are likely to attach an imprecise meaning to it and because it reflects a degree of intellectual sloppiness on the part of the expert. Variations of the phrase "people are impaired, test scores are not" were common reactions to this particular piece of jargon.

> *People use the words "impaired," "borderline impaired," or "mildly impaired" because that is what is in the book. But a score isn't impaired unless a person is impaired. A score may be low, it may be a meager performance, but impaired is very different than low; impaired is very different than short. Impaired means something went wrong. It doesn't mean that you didn't do very well. A lot of people don't do very well in golf. I went out last time and shot a 95. That's a pretty damn poor*

performance. But I'm not impaired. I had a very bad day. It doesn't mean I have impairment. The guy I played with shot a 114, but the week prior he shot an 84.

I am paid not to give the tests, not to give the scores, but to interpret the patient's evaluation. Just because the normative table says "impaired," I won't put down the word "impaired." Once a table is telling you someone is impaired, and they have no idea who the patient is, it is misinformation, and more than not helpful.

Borderline

Many interviewees point out that the term "borderline" to describe a test score is very confusing for non-psychologists. Borderline normal? Just missing average? Because it has no clear meaning outside of the world of standardized assessment, it becomes a projective screen, potentially conjuring up 12 different impressions for 12 different jurors when it is used. Experts may feel they have to use it because it is in test manuals.

> If an expert testifies that something is borderline, it seems like the person is saying, "You are almost there." I have not asked experts to use another term, but how I handle it is ask,
>
> *Q: Where does the term "borderline" come from?*
>
> *A: It comes from a historic test. Really what it meant was "borderline mentally retarded."*
>
> Then the term makes more sense. There is a context.- Attorney, Anonymous

While providing a broader context for the word "borderline," is helpful, it is often better to avoid the word altogether. When a specific test performance is described to the jury, the full context of the score, rather than a descriptor like "borderline" can be better utilized. In my own practice, I might say,

> *Her score was surprisingly low for a person who worked as an English teacher all of her life. If you put 100 people in a room her age, she was worse than 95 of them on this vocabulary test. That is clearly a change from her lifelong function . . .*

Average

What does the word *average* mean to the typical juror? A "C" grade? Good? Not impaired? Cheryl Weinstein defines it for jurors as "Average is a beautiful word. It means normal."

Gait

We are so used to the formulaic opening phrase of a mental status exam that it's easy to forget the word *gait* is inaccessible to most people. It is an object lesson in using an inaccessible word when a plain word works equally well. Let's just all say *walked*.

Bilateral

"Mr. Liu's function was normal bilaterally." In my own practice, I try to eliminate words like *bilateral* from my reports as well as my speech. It is actually typing less letters to write "b-o-t-h-h-a-n-d-s."

Upper extremity

This is one of my favorite examples of meaningless jargon. "Hand and/or arm" is much more straightforward, and when laypeople realize that "upper extremity" means nothing more than "hand and/or arm," they should be annoyed at our field. In Chapter 21, "Reports," I advocate writing forensic reports that use the same vivid, clear, succinct language that we strive to use on the witness stand. Eliminating phrases like "upper extremity" is a good place to start.

Motoric

Using *motoric* to describe movements is almost always far too specific a term for communicating with the outside world. There is very little that we need to explain as psychologists and neuropsychologists that requires the distinction between *motoric* and *nonmotoric* movements. The convention of always specifying that a movement is motoric creates unnecessary access problems. Unless there is a good reason, *movement* is fine.

Lateralized

This is another impenetrable term. Try "There was a big difference between the language side of her brain, which was working well, and the non-language side, which was not working well."

Euthymic

Neil Pliskin makes a plea to the field, "Just say their mood was normal."

Affect

What is the difference between *mood* and *affect*? No one sitting in the jurors' box will be able to tell you. Blunted affect, constricted affect, restricted affect, discongruent affect: None of these phrases has any meaning outside of our field. Ira Packer notes that when explaining some forms of mental illness to jurors, experts need to bring up the concept of an inappropriate affect. He will use the phrase and immediately explain, "Mr. Collins has an inappropriate affect: For example, while he was talking about something sad, he started to laugh."

Although it is a longstanding convention in our field to comment on a patient's mood and affect, unless there is a clinically relevant difference between the two, there may be no good reason to bring up the term *affect*. An expert can more clearly and vividly say, "I directly observed Ms. Plaintiff to be upbeat and positive throughout our testing session. She frequently smiled and made appropriate jokes."

Executive function

Very few people outside of the field of psychology understand what *executive function* is. The phrase is particularly dangerous because it includes words with commonly understood meanings, so jurors may not recognize that this is a jargon phrase they don't understand. Rather, they will hear "executive" and "function" and may continue listening, assuming their thought bubble and the experts are in sync. Instead of *executive function*, experts can simply explain concretely what they mean: flexible problem-solving, planning, time management, and so forth. See Chapter 13, "Specific Psychiatric and Neurological Disorders," for vivid strategies to explain problems with executive function to jurors.

Defensive and Defended

Judge Harms notes that when she first encountered the concept of people being so *defensive* in their psychological test answers that the test is invalidated, the word just didn't make sense to her as a judge:

> *Finally a psychologist explained to me that the word means, "Basically, it's faking good." And I said, "Now I get it." Just say, "faking good" or "trying to look better than they are." When I am working training postdoctoral fellows in forensics, I tell them that they can write all they want about "defended" and "invalidated," but I make them drop a footnote that says, "This colloquially is known as faking good."*

In my own practice, instead of "defensive" I might say,

> *People who respond like this to tests are either trying to make themselves appear more psychologically healthy than they actually are, or they are the type of person who is not good at knowing how they feel- not in touch with their own emotions. In this case, Mr. Plaintiff's report to me in our interview that {a,b,c] indicates . . .*

Obscure neurological terms

No one will know what you are talking about when you use words like *anosognosia, reduplicative paramnesia*, and *encephalomalacia*. Ira Packer points out that depending on the strategy of testifying, it is okay to use words like these as long as you acknowledge that they are jargon and immediately explain them.

Some neurological terms are valuable to use because they signal the expert is describing something that is a known syndrome that jurors may not be familiar with. For example, when I have to explain that a person has anosognosia, I may choose to introduce the neurological term because the common everyday understanding of the phenomenon is inaccurate or imprecise:

> *Mrs. Plaintiff developed anosognosia. That is a brain-based inability to know that she has problems thinking. The part of her brain that keeps track of how well the rest of her brain is working—that part isn't working. People with anosognosia literally can't know that they can't remember. It's not that they are "in denial" psychologically or don't want to know. This problem of anosognosia is common with people who, like Mrs. Plaintiff, have Alzheimer's disease.*

But other neurological terms are simply fancy ways of describing common experiences. Using words like *hypophonic* to describe a plaintiff's soft voice, *phonophobia* to say someone is bothered by sound, or *photophobia* that they are bothered by light just makes you sound like you're proud of using fancy words. When you then explain to jurors that *photophobia* means "sensitive to light," you'll sound condescending. Jurors are likely thinking, "Really? That's what you meant? Why didn't you start with what you meant?!"

A good rule of thumb for experts is that if you can simply substitute another word or short phrase for a commonly understood experience that has a little-known neurological name, do so. Otherwise, you'll risk sounding pompous. This is a good practice for every aspect of clinical work.

Statistical terms

Attorney DeBofsky notes that almost no juror understands the term *standard deviation*, but experts will tell him they believe it's a common term. This speaks to how foundational an assumption the concept is to our field: We use *standard deviation* so frequently that it's easy to assume everyone will understand it. The problem is that there's no easy way to replace many of the statistical terms we use as psychologists and neuropsychologists. Statistical terms necessarily are packed with complex assumptions. When they absolutely must be used, language to clearly and vividly describe standard deviations, error rates, percentiles, base rates, and other statistical terms can be found in Chapter 22, "Explaining Statistics."

In addition to finding more understandable ways to define statistical terms though, we need to ask ourselves, when we are tempted to use one while testifying, "Do I really need to introduce the concept of standard deviation in the first place?" Why do I need that concept to talk about my opinion? Is the goal to say that the examinee's performance on the test was very, very low compared with the her expected lifelong function? Is the goal to say that when looking at people with similar disorders to the examinee, people vary widely in their ability to perform a task? Then we should just say that.

Psychological diagnoses

Attorney DeBofsky keeps an old "Far Side" cartoon on his desk:

> *The psychiatrist is sitting in a chair with a notepad and the patient is lying on the couch. And the notepad says, "Just plain nuts." Sometimes it is okay to say it that plainly. Obviously not in those exact words, not that gross. But maybe,*
>
> *"This person is severely mentally ill. Psychologists use the term 'major depression.' That diagnosis is clearly supported by these test results."*

When we describe our diagnoses, we should do so in a way that opens the door for the jurors to better understand the experience of the plaintiff/defendant rather than shutting that door or reducing their access to the human experience behind the words. See Chapter 13, "Specific Psychiatric and Neurological Disorders," for clear, descriptive language we can use to describe psychological diagnoses and syndromes.

May

Some terms have legal consequences, and when experts unwittingly use the term, the court interprets their testimony in a way that they do not intend. Attorney Daniel

Corrin gives the example of the word *may* because it unwittingly brings up the legal balance-of-probabilities test:

> *I insist that trainees do not use the phrase "may" in forensic reports. "May" is no different than "may or may not." That doesn't help anybody: It doesn't help the judge; it doesn't help the lawyers. It opens up a whole pot of cross examinations. The trainees score the tests and then they say, "This profile may reveal that she is decompensated" or "These testing results suggest that she may struggle with interpersonal relationships."*
>
> *I finally persuaded the psychologists in the team that they just should go through their whole report and take out the word "may." It doesn't tell you anything. You've got to at least say "likely"; I can live with "likely." I totally get that the test results are not as definitive as a litmus paper test which definitively establishes—I know that, but you've got to at least make it "more likely." I don't even make them say "more likely than not" because that is a legal standard. I just say "likely" or "more likely" and I am satisfied. If the test results are much stronger, use stronger language, but I recommend going through these reports and take out the word "may."*

Disabled

Psychologists or neuropsychologists who use the word *disabled* in their clinical practice may continue to use it in their forensic work without realizing that it has very specific legal meaning. It is often better to describe any impairments that you have identified during an assessment and any limitations that result from them. For an excellent discussion of the issue, see Shane Bush and Grant Iverson's *Neuropsychological Assessment of Work-Related Injuries.*[1]

WHEN JARGON HAS INVADED VERNACULAR LANGUAGE

An attorney who preferred to remain anonymous notes that psychology experts run into trouble when they use words that are diagnostic labels but also are used in common parlance. Using these diagnostic labels without clarification may create a cross communication because jurors have one thought bubble in their head when a term like *OCD* comes up and mental experts have another. Both groups may not realize they have different definitions.

> *"He's kind of OCD." Those tend to be words that need much better clarification, because people will import their own beliefs: "Just like my brother. My brother is OCD because he likes to clean the counter four times a day." As a lawyer, those words worry me. Those words require a good lawyer to take the time to ask the expert, "Can you explain what you mean by that term?"*

Other phrases, like PTSD and even depression, can create these cross communications. See Chapter 13, "Specific Psychiatric and Neurological Disorders," for strategies to clarify these terms.

FINALLY, STRATEGIC USE OF JARGON

Attorney Brian Pomerantz tells the story of a particular judge he tried cases in front of whose personality was such that he made a conscious decision to have his experts use jargon. The take-home message of this story is that the use of jargon was a conscious, strategic decision designed to strengthen the relationship between the expert and the trier of fact. When using jargon, be in the driver's seat.

> *My philosophy is "Know your audience and prepare your expert accordingly." I had a case where the judge was known to be conservative and not someone who gives relief a lot. He is smart, really smart, and he knows your case better than you when you walk into the courtroom. It is daunting. He works very hard and he is egotistical. He thinks he is the smartest person in the room and he wants you to* ***know*** *that he is the smartest person in the room. So, that's how he acts. He is not afraid to do his own thing. He is not just going to vote party line against you. If you convince him, he will do something unusual, because he wants to show people he knows better.*
>
> *In preparation, I talked with my witness about the judge, what he is about, and how we appeal to that. I instructed my expert in the case, "Talk to him like you would talk to a colleague in your department. Don't dumb it down. Don't use lay terms. (Talk to me like that! I need it!) Talk to him like he is a board-certified neuropsychologist. If he needs definitions, he will ask you."*
>
> *In this particular case, my expert did that. It was a very high-level examination of her. She was not using analogies; she was not breaking it down. She was using jargon. And the judge liked her. She talked to him on a very high level, and that appealed to him.*
>
> *This goes to every case: Know your audience and cater to it.*

As another example, Nick Bogod notes that in Canada, attorneys have identified that use of occasional jargon can be helpful in expert reports as it is one of the only available doorways to ask the expert a question on direct testimony during a trial. It may have added advantages of drawing a judge's attention to an area of identified deficit (e.g., dysnomia).

> *The attorneys have said they like when I put some technical terms in reports, because in Canada, on direct, the attorneys can only ask you to elaborate on things that are hard to understand in your report. Your opinion basically has to stand for itself and they can't elicit any new testimony/opinion. But if you write things in jargon-y language, they can ask you to explain. For example, words like "dysnomia" or "prosody" or "hypophonic" may be able to be expanded on during direct testimony which otherwise is restricted to reviewing the written opinion only.*

NOTE

1. Bush, S. S., and Iverson, G. L. (Eds.). (2012). *Neuropsychological Assessment of Work-Related Injuries.* NY: Guilford Press.

8 Direct Examination

A JUDGE WHO prefers to remain anonymous described direct testimony as an expert's opportunity to shine: "This is your home base, your territory. You are being pitched slow balls down the middle, and you have the opportunity to hit each one out of the park." But with opportunity there is also risk: "Witnesses should know their direct testimony cold. If you are not prepared, there is nothing you can do to salvage it."

Following credentialing, the retaining attorney asks open-ended questions designed to draw the expert out about the nature of his or her opinions. Rather than cross examination's restrictive "Isn't it true . . ." questions that are designed to be answered with a yes or no, the questions on direct examination invite the expert to expand, "How did you conduct your evaluation?"

Ted Peck describes direct testimony as a dance, and just like any good dance, notes that the partners need to practice:

> *This is a dance where there needs to be a partnership. The attorney is leading. He or she has to be the one asking the questions upon which you can offer your opinions. If the attorney fails to ask key questions, you are not going to be able to offer the key responses that you feel are relevant.*

The questions the attorney asks on direct and the answers the expert gives form the heart of this chapter. While some attorneys have a clear vision for how they would like to draw the expert's opinions out, many attorneys rely on the expert to collaborate with them to structure the questions they will ask on direct. And of course, the goal is not just to present the information in an organized fashion. As discussed in Chapter 2: Setting the Truth on Fire, an important component of strong direct testimony is organizing the information into a narrative that is compelling, engaging, and holds jurors' attention.

In addition to Dr. Peck's analogy of direct testimony as a dance between the attorney and expert that must be practiced, consider the analogy of expert testimony presented in Chapter 2 as an engaging and informative Frontline documentary. Planning direct testimony then involves the expert and attorney as collaborative directors, determining the sequence of how the narrative unfolds; and as editors, determining where insert to breaks to move the narrative forward in the form of questions. This chapter focuses on the storyboard for direct: the sequence and goals of the overall narrative. The next several chapters focus on specific tools for presenting the content of direct testimony in an engaging and vivid manner, including strategies for telling the story of our assessment process, specific analogies, metaphors and concise descriptions of neurologic and psychiatric conditions, and importantly, how information can be shown as well as explained with use of visuals.

SEQUENCING DIRECT TESTIMONY

With the enormous amount of information in a typical case, including mountains of medical records, education and other developmental history, test data, relevant scientific literature, direct observations, critique of other expert's opinions, and countless other details, deciding where to begin in presenting that information in a coherent manner is a challenge.

Just as with a well edited documentary, whatever the sequence, the goal is to offer enough detail to explain a complex assessment without wading so far into the weeds that the jurors are lost. Attorney Sara Cohbra notes that those details should include information that "helps jurors understand that the methodology of the expert is really tight. The expert has to be able to explain that what he or she has done has been very carefully thought through and executed. However, we also need to make sure that the direct testimony is not so technical that the jurors disregard it as 'jargon-y.' This is a hard balance - a hard line to walk." Use of visuals, such as a table of results or timeline of history, as described in Chapter 10, is one way of showing the complexity of the foundation for our opinions without needing to wade through excessive detail.

How experts and attorneys like to organize the narrative and dance of direct testimony varies on the nature of the case, the type of neurological or psychological issue, and the personalities of the attorney and expert.

BEGIN WITH THE DATA

Almost no one suggested beginning with the data. David Hartman's advice was repeated by many interviewees.

> *The data should enter into your discussion only when it is clear how you see the patient and the larger picture of what happened to someone. If you start with the data, you are staring with the most boring and off-putting piece of the story. If you start with what happened to their brain and why things changed, you will then have a*

framework upon which to hang your data. If you don't have a framework, the data slides around and blows away in the wind.

Lead with the bottom line

Christopher Grote notes that in offering direct testimony, he likes to lead with the bottom line. And end with it. And repeat it as often as possible.

> Every case, clinical or forensic, starts and ends with a question and answer. For a murder case, the question might be, "Does the defendant meet the definition of insanity, having a mental disease or defect?" And if the answer was, "No, he doesn't," I would suggest to the attorney that we start with that.
>
> *Q: Dr. Grote, did you examine Mr. Smith?*
>
> *A: Yes.*
>
> *Q: Did you come to a conclusion?*
>
> *A: Yes, I did.*
>
> *Q: Does he meet the definition of insanity?*
>
> *A: No, he doesn't.*
>
> *Q: Does he have a mental defect?*
>
> *A: No, he doesn't.*
>
> *Q: Does he have a mental disease?*
>
> *A: No, he doesn't.*
>
> In my direct testimony, I am trying to tell a story. I lead with the bottom line and repeat the bottom line as often as I can.

Three points to my testimony. I start with them.

Every report and testimony should have three main points. People can remember three things. They have difficulty remembering more. (There can be two to four points, but not five!) I am trying to boil my testimony down to three points. What are the three things that we want the jury to understand or to come away with from my testimony? We decide what those three things are. Then I say to the attorney, "These are the kind of questions I would ask so that we lay out these three points." I start with the points.—Rodney Vanderploeg, PhD, ABPP-CN

Start with the bottom line

I really try to give jurors the bottom line at the outset. "What we found in our evaluation is that despite the fact that Mr. Smith claims to have sustained a brain injury during the accident, we found no evidence for this." Then the attorney goes back, and we will go through three or four specific findings that lead to that conclusion.—Rus Bauer, PhD, ABPP-CN

Demonstrate the forest: the human impact of the injury

> *My goal on direct is to first paint the picture of how a neurological injury affects a person from multiple pathways. That's the bottom line. The explanation of the tests can come later, but we first talk about what the forest is: the human experience that has been impacted by this injury. I walk through all the ways I saw the impact of the injury: cognitive testing, personality and emotional testing, collateral interviews. Walking the jury through what the impacts have been from an adaptive, emotional, cognitive, deeply personal standpoint is the way to truly understand the impact of the injury.*—Anonymous

Lead with the injury

Michael McCrea prefers his direct testimony to start at the beginning, with the injury event itself:

> *I like to talk about the injury event first—what things looked like acutely, what we would predict based on the science (recovery time, outcome), then what my exam revealed, then my impressions. In many of these cases people are reporting symptoms years after the injury event. Over the years, the injury event itself is overlooked. My mentor says, "It starts in the beginning." You have to give jurors a detailed understanding of what the injury mechanism was, and then discuss the factors that lead from that.*

Rod Swenson describes a similar philosophy as a "funnel approach":

> I like to use a funnel approach. The jury needs to be educated in a general way. What is a traumatic brain injury? I tell attorneys, for the top part of the funnel, act like you don't have a clue about what brain injury is, and you want to know. A good lawyer will say,
>
> *Q: Dr. Swenson, first of all, how does a brain injury happen?*
>
> *A: (I talk about general concepts of how a brain injury happens.)*
>
> *Then,*
>
> *Q: Doctor, when you see these brain injuries, what do you see in people? What kinds of problems do they have?*
>
> *And*
>
> *Q: Doctor, can you have a permanent injury from this or can people get better?*
>
> *(Then we get down to the bottom of the funnel.)*
>
> *Q: Doctor, now tell me about our patient. You evaluated her. Let's talk about her.*
>
> Now you are going to talk about the person. The jury has this overview. They know you are competent, did a thorough job. I like to start very "big picture"—what is an injury, how does it affect people?—THEN talk about the person on the stand.

I typically start by recreating the precipitating event (e.g., a traumatic brain injury), defining the severity of injury that may have resulted, and discussing what the empirical literature suggests regarding the natural history of that type of injury. Based upon the scientific literature, I offer a summary of what we know to be true of injuries of a given severity, and discuss whether Mr. Smith's presenting course is consistent or not consistent with known or typical recovery patterns.—Nat Nelson, PhD, ABPP-CN

I start with the injury. For example, I have a case marching toward trial where a woman had a well-documented stroke as a result of a medication error. I personally get the DICOM files on all the imaging and identify the best images to show the pathology. Then I speak briefly about the brain: left hemisphere, right hemisphere, four lobes, neural systems and networks that relate to neuropsychological status. I briefly outline in a domain fashion what each part of the brain is responsible for and how neural networks function. Then I talk about the person:

This is how we look at it from a neuropsychological standpoint. And then, here is Mrs. Smith's brain. Notice where this damage is here that we can see objectively? Notice how it overlaps with these neuropsychological functions we anticipate are going to be affected? Now let's look at Mrs. Smith's neuropsychological data."

Then I can go to the data sheet and say, "Okay, this matches this, and this matches that".—Erin Bigler, PhD, ABPP-CN

I start direct testimony with a short, clear answer to "What is your opinion?" Three sentences: what the severity of the injury was, what the findings were, and my conclusions based on the findings. One, two, three. The most important is the first one: What is the history of the actual medical event?—Greg Lee, PhD, ABPP-CN

See Chapter 12, "Concussion," and Chapter 13, "Specific Psychiatric and Neurological Disorders," for engaging strategies to explain specific neurological and psychological conditions on direct.

Begin where the important information begins

David Hartman notes that the structure of direct depends on the history in the case. "The beginning" for some patients is the onset of illness or date of trauma. For others, the salient "beginning" is years earlier.

How I like to structure direct really depends on the pattern of issues in the litigants. With some litigants, you really have to start at the moment of the injury; their pre-accident presentation is not that unusual. In other cases, it is different. You have to start where you think the important information begins.

The important thing about this woman . . .

In one particular criminal case, I had to write a letter to the judge about how to understand the behavior of a woman jailed for theft. It was a bench trial and the judge was soliciting opinions. The woman's history was positive for fetal alcohol exposure, neglectful upbringing, previous head injuries, and her own substance abuse. She had exhibited psychologically impaired behavior and committed petty crimes since she was a child. She had a history of borderline intellectual functioning. She was now in court for a felony, even though she stole only $5. Because this was her third offense, she could be required to spend the rest of her life in jail.

I interviewed her in jail and asked her how she understood her situation.

She said, "Well, I'm getting out. Oh, yeah, they're going to let me out because they will see I don't need to be here."

I asked her what her plans were. She answered, "I will stay with my friend. He has offered me a place to stay."

I asked how she would spend her time, and she replied, "I think I will relax and go to the library. My friend likes to smoke pot. We will sit around and relax with pot."

Now this is a woman who is in jail and seeing a doctor appointed by the judge. She is telling the doctor that were she to be released, she would (in Chicago) be a chronic user of illegal substances. I have to be concerned about her level of insight.

Now her test results reflected intellectual impairment and various psychological abnormalities, but these are the veins on the leaves on the trees in the forest. The most important issue is that this woman's failure to learn from past experience and current lack of insight meant she will gain nothing from extended jail time. I told the judge:

The important thing to understand about this woman is that you can keep her in jail for a day or a hundred years; she will learn nothing from it. She will not be able to understand the reasons why she is there. She will not be able to morally reconstruct herself, and the day after she leaves she will recidivate. She does not have the neurological/ neuropsychological capacity to learn from experience, jail experience included. The best thing one can do for her is to put her in a supervised halfway house program to keep her out of trouble. She is not dangerous to herself or others but does not examine her behavior and cannot alter her behavior to avoid bad consequences. She doesn't even see the consequences."

There was very little "neuropsychology" in the report, but the judge understood those conclusions and was able to bend the rules and minimize jail time for eventual halfway house residency.

Start with the person

Lisa McDermott suggests that experts incorporate the client as soon as possible:

> *Jurors want to know why what the expert is saying is important to the client and the case. Although the expert needs to explain her qualifications and the key professional and substantive concepts, she should try to incorporate the facts as she goes. Otherwise, jurors may lose interest.*

Start with the expected hypothesis

When experts are contradicting a theory that has already been presented in a case, or when they are presenting information that goes against "common knowledge" that may not be correct knowledge, it is important to be respectful of the jurors' current cognitive set or narrative structure. Jumping in and saying something contrary to that narrative may be disorienting to the listener: "Wait. What?!" A better approach is to address the common knowledge first: "We were all concerned when an initial study showed there may be a link between immunizations and autism . . ." And then present the contradictory information: ". . . but it turns out that the last 10 years of very-well-designed research show us that initial early study was incorrect."

> If a person has a recognizable injury or condition—that is, what everyone involved is assuming is the problem—but if I find other information that I think is more salient, I will start by highlighting the expected information, then move to the unexpected. Let's say the person is exaggerating or malingering, but they really did have an injury in their life. I will make the point right up front that the individual had an injury:
>
> *Mrs. Jones was a high school graduate working successfully as a plumber until a date where she had a car accident."*
>
> I will start with the fact that everyone under the sun had concluded xyz. Then I will explain why I disagree it is the cause of all the complaints.—Robert L. Denney, PsyD, ABPP-CN, FP

Structure direct like a neuropsychological report

Manfred Greiffenstein noted that on direct he will begin by laying out the possible differential diagnoses in this particular case:

> *In this case, there was a car accident, and I was asked to assess Ms. Smith. And the question became, historically, did she have a head injury? Is she faking? There is a history of depression; could that explain the symptoms?*

He will then follow the logic of his neuropsychological report to structure the rest of his testimony: "My philosophy is that the preparation of direct testimony starts with the report. I like to start with history, then records review, then behavior observation, then test results."

Jerry Sweet notes that he uses his neuropsychological report summary as a roadmap for direct:

> *At the end of every report, I have a very clear, "plain English" section of my summary. I number the points and try to order them in a clear logical manner. My intention is that regarding my direct testimony, I can say to the retaining attorney, "You can ask me about these points, one at a time." And, unless I've missed something important in my summary, most often that will be everything the jury needs to hear.*

More about the use of forensic reports as a foundation for testimony can be found in Chapter 21, "Reports."

GOALS OF DIRECT TESTIMONY

Telling the story of the examination

Regardless of the sequence chosen to present the narrative of direct testimony, at some point on direct, the attorney should ask you to explain your assessment. Bob Denney notes that the expert must educate the jury about what an assessment looks like, because most jurors will have no idea what a psychological or neuropsychological evaluation consists of: "They need to understand what it is you did and why you did what you did it." See Chapter 9, "Explaining Assessment Methods and Tools," for engaging strategies for telling the story of the examination, including explaining specific tests like the MMPI and issues with interpretation such as normal variability.

Including doubts, atypical findings, and drawbacks of the data to inoculate for cross

Although at first it may feel counter-intuitive, acknowledging relative weaknesses in the case on direct allows the expert to share that information in an open-ended manner, fully discussing its context. In contrast, the same information would otherwise first be brought up on cross in the form of an accusatory, narrow question that is answerable by only yes or no. If brought up first on direct, when confronted with the information again on cross examination, rather than the jurors feeling like it is a "gotcha" moment, the expert can refer the jurors back to his direct testimony, "As I said earlier . . ."

One neuropsychologist who preferred to remain anonymous notes that because no set of data are perfect and no case is perfect, "You should plan proactively for the cross by identifying the case's weaknesses and discussing it first on direct. When the criticism comes on cross, concede the point."

Rod Swenson describes the process of identifying such issues to bring up on direct as "land mine analysis":

You need to do a land mine analysis in the case and have the attorney ask you about any weaknesses during direct. "What can blow up in my face if you don't ask me in direct about that?" Look at the weakness of the case, and nail it on direct. Then on cross, opposing attorneys look like they are just focusing on these things that you have already addressed.

Manfred Greiffenstein similarly recommended that experts address potential cross questions on direct:

> Your direct testimony should always anticipate cross exam. If you bring up a subjective finding on direct, always freely admit, on direct, that it is subjective. You have to anticipate that the issue will arise on cross, and it's better to be able to say, "Yes, as I said, this is subjective."
>
> *Q: So, you admit this is a subjective measure?*
>
> *A: Yes, as I said, this is subjective. It's based on my years of experience with a wide variety of patients. It's also based on logic. With a grip strength score this low you shouldn't be able to grip a steering wheel. Or grip a pencil.*
>
> *Q: So, you admit that someone else could disagree?*
>
> *A: Yes, but in my opinion only a fool would say a grip strength score this low in a person who drives could be valid. But, yeah, you're right, somebody out there could disagree with it.*
>
> I will actually say "only a fool." You have to find a line between confidence and arrogance at all times. With enough experience, you can find it.

Judge Lynne Battaglia points out the benefits of bringing up information on direct rather than waiting for a cross-examining attorney to be the one to bring out information that might weaken an opinion:

> *When I was a prosecutor for a time, I always felt it was better to bring out everything in direct that I thought would be cross-examined, so I would look like I am the person who is disclosing it. You want to be the person disclosing information to the jurors because you are the expert. I was the attorney for the state, so I had to look stately.*

On direct, experts have the luxury of spending as much time as needed to acknowledge information that does not support their opinion and to help jurors understand how they are weighing that contrary information. Bob Denney notes that it is important to share his level of confidence in his opinion on direct. He will discuss his concerns about his opinions and any information that is contrary to his opinion right up front:

> *I will follow the points I have highlighted in my report in my direct testimony. I don't in any way read the report, but I will go through highlighted information from a section n of my report I title "Clinical Formulation." In forensic work, it is important to explain why you came to the conclusion that you did. We don't want to have what*

> *we call "conclusory reports." When I write my report, the reader needs to understand how I came to the conclusion I did.*
>
> *I can think of many instances in formulating my opinion where I say to myself, "I know this person has schizophrenia." I then get out a blank piece of paper and a pen and say to myself, "Why do I think he has schizophrenia?" And I write a list. Then I have a list of all the reasons I believe what I believe, and I will put them in an order that makes logical sense. That is how I will dictate the clinical formulation part of my forensic report. Then I will make a new list: What information do I have that he does* **not** *have schizophrenia, or that he has something else (e.g., a prior evaluation has come to the conclusion of multiple personality disorder)? I will then write up a section acknowledging the "alternatives" and why I do not agree with each possibility. If there is any level of doubt, I will put it there. Obviously, I don't rule out every condition under the sun, but just those that have either already been voiced in the case or are reasonable possibilities that I considered.*
>
> *Every clinical decision we make has a different level of clinical confidence. I want to reflect in the report and in my testimony an accurate level of confidence. I want the jurors to know how confident I am. I might think, "Well, I really think it is schizophrenia, but it could be schizoaffective disorder, or it could be that the person is exaggerating." I will talk about the evidence that it could be other things, and why I did not weigh that evidence as heavily. We must communicate that we considered other reasonable possibilities.*

Related to acknowledging relative weakness in the data or the case on direct, Judge Battaglia notes that direct testimony is the place for experts to acknowledge that there are multiple theories in a case:

> *The expert does not lose anything by saying that there are different theories and acknowledging that. I think a good attorney puts it out in the expert's direct testimony. The rubber meets the road in why the expert chose this particular methodology as more reliable or more valid to reach the conclusion. And not just having the hubris to say, "I chose it because it is the best."*

> It's not always a cut-and-dried case. If you are 70% confident that this is the way it is but in your mind you have 30% that is plaguing you—"It could be this . . ."—I would much rather communicate, "Here is how I thought about this, but there is a possibility it could be this over here, and this is how I decided between the two."
>
> I believe that our role is not to win cases. Our role is to go into the legal forum and educate; explain our findings and explain why we believe what we believe. And there is a possibility we might be wrong. Hopefully we can acknowledge that. People will appreciate you for your thoughtfulness and your flexibility and willingness to acknowledge the other perspective. If there is a big issue in the

case that goes to the contrary opinion, I think it is best to get that point out up front. That gives you an opportunity—the trier of fact will say, "Well, wait a minute: Why didn't he/she consider this?" It's better to get it out in the open up front; that gives you control over explaining why or why not that information was meaningful to you and how it factors into your clinical formulation. It's simple to do: You just tell the retaining attorney that we need to cover this issue.

Q: Dr. Denney, were there any issues in this particular case that gave you pause? Or made you really stop and reconsider your thinking? Or maybe even suggest that the contrary opinion might be true?

Q: Do you have any hesitancy, or are there any issues that come to your mind that could potentially suggest to you that something else is going on?

A: There are some issues that come to my mind. There were one or two issues that gave me pause. I spent a lot of time thinking about them. I eventually concluded that because of xyz, those facts led me to conclude this way, rather than that way, although I will concede that the other conclusion may ultimately be the right one, but this is why I came to my conclusions.—Robert L. Denney, PsyD, ABPP-CN, FP

One of my principles in both my reports and in testimony is to put it all out there. When I am asked to address any particular forensic question or issue, I try to address all sides of that issue, so if I am asked to write a mitigation report, I try to write a mitigation/aggravation report; that is, I try to include aggravating factors as well as mitigating factors. If I am asked to say what is the evidence that this plaintiff has had a traumatic brain injury, I try to present the evidence that they have and that they have not had a traumatic brain injury. I would rather get that out up front because if I don't, and then it comes out on cross, it looks like I've been hiding data or that I've been selective or cherry picking or that I have been biased. I will volunteer as much as I can whatever evidence there is that goes to the other side of the question from the person who has hired me. I will even do that on cross examination and typically when I am giving testimony in that regard, I have done my job, I have taken into account all of the evidence, and I have arrived at my conclusion.

But there are limits to that. Any neuropsychological evaluation could go on indefinitely, and the evidence that is helpful on one side of a case can be very different from the evidence that may be helpful on the other side. We need to be even-handed in presenting the evidence we find and we need to be reasonably responsible in fully exploring the situation, but we inevitably decide to stop our investigation at some point, and we need not be exhaustive in exploring the case against the interests of the side that hired us.

The opposing attorney may ask me on cross,

Q: But Doctor, aren't A, B, and C true?

A: Yes, A, B, and C are true, and furthermore D, E, and F are true. I have taken all of that into account in arriving at my conclusion Z.—Tedd Judd, PhD, ABPP-CN

And, of course, if an expert realizes a mistake occurred during scoring, direct is a considerably friendlier venue to bring it out. When the error is brought up on cross, the expert will lose credibility because it looks like he or she was trying to hide the error. On direct, if the error was minor, the expert has the luxury of responding to open-ended questions to talk about the way in which one or two points on a single test will not make a difference with respect to most standard scores and how an assessment's conclusions are based on broad patterns of test scores, in the context of the nature of the injury, rather than on one raw score on one item on a particular subtest. The expert also has the opportunity to tell the jury that he or she went over the other test scores with a fine-toothed comb and is confident that there are no other errors. Obviously, it is best not to make any scoring errors during an examination, but if you discover an error of any sort when preparing for testimony, don't try to hide it.

> *A: I would like to take a moment to point out an error in one of my scores.*
>
> *Q: Does this small scoring error change your opinion in the case?*
>
> *A: It does (or does not). Here is why.*
>
> Of course, if the error **does** change the opinion, then that should also be addressed.—Paul L. Craig, PhD, ABPP-CN

Creating sturdy frames for opinions

As discussed at length in Chapter 9: Creating Access to Assessment Methods and Results, a foundation of competent psychological and neuropsychological assessment is the concept of convergent validity. As professionals, we feel confident in our opinions when multiple sources of data converge to support our conclusions. Would we diagnose based on a single test score or the content of a single statement from a clinical interview without convergent data from medical records, developmental history, and countless other factors? Of course not. But the typical juror has not been trained in our assessment methods and does not know this basic assumption of our field. An important goal in direct testimony is to share the sturdy nature of our opinions with phrases like "all of these factors together . . . ". Emphasizing the sturdiness of our opinions on direct helps support the opinion through the cross examination that will follow.

Bob Denney recommends using a "bookending statement" to inoculate against the "knock down the pillars" cross-examination strategy. First, what is the "knock down the pillars" strategy?

> In a situation where there are many facts that lead to a conclusion, but no single fact would in itself lead to the conclusion, the attorney on the other side will try to knock down each of the facts or "pillars of the argument." They will try to knock down the confidence in all the pillars, so your final opinion has nothing to stand on.
>
> But if I put in an introductory statement during direct that any one of these facts is not enough to lead me to the conclusion; however, the sum total of all of them leads me to the conclusions. I "bookend" the points in my opinion with that

statement. This goes for both report writing and for direct testimony. It is not any single one of these points that leads me to the conclusion, but it is the sum total of these points that leads to the conclusion. On cross, they can knock down a point or two, but it doesn't frazzle me. I can always come back to the statement:

A: As I said, it was not just the a, b, c, it was also the x, y, z. It is the sum total of all of these elements that leads me to this conclusion.

Helping jurors navigate complex cases

While people are complex and most forensic cases are complex, some cases stand out in their sheer level of complexity. There may be multiple neurological disease or injury processes overlaying one another, severe developmental factors, psychiatric and emotional factors, and larger cultural or systems issues at play all at the same time. When even experts feel overwhelmed by the complexity of the case, imagine what it is like for jurors! Jacobus Donders notes,

> A lot of cases are very complex. I was involved in a case with very significant lead exposure. The blood levels were in the 60s—more than trivial. The child involved also got run over by a car at the age of 8 with a hemorrhagic contusion visible on neuroimaging. No expert had even commented on that. In that case I was fortunate to be able to get cognitive testing records from before and after the brain injury. I will help the jury focus on the most relevant details in a complicated case:
>
> *Listen, I have pediatrician records saying this child was developing normally and met all of their developmental milestones until the day she got the lead exposure. After the exposure, she began to have significant problems. And she got some new problems after the car accident.*

In highly complex cases with multiple psychological or neuropsychological evaluations, experts can use visuals such as tables and graphs to organize and simplify communication—for example, a table comparing neuropsychological test data across five evaluations. If a case has a huge number of "trees," visuals help the jurors see the forest. See Chapter 10, "Visuals," for many examples and ideas to transform complex, overwhelming information into memorable graphics.

In highly complex cases, where etiology cannot reasonably be teased out, Nick Bogod will focus on the litigant's current neuropsychological symptom as a final common pathway:

> I assessed a patient who was in five accidents. The first caused a stroke. He then had four more accidents. By the time I saw him he had multiple symptoms, physical, cognitive and psychological as well as significant fatigue. In Canada, if you can't tell which accident is responsible, they are essentially all responsible. If you have a $2 million policy associated with one accident and another one with a $4 million policy, then both are accessible. "Indivisible" is the term used in the Canadian legal system used to reference injuries from various potential causes that cannot be separated from each other in terms of symptoms caused.

A: These scores are a final common pathway, after all of these events have occurred. I can't distinguish the relative contribution based on test scores, but according to the injured individual and collateral witnesses, a certain accident event (e.g., stroke) may appear to be the most significant factor while symptoms may have been worsened by the subsequent events. In reports we attempt to identify the relative contribution when there are multiple events but sometimes this is not possible. In a circumstance where two accidents occur in very short succession it may be impossible to separate their consequences from each other, leaving the cause inseparable (or in legal terms indivisible).

Explicitly presenting the concept of the "biopsychosocial model" can be very helpful to jurors because it gives them a framework on which to hang multiple, complicating issues. A neuropsychologist who prefers to remain anonymous notes,

Presenting a good biopsychosocial model is important. Oftentimes in court cases, you get into this funny dance—a black-and-white model of brain damage, "yes or no," causing ALL of the symptoms. The notion that we are human and that emotions and relationships in the environment can reinforce behaviors and contribute to symptoms needs to be addressed. It's important for a jury to understand that you are acknowledging the complexities of human behavior. It is dangerous to be lured in to the idea that it is all black and white; that is a very dangerous place to go. In fairness, if you look at motor vehicle accidents, it is possible that there is a trauma, or PTSD, or brain injury that is totally explanatory. But typically, why is concussion associated with catastrophic outcome in this case? The end picture usually can be understood as relating to pre-accident personality structures and complex current relationships, or ways of looking at the accident. When you are done explaining it in that way, jurors feel that it makes sense.

Bringing in research

Judge Christina Harms is a strong proponent of weaving research into one's testimony.

It is incredibly effective, powerful, and persuasive, both in written reports and in testimony, when you have the ability to fold in articles and research, to be academic. It's easier to do in a report because of course you have the time to look for the articles or refer to a book or chapter of a book. I think that's incredibly powerful, and I encourage experts to do it as much as they can. It's impressive and probably the top of the credibility mountain, especially under cross examination. The attorney says,

Q: Well, isn't it true that it's more likely than not that a child who is battered grows up to be a batterer?

A: Actually, the current best research by Drs. Jones and Smith at Berkeley published last year in the Family Law Quarterly *reveals that . . ..*

> That just says to the judge: "This person is a scholar; they actually follow the state of the art." And when you can cite an actual study and give details about it, the judge is going to sit back and say, "This person really knows their stuff." Knowing about the research is very helpful, but when you know chapter and verse, like, "This is Drs. Jones and Smith. They are both professors at Berkeley in California and their study in 2014 showed that . . .," you sound mega-credible.

Attorneys and experts have different philosophies about bringing up specific studies during testimony. William Barr notes that sharing literature seems like a bother to some attorneys, but other attorneys are always asking for more. That said, he believes that "Our ability to search through the literature, clarify the scientific basis for our opinions, is an asset we bring to the table."

Attorney Sara Cohbra notes, "Sometimes we introduce studies into evidence through the experts' testimony. But we consider how the fact-finder—the judge or jury—will tolerate or judge this kind of evidence when deciding whether to use it in the examination of an expert." She notes that there may be a strategic reason having to do with a future appeal that an attorney may want an expert to talk about, or try to talk about, research on the stand:

> *If we are pretty sure the judge will rule against us on an issue related to the expert's testimony, we want to build as robust a record as possible for an appeal. The more information the expert provides that the judge disregards, the better for our future appeal.*

Glenn Larrabee's perspective is that testifying generally about research is fine, but, "If I start mentioning a study by name, objections may be raised." When can an expert bring up a study? Judge Christina Harms clarifies,

> *If you are testifying because you wrote a report and the research study is referenced in your report, then of course you are allowed to discuss the research on the stand. That's why I would encourage experts to reference literature in their report. You are not allowed to just spontaneously bring up research. But you are certainly allowed to cite research if on cross examination a question is raised and you want to answer it by reference to research.*

Part of the issue with spontaneously bringing in research is the discovery process. If the study is cited in an expert report, the other side has "discovered it." Has the opposing side had adequate opportunity to review the particular research? Based on experience of sometimes not being allowed later to discuss research that was not disclosed early enough in the case, Jerry Sweet makes a point of asking the retaining attorney at the time the report is issued if relevant research that's expected to be mentioned during the discovery deposition should be disclosed in advance of the deposition, or instead at the deposition.

> *In some cases, I want to cite specific research studies. Experience has taught me to have a conversation with the retaining attorney about the best or preferred means of ensuring that I can later cite and discuss specific research studies during my testimony.*

If I don't do that, I may not be able to talk about it in court. In one case, I gave the attorney the reference months prior, but he never disclosed the material to the other side. Then when testifying, any time the word "research" came up and I wanted to discuss a specific study, I was not allowed to do so. Variations of this problem have occurred in a number of cases, all of which leads me to be assertive with the retaining attorney.

Judge Jay Blitzman clarifies,

What an expert can testify to is a lot broader than what a layperson can testify to. Laypeople must testify to what they have witnessed or observed, whereas an expert can rely on established treatises and research that is generally accepted in the field. And that is the key. The expert will not be allowed to testify unless the methodology s/he employs is generally accepted and the scientific principles are so accepted in the field that they are deemed to have validity and reliability. That is vetted in pretrial hearings. There is pretrial discovery, where both sides go back and forth in order for opposing counsel to get an idea of what information each other's experts are relying on. If you think it is a quack theory, you can challenge it pretrial at a Daubert hearing.

General research conclusions versus specific studies

Giving a general overview of the literature as opposed to specific studies has the benefit of not boring or overwhelming juries with too much detail. In short, keep your explanations of the research literature simple and general: a 36,000-foot view. Do not focus on the blades of grass. Robert Mendoza notes that when he testifies about research, he typically does not cite a particular study:

I use research in this way: "There is substantial research that suggests that . . ." I will use the term "research" because it makes people's ears prick up. I will not talk about specific studies; I will talk about what the studies have found and how that literature relates to my particular case.

Jerry Sweet uses the phrase, "The question you are asking relates to hundreds of studies":

The most common topic for us is concussion. I have a huge collection of articles that talk about realistic expectations after concussion, as well as non-injury variables that might be at play.

A: The question you are asking me relates to dozens and dozens of research studies that look at this very thing. That i, if you have a mild injury, what happens afterwards? Are there consequences for working? Are there consequences for handling finances or driving? Do people become terribly depressed? Is it a life-changing event?

I find that going in depth to explain particular research studies is not helpful. Jurors tune out. Summarizing the research is better.—Lynn Blackburn, PhD, ABPP-CN

> Introducing research shouldn't be done in a pedantic way. I am typically summarizing the literature as opposed to diving deep into a particular study.
>
> *Look, there has been a ton of research that looks at the outcome of injuries like this person had. Virtually all of these studies, of which there are many, demonstrate that this type of injury does not carry any serious risk of lasting thinking problems.*—David S. Bush, PhD, ABPP-CN

That said, an expert who brings up "the literature" in a general way should be fully prepared to get more specific. Not being able to quote passage and verse after making a general pronouncement would likely result in a big hit to one's credibility:

> *I don't ever quote research that I don't have in my case binder or on my laptop. If I am ever asked if I have a copy, I can say, 'It's right here, or on my laptop, and I would be happy to provide it to you within the hour.'"*—Robert Mendoza, PsyD

Are jurors' assumptions about research the same as ours?

When presenting research during direct testimony, remember that jurors don't necessarily share our basic assumptions about research methodology. A 2008 study entitled "The Seductive Allure of Neuroscience"[1] found that "neuroscience" explanations are highly persuasive to laypeople. But Nicholas Scurich and Adam Shniderman[2] qualified that finding, showing that when laypeople are given fabricated neuroscience articles, they believe the articles when their prior beliefs are supported and are skeptical of the "science" when those beliefs are contradicted. That is, their study found that people engaged in motivated reasoning about science research. If the bogus research supported their beliefs, they expressed great confidence in it. If the bogus research contradicted their beliefs, they expressed skepticism about its methodology.

What does this have to do with testifying? As scientists, critical reasoning about research is baked into our DNA. It is a fundamental and likely invisible assumption that we can know whether a study is of high quality or not. That is, we feel confident about our ability to tell good research from sketchy research. Is it a reputable peer-reviewed journal? Was there a control group? What was the methodology? Was it a meta-analysis? To us, all of these questions are straightforward and answerable. We don't need to be mistrustful; we can just resolve the issue by reading the article.

But most laypeople, and therefore most jurors, don't have these evaluative tools in their toolkit. They have had a lifetime of hearing news reports about scientific studies that are contradicted with the next science headline. (This is because most science reporting is sensational and presents headline conclusions without appropriate caveats about drawbacks in the research methods, like "This is a pilot study and we can't know if this hypothesis will hold up when broader research is conducted.") To nonscientists, the issue is not that scientific studies vary in the quality of their research methods but that science itself is random and contradictory. Remember that jurors' reaction to research may not be as positive as that of psychologists. Helping jurors understand why we think the study is strong may counteract their tendency to dismiss research that does not fit with their worldview.

Lisa McDermott prefers experts to focus on real examples rather than just research studies.

> *Being natural and using easily understandable language when describing traits or characteristics is important. Studies and statistics need to be related to the person. There are studies for just about everything and multiple studies that counter those studies. Focusing on the person is critical, so that person doesn't get drowned out by studies or numbers. The facts about the person demonstrate why the studies and statistics are valid in the situation at hand. For example, a trauma expert may explain intergenerational abuse. But police reports that show a succession of women in the family being abused That is proof the jury can see and touch, showing that the cycle is real and present in your case.*

Chapter 12, "Concussion," includes specific examples of bringing concussion literature into your testimony.

"Best-of-breed research"

Manfred Greiffenstein shared a vivid descriptor for research studies that are really well done—"best of breed":

> And, of course, make sure that the research you are citing is really best of breed. If I am asked an open-ended question, I like to use the term "best-of-breed research." Not all research articles are equal. There is good research and lousy research, and it gives the jurors that idea. I don't explain the term unless I am asked. I hold it for cross exam.
>
> *Q: What is "best-of-breed research"?*
>
> *A: Something called a prospective study, where you study people from the moment of injury and follow them over time. Lousy research is where you study people who are in a lawsuit. That's not representative.*

Explaining meta-analyses

In my own practice, this is how I describe meta-analyses:

> *When a particular topic has been studied a lot, researchers will perform a "meta-analysis." This means that they combine all of the well-designed studies ever done in the area to answer the question: When you put all of the studies together, is there still an effect? It helps us know if an effect was found in one study randomly, or if it is a really rock-solid finding, because many studies found the same thing.*

John McSweeny notes,

> *I believe I must to explain to the jury what a meta-analysis is to make it compelling: "And there have been six meta-analyses published. A meta-analysis is*

a study that takes all the literature in a given area and combines it all to make conclusions."

Discussing research on direct versus cross

Manfred Greiffenstein recommended waiting for cross examination to bring in research: "A principle is to hold your firepower. Wait for cross exam, and then hit them hard." William Barr also notes that he rarely brings up specific studies on direct:

> I typically discuss studies on cross, when my back is to a wall. But I set myself up to do that on direct. A lot of the stuff I look at before trial is epidemiological, not complex. In pretrial conferences, I will sometimes give attorneys a copy of the article. They don't want me to pull it out of my pocket. On cross, the attorney might say, "Do you have that article?" I will say, "I don't have it." The district attorney will interject, "I have a copy of that and I will share it with the Court."
>
> On direct, I will set it up by saying something emphatic, knowing I can back it up:
>
> *It is extremely rare for someone with schizophrenia to murder someone.*
>
> *Then on cross:*
>
> *Q: Doctor, isn't it true that you hav testified in 15 cases where people with schizophrenia murdered someone? Isn't that common?*
>
> *A: The research shows that it is very rare for someone with schizophrenia to murder someone. In a study where they looked at 200 people with schizophrenia, only 2 had murdered anybody. Remember, schizophrenia is only 1% of the population. When you are talking about 1% of 1%, it is a very small number.*

FINALLY,

Like any testimony, presentation of research is most engaging when it is tied to vivid, real-world examples. Mitigation specialist Lisa McDermott counsels experts to use vivid, emotional, real-life examples as much as possible during direct examination, not only because it makes testimony more compelling but because examples cannot be easily countered on cross examination by another research study:

> *The strongest experts use the mitigation materials that we put together. The knowledge of the person and the experiences in the materials can come out in the expert's testimony. For example, the materials might include an interview with the mother during which she was shaking when she was talking about the abuse in her own life. This detail—that she was shaking—creates a visual reality for the jury that cannot be undermined by studies and statistics. A trial can be a war of studies that isn't useful to the jury. When the expert has information that rings true, like police reports and interviews, the prosecution will stay away from that on cross. But if the expert presents a cold technical analysis of the case, then the cross will be, "You do realize there is another study?" Those experts that have not*

spent ample time understanding the detailed picture, beyond their scientific expertise, are not as strong as witnesses.

We turn now, in the next several chapters to specific tools for presenting the content of direct testimony in an engaging and vivid manner.

NOTES

1. Weisberg, D. S., Keil, F. C., Goodstein, J., Rawson, E., & Gray, J. R. (2008). The seductive allure of neuroscience explanations. *Journal of Cognitive Neuroscience, 20*, 470–477.
2. Scurich, N., & Shniderman, A. (2014). The selective allure of neuroscientific explanations. *PLoS ONE, 9*(9), e107529.

9 Creating Access to Assessment Methods and Results

MY FIRST REFERRAL as a newly minted neuropsychologist at a rehabilitation hospital was unforgettable: *Mr. Smith is a globally aphasic patient without reliable yes/no gestures. Please assess cognitive function.* Of course, unless I could read his mind, that request was literally impossible: Globally aphasic patients cannot understand spoken, written, or gestural language and cannot express their thoughts with words, writing, or gestures. That is, I had literally no way of asking the patient questions or explaining what tasks I wanted him to do, and he had literally no way of answering questions even if he knew what I was asking. Thus, I learned early on in my career that even our medical colleagues are not always clear about how cognitive and psychological assessment works.

While experts from other medical fields may have imprecise or occasionally magical ideas about how neuropsychologists are able to measure and understand thinking abilities, jurors may literally have no idea about how our assessment tools and procedures work.

In their book *Made to Stick: Why Some Ideas Survive and Others Die*,[1] Chip and Dan Heath point out that attorneys, accountants, physicians, and other professionals are so used to speaking and thinking with the basic assumptions of our professions that those assumptions become invisible to us. We forget that others are not familiar with our assumptions, and our messages therefore become inaccessible to people outside of our profession. Standardized testing and normative interpretation are a great example of this concept. After years of graduate school and clinical practice, when a neuropsychologist uses the word *testing* we have a very precise image in our thought bubbles of a set of valid and reliably constructed instruments, normed on appropriate populations, administered in a standardized fashion, and interpreted in the context of the larger assessment.

But what is in the thought bubbles of jurors when they hear the word *testing*? Some may conjure scenes from movies where psychologists use ink blots or "word associations." Others will picture a plaintiff spending 8 hours taking an SAT-like bubble test. Very few will have been exposed to the concept of normative interpretation.

Another foundational assumption of psychologists and neuropsychologists is the distinction between testing and assessment.[2] Attorneys, judges, jurors, and other experts not trained (or not well trained) in assessment may not know about this distinction and may incorrectly assume that there is a simple relationship between a test score and the presence or absence of impairment, or even between a single test score and the literal functioning of a particular area of brain tissue. Such simplistic interpretations of test scores divorced from the context of the assessment lead to ridiculous statements like, "This Wisconsin Card Sort Test score means there is damage to Ms. Choi's frontal lobe."

To ensure that jurors and triers of fact have access to our broader message regarding assessment results, we need to begin our testimony with a clear, accessible, and engaging description of our assessment tools and process. Judge Allison Burroughs shared a striking cautionary tale of what happens when experts fail to do so:

> *I saw a case that was about whether a woman had a minor concussion that should have taken 3 months to resolve or a traumatic brain injury that would keep her from working, taking care of her children, and so on. The experts went through and explained the tests. I could see the jurors and I were all doing the same thing: We were taking the little tests on our pads of paper while the experts were explaining them. It was impossible to resist.*
>
> *Both experts gave the plaintiff these complicated drawings and she was supposed to copy the drawing. I was looking at my drawing and it was no better than the plaintiff's; in fact, it was worse than hers. I thought the tests seemed ridiculous: According to the drawing I produced, I have a traumatic brain injury!*
>
> *The experts on both sides were saying contradictory things: "Look at this drawing, it's great" and "Look at this drawing: She has traumatic brain injury." I think the jurors just threw it all out. I don't blame them. My guess is that the jurors rejected all of the testing testimony from both sides.*
>
> *I still have that little drawing that I tried to do during the experts' testimony. I keep it on my bench just to remind me of that experience. It is a good check-in that you can't believe everything somebody says just because they are saying it. Because according to that piece of paper, I am arguably brain-damaged.*

This chapter addresses strategies for explaining psychological and neuropsychological assessment procedures, as well as specific tests like the MMPI, in a clear, accessible manner. Such thoughtful, thorough explanations will help to avoid more negative experiences like the one Judge Burroughs relays. For the type of "in the weeds" explanations of specific statistical issues that may come up on cross examination or in the context of capital cases addressing intellectual disability, see Chapter 22, "Explaining Statistics."

TELLING THE STORY OF THE ASSESSMENT

While explaining standardized assessment to those unfamiliar with it may be a challenge, attorney Mark DeBofsky emphasizes the benefit in helping the jury to understand our assessment procedure. He describes assessment as "the objective advantage" in the courtroom:

> *The difference between an MD expert and a neuropsychologist: With physician expert testimony, someone is giving their opinion. When the neuropsychologist is giving their opinion, it is supported by objective test data. Testimony is more believable if there is objective test data to back it up. This is an advantage for the profession of neuropsychology. When you have data to back up your opinion, it is that much easier to communicate your opinion. It is like a radiologist walking into court with a scan.*

Robert Heilbronner explicitly states this advantage in his introduction of the assessment process to juries:

> *Our tests have all been standardized with people of various ages, education levels, and ethnicities. We can compare Mr. Smith's score on a test to scores of large numbers of people his age, education, and culture. This is a strength of neuropsychological testing.*

Assessment is multidimensional

"Doctor, how did you assess Mrs. Plaintiff?" In my own practice, one of the most important things I want to explain to jurors is that neuropsychological and psychological assessment is not just about tests; rather, it's about putting together multiple sources of information so I understand the whole person.

> *A: When I assess my patients, I do four things. First, I carefully read the medical records. I want to understand what happened at the time of the accident and Mrs. Smith's symptom course over time, but it's also very important that I understand how Mrs. Smith was functioning before the accident. The second part of the assessment is a clinical interview. I sat down with Mrs. Smith for 2 hours and asked her to tell me about the accident and the symptoms she is experiencing. I also asked her all about her upbringing and education and family and emotional history. It's important that I get a good picture of the whole person. The next part of the assessment is testing. I gave Mrs. Smith tests of memory, attention, language, problem-solving, and mood. And that takes a whole day. Finally, and this part happens during the interview and testing session, I carefully observe my patients. Are they able to understand and remember test directions? Are they able to focus on tasks? Are they tearful? These direct observations are also an important part of the assessment process.*

Many experts share with jurors that the assessment they conducted for the case at hand was just like the assessments they conduct every day in their clinical practice. That is, in the narrative that the jurors are developing as they hear the story of the assessment, an important element is whether you as the expert were assessing the plaintiff/defendant in the same careful, fair, and thorough way you would any of your patients.

Robert Heilbronner notes that on direct, he tells the story of how the neuropsychological examination was initiated:

> *It's important to clarify to the judge or jury that sometimes I don't think a neuropsychological exam is necessary and sometimes it is. Importantly, it wasn't the attorney who wanted to have it done; I was the one who decided that it would be important to do in order to provide a better foundation for my opinions. "I was asked to review the records, and then after reviewing them I determined that a neuropsychological evaluation would be helpful and I made the request . . ."*

Well validated, standardized, and normed

"Doctor, what are neuropsychological (psychological) tests?" Here are multiple strategies for explaining the nature of our tests on direct examination.

Robert Mendoza notes that it is important to let the jury know that our tests are well validated, well researched, and very well accepted. He will typically say:

> *I administered a number of tests that are globally accepted in the scientific community. They have been well researched, in some cases for decades. And the tests have been compared against populations very similar to the individual I assessed here today. The tests are commonly used and accepted both in courtrooms and in clinical practice."*

Jerry Sweet gives a beautiful description of the basis of normative testing, taking jurors through the difference between just asking someone how they feel, and asking in a systematic, detailed manner, turning the responses into numbers, and then comparing those numbers to other people:

> *We can ask people in the interview, "How are you feeling? Are you feeling depressed or anxious or worried?" And we will get a general sense of that. But in our psychological tests we have a much more specific sense of symptoms that they either have or don't have. We are also able to turn those responses into numbers and look at the numbers compared to people who are known to be very depressed or not depressed at all.*

This is how I explain in my own practice:

> *Many people are concerned that their memory isn't so good anymore. A lot of us start to misplace our keys more after age 40. Neuropsychological tests help us answer the question, "Is my memory any better or worse than anyone else my age?" The tests are standardized—that means the exact same directions and test items are given to everyone in exactly the same way. And they are normed, meaning the same memory test is given to thousands of people, of all different age categories. That means that when I take the test, we can compare my score to others my age. I may feel like my memory*

> *is not so hot, but by taking this objective test and looking at how my score compares to other people my age, I can actually get a concrete answer to that question.*

Test names are not necessary

When talking to colleagues, the names of tests are a rich source of information. Can you imagine talking to a colleague and saying, "You won't believe the score my patient got on a test of drawing and copying!" Huh? Which one? We include the specific test names when we are speaking with each other because the names are meaningful to people in the field. But test names are not meaningful to jurors. Saying "Logical Memory" to them conveys no information about the memory test you gave, and a good case can be made that it makes it harder for them to understand the test because they will be thinking, "*Logical* Memory? Was this a reasoning test, too?"

While there may be occasions when using a test name makes sense, Jerry Sweet notes that he tries not to use test names during testimony:

> *We have measures that look at learning and memory. We have others that look at simple and complex attention, language functions . . .*
>
> ------------
>
> Rather than use test names, I will often describe the nature of the tasks I am doing with the plaintiff and at the same time try to make a transition from the test to everyday life.
>
> *A story recall measure is very much like being involved in a conversation. There is a narrative going on. One is trying to remember the gist as well as the bits and pieces. Remembering the basic gist is often easier. Recalling the details is also important.*— Rodney Vanderploeg, PhD, ABPP-CN

TELLING THE STORY OF THE RECORDS REVIEW

Wendy Marlowe explains to jury members why it is important to review records:

> *I look at all the past medical issues and problems someone has had over his/her lifetime. In order to really attribute the current complaints to this accident, I need to rule out whether the complaints or problems were present prior to the accident. People often do not remember whether these things were preexisting; they focus more on the current accident. They may not mean to mislead us, but sometimes they misremember. We really need to review all of the records in order to be sure.*

David Bush also emphasizes the importance of the records review and recommends transforming that review into a timeline as tool to help jurors understand his testimony narrative:

> *I try to develop my cases along narrative lines: Who was the person before the incident/accident happened? How did they change? To what extent were they affected by the incident? Who is the person now? It is very important to construct a timeline*

of the history and to organize it into a narrative so that when you testify, you are describing the story of a three-dimensional person. You know who the person was, what their strengths and weaknesses were, and how that has changed—the kinds of relationships they had, the way they lived their life, and how all of that has been altered by the injury or whatever event is the basis of their claim, if it has changed at all.

For a discussion of creating a visual timeline to accompany direct testimony, see Chapter 10, "Visuals."

As experts describe their records review, they have the opportunity to frame and reframe inconsistencies. Wendy Marlowe notes that she frames many inconsistencies she finds in examinees' records, such as inaccurate grade estimates, as "misremembering."

Q: Can you tell us what you did to assess Mr. Smith?

A: The first thing I did was to review all of his records. I gathered every record I could find. I went back to his high school transcript (yes, you can still get that!) Why do I want to look at his high school transcript? Well, some people mistakenly remember themselves as having been better students or more intelligent than they really were. Some may have indications of specific learning disabilities. Also, most transcripts have group IQ measurements on them as well as grades. Those IQ scores give us information about the individual's past abilities. As a good example of people misremembering things, when I give workshops for attorneys, I ask, "Will anyone who did not get straight As in law school please stand up!" And you know, no one ever does.

TELLING THE STORY OF THE BEHAVIORAL OBSERVATIONS

An important concept to emphasize to jurors is that the assessment is not just about test scores. What we observe clinically over the course of an entire day, or throughout multiple days of assessment, hour after hour, is critically important information that is either *consistent* or *inconsistent* with the test scores and medical records. The fact that Mr. Defendant frequently needed test instructions repeated because he drifted off in the middle of long tasks and that he lost his train of thought multiple times when answering interview questions are important data points that are consistent with his low scores on attention tasks. The converse is true: If Mr. Defendant never needed questions repeated and never lost his train of thought during the interview, and drove himself to the appointment without an accident, then his Digit Span scaled score of 5 would be noncredible. In my own practice, I always let jurors know about both the consistencies and the inconsistencies:

And my direct observation of Mr. Defendant, throughout all those hours of testing, was consistent with the test scores. He has a really significant attention problem.

See Chapter 11, "Performance and Symptom Validity," for clear, vivid strategies of presenting inconsistencies between behavior and test scores to jurors.

TELLING THE STORY OF COLLATERAL INTERVIEWS

In addition to a clinical interview, forensic cases may also involve collateral interviews. In some forensic cases, it's not practical, it won't be allowed, or it's not necessary to interview other people, particularly when deposition testimony is available for major stakeholders in an examinee's life. But if they are done in a case, collateral interviews represent another potential leg of the assessment stool. Sharing the fact that part of one's opinions were based on interviews of parents, teachers, supervisors, or other observers in the examinee's life can be helpful for jurors when such contacts are allowed, necessary, and practical.

Depending on the nature of the interview information, sharing this information directly with the jurors adds depth to their understanding of the case. Lynn Blackburn will say,

> *Sally's parents are concerned that she can't learn anything new. I want to share with you what they are seeing.*

TELLIN THE STORY OF THE OBSERVATION

Pediatric forensic cases may involve classroom observations. Just as rich clinical information is gathered by watching one's young patients at school, the same is true for forensic assessments. In some cases, an opportunity arises to spend a day at the examinee's education setting, where I directly observe the child both in the classroom and in the lunchroom/playground. This also gives me the opportunity to directly interview teachers. If an observation is completed, it is a step in an assessment that jurors can immediately relate to as producing relevant information about the child. When an observation has taken place, I weave in my direct observations with the test results:

> *Before I met Jane for our two testing days, before she knew who I was, I visited her school for a day so I had the opportunity to see directly how she functions at school. I sat in the back of the classroom all day, and also followed the kids to the lunchroom and out to recess. It was a really valuable opportunity to see how she learns, but also to see if she has friends, and how she functions in structured classrooms and during free time. Just like I would expect with her strong scores on attention tasks when she came to my office, Jane was well behaved and focused throughout the school day. When the teacher asked a question, she was often the first to raise her hand, and her answers were right on point. When I had a chance to speak with her teacher, Ms. Peterson, she confirmed that what I saw in the classroom was Jane's typical behavior. Compared to the other kids in the class, her teacher described her as in the top 25% for good behavior and academic skills. She is doing really well.*

GETTING MORE SPECIFIC

"Doctor, what did you find as a result of your assessment?" Once the story of the assessment methods has been told, the attorney will ask for the story of the assessment results. The timing of the description of test results depends on the specific narrative in the case. This section presents engaging strategies to share information about tests and test interpretation.

Communicating test scores in court

Mike Chafetz has a pet peeve about neuropsychological reports: "It is a disservice for neuropsychologists to be over-inclusive about presenting all the different kinds of test scores in their reports: standard scores, T-scores, z-scores, scaled scores, and percentiles. Readers of these reports can't put it all together into a coherent whole, and I would argue that it is difficult for even neuropsychologists to compare across the different kinds of scores easily." Chafetz believes that jurors simply have no access to this kind of thinking, and to have numerous kinds of scores only creates higher hurdles. His reports use only percentiles in the narrative, as these tend to communicate well to lay persons. However, in graphs and tables, he uses standard scores, translating all the scores to this one metric. This method puts everything on one level playing field, so that it is easy to compare across domains. On the witness stand, communication is easy. For example, when asked about a standard score of 75 and what it might mean, he translates and says, "That score means that 95% of people the same age obtained a higher score than this individual."

Summarize, don't itemize

Manfred Greiffenstein advised, "If you present each test individually, you will put the jury to sleep. I would put myself to sleep!" Attorneys and experts almost universally caution against a long recitation of the results of each specific test given. Instead, many recommend summarizing test results by domain and creating a clear, vivid visual such as a table or graph to enlarge and show the jury as you are giving an overview of the test results. See Chapter 10, "Visuals," for examples of this strategy.

Explaining test interpretation

Normal variability

How would Ms. Jones have performed on our tests prior to her brain injury? The well-developed literature on normal variability tells us our answer must go far beyond our estimate of her average pre-accident intellectual function. The literature compels us to reframe the question: "How does a typical person with average intellect, who has never had a neurological injury or disease process, perform on a large set of cognitive tests?" It's a challenge to explain that answer to jurors who have no background in either standardized testing or statistics in an engaging, succinct manner.

David Bush notes,

> *I often see reports and testimony that overrepresent the specificity of cognitive tests, as if lower-than-expected performance on any given measure or within any given area can and does only mean one thing (i.e., acquired brain damage). This really does reflect a kind of overly concrete and magical thinking. Of course, people do poorly on our measures for many possible reasons. The differential diagnostic process requires the neuropsychologist to consider all possible alternatives on the basis of test evidence, history, extra-test behavior, and knowledge of the way different illness and injury patterns unfold and make their presence known. This is, inevitably, a very complex and sophisticated reasoning task that requires the flexible integration of multiple data sources.*

Here is how he approaches explaining the concept to jurors:

If I were to test everyone in your law firm

The analogy is a way of complimenting the attorneys. It breaks their set. They expect you to be afraid of them or want to put them down. The analogy has an element of surprise that comes from a compliment. Surprise like that in testimony is a good thing. When they expect a witness to be cantankerous, but the witness bends over backwards to be a gentlewoman or man, it breaks set.

If I came to your firm, and gave you and all of your partners (who I assume are quite bright with high IQs and neurologically healthy) a big set of tests, the vast majority of you are going to produce a number of test scores that technically fall in the abnormal range, even with a group of really bright and reasonably healthy people. And a fair number will have scores in the impaired range. Abnormal neuropsychological test scores are not synonymous with brain damage or neuropsychological impairment. Some abnormal scores are the rule and not the exception. You have to interpret patterns of scores and integrate that with the history and extra-test behavior to develop and support the basis of a brain damage diagnosis.

We all know that we are better at some things than others. We all have strengths and weaknesses. And thank God: That's what makes us unique. It is not a sign of brain damage. The fact that Mr. Smith has a few relatively low scores, this is a perfectly normal finding.—David Schretlen, PhD, ABPP-CN

If you give someone 30 tests that include 50 measures over a lengthy neuropsychological assessment, the person will get some higher and some lower scores. Nobody ever gets closely matching scores on every measure. If you don't understand how much variability in scores is present in the average, normal person, you will almost always conclude that impairment is present.—David Schretlan, PhD, ABPP-CN

Would you rather have a surgeon who is doing your heart surgery have a higher verbal IQ or a higher visual IQ? There is a huge literature that points out that scores of a certain nature may represent a real difference in people's abilities, but they don't necessarily indicate that the statistically significant difference in tested skills actually or always represents brain damage.—Ted Peck, PhD, ABPP-CN

When you give a set of neuropsychological tests to neurologically normal people, only about 10% of people have ***no*** *scores below normal. About half of neurologically normal people will have as many as three or four scores below normal, and one in five have 10 or more scores below normal. It's common to see scores below normal in a whole set of tests. In fact, when someone scores completely normal on every test across the whole set, that's actually abnormal in that it's unusual, because they are* *doing so well relative to other neurologically normal people.*—Nancy Hebben, PhD, ABPP-CN

There is a lot of variability expected in any one set of tests. In studies that have been done on normal individuals, in more than half of the cases, the biggest difference between the lowest and highest test scores is huge—greater than the 2nd percentile to the 84th percentile, for example. It is very common to see variability in normal people. Now let's look at Mr. Smith, let's see what we have: He has one score in the low average range and several in the high average range. That's normal. There is nothing abnormal here.—Nancy Hebben, PhD, ABPP-CN

We are not all above average. And even for average people, no one is average across the board. There is a normal, natural variation in skills. We all have strengths and weaknesses, and what you see with Mr. Thomas's test performances is still within the range of expectation for someone who has a normal healthy brain.—Glenn Larrabee, PhD, ABPP-CN

The literature is very clear that people naturally have a specific set of skills. For example, a high average IQ in an attorney with an average nonverbal IQ: That may simply mean he was born with better verbal skills and he was led into law as a career, as opposed to becoming an engineer. It doesn't necessarily mean he is brain damaged.—Ted Peck, PhD, ABPP-CN

With a God-given IQ of average to low average . . .

In a healthy person whose God-given IQ is around 90, you would expect to find most other scores in the low average or average range, but a few that are higher or lower, and maybe one or two that are abnormal or superior. And that is exactly what we found with Ms. Smith. (I will put up a visual of 1 superior; 6 high average; 22 average; 12 low average; 4 borderline; and 2 abnormal scores as I explain this).—David Schretlen, PhD, ABPP-CN

Most of us were trained to look at differences between subtest scores as having a lot of meaning. Now we know that clearly those differences do not have meaning—although some of my colleagues continue to make a big deal of the differences in subtest scores. [I might say:]

You know, one of the things that happens in the world is that technology changes and our understanding of things change. Even our understanding of the brain changes. We used to think that small differences in test scores made a difference. But there have been a number of studies that looked at the people who were tested when the tests were designed (standardized). These studies demonstrated that there was much more variability among the normal people who took the tests than we expected. That has really changed how we think about and talk about test scores."—Wendy Marlowe, PhD, ABPP-CN

If you are administering a big set of 30 tests to a healthy group of individuals, even healthy individuals will have a handful of low scores on the tests.—Michael McCrea, PhD, ABPP-CN

We have these tests. They are given to lots of people. We match the person being tested to similar people based on age and education. We compare the scores of Mr. Smith to a group of his peers, and we know how different he is from them. But at the same time, everyone has strengths and weaknesses. There is a lot of variability in the normal population. People do some things better than others. And sometimes you are really focusing in on a task and do it great, and other times you are not focusing in on the task the same way and you don't do it so well. People are variable in how well they do the same tasks over time. So if you give a large amount of thinking tasks, just by chance alone you are likely to get some times when a person isn't 100% engaging in on a task, and their scores will be relatively low.—Robin Hanks, PhD, ABPP-CN

Relative deficits

People vary in skills. Some people have good handwriting. Some people are fast runners. Some people have issues where they can't inhibit their behavior. We all know people who say what is on their mind and it gets them into trouble. And then some people have that problem at another level, and they get in trouble with the law. That's different than someone who has lived their whole life a certain way, then because of a brain injury or developing seizures now have lost the ability to maintain control and have gotten themselves into trouble because of this new neurological problem.—William Barr, PhD, ABPP-CN

Far be it from me to say his high score was caused by the brain injury.

One of the things that often happens is that someone does really, really well on one of the tests. If you give someone enough tests, they are bound to do really well on one of them. I will say,

Far be it from me to say that the brain injury produced this significantly increased ability. Just like I would never say that if he scores really badly on something; I wouldn't say a single low score was caused by the brain injury. That's what you call variability.—Tom Boll, PhD, ABPP-CN

Johnny Bench and the definition of "impairment"

Johnny Bench was an amazing hitter. He was an amazing hitter and an amazing catcher and an amazing fielder. But he wasn't a great runner and he couldn't pitch. He could pitch better than me and run faster than me, but compared to other major

league players, he had relative weaknesses in those areas. But that's normal. We wouldn't call him "impaired" in any of his baseball-related skills.—Christopher Grote, PhD, ABPP-CN

We will see a lifelong pattern

We are better at some things than others. Some people are very verbal but can't solve a third-grade puzzle. Some people are great with mechanics but their verbal skills aren't good. And you see that in the records. You see it in the school grades and you see it in the testing. This is what this guy is; he is a welder. He is probably a superb welder, but wouldn't be much of an English teacher—and he never was. Don't hold bad verbal skills against him when he is good at other things. That's just who he is.—Tom Boll, PhD, ABPP-CN

Base rates

Closely related to normal variability is the concept of base rates. Here are some clear methods to describe the concept to jurors.

Using base rates on the stand

When they developed the test, a quarter of the people who they used to standardize it, who never had any kind of neurological injury, got this same score. —Robin Hanks, PhD, ABPP-CN

Explaining base rates for risk assessment

The first time I was asked this on the stand, I just tried to discuss base rates, but it was hard for the jury to understand. Over time, I came up with a more succinct way to say it:

Q: Isn't it true that when you look at the outcomes for risk assessment, you are only right 50 to 55% of the time? Isn't that the equivalent of just flipping a coin?

A: That would be true if 50% of the population is violent. If 50% of the population is violent and I am only guessing 50% correctly, that **is** *like flipping a coin. But the base rate for violence is 25%. That's a like a four-sided die. If I can tell you which number will come up on a four-sided die 50% of the time, that's pretty good, because you should only be able to figure it out one out of four times (25%) on that die if you were just guessing. It is true that risk assessment is not perfect, but it is much more accurate than if we were guessing.*—Ira K. Packer, PhD, ABPP (Forensic)

Considering base rates of reported activities of daily living

Q: Isn't it true doctor that Mr. Plaintiff's wife confirms on this checklist that he does not to do housework since his concussion?!

A: There is no neurologically based reason why a concussion would cause a change in a person's ability to do laundry or scrub a toilet. This is where it is important

to have good base rate research. If I were to give that checklist to 1000 women, how many would tell me their husbands are doing an appropriate amount of housework?

A consistent pattern of test scores

Christopher Grote uses a "smoke and fire" analogy to explain the importance of multiple converging sources of information guiding an assessment conclusion:

> *It can be "normal" to occasionally score in the abnormal range if you give a very large number of tests; a bad score may well pop up eventually. If you see smoke, it doesn't necessarily mean there is a fire; you don't necessarily need to call the fire department. You should look closer. Are you seeing black smoke? In the same way, are you seeing a flame through a window? Are you are getting more data suggesting there is something real here, not just a false alarm?*

You wouldn't want your MD referring you for bypass surgery based on one test!

What I do is explain that the whole point of what I do is to assess those numbers and determine what the pattern means:

Just like you wouldn't want your physician referring you for bypass surgery based on an isolated lab result, you don't want me concluding you have brain damage based on some isolated scores that may have no meaning.

You can personalize this by noting how many false-positive tests you have had yourself, so for me I could note a false-positive mammogram, ultrasound, blood test . . . I could go on . . .

We know if you give, say, 15 tests to a healthy person, about half will have at least one 'abnormal' score. If I give a bunch of tests to someone (I insert the opposing doc's number of tests here), about 90% of people will have these so-called abnormal scores! Even more if the person is elderly, or depressed. So random low scores don't mean much to me. The hard part is what makes me a board-certified neuropsychologist: I interpret the pattern of scores as it relates to brain functioning and neuroanatomy, and this person's medical records and behavior."—Tannahill Glen, PhD, ABPP-CN

The one thing brain damage isn't is a grasshopper.

Usually, what happens is we are testing someone more than once. Or another expert is testing them on another occasion. And the low scores that some expert landed on with both feet and waved a flag over aren't there anymore. The next time, the person does fine on those tests. And the first set of scores, with a low nonverbal IQ, the expert concludes, well, it must be right hemisphere damage (even though there is no evidence in the world that a mild concussion produces any variability in nonverbal IQ). The next time his nonverbal IQ is 10 points higher than his verbal IQ.

The one thing brain damage isn't is a grasshopper. It doesn't jump from side to side. If it is there one day and not the next, it was never there.—Tom Boll, PhD, ABPP-CN

Medical lab test metaphor for normal variability

When an examinee gets a great score on one delayed memory test and a bad one on a second test, some neuropsychologists will claim that the score "proves executive dysfunction!" In that situation, I will get into intra-individual variation—that is, the more tests you give, the more low scores you get. Experts can spend 2 days in testing, and one abnormal score or three forms the basis for their opinion. Depending on how I am asked, I might introduce the concept this way:

Sure, if you test a person long enough, they will produce an abnormal score. They are tired. The score gets at an individul's weakness. If a doctor runs enough tests, eventually one will be abnormal by chance. Neuropsychological testing will be the same way; you have to expect a few abnormal results by chance. What's important is the pattern. Does the person consistently do poorly on the same type of task? Or is there a lot of variability?—Manfred Greiffenstein, PhD, ABPP-CN

Babe Ruth

Babe Ruth had more strikeouts than homeruns. We all remember him for his homeruns. And the string of 59 homeruns he had in one season? He had more strikeouts than homeruns. Are we going to look at his strikeouts and conclude he was a bad player? No, we are going to look at those strikeouts in the context of his overall play.—Jacobus Donders, PhD, ABPP-CN

Baseball pitcher analogy for variability

A guy pitches a no-hitter today, and then 4 days later he gets knocked out of the box in the fourth inning. Is he brain damaged? No, sometimes we are really good at things, and sometimes we are not on our game. There is huge variability.—Tom Boll, PhD, ABPP-CN

Eli Manning

Last night, the New York Giants played [other team]. In the first quarter Eli Manning threw two interceptions. He also threw three touchdowns. If you look at the quarter, Eli Manning had two poor scores, but the Giants still won the game. Are you going to say that based on those two scores, Eli Manning is a bad quarterback or has a bad arm? Or are you going to look at the totality of the game?—Jacobus Donders, PhD, ABPP-CN

Inconsistent test results: not a crack in the engine

A brain is like a Porsche. I start up my Porsche and the engine purrs. I can take it on the highway and drive it 100 miles an hour. It works great. Yet another time I take the Porsche out of the garage it sputters and I can only get it to go 40 miles an hour. When that happens—the fact that the car purrs and goes 100 miles an hour one day, then not the next day, then purrs again on the third day—that tells me that there isn't a crack in the engine.

The problem is like bad gasoline. Not a crack in the engine, just bad gasoline. What are the factors that go into that bad gasoline? Poor sleep, mood issues? Figuring out the answer to that tells us how to get the engine running more consistently.—Neil Pliskin, PhD, ABPP-CN

Explaining why I give multiple measures of a single domain

I always give more than one test to measure a brain function. I don't know about you, but if I am going to do work to my house, I wouldn't just take the first guy who comes out and gives me a price. No. You get multiple estimates. So when I am trying to understand how a child's memory works, I want to get three estimates to compare and make sure that I am consistent and know what I am doing. .—Lisa Stanford, PhD, ABPP-CN

Many clinicians will claim that inconsistent test scores in one domain somehow prove there is executive dysfunction. I will be all over that.

If it's not consistent, it's not neurologic. Inconsistency tells me it is due to extraneous factors. If Mr. Smith's performance on memory tests is great one day and terrible the next, I know that it is usually something other than a brain cause.—Lisa Stanford, PhD, ABPP-CN

You can't turn a brain injury on and off

I like to tie specific testing behaviors to concepts I am explaining. So, if a person has extreme slowing but only in the first half of the exam and looks normal at other times, that is inconsistent with brain injury:

You can't turn a brain injury off and on. Either you have the deficit or not. A major problem will unfortunately just be there, all the time. It may be more, or less, noticeable at certain times, but the deficit is still there.—Tannahill Glen, PsyD, ABPP-CN

Extraneous variables

Another foundational concept of assessment that often needs to be explained to juries is the effect of extraneous variables on test scores.

It's easy to fail a test

It is easy to fail a test and do poorly. Think of when you were in school. If you didn't sleep the night before, or didn't study, it would be easy to get an F. It's hard to get an A. To get an A you have to study, you have to sleep well, you have to be prepared. There are many reasons to do poorly on a test that have nothing to do with "This person is brain damaged, or impaired, or doesn't have intact functions."—Rodney Vanderploeg, PhD, ABPP-CN

Explaining low scores on timed tests

Although the majority do not, some folks with anxiety move really slowly to be very precise, to manage their anxiety. Also, some people tend to move slowly and precisely as a longstanding habit. If you were tracing something with your kid, you didn't go "zip!" like that (makes a hand motion of quickly scribbling). You do it kind of slowly, because you aren't doing it for time. Sometimes people when they do these tests, they want to make really sure that they are really precise. Even when you tell them to just go as fast as they can, they are like, "No, you don't understand; it's got to be really, really precise." Most of us know people like that. With them, some of the tests which rely on time are going to be slower. It's just about their test-taking style.—David Williamson, PhD, ABPP-CN

Effect of multiple extraneous variables on cognitive performance

To really know what's going on, you have to get these other things cleared up because they can influence people's test performance. For example, you can think less efficiently and be more forgetful if you are not getting enough sleep. In Ms. Taylor's case . . .—Kristie Nies, PhD, ABPP-CN

Negative thinking affects test performance

The pessimist, the person who always sees the negative side of things. The glass is always half empty. There is always something wrong. That is how the person moves through life and sees things. They experience their symptoms as one more example of a problem. That negativity unfortunately results in them being not only unhappy but also in having difficulty processing information and responding to life in a way that allows them to function well.—Rodney Vanderploeg, PhD, ABPP-CN

Effects of chronic pain on the test battery

Chronic pain can be really fatiguing. If you have to slog through the day dealing with pain it can really sap your energy. We know pain doesn't make you dumber. Pain doesn't cause brain damage in and of itself. But it can make the experience of taking the tests more draining.—David Williamson, PhD, ABPP-CN

Emotions affect mental processes

Strong emotions can definitely affect mental processes. We have all been there: When we get angry, we can't think of anything else than being angry. Everyone has had times when we are depressed, don't care, when we just don't pay attention.—Manfred Greiffenstein, PhD, ABPP-CN

Why is she reporting memory problems, then, Doctor?

Q: Why is she reporting memory problems, then, Doctor?

A: A lot of things can affect people's idea of how well their memory works: poor sleep, stress, even the idea that you have a memory problem. It can be a self-fulfilling prophecy.—Robin Hanks, PhD, ABPP-CN

Nonspecificity of test scores

There are a million reasons why a child would have done poorly on a test

There are a million reasons why a child would have done poorly on a test. It is my job to figure out why. Here are all these records that I reviewed. They are just as important as the time I spent with the child in front of me.—John Kirk, PsyD, ABPP-CN

Like a piece of artwork from a 4-year-old

It's like a piece of artwork your 4-year-old brings home. There's a big blob of brown on the page, and you know that a lot of coloring went into that blob. And if you are asked which part of that blob is explained by the orange crayon, well, it's really unclear. Sometimes along the edges, you can tell. But the big blob in the middle, you can't pull the orange out of that. That's what Mr. Smith's neuropsychological testing was like. There's some really low scores. You can probably list the factors that might have contributed to those low scores, like depression, medication side effects, his history of learning disability, his recent stroke, and his substance abuse, but exactly which score was explained by which factor—you just can't do that.—David Williamson, PhD, ABPP-CN

It is important to educate the jury that it is not a one-to-one correlation between positive neuropsychological test findings and the presence of brain injury.

Neuropsychological test scores can be low for many reasons. The person taking the tests might not have slept well the night before. They may have had a relative weakness in one thinking area all of their lives; we call that a learning disability. They might have a head cold on the testing day.—Nancy Hebben, PhD, ABPP-CN

Holistic rather than single-test-score–centered approach to interpretation

Neil Pliskin makes it a point to focus on a holistic interpretation strategy:

When I am communicating psychological findings, my goal is to communicate that it is the combination of tests plus my judgment plus behavioral observations plus the medical records. My cases don't usually rest on an elevation or lack of elevation on the MMPI.

In my own practice, when I am asked whether I relied on the MMPI or another specific psychological inventory alone, or on any one piece of information, I like to use the analogy of a puzzle:

Psychologists rely on multiple sources of information that we put together to form a picture of the person. It's like a jigsaw puzzle. It is very important that the pieces fit.

In Mr. Plaintiff's case, I directly observed him to have a normal mood during our day-long testing session. He smiled often and made several jokes. He did not appear depressed or anxious. In contrast, when he filled out the Beck Depression Inventory, he endorsed very severe levels of depression. His score was what one would expect if a patient with severe major depressive disorder was filling it out. Those puzzle pieces just don't fit—until you look at the results of the personality test I gave him, the MMPI-2. This is a psychological test with validity scales that are designed to measure a person's test-taking style. Are they overreporting or underreporting symptoms? In Mr. Plaintiff's case, the MMPI-2 validity scales showed that he was dramatically overreporting symptoms. Now the puzzle pieces fit. Here is a man whose MMPI-2 test shows that he is exaggerating symptoms, and this same man has a normal, upbeat mood, but endorses severe depression on the Beck Depression Inventory. Those puzzle pieces fit together.

Explaining practice effects

Practice effects are information.

What are practice effects? Practice effects are learning. If you can learn, how impaired are you? If someone took the test 8 months ago and were able to recognize all the tests and figure them out because they saw them before, then they have a pretty good memory skill, don't they. Practice effects are information.—Tom Boll, PhD, ABPP-CN

Testing someone temporally close to another expert

People get tested a lot. People say, "Well, you can't test him, because he was just tested." One guy, a well-known neuropsychologist, and I agreed he would see the litigant on day one and I would see him on day two. There isn't a problem with that. We are paid to interpret the data. So, if the data don't change, we interpret that. He just took these tests yesterday and they were very similar, I wonder why, when the tests were so similar. If the data does change, is he more comfortable with the testing situation? Is he learning?—Tom Boll, PhD, ABPP-CN

It's like hearing a joke for a second time: You know the punch line.

First of all, this person did worse for me on the same test that they did 6 months prior for this other doctor. Now, I don't know any way to explain that for a medical issue that occurred 2 years ago and is not supposed to get worse over time. Now if she had Alzheimer's disease, yes, that would make sense that her scores were getting worse over time. But she doesn't have Alzheimer's disease. They are claiming a TBI. That gets better over time. It's like hearing a joke for the second time: You know the punch line.—Jacobus Donders, PhD, ABPP-CN

Explaining shortened or brief assessments

In some circumstances, the court will order an Independent Medical Examination to take place in a limited amount of time. In my own practice, I had a case where the opposing attorney motioned the court to limit the number of hours a plaintiff could be evaluated. The judge ordered the assessment to be completed within 2 hours, even though the assessment was originally scheduled for a full day. Of course, in some situations, there is enough good testing data available from previous evaluations where a full-day assessment, or any assessment, is not necessary, but in this case, there was no valid, credible testing data available:

> *It's like turning off an MRI scan of the brain, which usually takes 45 minutes, after only 5 minutes. You can't expect to get a valid picture of the brain when you don't leave the scanner on for the full 45 minutes. It's the same with a neuropsychological assessment. In this case, where we don't have other valid data about Mr. Smith's thinking abilities, we can't get a clear picture of the claimant by stopping the assessment after only 2 hours.*

Explaining test findings in context

Robert Mendoza notes that he introduces specific test results to the jury in the context of the statutory question at hand and simply as a discussion about the data itself. In other words, he connect the test results with the question—for instance, "Is this person competent to stand trial?"

> I talk about test findings and how they might be helpful or relevant, but only in the context of the statutory question. If you start talking about tests and you are not linking them specifically to the legal question, people's attention tends to wander. For example, in a competence-to-stand-trial hearing, an exchange might be:
>
> *Q (opposing counsel): Dr. Mendoza, you said that this person has problems remembering. You even said they have this thing called mild cognitive impairment. But the Court clinician saw him, and he was able to remember things from their conversation.*
>
> *A: When I read him a story that had context—a beginning, middle, and end—you are right, his performance was much better. But when I gave him a memory test where he had to learn a list of words, his performance was terrible. In a criminal proceeding that requires the defendant to attend to and remember information without cues and or a familiar format, his performance is not going to be as efficient as in a short interview in a jail cell where he is not required to follow or respond to complicated matters.*

Discussing test results in context is the reason why almost no experts suggest a narrative strategy of starting with the test results. As discussed in Chapter 8, "Direct Examination," most strategies involve beginning with the larger context of the case and then discussing specific test results in that context.

DESCRIBING SPECIFIC TESTS

Psychologists and neuropsychologists have a huge advantage over jurors in making sense of assessment information because we have a clear, vivid picture of what each test is like to take.

Even if we haven't ever seen the Miller List Learning Task (because it doesn't exist), we will automatically visualize some version of hearing a list of words and recalling as many as we can over multiple trials. Jurors do not have this advantage. Our familiarity with what various assessment measures of confrontational naming, abstract reasoning, visuomotor construction, working memory, and so on, is so foundational that it's easy to forget that members of the jury have no idea what any of these tasks are like.

In some cases, there is a good strategic reason to take the jury into the weeds to help them understand the nature of a particular test. Telling the jury, or even better demonstrating for the jury, what it is like to take the tests helps ensure that they are "with us" as we talk about the meaning of the particular test score. If we craft the test explanation well, jurors will have an opportunity to "take the test themselves" as we are explaining. This is so much more engaging than simply listening to abstract explanations of tests.

One key thing to remember, given Judge Burrough's cautionary tale at the opening of this chapter of a demonstration of the Rey figure that left the courtroom bewildered: It's important to preface your introduction of specific tests with a careful explanation of the multidimensional nature of assessments as well as information about norms and standardization described above, and then to follow your descriptions of tests with thoughtful explanations of test interpretation, as described in the following sections.

In my own practice, if there is a strategic reason for talking about certain tests (for example, an examinee had been diagnosed with a severe attention deficit but aced attention tests in my office), I might take the jurors down for a brief "deep dive" and share a clear picture of one of the tests the examinee was able to ace. Once jurors have a clear picture in their mind of the experience of taking a test, they will not have to rely solely on the expert's word that the plaintiff's score was normal (or abnormal) based on abstract norms; rather, they will have a firsthand, common-sense perspective on the plaintiff's ability using themselves as the normative base. When I share test experiences, I will do so in a way that does not give specific items away. A good example of this is the Digit Span subtest of the Wechsler Adult Intelligence Scale-IV:

> *I gave Mr. Plaintiff a test that measures attention. Can he keep information in his mind long enough to do something with it? For example, I read him strings of numbers and he had to repeat them: 2, 5, 3, 8, 7. He needed to repeat those numbers. The strings of numbers got longer and longer. He was able to repeat a string of seven numbers: 5, 3, 7, 5, 2, 4, 9. That's a normal performance. Then I made it harder: I asked him to listen to strings of numbers and then say them backwards—tor example, 5, 3, 6, 8. He would answer 8, 6, 3, 5. He was able to repeat six digits backwards—that's really good! 5, 2, 3, 8, 4, 1 . . . he did it. That tells me his complex attention is intact. And that is consistent with what I directly observed as I sat with him all day. He had no difficulty following instructions, even when there were multiple steps. He could keep them all in mind. He didn't lose his train of thought; he showed normal attention.*

The benefit of choosing a test like Digit Span to explain is that jurors will naturally be inclined to take the test in their minds as you demonstrate the number strings. The Paced Serial Attention Test (PASAT) is another example of a test that people will naturally want to take in their minds. I have come across many instances when an opposing expert's neuropsychological assessment battery is completely normal, including all attention measures, except the PASAT. Juries need to be educated that while a good PASAT score clearly shows intact attention, a low PASAT score does not necessarily mean impaired attention is an issue.

> *This is a really, really hard test that makes most people very frustrated. It is so hard that in one study well-rested medical students—really smart, high-functioning folks—only got 50% right![3] That's really hard! The researchers concluded that the test is mostly measuring how anxious people get taking it rather than complex attention.*
>
> *When you take the test, you hear numbers one at a time on a recording. You have to add the first number to the second number and say it out loud, while you are listing to the third number. You have to then add the third number to the second number and say it out loud while the fourth number is being played. This is REALLY hard. You hear 5 . . . 8 . . . and you say 13, while the next number comes up, 7. You have to add 7 to 8 and say 15. Then the next number comes up 9. And you would add 9 to 7 and say 16. And the test keeps speeding up. I stopped giving it in my practice because so many people quit the test because they were so frustrated. When I reviewed Dr. Other Expert's test answer sheets in the case, it turns out that Ms. Plaintiff got a low score because she quit after the first 10 items. There was a notation in the margin of the test, "really frustrated." I don't blame her!*

Explanation of PASAT

> *I asked Ms. Smith to add these numbers sequentially and say them out loud. This is hard! She got a great score on this test. If you are able to do this hard test well, I don't understand how one does it and still has an attention problem. With her score at the 80th percentile, she will be able to pay attention to common things at home—the stove is on, her children are pulling at her.*—Cheryl Weinstein, PhD, ABPP-CN

> *This is an example of a test I might give to measure someone's ability to keep focused. I read some numbers. I ask the test-taker to add each number to the one before it and tell me what the sum is. You as members of the jury could try this: for example, 1 . . . 2 . . . 1 . . . 8 . . . 1 . . . 7.*—Rus Bauer, PhD, ABPP-CN

In my own practice, I occasionally describe the Wisconsin Card Sort Test:

> *This is a test that measures people's ability to solve problems flexibly. The IQ test has hard problems, but the directions tell you how to solve the problems. It's just that the problems get harder and harder and harder to solve. The card sort test is different. It doesn't tell you how to solve the problem. You have to figure it out.*
>
> *You are given a deck of cards to sort and you are not told how to match the cards. Mr. Plaintiff was just told "right" or "wrong" after he matched each card. He had to come up with an idea for how to sort the cards, and use the feedback to test the idea. Then, I didn't tell him in advance, but once in a while the rules change. He has to figure out that the rules have changed, and figure out the new rule. To do this test well, you have to have flexible problem-solving. In real life, this means that you can try a solution*

to a problem, and if it doesn't work, you won't just get frustrated and bang your head against the wall, but you will be flexible, and try different solutions. Mr. Plaintiff did really well on this test.

It's a test that looks at how well you can figure out how things go together without being told. And then switch away from that idea when the situation changes.—David Williamson, PhD, ABPP-CN

Cheryl Weinstein notes that she will often bring in tests to show the jury. The Tower of London is one of those tests:

These tests are hard! With this one, you need to solve the puzzle in as few moves as possible. There are rules about how you can move each of the disks. You really have to plan ahead. If you can do it, and Ms. Smith did it, it tells me that your planning ability is pretty good.

Clock drawing

When I am explaining someone has a dementia and the degree of difficulties that the person is experiencing, I may talk specifically about the Clock-Drawing Test. *There are some tests that measure organization and planning and long-term memory. For instance, one of the things we have folks do is draw a clock. We give them a blank piece of paper and say, 'Draw a clock and set the hands to 10 past 11.' We can all relate to drawing a clock, and we can all relate to setting it to a specific time. This person couldn't even put the numbers in the correct order or correctly space the numbers even though they have probably seen a million clocks in their lives. When I asked him to set the time, he drew circles around the numbers.—Robert Mendoza, PsyD*

Rey Figure

I gave him a complex picture to draw that has rectangles and some crosses in it. I left it in front of him to draw. Not only could he not draw it, but when I looked at the original and his copy you couldn't tell they were the same thing.—Robert Mendoza, PsyD

MMPI-2/RF

The MMPI-2 and MMPI-2-RF are frequently used in forensic assessments. The nature of the test, though, makes it difficult to grasp for those outside the field. Yossef Ben-Porath, shares how he explains the MMPI-2 in court:

The MMPI is made up of a series of statements. We ask the individual taking the test to indicate whether these statements are true or false as they apply to them. And we call these statements Items.

(In this way, I start defining the terms that I will use later. I don't want to use technical terms. Jurors might not know what the word item means. I will define the words, and I usually do it more than once, as once may not be enough for everyone. But eventually I will be able to slip into using "items" rather than statements).

The way we use the responses, is we group them together as research tells us which items or statements go together. The reason we do that is that the response to any single item may not always be accurate- or the term we use for that is- reliable (Now I have introduced the idea of reliability) *because someone may misunderstand a certain item or read it in a way that it was not intended. But when we combine the items, or several that mean the same thing then we are going to get more accurate information. We call those combined groups of items scales. And when you hear us refer to scales- the scales are nothing more than responses to groups of items that measure a certain thing we are interested in, such as a person's level of depression or anxiety.*

(There are two reasons I do that- one is to define what a scale is, the other is to establish right off the bat that responses to individual items are not reliable. Because that's a favorite ploy of cross examiners is to try to go to the item level and ask jurors to conclude that because the item is answered in a certain way, the scale is meaningless. I can say: "As I explained earlier, we don't interpret responses to individual items, rather we interpret scales. So any one of these individual items isn't the important piece of information, but rather how the individual responds to all of the items on the scale." Now I have defined items, I have defined Scales, then I will go on to explain:)

The way we interpret these scales is to count of the number of items within the scale that the person answered in either a true or false direction. This gives us a score. But then what we do is compare the score with a sample of the general population. A sample of individuals who took the test across the United States. We call this our normative sample. And we use that sample in order to tell whether someone's level of depression is average for the general population. Above average, below average. We can compare scores between different scales with reference to our normative sample.

(If I am talking about the MMPI-2 RF, I will also add:)

We also have samples we call comparison groups. Comparison groups are individuals tested in different settings, psychiatric inpatient, mental health outpatient, disability applicants. These comparison groups allow us to compare how this individual's scores compared not just with the general population but with other people assessed in the more specific setting.

(Now I have talked about items, scales, and norms. The final piece of foundation:)

We have two different types of scales on the MMPI. One is the type of scale we already talked about. A scale that tells us something about the individuals psychological functioning. The other type of scale is called a validity scale. These validity scales tell us about the quality of the information, how accurate the information is that we receive from the individual examinee. How they were able to read, comprehend and respond accurately to the items. The validity scales provide information about whether the person was able to respond consistently to the test items, or whether there were indications that they over reported problems, exaggerated them, or underreported the problems.

Depending on the narrative strategy of the case, a more compact explanation may be indicated. Jacobus Donders offers a vivid, concise explanation:

> *Basically, the MMPI asks you questions about anything: what you like, what you don't like; what you are interested in, what you couldn't care less about; what makes you happy, what makes you upset. And eventually it will address any type of problem that people can have, from anger to anxiety to asthma—and that's just the A's! What we do is we look at, compared to the average citizen, did the person endorse more or less symptoms in a certain area? And is it clinically significant—meaning, does it meet the level of something that would cause a problem for the person? And there are checks and balances in there: Did the person pay close attention to the test? Did they take it seriously rather than fill it out haphazardly? And there are checks and balances about responding: Are they responding in a straightforward manner? Some people don't like to talk about their feelings; they present themselves as better adjusted than Mother Teresa. Other people really want to emphasize how much they are suffering. You have the checks and balances, so if someone is saying, "My life is worse than Job in the Bible," then we raise at least one eyebrow.*

Subjective versus objective

> *Some tests ask directly what your experience of depression has been over the past couple of weeks. The MMPI also asks questions like that, questions that are obvious. But it also asks questions that are not obvious because it is based on studying groups of people with known conditions. Sometimes groupings of answers go together in a certain condition that if you looked at it you wouldn't think they would go together. The MMPI has built-in validity indicators. If someone says, "I love my mother" (true) and then later in the test says, "I hate my mother" (true), then that is an inconsistency in responding. And if there are enough inconsistencies in responding, then it calls into question whether the person was being straightforward in answering.*—Neil Pliskin, PhD, ABPP-CN

Introducing the MMPI

> *The MMPI tests are some of our best-validated tools that has been around for many years. People are given the same standardized questions and we compare their scores to others' profiles with known symptoms or traits, like people with depression. It has been updated regularly, and the MMPI-RF is the most recent variation. The test has been studied with lots of different populations so we can say that if someone scores high on a scale, they are similar to people who have a known problem or set of problems.*—Ira K. Packer, PhD, ABPP (Forensic)

Explaining the MMPI

> *It's a true/false inventory of scales that measure anxiety, depression, PTSD symptoms, and other psychological conditions.*—Kyle Boone, PhD, ABPP-CN

Explaining MMPI-RF

When I was trained years ago on the MMPI, it was all configurational patterns. It was really hard to explain to juries. Now, the MMPI-2-RF is more substance- and content-based:

This has been well researched. People who score high on this scale tend to have [this]. In Mr. Smith's case he scored high on a scale indicating paranoia, and that is consistent with my observation of him in our interview and with [xyz]records.—Ira K. Packer, PhD, ABPP (Forensic)

Issues with nonstandard MMPI administration

In some cases, it becomes important to explain the concept of problems with nonstandard administration to juries.

MMPI nonstandard: read aloud

It is very important that tests be given in the same way each time. That's called a standard administration. Then you can be confident that the research on the test would apply to Mr. Jones, because he was tested the same way as the people were when they developed the test.

The way people are tested is they have a test booklet that has all the items printed, and they record their response on a sheet. Or there is a computer version, where they read the items to themselves and answer directly on the computer.

There is research (and I bring the articles) that if you are administered the test a different way, then the scores may not turn out the same and therefore do not have the same meaning. There is research that if you read the test aloud to people or have them say their answers out loud, that can affect the score results. You can't rely on the norms to properly interpret those scores.

There is a big difference between a person interacting with a test and a person interacting with another person. When there is an interaction with another individual, when there is an interpersonal exchange involved, it significantly changes how people might respond.—Yossef Ben-Porath, PhD, ABPP

See Chapter 11, "Performance and Symptom Validity," for strategies to explain the MMPI-2/MMPI-2-RF validity scales.

Explaining checklists/adaptive scales

John Kirk notes that it is important to get checklists in a pediatric forensic case because the psychometrics of tests with younger kids are not always that stable:

Checklist data is an important additional source of information from parents and teachers. I like to use the BASC and the BRIEF because they have some internal validity. Are they consistently responding to questions? Are they overly negative?

We are all more than one dimension: checklists

I only get to see Elizabeth in one context. I want to make sure I have as much information about her beyond the assessment room that I can. I want to know her experience. I also want to understand her parents' experience of her at home. And her teacher's experience of her at school. We are all more than one dimension. Having all of these multiple perspectives helps me understand her better.—Lisa Stanford, PhD, ABPP-CN

Relationship is important when looking at checklist data

In a forensic case, there might be multiple adaptive function scales or checklists that, depending on how they are filled it out, you can get vastly different scores. What does that mean? That the test is invalid?

It means you have to consider the relationship and the context. A parent might be talking about the daily function of the child. They say, "Oh my God! I have never seen them do their laundry or cook their own meal." When they are at college, though, they cook. They are doing laundry competently. Or, for example, the wife that says, "My husband never talks. He is not social." But then he talks to his buddies he is playing football with—he's talking the whole time. When you are given information about how someone is functioning, you have to look at the relationship between the informant and the examinee.—Bernice Marcopulos, PhD, ABPP-CN

Explaining violence/risk assessment

Robert Kinscherff works out this sequence in advance with the attorney who brings him to court so the introduction of risk assessment tools can become a teaching moment on direct:

Q: And did you use any instruments in assessing the violence potential of Mr. X?

A: Yes, I did.

Q: What instruments?

A: x, y, z.

Q: Why did you use those instruments?

A: I used these instruments because they are specialized tools. These instruments have been developed because research has shown that mental health clinicians tend to significantly overpredict violence amongst mentally ill people. So, these tools tether my judgment by tying it to factors that have been demonstrated to actually be related to violence. (It's a powerful statement: "research shown that we overpredict.")

Q: How tethered is your judgment?

A: It depends on the tool, including whether the tool that I have relied upon has been validated for use for particular populations or circumstances. For example, some risk assessment tools are valid for use if you are concerned about community violence but would be misleading if used to assess violence risk for intimate partner violence.

Violence Risk Adjustment Guide VRAG (auto risk analogy)

The violence risk assessment guide merely asks me to determine whether or not these factors have occurred in a person's history. And it scores them up and gives a probability estimate, much in the same way that insurance companies don't need to know you personally in order to statistically decide what insurance risk you pose as a driver, or a doctor doesn't need to know you personally to know the fact that you have been smoking for 20 years and are 40% above your ideal body weight and are largely sedentary is going to put you in a higher risk group for heart attacks. Instead of worrying about auto accidents or heart attacks, this tool is intended to compare the risk of violence of a mentally disordered offender to a group of others whose risks of violent reoffending are already know. It offers a probability of violent reoffending but cannot specifically tell you whether or not an individual will actually reoffend—that takes more careful assessment of other factors, but is a more reliable starting point than unstructured clinical judgment of violence risk.—Robert Kinscherff, PhD, JD

Case Management/Level of Service Inventory

These are called structured clinical judgment tools. They require some judgment on my part as to whether or not specific factors are present and, if so, to what degree. But they still tie me to factors that are associated in research and with the tool's psychometrics with risk of violence. These tools also include protective factors and individual factors that would work against violence. The tools offer research-based guidance as to what risk factors need to be specifically addressed, what protective factors need to be supported, and what individual factors need to be taken into account when matching and implementing interventions, such as cultural, language, or cognitive factors.—Robert Kinscherff, PhD, JD

Explaining risk assessment

The beauty of Historical Clinical Risk Management (HCR) is that it allows you to explain the findings in narrative form. With a purely actuarial measure, you might say, "People who score this way are 55% likely to . . ." The HCR allows you to use a scientific method, but you are not trying to sell a blood test that shows a certain score means x. Rather, you are telling a story. With the HCR, you can say,

Here are the reasons I am concerned. He scores particularly high on a scale measuring lack of empathy. He still has paranoid beliefs about people victimizing him, and he continues to blame the victim. That's why I consider him high risk."

The benefit of the third version of HCR is that there are no numbers generated. Instead one scores each variable as N, P, or Y—no, probably there, or yes, definitely present. Then there is a fourth category, relevance. One can say, "Not relevant to person." For example,

Yes, there is a history of alcohol abuse, but he has been sober for 10 years. Even though I scored him yes on this historica variable due to his past use, this variable is not relevant today.

Here is how I introduce the measure:

> *The field has evolved to the point where we can identify factors that are associated with the risk of an individual committing another violent act. None of these things are perfect, they don't identify every single person, but they help us figure out which people are more likely than others to commit another violent act, and they allow us to indicate which particular factors are relevant to risk management for this individual. Perhaps the most frequently used tool is the HCR-20 version 3. It is a Structured Professional Judgment tool that directs the evaluator to consider specific factors that are known to be associated with violent recidivism. It has been shown in the literature that it can be reliably scored and has reasonable predictive validity. I am not saying that it tells us this person is 100% likely to be violent again, or 0% likely, but allows us to articulate the reasons that we think this individual is at [higher/ lower] risk.*—Ira K. Packer, PhD, ABPP-CN (Forensic)

Structured professional judgment

> *In the area of risk assessment there are three broad clinical approaches: (1) pure professional judgment, which science tells us is the least accurate; (2) actuarial judgment: if one does it in the purest sense, there is no discretion in decision-making; (3) middle ground: structured professional judgment. The structured professional judgment measures are like actuarial measures in terms of how they are administered. We have you score people on certain items to make sure you were considering factors that are known to be important, but ultimately it is up to you to come to the conclusion about risk. Those approaches have become popular with clinicians. One study compared testimony based on the actuarial and structured clinical judgment methods and found that jurors see the structured professional judgment come out similarly to clinical judgement. If you have such a measure, you can expect it to resonate with jurors. Again, based on one study.*—Marcus Boccaccini, PhD

FINALLY, TEST SECURITY ON THE STAND

While there is a clear advantage to concretely explaining how our tests work, like giving examples of strings of numbers on Digit Span or describing being read paragraphs on Logical Memory, there is a distinct disadvantage to disclosing specific test items. Recall that court records are public domain if they are not specifically sealed by the court, so individuals reading the court record could have access to the test items. With regard to performance validity tests, even if specific items are not disclosed, a detailed description of how the test works might allow individuals later reading the court record to learn how to distinguish a PVT from a non-PVT. Each time psychologists and neuropsychologists discuss the nature of a test or share specific information about what it is like to take the test, they must make a judgment call about the risk to test security versus the benefit to jurors' ability to understand the assessment. Bob Denney explains the conundrum this way:

> Either in your report or in court, there are times when you have to spell out how the PVTs work. I try not to give specific cutoffs, but you have to provide enough

information to triers of fact that they can understand how the tests show what you say they show. Otherwise, you look like you have a conclusory report or a conclusory opinion. The judge has to know the basis upon which you came to your conclusion. It's a legal requirement. I tend to have to give up the process more thoroughly on a forced-choice test.

In my reports, I include descriptions of the tests so readers can understand why a particular performance indicates lack of compliance with test instructions to try their best. I will name the test and say,

On this particular test he did worse on the easier subtests, even worse than individuals with dementia who are confined to a nursing home. And yet she performed better than individuals with dementia on the harder subtests, and that does not make any clinical sense. This pattern is more consistent with the types of patterns made by simulators rather than people with real neurological deficits.

Test security on the stand

If an attorney or judge wants you to give an example of a test while testifying, be careful of releasing actual items. I have seen clinicians include word pairs from similarities in their reports. I think that's a bad idea. It's always tempting to give an example of the actual items. I have had judges ask me to give an example. Instead of an actual test item, you give a story like, "John Doe and his friend walked home from work together and they both stopped for a Coke on the way."—*Robert Mendoza, PsyD*

Asked about specific WAIS questions

In the deposition in this one case, I had been asked by the attorneys that were representing an individual on death row for my raw data. I let them know that I couldn't give it directly to them, but I could give it to the state's expert. I did so, in a sealed envelope, at the conference hearing, when we were all sitting around a table, and the state's expert simply then handed it to the state's attorney—right in front of me! He was not ashamed to do so. At trial, the state's attorney began to read individual questions from the Comprehension subtest of the WAIS.

Q: How you can claim that Mr. XYZ has no rational understanding when he got credit for this question?

I could have answered, "Because it was a one-point response," but there were members of the public in the gallery, including two other death row inmates. I can't sit there and talk about what will get you points or not on an item! After I picked my jaw up off the floor, I said,

I can't speak about a particular item, and particularly what answers might lead to specific scores.

In hindsight, wish I had spoken briefly about the purpose of test security, even using the death row inmates in the gallery as a prime example of the risks.—Leslie Rosenstein, PhD, ABPP-CN

I try not to coach people on how to take the MMPI

I try not to go into specific scales for the jury. You don't want to be coaching people inadvertently on how to take the test. I usually don't go further than saying how common or uncommon certain problems are. Cross examiners can ask questions and I have to respond to them, but I don't volunteer too much on my own.—Yossef Ben-Porath, PhD, ABPP

Being asked about specific test items in a deposition

In one case I was told I would have to supply my raw materials to the attorneys in the case, and I said I wouldn't do it. When they supplied me with the judge's protective order that the data would not be further disseminated beyond the immediate aspect of discovery, I eventually agreed.

During the deposition, the attorney started requesting material (e.g., manuals) that were not in the original protective order. The attorneys agreed to place it all under the protective order, including the deposition transcript from that part onward. I was uneasy but agreed. Under this agreement, I started answering questions about the BHI2, particularly from the manual, which was fine. However, he then abruptly switched to the MMPI-2-RF and asked about particular items on the FBS. I thought this was odd, as the scale was not especially elevated. I started asking about the protective order, and again I was assured that the agreement was in place. We started with the first two FBS items, and then it dawned on me exactly what was happening. I asked again how far this material could go and whether it could get out into open court. The attorney then admitted that discovery was different than what the judge might order in court.

A: I am not going to release the most sensitive material in neuropsychology with the potential for it to be presented in court testimony.

Q: Doctor, are you refusing to give me the information that is necessary to prosecute my client's case?

A: Yes, indeed, test security is far more important. Particular items are never used to form opinions.—Mike Chafetz, PhD, APBB-CN

Unfortunately, I can't release that data

I have had situations where I am asked to provide raw data while I am testifying. In those situations I say,

Unfortunately, I can't release that data, due to copyright infringement and ethical concerns. I am happy to provide alternatve possibilities to the court, including an in camera *review, sealing the data, or I am happy to release the data to a qualified individual that can be identified and that can appropriately interpret the results.*—Robert Mendoza, PsyD

NOTES

1. Heath, C., & Heath, D. (2008). *Made to Stick: Why Some Ideas Survive and Others Die.* New York: Random House.
2. Matarazzo, J. D. (1990). Psychological assessment versus psychological testing, validation from Binet to the school, clinic and courtroom. *American Psychologist, 45*, 999–1017.
3. Brooks, J., Brooks, J. B., Giraud, V. O., Saleh, Y. J., Rodrigues, S. J., . . . Fragoso, Y. D. (2011). Paced Auditory Serial Addition Test (PASAT): A very difficult test even for individuals with high intellectual capability. *Arquivos de Neuro-Psiquiatria, 63*(9), 482–484.

10 Visuals

IF THE GOAL of direct testimony is to present the narrative of our opinions in an engaging, accessible, and vivid manor, visuals are one of our most powerful tools. Pictures, charts, graphs, videos, and other visual media invite our listeners to actively engage with the material we are sharing.

Humans are visual creatures and metaphors such as "I saw it with my own eyes" and "seeing is believing" that link sight to truth abound in our culture. The association between truth and visuals is so profound that one very common (if annoying) verbal preface when someone is about to *tell* someone else their interpretation of events is "Look . . ." Lisa McDermott notes that—in the courtroom—pictures say, "I am not making this up; this really happened to this person."

> *Visuals are very important. I had a client whose child died. He had to bury his baby. When the expert is talking about the trauma and is going through a checklist of things he might have been experiencing during the trauma, I will include photographs of him with the child at the hospital. I will include photographs of the funeral, depicting the size of the coffin, the family grieving, flowers at the cemetery, death certificates.*
>
> *There are many different documents that can validate the information. I might also include slides of family pictures, school records, or domestic violence restraining orders. Documentation that allows jurors to say, "You are not making this up. This really happened to this person."*

At the same time visuals invite our listeners to actively engage, the act of creating the visuals forces us to summarize. Neuropsychologists like to "hang out in the trees." We are detail oriented in our work and often in our testimony. Visual aids help describe the forest. That is, using a visual aid forces us to synthesize and describe the big picture.

Finally, recall from earlier chapters that the strongest testimony gives jurors tools to make their own decisions rather than telling them what to decide. Visuals allow jurors to see the data or other information and come to their own conclusions. They are not solely relying on the expert to tell them.

Judge Lynne Battaglia counsels that the more visuals experts use, the better:

> *I think the more visuals, the better. Whatever visual the judge will allow is helpful. I think charts, PowerPoints, anything, as long as they are not dense, are the way to go. If you are going to use something, though, you have to simplify the data and make sure the presentation is not dense.*

This chapter is about the use of visuals in testimony: the benefits, some cautionary tales, and strategies for using visuals in specific testifying circumstances.

GENERAL THOUGHTS ABOUT USING VISUALS

Judge Allison Burroughs notes that experts should be aware of the fact that visuals usually go back to the jury room during deliberations. The visual becomes another tool for the jurors in helping them remember the highlights of the expert's opinion. What information does an expert (literally) want to stay with the jurors? Turn it into a visual. With that in mind, though, Judge Burroughs cautions that experts need to make sure that they have constructed the visuals to be independently decipherable hours or days later when the jury looks at them again in the jury room:

> *The exhibits go back, and I will let demonstratives (visuals) go back if there is no objection. A lot of times the visuals are useful when somebody is testifying, but then they go back to the jury room and you can't look at it and make sense of what somebody said anymore. Experts should label their visuals with that in mind. When an expert shows a visual and says, "Here is where the trauma happened," and points, when the visual is back in the jury room and you just have this picture of the brain with no labels, it isn't helpful. Instead, experts can make an X on the visual, and label "trauma" or "injury."*

Judge Battaglia notes that it is important to strike the right tone with visuals: "Some experts can be patronizing in PowerPoints, making stick figures. Others find the right tone, not dense but broken into colorful, understandable slides." Martin Rohling also offers some cautions about visuals: "A picture is worth a thousand words; I am constantly drawing pictures. Don't bring pictures in, though, that are too complicated, or have small writing."

Attorney Mark DeBofsky cautions that visual aids have to be practiced:

> *Visual aids always pose a danger—if they are not mastered well enough; if you are using a computer and there is a glitch; or if a poster board falls down. Visuals are*

the kind of things that have to be practiced. If they do not go off smoothly, it can be annoying.

Once entered into testimony, a visual aid can be used during cross examination. Mike Chafetz tells the story of an opposing attorney changing his visual:

> *In a capital case in which I was retained for the prosecution, the defense attorney put my graph up on a slide, asking me if I minded that he had shortened the x-axis. Inwardly I smiled, recognizing the ploy that all the scores would now look lowered to the jury. I said: "I don't mind, because no matter what you do to the axis, the relation of the scores stays the same, and you can still see that mostly all the scores are above a standard score range of 75, indicating that the defendant is certainly not intellectually disabled."*

Nancy Hebben points out that visuals will not always be allowed during testimony. To increase the likelihood that a visual will be admitted, she puts them into her expert report:

> *There are limits to what you can and cannot do in your testimony based on what court you are in. In federal court, there is a rule that if it is not in your report, you cannot go there. There may also be limits as to what you can testify to. Sometimes you will be limited by a judge even outside of the federal court system, where it is a little bit looser. It's a good policy: If it's an opinion you have, or a visual you want to use, put it in your report.*

Of course, the argument for putting compelling, synthesizing visuals in a report also includes the fact that visuals will allow attorneys, who are report consumers, to better engage with and understand the report contents. This is discussed further in Chapter 21, "Reports."

VISUALS THAT ALLOW THE EXPERT TO LEAVE THE WITNESS BOX

Another benefit of using visuals, including flip charts and enlarged visuals on easels, is that they provide an opportunity to leave the witness box. Ted Peck points out that if you are the fourth, fifth, or twentieth expert sitting in the same witness box not moving,

> *Let's face it, anyone is going to get a bit tired of the lack of drama, listening to talking heads. Experts should maintain a professional decorum, but try to arrange for visual material to be presented to the jury that will allow them, with permission, to get out of the witness box, to stand next to the jury, while explaining the visual materials leading to your opinions.*

As noted in Chapter 1, "Disrupting Our Academic Communication Style," Judge Allison Burroughs is a strong proponent of getting in front of the jury to explain a concept:

> *When you get out of the witness box and you stand in front of the jury and just talk to them, it's very effective. You are teaching them something that they feel like they might need to know instead of trying to tell them what they should conclude. When you are directly in front of the jury, out of the witness box, you own the space. You walk out there and you, instead the lawyers, are running the show. All of a sudden the expert's in charge and looks authoritative just because he is running the presentation.*

John Kirk is another strong proponent:

> *Visual displays are very helpful. On a personal injury case jurors could be there for 2 weeks. If I am the defense expert, I am testifying at the end of those 2 weeks. If I am just sitting in the witness box at a microphone, even if I am making eye contact, it is really hard to keep jurors' attention. In contrast, it's really hard* **not** *to get their attention if I am standing in front of them with a visual display. I will do anything to get out of that witness box in order to more personally connect and effectively communicate with jurors.*

In my own practice, the first time I stepped down from the witness box to walk to a chart on an easel set up in front of a jury, it was a revelation. I felt literally and figuratively closer to the jurors. For those moments, the formality and distance disappeared and we were just people, trying to understand what was going on with the plaintiff. I like it much better when I am standing next to jurors than when I am sitting up and away in the witness box.

Let's turn now to specific uses of visuals.

TABLES

Explaining individual test scores can put jurors (and attorneys and judges) to sleep, but failing to describe the rich data that is a foundation of our opinions is problematic as well. Creating tables to share data with the jury circumvents the tedium and also empowers juries to come to their own conclusions about the test results. Ted Peck notes,

> *Jurors might have preconceived notions that the facts we provide are like trying to hold steam in your hand, that there is no substance. The use of blown-up tables with tests and standard scores or percentiles and descriptors shows that you are not just giving an opinion; you are giving substance. They can literally see your basis for the opinion. It creates a more difficult task for the cross-examining attorney for them to say that this data is not what you say it is. If a picture is worth a thousand words, a table is a good way to show a jury that you are not just pulling an opinion out of your ear.*
>
> *I will spend a moment or two explaining the nature of the test: "This test measures memory. The data here are showing that the scores are in a range that are consistent with average, normal functioning. Here is [language, sequencing, attention]. Mr. Smith's score was also average: 58 out of 60 subtests fell within the normal range.*

The two that were a little low may well have occurred by chance. The presence of an abnormal finding does not necessarily mean there is brain damage, particularly in a case that would not have been expected to produce a focal injury."

Nancy Hebben notes that tables do not need to include specific scores or percentiles; most of these numbers mean little to people outside of our field. Rather, broad descriptors like "average" can be much easier for jurors to understand.

I put up a table with each thinking domain that says, "average, average, average, high average, superior," while I am explaining to a jury that the plaintiff's testing was normal. When scores are so low—in the absence of any injury that would have resulted in low test scores—as to be completely and utterly noncredible, I put up a table that says, "Noncredible, noncredible, noncredible." That chart is up as I explain the data was not reflective of his/her true level of functioning.

When describing performance validity test performance, or scores in a battery that are so low as to not make any neurological sense given the nature of the injury at hand, Dr. Hebben's specific use of the term "noncredible" instead of "low" "or fail" is particularly helpful for the jury. Imagine seeing a table of tests with the word "fail" after them and then being told the person has normal brain function: That would be confusing.

Tables can also be very helpful for showing focal deficits in thinking abilities. Tables give jurors a visual that helps them come to the same conclusion as the expert- that there is something abnormal in the pattern of test scores. Ted Peck also makes the very good point that when you have shown a table of scores on direct to the jury, where visually it is very clear that all of them or 18/20 are normal, this helps inoculate against the strategy on cross examination where an opposing attorney will try to chip away at the idea that the person has normal brain function by selectively highlighting slightly less efficient scores.

An attorney might start hammering you on cross for the subtly lower Similarities subscale on a claimant who left school in the ninth grade and failed the GED twice. But when the jury knows all of the other scores are fine, because on direct you showed them a clear table of scores, the jury will literally and physically have a picture of what is going on.

Tables for performance validity tests

Graphs showing performance validity test scores of patients versus comparison groups can be very compelling for jurors as a visual. Kyle Boone notes that she regularly includes such graphs in her reports and will also use them during testimony. Many experts share this practice.

To make the point that even people with very severe injuries can easily pass the TOMM, I have put up the chart from the TOMM manual of the patients who had severe TBI who passed the TOMM. One of those was in coma for 3 months, with a penetrating gunshot wound.—Nancy Hebben, PhD, ABPP-CN

Table of effort tests

Here are nine ways that I measured effort. (I will list the tests: computer-administered, pencil-and-paper, MMPI, Digit Span, GWMT, TOMM.) Here are all the ways I measured it, and they failed all of them. This helps bring home the point. This is straightforward.—John Kirk, PsyD, ABPP-CN

Using graphs to compare scores when PVTs are failed

When someone is failing three, four, five, six PVTs and their MMPI is exaggerated and there isn't an injury that can account for the level of symptoms, it can be helpful to develop a simple table to show the jury: This is how an individual with severe brain injury would perform; here is how someone with dementia would perform; here is how a blind person would perform; here is the examinee's score.—Anonymous

In my own practice, I had an examinee score a very impressive "0" on a performance validity test. I created a table to show the jury as I explained what the score meant:

Score of people with severe TBI	Chance (not even looking at items)	Below chance	Ms. Plaintiff
xx/xx	xx/xx	x/xx	0/xx

I stepped down from the witness box to explain this chart that was enlarged on a poster to jurors.

This is a really easy test that is designed to look difficult. It is so easy that even people with the type of severe traumatic brain injury that leaves them in a coma for 2 weeks can get almost every item right. You answer in an either/or way. The answer is either "this item" or "that item." Each time you answer, you have a 50/50 chance of getting it right, even if you closed your eyes and didn't look at the test—like flipping a coin.

Here are the scores of people with severe head trauma. They get about [this many] right; it's that easy. Ms. Plaintiff had a concussion, at most. She should have scored way better than a person who had such a severe injury they were in a coma.

And here are the scores of people who closed their eyes and didn't even look at the test. Just by chance, they get about half right, or [this many].

Of course, when you flip a coin, it doesn't always land exactly 50/50; just by chance it may not be perfectly even. By chance, when randomly guessing, you could theoretically get a score as low as [this many].

Here is Ms. Plaintiff's score. She got ZERO correct. That is dramatically worse than if she literally closed her eyes and didn't even look at the test. In fact, she got a

PERFECTLY wrong score. There is only one way that could happen: She knew the right answer (for at least some of them) and said the opposite.

The jurors were nodding as I was explaining that the test was so easy that people with severe TBI did it well. They were vigorously nodding when I explained about just closing one's eyes and getting half right. They had outraged looks on their faces when I presented the plaintiff's score. I do not believe that the explanation would have worked as well without a visual to help the jurors track the various scores. And when they deliberated, the visual went with them into the jury room.

Another type of table I have used in my own practice is a "discrepancy table." This is a table of test scores and how the scores differ from my direct observations of an examinee and the possible effects of the injury or illness at hand. In this example, the articulate, clearly bright plaintiff failed multiple performance validity tests and produced some spectacularly low scores that were noncredible from both the perspective of "the person who walked in my office" and possible effects of a concussion.

	Different from observed behavior?	Possible consequence of concussion?
IQ = 62 Intellectually disabled range (previously known as Mental Retardation)	Yes	No
Memory <1st percentile	Yes	No
Attention 3rd percentile	Yes	No
Naming <1st percentile	Yes	No

The benefit of using a table like this is that the jurors can use the table to "hold" the information as all of the facts are presented. They are not being asked to hold the first three pieces of information in mind as you present the third. Particularly as the information is new to them, holding it all in working memory will be hard. As noted in Chapter 9, "Explaining Assessment

Methods and Tools," presenting the test results/scores in the context of the opinion, rather than as a separate part of testimony, is more engaging and more comprehensible.

GRAPHS

Rather than tables, graphs can be used to present a set of test performances. Mike Chafetz uses graphs rather than tables when he testifies:

> *I like to make a graph of all my findings in which everything is put on the same standard score scale. It is easier to see all the findings in relation to one another when they are all on the same scale. Tests are on the y-axis, standard scores on the x-axis. Then I have a line that represents the expectation. I have landmarks that are easy for the layperson to see. I can point to it with my laser pointer: "Here is what you would expect for the general population. This is the 50th percentile: 50% are above you and 50% are below you. But this individual has an expectation of 110. You know, that is better than 75% of people their age."*

TIMELINES

Many attorneys will help jurors understand complex facts in a case by creating a visual timeline. When jurors have the events laid out for them visually, they will be able to use the information to draw their own conclusions. Nancy Hebben makes a compelling argument for using a visual timeline in cases where multiple factors are likely at play to create changes in thinking ability:

> I think of my role as conducting a neuropsychological investigation rather than just a neuropsychological assessment. I look at every record I can get my hands on and explore them chronologically. The more history, the better: school records, work records, depositions. It helps me understand how the person got to this moment. For example, I saw a woman with a history of sexual abuse/trauma, multiple suicide attempts, and diagnoses of major depression and borderline personality disorder as well as cannabis abuse. She then has a motor vehicle accident and is certain she had a brain injury (when the records suggest a concussion at most). She saw a psychiatrist who agreed she had a traumatic brain injury, and her "brain injury" narrative was off and running. I did a chronological timeline of the records and italicized all the cognitive complaints that were present prior to the MVA. Literally, everything she was complaining about following the accident was present prior to the accident. That type of investigation helps me as a neuropsychologist understand the origins of her symptoms, and it helps me explain it on the stand. With the timeline up on a visual I will say,
>
> *I read Ms. Smith's medical record, and the symptoms she is currently complaining about have been there for years prior to the concussion. There is no evidence to support that these symptoms were caused by a concussion.*

Scott Millis notes that timelines can help the expert tell the story of the case that includes many complex elements:

> *Stan Brodsky has this great concept about telling a compelling story. In a particular case, can you tell a story? Sometimes it helps to look at timelines as a way of presenting a complicated history. Most of my cases have involved litigated brain injuries. Many plaintiffs have very complicated histories and jurors may find it difficult to keep straight what happened when. So a timeline can be really useful, when this incident occurred, you can see prior there were problems in school, episodes of abuse, and so on.*

Wendy Marlowe also relies on visual timelines during testimony. She points out that timelines can be used to demonstrate complex medical factors but also patterns of behaviors that speak to psychological traits. She notes that she will make a timeline in her office but then give it to the attorney so the office staff can create a professional-looking visual.

> *I really like using timelines. I had an examinee that had three separate accidents: 1983, 1996, and now current one. Each one was a minor fender bender. In each instance, the person turned a minor fender bender into a very extensive, expensive injury and collected big bucks. These accidents were like a career for her! She would run out of new funds, and thus had the new accident.*

John Kirk offers another clinical situation where a timeline was helpful in contextualizing a plaintiff's behavior, "In a particular case, a child had seen 50 doctors over 10 years, but he was suing one of the doctors. A chronology was put up: Here are all 50 doctors this kid saw. The visual made a compelling argument."

Attorney Wayne Miller notes that visuals can help rebut expert testimony that distorts the history of his client. In other words, the visual timeline sets the records straight.

> *I had a case where the defense neuropsychology expert was focused on grades my client earned 5 years prior to his injury rather than 6 months prior. I needed to show what the true baseline was. We had a series of charts that put these findings in a kind of a timeline, and we were able to say, "No, the true baseline, the better baseline, was the one right before that would show really how he was functioning in the months leading up to the accident, not years before."*

DIRECT QUOTES FROM RECORDS AND INTERVIEWS

One of the most compelling use of direct quotes on a visual that I have seen was in a lead poisoning case where the defense attorney enlarged two quotes from the plaintiff's expert side by side, describing the WAIS-IV Perceptual Reasoning Index of the plaintiff and his sister (who had no lead poisoning but was tested as part of the case). Both scores were 90. The plaintiff's 90 PRI was described as demonstrating weakness in visual perceptual processing and his sister's 90 PRI was described as solidly average, well-developed visual perceptual skills. Point made.

A neuropsychologist who prefers to remain anonymous notes that he will put up quotations from collateral interviews as visuals during his testimony:

> *Quotations from collateral interviews can be helpful in visuals. When you do collateral interviews and the interviewees have rich examples of memory lapses or difficulty attending or impulsivity, you can take direct quotes from those interviews.*

This might be particularly compelling after enlarging scores from the Frontal Systems Behavior Scale (FrSBe) or Behavior Rating Inventory of Executive Function (BRIEF) checklists that the family or teachers filled out.

Attorney Sara Cohbra notes that specific records make powerful visuals:

> *For example, a school record may lay out a client's impaired functioning and symptoms really well. It is a document from a time before the crime that clearly was not created for the purpose of defending the client at trial. That can be a powerful basis for the expert's opinion. Jurors also can see this data for themselves and draw their own conclusions.*

Similarly, when describing pre-accident or lifelong thinking abilities in a case, report cards showing straight A's (or D's and F's) make a compelling visual argument.

Another type of record that can be powerful is checklist data. In many concussion cases, rather than the expected course—that any symptoms will present immediately and improve rapidly over the first few weeks after the injury—many plaintiffs' symptoms do not appear for months or years and accelerate over time. This symptom course is inconsistent with the possible effects of a concussion. As this phenomenon is described, a copy of a review of symptoms checklist from medical records close to the time of injury with "memory problems, attention problems, irritability, poor sleep," etc. checked off as "no, no, no, no" is helpful.

FLIP CHARTS/WHITEBOARDS

Rod Swenson prefers flip charts to a premade visual:

> *I like to have a blank piece of paper. I feel it is simple. If an attorney walks up with a fancy exhibit, premade, it looks too slick. On direct, I will say, "It would be easier to answer your question if I could draw on this paper here." The attorney will ask the judge if that is okay. The judge will say, "Sure."*

David Williamson uses a flip chart to explain the emotional contribution in persistent postconcussion syndrome. He will draw a graph with time as the bottom axis and "how bad the symptoms are" on the vertical axis. He will say as he fills in the visual,

> *One of the things we know about concussion is that the symptoms that you have right after it happens (the symptoms you have because of actual temporary changes in the brain) get better over time. It is worst right at the time of the injury, and then the*

number of symptoms and the severity of symptoms goes down like this. (He draws the expected recovery curve.)

There are some people who have some problems, and if no one has bothered to explain to you that the symptoms will naturally go down/get better over time, it can be upsetting. (He takes out a different-colored marker to draw a curve showing emotional upset increasing over time.) You have to go back to work or school. And it is more upsetting for some people than others, because some people tend to get more upset about things than others. If you are here early in the recovery and you are terrified—"Oh my God! I have to do well!"—initially, the emotional stuff is not that much, but the emotional thing can build over time.

Now, a year later, you are still feeling "this level" of bad. But the contribution of the brain injury itself is gone; it's way down here. The emotional reaction is still there. You are feeling just as bad, but now it's for different reasons. We know that nothing bad with brain stuff is still happening to you, but you are still feeling bad. And we can help improve the emotional reaction.

If using a flipchart, recall that it may go with the jurors into their deliberation room. Make sure that whatever is drawn is clearly labeled so the jurors are not just looking at a set of squiggles that made sense at the time you were describing it, but now just look like squiggles.

USING THE BELL CURVE

The bell curve is familiar to many jurors and is a widely used visual by expert psychologists and neuropsychologists. Just like many psychologists and neuropsychologists will use the bell curve during a clinical feedback session, experts use bell curves to contextualize test scores in an easy-to-understand, visual way.

Some of the most effective testimony I have seen uses visual aids. To just say, "My client has an IQ of 75" doesn't mean a lot to most jurors. It is a lot easier for someone to look at a bell curve and have the expert say, "This is where an average person is. This is where my client is."—Lisa McDermott

----

When relevant and helpful to the jury, I have the attorney make a blowup of the bell curve and I say,

This is how we turn behavior into numbers. At the end of my report we have a whole page of numbers. It's really like a spreadsheet. We have counted behaviors and errors, and then we compare how this person does compared to others in their age bracket and education bracket. Just to be clear, if we found that a person had an average IQ, exactly 100, that doesn't mean we are going to expect all the other scores, from memory to processing speed, to line up exactly with that. We expect that normal people have quite a bit of variability." I would then talk about how this person fits into our understanding of normal or abnormal abilities.—Jerry Sweet, PhD, ABPP-CN

> I use a simple bell curve to explain what scores mean and also to compare my scores with other experts' scores or my scores with typical functioning: "They found this on the curve, and I found this." Or if a person is claiming he is super-impaired but then you look at all of his other historical test scores and that doesn't fit. I will say,
>
> *This big curve here is where most people fall. The big hump here, you are functioning like most other people. If you are in this tail end, you are different; fewer people function like you. If you are in the little tail on the right, that means you are functioning way better than the typical person. And if you are in this little tail section to the left, that means you are functioning way lower than the typical person."*—Bernice Marcopulos, PhD, ABPP-CN

Erin Bigler will use a flip chart to draw a bell curve. He prefers to use letter grades that everyone on the jury can personally relate to rather than standard scores or percentiles. He will say:

> *Here is a bell curve. You've all been graded on this in school. There is more to it than just an A, B, C, D, or F, but think of it that way. Here in the middle is the average, and if we assume some average ability, as long as your test scores are in this range, then it's consistent with average abilities. But as soon as your scores start to move to the left side of this curve, then we know that it is moving away from what was average.*

MMPI-2 AND MMPI-2-RF

Yossef Ben-Porath will put an MMPI-2 (or RF) profile up on a screen for jurors. This is a common practice for psychology and neuropsychology experts. The way the profile is organized is intuitive for most jurors and allows them to enter, with the expert, into a collaborative process of looking at the profile together to understand the meaning of the test.

Robin Hanks notes that she will ask the attorney to show the MMPI graph as a visual and say,

> *This is the line where most people who are not exaggerating their symptoms fall; they have credible symptoms. As you can se, Mr. Smith falls all the way up here. He is clearly exaggerating symptoms.*

Nancy Hebben notes that she will use comparison groups on the MMPI-RF and display the results on a visual. For example, the plaintiff is reporting a lot of pain symptoms, but the comparison chart shows that compared to typical chronic pain patients, he is reporting far more symptoms. This inoculates against a cross-examination strategy of dismissing MMPI results as "not fair" because the plaintiff is reporting actual pain symptoms. Dr. Hebben notes that it is striking to juries when a plaintiff's symptoms are well above patient groups.

CRITERIA SETS

Displaying criteria sets as a visual is another compelling way to invite the jurors to enter into their own decision-making process about whether a plaintiff or defendant meets criteria for a particular syndrome or disorder. Christopher Grote gives an example:

> *"I had the criteria for Antisocial Personality Disorder on an overhead projector. I made it clear that the litigant did meet criteria. This made it easier for the jury to understand why this, and not other diagnoses, was most appropriate."*

Ira Packer displays the DSM-5 criteria for PTSD on a slide:

> *PTSD is complicated, and it is a good topic for a visual or slide. Criterion A is easy to explain, but then you have B, C, D, E—all of these different categories, hypervigilant, negative affect, etc. This is a lot for a jury member who has never been aware of the specific PTSD criteria to take in. Then once you explain it using the slide, you can go back and say, "In Ms. Smith's case, she has . . ."*

Other experts will display criteria for concussion or major depressive disorder. Jurors are literally able to see for themselves when a plaintiff or defendant meets or does not meet criteria. Recall that the visuals may be allowed to go back with the jurors as they deliberate. It is therefore important not just to have the criteria on the visuals but a clear statement about whether the defendant/plaintiff met each part of the criteria.

Here is a table I have used in a case where there was no evidence that the plaintiff had a concussion but had been treated for years with the assumption by multiple clinicians that a concussion had taken place based on the word *concussion* in other doctors' medical records. On the left I listed the criteria for concussion from the Department of Defense, Centers for Disease Control, and American Academy of Rehabilitation Medicine.

Criteria for concussion (Department of Defense, Center for Disease Control, American Academy of Rehabilitation Medicine)

Loss of consciousness?	No
No memory for the event? "Posttraumatic amnesia"	No
Confusion or problems reasoning/thinking after the event?	No

PEDIATRIC DEVELOPMENT

Pediatric psychologists and neuropsychologists have the difficult job of explaining not only the presence of current thinking and emotional deficits but the changes in developmental trajectories the deficits may trigger. Many rely on visuals to compare a child's development before the injury or medical event to current and projected function.

John Kirk notes that explaining an injury's impact on development distinguishes child from adult psychologists and neuropsychologists: "We are assessing a moving target." He uses a visual to explain the concept of "growing into deficits." He will draw an x- and y-axis on a flip chart and say,

> *Look, here is a graph of typical development, from birth to early adulthood. Let's say we are talking about reading. Here's where a typical development might be from birth to adulthood. (He draws an upward-sloping line.) We are here at age 6. And we are comparing this 6-year-old to other 6-year-olds. When you are 6 years old, what you are expected to know reading-wise is very different than what you would be expected to know at 16. Look, this is a normal trajectory.*
>
> *Now, with Jane, after the severe traumatic brain injury, she is here, slightly below normal, but over time that could be more problematic. She is still making gains, but because of the memory and attention problems she now has, as time goes on that gap might widen. Typical development might look something like this (points). She continues to develop, but because of the thinking problems, it is a slower process (draws another less steep slope, with another color). This is a dynamic process. We have an injury at this point, and I am seeing Jane a year out from her injury. But my concern is that as they continue to develop, the gap is widening. This is what we call growing into deficits.*

PROPS AND BRAIN MODELS

Attorney Mark DeBofsky tells the great story of Jerry Sweet using a stack of books as a prop during a deposition:

> *Jerry Sweet walks into the deposition carrying a stack of books. When he was asked, "Didn't [the performance validity test] show that Mr. Smith was malingering?" Dr. Sweet said, "Absolutely not." Then he went book by book, showing that all of them backed up his interpretation. The case settled within a week.*

Wendy Marlowe used a very specific brain model in a case where there was a penetrating brain injury from a gunshot:

> *I will often use a regular brain model to show different parts of the brain during testimony. In one case, I had a guy with a penetrating brain injury from a gunshot. The model was very helpful. I found an old brain model at Goodwill. My son drilled holes in specific spots, corresponding to the trajectory of the bullet. I held the model, stuck my finger in it, and pulled it apart in front of the jury. It was very effective! Of course, I can't ever use that model again unless I have another patient with an injury in the same location.*

Rod Swenson notes that during his direct testimony he has literally walked over to the jury box and handed them a brain model: "It might be helpful to the jury if they could see this. Do you mind if I show them?"

But Scott Millis notes that in some types of cases, like concussion cases, he will not use a brain model: "I find it less helpful, because a lot of these mild TBIs are not about the brain per se."

PUBLISHED GRAPHS AND FIGURES

Martin Rohling uses a visual from his 2003 article "Neuropsychological Impairment Following Traumatic Brain Injury: A Dose-Response Analysis."[1] Kyle Boone and many other experts I interviewed use Grant Iverson's graph[2] and/or Martin Rohling's graph[3] for cognitive effects of various medical conditions and legal and illegal drug side effects, all converted into the same standard score metric to contextualize the expected effect of concussion of thinking.

> *The graph is very helpful for juries. These are all the conditions that have a powerful impact on thinking: ADHD, bipolar, benzodiazepine use, litigation, depression. These are the conditions that we know affect thinking. As you can see, the other conditions have a much more significant effect than concussion/mild traumatic brain injury.*

I like to use the chart from Michael McCrea's classic book *Mild Traumatic Brain Injury and Postconcussion Syndrome*[4] showing the base rates of postconcussion syndrome symptoms in healthy college students, depressed individuals, and other groups as a visual as I describe the natural history of recovery and "PCS" to juries. Bernice Marcopulos uses a table from a book by Roger Tourangeau and colleagues *The Psychology of Survey Response*,[5] to create a visual demonstrating that people's memory for autobiographical data declines over time:

> *I use a slide that shows typical memory loss for past events. The timeline shows how long people remember past events—that is, how retrospective memory declines over time. Someone in their 40s says they were a "straight A student" in high school, but maybe they didn't remember their grades accurately. Normative data from survey research shows people are not that good at remembering stuff.*

VIDEOS

Videos can be a vivid and compelling method of sharing information in a case. Antonio Puente and Lisa McDermott have collaborated on death penalty mitigation cases to create videos that allow jurors to empathize with a defendant's experience of extreme poverty that is otherwise almost impossible for Americans to imagine.

Lisa McDermott notes that videos allow jurors to meet people in the defendant's life in a way that is natural for them, as opposed to the nervous, stiff people jurors might see if the information was conveyed on the stand

Think about the grandmother that is on the stand. She has come in her Sunday best. She is nervous and quiet. Think about interviewing her in her housecoat and rubber boots in a chair that is made out of ripped Styrofoam with pigs yapping in the background. It is a different visual. This is her everyday life. The person jurors see on the stand is not the person they'd meet any other day of the year.

I had a client's son who was too young to testify. He was comfortable with me though, hanging out in the family's living room. We colored on camera. He showed me a picture of his dad. He talked about how much he loved his dad, and what they liked to do together. He shared words and feelings that might not have been conveyed if he'd been in an unfamiliar courtroom full of strangers.

Additionally, videos show jurors a level of poverty that they will have had no experience with previously.

You can say someone is poor, but if you see the buckets used to bring in water to the house, or the roof made of tin, or the dirt floor—that is different. Most of the videos are interviews, but they are usually interviews in the environment where the client was raised.

When you say someone is poor, how do you define poor? You can define poor by using examples: "In order to brush his teeth every morning, he had to go outside to get water. The defendant's brother would keep his Twinkie locked up in a box; it was that special."

We have also done mapping using demographics. We will get census data that says that, in this particular community, 70% of the population did not have more than a seventh-grade education. Or this particular community, in a 6-month span of time, had 27 murders. We or someone on the team will create colorful graphics that give meaning to the data in the context of the family history.

Tony Puente and I made a recent video. At the parent's house, in the backyard, they kept six pigs. They kept them because the only way to make money is to sell pigs at Christmas Eve. They can get $150 a pig. This was the only source of income at the time. Anything they could find to feed the pigs, they would. We documented this by video.

On another case, the client was from Cuba. The river, which was filled with waste from the nearby meat factory, would overflow. It would overflow up to an adult's knees, and the smell would persist for months. Every other month, all of the family's belongings were ruined, even though they tried their best to keep things off the floor. We were able to not only talk about it but show the videos so that the jury has an accurate visual —Lisa McDermott

Erin Bigler will use video clips from parts of his evaluation to demonstrate problems litigants are having that may not be familiar to jurors, like apraxia. He has also shown a video to dramatically demonstrate anosognosia, the lack of awareness of deficits:

Doing my clinical interview and mental status exam:

Q: How are you doing?

A: Great!!

Q: Can you please explain your deficits?

A: Well, I think I'm doing pretty well! Things aren't bad!

There she is in a wheelchair, paretic arm, and telling me things are great. An unscrupulous defense witness could say, "No complaints." The video is really valuable.

Attorneys may also use video clips from surveillance during the expert's testimony to demonstrate inconsistencies between test scores and everyday function.

I had a case where surveillance video showed the plaintiff pulling out car keys from his pocket, counting change easily. His finger tapping was severely impaired. The Rey Figure was severely impaired, just a jumbled figure—and yet the surveillance tape showed him driving with no difficulty and making a U-turn. Another patient claimed that numbers made her nauseated and had made large retching noises in the office during tasks that involved numbers. She was shown putting coins into a machine on surveillance. I have used clips of surveillance in these instances to demonstrate the lack of credibility in the neuropsychological findings.—Anonyomous

Robin Hanks notes that in many cases she has access to surveillance on people who say they cannot do things and the videos show they can. She will say to juries after they watch the video clips, "These are inconsistent behaviors. It doesn't make neurological sense." David Hartman explains the value of surveillance footage:

When you have a situation in which a person's credibility is low, 1 minute of surveillance speaks a thousand words. Someone who says that they are too disabled to walk and drive and shop who is caught on videotape walking, driving, and shopping. Their behavior is extremely discrepant from their claim. That goes to common sense. Some neuropsychologists take umbrage about including surveillance results in their reports, but surveillance is just observational data on behavior outside the clinician's office. It can and should be incorporated.

Experts also use videos to explain brain phenomena like the effects of stroke and severe TBI. Lisa Stanford noted that in one case, she partnered with the attorney to create a video to explain the effects of lead in the brain.

Legal teams may also put together "day in the life" videos to vividly describe a plaintiff's current function or to create contrasts using old family and other videos between the person's function before the accident and now. Erin Bigler notes,

In some high-net-worth cases, attorneys will put together a "day in the life" video, showing pre- and post-accident function. They use videos prior to the accident: family videos, activities. And then show post-injury. The "day in the life" videos are not typically

> *introduced at trial because there are some legal hurdles. They are usually used pretrial, in settlement negotiations. If the case goes to trial, the videos may be used in part; typically it will be a little snippet that the attorneys have approved for the actual trial.*

In my own practice, I have consulted with attorneys about what types of daily activity would be helpful to film in order to illustrate various thinking deficits in very severely impaired plaintiffs. Experts may be interviewed for these types of videos to help explain what the viewer is seeing.

ACTING SYMPTOMS OUT

At times, the expert's body can be the visual. Erin Bigler notes that when he does not have a video of a clinical symptom, he will demonstrate it himself. For example, he might demonstrate apraxia or a slow rate of speech.

Glenn Larrabee will sometimes explain behavioral inconsistencies during the examination by acting them out on the stand:

> *I will sometimes act it out, if the inconsistencies are egregious. I examined a guy in a toxic case. He came in with a cane. At the end of the exam, he gets up, walks over and shakes my hand, walks to the door, entirely normally, touches the doorknob, and says, "Oh, doc! There's my bad memory; I forgot my cane!" He bent over double to hobble back to get his cane. I acted out that story for the jury.*

POWERPOINTS

Some experts will create a PowerPoint presentation for the jury. Ira Packer cautions experts to be very thoughtful about how the slides will be used in direct testimony:

> *I saw testimony from an expert who had his whole direct testimony presentation on PowerPoint. The attorney would ask him a question; he would then answer with the aid of a slide. He was asked the second question, then answered with the next slide. The problem was it was so obviously rehearsed and coordinated with the attorney that it impaired his objectivity.*

PowerPoints as a medium can also seduce experts into creating too many slides. Bernice Marcopulos recommends keeping the number of slides to a minimum: "I have seen experts have a hundred-slide PowerPoint presentation. That is overkill. It is better to have two or three visual aids to come back to that buttress your points."

SERIAL TESTING

When plaintiffs or defendants have been tested multiple times, visuals may be the only way to cogently share this information with the jury. Otherwise, verbal descriptions of score sets over time will be overwhelming. Antonio Puente uses multiple testing sessions over time to establish examinee-centered reliability and validity:

> *I worked on a case in Puerto Rico where we gathered test data over a 10-year period. In this situation, there was a possibility of dementia. We did 60 tests over a 10-year period. There was a lot of information that had to be taken into account from both a developmental and a clinical perspective. It was important to present the information by making it into tables and graphs in an understandable and useable fashion. Then you can really speak to validity and reliability.*

Comparisons of neuropsychological test data from different assessments following the onset of illness or injury can likewise be used to demonstrate deterioration (which can in some cases indicate dementia syndromes), consistency (which suggests a plateau has been reached in recovery), or improvement.

In some cases, neuropsychological test results are available from prior to an injury. A table comparing the results from before and after the injury/illness can be helpful for juries, both in demonstrating changes in scores over time and in showing the big picture.

In one case I saw, a plaintiff had been assessed neuropsychologically while in college. Ten years later, after a concussion, the plaintiff's expert witness concluded that there was good evidence for brain damage based solely on a decline in the plaintiff's Wisconsin Card Sorting Test compared to her previous assessment. To help explain the concept of normal variability, I created a table comparing all the scores from both assessments. It showed the decline in WCST performance but also the improvement in memory and attention scores. I made the point that the WCST has been shown in research not to show any long-term effects due to concussion, so the change in the score was likely due to chance alone. I also made the "big picture" point that if the expert was concluding that the concussion caused the change in the WCST score, was he also claiming the concussion caused the improvement in memory and attention?

BRAIN IMAGING

While static MRI and CT scans are common in courtrooms, functional neuroimaging is still not often seen. Judge Jay Blitzman notes that certain types of imaging studies are often kept out of evidence based on the belief that they are not definitive enough, the science is not widely accepted, and they can have an inappropriate emotional effect on the jury:

> *As David Eagleman notes in his book,* Incognito: The Secret Lives of the Brain, *with regards brain imaging and neuroimaging, we are back where it was when Copernicus challenged the ethnocentric conception of the universe and the Ptolemaic theory was threatened. We can run to the caves and hide or we can be really excited and look at it with awe and wonder. We are going to know so much more 20 years from now, even 5 years from now. But right now, to get that science into an individual case is very challenging.*

Many neuropsychology experts will use CT or MRI images as visuals for their direct testimony. Others may be asked to comment on brain scan images that have been shown by experts on the opposing side. The decision to use brain imaging as a visual or to comment on brain scan images begins with an expert's evaluation of their scope of practice.

Tom Boll will ask attorneys to call in a radiology expert when brain imaging is likely to play a role in the case:

> *Some neurology experts in concussion cases will admit that the person only had fleeting loss of consciousness, but then state that using their very fancy MRI diffusion tensor imaging technique, they know that the plaintiff sustained diffuse axonal injury. Of course, that is ridiculous, but it is not my area of expertise. If I see records in a case that indicate imaging will be used in this manner, I will tell the attorneys, "You are going to have to get someone in there, someone to testify about it who is credible. I can talk with you about the issues, but I can't be a credible witness on the stand because it is not my area."*

Bob Denney notes that some neuropsychologists truly have neuroimaging as part of their scope of practice. In his case, he had independent neuroimaging privileges as a medical staff member of his prior forensic medical center. Jacobus Donders notes that interpreting scans is not in his scope of practice, but when a radiologist has found that a scan is abnormal—for example, in a DTI analysis of an MRI brain image—he will comment on the research literature showing the nonspecificity of DTI findings. That is, he will not claim to be able to determine whether a scan is normal or abnormal, but he is qualified to comment on the literature that discusses how common abnormal scans are in various conditions neuropsychologists treat.

> *I will let the radiologist tell me if there is any abnormality in the scan. It would be helpful to have a second radiologist interpret the scan because in the field of radiology, the reliability is poor. But the radiologists interpret the scan.*
>
> *When the question is to what is the abnormality due, that's an area that it is possible to testify, because I know the literature about what abnormalities are common in certain psychiatric and cognitive conditions. And no one, to my knowledge, has written a paper, done a study, that can discriminate on the basis of just looking at DTI scan whether a person's symptoms are because of concussion, PTSD, or both, or neither.*

Rus Bauer notes that he has used visuals of a normal human brain and the plaintiff's or defendant's brain as visual on direct examination:

> *I have put up a good representative image of a normal human brain and a picture of the patient's brain. There have been judges that have allowed me to make a comment. I do not interpret; I rely on the interpretation of board-certified radiologists. I have sufficient experience with brain scans. My research involves quantitative measurement of brain scans with TBI. I won't render a medical opinion, but I am going to use that data in formulating my opinion. Frankly, the fact that I do structural MRI*

in my research has been enough not to disqualify me. In one case, there was a plaintiff with a deep cerebellar bleed. We put an image of his scan up for the jury.

Erin Bigler notes that he likes to relate brain imaging to his neuropsychological findings to create a solid anatomical and neuropathological basis for the conclusions of the neuropsychological assessment. He notes that he works frequently with functional neuroimaging in his research and teaching but does not currently use it in court. He will use static brain images and often has them reproduced as three-dimensional images to assist the jury in understanding what they are seeing.

I don't use functional neuroimaging in the courtroom now because I think it is premature. In the not-so-distant future, we will have some standard neuropsychological measures that are reproducible in the imaging setting and we will be able to integrate that with the patient's 3D image of their brain, in real time. For now, I am using static CT, MRI. The problem with day-of-injury CT scans is that they are done quickly and are clinical. You generally get a basic 2D or 3D image of the brain. Quantitative neuroimaging is now available if the proper 3D MRI is obtained. With the proper MRI acquisition in addition to the standard clinical neuroradiological report, it is very straightforward to request generation of a 3D image and quantitative image analysis of the MRI from the radiology lab. There is no reason that every neuropsychologist shouldn't be using these programs that are now available. For example, in assessing a memory condition, current neuroimaging information provides relevant objective quantitative information about mesial temporal lobe and hippocampal volumetrics. To have this information as part of their presentation in a legal case only provides additional objectivity. A typical private-practice neuropsychologist would have to educate themselves a little bit on image acquisition, what to request and how to work with neuroimaging colleagues.

One neuropsychologist who prefers to remain anonymous describes the following three-slide strategy to clearly integrate the brain imaging with the neuropsychological test findings:

In some cases, people have undergone multiple MRIs, EEGs, fMRIs, etc. Sometimes we use a three-slide strategy. The first slide is a graphical depiction of the brain. Oftentimes you have a convergence of evidence from the multiple imaging studies. The visual of the brain can show where the multiple studies converge on the same finding. On the next slide, we take those areas of the brain and we talk about research involving those areas that implicate behavior. An easy example is impulsivity or difficulty with mental flexibility. Jurors see the first slide, the convergence of the evidence that there is damage in a particular area. The next slide is a tutorial in functional neuroanatomy. The third slide is a description of the problem behaviors in the trial. This usually involves them engaging in aggression and impulsivity. With the triad of slides you can bring a jury from complex brain imaging, to neuroanatomy, to the actual behaviors they are thinking about in the trial. Juror feedback has indicated that those slides are very helpful.

When asked to comment on other experts' use of brain images, Martin Rohling offers a powerful analogy explaining why static measurements of structure do not necessarily tell us about function:

> *You may not know who Spud Webb is. Spud Web was the shortest player to play in the NBA. He was 5-foot-7. And his rookie year he won the dunking contest. Now, Spud Web, at 5-foot-7, looked impressive dunking a basketball, especially as compared to the other guys, all of whom were 6-foot7 and 6-foot-9. The fact that was so short and he could jump so high was part of the athleticism that won him the All-Star Slam Dunk contest. It was harder for him, but he could do it. If you just had them standing there, and imaged them, would you predict that Spud Webb would win the contest? No! So, function is what we need to focus attention on. And you can't have static colored pictures that allow you to predict function.*

The issue of DTI findings is so common in concussion cases that several experts offered strategies to address DTI evidence on cross examination.

DTI limitations

Q: But aren't DTI scans objective?

A: You can have scans like this not only in mTBI, but these DTI scans show abnormalities in people who are anxious, people who have ADHD, people who have autism, and that's just the A's. Or fat kids: There was a recent article showing that obese kids showed DTI abnormalities. These are extremely sensitive scans, and they pick up issues when anything is not quite right. But are the abnormalities due to this accident? We can't say that.—Jacobus Donders, PhD, ABPP-CN

DTI not used in outcome research

I am not going to get in the trenches and argue whether DTI scans were normal or not.

Q: Doctor, didn't the DTI scan show there was brain damage?

A: When they did the outcome research for recovery after concussion, they were using the traditional scans. The outcome data is based on normal CT and normal MRI. If minute changes were present but not detected on CT and MRI, it did not affect the outcomes.—Kyle Boone, PhD, ABPP-CN

DTI non specificity

I am careful not to interpret MRI/DTI in terms of results; that is beyond our scope. But I am comfortable talking about what I know from the existing literature about the evidence of mTBI and DTI. Nonspecificity is a big deal. The picture is worth a thousand words; it's hard for the thousand words to undo. It is important to provide context, a balanced interpretation, so that the jury is aware that the scientific evidence on the application of this.

These tools are evolving. They are not the standard of care in brain injury assessment diagnosis and management. We are very limited in our ability to use them for diagnostics. It turns out that these findings are reported in uncontrolled studies of concussion. But the same findings also show up in studies of people who are overweight, or underweight, or kids with ADHD or diabetics, or have had childhood abuse or hypertension.—Michael McCrea, PhD, ABPP-CN

Q: But, Doctor, there is blue and yellow on the picture!

A: So far, the position papers indicate that DTI is not a useful technology for diagnosing concussion because it is so nonspecific.

(I will not comment on the scan itself but will on the status of the research regarding concussion)—Scott D. Bender, PhD,ABPP-CN

Explaining variability in brain scan findings

In the situation in which there are some abnormal findings on the brain imaging scan, but the patient is functioning well,

If we go out to the parking lot and we find a dozen cars that are 10 years old, some of those cars will have a lot of rust on them. But even with rust, some of the engines will be in remarkably good shape, and some of them will not be. The outside structure of the car does not necessarily tell us how it will run."—Jacobus Donders, PhD, ABPP-CN

Explaining the "so what" small vessel ischemic disease

You are probably familiar with an MRI. It looks at the structure of the brain but it doesn't tell you anything about function. I have seen people with extensive, very extensive, white matter disease who do great on testing, and people with no white matter disease who do horribly. Not everything shows up on the scans. We really need both pieces of information.

I use my hand to demonstrate the vascular system, where the tip ends of my fingers represent the tip ends of the blood vessel where they touch the brain tissue:

If that little spot is not getting blood flow because the blood vessel has shriveled up, that might cause a tiny bit of damage. If you get enough of that type of damage, it might affect brain function."—Kristie Nies, PhD, ABPP-CN

Explaining hypointensities

People have common experiences in the sense of driving or cooking dinner or taking kids to school. I try to use those common experiences in my analogies with jurors so they can connect what I am talking about to their everyday knowledge.

For example, I live in the Bay Area. I assume that jurors have been living here long enough to know what being in traffic is like. When I want to explain how white matter changes might affect or eat into cognitive reserve, I use a traffic analogy:

A hypointensity on a brain scan represents a little block in the brain's blood flow and information flow. It's like traffic. Maybe a little detour here and there, like a few hypointensities, will slow the traffic down a little bit. Probably not a noticeable amount. But if you have several of them, it adds up and everybody knows that the traffic gets a lot worse when there are several detours or a lot of construction. —Shelley Peery, PhD

FINALLY, HIRING GRAPHIC DESIGNERS

I was intrigued to hear that one neuropsychologist (who prefers to remain anonymous) hires a graphic designer in his practice to create beautiful, clear visuals. I think this is a great idea, particularly if a designer agrees to work with a neuropsychologist to create a few visual strategies that might work in a variety of different cases whose format might be used more than once.

Part of being productive in thinking about how a jury will react to your testimony is staying away from boring scores. Attorneys will immediately tell you that scores will put the jury to sleep. A good way to avoid the minutiae of scores is to create visual aids. It's a way of talking about the data without getting lost in the scores. In our practice, we will work with a graphic designer to make 3-foot by 4-foot exhibits. We hire the designer in house but include the cost in general billing to attorneys. Whenever attorneys interview the jurors after the cases, jurors always give clear feedback that the visuals are very helpful.—anonymous

NOTES

1. Rohling, M. L., Meyers, J. E., & Millis, S. R. (2003). Neuropsychological impairment following traumatic brain injury: a dose-response analysis. *Clinical Neuropsychology, 17*(3), 289–302
2. Iverson, G. L. (2005). Outcome from mild traumatic brain injury. *Current Opinion Psychiatry, 18*, 301–317.
3. Rohling, M. L., Larrabee, G. J., & Millis, S. R. (2012). The "Miserable Minority" following mild traumatic brain injury: Who are they and do meta-analyses hide them? *Clinical Neuropsychologist, 26*(2), 197–213.
4. McCrea, M. A. (2008). *Mild Traumatic Brain Injury and Postconcussion Syndrome: The New Evidence Base for Diagnosis and Treatment*. New York: Oxford University Press, p. 160.
5. Tourangeau, R., Rips, L. J., & Rasinski, K. (2000). *The Psychology of Survey Response.* New York: Cambridge University Press.

11 Performance and Symptom Validity

POSITION PAPERS FROM the American Academy of Clinical Neuropsychology[1] and the National Academy of Neuropsychology[2] define assessment of symptom and performance validity, using well-validated assessment tools, as a critical component of a competent neuropsychological assessment. Paul Green articulates the well-accepted, compelling argument for determining whether the data we collect as psychologists and neuropsychologists are valid:

> *It is very important for us to make sure that when we present data to the court, those data are valid, that they reflect the person's actual ability. Using performance validity tests to ensure our data are good is the same as the question anyone would ask about the validity of DNA data: Are the test data accurate? It is a fundamental question for neuropsychologists: Do these test scores really reflect day-to-day functioning?*

Nancy Hebben explains the need for performance validity testing (PVT) this way: "We can only see cooperation, not effort."

> *Performance validity testing is very important to neuropsychology because we cannot see a person's effort in testing; we can only see their level of cooperation. Neuropsychological tests are dependent on a person doing their best. If you come in and don't try your best, I cannot make any valid statements about what you are truly capable of. I can make statements about the minimum that you can accomplish, but I can't talk about the maximum. And that's what neuropsychological testing is about, learning what you can do. So, we have tests that we use on which a person could have a documented hole in their brain and would pass this particular test.*

Dr. Hebben describes the difference between performance validity tests and symptom validity tests (SVTs) this way:

> *Symptom validity tests help me understand whether someone's self-report of their experience, their complaints and symptoms, is accurate. Performance validity tests help me understand whether the test results can be viewed as reliable and valid measures of what the examinee is capable of doing.*

The ability to provide information to the court about whether defendants/plaintiffs are providing accurate information about their symptoms and abilities is a unique and valuable contribution our field brings to the forensic arena. This chapter addresses strategies to assist jurors in understanding concepts of effort and exaggeration through evaluation of noncredible symptom patterns and PVT/SVT performance.

LABELS

This first section addresses language that experts use to describe problems with performance validity and symptom report. Subsequent sections will address strategies to introduce and interpret PVTs and SVTs.

Using the word *malinger*

Attorney Mark DeBofsky points out that the word *malinger* may have a very different meaning in the courtroom than it does to neuropsychologists:

> *There have been cases where neuropsychologists have been barred from giving testimony using the term* malingering *because of the potential for the juror considering the term to mean lying. It is really critical where there is a situation involving malingering that the neuropsychologist be very careful in explaining the meaning of that term.*

As noted in Chapter 3, "Relationship with the Attorney," some jurisdictions do not allow experts to use this word. It is always important to discuss specific rules about using it with the attorney who brings you to court as part of pretrial preparation.

Many experts avoid the word on the stand. One expert who preferred to remain anonymous notes, "I do not use the term *malingerer* on the stand. I want to avoid appearing to beat up on the litigant. Jurors can connect the dots themselves."

Others note that when appropriate, they will use the word, but they reserve it for extreme, very clear-cut cases. Tom Boll notes that he is very reluctant to call someone a malingerer:

> *That tells me that I know what is in their mind. I am not comfortable with using the word* malingering *unless it is absolutely clear. I have only used the term once in court. It is such a big hammer. I don't find beating up on a plaintiff will get me anywhere.*

When the term is appropriate, Yossef Ben-Porath explains malingering this way:

> Malingering *is a term found in the DSM-5, our manual for diagnosing behavior, thinking, and emotional problems. The DSM-5 defines* malingering *as a gross exaggeration or fabrication of psychological symptoms or complaints in response to an external incentive. In fact, one of the examples the DSM gives for an external incentive is litigation.*

He notes that he will often tell juries about the Slick[3] criteria for determining whether someone is malingering:

> *The Slick criteria are a specific set of criteria or questions that experts can rely on to focus on malingering of thinking difficulties. They are more detailed than the DSM-5 criteria and they indicate when there are very strong indications of malingering, or indications of possible malingering, or situations in which there are no indications of malingering at all.*

Enlarging the Slick criteria set as a visual can be a clear, concrete method of assisting the jury in evaluating whether a plaintiff or defendant is malingering.

Using polarizing words like *liar*

In his book *Polarizing the Case*[4] Rick Friedman lays out a strategy for "wrapping the malingering defense around the neck of the defense lawyer and strangling him with it." His strategy? Using inflammatory language that polarizes the question of performance or symptom validity into words like *liar* and *faker*. He suggests this strategy because jurors may feel uncomfortable with experts appearing to be unkind to plaintiffs. He notes that his strategy is to force experts to describe his client as either telling the truth or lying. While there may be compelling cases where the word *malingerer* is the most appropriate label, the word *liar* never is.

Liar *is not a term you will find in the medical literature*

Q: Are you calling my client a liar?!

A: Liar *is not a term you will find in the medical/psychological literature or in our diagnostic manuals. It is not a term I find useful in my clinical practice. My tests document failure to perform to best of ability.*—Kyle Boone, PhD, ABPP-CN

***I never use the word* lying**

I would never use the word lying. *I am not a lie detector. I avoid saying they are not having the symptoms. I can't tell if someone has a headache. That's their own personal expedience. I have reason to believe that they do have a headache. The issue here is what is causing it. I can't say for sure, but with a reasonable degree of scientific certainty, it is not associated with that pack of paper towels that fell on their head at the grocery store.*—Martin Rohling, PhD

I'm not saying he is lying; that is for the judge or jury to decide

Q: Are you calling my client a liar?

A: No, I'm not saying he is lying. That's for the judge or jury to decide.—Jacobus Donders, PhD, ABPP-CN

Are you calling my client a liar?!

Q: Dr. Millis, are you calling Ms. Smith a liar?!

A: I am a neuropsychologist. I am not a lie detector.—Scott Millis, PhD, ABPP-CN

Are you calling my client a liar?!

Q: Dr. Expert, are you calling Ms. Defendant a liar?!

A: You know, I know that I can't really ask the jurors this, but if I could, I would ask, how many of you as a kid faked a stomachache to get out of a test? It is not calling someone a liar. At times, there can be incentives not to do your best.—Anonymous

----

Q: Doctor, are you calling my client a liar!?

A: I am not here to engage in name-calling, and we don't really use terms like that. The professional terminology that we would use, as opposed to the colloquial term, is malingering, *and malingering is when we believe that there is significant intentional exaggeration of physical or psychological symptoms or signs due to some type of external incentive.*—Dominic Carone, PhD, ABPP-CN

Q: Well, Doctor, are you calling Ms. Smith a liar!?

A: No. That is not clinical terminology. Clinical decision-making involves identifying whether a person is presenting in a credible manner but does not involve judgments related to morality or ethics. As previous writers and researchers have discussed, there are many occasions, if given the right set of circumstances (e.g., financial hardship; lack of enjoyment in a work setting), when it makes sense that an individual would feign impairments or exaggerate symptoms, in an effort to improve one's quality of life.—Nat Nelson, PhD, ABPP-CN

Q: Doctor, did you say you have a lie detector test that you use?

A: No, but we know when people are not trying hard.—Neil Pliskin, PhD, ABPP-CN

Of course, there is always the exception to the rule. Jacobus Donders notes,

> I rarely if ever talk about people lying or not telling the truth. The fact that Mr. Smith claimed he was sober for 6 years is not consistent with medical records or sworn testimony in a deposition by his own father. Sometimes I will say,

Q: Are you calling my client a liar?!

A: Well, you will have to ask Mr. Smith.

Sometimes I will say,

I do think that he was lying when he told me, face to face, that he hadn't had a drink in x number of months, and it turned out that he was drinking heavily during that time. He claimed to me that he had not been drinking when the medical records indicate that he was forcibly hospitalized a couple of times for heavy drinking. So yes, that was a clear lie. Now on my test, all I can tell you was his scores were not consistent with who he really is. He was at least engaging in exaggeration or magnification. For whatever reason. We will let the jury decide if he is a liar.

Other language to describe effort

In some cases, the pattern of performance validity testing, interview, behavior observations, and medical records review clearly indicate symptom exaggeration and poor effort, but without the "smoking gun" of significantly below-chance performance on a PVT that would meet Slick criteria and trigger the potential use of the word *malinger*. In these instances, experts shared strategies to explain their assessment of effort to juries.

There are a high percentage of people involved in legal cases that have been found to have exerted poor effort. One reason is that the p believes they have a problem that is objectively not present. But they believe it to the extent that they are performing less than optimally on the tests. They may desperately want you to believe it. It may be simply a way of saying, "I have to get this guy on my side. I have to convince him I have a problem. And if he says this is a memory test, I am going to really let him know."

This is not Ms. Smith's best effort. She may have not tried as hard as she could in order to make me believe she has a problem, or because she genuinely believes she has a problem, but she was able to do [this] and [that] on the other tests, which shows this brain function is intact.—Tom Boll, PhD, ABPP-CN

Robert Heilbronner simply and clearly states, "This person wasn't trying their hardest."

Not trying hard

Did the person try their hardest, or did it look like they were attempting to come across as worse than they are? We have specific tests in the battery that look at whether or not someone was trying their hardest.

David Schretlan notes that most people don't give 100% effort over an 8-hour assessment.

Effort as a continuum

We all know people who try hard all the time. Other people coast. I always tell my patients to do their best. This doesn't mean I expect them to give 100%, and it definitely doesn't mean they will give 100% on every measure administered. After a few

hours, your stomach begins growling. You start thinking about other things. Many different factors go into how hard someone tries on a particular test. In many cases people try harder on tasks they think they are good at. We tend to over interpret normal variability in test scores across a long battery as reflecting the effects of an injury. But not many people can maintain full effort over several hours.

Engaged

It's like when you are talking to a teenager and they pull out their iPhone. They are obviously not engaged in the conversation any longer. Not that they can't, they just aren't. This can be true with someone who is depressed. They are not engaging in the testing. Low memory scores don't mean they can't remember, just that they were not engaged in the task.—David Williamson, PhD, ABPP-CN

I personally like to use the analogy of riding a bike because all of us have had the experience of pedaling hard—or not so hard.

Effort is like riding a bike

Effort on tests is like effort when riding a bike. You can pedal really hard. Or not so hard, depending on the situation.

If you are in a bike race, you are going to be pedaling your heart out. As hard as you can. People taking a high stakes college entrance test might be "pedaling" that hard when taking test. Really strong effort.

Or maybe you are just riding your bike on a weekend to for a relaxing ride. You are putting in effort, but not killing yourself.

In some cases, it is clear that someone isn't pedaling the bike hard. It is clear that they are just coasting. Performance validity tests are able to pick this up. The tests scores are so low, it doesn't make neurological sense. It is clear they are not trying to perform well.

Sometimes the scores on performance validity tests are so low, near chance, that it is clear the person has gotten off the bike. They are literally putting in no effort to pedal. Their scores are at chance—the same as if they weren't even looking at the test.

In extreme cases, like Mr. Plaintiff, scores on performance validity tests are substantially below chance. That means that the he would have gotten a way better score if he didn't even look at the test items. That's like getting on the bike and pedaling really hard in the opposite direction. He was not trying to win the race, he was trying to lose. To get a below chance score, you have to know the right answers, but give the opposite answer instead. That's a lot of effort, but effort to look worse than you are.

Martin Rohling uses the analogy of having a good engine in their car, but just not driving it.

Just not driving the car

To explain PVT failure, I will use a car engine/ brain metaphor and say,

Mr. Smith has a good engine, he just isn't driving it. During testing, he wasn't motivated to do well.

Nancy Hebben notes that she doesn't come to conclusions about why someone fails PVTs. "I lay out the possible explanations, then let the jury decide."

> *Putting this all together, the neuropsychological data lead to one of two conclusions. Mr. Smith might have been creating symptoms for secondary gain. Here is the data that support that. Second, he may have been somaticizing or performing so low because he believes he is impaired or without realizing it because he is being reinforced for his symptoms. Here is the data that support that conclusion.*

Rus Bauer similarly leaves the final conclusion to the jury.

> ***I can't look you guys in the eye and tell you I know why they failed the PVT***
>
> When patients put forth poor effort, there is usually a negative emotional reaction from the psychologist. I bend over backwards not to disparage the person but to simply talk about "When you don't try or you think this is too much for you that you give up early." Or "For whatever reason you are not there 100%." The test scores that I get are clearly useless. The really difficult thing comes in with the conclusions an expert will come to. Some people might take a completely value-neutral approach: "Well, it's worthless data and I can't say anything about it." And others don't. They might say, "This person was trying to exaggerate for gain." I suspect but don't completely know. So, I will say,
>
> *There are three possible reasons this person did it. (1) They are convinced on the basis of things we talked about earlier [iatrogenic] that these tests are beyond their capability because they have 'brain damage.' (2) They want to convince me that they have a deficit. Put yourself in that situation. You go to an opposing doctor, who you feel doesn't believe you. You have a problem, and you 'jack it up,' kind of like talking louder or shouting to be heard. (3) They don't have a problem; they are making it up. I can't sit here and look you guys in the eye and tell you I know which one it is. It could be a combination of those three. In any case, it reduces my ability to precisely tell you what the specific pattern of brain function and dysfunction is.*

NON-PVT/SVT INDICATORS OF PERFORMANCE AND SYMPTOM VALIDITY

Inconsistent/noncredible scores and symptoms

There are many cases where, even before PVTs and SVTs are administered, the facts of the case do not add up. David Schretlan notes that he likes to ask rhetorical questions in these situations to engage the jury in their own evaluation of the inconsistencies: "Does that make sense to you?"

When someone's overall performance on the neuropsychological battery is much lower than what would be expected given an alleged injury, Cheryl Weinstein will share her concern about the inconsistencies with jurors by stating, "I'm going to wonder what else is going on." This invites jurors to engage in their own wondering.

Ms. Smith had very, very poor performances on these tests. She couldn't put numbers on the face of a clock. She couldn't remember information on my memory test. And yet she spoke with me for 8 hours in my office and did not have any problem remembering details from her history. In that situation, I'm going to wonder what's going on. It doesn't make sense. It just doesn't make sense. I go to the literature. This is not consistent with what we know can happen after a concussion.

Robin Hanks frames inconsistent presentations for jurors as "not making neurological sense":

This does not make neurologic sense. There are other factors at work.

It is not neurological

This test pattern tells me it is not neurological. I am not a mind reader. I can't say for sure if it is secondary gain, or belief in impairment, but I can tell you for sure that this is not a neurologically based pattern.—Kristie Nies, PhD, ABPP-CN

Scott Millis talks with juries about "fingerprints" of disorders:

Head injuries have a fingerprint, just in the same way fingerprints can identify people. The neuropsychological examination is like taking a fingerprint. Certain diseases and disorders have a unique fingerprint. We expect certain patterns on the tests and certain patterns of symptoms. The fingerprint that this person gave me is not the head injury fingerprint.

In my own practice, I had an examinee who, after a low speed MVA, claimed a concussion that impaired his ability to speak his native English, but left his second and third languages, French and Spanish, intact. He spoke English haltingly, with a very thick French accent after the accident. Another neuropsychologist, a speech therapist, her primary care physician, and a board-certified neurologist all accepted that impossible, non-neurologically based presentation at face value. Here is how I explained it.

Just because a physician agrees with the symptom, does not make it so. Loss of language function is not a possible symptom of a single, uncomplicated concussion. Even when a catastrophic neurological event like a massive stroke or a severe traumatic brain injury disrupts language function, ones first language is the best preserved. This pattern is clearly not neurologically-based.

Ted Peck notes that it is important to start with the fact that symptoms are preposterous given the injury characteristics, rather than starting with scores.

For patients who are deliberately malingering, with completely preposterous claims, you have to start with,

This is why I think this claim is preposterous. . . (Not: They scored 5 SD below the mean on this test.)

This is important, because jurors will not have the same emotional/ visceral reaction neuropsychologists will to hearing that a plaintiff with a concussion scored 6 standard deviations below the mean on a memory test.

When there are clear inconsistencies between an examinee's self-report and their observed behavior, Manfred Greiffenstein suggested using his concept of compelling inconsistencies:

> I always have a separate section in my reports, "reliability as a historian." It is a mix of the examinee's subjective report and my objective behavior observations. I will include my clinical judgment about how well their subjective symptoms match their mental activity implied by their speech.
>
> If people are exaggerating memory problems, most already get caught at the mental status exam: "My memory is terrible! Last Monday I was talking to my sister, and I forgot my dentist appointment at 3 o'clock that day! I had to call them! I was so embarrassed. Doctor, that's an example of what I am talking about!"
>
> That's an extreme example. More often than not, and in almost every mTBI case, there is a gap between expressed symptoms and observed behavior.
>
> I don't limit the section to mental behavior; I include motor behavior. I believe there is an important phenomenon—a malingered motor deficit. You see that a lot in patients who are claiming pain symptoms along with their reported cognitive symptoms. I can press only 2 kg on grip strength, and yet I have a firm handshake and I can grip a pencil and a cane. I pay a lot of attention to musculoskeletal issues, with the intention of matching it up with the objective motor scores. Then I make a clinical judgment about the subjective distance between observed motor scores and self-report. I will use the phrase "compelling inconsistency"—"it's so obvious you can't ignore it."
>
> On the stand I might say,
>
> *Look, she shook my hand, she drove to my office, so logically she gripped the steering wheel. And yet her grip strength scores are incredibly low. In my professional opinion, this is a compelling inconsistency.* (Not just an inconsistency, a compelling inconsistency. Make sure your example is really clear, major.)

> ***This gentleman can drive and button his shirt. Something else is going on.***
>
> On direct, you can start with whether the test results are reliable, and then use that as a context for discussing the meaning and quality of the test performances, not just the scores out of context.
>
> *Q: Go on and tell me how they did on testing.*
>
> *A: Well, okay, on this test of his ability to copy a design, he performed at the very bottom level, but that doesn't make a bit of sense: This is a gentleman who drives, and buttons his shirt, and manages his finances. There is absolutely no reason. His brain imaging is normal. There is no reason from him to have this problem. There is clearly something else going on here.*—Tannahill Glen, PhD, ABPP-CN

When I looked at the records prior to the evaluation, this is what I expected to see

After I read these records, this is what I was expecting before Sam came in. I was expecting someone who is having daily headache pain of an 8/10 or 9/10. I would have expected that we would take a lot of breaks in a 6-hour evaluation. And the reality is that I needed to take more breaks than Sam! I checked in with him, and he was still saying that he was having an 8 or 9/10 headache pain.

[or]

he needed to take frequent breaks, he was shifting constantly in his seat, and he was clearly in pain.—John Kirk, PsyD, ABPP-CN

David Bush notes that he will testify about extra-test behaviors:

> I recently consulted on a case with a severe TBI. The plaintiff had a bad outcome. The party line from everyone was, "He has no executive functioning" and he needed 24/7 attendant care. I was going over the video consent form process. Before he was willing to sign, he wanted his attorney to advise him. I included that in my report. His request to have his attorney review the form demonstrated a capacity for abstract reasoning, the ability to anticipate future consequences, and good judgment. Extra-test behavior like this is important to include in our formulations. It is common sense. If somebody gets a 5 on the RAVLT recognition but comes in on day 2 and says, "Remember when you were asking me about that medication?" I am always keeping my eyes open for things like that. Does the person need directions constantly repeated, as they would if they had a truly severe memory deficit?
>
> *This incredibly low score that falls in a range of elderly adults with Alzheimer's disease cannot possibly be valid because there were several instances throughout my exam when Mr. Jones demonstrated entirely normal memory function. For example, when he came back from lunch he told me that his hamburger was burned. Or he had no trouble remembering where the bathroom was. He remembered directions."*
>
> *You have to be collecting data over and above the formal testing setting.*

Experts can help jurors understand when test scores fall way below expected levels given a particularly mild injury by comparing their performance to severe traumatic brain injuries. For example, Glenn Larrabee will say,

> *He performed like someone who had spent a month in a coma, and yet he never even lost consciousness from this concussion. That just doesn't make sense.*

Similarly, Jacobus Donders will help jurors understand patterns on cognitive tests that are not patterns we expect from a brain injury:

> *There are also checks and balances in what we call the pattern of the tests. If I have you learn a shopping list, and we really practice it—I give you that list three times,*

> *four times, five times—then I say, "Now what I want you to do is, you are going to go shopping on a different day," a lot of people have difficulty shifting from one list to another because they are so used to the first list. Now if someone all of a sudden does 3,000 times better on that second list than the first shopping list, that's unusual. That's not something we would expect on the basis of a brain injury. That does not mean they're lying—maybe they are nervous with the first list—but it's not a pattern that we expect with a brain injury.*

He could recite five digits backwards but only got three words on CVLT

> Using a concrete example is effective to point out inconsistencies in test results.
>
> *This man was able to repeat 5 digits backwards on a test I gave him. 6-7-4-3-8 would be 8-3-4-7-6. He could keep five numbers in his head long enough to mentally rearrange them and say them backwards correctly. Yet when I gave him a list of words and asked him right away to tell me as many as he could, he only said three. That just doesn't make sense.*—David Schretlen, PhD, ABPP-CN

Similarly, Glenn Larrabee notes that it is important to engage jurors in using their own common sense to come to a conclusion about whether the plaintiff/defendant's test performances were credible. Making tests real to jurors with concrete examples and using the concept of graded difficulty is one way of doing so.

> You can look at tests with graded levels of difficulty. Grip strength, you squeeze as hard as you can. That's all you have to do. Finger tapping, you have to tap a lever quickly. But the Grooved Pegboard, you have to pick up these little pegs, and put them in these little holes that are angled in different ways as fast as you can. (I put my hand up and demonstrate.) Why would this person do that better, then tapping on a lever? That makes no sense. When you talk about graded levels of difficulty, you allow the jurors to come to their own conclusions. And you also make the tests real to them. The other expert is pontificating about "The impairment index says . . ."
>
> *What kind of brain damage would make you count from one to forty by threes better than you can say the alphabet?*
>
> *My colleague, Dr. Kevin Greve, had an attorney react to his description of performance inconsistency by saying "Ah, it's like being able to lift 20 pounds but not lift 5 pounds."*

Manfred Greiffenstein shared a similar strategy for explaining inconsistent test scores. He noted that experts can apply the concept of compelling inconsistencies to the test scores as well as behaviors. For example, if processing speed is dramatically impaired and memory is normal.

> *The Processing Speed index is severely impaired. But her delayed memory was average. How can you possibly remember information if you process that slowly?*

Noncredible family reports

Robin Hanks notes that she always tries to get collateral interviews from family members of examinees as it gives her an understanding of their social references and home life context. If the collateral report makes no sense, she will tell that to the jury:

> *Mr. Smith's wife told me that over the year following the concussion, none of his symptoms have improved to any degree. This just doesn't make any neurological sense.*

Cheryl Weinstein notes that families will fill out behavior rating forms like the Behavior Rating Inventory of Executive Function-Adult Version (BRIEF-A). Many times, the scores are noncredible given the alleged injury:

> *These ratings don't make sense. Mr. Smith's family checked off so much impairment on this questionnaire, it is a level that you see after someone was in a coma for weeks and woke up with severely slurred speech and not able to coordinate their movements. These scores are at the 99th percentile of possible impairment. It just doesn't make sense. If I had a bad day with my husband, I might rate him at the 99th percentile!*

EXPLAINING PVTS

Introducing PVTs

Tannahill Glen uses an analogy to something jurors are familiar with, Nyquil, to explain the need for PVTs:

> The first thing I want to establish in my direct testimony is the reliability of the results.
>
> *Q: How do you know you can rely on these results?*
>
> *A: We have to know we can rely on these results when I do any form of evaluation, whether it is in my regular clinical or in one of these cases, it doesn't matter. I need to be able to know that the results I get are valid. The reason is that just "low scores" by themselves don't mean anything out of context.*
>
> *For example, would you want me to give you a bottle of Nyquil to drink and then the next morning give you a competency evaluation in which I made a determination about whether you could ever use a checkbook again? Would you be confident in your ability to perform at your best on the test? Probably not!*
>
> *It is vital that we have confidence in the scores from our tests, so over the years we have built indicators that these are valid and reliable scores, or if there is something else going on. In the case of the bottle of Nyquil, you would have your head on the testing table and looking half-asleep, so that would be all I would need to know to say that these poor results are not necessarily an indicator of brain dysfunction. It helps me say, "There's something else going on here, so hold up, let's check this out."*

Jacobus Donders introduces the concept of performance validity tests to jurors this way:

> *It is now the standard of care in our field. That is, everyone who does our job has to do this in some way or another. We have to look at whether people are doing their best. Because face it, not all of us are doing our best every time. That doesn't necessarily mean we are throwing the game like they did with the Chicago Black Sox game in the 1930s; that's the extreme version of it. But sometimes we are not working hard enough, so we have to have checks and balances.*
>
> ------------
>
> *On the performance side of it, we have two sets of tests. One set is developed solely to determine whether patients are performing in a valid way; by valid I mean they are producing an accurate performance reflecting their actual ability. Those tests are designed to mimic real tests. They look like they are measuring memory or other abilities but they are really not. They are so easy that people with real memory disorders caused by a stroke or a severe traumatic brain injury can perform almost perfectly on them. So, when you see bad performance on a very easy test that only mimics a real memory test, so easy that brain-damaged people can pass them, that tells you that the patient is not performing adequately. Those are called freestanding performance validity tests.*
>
> *We also have tests that are derived from actual tests that we use in our everyday practice. For example, a person might have to learn a list of words, and then you come back and test their delayed recall and recognition—a real memory test. People with real memory problems usually have better recognition than free recall. People who are feigning or exaggerating memory problems can show abnormal responses on recognition trials compared to learning trials. Or they may fail to recognize words that they have been shown to consistently recall during the learning trials.*
>
> *Sometimes examinees will show better memory than learning; for example, they'll provide six words on the fifth trial of a list-learning test but then produce nine words at delayed recall one half-hour later. How can you remember more than you have learned?*
>
> *Others may show evidence of very poor attention but produce a superior performance on memory testing. How can you have a superior memory when you have impaired attention?*—Glenn Larrabee, PhD, ABPP-CN

Christopher Grote points out that it is hard to know how much to get into describing PVTs, "because (A) it may not matter, or (B) you are giving away trade secrets, or (C) it's too much minutiae." He might instead say,

> *There are ways we can tell whether a person is able to give us their best effort. On at least one test, this person didn't get the score he needed to convince me that he was putting forth good effort at that particular time.*

Cheryl Weinstein gives a general description as well, with a compelling comparison group:

My little granddaughter could do this test!

We give measures that my little granddaughter could pass. They are simple tests, and very easy, but they look like they might be hard. A second grader can do them! Here is a person, who performed so low on these easy tests. I just want to know what else is going on.

Explaining below chance on a PVT

Ira Packer explains forced-choice PVTs using an example of someone taking a test where they genuinely do not know the answers:

Look, it's a forced choice. If someone is significantly below chance, it is a clear indication that the score is not credible. For example, if you gave me a test on nuclear physics that is true/false, I am probably going to get about 50% right. A random score, because I don't know the answers. But if I do significantly worse than random, how is that possible? How did I only get 7 out of 100 answers right if I was just randomly guessing unless I knew the right answers and was deliberately answering incorrectly?

In my own practice, I compare at-chance performance to just closing your eyes, and below-chance performance to *worse* than closing your eyes.

If she had been literally closing her eyes she would have scored higher.

I gave Ms. Plaintiff a really easy test that was designed to look difficult. There were only two possible answers for each item. Was it this? Or that? Ms. Plaintiff's score was substantially worse than if she just closed her eyes and had not even looked at what I asked her to remember. Worse than a blind person who couldn't see the test items. A blind person would get half right, just by chance—the flip of a coin. The fact that she was significantly worse than chance tells me that she knew the right answer but gave the wrong answer. If she had been literally closing their eyes she would have scored way higher.

Below chance PVT

You can't get below chance scores unless you purposely choose the wrong answer on at least some items.—Nancy Hebben, PhD, ABPP-CN

Look, if it's a forced-choice situation, if you were closing your eyes and responding, you would get about 50% right. And he is getting 10% right. This is noncredible performance. There is no question. In the world of what I deal with, where sometimes

things are not black and white: This is black and white.—John Kirk, PsyD, ABPP-CN

These are tests that ask people to perform tasks that appear to be difficult but are actually very easy to do. Most people score 90 to 95% correct on these tests. If someone scores much below 95 to 100% you have to begin to question how much effort they put into their responses. Of course, if someone is just wildly guessing, or had no memory at all, we would expect them to get 50% right. If someone gets much below 50%, then we can calculate the probability of them doing that. There is a very low chance that this person didn't give the wrong response on purpose.—Yossef Ben-Porath, PhD, ABPP

Attorney Mark DeBofsky finds that when experts connect PVT scores to patient's actual test scores, it makes the opinion that the examinee is not trying hard much more persuasive. See Chapter 10, "Visuals," for strategies to create tables of scores and effort indicators.

Explaining graded performance expectations on PVTs

Paul Green notes,

Most people think the basic principle of a performance validity test is that it is really easy and that, unless you've got dementia, you will pass it; it's so easy that anybody can get 100% on it. That is an important principle. But another equally important feature of performance validity tests is graded difficulty. Can you produce results which are internally consistent on these tests when some subtests are a lot easier than others?

When he describes the concept of graded difficulty levels in court, Dr. Green will talk about the Green Word Memory Test or Medical Symptom Validity Test as having multiple subtests with different levels of difficulty:

It is like a flight of stairs. I know, because of doing testing on people with genuine impairment, that the top flight is the easiest test, the next flight is the next easiest, and so on. It's just like a flight of stairs until we get to the bottom, and now we are looking at the most difficult test. The subtest scores come in order because objectively there is an order of difficulty contained within those subtests, and when we give the test, the patient does not know in which order the subtests are being given. For them to produce a credible flight of stairs is very easy if they've genuinely got dementia because they will score higher on the easy subtests than they do on the hard subtests; they will produce a flight of stairs if they try their best.

But somebody who is trying to fake impairment has difficulty producing that flight of stairs. When I tell you about it, the principle is easy to understand. However, in practice, it is very hard for somebody to fake even if they have been coached to come in and produce that flight of stairs. It is very difficult because they do not know what order the subtests are in. It is very, very hard for them to deal with lots of tests in this way, multiple subtests which are of different levels of difficulty.

Dr. Green shares the story of a recent case where he was asked to testify about the Medical Symptom Validity Test results of a man who was producing dementia-range scores following a very mild concussion:

> *On the very easiest measures in each of these tests, he scored worse than the average patient with dementia, but on the more difficult subtests, he scored higher than patients with dementia. Therefore, there was major internal inconsistency in these test results. One example of his performance: On an immediate recognition trial, which is very easy, he scored only 40% correct, and yet on a later trial where he had to come up with a word on his own, which is much more difficult for people with dementia, he scored 100% correct.*

Dr. Green notes that in his decision, the judge in the case said that with regard to the validity test data, this man was scoring worse than dementia patients on the easy subtests, but when the subtests got progressively harder, he did better and better and so these results are not valid. It was clear to Dr. Green from the text of the decision that the judge "got it."

Failed PVTs do not necessarily rule out impairment

David Williamson's vivid, compelling analogy of black paint on the windows makes the point that in cases where the nature of the injury is such that genuine impairment could result, PVT failure means we cannot know if there is true impairment.

Like painting the windows black

> In situations where I know the examinee was severely injured—for example, they were in a coma for a week—but they fail the PVTs, despite the fact that the PVT failure means I can't get a read on their function, I can't say there are no residual thinking problems.
>
> *Neuropsychological assessment is like being asked to make a map of the inside of a house by looking through the windows. Of course, as doctors we can't walk directly inside the house to see everything, but using our tests as windows into the brain, we can make a pretty good map of the inside of the house. There may be some rooms in the interior you can't see from the windows, but we can get a pretty good map.*
>
> *What happens when someone fails PVTs? It's like they took black paint and painted over the windows. That doesn't mean that there isn't something going on inside that house. But I can't tell, because I can't see in the house.*

Spaghetti on the wall

> *Just because somebody is exaggerating does not mean they do not have some kind of genuine cognitive difficulty. So many people "gild the lily." They may have a genuine mild deficit from an injury, but they will exaggerate the problem on*

testing. I will go through the points about why I believe the person is exaggerating or malingering. Immediately after, I will often say, "Just because Mr. Jones is malingering does not mean that he does not have cognitive deficits, but his exaggeration makes identifying those deficits impossible. It's like the child who has thrown so much spaghetti up on the wall that you can't tell whether there is a picture under there or not. Mr. Jones is engaging in so much exaggeration (or malingering) that it is impossible to tell what is genuine and what is not. I can't tell the difference between the spaghetti that he has thrown against the wall and the potential picture that might be hanging there."—Robert L. Denney, PsyD, ABPP-CN, FP

When severely injured people fail SVTs

An individual can have a very real injury or illness that affects the brain and can have a genuine impairment. The fact that they perform poorly on measures of validity doesn't necessarily mean that there is not an injury; it just means that we have concerns about the data that we are obtaining—whether it is an accurate reflection of their best functioning.—Anonymous

Normal PVTs don't mean good effort

In some situations, performance validity tests will be passed by examinees who have noncredible scores on other tests in the battery or noncredible symptom patterns. Clarity about what PVTs can and cannot do is important.

These tests don't really measure effort. . . .

These tests really don't measure cognitive "effort," per se. Because they are so easy, it actually takes very little effort to pass them. So, if you pass the TOMM, it doesn't mean you are necessarily putting forth your best effort on a test.—David Schretlen, PhD, ABPP-CN

These tests detect poor effort. They don't detect good effort.

If you get a positive finding—that is, a failure on a PVT—it is meaningful, but if you get a normal finding it doesn't mean anything, because the tests are so easy. These tests are only useful in detecting poor effort or poor compliance with testing. Passing the extremely easy tests doesn't mean that a test-taker is giving their best effort.—Nancy Hebben, PhD, ABPP-CN

Some effort tests are better than others

There are some tests that are more rigorous; they are valid and really well studied. There are other tests that are not as sensitive in detecting poor effort. If those less sensitive tests are given, a person might pass them but still not be trying their best.—Robin Hanks, PhD, ABPP-CN

In my own practice, I will bring up the issue of sensitivity of the PVTs to address this issue.

> *Each performance validity test has data about how good it is at catching a person when they are not trying their best. This is known as "sensitivity." Research tells us that because the TOMM is so easy about 50% of the time, the TOMM misses a person who isn't trying hard. So when someone doesn't get flagged by the test, it doesn't tell us they were trying their best.*

Pediatric issues with effort

Lisa Stanford uses this very clear explanation for why it is important to test effort of children:

> Effort can be very different than malingering. Children, for a million different reasons, may have suboptimal effort. For younger children, we have the TOMM. For the older we use MSVT. We also interpret other embedded measures such as reliable digit span, forced choice, etc. . . .
>
> *"I don't know about you, but when I am anxious or worried or sad, I don't think as well as I usually do, and you probably don't either. And when I don't feel well or I have had a tough day or I don't want to be somewhere, I may not give as much effort as if I am doing something I love. And it's not because I want to be bad or I don't want to participate; it's because that's not my internal state. I am just not into this. Children are like adults in that they are internally motivated and externally motivated. I give performance validity tests so I can eliminate one more thing in an already complicated minefield. Assessing effort is another component of establishing rapport. I establish rapport and make sure the child is comfortable. I make sure they are trying as hard as they can. I make sure they understand what is happening so they can give their best effort. I don't see it as a separate part.*

John Kirk uses the concept of base rates to explain why using PVTs on children is important:

> *At Children's Hospital, we have a 17% failure rate on the performance validity tests. The majority were sports-related injuries, ages 8 to 16. That has not changed over time. These were clinical cases. And if that was in our clinical population, it is reasonable to think that in a court situation, it will be higher. When I see this in a clinical population, it is clearly not driven by money. The biggest thing is school avoidance. No one would argue that there are kids who don't want to go back to school: "If I don't get better, I don't have to go back!" So, when I see that high a base rate of not trying hard in a clinical population, I absolutely feel I need to do this in a courtroom situation.*

> ***Testifying when the other expert has not given PVTs to children***
>
> I don't ever use the word malingering; I use the term effort. There are a lot of studies out there that show that we are not very good at determining whether

someone is putting forth good effort unless we use PVTs. Some of my colleagues say, "Well, I can tell!" And I say, "Actually, no, you can't!"

It is a naïve assumption that children can't demonstrate less-than-optimal effort. We have to use objective tests to find out.—Lisa Stanford, PhD, ABPP-CN

Keith Yeates notes that using PVTs with children is standard practice:

> You just have to use PVT; it is standard practice. If you don't use PVT, you are asking for someone to discredit your assessment even though it may be a normal performance. You really can call into question an evaluation where someone didn't use this.
>
> *I routinely use PVT in a child 8 or older. It is important to be sure we have some confidence that the child is putting forth a reasonable level of effort. You can give a test that looks hard that actually isn't. People who are not putting forward enough effort are going to do badly, even though it is really easy. Kids with intellectual disability and adults with dementia can pass this test, and this kid did 50%. The only explanation is that they weren't trying. It doesn't mean that they weren't trying hard on everything, but it calls it into question.*

John Kirk notes that in the world of adult assessment, people know they need to give free-standing PVTs, but in the pediatric world, it is still common to see an evaluation without PVTs. The context that he provides with his explanation is important—he explains that he gives PVTs to every patient, not just in court-related cases:

> *Look, when we do all these tests, and you don't do well on something, I need to know that when you didn't do well on the tests it was because you had weaknesses in this area, not that you weren't trying your best. It makes sense to give these tests so we can know whether the data really reflects a problem. I have a wealth of information on this person—my interactions with the child, the medical record review. I am not giving these tests to try to trip them up or catch them. This is what I do with every patient I see, not just forensic cases. Maybe they didn't want to be here. They have been to a lot of appointments and they didn't want to be there.*

Some passed, some failed PVTs

It is common for test-takers to pass some PVTs even when they fail others. One of the reason for this is that cutoff levels for failing the tests are very conservative—that is, a person could be putting forth very little effort and still "pass" some PVTs. Kyle Boone will note this in court:

> *Q: The person failed six of your effort tests but passed seven. Why are you focusing on the six he failed?*
>
> *A: Cutoffs are set to protect patients. Therefore, they err on the side of failing to detect patients who are faking and exaggerating problems. As a result, test failures are going to be more informative than a passed test. Then there is the research on actual*

cognitively impaired patients in clinical settings. None failed four PVTs. When you get to four failures, there are virtually no clinical situations in which you would see that, aside from such severe conditions as dementia and/or extremely low intelligence, so it doesn't matter how many they pass. Also, patients are typically selective regarding what symptoms to fake; it is a relatively rare patient who fails every PVT administered. They are "picking and choosing" in the moment as to what to underperform on.

Q: Aren't you cherry-picking the evidence? Didn't Ms. Smith pass three PVTs?

A: In this situation, I am aware that she passed some PVTs. Yes, there are some performance validity tests that Ms. Smith did not fail, but these tests are designed to be more specific than sensitive, so they cannot rule out poor effort as much as they can rule in poor effort.—Mike Chafetz, PhD, ABPP-CN

The American Academy of Clinical Neuropsychology's position paper on effort, response bias. and malingering[5] contains the common-sense statement:

When inconsistent or variable effort is shown to be present at any point during an evaluation, a reasonable and conservative conclusion is that all performances and obtained test scores may underestimate actual abilities, even those that occurred during apparent periods of adequate effort.

Many experts reference this position paper in their testimony.

Failed PVTs, average test scores

In some test protocols, examinees fail PVTs but produce average test scores. In those situations, John Kirk will note,

This score is likely an underestimate of their best ability. But it is still average. It's not impaired.

Kyle Boonenotes that some examinees are trying to feign not a memory problem, but rather attention or processing speed problems. If only memory-based PVTs are given, they may pass the PVTs but produce noncredibly low performances on other tests in the battery.

Q: Why did the plaintiff do well on some tests if she was faking?

A: What that signals is the strategy of feigning. Ms. Jones was targeting processing speed and visual spatial skills for exaggerated deficits. She was not targeting memory or language skills. Embedded validity scales show . . .

Noncredible explanations

Paul Green and Thomas Merton wrote a compelling chapter, "Noncredible Explanations of Noncredible Performance on Symptom Validity Tests,"[6] where they describe common, noncredible explanations for why an examinee might fail a PVT other than poor effort. Many experts have been asked whether various factors, such as depression or chronic pain, could be the cause of the PVT failure. Familiarity with the research demonstrating that depressed people and those with chronic pain pass PVTs is helpful.

> *Q: Doctor. Isn't it true that Mr. Plaintiff failed the [PVT] because he was in pain?*
>
> *A: You know, that's a great thought. And you might think that, but the experiment has been done. And it turns out that even people who are given significant pain in the laboratory do not have problems passing these tests. They stick your elbow in a bucket of ice water. It hurts a lot. And folks still do well on the PVTs.*—David Williamson, PhD, ABPP-CN

EXPLAINING SVTS

MMPI validity scales

See Chapter 9, "Explaining Assessment Methods and Tools," for general strategies to introduce the MMPI-2. As noted in Chapter 10, "Visuals," creating a large visual of the MMPI graph is helpful to jurors, particularly if the expert orients them to what scores mean if they are over or under the "clinical significance line." As specific validity scales are described, they can judge for themselves whether the scales are elevated.

Yossef Ben-Porath notes that if the focus of a case is overreporting, he will provide a more specific information about the validity scales when he explains the MMPI:

> *We have different ways of gauging the accuracy of problems that people report. Some of the ways have to do with how common the problems are or uncommon. Other methods have to do with certain combinations that are more or less likely to occur. All of this is based on research that has been published in multiple peer-reviewed scientific journals. And the reason why we have these validity scales to begin with is that before we can reach any conclusion about an individual's psychological problems, we have to have a sense of the quality of the information we are getting—if someone is not processing the items accurately, or overreporting symptoms, or underreporting symptoms. Substantive scales tell us about an individual's psychological functioning. Validity scales tell us about the quality of information that we have to assess people's psychological function. If the validity scales show poor quality, then in some cases we can't reach any conclusions about the person's psychological function because the substantive scale scores are invalid. They are unreliable. That's why we have the validity scales.*

Several experts used the analogy of a thermometer to describe the MMPI-2 symptom validity scales:

> *People who are really experiencing problems can have a mild elevation on a scale like this, but it's like a thermometer: If the temp is 98.6, we think they are doing probably well. 101, we think they are probably sick. 102 we know they are really sick. But if we saw the thermometer, and they had a temp of 120, we would think there was something not right going on. (I use the number 120 because a T score on the MMPI of 120 is a good indication of malingering.)*—Scott Millis, PhD, ABPP-CN

> MMPI-2/RF as thermometer II: Johnny held the thermometer under the hot water too long

> *Our best tool to evaluate the accuracy of an examinee's self-report is the MMPI-2-RF. It has scales that tell us whether people are responding randomly or consistently. And if they are responding consistently, then we look for evidence to see if they are accurately versus overreporting symptoms. It's like a thermometer. There's a certain temperature that is normal, and that is a T-score of 65 or less. And there is a range that shows us elevated temperatures. The scales elevate when examinees report areas of major clinical concerns, like depression, anxiety, or chronic pain. Then there are temperatures that are so elevated they tell us, "Johnny has held the thermometer under the hot water for too long." This shows up as overreporting on the validity indicators which capture overreporting of symptoms. This is not caused by valid clinical concerns; you can't get a temperature that high.*—Glenn Larrabee, PhD, ABPP-CN

> *It's like a thermometer. You know that when you take a temperature, normal is 98.4. Anything above that would be considered having a fever. The higher you go on the scale, the higher your temperature, the worse you feel. Our symptom validity scales are like that: The more symptoms you report, the higher the scale goes. But you don't see temperatures above 105. You know it can't be real.*—Robin Hanks, PhD, ABPP-CN

Goldilocks analogy for MMPI validity

> *There are several levels of analysis. First, we have to determine whether the results of the tests are interpretable. To do this, we examine the consistency of responses—saying too much and saying too little. It's the Goldilocks Rule: You can't have too much and you can't have too little. Nobody has every symptom in the book; nobody has nothing going on with them. It is always a middle ground. What kind of middle ground is the person experiencing here? We often see extreme patterns on either end. Once we decide that the examinee's response pattern is consistent and not too biased, then we can go look and see what kind of symptoms they are experiencing.*—William Barr, PhD, ABPP-CN

Yossef Ben-Porath notes that there have been some attorney-focused publications that have singled out the FBS (Symptom Validity Scale) as an MMPI validity scale that should be subjected to rigorous cross-examination:

The FBS has a bullseye on its back. It tends to be one of the areas of scrutiny on cross. Some attorneys can be fixated on it. This is a scale, though, that has been particularly well validated in these types of evaluations, and is very salient.

A: It's a scale, like all other scales that is based on responses to items. The items in this case are ones that the developer of the scale, a neuropsychologist Paul Lee- Hayley, identified in his research, based on his own research and experience with people who he concluded were malingering. That was the starting point of development. After Lees-Hayley put together the scale, many studies, dozens of studies have since been conducted and published in peer review literature showing that people who have a score above a certain level on the scale are more likely, and the higher the score they are increasingly likely to be over reporting.

Another benefit of using a enlarged MMPI-2 validity graph as a visual is that you can point out that the FBS is a mainstream scale that is included on the computer printout with all the other scales that MMPI publishers have determined are valid, reliable, and helpful enough to include in their computer scoring program.

One strategy on cross examination is to read specific MMPI-2 items to an expert and examine whether in isolation each item shows that the claimant is exaggerating.

Is it beer number 6? He is an alcoholic because he drinks a 12-pack

A recent cross examination trend is to ask experts about the MMPI item by item. For example, items on the FBS scale might be read aloud one by one.

Q: Was my client malingering on this item? Or this one?

A: Let me explain to you why it doesn't work that way. This is the equivalent of saying, "Okay, here is an individual who I consider to be an alcoholic. And you ask me why I consider him to be an alcoholic; well, because he drinks a 12-pack of beer a day. Now we can argue, was it beer number 2 or number 6 or number 9 or number 11 that makes him an alcoholic? He is an alcoholic because he drinks a 12-pack of beer a day. The individual beers don't matter.—Jacobus Donders, PhD, ABPP-CN

Specific item cross gambit on MMPI

Some cross examiners will want to focus on specific test items, particularly with the FBS. Just because an examinee said true or false to [read specific item], most people will hear it and say to themselves, "Why is that evidence of overreporting?"

Q: Just because my client answered true to "x item," are you calling them a liar?

A: I haven't said your client is a liar; you said it. What I explained earlier is that we don't reach conclusions from responses to single items. We look at the score that represents the responses to all of the items. All of the research that we rely on, that has been published, is based on scores on scales, not on responses to specific items. It would be misleading for me to say something to the jury about this individual based on his response to a particular item.—Yossef Ben-Porath, PhD, ABPP

An item-by-item strategy is not unique to cross examination about MMPI scales:

I have seen attorneys use questions from mood questionnaires intended to elicit information about depression and anxiety. Attorneys can always use items that were endorsed or not endorsed and mock the expert for that. Any self-report questionnaire—you can pick one or two things and show that the specific question is odd or irrelevant. But the expert needs to return to the point of the whole questionnaire—to give an overall sense of the person's personality. It's not about the specific question. (Attorneys in my jurisdiction can ask questions about specific test items because all the raw data is produced in this jurisdiction prior to each case.)- Attorney, Anonymous

Other indicators of symptom validity

When an examinee endorses ALL symptoms

The extreme endorsement of symptoms makes the case. When an examinee endorses all symptoms, on any type of checklist, from a primary care review of symptoms, to a symptom validity scale, they appear to be hypochondriacs.

On a review of symptoms, they endorsed ***every*** *symptom . . .*—Nancy Hebben, PhD, ABPP-CN

We are all liars sometimes

Who among us is not a liar? We have all lied at some point. Have you seen the movie "Ferris Bueller's Day Off," starring Matthew Broderick? I have to admit there were times that I told my mom when I was in the fourth grade that I was sick so I didn't have to go to school that day. Is that terrible? Do we all learn that there are times we can feign illnesses to get out of something? You know what? It works so much better if you ate something that is not sitting well with you. In your head, you can say to yourself, "I really don't feel that well." Now if you were given the options to go to school or go to the fair, it would make a big difference whether you felt well enough to go. Ferris Bueller had a fun time on the day he skipped school. It is sometimes hard to tell, just from watching someone's behavior, whether he or she is feigning illness. We need objective measure.—Martin Rohling, PhD

David Hartman explains negative response bias in a common-sense manner:

Look, when Dr. Other Expert asked about all the severe symptoms in this area, Mr. Jones endorsed all of them. The problem with that is that Dr. Other Expert didn't check to see whether this reflected the examinee's tendency to admit to any problems that sound severe. I asked Mr. Jones questions that were preposterous, like, "When you stretch, does your vision change from red to green?" or "When you have double vision, do you still have it when you close one eye?" Both of those are extremely unlikely. They just don't happen with real patients, but Mr. Jones endorsed both symptoms. When patients endorse severe legitimate and severe preposterous symptoms, you have to understand their endorsements as evidence that they are willing to admit to anything that sounds severe that they believe will support their claim.

Explaining the SIRS

On the Structured Interview of Reported Symptoms-2 (SIRS-2) people whose scores are similar to Mr. Smith's are considered to be exaggerating their symptom. In Mr. Smith's case, here were the kinds of things he was saying on this instrument [I try not to give specific examples, but more general examples, but I will be specific if pressed]. (Or,) In Mr. Smith's case, he was saying "yes" to almost all of the symptoms, no matter how far-fetched.—Ira K. Packer, PhD, ABPP (Forensic)

Kyle Boone points out symptom validity scales are not equally sensitive:

The Detailed Assessment of Posttraumatic Stress and Trauma Symptom Inventory validity scales are weak and were not validated in a medical-legal context. They include questions for highly unlikely symptoms that would not be endorsed by, for example, people feigning symptoms in the context of concussion, such as extremely inappropriate social behaviors, markedly impaired visual perception, etc.

In cases where opposing experts are making conclusions about the validity of symptom report based on SVT scales that are not sensitive, the expert may need to have the sensitivity statistics at his or her fingertips to prepare for a cross-examination question like "Doctor, isn't it true that Ms. Plaintiff passed Dr. Other Expert's symptom validity measures?"

COACHING/PVT AND SVT TEST SECURITY

Manfred Greiffenstein noted that unless he has "smoking gun evidence" in a case, he will not introduce the idea of coaching:

I think coaching is hard. There are too many tests. It is asking for trouble if you indirectly ethically attack the plaintiff's attorney. There is not accumulated scientific data on this. Answering a question about coaching with "I haven't formed an opinion on that" or "There is not sufficient evidence one way or the other" is a powerfully ambiguous answer. You haven't ruled anything out. It gets the jury thinking about it.

There are some cases, though, where the fact of coaching is indisputable. For example, Bob Denney shares a case where an examinee learned from one round of his courtroom testimony about how he failed a PVT. The defendant was in the courtroom as the judge asked in-depth questions about the nature of the PVT and why the defendant's scores looked noncredible. Thus, he had clear, documented "coaching" on what not to do on the test in the future.

I had a case on a very-high-net-worth embezzlement case. The defense was that he had dementia. He was sent to me and he came in grossly exaggerating—noncredible stuff like not remembering his address of 20 years or his shoe size for a man who was otherwise cognitively intact for everyday interactions.

The issue was his competency to stand trial. I testified that on the Medical Symptom Validity Test, his pattern was the same as what simulators produce. It didn't match individuals with dementia; it was just the opposite. The judge wasn't fully convinced. He was halfway convinced and so he sent the patient to another evaluator who thankfully also gave him the MSVT, and this time the defendant aced it.

At first I thought it was a problem, but then I realized that this proved my case. Number one, it proved he did not fail the MVST because of dementia with me in my assessment session. It also verified that he could learn from my teaching in the courtroom! I wrote a follow-up report and testified again. The fact that he did well on this test proved the point that it was not because of dementia that he failed the MSVT during my exam, and it verified that he could learn from my courtroom testimony. The judge concluded he was competent to proceed.

PVTS WITH DEMENTIA PATIENTS

John McSweeny notes that he uses performance validity tests in workups for dementia. However,

It is difficult, though, because depending on how demented the people are, the tests may have false positives. It depends on the situation. Most people are very motivated to do their best in assessments for capacity. They want to retain capacity—that is, the legal right to make certain decisions for themselves.

Dominic Carone explains the use of PVTs in cases of dementia this way:

These are tests that to the vast majority of people are designed to look challenging or difficult, but objectively we know that they are very easy and that patients with significant neurological compromise can typically pass them. But there really is no way to create a performance test of effort and motivation that is completely devoid of some level of cognitive ability. And so, because of that, if a particular patient (and it typically would occur in an advanced dementia case) reaches such a severe level of neurological or cognitive decline, they very well may obtain some scores that fall below the cutoffs that we use for these particular tests.

There is a particular set of tests (and I don't necessarily say this in a deposition in terms of identifying them, but it would be Green's Word Memory Test or the MSVT) where research shows that there is a pattern of performance that is much more consistent with advanced dementia as opposed to a person who is not putting forth their best effort. I look for that pattern, and so when looked at in this way, some PVTs can actually help make a dementia diagnosis.

FINALLY, ESTABLISHING RAPPORT IN FORENSIC EVALUATIONS TO IMPROVE EFFORT

Tedd Judd points out that there is an enormous literature on detecting poor effort but little literature on fostering good effort:

> *I give assurance, not warning, about effort testing prior to forensic evaluations. For example, "You said that (Dr. X, your wife, the insurance company) doesn't believe you . . ." "In these kinds of situations sometimes (the court, the insurance company, the university) is concerned that you might not have told the truth or done your best on the tests." "That's why I include in the evaluation ways of measuring and knowing that you have done your best so that I can say with confidence that you did your best and that what I found really shows how your brain is functioning and the things you can and cannot do."*

NOTES

1. Heilbronner, R. L., Sweet, J. J., Morgan, J. E., Larrabee, G. J., Millis, S. R.; Conference Participants. (2009). American Academy of Clinical Neuropsychology consensus conference statement on the neuropsychological assessment of effort, response bias, and malingering. *Clinical Neuropsychologist, 23*(7), 1093–1129.
2. Bush, S. S., Ruff, R. M., Tröster, A. I., Barth, J. T., Koffler, S. P., Pliskin, N. H., . . . Silver, C. H. (2005). Symptom validity assessment: Practice issues and medical necessity. *Archives of Clinical Neuropsychology, 20*, 419–426.
3. Slick, D. J., & Sherman, E. M. S. (2012). Differential diagnosis of malingering and related clinical presentations. In E. M. S. Sherman & B. L. Brooks (Eds.), *Pediatric forensic neuropsychology*. New York: Oxford University Press, pp. 113–135.
4. Friedman, R. (2007). *Polarizing the Case*. Portland, OR: Trial Guides.
5. Heilbronner, R. L., Sweet, J. J., Morgan, J. E., Larrabee, G. J., Millis, S. R.; Conference Participants. (2009). American Academy of Clinical Neuropsychology consensus conference statement on the neuropsychological assessment of effort, response bias, and malingering. *Clinical Neuropsychologist, 23*(7), 1093–1129, p. 1103.
6. Green, P., & Merton, T. (2012). Noncredible explanations of noncredible performance on symptom validity tests. In D. A. Carone & S. S. Bush (Eds.), *Mild traumatic brain injury: Symptom validity assessment and malingering*. New York: Oxford University Press, pp. 73–99.

12 Concussion

MANFRED GREIFFENSTEIN POINTED out that concussion has become the driving force behind forensic neuropsychology practice:

> *Every medical specialty has a diagnosis that drives practice. For example, without BFGs (big fat guys) and sleep apnea, there would be no sleep labs. Rheumatologists see an enormous number of arthritis cases. Endocrinologists primarily treat diabetes. Concussion is the dominant driving force for forensic neuropsychology.*

In the course of interviews, almost all of the forensic neuropsychologists involved in civil litigation reported that their primary case type was concussion—therefore, concussion earned its own chapter. Moderate and severe traumatic brain injuries are covered in Chapter 13, "Specific Psychiatric and Neurological Disorders."

CONCUSSION VERSUS MILD TRAUMATIC BRAIN INJURY

In speaking with jurors and colleagues about concussion, many experts have followed the lead of the Department of Defense and Veterans Administration[1] and have specifically chosen the term *concussion* over *mild traumatic brain injury* (mTBI).

> *I follow the Department of Defense's recommendation to use the word concussion rather than mTBI. mTBI can be confusing to jurors and patients as it sounds worse than it is.*—Nancy Hebben, PhD, ABPP-CN

I don't use the term mild traumatic brain injury. *I use the term* concussion *because the connotations of mild brain injury sound more significant than they actually are.*—Robin Hanks, PhD, ABPP-CN

On cross, some attorneys will ask why you are not using the term mTBI.

Q: Why don't you use the term mild traumatic brain injury?

A: I prefer to use the word concussion. Because that most accurately describes the temporary nature of the injury.—Nancy Hebben, PhD, ABPP-CN

EXPLAINING WHAT A CONCUSSION IS

Many experts begin their direct testimony in concussion cases by explaining to the jury what a concussion is. Michael McCrea shares how he structures the flow of information:

> When I explain concussions in court I use the same format of the lectures I give at professional meetings. First, here is the existing science and what we know about the acute and subacute effects of concussions. Then, here is the common and expected time course of recovery. And here are the factors that predict normal and abnormal recovery. I then move to the specifics of the case: Here are the factors in this case that will affect recovery and outcome. Here is what I say for the immediate effects:
>
> *We know that mTBI or concussion results in a disruption of normal brain function at a cellular and metabolic level. It is a widespread chemical change. We can't say, where is the concussion on the CT scan or MRI- because concussion is not a lesion-based injury like stroke. There is a sequence of neurometabolic changes that occurs as a result of the concussion. And we are learning more and more about how that sequence of events play out. It is called the neurometabolic cascade. Almost immediately, the brain begins to return to its normal state.*

See below for subsequent components of Dr. McCrea's description of concussion. Here are additional, vivid ways of describing the acute effects of concussion.

Concussion is like a computer with the plug off

A concussion is a temporary interruption of brain function following a blunt force to the head. It is a temporary interruption in the working of brain cells, but there is no actual destruction of the wiring. A computer analogy can explain. If you shut off the power to a computer, that's a concussion. When you turn the computer back on, it works; there is no permanent damage. If you take a hammer to the hard drive, that's a severe traumatic brain injury.—Manfred Greiffenstein, PhD, ABPP-CN

What a concussion is

A concussion is a transient change in brain metabolism. We are not talking about a bruise on the brain or areas of dead cells. If you look at athletes with concussion, their

symptoms resolve within 1 to 7 days; with the general population, within 3 months. Everyone gets back to baseline.—Nancy Hebben, PhD, ABPP-CN

HOW DO WE DIAGNOSE CONCUSSION?

A concussion is diagnosed by neurological indicators at the time of the injury. Nancy Hebben will explain to jurors,

You can't diagnose concussion with neuropsychological tests

> *Just because a person has a low score on a memory test does not tell us anything about the initial injury. You cannot work backward from a neuropsychological assessment to tell whether a concussion happened. The medical records at the time of the event tell us that.*

A common error of clinicians not well trained in concussion management is relying on the presence and severity of symptoms months or years following a possible concussive event as a way to determine whether a concussion occurred in the first place—for example, concluding that if Ms. Plaintiff is complaining of memory symptoms 3 years after a slip-and-fall accident, it must mean she had a concussion, even though she never lost consciousness, had no mental status change, and vividly recalls the accident. Robin Hanks will help jurors understand that relying solely on people's complaints to make a medical diagnosis is not good medicine:

There are few areas of medicine where people's complaints alone are used for diagnosis

> *There are a lot of reasons why people experience complaints. There are very few areas of medicine where people's complaints alone are used for diagnosis. There's literature that shows that people's reports of their memory problems do not correlate with their objective scores on memory testing. Self-report is not a good indicator of true dysfunction. That's why to diagnose a concussion we have objective neurological indicators.*

Similarly, Michael McCrea will tell jurors that concussion diagnosis is based only on the acute accident mechanics:

> *The injury diagnosis is based on the reported mechanism at the time of the accident. That is different than what the diagnosis might be 3 years later when you are called in to a case. It is important to make that distinction. Some "concussion" cases, where there was no LOC, no alteration of consciousness, no symptoms for 3 months: Those are not consistent with a concussion.*

Here are clear explanations for jurors of how a concussion is diagnosed. In my own practice, I will put up a visual of the Centers for Disease Control,[2] Department of Defense,[3] World Health Organization,[4] or American Academy of Rehabilitation Medicine mTBI/concussion criteria[5] set while I am offering this explanation:

When someone has a bit enough hit to their head, their brain reacts with an immediate and dramatic change in cell functioning. It's temporary, but it's a very significant change while it lasts. This is known as a concussion. It takes a really big hit—a G force of about 90 or greater. That's a really big hit!

How do we know that the brain is concussed? We can tell because at the moment of impact there are three neurological changes we can see from the outside that reflect the temporary change in brain cell function. All three don't have to be present, but we need to see at least one to know that the cellular cascade of changes, the concussion, is taking place.

First, the person may lose consciousness. They are out cold.

Second, there is confusion. Serious confusion. The person is talking out of their head, not able to follow directions,

The third sign is what we call post traumatic amnesia—the person is so confused they can't create new memories for a period of time. The classic example is the football player who goes back to play in the game and cannot remember it afterwards.

The brain is designed to be protected from hits—think of little kids, they fall and hit their heads all the time without getting concussions—we have our own built in helmets—our skulls, and our brains are floating in liquid and covered with tough membranes—our brains are literally built to take big hits without any problem. Most of the times when someone hits their head they hurt their head- they may get a bruise or need stitches, or their head hurts, but they don't get a concussion. The presence of one of those three things tells us it is a concussion.

Robin Hanks' description of how a concussion is diagnosed educates jurors that there is a spectrum of severity of initial neurological indicators that all still qualify as concussion:

The only way that a concussion can be diagnosed is based on neurologic indicators at the time of the injury. Here are the indicators: loss of consciousness, alteration of consciousness, Glasgow Coma Scale score.

With the Glasgow Coma Scale, this is a measurement that is done with the ambulance personnel that looks at the level of alertness, the person's responsiveness to questions, and how they are moving their arms and legs. The scale is numbered from 3 to 15, and 15 is a score that you or I would get. For a concussion, you have to score between a 13 and a 15.

And with the alteration of consciousness, there has to be a significant change of consciousness so the person is knocked out briefly. You can actually have a loss of consciousness up to 30 minutes and still have a concussion. (Jurors usually say, "Ohh!")

With posttraumatic confusion, you may be disoriented and confused and not remember events while you are confused. But you can have that up to 24 hours and still have a concussion (at which point the 5-minute period of confusion claimed by the plaintiff seems minor).

But remember, it is not uncommon for people who have not had a concussion to not remember all of the events of the accidents. There are a lot of things happening at once, people are in shock, and our memories are not like video recorders.

How a concussion is diagnosed

A concussion is diagnosed by the injury characteristics: whether or not there is an alteration of mental status (for example, recalling the impact and/or being confused), whether or not there was a loss of consciousness, and the Glasgow Coma Scale score. These injury characteristics are often present in the records.—Nancy Hebben, PhD, ABPP-CN

Explaining mTBI diagnosis

There are different severities of TBI and they have different characteristics and different outcomes. The first step is to look at how severe the injury was. The way to do that is to look at the ER and ambulance records to see if there was a period of unconsciousness. And if so, how long and how deeply was the person unconscious. We also look for evidence of post-traumatic amnesia, or was the examinee confused and disoriented, as observed and documented by the emergency medical technicians or ER doctors.

One way to measure depth of unconsciousness is with the Glasgow Coma Scale. There are 15 possible points. A score of 13/15 to 15/15 is the range of mild traumatic brain injury. 9–12 is moderate. 8 and below is severe.

We also look at the duration of loss of consciousness. If the person is unconscious less than a half hour, are confused and disoriented less than a day, and have a normal CT scan, then they fall into the category of mild TBI or concussion.—Glenn Larrabee, PhD, ABPP-CN

The case wouldn't qualify for a research project

Over half of the cases I see that have been diagnosed with mTBI or concussion, the injury wouldn't even qualify for a research project on mTBI. They don't have any of the criteria.—Glenn Larrabee, PhD, ABPP-CN

You can't be like an economist assuming inflation

You can't do what an economist does and assume inflation. You can't assume a brain injury and then go from there. You have to prove there was a brain injury.—Tom Boll, PhD, ABPP-CN

I won't get into a squabble about a momentary loss of consciousness. It literally doesn't matter

Q: Was it a concussion?

A: As long as the loss of consciousness was not more than 30 minutes, Glasgow Coma Scale was 13 to 15, anterograde amnesia was <24 hours, and if standard brain

imaging was normal, the outcomes are very good. There is no permanent cognitive change. I will not get into a squabble about whether there was a momentary loss of consciousness. It literally does not matter.—Kyle Boone, PhD, ABPP-CN

On cross examination, the Zurich guidelines may be brought in as a way to claim that a person had a concussion, without any of the neurological indicators (no loss of consciousness [LOC], alteration of consciousness, or posttraumatic amnesia [PTA])required by the Centers for Disease Control, World Health Organization, American College of Rehabilitation Medicine, or Department of Defense criteria. The guidelines have been widely criticized for having low specificity due to utilizing a long list of nonspecific indicators that have high base rates in the general population and in people who have other types of injuries and illness.[6]

Q: Doctor. Isn't it true that Mr. Plaintiff does meet the Zurich Criteria for concussion?!

A: Look at the outcome research. How do they set up the groups? It is based on the CDC, WHO, ACRM research of loss of consciousness, alteration of consciousness, post traumatic amnesia. It is not based on the very nebulous, overly inclusive research of the Zurich guidelines.—Anonymous

Criteria I don't agree with

I have no trouble disagreeing with published books or articles. You are a professional. You have training and experience in the field and the ability to review the literature.

"In my experience and knowledge of the research, that doesn't fit."—Glenn Larrabee, PhD, ABPP-CN

In some cases, it is not clear whether or not neurological indicators were present as the plaintiff reports they happened, but they were so fleeting that the problem was not noticed by first responders. Tom Boll makes the point that the fact that the neurological indicators were so fleeting that no one was clear they actually happened speaks to the severity of the injury.

I think of neuropsychology and brain injury kind of like building a rocket ship. You have to have a certain kind of platform to get it off the ground. If you are shooting a little nickel-and-dime firework up, you just stick it in the ground and light it and it goes up a little bit. But if you want to shoot a rocket ship up to the moon, you are going to be shooting it up from a great big platform. And the brain injury is the platform. If the brain injury involves no unconsciousness that anyone can identify, and maybe or maybe not posttraumatic amnesia and retrograde amnesia, and no complications like bleeding or a skull fracture or a seizure, and the MRI and everything else is normal: You can agree, carefully, that none of those things are required to establish a brain injury. But after each one, you can also say that each time you take one away, you are taking away an amount of severity.

Q: Doctor, isn't it true that you don't have to lose consciousness to have a concussion?

A: No, you don't have to lose consciousness; you can still have an injury. If you don't lose consciousness, it tells you about the severity of the injury.

Q: Doctor, isn't it true that you don't have to have posttraumatic amnesia to have a concussion?

A: No, you don't have to have posttraumatic amnesia, but if you don't it tells you about the severity of the injury.

Q: Isn't it true that you can have a normal MRI scan and still have had a concussion?

A: You don't have any complications like bleeding or seizures, but if you don't have it, it tells you about the severity level.

You say, *"Yes, you can have a brain injury without these things, but it tells you about the severity level."* And in the end, you can say, *"He might have had some kind of an injury, but it couldn't be very much. And if this 'nothing burger of an injury' produces really bad scores, then those scores came from something else."*

EXPLAINING THE DIAGNOSTIC INDICATORS FOR CONCUSSION

Loss of consciousness

Often the story about the presence or severity of initial neurological indicators changes over time. For example, the defendant/plaintiff might tell the ambulance drivers and ER staff that there was no LOC. As the story is told over a few years after the accident, though, medical records show him telling clinicians there was an LOC of ever-greater duration. Because human memory is fallible, and often there are external and/or psychological incentives to exaggerate the severity of the accident, careful review of the day-of-accident medical, police, and ambulance records is very important to establish whether the indicators were indeed present.

When the story changes

When a plaintiff's story about whether they lost consciousness changes over time, it's much more helpful for the jury to hear an explanation for this that doesn't involve accusing the plaintiff of lying.

"People have to tell the story of their car accident over and over again, to many doctors and other people. When someone is asked over and over again whether they lost consciousness, they might eventually think, 'Well, maybe I did.'"—Nancy Hebben, PhD, ABPP-CN

Posttraumatic amnesia

Examinees are often very motivated to share specific details of the accident that they recall, like the fact that they noticed the other driver was on their cellphone, or the driver after the accident came over to the car and offered an apology. Eliciting this information in the clinical interview lays a solid foundation for an opinion about whether or not the

examinee had PTA. PTA is a confusional state so severe that the person cannot retain new memories. They may be conscious, walking, and talking, but they are confused and cannot remember events from moment to moment. When PTA is present, ambulance drivers will note that the patient repeatedly asked what happened, even after being told each time they were in a car accident. At the point where medical personnel note that the patient is fully oriented (that is, to person, place, time, and current situation), it is because the patient now has a good answer to "what happened to you?" They have emerged from PTA.

Explaining PTA

For PTA I rely on the Department of Defense management of concussion publication. I couldn't have written it better myself. It is really helpful and useful. I will send a copy of it to attorneys. One can refer to it on the stand.

It's a period of disorientation after regaining consciousness. The end of the period of PTA is when the patient becomes oriented times three. That means, oriented to who they are, where they are, and the time. During the period of confusion, the last component of orientation to return is orientation to time. Thus, the point of time in which they are documented to be oriented x three, is the end of PTA. During that time period of PTA you can't count on them laying down reliable memories. I used to watch a detective show as a kid. The detective gets hit on the head, is unconscious, wakes up, shake off the cobwebs, and gets up to chase after the bad guy. It doesn't work that way. When you wake up after losing consciousness from a TBI you are confused for a period of time. You might not remember there was an accident. You go through a process where you are confused and not processing new memories. That period of PTA tells you how severe the injury is. If PTA is less than 24 hours, that is classified as a mild TBI or concussion. If it goes beyond a day to 7 days, it is a moderate traumatic brain injury. If it goes beyond a week it is a severe traumatic brain injury.—Glenn Larrabee, PhD, ABPP-CN

PTA: bucket of foamy water

When you have a sufficient blow on the head, the parts of the brain that take in or imprint new information in the brain, the hippocampi, are temporarily interrupted at a chemical level, so they are not working properly. Then slowly but surely, the chemicals that control these processes slowly come back to working order. And it takes time to be able to imprint new memories normally. It's like if you shake a container full of water with soap in it, it will get foamy. While it is foamy it is hard to lay down new memories. It takes a while for the foam to dissipate and return to normal.—Greg Lee, PhD, ABPP-CN

That period of time where a person is confused and doesn't lay down new memories is called posttraumatic amnesia. Someone can come visit them and walk out of the room, and 5 minutes later the patient doesn't realize they have been in there.

(If I am opining that there is not PTA):

"The examinee has described details of the accident right before and after; there is no evidence of PTA."—Leslie Rosenstein, PhD, ABPP-CN

When people have a TBI and they are really struggling to remember the accident, they are often under the impression that the memory is just suppressed. "I can't remember the accident because it was traumatic." This can really bother people. I explain PTA like this:

With a TBI, it is like the tape recorder of memory in your brain was just turned off in that moment of impact. There is no recording.—Shelley Peery, PhD

Like a 2-hour delay saying "ouch"

Sometimes a person will have exquisite memories of what happened after an accident –who was at the scene, who said what to whom, they're refusing an ambulance, etc. Then they will say that several hours later, they have no memories for the rest of the day or the next two days.

Posttraumatic amnesia, if it occurs, starts immediately after impact. Saying you can remember events following the impact but not events 2 hours later is like bumping your elbow on a table and then 2 hours later saying "ouch!"—Nancy Hebben, PhD, ABPP-CN

The "2-hour delay saying 'ouch' " analogy can also be used in situations where symptoms that are attributed to a concussion appear months after a blow to the head.

One problem with determining whether someone had PTA months or years following an accident is that many people expect their memories to work like a video recorder. If a doctor says, "Did you lose memory for the hours or day after the accident?" Most people will think back and not have crisp, clear, detailed memories of that day: "Well, I can recall being in the ambulance, and kind of in the ER, but other than that, it is all a blur." Often clinicians write down, "Spotty memories for the event: evidence of PTA." But hold on: Think of the most memorable days in your life—your son's graduation from elementary school, the day you got a promotion. Do you remember a lot of details? What you ate? Who drove? Exactly what was said? Probably not. We all have "spotty memories" for specific days that occurred in our pasts.

If a person can remember information from immediately after the accident, such as police speaking to them, and what happened after they got out of the car, there is no PTA. Our memories are not like video players; no person will recall every single detail after an accident.—Nancy Hebben, PhD, ABPP-CN

"Patchy recall" as evidence for PTA

"Patchy recall" is a big issue. Many opposing experts will claim that a patient has "patchy recall" for events postinjury and use that as the sole criterion to document concussion. I spend a lot of time asking examinees about their recollections after the

accident: "What is your first memory after the accident? What do you remember next? What next? What next?" I often find very detailed memories that contradict "patchy recall." It is incorrect to assume that a patient will recall every single event after an accident 3 years earlier, just as uninjured people do not recall every aspect of a sequence of events from an experience 3 years ago. And when patients get to the hospital, they are often administered sedating medications while their orthopedic injuries are managed, and then end up with loss of memory for events in the hospital, but this should not be construed as posttraumatic amnesia.—Kyle Boone, PhD, ABPP-CN

Dr. Boone makes an important point. If an accident involves orthopedic issues, pain medication may be administered at some point after the injury. Powerful pain medication can alter consciousness and make it difficult to lay down new memories. A careful review of ambulance and ER records will provide a timeline for what medications were administered when.

HEAD INJURY VERSUS BRAIN INJURY

If the acute injury neurological indicators for a concussion are not present, experts can contrast the presence of a "head injury" versus a "brain injury." It is important to note that the brain is designed with a built-in helmet (or skull): It's wrapped in tough membranes and it's floating in liquid. It is literally designed to take falls and blows to the head in stride.

Some diagnosis codes are "head injury" and those can be used when there is a bump on the head but not necessarily a brain injury. We have all had bumps on our heads, or we have had toddlers with goose eggs on their head, and they are fine.—Leslie Rosenstein, PhD, ABPP-CN

First thing the doctors have to do is demonstrate that there was an injury to the brain. Not to the head, like "I cut myself shaving" or "I bonked my head on a counter." There are markers that show there was an injury to the brain—a loss of consciousness, no memory of the event, a change in mental status. You can't have zero criteria; you have to have at least one.—Tom Boll, PhD, ABPP-CN

g-force necessary for concussion

From research using helmet sensors, what we know is that it generally takes 90 to 100 g to cause a concussion in an athlete. If you translate that to a normal person's experience, that's like driving your car into a brick wall at 25 miles an hour. (The plaintiff had a roll of toilet paper fall on their head at a grocery store). The possible g-forces from this injury, it isn't even close to that.—William Barr, PhD, ABPP-CN

SYMPTOMS OF CONCUSSION AND NATURAL RECOVERY CURVE

Dose–response relationship

The dose–response relationship in TBI is summed up beautifully by Tom Boll: "Big injury, big damage. Little injury, little damage."

> *We have a lot of good science that shows us that there is a dose–response relationship in brain injury. For example, if you know that somebody has had a significant brain injury, they are going to have a lot more problems in the real world than people with a concussion. (I will draw a line on a flip chart.) It is a very clear relationship. The longer you are unconscious, the more significant your injury, the more deficits you have. (I will bring in Meyers/Millis paper straight line and draw it on the chart.[7]) Here are people who have had a concussion: This is where their thinking skills are, where their functioning is, and it is the same as people who have not had an injury at 1 year. This has been replicated over and over and over. . . .*—Robin Hanks, PhD, ABPP-CN

My severe traumatic brain injured patients don't report this many symptoms

I see a lot of brain injury. And my brain injury patients don't report this many symptoms. They don't have this level of impairment. They don't need the amount of supervision or treatment as Ms. X has with a concussion.—Robin Hanks, PhD, ABPP-CN

Is a bruise on the arm as debilitating as a compound fracture?

Is a bruise on the arm as debilitating as a hairline fracture versus a compound fracture? How much force does it take to create a bruise versus a compound fracture? This is like the difference between a concussion and a severe traumatic brain injury. A concussion is like a bruise: It goes away.—Martin Rohling, PhD

Expected recovery course

Natural recovery curve for concussion

The natural recovery process for concussion is 7–10 days. A few months at the most. We don't need any treatments. The symptoms spontaneously recover, at which point people have great recoveries.—Robin Hanks, PhD, ABPP-CN

How long does it take for concussion symptoms to clear up?

Studies have shown over and over and over that it takes 7 to10 days for symptoms of a concussion to go away. If you are older it can take a little while longer to recover. If you have had a more significant injury, with a longer length of unconsciousness, it could take a little while longer, but by three months, there are typically no effects.—Robin Hanks, PhD, ABPP-CN

Worse thinking scores 3 months pregnant than 3 months post-concussion

The research is clear, by three months, the effects of a concussion on thinking are approaching zero. To give you a comparison, the effects of being three months pregnant on thinking abilities are greater than those seen three months post-concussion.—David Schretlen, PhD, ABPP-CN

Explaining concussion

Everyone recovers within weeks to months. The literature shows that everyone recovers. That doesn't mean individuals 6 months or a year later people might not report having problems- but the problems, the medical literature indicates, are not due to concussion. The problems are due to anxiety, depression, or ADHD or other things. This is what the literature shows.—Rodney Vanderploeg, PhD, ABPP-CN

For a short period of time

Of course, if you have a concussion, you will have some problems—for a short period of time. It is very normal to be a little irritable, to have some concentration problems, to have a headache. For a short period of time. Research shows that those problems that arise after a concussion are present only for a short period of time.—Jacobus Donders, PhD, ABPP-CN

The typical course of recovery from a single, uncomplicated mTBI per the civilian literature is complete recovery in 30 to 60 days. Although athletes show evidence of complete recovery within one week.

For athletes, researchers take a whole bunch of football players preseason, and get a whole bunch of data on their thinking abilities, and balance, and symptom reports. Then they test them again right after a concussion, and every day for a week after the concussion. And they find that by a week out, their thinking abilities are the same as before a concussion, and their balance is the same as before the concussion, and their symptom report is the same as prior to being concussed. They have a complete recovery. In the civilian sector, there is full and complete recovery by 60–90 days. In multiple studies.—Glenn Larrabee, PhD, ABPP-CN

In my own practice, I like to bring in the Sports as a Laboratory Research (SLAM) model because the story of the research is compelling and interesting to jurors. I will put up the recovery curve graphics from Michael McCrea and colleagues' *Journal of the American Medical Association* article[8] as I am telling this story:

For a long time, we didn't have great research about what happened to people's brains after a concussion. We had great animal research, because we could do those awful studies where researchers would give a monkey a concussion, then measure what happened in terms of their brain function. Of course, we couldn't do that to humans.

Then a group of researchers realized, wait—we could use sports as our laboratory! In some sports, like football, players are pretty likely to get concussions. So the researchers enrolled thousands of high school and college and NFL players and gave them neuropsychological tests, like I gave Ms. Smith, before the season started, before the player got a concussion, so they knew exactly how their brains worked before a concussion happened. Then they would just sit and wait like spiders all season. As soon as a player got a concussion, they had researchers right on the sidelines, measuring symptoms like loss of consciousness or confusion or problems with balance. They even wired the players' helmets to see how big a force or hit was necessary to cause a concussion. Then they measured the concussed player's brain function with thinking tests—right away, then hours later, then the next day, and every day for a week, 2 weeks, 3 weeks.

They found that concussions cause a really big initial change in how the brain works—confusion, memory issues, balance problems. It's really a big deal. But almost immediately, the symptoms began to reverse. For players, most were 100% better within a couple of hours or days, and 100% were better within a week. By a week, there were literally no differences in how the player's brains worked compared with their teammates who didn't get concussion and compared to their own baselines.

Those studies were replicated with nonathletes, and the pattern was the same. It took a little while longer, but everyone was back to normal by 3 months.

"POSTCONCUSSIVE SYNDROME"

> *This is a clinical diagnosis based largely on self-reported symptoms, and the challenge we have is that the long list of symptoms are not only evident in a whole host of conditions other than brain injury, but they also have a very common occurrence or base rate in the general public population—college students and normal adults. Symptoms alone are very problematic in making the diagnosis of postconcussion syndrome.*—Michael McCrea, PhD, ABPP-CN

Many experts commented that they will put up a graphic from Dr. McCrea's book *Mild Traumatic Brain Injury*[9] showing how common postconcussion syndrome (PCS) symptoms are in healthy college students or people with depression as they are explaining the commonplace nature of these symptoms.

Commonplace nature of PCS

Several years ago, when I started at the VA in Tampa, I got funding for an aging and memory study. My colleagues knew about it. A physician colleague in his 50s got in the elevator with me and said, "You know, I'm getting a little worried about my memory." And I said to him, "How busy are you?" And a lightbulb went off over his head: A new group of med students had just started, he was worried they were going to kill somebody; he was running multiple grants; he had a heavy patient caseload. He made that connection right away.

But if you are someone who has been told by several different doctors that you had brain damage, and they tell you things like, "You have to rest your brain," and the first time you have one of these normal common symptoms, the first thing you will think is, "Oh no! That's my brain injury and I am never going to get better!" And then of course you get more stressed, and have more headaches, and are more distracted and forgetful. It's a vicious circle.—Glenn Larrabee, PhD, ABPP-CN

Fever and PCS symptoms

It's like a fever. Fever is a real phenomenon. It's a fact. You can die from too high a fever. But fever is nonspecific. There are certain diseases where a fever is more likely to be present. We use fever to indicate some underlying illness, and the problem is figuring out which illness. High blood pressure is the same way. When it is present, you have to figure out what is causing it. Some people have a naturally higher blood pressure, so it is premorbid. Just like someone can have a higher baseline body temperature. So, you need to figure out if these symptoms are just their baseline. It doesn't mean you ignore it; you don't say, "The fever is not important." You have to figure out where the fever is coming from. I see postconcussive symptoms the same way. They are not specific, and no one can argue that they are. My job as a neuropsychologist is to make a careful analysis of where the symptoms are coming from. Maybe the person has a mood issue. This is called differential diagnosis. And that's my job as a neuropsychologist.—Keith Yeates, PhD, ABPP-CN

HELPING JURORS UNDERSTAND AN ALTERNATIVE NARRATIVE

If a single, uncomplicated concussion isn't to blame for Ms. Plaintiff's report of multiple symptoms and inability to work a year after the accident, what is? Diagnosis threat, the "good old days" hypothesis, symptom magnification, and iatrogenesis are among the psychological phenomena that can account for persistence of symptoms in many cases.

Recall the importance of narrative in jurors' ability to make use of information in order to do their job in court. If one side is telling a noncredible narrative about a single, uncomplicated concussion causing catastrophic, permanent disability, the competing narrative should not be limited to, "That makes no sense." Rather, (just as in good clinical assessment work) the expert should help the jurors understand the often complex, interacting factors at work perpetuating the idea or experience of the symptoms. Nancy Hebben notes,

When concussion symptoms worsen over time or new ones develop, it is important to recognize that symptoms are just people's complaints. The neuropsychological investigation seeks to find out why is the person maintaining these symptoms: Are there psychiatric issues? family systems issues? Is the person trying to pull the wool over my eyes? Somatization? Technically, we don't have to come up with an explanation; we could just say, "This is inconsistent with the possible effects of concussion." But having a deeper and more complete understanding of what is behind the symptoms helps me with the picture of the whole person, even if I never share it with the jury. Telling this more complete narrative of a person helps make your testimony more accessible to a jury. They don't want experts just coming in and saying a person is feigning.

Robin Hanks begins with acknowledging and expressing empathy for the symptoms:

I have no doubt that Mrs. Jones is having problems . . .

I have no doubt that Ms. Jones is having problems. But the problems are not caused by a traumatic brain injury. Her problems need to be fixed by mental health treatment.

This is clearly not concussion.

There are some cases where I don't make the specific call, but rather share possibilities with juries.

This is not concussion. I can't tell you what it is. Here are the kinds of things you could consider it being . . . —Nancy Hebben, PhD, ABPP-CN

Here are strategies for describing common, alternate explanations to neurologically non-credible symptoms.

Diagnosis threat

Diagnosis threat, or the idea that people will act in stereotypical ways consistent with a particular diagnosis, was first applied to concussion patients by Suhr and Gunstad in 2002.[10]

Juries understand the idea of self-fulfilling prophecy. Wiley Mittenberg's research showing that if you ask people to imagine having a head injury, and then give them a symptom checklist, they will check off the same symptoms that people who really did have a head injury endorse. Or Julie Suhr's diagnosis threat research; this is particularly helpful in a somatoform case.

Not only do you start to mislabel these everyday common symptoms, but if you start to believe that they are from brain damage you will actually perform differently on tests. This one doctor at a university had everyone in the Intro to Psych class volunteer for a study. She found a subset where 100% said they had a prior concussion. She divided them into two, and said to one group, "Your memory, attention, and processing speed are getting tested to see how well you do." The other group was told, "We saw that you had a concussion/head injury, and we want to see the effect of this on your memory, attention, etc."

Guess which group did worse? This is known as diagnosis threat.—Glenn Larrabee, PhD, ABPP-CN

We know that if you tell people they are going to have problems in certain areas, or do worse in certain areas, then they will. You don't have to be crazy for that to happen; it's just a normal human behavior. When someone's been warned they're going to have trouble in certain areas, and then they do my testing and they in fact have trouble in those areas, it's something I have to take into account when I interpret my results. It can happen to anyone.—Tannahill Glen, PhD, ABPP-CN

Symptom amplification

Closely related to diagnosis threat is the concept of symptom amplification. Many people are told by well-meaning clinicians to keep a journal of any "postconcussion symptoms" they experience. Nancy Hebben explains to juries how this practice can actually produce symptoms:

> *When I wake up in the morning, I might have a pain here or there, but I don't pay attention to it because I don't think it is meaningful. And then something happens, and afterwards I have the same symptoms, but now I think, "Oh, wait, that is related to that!" And I pay more attention to it. People are told to keep a journal. And what is that? They are being told to super-focus on everything they would have just dismissed prior to the incident. They are being told to train their attention to every little thing that goes wrong during the day. And they will say eventually, prior to the accident, "I was perfect, but now I am a mess! I have terrible symptoms."*

> *There is one famous experiment that shows how people can develop symptoms just by focusing on a body part. In the experiment, the person is asked to hold their hand out and a piece of paper is placed on their hand. They are told not to let the paper shake. As they hear that, most people's hand starts to shake a little, and as they watch it, they become nervous, and it shakes more. It is like they have a tremor. But as they are engaged in conversation and are no longer focusing on the paper, the "tremor" disappears. This is similar to what happens when we ask people to journal about thinking problems.*—Robin Hanks, PhD, ABPP-CN

Dr. Hanks shares her clinical intervention with jurors when her patients have been engaging in symptom amplification.

> ***I tell people to focus on the times their brains are working***
>
> *I have my patients focus on all of the good things they are doing cognitively during the day. That is the intervention that is necessary when someone has been trained to over focus on symptoms.*

"Good old days" hypothesis

Another psychological concept that is helpful for understanding why people may tell doctors that they were never the same after a single, uncomplicated concussion is that they have an inaccurate picture of how they functioned prior to the accident. This phenomenon is known as the "good old days" hypothesis. Wiley Mittenberg described the phenomenon as "etiology as expectation" in 1992,[11] noting that after a concussion, patients underestimated how frequently they experienced the common "postconcussive symptoms" before the accident as compared to base rates of controls. Studies since that time have demonstrated that regardless of the type of injury sustained, people after a negative event tend to overestimate their level of health prior to the event.[12] Patients may see a doctor after a concussion and tell them that prior to the concussion, they had no problems with headaches, fatigue, depression, and poor sleep. The doctor writes down that the symptoms began after a concussion, and the patient has just been diagnosed with postconcussive disorder. One of the reasons forensic experts often come to different conclusions about patients than treating doctors is that experts have the opportunity to review medical records from prior to the concussion. In the course of reviewing the records, it is common to find pre-accident medical records documenting that the patient has reported the same set of symptoms to various doctors over and over again prior to the concussion. Is the patient intentionally trying to deceive the doctor? Maybe, or the "good old days" hypothesis may also be at work.

> *What I have seen with my own patients over many years (I have been doing this for 25 years), the grass is always greener on the other side. Everything was great until this accident occurred. They aren't lying, but it is a normal human tendency to look back and think that life was great before and it's all terrible now.*—Jacobus Donders, PhD, ABPP-CN

Misattribution

Misattribution is closely related to diagnosis threat and the "good old days" hypothesis. Common everyday symptoms are misattributed to a concussion. The classic example is chronic pain leading to trouble sleeping after a car accident. Patients who are not getting good sleep will feel less attentive and make more thinking mistakes. These symptoms are then misattributed to the presence of brain damage. The concept of misattribution can be applied to many neurological problems in addition to concussion.

> *There are days that I wake up with postconcussive syndrome. I have a headache, I feel tired. I can't concentrate. A person with a hangover could be diagnosed with postconcussive syndrome.—Anonymous*

> ***I got shot in the ear and my leg fell off!***
>
> I use this explanation if the impairment the patient is claiming is disproportionate to the nature of the injury.
>
> *I see a patient, and they come in and their leg is amputated, recently amputated, and bloody, and there is blood draining from their earlobe, just draining out. The guy says, "Doc! I've just been in a terrible situation! I got shot in the ear and my leg fell off!"*
>
> *Well, you are definitely bleeding from your ear. I believe that. And you definitely just had your leg come off. I believe that. But I don't believe that getting shot in the ear made your leg fall off. Let's talk about what really happened.*—Tom Boll, PhD, ABPP-CN

> ***Explaining attribution error***
>
> *Attribution bias is extremely common. It's a normal human behavior. We all do it. Back in my epilepsy clinic at the University of Florida, we saw loads of patients who would come in with their first-time seizure onset, and they would very often say*

things like, "I think it has to do with this bump on my head I got from hitting my head on a kitchen cabinet 2 weeks ago. I am pretty sure that started the epilepsy." As human beings, we have a tendency to attribute things that are going on in our lives to recent events, or events that have great meaning to us. This is a normal human process. As doctors, we have to take that normal human process into account when people tell us about their symptoms.—Tannahill Glen, PhD, ABPP-CN

Explaining base rate of everyday memory symptoms

You know, some people begin to worry about where they put their keys, or going into a room and forgetting their keys. They begin to attribute this to their brain injury. But we all do that. And actually, there is some good data on how often the general public does that. And you would be surprised how often people who have never had a concussion do that. . . .

Many people will say, "I can't multitask." But the reality is that no one can multitask. There is a book called The Teenage Brain. *The author was asked about her own brain and she says "Look, we all have these symptoms. fMRI study showed that the optimal age for multitasking is the late 30s, and after that it declines or plateaus. Patients will tell me, "I can't multitask!" and I tell them, "Neither can I."*—Robin Hanks, PhD, ABPP-CN

When you go beyond the normal recovery period, the very symptoms of "postconcussion syndrome" are the same symptoms we all experience in everyday life. There is a physical symptom cluster such as headache, an emotional cluster such as irritability, and a cognitive cluster such as forgetfulness and memory problems. The thing is, we all experience those symptoms in our everyday life. Those of us who haven't been told we experienced a brain injury, usually the first thing we think is, "I've got too much on my plate. I'm stressed, I'm irritable. I'm getting headaches because I am stressed. And because I am distracted by my headache and by my stress. I am forgetting stuff." When we were in a car accident, we might take those very same experiences and think, "I have brain damage."—Glenn Larrabee, PhD, ABPP-CN

Scapegoat for life's problems

The reality is that many people come to view relatively minor injuries as all-encompassing scapegoat mechanisms. They come to rely on their accident as a means of externalizing responsibility for lifelong frustration, disappointment, and bad outcomes. When I am confident this is what's going on, I will point that out to jurors: "Unfortunately, Mr. Jones has never been a happy person. Mr. Jones has not been effective in maintaining employment, or holding onto relationships, or living life as a responsible adult. The kinds of problems that he now attributes to the accident are the exact same kind of problems he has always had. This is why it's important to consider the effects of this accident from the perspective of how this man has always lived his life."—David S. Bush, PhD, ABPP-CN

When is the last time any of us have experienced PCS symptoms?

Juries have all had the experience of "PCS" symptoms.

When is the last time any of us had these symptoms? I had a head ache this week, I have been irritable, and I have forgotten some things. I have been under a lot of stress because I don't like going to court.—Glenn Larrabee, PhD, ABPP-CN

Reattribution

Yeah, it is true that people who have prior psychiatric problems complain of symptoms for longer periods of time. It doesn't mean their symptoms are associated with a brain injury. There are reasons why that is. A process called reattribution can occur. What does that mean? There is a tendency to blame or attribute all their current misery to that car accident. And that is not because they are lying or being dishonest, but typically it is a more socially acceptable way to say, "That's why I have problems." It's not dishonesty, it's not lying; it's the way people cope. But it doesn't mean that we should attribute all of these symptoms to the accident.—Jacobus Donders, PhD, ABPP-CN

Hanging problems on the concussion hook

It is clear from her medical records that Mrs. Smith had headaches, memory problems, irritability, and chronic sleep problems for years prior to the concussion. Now she is hanging all of those problems on the hook of concussion. She is calling them something else now—"postconcussion syndrome"—but they are the same symptoms.—Nancy Hebben, PhD, ABPP-CN

Iatrogenesis

Iatrogenesis occur when a medical treatment causes a disorder or problem. A classic example of this is a clinician who tells a patient that some people with concussion never return to their previous thinking abilities and helps them "mourn" the loss of their previous capabilities in psychotherapy. Robin Hanks notes that the "no-fault" insurance rules of Michigan have created systemic iatrogenesis:

Michigan has "auto no-fault" insurance. If anyone is in an accident, there are unlimited benefits for life: medical treatment, home modification, supervision services, etc. It is wonderful if you have a severe traumatic brain injury.

Unfortunately, the unlimited benefits have created a thriving rehabilitation industry to "care for" people who have had a concussion. Scott Millis has referred to rehabilitation "treatment" for concussion as "brain injury charm school" where people are taught to be brain injured. There are iatrogenic effects that are reinforced by the rehab provider networks. They only take auto no fault; the physiatrists, physical therapists, occupational therapists and speech language therapists only refer to each other. There are some people who are outright creating fraud, but for a lot of people there is a very strong attributional model of "brain injury victim." They have a confirmatory bias. They only see providers who are telling them they have brain injury and never see anyone who can tell them they are well. There are over 100 rehab programs in the state because there is so much money in it. There are no civil suits, but it is insurance company pitted against insurance company, in civil court. Residential programs are set up for people with a concussion. The rehab facilities are very entrepreneurial. Some rehab facilities were caught paying people to stay in the program, or giving them TVs. The physicians will testify that mTBI is forever. One of the facilities even had that slogan written on their walls, "Brain Injury Is Forever." The facilities are creating disability.

Explaining iatrogenesis

Iatrogenesis is something that you and I could agree on readily with a relatively small amount of information. But to advance a theme of iatrogenesis and the kind of conditioning that that implies to a nonpsychologist? That is a hard concept, a big leap, for a judge or attorney or jury to grasp. That is not something that will be immediately obvious or familiar to them, so you have to build that to help them understand what you're talking about.

I use a lot of quotes in my report. In many of the mTBI claims the person is being subtly conditioned when they are sent to a neurologist handpicked by a plaintiff attorney. And then cognitive symptoms that were previously denied are now appearing in the records.

(Start with nonspecific symptoms.) "Listen, the kind of symptoms that ordinarily get ascribed to concussion are very common. Sleep disturbance, headache, a little balance trouble, memory difficulty, irritability. These are the very same complaints that people will report with high levels of frequency going into their annual physicals, even if they have never had a concussion. These are the same symptoms that many college students endorse going into midterms and final exams. And recent law school grads also describe these very same types of symptoms prior to the Bar exam. These complaints are not specific or unique to mTBI. The symptoms are very common under conditions of stress, depression, sleep disturbance, and substance abuse. And somebody who is in pain and distressed and upset in the aftermath of an accident is going to be susceptible to influence. They can be led to believe that they have a condition, like permanent brain damage, which they really don't have. Unfortunately, they haven't gotten treatment for the condition that they actually do have. I am very optimistic that if Mr. Smith receives more accurate education about the usual course of concussion and treatment for depression (and/or chronic pain etc.), he will be fine.— David S. Bush, PhD, ABPP-CN

Empathetic doctors sometimes contribute to the problem

I also try to depict physicians as human beings. If you see me as a psychologist, I have my agenda, but I am also trying to respond to your concerns.

"Some iatrogenic or doctor-caused problems come from a doctor being overly sympathetic to a patient's problems, and inadvertently—not meaning to—but contributing

> *to the problem. What this doctor is really meaning to do is to sympathize with the patient and to say, 'Yes, you really have a problem. I hear you.' But then that can have the effect of further convincing someone something is wrong. The doctor is an authority figure. They have special knowledge and skills. When they state their awareness of your problems with memory, concentration, or thinking, do you listen to them? Of course you do. When the doctor says, 'Yes, you really have a disability,' you believe it. Many patients interpret physician statements as fact, even if the doctor was only trying to sympathize with you.*—Rus Bauer, PhD, ABPP-CN

Rus Bauer helps jurors understand iatrogenic problems by asking them, "Put yourself into this person's shoes."

> Attorneys are concerned with: Does this person have or not have a compensable injury or total disability? In many cases you will find deficits, but they are attributable to depression or poor effort or a year of disuse. I encounter what I consider to be iatrogenic disability quite a bit. I ask jurors to put themselves in the plaintiff's shoes, and I focus on what the plaintiff needs.
>
> *On direct*:
>
> *A: Suppose you went to a doctor and that doctor said you have significant brain damage and you will never work again. And you respond to that by not working. And then you spend a year in your house, and you don't see your friends, and you don't engage in activities that stimulate you and make you want to get up in the morning. Put yourself in this person's shoes. Ask yourself, "Would you be as sharp as you were after going through that?"*
>
> *Q: Can anything be done to alleviate this?*
>
> *A: Recreation therapy, antidepressant medication, activity therapy, vocational retraining, psychotherapy, physical therapy to try to get them more functional.*
>
> *Q: How long would that take?*
>
> *A: I would like to think that within 6 months, this person should have made visible progress, particularly if their family can become involved in the therapy.*

Other factors that can reinforce symptoms

> ***When family members are paid caregivers***
>
> *What is the most compelling reason for why this person is reporting all of these problems? Sometimes it is the social reinforcers. In Michigan families are paid care providers. They make $85,000 to be a paid care provider. These are people who lived marginal lives before. The whole family is living off this person's concussion. It's really hard. This is a poor family. People were not working. This accident happened and now they are getting paid a lot of money to take care of this person. It's hard for their*

doctors to fill out forms then saying Mr. Smith is doing well. It's hard for Mr. Smith to say to family and others, "I feel fine now."—Robin Hanks, PhD, ABPP-CN

Family context

Sometimes there are competing disabilities within a family. Maybe the plaintiff's spouse is on disability or their siblings are. Sometimes there is a competition within a family for who needs the most care. When I put all of this information together, when I look at what is maintaining Mr. Smith's symptoms, this context is important. Because the research shows that by 3 months, people are cognitively normal after a concussion.—Nancy Hebben, PhD, ABPP-CN

Other physical problems

Claims of lingering mTBI symptoms

In cases in which postconcussive symptoms linger and are clamed to interfere with function months or years after an injury, I will readily acknowledge the person has chronic pain and that is related to the accident, or they are depressed and I think the depression is related to the accident. Or sleep difficulties associated with chronic pain.

People who have chronic pain have problems sleeping and concentrating. Those problems will affect your ability to function during the day. That doesn't mean it is brain damage.—Rod Vanderploeg, PhD, ABPP-CN

A more likely explanation

I always consider if comorbid conditions have likely resulted in cognitive change, things such as diabetes, preexisting ADHD and/or learning disability, substance abuse, small vessel vascular disease detected on brain imaging, etc. If I don't know if a concurrent medical condition impacts cognition, I do a quick search in Google Scholar; within seconds you will have the information. If I find that a person has concurrent conditions that would explain cognitive inefficiency, that would be of more importance in explaining cognitive changes than a concussion in the past. Research shows that the remote effects of concussion on thinking skills are not significantly different from zero.—Kyle Boone, PhD, ABPP-CN

In my own practice, I have begun creating a visual in the form of a table with the PCS symptoms on one side, and the side effects from the medications the examinee is taking, their medical conditions like untreated sleep apnea, and their current mood issue as columns. This is a helpful way to show the nonspecific nature of the PCS symptoms and other, more likely reasons why the symptoms are present for the examinee than a remote, uncomplicated concussion.

“Post concussive syndrome” symptoms	Topamax	Amantadine	Melatonin	Ambien	Amitriptyline	Trazadone	Depression	Untreated sleep apnea
Headache		xxx	xxx			xxx		xxx
Dizziness			xxx			xxx		
Fatigue	xxx		xxx	xxx		xxx	xxx	xxx
Irritability		xxx	xxx				xxx	xxx
Anxiety	xxx	xxx	xxx	xxx		xxx	xxx	xxx
Insomnia					xxx		xxx	xxx
Poor concentration	xxx	xxx			xxx	xxx	xxx	xxx
Memory problems	xxx			xxx		xxx	xxx	xxx
Nausea	xxx	xxx				xxx		

Effects of depression and anxiety

Unhappy people report worse symptoms

In every disease state, people who are unhappy report more symptoms. We know when people are depressed they not only report more thinking problems, but also report they feel they can do less around the home. They are more pessimistic and assume they won't be able to do tasks. Being depressed prior to an accident doesn't mean they physically have a worse head injury, but it does mean they are likely to report more symptoms.—David Williamson, PhD, ABPP-CN

Good news, bad news

In very mild concussion cases, the research suggests a big overlap between depression symptoms and PCS symptoms. I like to frame this up as good news for the plaintiff because depression is very treatable, but the primary problem needs to be identified. I am cautious and careful about speaking directly to a plaintiff in court, but I will do it on occasion. "This may not be good news for Mr. Jones's lawsuit (look to Mr. Jones), but this is very good news for you, Mr. Jones. Your condition is very treatable. You can look forward to a very positive outcome when you receive proper treatment for your depression."—Paul L. Craig, PhD, ABPP-CN

Aware of the literature that shows people who had depression prior to a concussion report PCS symptoms longer than those who were not depressed, some attorneys will argue that having depression makes the effect of a concussion worse—that is, the brain will be damaged because of the presence of depression at the time of the concussion. Here are some thoughts from the experts about this issue:

Q: Doctor, isn't it true that because Ms. Smith had preexisting depression, her concussion is expected to affect her brain more strongly, and research shows preexisting depression results in longer postconcussion syndrome?

A: No, what having lifelong depression did is leave her as a perfect candidate to have persisting complaints of symptoms after a concussion because of misattribution and preexisting problems, not because her concussion was any greater or had any greater effect.—Nancy Hebben, PhD, ABPP-CN

Q: Doctor, isn't it true that because Ms. Smith had preexisting depression, her concussion is expected to affect her brain more strongly, and research shows preexisting depression results in longer postconcussion syndrome?

A: Ms. Smith was having a hard time coping prior to the concussion, and I would not expect her to cope well after the accident. No matter what the event—a slip-and-fall accident, or losing a job at work—no matter what it is, Ms. Smith does not cope well with events. This is why she has had a stormy recovery. It is not an issue of her being actually disabled, but fits with her lifelong pattern of problems coping with any events.—Robin Hanks, PhD, ABPP-CN

In my own practice, I point out:

A concussion will not cure lifelong depression

The reason why the idea of "postconcussive syndrome" is so criticized is that the symptoms are not specific. They occur in a lot of other conditions, particularly depression. Most of the symptoms of "postconcussive syndrome" Ms. Plaintiff reports, she was reporting for years prior to the car accident; she and her doctors were just calling it depression. Prior to the accident her primary care records and psychotherapy records show that she had problems sleeping, she couldn't concentrate, she wasn't motivated to pay her bills, she frequently lost jobs, she felt sad and irritable. After the accident, she was having the same symptoms, but now she was labeling them as coming from the concussion. There is nothing about having a concussion that would cure lifelong depression. It is not surprising to me that those set of symptoms continue.

Keith Yeates points out that sometimes concussions in teenage athletes are managed in a way that produces iatrogenic depression. Some doctors recommend weeks of "cognitive and physical rest" away from social media and friends and long periods where athletes are not allowed to exercise. This can lead to a reactive depression whose symptoms are often then interpreted as "proof" of a postconcussion personality change.

I don't think this kid's emotional distress is directly related to the brain injury, but it is related to the events following the injury, where they couldn't play their sport any more, they were isolated from their friends, and for better or worse they were kept out of school a long time.

Litigation effects

Just being in a lawsuit has significant effects on test scores

We know from research that just being involved in a lawsuit has significant effects on scores on thinking tests. It's the stresses of being in a lawsuit, the messages that they are getting from clinicians that they have suffered a serious brain injury that won't get better, pressures to continue reporting symptoms that may have cleared up.—Robin Hanks, PhD, ABPP-CN

Effect of litigation on mTBI

You are talking about the science, and the science is very clear that there is a different set of symptoms and recovery pattern following mTBI for people who are in litigation when compared to people who are not.

Our brain is a very, very important part of who we are, but we have to look at the whole context of our lives. Being involved in litigation is very stressful and has potentially life-changing consequences. If an examinee is facing a court proceeding, of course that has an effect on their behavior.—Darcy Cox, PsyD, ABPP-CN

The litigating process is stressful

In a case where the plaintiff is 3 or 4 years out and still not recovered, I try to get the judge or the jury to appreciate that the litigation process is a stressful one. The litigating process brings on its own symptoms whether you are injured or not. It's stressful. It can be hard to sleep. Some of the symptoms of being involved in litigation—headaches, sleeplessness, or you might have had some aches and pains. All this gets worse now. Litigation is stressful.—Martin Rohling, PhD

No cheerleader (effect of litigation)

And frankly, the litigation is going on, and Ms. Smith has people telling her she is impaired, and that takes its toll. My role as a clinician is to be a cheerleader and encourage people along. But many times, when someone is in the process of litigation, that is not present.—Leslie Rosenstein, PhD, ABPP-CN

Other life factors contributing to symptom maintenance

Third string quarterback on a team that never wins

If you are the starting quarterback for a team that has not lost a game and looks like they are going to the playoffs, how badly do you want to get back in the game? How soon after an injury do you feel "fully recovered?" But, if you are the third string quarterback, who got injured during practice, has never played in an actual game, have no expectations that you will ever play in a game, and your team has lost every game. How badly do you want to recover and how soon after an injury might you say that you are "fully recovered?" What if you hate your job?—Martin Rohling, PhD

I didn't like my job to begin with

I don't like my job. I was thinking of quitting it anyways. I ended up getting injured on the job. I thought it was a dangerous job in the first place, which is why I wanted to quit. Now, I have the prospect of getting paid to stay out of work. I get out of a job I didn't like in the first place. If I get better, I am going to go back to a job I didn't like. How fast is my attorney going to want me to say that I got better?—Martin Rohling, PhD

INTRODUCING RESEARCH

See Chapter 8, "Direct Examination," for general guidelines on bringing up specific research studies during testimony.

Listen, you don't have to just believe me when I say this. It's not based just on my own clinical expertise. If you look at independent studies from people who don't have an agenda, who looked at all the research that was out there, not picking and choosing, they sat around a table and came to an agreement, it is very clear that there are two conclusions about mTBI/concussion. One, most recover within a couple of weeks to months; rarely, symptoms continue for more like a year. And two, when it does continue to be a problem, there are usually one of two things involved: compensation seeking, or prior psychiatric history. And guess what? We have both in this case.—Jacobus Donders, PhD, ABPP-CN

Explaining mTBI literature

There may be several experts in the community who will get up on the stand and provide testimony that has no relationship to the facts of the case or current scientific knowledge. Even though because of courtroom rules I generally can't cite specific studies, I will say this:

Multiple studies with control groups have shown that when you compare people who have been in an accident who had a concussion with people in an accident with no concussion but who have orthopedic injuries (that is, you have controlled for the experience of being in an accident, you have an injury, you go to the hospital, the only difference is that the control group injury doesn't involve the head), when we look at those comparisons, we see no difference in outcome.—Glenn Larrabee, PhD, ABPP-CN

Show me any data that demonstrates significant cognitive deficits

If you get any expert on the stand who is saying three months later, they are finding big cognitive deficits—it's so easy to take that apart. I would never put myself in that position.

Show me any data that shows that in any group or individual study that any person has had significant cognitive deficits three months later- on standard cognitive testing three months after a concussion—there is no data, no scientific basis for making that claim.—Keith Yeates, PhD, ABPP-CN

Our best understanding from the scientific literature is that in uncomplicated mild traumatic brain injury there is a rapid recovery of function. There is 20 years of study of athletes, and adults in consecutive admissions to emergency rooms . . . I will bring the research in, but more functionally. I won't say, "Smith in 2012 did a study that showed . . ."—Neil Pliskin, PhD, ABPP-CN

WCST (specific tests) on mTBI

I had a recent concussion case and the plaintiff a couple years after the fact had seen a neuropsychologist who, based entirely on the WCST, diagnosed the person with mild cognitive impairment. There is actually a specific study looking at this particular

test[13] *that shows that uncomplicated minor concussions have no lasting effect on WCST performance.*—David S. Bush, PhD, ABPP-CN

Cross: What about the 10% to 15%?

While the research literature is very clear that people recover from concussions, generations of clinicians were trained to expect that 10% to 15% of people will become the "miserable minority" after a concussion. Experts address this clinical lore:

15% don't recover; Michael Alexander paper

Michael Alexander wrote the widely quoted paper in 1995 that stated that 15% of concussion patients do not recover. For research, he cites only two publications. When you look up these two publications, in one of them, the patients were complaining of symptoms but the testing was actually normal. The other research study included patients that the study authors identified as malingerers. This 15% failure to recover rate is very widely requoted, but it is based on clearly faulty research. To me the cautionary tale is "read the literature before you quote it." —Kyle Boone, PhD, ABPP-CN

I have never seen a patient like this

Q: What about the 10% who never recover from a concussion? You already made up your mind that this person didn't have thinking problems before you saw him, didn't you?!

A: I keep an open mind. But in order for me to consider that people have genuine cognitive problems from a remote concussion, three criteria have to be met. First, they can't fail performance validity tests. Second, there can't be evidence of hypochondriasis or a somatoform disorder, a tendency to magnify or distort normal physical and cognitive symptoms. And third, there can't be a more likely explanation for cognitive inefficiency, such as overuse of pain medication and tranquilizers, ADHD, learning disabilities, etc. In my experience, I have never seen a patient who meets all three criteria. And given that there are 80,000 concussions that occur in this country each year, if the 10% statistic were true, I would be seeing patients who met these criteria all the time. And I am not.—Kyle Boone, PhD, ABPP-CN

"Concussion causes somatoform disorder"

It feels like the age of whack-a-mole in court. There is always something new. In Los Angeles, performance validity tests have been a game-changer. The performance validity tests are so convincing. We no longer simply give test-takers the "benefit of the doubt" regarding whether or not they are performing to true ability because we now have objective data on the issue. A new tactic is for attorneys to argue that maybe the person is not performing to true ability, but that it is because the person has a somatoform disorder—that he or she believes that he/she is damaged, and acts it out, and that the accident caused a somatoform disorder.

However, there is no literature I am aware of suggesting that a concussion would cause somatoform disorder. Rather, the symptoms patients are having are solving life problems that otherwise could not be solved. In other words, the accident "came along at the right time" to solve a problem for the examinee. I bring up the study by Greiffenstein and Baker (2001)[14]*—they had MMPIs on folks pre- and post-concussion, and both showed somatoform predispositions.*—Kyle Boone, PhD, ABPP-CN

Concussion and risk for dementia

Some experts will say mTBI increases the risk for dementia. Current established science suggests that's unlikely. Moderate to severe TBI, particularly if it occurs much later in life? Sure, there is some increased risk. We can quibble about how much. But a single concussion early in life? No.

"When we are 85, all of us—me, you, a lot of us—will develop dementia. I can't say whether you playing high school football increased your risk a little bit, but the honest truth is that age is by far the single biggest risk factor for developing dementia. And if you're lucky, you will get to have a lot of age.—Darcy Cox, PsyD, ABPP-CN

Chronic traumatic encephalopathy

In the context of the highly publicized NFL concussion lawsuit, the sensational news coverage of the chronic traumatic encephalopathy (CTE) research literature, and the 2015 movie *Concussion,* many jurors conjure up the effects of an entire football career of dozens of concussions in their thought bubbles when the issue of the lasting effects of a single concussion is raised in court. Michael McCrea notes,

There is no question that the media exposure about concussion and long-term neurological health consequences and CTE has had a major influence on public perception of concussion in the United States. This comes from my experience in my clinic and my dealings with the public in general.

Many experts shared that they make a point on direct to have the attorney who brought them ask them a question that allows them to contrast the effects of large numbers of concussions with the effects of a single, uncomplicated concussion.

CTE versus single concussion

When we are talking about a single, uncomplicated concussion, it's different from someone who has had many, many concussions and hundreds of subconcussive blows over the course of their careers. It can be apples and oranges.—Christopher Grote, PhD, ABPP-CN

News media and concussion

The media tells us things that are not based on science. The news media and social media sometimes present information about concussion that is not scientifically

based. People hear this information and become concerned that the concussion they had will result in catastrophic changes in their life when the science tells us that is not the case.—Robin Hanks, PhD, ABPP-CN

Second impact syndrome

I am occasionally asked a question about second impact syndrome on the stand. I will say,

"It was once accepted as the main risk for consideration in the context of sports-related concussion. A number of critical reviews raised the question about whether there really is a second impact syndrome. These days, there are few references to it in the literature."—Michael McCrea, PhD, ABPP-CN

FINALLY, TALKING ABOUT ONE'S OWN CONCUSSIONS

How many members of the jury have had a concussion? How about the attorneys in the room? The judge? As an expert is speaking, the people in the room may be comparing the defendant/plaintiff's experience to their own concussion. Many psychologists and neuropsychologists have had a concussion or two, often prior to going to college and then graduate school. In sharing your own experience of concussion, you become the exhibit.

I personally had a concussion while administering cognitive tests during a WADA procedure as a postdoctoral fellow. Embarrassingly, I felt queasy and got rubber legs. I must have hit my head on the floor but made the mistake of asking people a few times if they had that part right, because I had no memory of hitting my head. That earned me a visit to the CT scanner.

I will occasionally explain the disruption of mental processes, loss of consciousness, confusion, and PTA in a concussion to jurors using my own experience. I was in a car accident, and after the accident, my first memory was, "Why is my head wet?" If anything, I was confused. I didn't realize I had just been in an accident. Later, pictures showed that my head shape was splintered on the windshield. Then my next recollection was of the EMTs showing up and asking them, "Who called you?"—Nancy Hebben, PhD, ABPP-CN

You know, most of us sitting in this room here today probably had a mild traumatic brain injury at some point in their lives. I know I did. I had two in college—and I still did pretty well for myself.—Jacobus Donders, PhD, ABPP-CN

NOTES

1. *VA/DoD Clinical Practice Guideline for the Management of Concussion-Mild Traumatic Brain Injury*. (2016). https://www.healthquality.va.gov/guidelines/Rehab/mtbi/mTBICPGFullCPG50821816.pdf

2. *VA/DoD Clinical Practice Guideline for the Management of Concussion-Mild Traumatic Brain Injury*. (2016). https://www.healthquality.va.gov/guidelines/Rehab/mtbi/mTBICPGFullCPG50821816.pdf
3. *Report to Congress on Mild Traumatic Brain Injury in the United States: Steps to Prevent a Serious Public Health Problem*. (2003). Atlanta, GA: National Center for Injury Prevention and Control, Centers for Disease Control and Injury Prevention.
4. Holm, L., Cassidy, J. D., Carroll, L. J., & Borg, J. (2005). Summary of the WHO Collaborating Centre for Neurotrauma Task Force on Mild Traumatic Brain Injury. *Journal of Rehabilitation Medicine, 37*(3), 137–141.
5. Kay, T., Harrington, D. E., Adams, R., Anderson, T., Berrol, S., Cicerone, K., . . . Malec, J. (1993). Definition of mild traumatic brain injury. *Journal of Head Trauma Rehabilitation, 8*(3), 86–87.
6. E.g. Cranton, N., & Oliver, L. (2014). Time to re-think the Zurich Guidelines: A critique on the Consensus Statement on Concussion in Sport: The 4th International Conference on Concussion in Sport, held in Zurich, November 2012. *Clinical Journal of Sports Medicine, 24*(2), 93–95.
7. Rohling, M. L., Meyers, J. E., & Millis, S. R. (2003). Neuropsychological impairment following traumatic brain injury: A dose–response analysis. *Clinical Neuropsychologist, 17*(3), 289–302.
8. McCrea, M., Guskiewicz, K. M., Marshall, S. W., Barr, W., Randolph, C., Cantu, R. C., . . . Kelly, J. P. (2003). Acute effects and recovery time following concussion in collegiate football players: The NCAA Concussion Study. *JAMA, 290*(19), 2556–2563.
9. McCrea, M. (2007). Mild Traumatic Brain Injury and Postconcussion Syndrome: The new Evidence Base for Diagnosis and Treatment. New York: Oxford University Press.
10. Suhr, J. A., & Gunstad, J. (2002). "Diagnosis threat": The effect of negative expectations on cognitive performance in head injury. *Journal of Clinical and Experimental Neuropsychology, 24*(4), 448–457.
11. Mittenberg, W., DiGuilio, D., Perrin, S., & Bass, A. (1992). Symptoms following mild head injury: Expectation as aetiology. *Journal of Neurology, Neurosurgery, and Psychiatry, 55*, 200–204.
12. Gunstad, J., & Suhr, J. (2001). "Expectation as etiology" *versus* "the good old days:" Postconcussion syndrome symptom reporting in athletes, headache sufferers, and depressed individuals. *Journal of the International Neuropsychological Society, 7*, 323–333.
13. Ord, J., Greve, K., Bianchini, K., & Aguerrevere, L. (2009). Executive dysfunction in traumatic brain injury: The effects of injury severity and effort on the Wisconsin Card Sorting Test. *Journal of Clinical and Experimental Neuropsychology, 32*(2), 132–140.
14. Greiffenstein, M. F., & Baker, W. J. (2001). Comparison of premorbid and postinjury MMPI-2 profiles in late postconcussion claimants. *Clinical Neuropsychologist, 15*(2), 162–170.

13 Specific Psychiatric and Neurological Disorders

THIS CHAPTER SHARES vivid, succinct strategies that experts shared regarding how to explain psychiatric illness, intellectual disability, cognitive effects of illness, chronic pain, and severe traumatic brain injury to jurors and other triers of fact. Many of the strategies shared in Chapter 12, "Concussion," such as misattribution error and diagnosis threat, can be applied to specific disorders described in this chapter as well.

Eliciting engaging methods of explaining every psychiatric and neurological syndrome that psychologists and neuropsychologists typically see in clinical practice was not the focus of this research. Rather, experts were asked to share what they actually say in court to describe the most common clinical phenomena that are the subject of criminal and civil cases. *Feedback That Sticks: The Art of Communicating Complex Neuropsychological Assessment Results*[1] is an excellent companion source to this chapter. Over 90 seasoned clinical neuropsychologists shared clear, vivid analogies, metaphors, and stories they use to describe a very broad array of mental health, developmental, and neurological conditions. Please see the *Feedback That Sticks* chapters on autism, dementia, neurological disorders, stroke, ADHD, learning disabilities, developmental disorders, and emotional function for additional, engaging pearls that can be used to describe additional clinical phenomena in court. See Chapter 14 in this book, "Cognitive Development, Premorbid Function, and Intellectual Function," for strategies to describe intellectual disabilities.

ADDRESSING THE KNOWLEDGE JURORS BRING TO THE COURTROOM

Whenever experts discuss psychological or neurological syndromes, jurors cannot help conjuring their own background knowledge and understanding of those disorders. The challenge for the expert is that the information jurors bring to the courtroom from their own personal experiences about mental health or neurological illness may not be accurate. For example, a juror might mistakenly believe, based on his experience with an elderly aunt with a mixed vascular and Alzheimer's-type dementia, that memory problems get worse and worse over time after a stroke, just like they do with Alzheimer's disease. Or a juror might connect the term *OCD* to the label her family always used for her mother's insistence that the kitchen floor be swept before the family went to sleep at night. The juror may consider "OCD" to be a minor personality trait rather than a mental illness that, in its worst forms, impairs functioning and is accompanied by substantial thought disorder.

Marcus Boccaccini notes that jurors are typically confused when an expert offers testimony that goes against their preconceived notions, and this confusion may lead jurors to reject the unexpected information. He recommends inoculating against this process by warning jurors upfront that you're about to offer unexpected information:

> *Jurors come into cases with preconceived notions. Sex offender cases, for example. Most folks think sex offenders reoffend. In actuality, that is not really the case. When you are a witness telling jurors that a sex offender is at risk of reoffending, they say, "Yeah, I get that." When you give them testimony that is consistent with their preconceived notions, they say, "Yes!! Great testimony; give me more of that!" If you give them testimony that says that there is a low risk of reoffending for sex offenders, they tell you, "I don't understand that; that's not very useful." If you are going to provide testimony that is likely to go against common sense, you will be facing an uphill battle. No one has yet studied the next step in that area: What are the strategies that you can use to tell them in advance that what you are about to testify to will go against their preconceived notion?*

> ***Tailoring examples can be a bridge to jury experience***
>
> I recall a jury trial in rural Georgia. It was a military town. Pretty much everyone on the jury had a family member in the military or had been in themselves. The question in the case was PTSD after a car wreck. I was testifying on behalf of the plaintiff. She had a huge psychiatric exacerbation after this wreck. It triggered a decompensation for her. I was asked on direct:
>
> *Q: What is PTSD?*
>
> *A: PTSD is what you all heard about back in the 1970s when people started coming back from Vietnam. They had these feelings that weren't well described. People just had to live with it. It has a huge impact on veterans.*
>
> *I saw people on the jury violently nodding their heads: "Yes! I was there. That was me!" And from that point on, the jury was transfixed. The military example became*

a bridge for their personal experience and the experience of the jury.—Tannahill Glen, PhD, ABPP-CN

EXPLAINING SOMATOFORM DISORDERS

Most jurors will understand the idea of a hypochondriac, someone who is anxious and fearful of becoming sick. Here are some vivid, empathetic ways of helping jurors to connect that basic understanding of the relationship between anxiety and perception of illness.

> *We all experience anxiety and other forms of emotional distress that may be expressed in many different ways. Some people tend to develop physical symptoms in response to life stressors, and for some, those symptoms can be mistaken for the results of a medical problem or injury.*—Nat Nelson, PhD, ABPP-CN

Somatoform disorder

> *There are people in the world who physically react to stress, and they notice when they get stressed their stomach tightens up or they feel a tightness in their breathing. Such individuals will frequently take that stress and their body reacts. They become more hyperaware of symptoms. The more they are aware, the more the symptoms bother them. Have you ever noticed that when someone in the room is coughing, you become aware of your throat, and you might start coughing? Then you think, "Oh, no! Am I coming down with a cold?" It is very common.*—Robin Hanks, PhD, ABPP-CN

Somatization spectrum

> *In my practice, I have seen patients at one end of the spectrum of somatization. These are patients who are absolutely convinced they are blind, even if there is nothing wrong with their vision. Or some people who are convinced their legs don't work anymore. If you pick them up out of their wheelchair they will fall down, because they are absolutely convinced they are paralyzed from the waist down. But there is absolutely nothing neurologically wrong with them. Those are people at one end of the spectrum.*
>
> *At the other end of the spectrum you get me. If I have a migraine or sore throat, I have three kids, I am toiling, going 100 miles an hour. You have to. But if my husband walks in, suddenly I am limping, with my hand on my head, with this really pained expression on my face. Because otherwise he would never know how I am doing, because I have to get things done. I send out signals that let people know what kind of discomfort I am in. I am not exaggerating anything; I am just sending signals in a way that frankly doesn't need to be done, but emphasizes my level of distress. And hopefully my husband will pick up on those signals.*
>
> *So I describe somatization as a spectrum, and you can fall somewhere on that spectrum. Everyone does it to some respect, but we only diagnose it when it is getting in the way of your ability to do what you need to do every day.*—Tannahill Glen, PhD, ABPP-CN

Explaining somatization

I genuinely feel empathetic to the patients I see. I work primarily on the defense. Almost every patient I see I wish I had seen them a year prior clinically, because they wouldn't be in the position they are in now. I trained in systems therapy and family therapy in graduate school. In my era, we had to be in therapy, we had to do therapy. In internship, I had great psychoanalytically trained supervisors. That is more useful to me than CBT. The analytical and systems work helps me with empathy and understanding.

"We all know individuals we may call hypochondriacs. They have lots of physical symptoms. They frequently have headaches. They frequently call in sick to work. They genuinely believe they have a cold. Or their headache is such that they really need to stay home and take care of it. They genuinely feel that way. But these beliefs and behaviors essentially result in them attending to normally occurring symptoms like a headache and believing that it is far more severe or significant or disabling than it actually is. That's simply how they go through life. And it is a difficult way to go through life, because you are always feeling sick and you are always distressed by something. Those kind of symptoms and that kind of belief pattern affects your whole life. It affects your ability to learn and remember, and to concentrate, and to perform your job. That's what we saw here on the testing, that these difficulties and that way of responding to the world undermined their ability to perform well on the memory test."—Rodney Vanderploeg, PhD, ABPP-CN

Some psychologists argue that we cannot diagnose a somatoform disorder unless a physician has ruled out a medical cause for symptoms. But many physicians feel that diagnosing a somatoform disorder is out of their area of expertise, so they will refer patients to psychologists to make that call. Most physicians do not consider a somatoform disorder because they uncritically accept a patient's self-report of physical symptoms as accurate, and somatoform patients of course do not say they have somatoform symptoms. We need the test results from personality testing to help us diagnose somatoform disorder. If the treating physician doesn't do personality testing, how would he/she know?—Kyle Boone, PhD, ABPP-CN

I'm not saying he does not have pain

I recall one case, we now call it somatic symptom disorder. It came down to:

Q: How do you know that this person doesn't have pain?

A: I am not saying this person doesn't have pain. I'm saying that this person very well might be miserable. But although this person's pain, at least in the beginning, most likely had a biological or bodily cause to it, right now the pain is influenced by, and kept going by, psychological factors. I am not saying they don't have pain. I am saying there are reasons other than the original injury that this person is so miserable at this time. And those reasons are what we call psychological factors, related to how angry they are at the world, related to how they feel they have been mistreated, related to having too many narcotics prescribed to them.—Jacobus Donders, PhD, ABPP-CN

CHRONIC PAIN

We have all had the experience in our lives of being in pain. How many people on the jury might have fibromyalgia or chronic pain syndromes themselves? It is important to help jurors connect with their own experience of pain and maintain respect and a humble attitude toward our ability as clinicians to appreciate the plaintiff/defendant's experiences with pain. At the same time, our science allows us to compare expected symptom patterns and identify situations in which the pain report is not consistent with observed behavior or the typical experience of those with similar medical conditions. Explaining the science while maintaining empathy is important.

A general misery index

I get plenty of cases where pain is the primary complaint but there is no objective evidence of a basis for that. To me, that is one of the most difficult things to explain to a jury, to explain pain-related behavior that really doesn't have an objective basis. In somatoform disorders it's easy because there is a psychological issue there, and jurors can relate. When there is ***not*** *a somatoform issue, it is more difficult. Jurors tend to be swayed by evidence like a slipped disk or degeneration. If they can see it in a picture, they tend to be swayed. It's a bit of a challenge. Less is more in those cases. If I can avoid talking about MMPI profiles and psychological testing, I will; it's better to focus on the big picture, which is your summary. What I would rely on, when I have to describe someone who is reporting a tremendous amount of pain, is to say: "I'm not here to say whether or not there's* ***any*** *pain—it'll be up to others here to determine that. What I* ***am*** *saying is that this reported level of pain is at a level we don't even see in pain patients. And also, it doesn't fit with what we see Mr. Smith doing—he is out there washing a car on that surveillance video. And this is a person who says he can do nothing, not even sit at a desk for 5 minutes. It just doesn't add up. But for some people, a pain rating is like a misery index: It's more like a statement about general unhappiness rather than pain per se."*—Tannahill Glen, PhD, ABPP-CN

Pediatric pain

When I am talking about new pain from an event, I will say,

"Pain can get in the way of kids' ability to focus and be functional. That's the way I look at pain. It's a different kind of story if you have persistent pain but you are still able to do the things you need to do."—John Kirk, PsyD, ABPP-CN

Chronic pain

The person's complaints of pain are beyond what you might expect for people who have legitimate, verifiable causes of their symptoms and complaints. Secondary gain may not be entirely conscious and could be a product of a number of other psychological, emotional, or situational factors and conditions.—Robert Heilbronner, PhD, ABPP-CN

Use of chronic pain inventories

I like using the Chronic Pain Coping Inventory (CPCI) and Survey of Pain Attitudes (SOPA) by Mark Jensen at the University of Washington. They are normed on chronic pain patients. It is broken into adaptive and maladaptive coping strategies and coping methods and normed on chronic pain patients. When the examinee has elevations, [I might say:] "

These are exaggerated complaints. Even people who have been diagnosed with chronic pain syndromes do not report these symptoms" or "Ms. Jones shows adaptive coping strategies and attitudes about the pain she is experiencing."—Robin Hanks, PhD, ABPP-CN

It's hard to measure pain

Pain is a problem because it is subjective. We don't really know if Mr. Smith experiences pain; we just know that he says he does. It becomes important to do a comprehensive evaluation and look at how he handles other things that we can measure because we really cannot know if he is reporting more pain than he is feeling. And we can't ask directly. So we have to measure it by looking at related tests. There are some people who report much greater pain than we know occurs in people who have illnesses that closely correspond. If this person reports more extreme pain than somebody who is dying from a painful cancer, then we have to really look at whether there is exaggeration. The MMPI is a test that allows us to compare Mr. Smith's responses to people who are medically ill. It allows a good comparison.—Wendy Marlowe, PhD, ABPP-CN

McGill Pain Questionnaire and MMPI

I go back to the literature and I will talk about the studies based on the MMPI and other pain measures. What is the research with the comparison groups? I will go back and look at that and include it in my testimony (e.g., MMPI scale 1 and 3 compared with patients in the hospital). "

The McGill Pain Questionnaire has been very well validated with different groups of patients. I compare the injury and pain complaints of Mr. Smith with those having bona fide pain disorders in the standardization samples."—Wendy Marlowe, PhD, ABPP-CN

Pain affecting performance

If you've got a migraine, you can't do as well as you would normally do, or if you had shingles during testing, or phantom limb pain from an amputation. It can be pretty constant, and intrusive, and puts people in bad moods. That can affect one's performance.—Tannahill Glen, PhD, ABPP-CN

People can have headaches for many reasons

With chronic headaches after a concussion, I will suggest an IME by a physiatrist who is a headache specialist.

> *"People can have headaches for many reasons. This includes problems with the cervical spine, overuse of medications, stress, anxiety, depression" (list multiple factors).*—Robin Hanks, PhD, ABPP-CN

Experts often need to explain the effect of chronic pain on the plaintiff's experience of chronic thinking and memory problems. Concepts like "fibro fog" have become commonplace. Unfortunately, people often misunderstand the dampening of attention that may accompany the distraction, poor sleep, and medication side effects that go hand in hand with chronic pain for a neurologically based brain disorder.

Chronic pain drains brain resources

> *Have you ever seen that thing on the computer that shows how much space is allocated for certain things? Like a pie chart. Even if you are not constantly thinking about your chronic pain, your brain is monitoring it, and it is pulling off resources that could be allocated to thinking and remembering.*—Kristie Nies, PhD, ABPP-CN

Effect of pain on thinking

> *With many chronic pain situations, I express empathy and understanding. I acknowledge that it could be influencing the plaintiff's day-to-day experience of thinking problem.* Nick Bogod, R.Psych

Chronic pain doesn't make you dumber and it doesn't cause brain damage

> *Chronic pain can be really fatiguing. If you have to slog through the day dealing with pain it can really sap your energy. It doesn't make you dumber, and it doesn't cause brain damage. It can make the experience of taking genuinely difficult thinking tests more draining.*—David Williamson, PhD, ABPP-CN

SLEEP DISORDERS

Problems with sleep are very common in society at large, and even more common in populations of people with chronic pain, psychiatric issues, and neurological disorders. Explaining the effects of poor or restricted sleep to jurors on thinking and mood is often an important component of testimony.

Remember when your kids were little, and you got no sleep?

> *Remember how you felt when your kids were little, and you had to stay up all night? We all know that it's a miracle that mothers function. Lack of sleep affects how we think.*—Kristie Nies, PhD, ABPP-CN

Less than 4 hours sleep is the equivalent of drunk driving

> *I've heard that if you have less than 4 hours of sleep, you should not drive a car. It is the equivalent of drunk driving.*—Kristie Nies, PhD, ABPP-CN

When a person has thinking problems far past the time expected after a concussion, or excess disability from another type of neurological insult or illness, the effect of untreated sleep apnea is often high on the list of suspected causes. Many people are aware of sleep apnea but see the problem primarily as loud, annoying snoring and the treatment mainly to fix that symptom. Educating jurors about the cognitive "so what" of sleep apnea is important. In my own practice I will say,

> *As all of us age, our airways fall in a little easier at night when we lie down and can make it difficult to get enough oxygen. If we gain some weight, it often goes to our necks, and that presses down on the airway even more, making the situation worse. So, as we are sleeping, we are breathing, and when we can't get enough air in, it often sounds like (make loud snoring sound).*
>
> *Our brains can't store oxygen; we are totally dependent on what is in the bloodstream at the moment. As we are "breathing" (make snore sound) and our oxygen level goes down, when it hits a certain low point, our brain won't let us suffocate. It wakes us up (make snorting, choking noise). Then we can take a few deep breaths and get our blood oxygen level back up (demonstrate). We fall back asleep, and guess what? (Demonstrate snoring again.)*
>
> *All night long, people with sleep apnea aren't getting enough air, their blood oxygen gets really low, their brains wake them up, they take a few breathe, and the cycle repeats itself. Over and over, sometimes 50 to 60 times an hour.*
>
> *What happens the next day? Folks might not have any memory of waking up a million times, but they wake up still tired, and because they have been deprived of oxygen all night, they aren't thinking straight. Their reaction time is slow; their attention and memory are off. Every time the brain has to wake us up, it also interferes with how long we are in REM sleep. This is the deep restful sleep that sets memories from the day before. Normally we start in stage 1, go deeper to stage 2, then deeper to stage 3 and 4 (REM sleep) (use hand to demonstrate). Then we go back up through the stages. This natural sleep cycle continues in healthy people all night. When the brain is oxygen-deprived and waking us up (use hand to show going to stage 2 then abruptly higher to the waking stage with the sleep apnea sound), we might not ever make it to the REM stage.*

I will also point out,

> **_Sleep apnea vs. drunk people_**
>
> *Sleep apnea affects how quickly the brain processes information- it affects reaction time. Compared to drunk people –people over the legal limit for intoxication– guess who are the safer drivers? People with untreated sleep apnea or drunk people? Drunk people. It affects thinking that much.*
>
> **_Effect of sleep apnea_**
>
> *Let's think about how the brain works. It lives on oxygen. If it doesn't get oxygen, certain parts of the brain are going to be more vulnerable than others. Lack of oxygen*

might not show up on an IQ test, because those functions are pretty well set. The areas that control memory are going to be more vulnerable, and that's where we can expect problems to show up.—Kristie Nies, PhD, ABPP-CN

Mild sleep apnea is like being a little bit pregnant

When you hear the word mild *to describe sleep apnea, it's confusing. It's like saying someone is "a little bit" pregnant. If you are diagnosed with sleep apnea, you are having many events in the night when you are not getting enough oxygen. This will affect your thinking the next day. There are mild, moderate, and severe degrees of lack of oxygen, but even with mild apnea, you are not getting enough oxygen.*—Cheryl Weinstein, PhD, ABPP-CN

MENTAL ILLNESS IN GENERAL

Attorney Mark DeBofsky stresses that the bias of the general public against mental illness finds its way into the courtroom. For example, he notes that many disability policies limit benefits for psychiatric conditions but not for physical conditions. Experts often face an uphill battle to connect the jury to the condition and experience of the plaintiff/defendant when mental health is at issue.

Lack of insight on the part of the plaintiff/defendant is also often a significant barrier to helping jurors understand the litigant's experience. When litigants cannot accurately describe their own experience, this is distancing to others (including experts and jurors). David Hartman points out that plaintiffs/defendants fall somewhere on a continuum of accuracy, from exact accuracy through extreme feigning or unawareness. Inexact self-report, whether from lack of awareness or malingering, can mislead and confuse both experts and jurors.

> *A person can have just what they say they have. They can also be completely lacking insight into how they are. When you examine a demented person, that person will tell you they are fine; nothing's wrong! They have no insight into their level of impairment. People with psychotic disorder may have very little insight into their disturbance.*
>
> *Finally, you have groups of people who know full well that what they say they have, they don't have. They are trying to grab a set of brass rings from a litigation context.*
>
> *There is a spectrum of presentations from exactly what they say it is to completely different in every way.*

Robert Mendoza notes that even with a major mental health diagnosis, people can look normal on the outside:

> *People with significant depressive disorders go to work, have friends. We have all had friends who have been diagnosed with depression, who take medication and they still manage to sort of get by. We don't think of them as abnormal per say.*

Many experts noted that a goal on the stand is to help jurors empathize with the experience of mentally ill plaintiffs/defendants.

Mental health can destroy life of victim and defendant

> *My mindset in court is to tell people how mental illness can destroy lives; not just the victim, but also the person sitting in the defendant's chair. Mental illness has destroyed his or her life too.*
>
> *I try to remind jurors of folks they have known with mental illness. Seven out of ten people have experienced depression in their lives. If someone has been to a NAMI meeting, it's amazing how many neighbors they will see.*—Robert Mendoza, PsyD

De-stigmatizing mental health

> *Bring in awareness of defendant's family to help humanize. I literally want to put a human face on mental illness. For example, I might say,*
>
> *"Mr. Jones' mother has made valiant efforts to keep him on his medications; leaving work early, even getting fired from a job because she had to take care of him. But it wasn't enough. We can't blame mom. I guess to some extent we can blame the individual who didn't take the medication- but as I just described to you his ability to think clearly and organize and rationally respond to things is pretty limited. Understanding the consequences of his behavior when he is not taking his medication is impossible for him. Unfortunately, all you have to do is ask his mother about the effect that it has had on both of their lives.*—Robert Mendoza, PsyD

An issue that frequently arises in testimony about psychiatric illness is medication compliance.

> *When someone with mental illness has generally been doing fine, then commits a crime, people might say, "Well, he's been functioning fine. Why should we excuse this behavior?" I bring up an analogy of medical illnesses.*
>
> *"Sometimes, not taking medication has a specific, measurable response. How many times have you known someone to forget to take their blood pressure medication one day—and sure enough, their blood pressure goes up. With psychosis, if a person is not taking medication there will be similar outcomes, and usually not good ones. We can all relate to the importance of taking medications, and the importance of taking psychiatric medications is no exception.*—Robert Mendoza, PsyD

In some forensic situations, although a plaintiff/defendant does not meet full clinical criteria for a disorder, there may be a reason to comment on a subclinical symptom picture.

> Even though I may not have someone who meets full criteria for an Axis I disorder, they may show tendencies that would lead me to be concerned about that down the road.

I don't think Samantha has a full-blown anxiety disorder or depression, but she does have low self-esteem. She is very awae of her deficits. She is very concerned about doing well in school. If this isn't addressed now, my fear is that there may be an anxiety disorder down the road."—John Kirk, PsyD, ABPP-CN

SCHIZOPHRENIA AND PSYCHOSIS

A foundation for being about to communicate the experience of psychosis to jurors is understanding it ourselves.

David Schretlen asks, as clinicians, are we asking not just about symptoms, but what it feels like to experience those symptoms?

Get examinees to tell you how their symptoms feel

Explaining severe mental illness is tricky because the psychotic experience is so far from the mean. We are not good at empathizing with it. For example, a T of 90 for depression- we probably can empathize up to two standard deviations but not much farther. What does it feel like to be <u>that</u> depressed? With schizophrenia, the experience is so frightening and so unsettling, and so far out of people's daily experience it is very hard to explain and understand. Just saying that a person hears voices or has disordered thinking doesn't capture the experience in a way the jury can really grasp. So, I like to get a few specific examples of how psychotic experiences felt to the patient when I interview him. When you were manic and took off your clothes, how did you feel at the time? And later?" If you can get the feelings associated with a psychotic experience, you can communicate how the defendant experienced it since we can all relate to feelings.

Strategy for presenting psychosis

I back away from accepting the premise that just because a person is organized enough in other ways in their life and they might seem normal, they must be in control of their behavior all the time. I say, "Let's look below the surface to the crazy behaviors. Here's how the delusions can impact a person's life.... This person, in every other area of their life, is absolutely normal, but he has this delusion that this actress is in love with him. You don't see that in the rest of his life. People who are delusional often look normal on tests, because every other part of their life is in fact intact. This extreme, odd behavior that you are seeing about letters and pictures and poems are in fact very disturbed but explainable. So yes, this person went to work every day, had a family, they engaged in friendships. But here's the other side of this person's life. These pictures are the tip of the iceberg.—Robert Mendoza, PsyD

Leslie Rosenstein points out that in many court contexts, a big component of the hearings is for the judge to determine if the patient is faking mental illness. Her testimony therefore includes not just descriptions of symptoms the defendant is experiencing but information (if true) that the symptoms the person is experiencing are consistent with expected symptoms given the diagnosis.

Explaining schizophrenia

The pattern of test findings is consistent with what the literature tells us arises in schizophrenia.

When Robert Kinscherffis explaining psychotic symptoms to juries, he makes a point to tie the explanation to things that are straightforward, understandable, and directly related to the experience of the defendant:

> *A persecutory delusion is when a person perceives a threat that most people would not be able to perceive at all or, if they did, they would think the person is wildly exaggerating. We all know, for example, that the Chinese have nuclear weapons and could conceivably on any day attack the U.S. The defendant believes that the Chinese were specifically tracking him, and, depending on where he was, were targeting their nuclear armaments to destroy the city in which he was staying. Which was why he never stayed in a city for more than 24 hours over a period of 7 years, and why he panicked when he was arrested and assaulted the officer in an attempt to get away—here, because he feared that if he were detained it would prompt a nuclear strike upon the city where he was being held.*

Explaining delusions

He has delusional beliefs: In this particular case, that means that he has paranoid thinking that the CIA is out to get him.—Ira K. Packer, PhD, ABPP (Forensic)

The brain makes mistakes when tired

Sensory indiscriminations fall into two categories: hallucinations and illusions. If there is no external reference, it is an hallucination. If there is an external reference, it is an illusion. We have all experienced this. You are sleeping or almost sleeping in the middle of the night and you open your eyes and you start because you think someone is standing over you until you realize that "Duh, it's my jacket I threw over the back of my chair." That is an illusion—because your brain is not fully functioning, because you were almost asleep. Or when you are really tired and driving, you might think you see rabbits jumping in front of the car, but it really is simply the movement of the ground and the vegetation passing by your line of sight rapidly, and your brain is tired and not able to rapidly process that visual information. It doesn't happen when you are well rested. Your brain knows that movement is there and inhibits it, takes your attention away from it. Those are not indications of pathology, but it is an indication that your brain is not working at peak efficiency.—Robert L. Denney, PsyD, ABPP-CN, FP

Robert Kinscherff notes that communicating about legal insanity is very difficult because you have to work against misconceptions.

> Americans have a lot of misconceptions about the insanity defense like "lots of people get off" when actually they don't. They believe that if the person is found

insane, then some naïve doctor in a tweed jacket will let them out in 6 months. Actually, if a person is found legally insane, many tend to spend a significantly longer amount of time behind locked doors in a forensic hospital than bars than they would if sentenced to time in a prison.

In preparing for direct examination for a case where the insanity defense is in play, I will ask the attorney to walk me through the legal test for legal insanity—which is about the defendant's mental state at the time of the alleged crime.

Q: At the time of the defense, did this defendant suffer from a mental illness?

A: Yes.

Q: What was the mental illness?

A: Capgras syndrome.

Q: What does that mean?

A: This is a condition in which an individual becomes convinced that an individual known to them is not really that person. This is a delusion and is not readily changed by offering information to the contrary.

Q: Did he lack sufficient capacity to appreciate the wrongfulness of his act? (if the facts are there . . .)

A: Things that would suggest he did not appreciate the wrongful nature of the act include: He sat by the body of his friend—whom he had killed—for a day and a half and called neither the police nor an ambulance. When he and his dead friend were next seen—by a neighbor who came by to borrow a cup of sugar—the defendant had apparently not eaten or drank anything during that time. He made no effort to keep the neighbor from seeing his friend on the floor. When the neighbor screamed, he looked up and asked in a childish way, "What is wrong?" He did not try to stop the neighbor from calling police on her cellphone.

When the police arrived, he did not attempt to flee and seemed puzzled as to why the police were there. When they asked what happened, the defendant said that he had become aware that his friend was not really who he seemed to be. He became aware that his friend was an alien creature that had inhabited his friend's body. The defendant had worried about this for some days and had told others of this concern (who unsuccessfully tried to dissuade him). Eventually, the defendant concluded that he had to kill this alien before the alien killed him to protect this change in identity. And, the defendant told the police, he was certain that his friend would want to be "put out of his misery" rather than live his life as "a husk."

In some cases, the fact pattern calls for a distinction between mental health conditions and the actions of the defendant. William Barr will say,

It's not schizophrenia that causes someone to murder someone. It is the situation and context that causes someone with schizophrenia to murder someone, just like anyone else. It is not the condition that is doing the murder.

PTSD

It is always startling to see a low-speed motor vehicle collision produce a claim of debilitating PTSD. When I talk with attorneys about PTSD I always share a case I was involved in some years back where a plaintiff was hit at high speed on a high bridge spanning a major waterway. His car was slammed against the side rail. The rail buckled on impact, leaving the car tipping over the edge of the bridge. His driver's door had been deformed to the extent that he couldn't open it to escape the car, and a fire erupted in the engine, producing copious smoke. Bystanders were screaming, warning him that he had to get out before the engine exploded. That person developed PTSD. The plaintiff who had another car bump into hers at 10 miles an hour at a stop light? Let's look at what other factors might be at play.

Claims of PTSD often develop in the context of treating clinicians using the diagnosis the way a layperson would—that is, to signify significant upset about an event and/or caution about placing oneself in a position where the event might recur. Those are normal, appropriate reactions to injury or illness. Unfortunately, the original misdiagnosis might be recorded and re-recorded in multiple clinicians' diagnoses lists without ever reflecting a moment where a clinician sat down with the person to ask about the presence, frequency, duration, and effect of any PTSD symptoms on her daily function. The patient, having been told that she has PTSD and not understanding what PTSD means in the true clinical sense, may genuinely believe that she has it and will feel offended and misunderstood when an IME concludes that she does not.

Here are some clear, vivid strategies to help juries understand the diagnosis—or misdiagnosis—of PTSD.

Explaining PTSD

> I actually like the DSM-5 criteria. It makes it a lot easier to explain. I go through the criterion ABCDE, first giving a general description.
>
> *PTSD is a specific set of reactions that can occur when a person has gone through a very traumatic experience that is life-theatening or threatening severe bodily harm. Examples are [use examples relevant to case]. There is a characteristic pattern of responses [give examples based on the criteria]. And in his case, this is what happened. He had [give examples from each criteria].*—Ira K. Packer, PhD, ABPP (Forensic)

As the diagnosis of PTSD involves multiple criteria, many experts indicate that they display the DSM-5 criteria as a visual as they are explaining the diagnosis to the jury. A table with each criterion on one side and whether the plaintiff/defendant meets it on the other is particularly helpful as jurors will likely be able to refer back to the chart as they deliberate.

The thermostat is broken

> *Sometimes someone can have an experience that so affects them that it causes a tsunami of chemicals to get released into their system—the fight-or-flight response. And in some people, that alters their emotional thermostat. If you are cold in the room, you set the temperature a little higher. If a small thing happens, you have a small*

emotional response. If you are really cold, you set the thermostat a lot higher. If something really big happens, you have a bigger response. People who are exposed to significant trauma, who get that jolt of chemicals and adrenaline in their system, it's like their thermostat gets stuck on high. Everything becomes a big emotional response, so that even small issues may have big emotional responses, problems with emotional control. And when the thermostat is broken, a lot of treatment is about trying to recalibrate the thermostat so you don't overreact emotionally.—Neil Pliskin, PhD, ABPP-CN

What is PTSD?

Humans are built to take only so much stress. There are certain situations in our lives, may we never encounter them, where there is too much sensory and/or emotional overload. Situations like combat, rape, or a terrible accident, it may be too much. (Then talk about issues of the case).—William Barr, PhD, ABPP-CN

Part of the trend in the large numbers of cases of claimed PTSD is the fault of our profession. Look how DSM-5 has watered down criteria, My mother is 86 years old. One day I will find out she has died. If she has a fall or gets run over by a car, and my brother calls me to tell me about that, I would qualify for having PTSD.

I am not going to pretend to understand what that feels like. Because I don't, I can only tell you what dozens of people that I have worked with over the years have told me. And typically, what they describe is a pattern that they feel constantly on edge. They are very jumpy. When we started our treatment program for veterans, I told my treatment team, "Never approach them from behind. You will probably get hurt." The other thing they often have is what's called re-experiencing; it feels like it is happening to them all over again. It might be a flashback that happens during the day, and they feel like they are there again. Because a car backfires and they think it's a bomb. Or at night when they have horrible nightmares.

A good example would be one person I worked with who was so on edge, every night before bed he would walk the perimeter, just like when he was in Iraq. The problem was that his perimeter was now his house, and he would walk the house checking all the doors and all the locks and all the windows. With his sidearm.

One night his 4-year-old daughter came out of her room. He almost killed her. He had the gun right in her face. The girl said, "Daddy! Daddy!" And he snapped out of it.

That is what PTSD is. This man was not mean. He was not trying to hurt his family; he was trying to protect his family. And here he finds himself with a gun down his daughter's throat. You imagine how he feels.—Jacobus Donders, PhD, ABPP-CN

Explaining PTSD

PTSD is a reaction to a definable traumatic stressor. Unfortunately, the criteria have been watered down over the years. PTSD occurs after something very traumatic has

happened. You have had a threat to your own life, or a threat to the life of a loved one. Or you see something horrific, like someone dead at the scene. There is a disorder. You re-experience the traumatic event, you try to avoid thoughts of it, you might forget parts of it: Those are some of the features. The key is the re-experiencing.

The first thing I do is when I examine someone, I ask them in detail about what happened. And in the entire half-hour where Mr. X was describing the accident, I saw no unusual emotional reaction. And to me that is very significant. Even if they have recovered from PTSD, someone would have a reaction to describing the event in detail. I have had people who I have looked carefully at their medical records, and it was clear they initially had symptoms of PTSD and then recovered. But for those people, when discussing the event with them they became more emotional. That was not the case for Mr. X.—Glenn Larrabee, PhD, ABPP-CN

Suggesting symptoms

So many PTSD checklists and tests are out there. They are so transparent. When people are filling them out, symptoms are suggested. Jim Andrikopoulos, in his chapter on PTSD, questions whether the nightmares are real symptoms of PTSD or Hollywood. When clinicians sit down with patients and say, "Do you have trouble thinking about the event?" there is a pull to say, "Well, yes"—and when you are asked that question 100 times, it becomes real. The big thing is nightmares: "Do you find you have nightmares?"

To avoid suggesting symptoms to patients, I use an old Harvey Levin semistructured interview. Do you have problems with your sleep? Yes. Okay, what's wrong with your sleep? I have a hard time falling asleep. Okay, anything else disturb your sleep? Well, I have trouble breathing . . . Anything else? No. If the person was having recurrent nightmares that are a significant problem in their life, and you asked him multiple in-depth questions about sleep, it should come out.—Glenn Larrabee, PhD, ABPP-CN

You have to step back from these tests

I had one case where a claimant was 6 months pregnant. When they hooked her up after the MVA to a fetal monitor, she said, "I'm bored. You can let me go." There was all this data showing no abnormalities in the ER—then she claimed PTSD. And I said to the jury,

Not only does she not meet criteria for PTSD, but if you look at the ER records, she is not showing any emotional response. And they had her hooked up to monitors. If there really was a traumatic reaction, she would have shown a reaction then. They [hospital staff] were really paying attention."

On cross,

Q: But she failed the PTSD test!

A: Well, you have to step back from the tests. They ask leading questions. I spoke with her for a half-hour about the MVA; she didn't get upset once. Look at the ER records.

She was hooked up to a monitor and bored. You are not bored if you just had an acutely stressful event.—Glenn Larrabee, PhD, ABPP-CN

Statistics on PTSD

There are times when numbers are useful to help jurors understand the likelihood of developing a condition. For example, PTSD would not typically result from passing by a building and hearing gunshots, but therapists will often suggest that PTSD is the inevitable result of any potentially traumatizing experience and that such an experience is inevitably disabling. These are times when numbers help. You can say,

Look, a lot of people believe that any trauma precipitates PTSD. But in fact if you look at the national statistics, that in a lifetime, only about 2 to 5% of individuals exposed to psychological trauma will develop PTSD. Even among those whose injuries are so severe they require treatment in a Level 1 trauma center, only about 20% will develop PTSD. PTSD is the exception, not the rule."—David Hartman, PhD, ABPP-CN

Being upset does not mean it's PTSD

Of course it was upsetting; of course it was. But PTSD isn't just being upset or experiencing a nightmare once in a while. It is a serious psychiatric condition where the horror of experience ruins your ability to work, to be in a relationship. It was clear from interviewing Mr. Smith that he has occasional nightmares (as we all do). And he flinches when he hears loud noises (as we all do), and thinking about Bosnia upsets him (of course; anyone who has been in war will tell you that it is an upsetting thing). But that doesn't mean that he had PTSD. If that was the case, every soldier retuning from war would have PTSD, and that is not correct.—Anonymous

Nightmares and PTSD

It's important to indicate to the jury [that] clinicians should not limit themselves to a checklist. In psychological disease, the timing is important, not just whether symptoms are present. It's when they appear, and how long they last, and their intensity. So, for example, this is where the neuropsychologist has to bring in a well-developed knowledge of PTSD. If you don't have a well-developed knowledge base of PTSD, you shouldn't be evaluating folks or testifying on the issue of PTSD.

Let's take nightmares. The best research has shown that nightmares and other re-experiencing symptoms are the first to drop out. This is shown with the Oklahoma VA bombing. The survivors were tracked for years. Carol North, a psychiatrist, did the landmark research. After the first year, chronic PTSD was characterized by psychic numbing, but the nightmares and re-experiencing had dropped out. So, if you have someone who is reporting PTSD and they are saying they have nightmares every night, be suspicious—very suspicious. You don't have to agree with Carol North's findings; there might be other research. My point is that you have to bring in a research database as the context in which to understand symptoms.—Manfred Greiffenstein, PhD, ABPP-CN

Confusion between PTSD and actual learning

> *There is confusion between PTSD and learning. I have tested people who had an accident on a freeway with a big rig, and forever into the future, they are nervous when a big rig comes up beside them while they are driving. But this is appropriate. Learning is a process whereby humans become aware of what is dangerous, and remember and act on it in the future. This is not a mental disorder. It is a situation of shaping behavior in response to learning. If the reactions do not cause significant disruption in social and occupational function, it would be appropriate to say that the fears are an expected and adaptive reaction and not a psychiatric diagnosis.*—Kyle Boone, PhD, ABPP-CN

In my own practice, I often see cases where a plaintiff has been diagnosed with PTSD when they actually developed an acute driving phobia from tan accident. Unfortunately, misdiagnosis often results in years of unproductive psychodynamic psychotherapy when eight sessions of graded exposure with a CBT therapist would have gotten them back on the road. I will explain the difference to jurors:

> *Many people develop driving phobias after a car accident. That accident may have been the first time someone realized, really realized, that we are all driving 3-ton metal contraptions at 65 miles per hour down highways. Developing fear after a car accident is normal, and it is adaptive. Fear is our body's way of protecting us, to make sure we are safe.*
>
> *Most people are nervous drivers for a little while after an accident and eventually get back on the road. They may always be more careful, but that's not a bad thing. A much smaller number of people are so afraid, they can't get back on the road, or if they drive, they won't drive on highways. This is known as a driving phobia. Luckily, there is a great treatment for driving phobia called graded exposure. It's like treating any phobia. The person learns to relax while being exposed to just a little of the thing they are afraid of. Eventually, they learn to relax sitting in the car, then driving in a parking lot, then they graduate to back roads and finally highways. Therapists will actually drive with people, or some have virtual reality sets. It has decades of great research, and it works.*
>
> *A lot of people who have driving phobias after an accident are misdiagnosed with PTSD. Ms. Smith does not meet criteria for PTSD. That is a really severe mental disorder that affects every area of functioning. For Ms. Smith, she never got the really good, evidence-based treatment for driving phobia. Once she does, if she is like the vast majority of people who get the well-researched treatment, she will be back on the road.*

Not full PTSD criteria

> *In one case, the examinee was a gentleman who was molested for years by a priest. When the examinee confronted the priest when he was a teen, the priest said, "It's fine if you want to stop, but because of you, I have access to all these other kids." That*

completely shut down this guy, who never disclosed the abuse. He went on to have a successful career. At midlife, he got divorced. His wife had a new partner. They had a high-conflict divorce. He got it in his head that the new boyfriend was molesting his child, and he threatened his life. He ended up with a felony.

My goal on the stand was trying to help people understand how this could come to be—how someone might not disclose childhood sexual abuse but in the right circumstances would have a set of core beliefs that led to certain behaviors; how he could be successful in the right circumstances, he could keep his experiences in the box, until the box broke.

This is somebody who didn't meet the diagnostic criteria for DSM-IV-TR PTSD. For all those decades, he wasn't having nightmares about the events; he wasn't being hypervigilant or having intrusive thoughts. He was avoiding it. He had some features, but he didn't meet full DSM-IV-TR PTSD criteria. His actions were in response to this situation where a strange man had access to his children. For all of these decades, he believed that the abuse was his fault, not the priest's fault, and when he felt that it was his fault his children were under the control and influence of a man he didn't trust, it all came spilling back out.—Darcy Cox, PsyD, ABPP-CN

He should be ashamed.

I had a case where a few years after 9/11, there was a guy who worked as a cook on a boat. He was going on the stairs between decks. While on his way down, he fell on his butt and ended up claiming TBI and PTSD as effects of the fall. My testimony was:

In this city, 2 years after 9/11, for this man who has fallen on his rear end to be claiming PTSD is a total shame in lightof all of our heroes encountered in this city who developed PTSD as first responders." The jurors were outraged.—William Barr, PhD, ABPP-CN

I was offended by this PTSD claim.

When examinees claim PTSD from a minor fender-bender [I might say],

Frankly speaking, I was offended by this claim. I am old enough to have treated Holocaust survivors. Not many, but a few. I am also current enough to have seen men and women in uniform coming back from Iraq and Afghanistan with real PTSD. And for anybody to equate being rear-ended at 5 miles an hour with the horrors of the Holocaust, or service members who were seriously injured while serving our country, to me is offensive.—Jacobus Donders, PhD, ABPP-CN

DEPRESSION

Depression is another psychiatric phenomenon that most laypeople are familiar with. The problem is, when a psychology expert says "depression," there are likely to be 12 very different thought bubbles produced in reaction to the word. Juror 1 experienced severe depression in her teenage years requiring medication and years of therapy. Juror 2 had an aunt who was hospitalized for bipolar depression. Juror 3 relates to characters on TV saying they are "depressed" about a bad date. And so on. The challenge in the courtroom is to ensure that everyone is on the same page with their understanding of depression as a serious clinical condition.

Depression is not just a sad mood

> *Depression feels different from sadness. It's more intense. The impact is greater. It involves a large and lasting change in mood and always in the same direction—and that is down. It is sadness turned up all the way to 10. Imagine that experience; then imagine what that would do to your thinking abilities.*—Scott D. Bender, PhD, ABPP-CN

> *Depression is not just a sad mood; it is a systemic illness. It can affect how you think and remember. We need to get the depression treated before we can figure out what is going on with Ms. Jones's thinking.*—Kristie Nies, PhD, ABPP-CN

When the diagnosis of depression is at issue, many experts will display the DSM-5 criteria for depression as a visual to underscore for jurors the severity and pervasiveness of the symptoms required for diagnosis. The other benefit of the criteria set is that jurors can see firsthand that problems with concentration are so common in depression, it is literally part of the criteria for diagnosing it.

Effects of depression on cognition

> *Sometimes depression generates a "what's the use?" thinking. In many cases, if you are depressed, you feel, "I can't do this." You feel hopeless. When encountering a challenging situation, you feel, "Well, it doesn't matter what I do." Put yourself in the person's shoes. If that person encounters a test of mental ability, they may feel, "I can't do this"—so they give up. And that's what the research says. The most significant effects of depression on thinking are on motivation and effort to produce and succeed.*—Rus Bauer, PhD, ABPP-CN

Depending on the fact pattern of the case, an expert may need to help jurors understand various types of depression. Manfred Greiffenstein noted that he begins his description of bipolar disorder with something almost everyone can relate to:

> *Look, we have all had mood swings. But with bipolar disorder, the mood swings are particularly wide and particularly intense.*

Chapter 2, "Setting the Truth on Fire," includes advice regarding person-centered testimony that is worth restating here. That is, jurors will quickly zone out if testimony is centered on diagnostic categories and abstract criteria sets. While addressing criteria and diagnostic categories may be required due to the legal question at hand, experts can move quickly to concrete examples of the symptoms for the plaintiff/defendant and, importantly, how those symptoms are experienced by them and the people they interact with.

MODERATE TO SEVERE TBI

See Chapter 12 for clear, engaging strategies to help jurors understand concussion. Here are strategies to explain the effects of moderate to severe traumatic brain injury.

Hammer vs. chisel metaphor for encephalomalacia

> *Encephalomalacia means that this is brain damage that happened a long time ago. The analogy would be if you hit yourself on the thumb with a hammer while you are trying to hang a picture. Your thumb is black and blue; it's bruised. That is a bruise that will eventually go away and your thumb will go back to normal. If you are working with a chisel, and you cut your thumb off, you don't grow a thumb back. Encephalomalacia means brain damage, with a loss of brain tissue. It means we can see that there is damage in the brain and it is not repaired.*—Jacobus Donders, PhD, ABPP-CN

TBI outcome

> *There is a relationship between how severe their injury was and their outcome, things like their oxygen saturation on the scene, were they in shock, did their blood pressure drop too low, did they have respiratory issues. All of these things impact outcome.*—Leslie Rosenstein, PhD, ABPP-CN

Like a downsized car engine

> *You can think of the brain like the engine of a car. What happened here, because of the severe brain injury, Mr. Hernandez has had his car engine downsized. He might have the same motivation, but he may not be able to go as fast or as far as he used to go. He will get tired and probably frustrated. And he will have to devote more time to the task than he used to do.*—Martin Rohling, PhD

A football team metaphor

> The brain is made up of neurons. Brains are like a football team with 11 players. (Obviously, there are more neurons than that, but let's stick with the analogy.) We'll also say that the rules say you cannot replace the player. Now, if one player gets injured, your team has to play not only the current game one man down, but all the remaining games in the season with just 10 players. To do as well as you want to, you are going to have to play differently than before. Maybe your players are not very well conditioned. If you beef up your 10 players, they can run faster and play stronger. They may be able to do as well as when the team had 11 players. You will also have to change your playbook. The whole playbook was built around having 11 players on the field. The plays that worked with 11 players may not work with just 10 players. And what about the quarterback? If

the player you lost is the quarterback, who will be calling the plays? You have 10 well-conditioned players, but they are standing around not knowing what to do. The quarterback does executive functioning. When you get into the huddle looking at each other standing around: "What are we going to do? We need someone to call the plays!" You may need help from a coach. Maybe the guy who was the tight end becomes the quarterback. That's neuroplasticity.—Martin Rohling, PhD

Football team metaphor extended

Now you used to play in the Southeastern Conference. The SEC is a really tough league in which to play. I don't care how good your 10 players are, you can't win in the SEC with 10 players, no matter who the 10 players are. You will have to play smaller schools. An example would be, instead of being a neurosurgeon, you will have to be a cashier. Still challenging to you, since your brain injury—but not too challenging that you can't stay in the game.—Martin Rohling, PhD

Football team metaphor extended II

So, what we are talking about here is aging. Some players on your team are older, and they will retire sooner than you think. You were already down to 10 players, what are you going to do when another player leaves?—Martin Rohling, PhD

Football team metaphor extended III

This person only has 5 players. They have lost a lot and can hardly play anymore against an opponent. But those players still want to play. How can we help them feel like they are still in the game? Even if all they can do is cheer for their former teammates, that will make them feel like they are part of the game.—Martin Rohling, PhD

Mental traction

Severe brain injuries are often invisible. If you had someone with a broken leg and they had a cast on their leg, you wouldn't expect them to run a race. With brain injury, there are no casts. Sometimes there are too high expectations. The person looks fine, they sound fine: They must be fine.

But you can have a very accomplished long-distance runner. Take them off of the concrete and put them on the beach so they are running on sand. They can churn their feet as always, they can expend as much energy as always, but they are not getting the same kind of traction.—Neil Pliskin, PhD, ABPP-CN

Brakes and gas

The frontal lobe is the part of the brain that puts brakes on our emotional response: "Whoa! Too much anger, better slow down!" Or allows us to feel an emotional response: "Hey! This thing over here happened; time to respond with some emotion!" It's like a brake pedal or a gas pedal.

After the severe brain injury, Mr. Smith had damage to this part of his brain. What you have here is a guy with no brakes and a heavy lead foot. When he is feeling a lot of emotions, when he is overwhelmed, he can't hit the brakes, and instead he hits the gas. And we have a problem. And I'll tell you what: If you ask his wife, she will say that every time it happens, he feels so bad about it.—Rod Swenson, PhD, ABN

Psychosocial factors in TBI outcome

Outcome in severe TBI is influenced by a number of vulnerabilities, some of which may be neurological and some psychosocial. If you look at the outcome studies of TBI, one of the strongest factors in outcome is how intact and supportive the family is. Factors like life stressors, like trouble at work, depression and anxiety, will influence outcome.—Michael McCrea, PhD, ABPP-CN

Depression and recovery from severe TBI

We know that people with depression, in every disease state that has been looked at, people who are unhappy report more symptoms. It could be multiple sclerosis, surgical recovery, traumatic brain injury. People who are depressed, they report more symptoms, but they also genuinely feel like they have more trouble doing things around the house and at work competently. It's that way for so many medical conditions. It's because what depression does, it makes you less optimistic. You assume your medical condition is going to have worse consequences. You just feel worse about yourself and about your future, how you evaluate things and how you think things are going. There is no data that depression makes people have a more severe brain injury in terms of the neurons and pathways in their brain, but if you tell me people with depression report more symptoms after brain injury, I would say that makes sense. Because that sentence works for just about every medical condition.—David Williamson, PhD, ABPP-CN

Severe TBI

Listen, I looked at this person's medical records. And if you were to look at his CT, which is really an x-ray shown in slices, if you put it up there, my grandmother, God rest her soul, who had a sixth-grade education, could say, "Hmmm, something is not right here." That's how bad it is, even though this person is not drooling, not missing an arm or a leg. But there is an injury here, inside the brain. This person clearly is missing some brain cells. Now we can lose **some** *brain cells; we have extra ones. But this goes way beyond what we have in our reserve tank.*—Jacobus Donders, PhD, ABPP-CN

A work in progress

I recall a case involving a 20-year-old young man who was premorbidly very smart, had graduated with a degree in economics. He had a horseback riding accident and sustained a severe TBI. He was left with some subtle frontal changes, reduced processing speed, and a flattening of his affect and personality. There was some real injury there. At the time I saw him he was 3 years out from his accident. He was seen by a plaintiff-friendly neuropsychology expert who wrote a report that predicted dire consequences for this young man: He will never work, he will never have friends, he will never marry, he will have a very limited life. It was way over the top pessimistic. I made the point in my testimony that:

> *This young man is a work in progress. It has only been 3 years. Yes, he had a life-altering injury, but he had a lot of assets in his column. He had insight into the nature of his difficulties. He had a wonderful, supportive family. He had many friends who cared about him. He was well educated. He did not have any physical disability.*
>
> *Recovering from a TBI is a dynamic process. People grieve the loss of their former selves. When it goes well, they formulate new goals that fit their current ability structures. This process does not happen overnight. It is a very challenging experience that is, ultimately, best understood as a reorganization of one's sense of self. Of course, sometimes this process doesn't go well. But even when it goes, well, which I think it will in this case, it takes years, maybe 5 or more years, to move from the life they had to the life they will live out in the future. When you look at the severe TBI literature, this man has a lot of positives.*—David S. Bush, PhD, ABPP-CN

Paul Craig, will speak with juries about the issue of returning self-awareness after a severe traumatic brain injury:

> *Awareness of their impairment, or lack thereof, can be so frustrating, challenging, and humiliating. At first, it is common to have no awareness there is a problem, a phenomenon referred to as anosognosia. Then, as self-awareness begins to return, the person begins recognizing the impairment and can become increasingly disengaged with the social world around him. We see that with Mr. Jones.*

Indy 500 analogy

> Another thing I won't accept, and I won't even look at, is pictures. A lot of attorneys want me to look at pictures. "You want to see the pictures?" No, I don't care what the pictures look like. I use the analogy of the Indy 500.
>
> *Have you ever watched a sports car race where the car goes into the wall, and it is sliced and diced, and the guy climbs out of the wreck and waves his hands and walks off? That's because the car did its job. Remember those old cars you had when you were a kid, and you could drop it on the floor and it just bounced? Well, if there were people in there, everyone inside the car would be dead, because all of the energy of the impact went right to the inside. Your car is all smushed and bunched. Energy is finite. If you expend a bunch of energy busting up your fenders, the car is doing what you bought it for. It is saving your life; it is protecting you. You want your car to be crumpled, because that gives you a fighting chance inside the car.*—Tom Boll, PhD, ABPP-CN

PROBLEMS WITH EXECUTIVE FUNCTION

Psychologists and neuropsychologists are so familiar with the phrase "executive function" that we forget almost no one outside the field knows what it means. Here are strategies to explain the term to jurors.

> I don't like to use terms like executive function. That is inaccessible. I say,
>
> *The frontal lobes control how you do things, as opposed to what you know. Part of the back of the brain is about getting knowledge, and understanding things. The front of the brain is about what you do with that knowledge. Can you plan ahead? Solve problems? Make an appropriate response to a situation?"*—John McSweeny, JD, PhD, ABPP-CN

Corral/gate metaphor

> After a 5-week trial, this is the take home for juries:
>
> The frontal lobe [executive function] is like a gate in a corral. We are all born with a "gate" which is our brain and our behavior and our mouth. And the gate is wide open. Think about it. If you have a gated area with lots of animals in it, and the gate is open, they all come out. So when we are younger, we have poor impulse control. Our corral's gate is wide open. Everything we think comes out of our mouth, everything we see, we react to. It just comes out because the gate is wide open. As we get older the gate closes more and more. Or maybe it closes more slowly because you have an injury, or something happened to you. And then you think about adolescents, and their gate is sort of opened and closed and maybe fewer animals get out, but it is not ideal. And then when we are adults, the gate is closeable. So think about your kids at home, all the horses are coming out of the corral. So you have to be the one to keep the gate closed and monitor the gate. You have to be your child's frontal lobe [executive function].- Lisa Stanford, PhD, ABPP-CN

It's like the judge

> I feel a striking beginning gets everyone's attention. Part of my strategy is to grab the attention of the jury. To do that, you might say something outrageous:
>
> *It's sort of like the judge sitting here. Most of the time, it seems like he is not doing much of anything. But when ther is any question or problem or disagreement, the judge has to come in as the executive and weigh issues, make decisions, and is the decider about what needs to be done next. That's what the central executive is like. Much of the time when things are automatic and proceeding well, it doesn't seem to have much involvement. It's when there is a problem, error, or contradictions that executive functions come into play. If you are not aware of the errors or attending to them, then you make mistakes, but a good executive catches the errors and makes adjustments and corrections."*—Rodney Vanderploeg, PhD, ABPP-CN

Explaining higher-level executive function

Executive functioning is like the conductor of an orchestra. S/he is not playing any instruments. But s/he is standing in front of the orchestra and organizing the musicians, keeping the tempo, guiding the mood and the message of the music. S/he is not playing but is guiding all components of the orchestra in an integrated manner. The conductor is to the orchestra what executive functions are to the management of other brain functions—Paul L. Craig, PhD, ABPP-CN

Frontal dysfunction doesn't affect learning a fact, it effects how you use a fact

Frontal dysfunction doesn't affect learning a new fact. It affects how you use a new fact. It doesn't affect knowing a rule, but it affects your ability to follow the rule.—Lynn Blackburn, PhD, ABPP-CN

In my own practice, I like to use an example of frontal executive function that everyone can relate to: a diet. Few jurors will have experienced frontal impairment but most will have been on a diet:

Frontal dysfunction is like dieting. It's a performance issue. When we are dieting, we know what we are supposed to do: We shouldn't eat sugar, we shouldn't eat French fries. But it is hard to make ourselves stick to it. Ms. Smith's frontal lobe deficit doesn't prevent her from knowing what she should be doing, but it makes it very hard to carry it out.

Defining executive functions

Q: Doctor, what is executive function?

A: The executive functions are the adaptive functions of the brain. When we deal with new things, we have to use our executive functions. For the stuff that you do every day (that is, automatic behavior), you don't use your executive functions.

Now there are lots of different kinds of executive functions, likely mediated by different regions of the brain: Can you pay attention to something? Can you prioritize by importance, by timeframe? Can you shift from one thing to another as necessary? Can you make reasonable decisions for circumstances, considering all of the pertinent factors? Can you solve life problems?—Wendy Marlowe, PhD, ABPP-CN

Explaining executive function

***Executive functions** refers to your ability to manage and complete complex tasks and monitor how you're doing, and change it up if need be. An example is birthday party planning: I have to choose the date, then see if it is a good date for everyone (not a football weekend), then choose the invitations and send them in advance, then plan the activities and location and menu. And buy a cake or order it in advance. On the day of the event I have to lay out the serving dishes and be sure they are clean, and heat up hotdogs at different temps than the French fries, etc., etc., etc.*—Tannahill Glen, PhD, ABPP-CN

Explaining disinhibition

It's like walking past a fruit stand. We could take a piece of fruit, but we don't. We stop that response in ourselves.—William Barr, PhD, ABPP-CN

Explaining poor problem-solving

When I speak to a jury I think of the varied experiences they have had as sort of an average American; everyone faces traffic; everyone has had those situations where AT&T messes up your bill or the bank charges you something. When I am explaining when people aren't at the top of their game anymore, they have issues with executive function or new problem solving, I will use typical problems the jury can relate to. It is less of an explanation of how they do on a particular test, and more I am talking about the cognitive domains and how that affects the person's everyday life because that's the only thing people relate to.

Everyone knows that when there is thick black smoke coming from your neighbor's home, you call 911. That is what we do, but that means that you are safe for sort of well-known emergencies or problems but when it comes to something more nuanced like say the bank has charged you twice for overdraft protection when one of the charges was reversed, they need to fix that. And this individual can't handle a problem like that but we all face those kinds of problems. Those problems come up.—Shelley Peery, PhD

Mr. Smith had the ability to inhibit his impulses but chose not to.

This was a criminal responsibility case. The question: Was there an executive dysfunction that caused someone to act on an impulse to kill someone? On all of his tests, Mr. Smith seemed to have the ability to do that, but in real life, he obviously did not inhibit his impulse to kill. It is my opinion that Mr. Smith had the ability to inhibit his impulses but chose not to.—William Barr, PhD, ABPP-CN

Everyone in prison has something wrong with their frontal lobes

The frontal lobe is the part of the brain that tells the other parts of the brain what to do. It is the highest level of functioning that we have as humans. It makes us different from the apes. It enables us to solve complex problems, to make plans for things down the road, and importantly it plays a key role for inhibiting behavior.

All criminal behavior is the result of some type of frontal lobe activity or inactivity, in my opinion. If you look at the research on antisocial personality, those samples all have frontal lobe dysfunction. If you say these people are not guilty because of frontal lobe dysfunction, you are going to empty the prisons. They are all in there because their frontal lobes are not working well. The question is, "Is there a mental disease and defect over and above general criminal behavior that is relevant in this case?" You have to hold the level of dysfunction to a higher standard, beyond ADHD, or even multiple mild brain injuries from bar fights; you have to have a brain tumor or seizures, that next level of neurological believability. Everyone in prison has something wrong with their frontal lobes or they wouldn't be there.—William Barr, PhD, ABPP-CN

ANOSOGNOSIA

Anosognosia is a neurologically based unawareness of deficit. One neuropsychologist who prefers to remain anonymous notes that when he sees a plaintiff who is densely anosognosic for their deficits,

> I focus on the importance of collateral interviews and treatment records—for example, OT, PT, and speech therapy. The direct observations of the people around the plaintiff are critical. The direct testimony should be about building the picture about "this is how the world views the person." The jury has to be educated that the capacity for self-awareness is part of their thinking deficit pattern.
>
> *The part of the brain that contributes to a person's understanding of how well their brain is working, that part is not working well, so Mr. Smith's self-report is not accurate. His statements that he is fine is absolutely a function of brain dysfunction.*
>
> ------------
>
> *The brain has a lot of jobs, and one of the jobs of the brain is self-awareness. When certain parts of the brain are injured, self-awareness is also injured, so the person may not notice things that they are doing wrong. It actually mostly has to do with the things that Mr. Smith now cannot do that he used to be able to do. And it is very distinct from denial, from the sense of denial, "I'm just not ready to face up to this; I'm not ready to accept it."*—Tedd Judd, PhD, ABPP-CN

In my own practice, I make the distinction between "can't" and "don't want to":

> *With this injury, the part of the brain that tells him how his brain is working, that part isn't working. He* ***can't*** *know h has deficits. It's not a psychological denial, he doesn't* ***want*** *to know. Its neurologically based. He literally can't know.*

ANOXIC INJURIES

> ***Explaining microvascular versus hypoxic/anoxic injury***
>
> In one case, the claim was an anoxic issue. The plaintiff was a lady in her 60s, with diabetes, obesity, and high blood pressure- lots of cardiovascular risk factors for subcortical microvascular ischemic changes. The issue at hand was are the problems consistent with anoxia/ hypoxia or with these subcortical micro vascular ischemic processes? My strategy was to ask,
>
> *What does the literature tell us that are the problems we see with hypoxia? Memory problems with keeping information over time. What are the problems we see with subcortical microvascular issues? Speed of information processing and getting information in in the first place. Do we have a pattern of rapid forgetting vs. trouble getting information in, but normal retention?*

This is what I found . . . . (I am educating the jury about the two alternative explanation for a problem, and saying my data is most consistent with this or that.)—Rodney Vanderploeg, PhD, ABPP-CN

Anoxia

Anoxia is a very fancy term for not getting oxygen. Everyone understands we need oxygen to breathe, and the brain can go without oxygen for only so long. After a couple of minutes it really becomes problematic. Cells start to die. The brain starts to die. There are parts of the brain that are more vulnerable to that. [I show with my hands, fingers spread apart.] There are several blood vessels that feed the brain, an area of overlap that we call the watershed zone. Those are the most vulnerable to lack of oxygen. Now those also happen to be the areas of the brain that are very involved in memory, so a lot of people with anoxia tend to have memory problems. The funny thing is that they can remember things from way back, but they can't remember anything new.—Jacobus Donders, PhD, ABPP-CN

How can it get from the heart to the brain?

How could a heart attack lead to cognitive impairment? What is the mechanism of action?

How can it be that someone would have a heart attack and it caused problems with thinking? How can it get from the heart to the brain? The most likely cause would be if you stopped breathing. We know that if you don't get enough oxygen, certain areas of the brain, which are more vulnerable than others, may be damaged.

An important question to ask, though, is did Mrs. Smith in fact stop breathing? There is no other mechanism that would account for cognitive changes from a heart attack. If she didn't stop breathing, it doesn't matter whether she had a heart attack. Because there is no other variable than lack of oxygen that could account for problems with thinking. When I went through her medical records, there is no documentation in the records that she stopped breathing. Instead, her cardiologist wrote that there was no issue of lack of oxygen . . .

There are a lot of other things than not breathing in a heart attack that could cause the problems Dr. Other Expert found when she tested Mrs. Smith 5 years after the heart attack, like the fact that she has insomnia, she's depressed and she has chronic pain.—Kristie Nies, PhD, ABPP-CN

Manfred Greiffenstein noted that his explanations to jurors about anoxic injuries depend on the facts in the medical records:

> Hypoxia *means deficient, less-than-normal oxygen in the lungs.* Anoxia *means no oxygen in the lungs. Episodes of hypoxia are common; if you snore severely, you will have hypoxic episodes. The key concept, though, is ischemia, which is insufficient*

oxygen to tissue. That is different from insufficient oxygen to lungs. I look for evidence in the medical records for ischemia and not just look at pulse oximetry.

APHASIA

Explaining anomia

When I showed him pictures, he really had trouble coming up with the names of objects to a degree that is abnormal for his age group. You have probably all had the experience where you see someone whose name you should know coming towards you and thought, oh God! I'm not going to remember their name. You can't get it when you need it. In the case of this individual it happens a lot more than the average person, and it can be very uncomfortable and embarrassing and have an impact on their social functioning—Nick Bogod, R.Psych

Demonstrating Broca's aphasia

It is hard to generate the jibberish to demonstrate Wernicke's aphasia with classic jargon. I If it is Broca's aphasia, I will demonstrate the problem with my own speech,

I . . . Will . . . slow . . . things . . . down . . .—Erin Bigler, PhD, ABPP-CN

Alexia without agraphia

Alexia without agraphia is simply being able to write without being able to read, which obviously sounds like a very counterintuitive condition. No one would think that you would be able to do that, but that's one of the fascinating things about the brain that the networks that work to help us read are somewhat distinct from the networks that help us to write. Fortunately for Mr. Plaintiff, he did retain the ability to write.—Shelley Peery, PhD

Explaining dyslexia

Dyslexia is a specific reading disorder. It makes it hard for people to put together and take apart sounds within words. People with dyslexia have a very common pattern on testing, and it is exactly what I found for Mr. Smith.—Robb Mapou, PhD, ABPP-CN

SEIZURES

Explaining phases of seizures

In most of the cases where there has been a crime with epilepsy, it is in the post ictal phase. Jurors need to understand the difference between pre-ictal, ictal and post ictal phases.

There is a period where the person gets a warning that there could be a seizure, there is the seizure itself which lasts from seconds to a few minutes, and then there is a period in which the brain is trying to reorganize itself. The person can be

confused during any of these phases. And that is what happened here. Mr. Smith was confused.—William Barr, PhD, ABPP-CN

Postictal violent behavior

I had a murder case where an epileptic was post ictal. He beat up an old woman. Terrible. He was convicted in the end. Another case, a guy had a seizure behind the wheel of a car and drove up the courthouse steps.

There is a period of confusion after having a seizure. People respond in a confused way to what is around them. It's like you are knocked out. And you wake up, and someone is pressing down on you. You want to get them off you. That lapse in awareness, and confusion upon waking is what explains most post-ictal violent behavior. People are trying to administer to them- but, they react against that out of confusion.—William Barr, PhD, ABPP-CN

Misconceptions of seizures

Q: Aren't all seizures characterized by moving your arms and legs?

A: No.—William Barr, PhD, ABPP-CN

A group of neurons going wild

Epilepsy is a group of neurons going wild. A group of neurons sets up a disruptive pattern. Afterwards, many of the kids need time to reboot.—Lynn Blackburn, PhD, ABPP-CN

ELECTRICAL INJURIES

The truth is, no one really knows what electrical injury does to the brain. There is various research that has been done, but at the end of the day, when someone comes into contact with an electrified power source, unless their head is a direct point of contact, you don't know where that electricity is going to go. You don't know how it affects the person.

In my career, I have worked with over 250 people who have had electrical shock injuries. I have written book chapters and spoken all over the world about electrical injury. And I am telling you that there is a lot that is still not known. Somebody that tells you that they do understand it, they must be much smarter than me, or spending more time studying this issue than I do, because I am not aware of studies that show that.—Neil Pliskin, PhD, ABPP-CN

VIOLENCE

Tedd Judd shares a vivid analogy for predatory versus reactive violence:

This is the story of the cat, the dog, and the bird. Imagine a walled garden and there is a cat in that garden and the cat is in the corner of the garden and there is a dog in

the garden barking at the cat in the corner. What does the cat look like? Its back is up; its tail is big. What's the cat doing? It's hissing, its fur is all standing up, it may be putting its claws out and showing its teeth. What's the probability of violence in that situation? Fairly high.

Okay. Same cat, same garden. There is a bird in the middle of the lawn. The cat is approaching the bird. What does the cat look like? Its fur is all sleeked down, it's as close to the ground as it can. Is it making any noise? As little as possible. What's its movement like? Very slow and cautious. What's the probability of violence? Pretty high.

But those are two very different kinds of violence, and as it turns out different parts of the brain are active during those two different kinds of violence.

[Specific to TBI:]

Almost always the irritability and the anger that you see after a TBI is the reactive sort and has several specific characteristics. It is usually an overreaction to the situation. Something has to have happened to trigger it; it doesn't just arise out of the blue. It's out of character for the person, and they usually calm down pretty rapidly afterwards

Explaining an opinion about violence

To go to Bridgewater State Hospital a person has to be male. He has to be forensically committed, has to require the "strict security" of Bridgewater. From time to time I will do a case where someone has been found not guilty by reason of insanity for a homicide case 20 years ago when they were acutely psychotic. Unfortunately, they have not accomplished full remission from psychotic symptoms; they may retain some delusional thoughts about weather patterns, or the Kiwanis club, or the pope. You use specialized tools and score them on the basis of information that they don't have a delinquency history or criminal history prior to the homicide. They have little or no history of substance abuse. Their institutional incident reports are limited to the first year, when doctors were trying to get their acute psychotic symptoms under control. When you go through their records, all of their disciplinary reports involve incident reports when they were hit by others, didn't strike back, and told a guard. The mental health staff at the hospital opine that he still needs strict security because of the unresolved psychosis and argue that nobody knows whether or under what circumstances he might become violent again because of the incompletely psychosis.

Fair enough, but we are now driven by a single murderous act that occurred while floridly psychotic 20 years ago—and with no other history of threatened or actual act of violence before then or subsequently. On the Violence Risk Appraisal Guide he scores very low. On the Historical Clinical Risk Management-20 test (HCR-20) he looks low risk and readily manageable in terms of violence risk. My opinion is that he can be safely transferred to an inpatient unit operated by the

Department of Mental Health unit and no longer requires the strict security of Bridgewater State Hospital.

Here we are looking at how much violence risk, to whom, and under what circumstances. My opinion is that in a state hospital locked mental health unit the threat to the community would be low because he is not in the community. He is unlikely to pose risk to the other inpatients or to staff as he has not acted in a threatening or aggressive manner in 19 years, although symptoms of psychosis are not fully resolved.

Can I tell you at 100% probability that he would never become assaultive again? No, I can't tell you that. Once you manifest a behavior it is virtually impossible to say it would never happen again, especially since his is associated with psychosis and he continues to percolate a psychosis. On the other hand, but for the incident that occurred when he was floridly psychotic, he does not show a prior or subsequent history of predatory/instrumental or reactive violence—even though he has continued to show some psychotic symptoms. His only known incident of violence—although admittedly lethal—occurred when he was floridly psychotic, and he is no longer psychotic. And he has percolated a less acute psychosis for the better half of a quarter-century. And, other than a time when he might again be floridly psychotic, it approaches sheer speculation untethered from research-based violence assessment approaches that he might attack someone again, someday, under some circumstances that it would be virtually impossible to identify in advance.

That's probably as far as I would go. I would hope that the attorney would stress to the court that the standard for commitment in this jurisdiction is "beyond a reasonable doubt." I would not except at the point where I need to offer an opinion that includes reference to the legal standard for continued commitment.—*Robert Kinscherff, PhD, JD*

TOXIC EFFECTS

Depending on one's area of expertise, some experts feel comfortable testifying about toxic mechanisms and others will not. David Schretlan makes a distinction on the stand between the pathophysiology of carbon monoxide poisoning and the thinking effects of carbon monoxide:

> *The pathophysiology of carbon monoxide is not my area of specialty. I know a lot about the effects of carbon monoxide poisoning on thinking, but my area of specialty is not the neurological mechanisms.*

Robert Heilbronner notes that while he is familiar with toxic mechanisms of carbon monoxide poisoning,

> I am not a chemist and I don't want to go beyond my expertise. I will make general statements rather than comment on the toxic mechanisms.

> *Studies shows that carbon monoxide affects mostly hippocampal and basal ganglia structures.*

Lisa Stanford notes that when testifying about the effect of organophosphates on the brain, she requests to testify last:

> I never go first; I go last. The physicians have already discussed causation.
>
> *Information is carried around in our brain chemically. When some disease or substance interferes with those chemicals, then the brain doesn't communicate with itself efficiently. Organophosphates are substances that can interfere with those brain chemicals. I am not talking about a 'chemical imbalance' like you sometimes hear; I am talking about when the natural production and use of neurotranmitters gets disrupted by some other element, then it can have a wide range of effects. In this case . . .".*

Martin Rohling uses an analogy that came to him from Paul Lees-Haley:

> *Everything is toxic if you take too much of it. Water will kill you if you drink too much of it. There was a radio station who had a competition to see who could drink the most water without peeing. One woman drank about 3 gallons in 2 hours. She went home and died. The electrolytic imbalance created hyponatremia, which killed her. Even things we don't realize are toxic in a high enough dose will kill us. What we need to take into consideration in this case [lead, mercury, etc.] is not whether any of these things could kill you (they can; water can kill you), it's whether the dose was sufficiently high to cause the injury the person is complaining of.*

FINALLY, A NOTE ON EXPLAINING SUBSTANCE ABUSE

Lisa McDermott notes that jurors often have a lot of background information to draw from when experts talk about addictions on the stand. She emphasizes how important it is for experts to personalize the plaintiff/defendant's experience of substance abuse lest the jurors fill in the blank spaces with their own or their family's experiences.

> *In almost everyone's family, at some point, there is someone who had a substance abuse problem—did drugs or drank too much. That will come into the jury room: "I recall my uncle. He was an alcoholic, and he never behaved like that!" Jurors must understand not only that each person may act differently in the context of their substance abuse, but how that manifested in* this *case.*

NOTE

1. Postal, K., & Armstrong, K. (2013). *Feedback that sticks: The art of communicating complex neuropsychological assessment results.* New York: Oxford University Press.

14 Cognitive Development, Premorbid Function, and Intellectual Function

PEDIATRIC TRAUMA, MEDICAL malpractice, teen criminal cases, and capital cases often require explanations of normal and abnormal cognitive development, and almost any case we see as neuropsychologists requires some level of communication about how we assess "premorbid" intellectual or cognitive function. This chapter shares clear, vivid strategies to explain concepts of cognitive development, premorbid intellectual function, and current intellectual abilities.

As noted in the introduction to Chapter 13, "Specific Psychiatric and Neurological Disorders," eliciting engaging methods of explaining every psychiatric and neurological syndrome that psychologists and neuropsychologists typically see in clinical practice was not the focus of this research. Instead, experts were asked to share what they actually say in court to describe the most common clinical phenomena that are the subject of criminal and civil cases. *Feedback That Sticks: The Art of Communicating Complex Neuropsychological Assessment Results*[1] is an excellent companion source to this chapter as well, with many specific strategies for explaining the myriad clinical conditions that arise when cognitive development goes wrong.

THE DEVELOPING BRAIN

Judge Jay Blitzman notes that experts are frequently asked to inform the court about the developing brain, particularly the adolescent brain:

> *This comes up with great regularity in terms of the ability to form specific intent, jurisdiction, degree of culpability. The Supreme Court has said that children as a*

class are constitutionally different from adults. Does that mean every child? Every adolescent? Are these concepts so universal that we can make assumptions about every defendant? Science is probabilistic. But what does that tell you about the specific adolescent? You may have a 15-year-old that is very precocious, or one in front of you who is the same as any 15-year-old.

Judge Blitzman notes that the age at which a culture draws the line between who is a juvenile and adult is artificial: "This is a fluid proposition, and recent court decisions and legislation in various states is resulting in the creation of sentencing that has flexibility."

An expert's ability to help the court understand not only adolescent brain development in general but the specific development of the defendant in the particular case is therefore highly valued. The problem is that it's hard to explain the complex mechanisms involved in neurocognitive development to even graduate students without losing their attention, so how do we do this in an accurate but engaging manner with members of the general public? One strategy is to connect our explanations to the experiences of the triers of fact. After all, we have all personally experienced cognitive development and many us have had a ringside seat for our children's development as well.

Another point to consider is that we don't need to give a comprehensive, abstract lecture about brain development on the stand. Instead, we only need to help jurors understand the aspects of brain development that are important to their decision in the particular case at hand.

One common context for experts to be asked to explain cognitive development is criminal cases involving impulsive behaviors. Tannahill Glen notes that she grounds her explanation in the fact that we all instinctively treat adolescents differently. Connecting this instinctual knowledge with neuroscience helps jurors understand the predisposition of the adolescent brain for impulsive behavior. She will say,

Instinctively, we treat adolescents differently. For instance, as psychologists, we don't even diagnose certain conditions until adulthood is reached because what we would later call abnormal impulsivity is normal for adolescents. And research has further informed our practice. Specifically, research has shown us areas in the brain where adolescents are different from adults. Two important ones are the prefrontal cortex (an area that is all about reasoning and self-regulation) and the limbic system (an area that is all about emotions and reward). The problem for teens and their control over their behavior is that these two regions develop at different rates.

Depending on the strategy for direct testimony, Dr. Glen notes that she will describe three specific ways adolescent brains are different from adults:

During development, a process of pruning back occurs after a period of wild growth, and like a rose bush that has to be pruned back, this allows for more efficient communication between the two areas, the thinking/reasoning area and the emotional area. This process is ongoing for many years and results in more adult-like communication and balance between emotions and reason. But during adolescence, the areas

> *for experiencing emotions and reasoning about those emotions are not talking to one another like they will in adulthood.*
>
> *Another thing that is different is neurotransmitter levels, the chemicals that help our brain cells work well. The chemicals in the brain that have to do with reward and motivation increase, while the chemicals that have to do with thinking and putting the brakes on actions stay relatively lower, so a teen's "reward" system is full speed ahead while their manager is on break.*
>
> *The third difference is that the adolescent brain activity is less efficient and less concentrated in important areas during reasoning tasks as compared to adult brains. Problem-solving is taking up a lot more resources.*
>
> *If you put this all together, thinking is online in teens but self-regulation is often not at "adult" level until mid-20s. (At this point I make a self-effacing joke about how in some cases, like my own, it wasn't online until even later, my late 20s.) This is why adults are known for their ability to plan, consider consequences, regulate emotions, ignore what other people think, etc., while teens are known for just the opposite: overvalue of reward, response to peer pressure, not considering long-term consequences, etc. And not only that, but when we see a teenager who is calm and polite and industrious, we all nod appreciatively and talk about how "mature" he or she is—because we understand it is not the norm!*

As discussed in Chapter 2, "Setting the Truth on Fire," during testimony an expert would want to immediately connect each of these three areas to specific behaviors of the plaintiff/defendant. In other words, anchor each abstract concept to concrete, clear examples in the life of the person you have examined.

Also depending on the nature of the case, Dr. Glen notes that she may expand the rose-pruning analogy for "broad-brush" descriptions of brain development:

> *What we see in the developing brain is that you get this exuberant growth of connections between brain cells. And it's just like your rose bushes at home: In order for them to thrive, they really need to be pruned back, because that's what's going to make them the most effective at growth and flowering. Your brain does the same thing over time. We used to think that was done and adjusted by age 16 or so, but now we know that this is a process that goes on through the early to mid-20s.*

Robert Mendoza shares an example of a targeted narrative about neurocognitive development that is grounded in everyone's direct experience:

> The defendant was 18 at the commission of the crime. He served 15 years in prison. My job was to describe for the jury why, in his 30s, this person has a different brain than the one he had at 15. I said,
>
> *Let's all think of ourselves at age 18, and then let's think of ourselves at 32. Let's make the assumption that all of us in this room probably think they were a little different at 15 compared to 32. I am going to say most of us are different at age 32 in some specific,*

predictable ways. We are probably different in that we don't take as many chances; we probably have more insight; we probably do a lot of things differently in our lives, especially if we have children and families.

These predictable changes in our behavior go along with changes in our brain. We change because our brain has changed along the way. We are fortunate in the past decade and a half: We have the technology now to witness this transformation. We don't have to assume; We can literally see the very specific ways in which our brain changes during the teenage years.

So let's talk about Mr. Defendant, here in this courtroom. Here are some behaviors that he demonstrated at age 17 or 18 that were prevalent and problematic, and here's how some of the expected developing brain changes may be relevant to different behaviors now."

PROBLEMS EMERGING LATER ON

Experts are often asked to make predictions about how well children will do as they grow up: Will they be able to go to college? Get a job? Live independently? Keith Yeates, notes that the issue of predicting future outcome is important in pediatric forensic work, but the younger the child, the worse we are as experts at predicting outcomes. He recommends educating attorneys about the benefits of waiting as long as possible to try the case.

I will say, "You are sending me a 4-year-old. Unless they are pretty devastated, we can't say with any degree of certainty what the outcome will be. There is a lot of variability here, and we have to acknowledge that that is the case." I will ask attorneys, "What is your statute of limitations? How long does the family want to wait?" If we wait until the child is 7, we can say a lot more about the outcome. You need to be clear with the attorneys.

Even older children have variability in their outcome. Dr. Yeates goes on to note, "The reality is that kids have a lot of variability in their outcomes, and anyone who pretends otherwise is not looking at the research. Unless a child is totally devastated, we can't know for certain."

Educating the court about the usefulness and also the limits of experts' predictive powers is an important task on the stand.

The crystal ball is foggy

Some homespun modesty is important where the research is genuinely not helpful in predicting outcome; you don't look like you are overstating things. Then when you **do** get definitive about something, it isn't in the context of "he says everything is a certainty."

Our crystal ball is a bit foggy. If you ask me what a kid will be like a year from now, I can do that. 5 years? 10 to 20 years? Things get foggy. I don't want to claim that we have this amazing ability to predict the future that no other profession can claim. We have data, and multiple pieces of data that are relevant.

Can the child go to college?

Q: Will Jane go to college?

A: We don't have a whole lot of research to base that prediction on. "If you get this score, on this particular test, you can go to college." I think that it is possible that Jane could get a college degree, but if she is to succeed, these [x,y,z] supports would need to be in place.

Q: But what is probable?

A: If these things are in place, it is likely she could get through college. If these things are not in place it would be unlikely.—John Kirk, PsyD, ABPP-CN

I know from the social security administration that if you have an IQ of 70 and below you are considered unable to participate in "substantial gainful employment", and you would need financial support. With an IQ now of 68, Charlie would likely be unable to go to a four year college and be successful. Instead, he would need to think about a sheltered work situation [explain] where there are ample supports and repetition of a learned skills in a protected environment.—Lisa Stanford, PhD, ABPP-CN

There is a continuum of care available to someone after injury and after they have left the home of their parents. That can range from someone with them 24 hours a day with a very specialized routine to someone who drops by once a day for medication checks. Some people can learn to drive and some can't. Some people can learn to use public transportation and some can't. This child fits [here] because of [their memory loss, intellectual function, executive function].—Lisa Stanford, PhD, ABPP-CN

Like taking a photo in time

During the neuropsychological evaluation, it's a lot like taking a fancy photograph of somebody. I can take a picture of someone. I can look at that photograph. I can say, "I think I know what they might have looked like 2, 4 years ago." And I can say, "I think I know what they are going to look like down the road from now." But at the end of the day, what I have is a special photograph of how they look now, at this point in time.—Neil Pliskin, PhD, ABPP-CN

A farming analogy

When you grow up on a farm there is a lot to learn about nature. This child had a severe brain injury. Outcomes are hard to predict. The seeds are planted; now it is up to God.—Lynn Blackburn, PhD, ABPP-CN

Lynn Blackburn notes that in addition to helping jurors understand the immediate, measurable effects of a severe injury or illness, experts must help jurors understand that some children might experience problems later, as they "grow into a deficit." She notes,

> *You can have early insult to the brain but not show early deficits in those areas, because your brain hasn't developed to a point yet where you should be exhibiting those skills, or they can be reasonably measured. For obvious reasons, experts can't measure those yet-to-be-developed skills. Even though I think that's a basic point that is well founded, in my experience it is very difficult to covey to a jury.*

Tannahill Glen shares the example of a 7-year-old who had a severe traumatic brain injury at age 3. She notes that how well an explanation about future, currently unknowable deficits goes over with jurors is directly related to her credibility as an expert.

> *Q: Sally did okay on most of her testing, so why are you suggesting that she is going to have trouble later on?*
>
> *A: We know that when brains are young at the time of a severe traumatic injury, kids may look initially like they are recovering beautifully. And in fact, 20 years ago when I first went into this field, we thought that was the age to have an injury, because everyone looked so great coming out of it. Unfortunately, we have since learned that some of the patients have worse outcomes when they get a TBI at this age than if they were older, because it is such a critical time of development. It is just that you can't measure the skills like complex problem-solving when they are that young, before the skills are expected to come online. Essentially, you can't test for something that isn't there yet. As Sally's brain continues to mature, that's when we might see her start to falter in terms of complex problem-solving or complex social skills.*
>
> The explanation sounds rational, and jurors seem to pay attention, but the "smell test" part is that if they see someone functioning normally, it is very hard for them to believe that the child may not be normal 10 years from now.

Lisa Stanford uses a "bunny" metaphor to help jurors understand the concept that a slowed rate of learning after an injury or illness can result in widening gaps between a child and his or her peers:

> *You have two bunnies (use fingers for ears). The first bunny is the child. He has something happen, the injury, but his brain will still keep growing and maturing, and he will keep hopping forward. And this bunny is his friends. They are also continuing to grow and mature. They are hopping forward, too, but faster. And over time, the gap between [name] and his friends gets bigger and bigger (bunny ears/hands move further apart). Your bunny is still growing and learning, but he is not moving as fast. So, if I test your bunny now, he is low average compared with the other bunnies. 5 years from now? He may be much lower compared to where the other bunnies are.*

If hopping bunnies do not fit with your personality as an expert, the explanation can be adapted for use with a flip chart and graph with two lines—but the moment when the expert with serious gravitas goes against type and makes the bunny ears might be the one that stays with jurors as they go through deliberations. See Chapter 10, "Visuals," for a description of explaining developmental trajectories with graphics.

PRENATAL INJURIES

Medical malpractice cases might pull for an expert to discuss insults to fetal development. Lisa Stanford, like many experts, cautions against being caught in the "causation trap" during such cases. Rather than testify about why a child has a particular set of thinking, behavior, and emotional difficulties, the cleaner approach is to simply explain the strengths and weaknesses.

> ***Avoiding getting into the causation trap***
>
> When the issue is perinatal injury, attorneys always want me to discuss causation. Instead, I will say,
>
> *A: I am dealing with [known entity], and what is the impact of that [known entity] has already been well documented by other experts in the records. I am not here to talk about the diagnosis of [known entity].*

> ***Standard of care***
>
> I do not get into standard-of-care issues in medical malpractice cases. Most medical malpractice cases are not neuropsychological malpractice; they are medical malpractice, with a neuropsychological outcome. I talk about the outcome, not the malpractice issue. I am the expert helping the jury understand about cognitive ability and mental health.
>
> *A: Here's the shape the person is in now. They can do this; they can't do that.*
>
> *Q: Why do you think that is?*
>
> *A: On my review of the objective information and what I know about this person, it is the aneurysm that did it.*
>
> *Q: Well, Dr. Pliskin, do you have an opinion about whether the standard of care was met?*
>
> *A: No, I do not.*—Neil Pliskin, PhD, ABPP-CN
>
> ------------
>
> *I always stay away from the question, "Did the physician do something wrong?"*
>
> *A: I don't know. Something went wrong somewhere, because I am looking at this problem. Now whether that problem is due to something that happened at birth, or something else, that's debatable.*—Jacobus Donders, PhD, ABPP-CN

PREMORBID FUNCTIONING

"But, Doctor, how can you know what he looked like before the [fill in the blank]?" That is actually a really good question. The issue of "premorbid" cognitive function, "preinjury," "pre-dementia," even "pre-anoxic injury at birth" function, is foundational to our opinion that something has changed. As Rod Swenson reminds us, "People bring their brains to the injury. Everyone is different." As psychology and neuropsychology experts, we must be prepared to explain to jurors our methods of estimating what kind of brain was brought to the accident or injury.

Explaining premorbid cognitive function in children

When a child is injured at age 9 or 10, pediatric neuropsychologists can use school records to estimate pre-accident or pre-illness intellectual function. Predictions are very difficult to make, though, when the issue for the court is how children would have functioned before they were injured or ill at a very young age; that is, before they had time to develop a track record of their thinking abilities at school or develop "hold skills" like reading or vocabulary.

In some cases, the question is even more difficult: How was this child functioning before they were even born? Keith Yeates notes, "There is no way to have a premorbid measure for a kid who was injured at birth. Even school-age kids, you have a lot less to work with than adults." He will say to jurors,

> *We don't have a long history before the injury, but we have a reasonable basis to estimate what the child would have looked like prior to the injury given their socio-economic status, given the absence of any other medical factors, given the absence of a family history of neurodevelopmental disorders . . .*
>
> Or if the factors **were** there, it is important to acknowledge they are present and temper your conclusions.

Lynn Blackburn notes that in her pediatric forensic practice she will test siblings in order to have a benchmark for baseline intellect: "When I am asked to testify on an anoxic injury at birth, I feel fortunate if there are siblings. I will test the siblings and they give me a good understanding of where the examinee should have been." Similarly, Lisa Stanford regularly tests the IQ of the mother (and her preference is for both patents if they are available):

> I test the IQ of the mother in every forensic case. It's the best predictor I have. Male attorneys hate it and ask, "Why not the dad?" The correlation is close but generally not as good. Here is what I say during testimony:
>
> *Had the child not sustained this injury I would have expected them to be about this level because research indicates that a mother's intelligence is a highly predictive factor in determining a child's later intelligence.*

Erin Bigler cautions, however, that the presence of developmental disorders in siblings or other extended family members does not mean that the child in question would necessarily have inherited the condition. Having base rates of heritability at your fingertips in such cases to share with jurors can help them understand the "so what?" of a person with autism, intellectual disability, or other conditions in the family tree.

Heritability with child plaintiffs

> If a case involves the heritability of intellectual and academic abilities and neuropsychiatric conditions, it is important to acknowledge that and bring in the

research. For example, in some cases, an expert will introduce the idea that because there is a family history of autism, there is a greater likelihood of low IQ in the plaintiff. I will go right to our publications and say,

> *On many of these domains there is no difference between the IQ of autistic individuals and healthy control samples. Just because there is autism in the family does not mean there is reduced IQ in the patient.*

Keith Yeates notes that in many cases, the best bet is "average":

> *A: Our best prediction, probabilistically in any circumstance, unless we have data to suggest otherwise, is that the child was average. 50% of all kids are going to have an IQ between 90 and 110. If you have a kid whose parents were college-educated, whose siblings are average, with no history of perinatal difficulties, you are safe to say that the child was at least average. Our ability to predict at an individual level is not perfect, but it is reasonable to say this child was average.*
>
> *Q: Are you saying more likely than not?*
>
> *A: Yes. Tommy, more likely than not, had average intellect.*

Explaining premorbid IQ in adults

Cheryl Weinstein introduces the concept of premorbid intellect to jurors by reminding them that it is our job to look at the whole person, not just the injury or illness characteristics:

> *The research shows that (moderate TBI, long-term alcohol abuse, anoxic injury, fill in the blank) can cause changes in the brain. But what did Mr. Smith look like to begin with? A neuropsychologist looks at the whole person.*

When neuropsychologists predict premorbid intellect, one of our tools is to use demographic information such as number of years of education. Kristie Nies notes that talking about the connection between premorbid education and IQ to a rural jury, where education levels are low, can be touchy. That is, an expert with a PhD gets up on the stand and blithely says to a set of jurors with high school educations or lower that one of the best ways to tell how smart someone is how many years of education they have. And Mr. Plaintiff, who only went to the 11th grade, was likely "low average." That's an easy way to alienate a group of people. She will make the distinction between years of education predicting how well one will do on an IQ test versus years of education predicting "street smarts":

> *You have heard of people who have "book smarts" and "street smarts." We are not going to worry about the fact that these scores are pretty low. I knew they would be low because Mr. Smith had a GED. These tests are higher depending on how much education people have had. And if you have not had a lot of formal education, these tests will be lower.*

Desiree Byrd points out that small word choices can make a difference in how experts' explanations are received:

> When I have to explain how demographic factors affect IQ, I emphasize test performance and not the construct of intellect itself. I also use empathy-building language, small word choices that reduce the likelihood of a juror becoming defensive about the specifics of the demographics. It's small things that I think reduce a juror's defensive systems, so the likelihood of them feeling attacked by people who had the opportunity to finish high school or go to college is lessened. Saying "didn't have the chance to finish high school" is a very different from saying "high school dropout."
>
> *How far someone goes in school can influence their score on this test [rather than saying their IQ level]. This isn't a precise discipline. There is a lot of room for error, and some of that error is due to how far we went in school. Some of us didn't have the chance to graduate high school [not "dropped out"], so our scores may not be as high as those from people who went to college.*

> ***Explaining premorbid IQ in low-education populations***
>
> It's hard when the plaintiff/defendants are fourth-, fifth-, sixth-grade-educated folks working on a farm. The premorbid estimates are so low. The verbals are all very low and the nonverbals are normal. The difficulty is how to explain this to the jury in a way that doesn't alienate the three jury members who also have low educations.
>
> *Your intellectual functions are mostly genetic, around 60% genetic. For your verbal intellect, your ability to reason through things with words, your exposure to school is probably the next major factor on how you will do on an IQ test. Mr. Plaintiff really didn't have the opportunity to acquire a higher score by exposure to education, so this is my best estimate is for what his lifelong expected levels should be on these types of tests.*—Greg Lee, PhD, ABPP-CN
>
> ------------
>
> *Jurors have a fairly reasonable understanding of ability related to education and profession. You have to approach this sensitively, because if you have everyone in the jury with a high school education, you don't want to be saying, "If you don't have a college education, that's a problem." So in addition to just educational attainment, I also often use the broader concept of individual skill and talents.*
>
> *In some cases, you can describe specific job skills in a non-college-educated person that makes it clear they had at least average or better cognitive function. In one case I was involved in, the plaintiff was the companywide supervisor for the crane operators in a large construction company working with high-rise and complex commercial buildings. He only had a high school education. The attorneys in the case made sure to bring in for the jury some of the technical things he had to understand in terms of*

> *weights and angles and what you can and can't do with these cranes and the motor skill level required to operate the cranes.*—Erin Bigler, PhD, ABPP-CN

Keith Yeates points out that another demographic variable in predicting IQ is socioeconomic status (SES). Explaining this to jurors with a low SES can likewise be alienating.

> Most juries are not made up of high-SES folks; it's hard to say that the person is low average because his parents are poor. That can be touchy, but you can say that in a way that is not offensive:
>
> *He is not far off from what you would expect given his parents' level of education.*

As our field's understanding of normal variability has improved, it is clear that some methods of estimating premorbid intellect are inaccurate. In my own practice, I frequently come across opposing experts' use of the "best performance method" to estimate preinjury function. The idea goes like this: Let's take the examinee's best test score and then assume that every other test score would have been that good had it not been for the brain injury. For example, if someone had a high average score on a test, then unless every other test in the battery was also high average, we should consider that proof of brain damage. Here is how I explain the problems with this during testimony:

> *Q: But didn't Dr. Other Expert tell us that Mr. Plaintiff should have gotten high average scores on everything?*
>
> *A: The method of taking a person's best score, in Mr. Plaintiff's case his high average Block Design score, and then assuming that every other test score should also be equally high average, used to be widespread in the field. Then, researchers said, "Hold on. What if we tested a bunch of normal people, people who have never had a brain injury or neurological disease. What do they look like when we give them a large set of tests?" It turns out that normal people have strengths and weaknesses: We are good at some things and less good at others. It's one of those common-sense things that the research says, "Yes, that is actually true."*
>
> *If any of us in this room were to take neuropsychological tests today, we would have some great scores (we are really good at some types of thinking tasks), and some okay scores, and a few relatively low scores—because we are human.*
>
> *What if I said, "Okay, I am going to look at your best score and then any score that is not that good, I am going to consider evidence of brain damage"? I will tell you that all of us in this room would be considered brain-damaged using that method—and obviously that's not true. This is why the "best performance method" is no longer accepted as an accurate way of understanding pre-accident brain function.*

Another issue that experts often need to address during testimony is the difference between premorbid intellectual function and premorbid cognitive function. We may not be intellectually rigorous at times and use the concepts "premorbid intellect" and "premorbid cognitive ability" (e.g., premorbid memory, attention, language, and other thinking skills) interchangeably. While research focuses on predicting premorbid intellect from specific demographic formulas or "hold tests" like irregular word reading, we often use those IQ predictions to not just compare pre- and postmorbid IQ but also to compare pre- and postmorbid "everything else." That can create some significant mischief. In my own practice, if the issue arises I will say,

> *We know from IQ tests that Ms. Plaintiff took during high school, as well as the formulas I talked about earlier, that a good, solid estimate of her lifelong IQ is high average. What we know from research, though, is that knowing someone's likely lifelong IQ doesn't tell us precisely what their lifelong memory skills or language skills or attention skills were.*
>
> *When you give normal people who have never had a brain injury IQ tests and also tests of their memory and attention and language and other thinking skills, the scores are not all even. If we grab someone with a high average IQ in this courtroom and give that person tests of their other thinking abilities, some of those scores would be high average, but a lot would be average. In fact, the higher a person's intellect, the more likely that there will be a pretty big difference between their intellect and many of their other thinking abilities, like language or memory. In big studies of people who never had a brain injury that compare intellect and memory abilities, large numbers of perfectly normal, really smart people had average memories.*

See Chapter 9, "Explaining Assessment Methods and Tools," for more strategies to discuss normal variability.

In some cases, other available records contradict the predictions of demographic formulas or single word reading tests. For example, I had a case where demographic formulas indicated average intellect. However, I had reviewed elementary through high school transcripts documenting special education services, a 1.3 GPA, and several failed classes. It is hard to "unsee" that information and opine that the examinee has lifelong average intellect and/or cognitive function. What I say in those situations is,

> *We all went to high school, and there were some really smart kids and some kids who really struggled. If you use these formulas, everyone who went to high school is categorized intellectually as the same. 12 years of education gets you the same score, whether you got straight A's or you took a couple of extra summers to finish, and that just doesn't fit with common sense. Some kids have learning problems or attention deficits or were in special education classes. The formulas that predict IQ based on whether you graduate from high are helpful when that's all you know about someone, but when you have actual records of how someone* **did** *in highschool, not just whether they graduated, like we do in this case, we can make even better predictions.*

Robin Hanks notes that some groups, based on their educational attainment, are automatically assumed to have superior intellect. She gives the example of a case where a plaintiff has an medical degree, has the type of injury that is not expected to change IQ score, and yet has an IQ in the average range.

> When an MD has an average IQ and an expert said, "It has to be a decline. There is no other explanation," [I could say],
>
> *Absolutely it is possible for a person with an advanced degree to have an average IQ. I have tested many medical students with average IQs. People find many ways to succeed: motivation, opportunity, persistence, home life. There are so many other factors to success than IQ.*

And of course, there is the issue of people with low premorbid intellects who sufferer more deficits as a result of an injury or illness. In these cases, it is often factors other than testing, which might have hit a floor effect before the accident, that build a case, or contradict the case, for change in cognitive status. John McSweeny will help jurors understand that the interpretation of test results does not end with a determination of low premorbid intellect.

> One malpractice case I was involved in, an ENT doc's surgical instrument pierced the cribriform plate and entered a 14-year-old's frontal lobe. In that case I talked about the functions of the frontal lobe. And what was the evidence according to the defense expert that she had no impairment? The fact that she wasn't bright to begin with.
>
> *Q: Isn't it true that the defendant was never bright to begin with?*
>
> *A: True, but she is worse now. A low IQ doesn't protect you from brain damage.*

COMMUNICATING INTELLECTUAL DISABILITY WITH JURORS

When a psychologist or neuropsychologist hears "IQ of 65" or "IQ of 110," we get a very specific picture in our thought bubbles of what that means. The label "intellectually disabled" or "high average" pops into our minds, as well as what the label means, functionally, in the real world. We are so used to this number-based code that it is easy to forget that jurors likely do not share this knowledge. Jurors may not know that an IQ of 100 is "dead center" of average. Instead, they may have taken an online IQ test and picked up the idea that a good IQ hovers around 200, so 100 looks pretty bad. Jurors may think of IQ scores in terms most familiar to them: like percentages for a math test. To a juror who got a few C's himself during high school, an IQ of 70 doesn't seem that bad. Conversely, an IQ of 95 feels like it's pretty much as high as you can get—an A.

Anecdotes and comparisons are powerful tools as experts help jurors understand what a low IQ score really means.

> Giving jurors real-world examples of what a very low IQ would look like in everyday life, contrasted to the claimant's observed and reported behavior, can be effective on the stand:
>
> *If this guy really had an IQ of 65, he wouldn't be driving a car, he wouldn't be working, he wouldn't be able to tell you what happened to him. He would appear to a casual person to be very impaired. If his memory scores were really this bad, he*

would act in everyday life like an Alzheimer's patient. And yet he can tell clinicians his medical history without a problem.—Glenn Larrabee, PhD, ABPP-CN

Lisa McDermott notes that sometimes helping jurors understand a defendant's IQ is difficult as they may have been functioning in a semi-independent way in the community prior to a crime. The key is to ask very detailed questions about functioning within specific roles, not just about the roles themselves. She notes that young people with intellectual disability on the street often mask their disability:

> *Kids with disabilities who lack support systems may mask, disguise, their limitations. Because of that, most people would not recognize their disabilities. We assume that if a kid can have sex, use a gun, deal drugs, then they are fully capable. This is not true; you cannot judge someone's overall functioning from one action. Many of those with even the most serious of disabilities are able to work, get married, have children, and do many other things that one might consider "normal." It is up to an expert to help people understand how to recognize a disability, and it is up to us to give them the facts in support.*
>
> *A great real case example is a kid who sold hot dogs from a cart on the street. Sounds functional, but, it turns out he couldn't make change. To help him, the owner of the stand gave him a chart so all he had to do was follow directions: If someone gives you $2, give them two quarters. If they give you $5, give them $3.*

Not roadworthy

I had a judge ask me, "Is this something where we could take this car and get a new part for it, or is this something where if you give it better fuel, it will start running better?" The examinee was in the room, so I wanted to choose my words carefully and not compare him to a clunker but make it clear that in the judge's analogy, the kid was a car that really isn't going to be roadworthy.

This individual is not like a Honda that just needs a part or better fuel. He is not able to work, he has been in small special ed classes his whole life, so that's not a car that is really truly roadworthy. That's really a car that maybe you keep it to drive on private property. Just like with this kid, who is only getting job opportunities when friends or family take him along and have them be his assistant but he has never gotten a job on his own, so it is that kind of car that you might keep for driving on private property or for specific short trips but not something you would take on the highway or take on a long trip.—Shelley Peery, PhD

Technical issues with intellectual disability

Many experts note that the phrase "intellectual disability" sounds a lot better than "mental retardation," but it also carries a lot less information. In my own practice, I will say to jurors, "This is what we used to call *mental retardation*. We now use the words *intellectual disability*, but it means the same thing."

Use terms jurors will know

> I don't use the term *intellectual disability* because nobody knows what that is. If you say mental retardation, people know what you mean. I try to use terms that jurors will be aware of. Intellectual disability may be the correct term in our field, but it will not communicate anything. *Mental retardation* feels very awkward, and I have an internal reaction when I say it, but my job is to communicate.
>
> *We know that people with IQ scores less than 70, people in the mental retardation range, fail 40% of validity indicators across an exam, but the plaintiff failed 70%. So he performed worse than a person with mental retardation. And we know that that doesn't fit his clinical picture.*—John McSweeny, J.D., PhD, ABPP-CN

Mike Chafetz notes that the term *intellectual disability* can be problematic in some forensic contexts because it has the word *disability* in it:

> *Intellectual disability presumes a disability, where the word* disability *is actually a specific legal term. It potentially muddies the waters for those of us who do disability exams. In disability examinations, the term* disability *is a contractual term. If you meet the requirements for disability for SSDI, you meet the criteria of the law. If you meet the requirements of disability for a private insurer, you have met the criteria of the disability contract. The term* disability *embedded in the diagnosis becomes a problem when it conveys a legal definition that may not be true.*

Many experts will use bell curves to help explain the meaning of a plaintiff/defendant's IQ score. See Chapter 10 "Visuals," for a description of specific visual strategies. Antonio Puente notes that he will frequently use the metaphor of walking through a mall to help jurors understand the idea of a normative sample as he explains intellect:

> I put a bell curve on the screen and say to the jurors:
>
> *Imagine if you went to a mall, you are going to come across people with different levels of IQ. Think about meeting 100 people walking through the center section of the mall.*
>
> Then a new slide superimposes the score of the defendant. It visualizes for jurors what an IQ means in a larger social context.

Many experts use both percentiles and standard scores to help jurors understand the IQ number.

> *The instrument is designed to give an IQ number, but intellectual function is much more than what a single test score or scores can tell you. [For instance, in a mental retardation case, I might say:] "This person's score is below the 2nd percentile. That means that over 98% of the people in this courtroom will score higher than he does."*—Robert Heilbronner, PhD, ABPP-CN

Culture of intellectual disability

Medical anthropologist Robert Edgerton characterized mental retardation in the 1960s as (in part) a sociocultural construction that affects how people with low intellect see themselves and how others interact with them.[2] A research literature has since developed addressing cross-cultural aspects of these social constructions.[3] Experts should consider that members of the jury have varying degrees of familiarity with the culture of intellectual disability, ranging from no experience to intimate experience through their work settings or through family members. If the issue is likely to rise in the case, attorneys may ask potential jurors as part of the voir dire process if they have had any personal experience with people who have very low IQ. Understanding where jurors are starting in their understanding (e.g., a retired special education teacher may be sitting on the jury, or a man with a brother who has Down syndrome) will help you come up with appropriate examples that are likely to connect with jurors' lived experiences. If there are members of the jury from non–European-American cultural backgrounds, you will want to familiarize yourself with available sociocultural literature on how those cultural groups construct, understand, and typically interact with "intellectual disability."

Shelly Peery brings up an important point: Individuals with intellectual disability may engage in behaviors or have attitudes that are shaped by their reaction to society's reaction to their low intellect. Using the frame of a "culture of intellectual disability" is helpful in understanding the dynamics that may play out.

> I recall one case where there was a wiretap and the woman with an IQ of 75 was saying how smart she was to drive across the parking lot to avoid the police.
>
> *Q: Isn't it true that even Ms. Defendant says she's smart?*
>
> *A: There is a little bit of a different culture with people who experience different disabilities. When you have low IQ your whole life, you may be more prone to try and stick up for your own intelligence and say, "See how smart I am?" because it's a point of contention for you, it's something that you are sensitive about. That's one of the cultural things that people are sensitive about when they have low IQ.*

FINALLY, WHEN DISCUSSING INTELLECTUAL FUNCTION, BE PREPARED

In many forensic contexts, a defendant/plaintiff's IQ number can have very profound consequences; a case may literally hinge on accurate measurement of that number. Attorney Sara Cohbra cautions experts to be prepared when IQ is discussed in court: "We want experts to be very prepared to answer questions about statistics, normative data, and any issues regarding the validity of standardized intelligence testing. We want the expert to be able to point to specific studies or literature to support everything she is saying." See Chapter 22, "Explaining Statistics," for strategies to clearly and vividly describe statistical concepts to jurors as you face cross examination about your IQ calculation.

NOTES

1. Postal, K., & Armstrong, K. (2013). *Feedback that sticks: The art of communicating complex neuropsychological assessment results.* New York: Oxford University Press.
2. Edgerton, R. B. (1967). *The cloak of competence: Stigma in the lives of the mentally retarded.* Berkeley: University of California Press.
3. Skinner, D., & Weisner, T. (2007). Sociocultural studies of families of children with intellectual disabilities. *Mental Retardation and Developmental Disabilities Research Reviews, 13*, 302–312.

15 Cross Examination

IF YOU HAVE a pulse, cross examination will get your heart rate up. After the attorney who brought you to the courtroom asks, "Doctor, can you please explain your competent and wise opinions?" the attorney who is conducting the cross examination will ask, "Doctor, can you please explain to the court whether you are crooked, or stupid, or both?" There are few other professional situations where one willingly subjects oneself to the latter set of questions in a public forum.

Bernice Marcopulos points out that compassion for the cross-examining attorney can help slow our heart rate down: "The scary attorney who is asking aggressive questions—they are nervous too." Mike Chafetz notes,

> *With few exceptions, I have great respect for lawyers who are cross-examining me. They are the ones with the more difficult job. While advocating for their clients and conducting the fight in the courtroom, they must also learn to appreciate a complex interplay of neuropsychological facts. Some do this better than others. Some get better help than others.*

While anxiety-provoking, many forensic neuropsychologists enjoy the challenge of cross examination. Mike Chafetz notes,

> *While I sometimes compare a cross-examination to a "dance" or a "game," I look at it as a serious undertaking that I usually enjoy. One has to understand that the examiner's role is to undermine your testimony in some way, make you appear biased, or to throw you off your game by the use of techniques. If you listen carefully*

and understand what the examining attorney is trying to do, it is usually fairly easy to respond.

David Williamson puts it this way:

It doesn't bother me to be cross-examined. Someone is getting paid a lot of money to make you look like a monkey. And that's their job. And if they don't do that, they are not doing their job. And if it was you in their shoes, you would be trying to do the same thing. So, okay, it's my job to make it hard for them to make me look like a monkey. No harm, no foul. It's nothing personal. It's my job to defend why I did what I did and what I think it means. And if I cannot do that, then I put myself in a bad situation. They might make you feel like it's personal to throw you off, but that's their job too.

This chapter addresses how we can remain productive as experts in communicating our opinions during cross examination by shining light on common techniques and strategies used by cross-examining attorneys and hearing from attorneys, judges, and experts about best practices for maintaining our credibility and clarity through the process. See also Chapter 16, "Relationships with Other Experts," to address the issues of being asked to comment on other experts' work during cross. Also, see Chapter 9, "Creating Access to Assessment Methods and Results," for specific cross-examination issues that may emerge when testifying about the MMPI-2 and MMPI-2-RF.

WHAT IS CROSS?

During direct examination, attorneys ask open-ended questions. In contrast, on cross examination, attorneys are expected to ask very specific, leading questions like, "Isn't it true that . . ." Judge Fader notes,

The situation in cross examination is that the lawyer on the other side is told in law school to ask questions that you just give a "yes or no" answer to. You are not to let that witness expand. So the professional witness has to keep that in mind. If the expert has a point that she or he wants to make during cross examination, they are not going to be able to make it because they are going to say "Yes, but . . ." and the cross-examining attorney will shut them down. That said, saying "Yes, but . . ." will give your lawyer the message that you have something more to say about that. Even though you have been shut down, it is a communication with the lawyer that brought you that he or she should take up the issue on redirect.

That is, the attorney who brought you to court is listening very carefully to the way you respond to cross-examination questions. The attorney is listening for a sign that they will need to go in and ask additional questions to allow you to "clean up" something you said during cross. This is also called "rehabilitating the witness."

After the opposing counsel completes cross examination, the attorney who engaged you can ask "redirect questions," but it's not always clear to the attorney what he or she should ask. Hearing, "Yes, but" is one signal. Lynn Blackburn offers this advice: "Create a signal with the attorney who engaged you that you can use with him as you are being cross-examined to tell him that this is a place where he should follow up with a redirect question."

While some experts prefer to answer as fully as they can (see later in the chapter for strategies regarding how to do this), other experts advocate responding succinctly and in the most straightforward manner possible, keeping their answers short and simple, with the expectation that the counsel who brought them in will give them an opportunity to give more context to their "yes" or "no" answer on redirect. This strategy requires trust on the part of the expert witness, as Robert Mendoza tells us:

> If I respond to cross-examination questions correctly, I am giving very short, specific responses. My fear is that the attorney that hired me will not follow up on direct. For example,
>
> *Q: Dr. Mendoza, isn't it possible that the defendant wasn't suffering from a delusion when he stabbed his wife?*
>
> *A: Yes.*
>
> *That's the last thing the jury will remember. If I have done my job right, on cross I will not give any additional information. The jury could be left with an inaccurate view. That goes to strategy. I tell attorneys, "I will be very specific and short on cross. Ask me to explain on redirect." The opposing counsel will not let me talk about things that are not helpful to their case. The minute I say, "Possible but unlikely," they will say, "Thank you, Dr. Mendoza. You have answered the question" and move on. Why not have that "unlikely" statement come out on redirect? Now I can say that it is unlikely, but also I can say why.*

The process of cross examination is begun by the attorney from the opposing side, and then the attorney who brought the expert has a chance to "redirect." Questions during redirect are limited to areas discussed on cross examination. At times, a "recross" is allowed where the opposing counsel asks further questions about issues discussed even more narrowly on redirect. Subsequent rounds of redirect and recross can follow, sometimes for multiple iterations, each one ever narrower.

DRAWING EXPERTS OFF SIDES

Don't be arrogant

If an important goal of direct examination is creating rapport with a jury, an important goal of cross-examining attorneys is to damage that rapport. One of the most effective ways of doing so is to "expose" the expert as arrogant. One judge who preferred to remain anonymous noted that attorneys will bait an expert, hoping that the expert will take the bait and respond with anger or demands to be respected. This is always alienating to the jury. Baiting is the real reason for the "You aren't a real doctor, are you?" questions or why attorneys use "Ms. Expert," not "Dr. Expert," when beginning their cross examination. They aren't really going after the "you're not a real doctor" as in "I want the jury to know you're not a physician" or "you're not qualified." What they are after is to try to get you to look arrogant and defensive. Cross-examining attorneys do this with police officers as well, calling them "Mister," not "Officer."

All agree that the best way to ruin the ploy is to not comment at all. The jurors will have heard you referred to as "Doctor" by the attorney on direct, and if they notice, they'll think the cross-examining attorney is being impolite.

> *Experts are accustomed to deference. People of all sorts, whether they are secretaries or coworkers or nurses, are accustomed to deferring to experts in the workplace and in their everyday life. In a courtroom, everybody is on common ground and there is no automatic deference to an expert. Really good cross examination needles the expert witness into believing that the lawyer believes the expert is sort of stupid and unqualified. In response, the expert witness, sometimes overdoes it trying to reassert his training, expertise, and credibility. Cops and agents have the same problem because they are accustomed to deference anywhere and everywhere. They carry guns and badges and they are the law. So when a defense lawyer suggests that the agent is crooked or lazy or that he didn't see what he says he saw, the agent gets angry. The questioning threatens his foundation and self-respect, which is the same thing that happens to a medical expert who isn't deferred to on cross examination. It threatens his self-image.*
>
> *When an attorney wants you to look arrogant she will purposefully refuse to defer to you, hoping you will respond by demanding deference. And then you look arrogant. So don't fall into that trap.*—Judge [Redacted]

Judge Christina Harms agrees:

> *Many lawyers will start out very early saying, "Now, Ms. Jones . . ." and of course the question is, do I jump in and say, "It's Dr. Jones," or do I let it go? I've always counseled: Let it go. Unless you think it's important to you and you've got some kind of point to make (which I hope you don't), let it go. They are baiting you. If you start out in the first 2 minutes saying, "Oh, no, it's Dr. Jones to you!" you set the wrong tone. That's not the place to pick the fight. The place to pick the fight is if they try to put words in your mouth or try to get you to admit something that you don't want to admit.*

> *Q: You are not a real doctor.*
>
> *A: I am not a medical physician. I am a psychologist.*—Antonio E. Puente, PhD

> You want to be factual and not defensive.
>
> *Q: Isn't it true that you are not an MD?*
>
> *A: That's true.*
>
> *Q: You don't treat medically, right? So you aren't a doctor, right?*

A: I am a PhD doctor, a PhD neuropsychologist. This is what I am trained to do.— Greg Lee, PhD, ABPP-CN

Just answer them very kindly.

Q: You're not a real doctor, are you?

A: I am not a physician. I have a PhD, not an MD.

Q: You can't give medications?!

A: That's true.—Rod Swenson, PhD, ABN

Don't take it personally

Attorney Sara Cohbra asks witnesses to find a way to endure being needled:

We want to prepare experts to expect to be attacked and to not take it personally. We want them to make sure to figure out a way to endure being needled, and not to react negatively. That is probably the hardest thing to do. But reacting sarcastically or in anger makes the expert seem defensive, not objective, and not certain of her opinions, even when the expert is justified in getting angry over the questions posed. It is really important to keep cool.

All of us have enough pride to wish that others will agree with our opinions. But you have to realize that the other side is never going to agree with you, at least not officially. You may be standing in the way of their ability to get a larger verdict, or you may be a factor in whether they are sentenced to prison. The stakes are high. Sometimes, they may secretly agree with you. Other times they really may be upset for they have a very different opinion, but rarely do others express personal enmity toward the expert. I try to remember this, and just try to focus on answering the questions as honestly and competently as I can.—Christopher Grote, PhD, ABPP-CN

He's just lawyering, so you have to expert him back.

You can't take cross examination personally. The attorney has a client to protect. He will try to undermine you. He's just lawyering. So you have to expert him back.— Mike Chafetz, PhD, ABPP-CN

Handling countertransference

Neuropsychologists need to manage countertransference. You have to not take the attorney's attacks, slights, criticisms, and sarcasm personally. At this point in my career, it helps that I have heard it all. Like the line from The Godfather Part II: "This is the business we have chosen." It goes with the territory.

You are being well compensated for this. You are not married to this person. You do not have them in your personal life. This is the way they play their game, do their job, and earn their living.—David S. Bush, PhD, ABPP-CN

I try as much as possible to be neutral and stick to the facts and try not to get drawn into taking a side and getting emotional and defensive about things. There are a lot of reasons why experts get emotional and defensive. People feel that they have an opinion and that there is going to be one side that is going to go at them and try to diminish what their interpretation is. This leaves them prone to getting defensive about that and not wanting to acknowledge some of the limitations that might be there in terms of their interpretations.

How do I avoid getting emotional? I literally remind myself not to get emotional. I say those words to myself: "You can't get drawn into emotions."

The reason I went into neuropsychology was to be into a field that uses more objective, factual, evidence-based data to pull in information from research to tie into what we are finding in the particular case. I remind myself that if I don't present it in that kind of factual way, it is going to look like I am biased.—Dominic Carone, PhD, ABPP-CN

While some attorneys adopt an angry posture, Nancy Hebben notes that when an expert takes the bait and gets angry in response, the expert looks bad.

Sometimes it is best to meet hostility from the cross-examining attorney with nondefensive postures. Juries do not like to see experts beaten up. A "pissing match" looks bad for you. On the other hand, if you get angry, you look bad. Take a deep breath.

A judge who preferred to remain anonymous noted that doctors on the stand will often appear arrogant because in their work life they are used to being at the top of the hierarchy.

Others on the jury don't share your frame of reference and things you take for granted. When you are cross-examined, these issues bubble up. If you are an attending physician at a teaching center, you are a god. In the courtroom, doctors will respond in ways that are unfortunate. A doc on the stand might answer a cross question:

Q: Did you forget to write [the important detail] in the patient's chart?

A: Of course I didn't write the note in the chart. The interns do!

Better answer:

A: The chart is important and we are trained to keep as much in there as possible, not every fact gets in. We try to be complete, but if we were writing an encyclopedia of the case, I would never be able to treat the patient.

A neuropsychologist who prefers to remain anonymous notes that it is always best to be humble on the stand:

> If an attorney is being snarky or bombastic, just respond in a very calm, humble fashion. Years ago, I was asked a question by a plaintiff attorney on cross. After my response, he said,
>
> *Q: And you didn't know that when you were deposed, did you?*
>
> *A: No.*
>
> *Q: What did you do, look it up between the deposition and now?*
>
> *A: As a matter a fact I did. The deposition lasted 7 hours. And there were times that you were better at asking questions than I was at coming up with answers. So I did some homework between then and now. (The attorney felt the jurors loved it. "Okay, you got me on that one.")*

While it is important not to be difficult or arrogant on the stand, Judge Christina Harms does not want experts to be pushovers, either:

> Some experts feel like they have to be so polite and cooperative (because psychologists are polite and cooperative) that they get beat up on the stand. I want experts to have some backbone and not get beaten up, but I also don't want witnesses who feel like they have to get into it with the questioner- have a fight with them.
>
> I want a nice middle line so that if the question was:
>
> *Q: You do agree with me, Doctor, don't you, that the tone of that paragraph suggests that you are angry at my client?*
>
> And that's a tough question and I wanted the witness to either stick up for herself and say
>
> *A: No, I don't agree with that, (but nicely)*
>
> Or
>
> *A: Well that certainly wasn't what I intended.*
>
> Not:
>
> *A: No. I can't imagine why you think that and I am offended at your suggestion.*
>
> I have seen witnesses who think that cross is the time to push back really hard, and that's never the right answer. You need to keep your cool. You need to never get angry, never show that you are insulted or say that you are insulted, but at the same time, I didn't want the expert to say
>
> *A: Oh, I can see how you could take it that way, or*
>
> *A: Yes, now that I think about it I guess the tone is a little insulting.*
>
> I didn't want experts to get pushed around but I don't want them to push back too hard and there is a lot of that opportunity to just try to stay in the middle.

Ira Packer sagely advises experts not to be difficult on the stand:

> *At a Harvard Law School mock trial, I recall watching one student being cross-examined. The student cross-examining her said, "And you didn't interview the defendant's wife." Her response: "Is that a question?" There were some laughs in the courtroom, and technically the law student cross-examining her had not asked a question, but the feedback from the law professors was that it came across as snarky. The witness should have taken the high road.*

RIPCORD ANSWER

When the attorney has needled us, our patience is frayed, or we do not know what to say, a judge who preferred to remain anonymous noted that one of the most important things for an expert witness is to have a "ripcord answer" for each case:

> A ripcord answer is an answer you give on the stand when you are uncertain, confused, or angry. This is a natural occurrence in a pressured situation, but you don't want the jury to experience you as uncertain, confused, or angry.
>
> Before I was a judge I used to work with a police officer who could get rattled on the stand, particularly when the defense needled him and suggested he was sloppy. When he got rattled, his default answer was, "Are you f***ing kidding me?!" We had to coach him to avoid some version of that answer being given in court. What are the alternatives? In a particular case he was testifying in, there had been a seizure of cocaine after a wiretapped meeting. A firefight broke out and no photographs could be taken. The defense attorney had identified the fact that there were no photographs as the signal weakness of the officer's testimony. The first step is to identify the signal weakness: "Where will they come at me?"
>
> Once you figure out where you are likely to be challenged in your testimony, you develop your ripcord answer. Pack a lot of opinion-serving and truth-serving info into your ripcord answer. This is what he practiced.
>
> *A: In the 2 nanoseconds after I got out of the car at the scene of the meeting and identified the defendant and heard the gunfire, I would have been violating all of my training had I stopped to take a picture.*
>
> *BOOM!*
>
> *A less experienced answer:*
>
> *A: No, I did not take a picture.*

CHIPPING AWAY AT CREDIBILITY

Attorney Kate Nemens describes the typical strategy of attorneys during cross examination as trying to chip away at a witness's credibility with a thousand tiny cuts. She points out that the process of redirect is an important tool to demonstrate confidence in your opinions.

As an attorney cross-examining an expert, you know it is unlikely you will be able to get the expert to change their opinion. If their conclusion is bad for your client, you are not going to get them to say the opposite through cross examination except in a really rare case. In fact, often by challenging their position through cross examination, an expert might become even more wedded to their opinion as a result.

Cross is therefore usually a matter of undermining the expert's credibility. And assuming that the expert is basically credible and didn't rely on methods that have been totally debunked, the job is to undermine their credibility by a thousand tiny cuts. Are there things they did not consider? Did they come to their conclusion without all the information? Is there a piece of information that might have changed their mind, like had they known X, could they come to a different conclusion? Can you test the bounds of their opinion through your questioning?

I think most of the time that is that middle space that the attorney is trying to get to. The strategy is a slow, methodical undermining of credibility.

If you have an expert up there who is going to stand up to cross examination and is feeling confident in their conclusion and the method in which they reach that conclusion, then they should feel confident enough to say,

A: No, I didn't interview that person.

And then on redirect, the attorney who hired them can say,

Q: Why didn't you interview that person?

A: [Reason why].

And they get to say their reason why.

I think an expert's degree of confidence in their opinion and how they came to that conclusion can also be communicated through body language and the way that they respond to the cross examination. It would certainly make me feel like I did a great job of cross examination if they kind of crumble just being asked why they didn't interview Mom's third cousin's neighbor about that one time in the park. That's not the sign of an expert that inspires a great deal of confidence to trust their opinion.

See Chapter 6, "Social Pragmatics of Testifying," for an in-depth look at how confidence is projected or undermined through experts' nonverbal communication.

Rod Swenson has a similar perspective to that of attorney Nemens:

Good attorneys, when they cross-examine you, should never ask you anything about neuropsychology. What they should ask about is what you didn't do. Why didn't you talk to his boss? His treater? Attorneys ask experts about what they don't know, what they didn't do, what they left out. Why didn't you do this particular test? Is there any reason that you didn't want the jury to know the information that test would have shown? Is there a reason why you didn't want the jury to understand that?

Attorney Wayne Miller describes his line of questioning defense witnesses to make the point that they did not speak with enough family members or friends or spend enough time with his client:

> I try to use lay witnesses a lot—people who know my client. Neuropsychologists of course are also supposed to use lay witnesses—collateral interviews. They are supposed to buttress their test data, put their test data the context of collateral data, interview data, and other records. But neuropsychologists a lot of time have a disdain. I don't how else to describe it. Because the literature is so clear that you must integrate your data into the real-world experiences: ecological validity. Many of the experts just don't have that. I can say on cross examinations:
>
> *Q: The sum total of your involvement with this patient was six hours in testing and 45 minutes of interviewing on one day, right?*
>
> *A: Yes.*
>
> *Q: And of course, some medical records that were provided to you that took you another hour to review, right?*
>
> *A: Right.*
>
> *Q: And the interview that you did was exclusively with the patient, right?*
>
> *A: Right.*
>
> *Q: And you did not bother to talk with the patient's wife, did you?*
>
> *A: No.*
>
> *Q: Did the insurance company bar you from doing that?*
>
> *A: No.*
>
> *Q: Did you ask to do that?*
>
> *A: No.*
>
> *Q: It didn't matter to you then to interview the patient's wife. It wasn't important to do that. Did you get the employment records?*
>
> To the Jury: *This guy that the insurance company hired spent the same amount of time that you spent on this case in the first day of trial. We have been here eight days. You've heard far more about my client from far more people, people who know exactly about what my client is all about, how my client lives, what my client's style and attitude toward his work is, what my client's hopes and dreams and aspirations are. In other words, who my client is and this fellow hired by the insurance company has just not done that. Why? Because he didn't want to. He didn't feel he had to. He didn't care enough.*

When confronted with this type of questioning on cross, many experts will respond with some version of:

> *A: I had the opportunity to read 8 hours of deposition testimony from Mr. Plaintiff's wife, sister and mother. That gave me a very detailed account, from their perspective,*

of the changes they are reporting in Mr. Plaintiff after his car accident. Because I already had that information, interviewing them in my office was not necessary.

Another strategy is to note that an expert could not possibly know the plaintiff/defendant as well as the treating clinician:

> *Q: Doctor, are you saying you know my client better after meeting her for 6 hours than Dr. Treating Clinician, who has known her for 5 years?!*
>
> *A: She is not my patient. That means I am able to be impartial.*

See Chapter 9, "Creating Access to Assessment Methods and Results," for strategies to clearly explain assessment techniques and address these types of questions.

Yet another strategy to chip away at credibility is to try to get the expert to agree that a narrow area of practice (that falls under the broad scope of competency for psychologists and neuropsychologists) is not in the expert's scope of practice. The logic usually goes like this: Because you don't hold a narrow certificate or specific master's-level degree that requires far less training, you are not qualified to do the thing. An example is the recent bizarre phenomenon where master's-level behavior analysts (who are typically trained in their schools by doctoral-level psychologists) ask licensing boards to restrict psychologists from practicing behavioral psychology because they don't have a master's-level "behavior analyst certification." Of course, experts must be scrupulously clear about their scope of practice, but when something falls within your wheelhouse, it is important to clarify that for the jury. This is one of the reasons that defining oneself during the credentialing phase of testimony as a neuropsychologist as "first a fully trained and licensed psychologist who received additional training in neuropsychology" is helpful if a cross examining attorney attempts to define assessment of depression as possible only by a defendants'/plaintiff's therapist and not by a neuropsychologist.

> It is common for attorneys to try to get a neuropsychologist's opinion about vocation excluded. They are trying to use a vocational expert criterion to limit your neuropsychological testimony. In your answer, you need to step back and clarify your broader training, which includes vocational assessment issues.
>
> *Q: Doctor, you are not trained as a professional vocational counselor or as a vocational rehabilitation counselor, are you? You don't give vocational tests, do you? You don't work at a vocational agency, do you?*
>
> *A: Part of my job is to interpret my assessment data to determine whether my patients have the requisite cognitive and emotional capabilities to resume their jobs.*—Ted Peck, PhD, ABPP-CN

It is interesting to hear a judge's perspective on these types of "chipping away" strategies during cross examination. Judge Christina Harms notes that attorneys are often just "flailing away" at experts, and if judges become sufficiently annoyed, they will move the process along.

From the perspective of a judge, flailing away at a witness (which is what much of cross examination is, just flailing away) is so annoying. And it quickly gets the judge to start saying things like, "Move it along, Counsel." I train lawyers and say, "Just because you can cross-examine doesn't mean you should, and just because you can cross-examine for 2 hours doesn't mean you should. What you should do is make strong points and then sit down when you're done." What I do say to a lot of psychologists when I try to ease their nerves about testifying is, if it feels like someone is just flailing away at you, they probably are, and don't let that worry you. It's annoying the judge, but it's not scoring any points.

Rigid ideas about assessment protocols

Attorneys may also try to impeach the credibility of a witness by implying that not giving all possible subtests in a battery constitutes a subpar assessment. This is one of those instances where jurors look to psychologists and neuropsychology experts to guide them via their response about whether this is in fact a big deal. Responding calmly and matter-of-factly that one does not need to give an entire large battery is important.

Q: Isn't it true that you didn't give the entire Wechsler Memory Scale?!

A: Yes. I gave a thorough set of memory tests, including others that are not part of the Wechsler Memory Scale.—Laurence Binder, PhD, ABPP-CN

The best response to the challenge, "You didn't give every subtest of every battery!" is to nondefensively say, "No, and this is why." (If you don't know why you didn't do it, then don't not do it.)

Q: You didn't give all of the IQ subtests.

A: I didn't give the tests to establish an IQ. That's not my point. My point is to establish a baseline.

(Variant)

Q: You didn't give all of the Halstead-Reitan battery, Doctor!

A: No, I didn't; you don't have to. There are a lot better uses of the time I have with the patient than giving some of the very narrow tests in the battery. I would rather give more memory tests.—Tom Boll, PhD, ABPP-CN

In my own practice, I will say,

Q: Dr. Postal, you gave only two subtests from the Wechsler Memory Scale!?

A: Correct. Many tests include a large number of subtests that do not all have to be administered. If I were to give every subtest from every test, I would have had Mr. Reyes in my office for 3 days. Instead, neuropsychologists choose a set of tests that thoroughly measures each area of brain function, without exhausting the person being tested.

TBI battery from Model Systems

> This is a very brief battery, but it is validated and it predicts real-world behavior. For folks who have non-substantiated concussion, I don't overtest.
>
> *Q: Why didn't you give xyz test? Why didn't you test for 2 days?*
>
> *A: I used the TBI Model Systems battery. This is well validated and has excellent data that correlates with real-world activities.*—Robin Hanks, PhD, ABPP-CN

Attorney Wayne Miller notes that he will use the following "bad tools in a toolkit" analogy when cross-examining experts about not using what he will later present to the jury as the best assessment tools—for example, if an expert is using a very outdated version of an IQ test or is using tests that were not normed for a person of the plaintiff's language background.

> I think the juries think of experts as walking around with a wizard's cap. They just think that experts have special knowledge, and I think for us, people who work with experts of different disciplines or who are experts within certain disciplines, we know that we have a methodology and our opinions are only as good as the data and the methodology used to process the data. Garbage in, garbage out, or good data in through bad methodology, garbage out. So sometimes I often use a hammer and saw analogy and ask neuropsychologists this question:
>
> *Q: I don't mean to be facetious by this question, but you are not a magician, are you? You're not a mind-reader, are you?*
>
> *A: (And of course)No, no, I'm not.*
>
> *Q: You draw your conclusions on the basis of data and on the basis of a methodology you employ. So, you are just like a carpenter, you use tools, and if your tool, your saw, has dull teeth, it's not going to cut, and if the wood is flawed, you might break the hammer when you try and use it. That's fair, isn't it?*
>
> *A: Yes.*
>
> *Q: So, I would say if your data is bad, your results may be bad. If your methodology is bad, your results may be bad?*

Of course, responding to this line of questioning involves (appropriately) recognizing that bad data will not help us understand brain function. As noted in Chapter 19: "Preparation and Managing Anxiety," good testimony is predicated on a thorough, solid assessment with a foundation of evidence-based medicine. Otherwise, an expert should dread cross-examination. If an expert's assessment strategy is based on anything but evidence-based practice, there is literally no good response to Attorney Miller's line of questioning. Otherwise, this type of questioning ideally gives the expert an opportunity to explain to jurors in a non-defensive manner, why the assessment strategies s/he used were appropriate given the particular characteristics of the case.

Fees

Another way to chip away at the credibility of experts is to imply that their opinion was bought. Judge Allison Burroughs notes that jurors frequently ask themselves the question "Why do we make $40 a day in jury pay and the experts make $900 an hour?"

> *What I think bugs jurors the most about expert witnesses is how much they are paid. I went back and talked to a jury fairly recently, and I always tell them I am not going to talk to them about the case, but if there is anything that they want to talk about or any way that we can make their service more pleasant or more productive, they should let us know. The very first hand that shot up was, "Why do we make $40 a day and the experts make $900 an hour?" Which is not an unreasonable question.*
>
> *The fee issue just looks bad. I think there are ways to soften it a little bit with responses to cross examination, but it's a lot of money. It's a lot of money for your average juror. It's a huge dichotomy between what they are making to be jurors, what they are making in their regular life, and what these experts are making. And I think the best way to sort of soften it is to say is, "I'm taking time away from my regular activities and I need to be compensated for it." It's a tough thing, though.*
>
> *But the people that just look like hired guns are the worst, and I don't think that jurors like to hear about people with tons of training and expertise who could be saving lives or doing whatever they could be doing and instead they are doing this legal work full-time because it's easier and more lucrative. To the extent that people are still practicing or do some pro bono work on the side, just to sort of humanize it a little bit, it is better, instead of the jurors just thinking you're some arrogant rich jerk.*

> **_Pure forensic practices_**
>
> *Experts are less credible when they are engaged in doing pure forensics and not currently engaged in any kind of clinical practice. By the time you start getting into the meat of their testimony, you have already blown away their credibility by asking them about their income and how often they do this work. One particular neuropsychologist who I did the math with in deposition was earning $700,000 a year. No clinical work anymore. He became really defensive.*—Mark DeBofsky, Esq.

Judge Allison Burroughs recommends having a single hourly rate:

> *There are experts who charge $400 an hour for preparation and then $900 an hour for the actual testimony and, in my opinion, that hurts an expert's credibility with a jury. Your hourly rate should be your hourly rate. I just think it looks like what they sell to the jury in the courtroom is more important than the preparation or the deliberative process that goes into it.*

> *For me it brings credibility that my hourly is the same for any clinical or forensic referral, and hourly for deposition and trial testimony is the same. I think there are a*

lot of reasons to justify that, but it feels straightforward to say, "This is my hourly rate for any task I do."—Anonymous

When the subject of fees comes up on cross, Antonio Puente reminds the jury that attorneys are being paid as well:

Q: How much money did you get paid to testify?

A: Like you, I have a family to feed. I was paid . . .

Several experts note that attorneys often frame fees as being "paid to testify." In their answers, they are sure to reframe the fees as being paid for their time.

Q: How much are you being paid for your testimony?

A: I am not being paid for my testimony; I am being paid for my time in this case.— Lynn Blackburn, PhD, ABPP-CN

Q: Well, you are hired by the defense for your opinion. They paid for your opinion, correct?

A: They paid for the time that I spent evaluating this patient. Really, that puts me in a unique position. I just have one job here. My job is not to be an advocate for the patient, or look out for the plaintiff. I have one job here. And that is to provide the most objective and scientifically sound opinion I can.—Tannahill Glen, PhD, ABPP-CN

Juries know that experts are paid for their time. You do not need to get defensive when asked about it on the stand.

Q: Doctor, how much were you paid to testify?

A: Of course I am charging for my time here. It is part and parcel of the work I do. I am charging [insert hourly fee here] for my time and work in this case.—Nancy Hebben, PhD, ABPP-CN

Manfred Greiffenstein notes that attorneys often ask questions along the lines of, "Doesn't secondary gain apply to you?"

Q: How much do you get paid?

A: So far, I have charged this much.

Or:

Q: After court is done today, how much will you have made on this case?

A: Well, that depends on how long you cross-examine me.

That almost always gets a laugh. I have used it so many times I am surprised it still works. Even judges crack up.

Tannahill Glen notes that she has seen nonrefundable retainers recommended against in the literature sometimes, but she uses them and has never had a problem explaining her reasoning to jurors like this:

> *Q: You charged the attorney who hired you $4,000, a flat fee, for this exam. So, they paid $4,000 for your opinion in this case.*
>
> *A: No, they are not paying for my opinion. Just like everybody else in this room, except for perhaps the jurors, I am being compensated fairly for my time in this case. Over the course of many years in doing these examinations, I know about what it costs to conduct a thorough records review and testing as well as deposition in most cases. That's how I estimate my retainer. But because I have a retainer up front, I am truly divorced from the outcome of this case. I get paid whether Mr. [attorney who hired me] likes my opinion or not. That frees me up to be completely objective.*

Some practitioners do not see any change in their salary based on forensic activities. Rus Bauer has the advantage of telling jurors that he doesn't personally make any money on any case.

> Particularly in some jurisdictions, like Levy County, that is one of the poorest counties in Florida, when you say you are billing $400 per hour, and you are billing $5,000 in total for the case, that is stunning for jurors. I can tell the cross-examining attorney what I have billed, but I personally do not make any money on the case. We consider this part of our public service duties as employees of the state of Florida. It's very powerful. When jurors realize that you are not personally profiting from your work on the case, most ideas about "I have a dog in the hunt" are gone.
>
> *Q: Dr. Bauer, precisely how much are you making in this case?*
>
> *A: In my practice, I am not allowed to accept a per-hour fee. I charge a per-hour fee, but it goes into the Florida Clinical Practice Association and goes into the practice general fund to support training and other departmental activities.*
>
> ------------
>
> *Q: How much are you getting paid for your opinion today?*
>
> *A: I am not getting paid for my opinion today.*
>
> *Q: You do this for free?*
>
> *A: No, I get paid for my time. And my time will be spent answering questions to the best of my ability. But I am getting paid my regular salary by the hospital for my time. That big fat bill that you will get from the hospital, I don't see that; I wish I did! I get paid the same amount if I see a kid on Medicaid, which doesn't pay anything, or I have one of these pleasant conversations with you ladies and gentlemen. I don't get paid a penny more or less.*—Jacobus Donders, PhD, ABPP-CN

Laurence Binder notes that he simply and nondefensively states his fees: "I just tell them the answer. Rules are different in most states, but I am required to tell them the answer. Attorneys tell me that it doesn't matter. But I am required to answer."

Keith Yeates notes that some attorneys will badger you or try to rattle you with questions about fees that are not always based in real issues.

> *Q: What do you mean you haven't registered your outside income with your university?!*
>
> *A: Because I am not required to.*

Irrelevant background experience

Nat Nelson points out that another strategy cross-examining attorneys might use to undermine an expert's credibility is making irrelevant or illogical conclusions about the fact that the expert did not have a particular life experience:

> In recognizing the attorney's role as a "zealous advocate" in cross examination, it can be helpful for neuropsychologists to recognize that attorneys may adopt various strategies to undermine one's credibility. This can include logically fallacious reasoning, such as ad hominem argumentation. As an example, during one cross examination, an attorney reviewed some of the research that I have completed with veterans and outcomes following blast concussion. The cross examination went something like this:
>
> *Q: Isn't it true, Dr. Nelson, that you never served as a soldier and you are not a veteran?*
>
> *A: Yes.*
>
> *Q: Isn't it true, Dr. Nelson, that you have never personally encountered a blast injury?*
>
> *A: Yes, that is also true. I would add that your line of questioning is not related to the issues at hand, and is in fact illogical. My veteran status is not relevant to the source and severity of impairment in this case. Extending your line of questioning to a different example, if a clinical neuropsychologist has never been diagnosed with Alzheimer's disease, would this limit her ability to conduct Alzheimer's research?*

Prior testimony

In her book *Talking Power: The Politics of Language*,[1] Robin Lakoff notes that "testimony is addressed not only to the lawyer; not only to the jury; not only to those present in the courtroom; but, via the court reporter's record, to the public at large, present and future." An expert's previous testimony, if it contradicts their current testimony, may well be brought up in cross examination to cast doubt on an expert's credibility.

"The key to successful testimony is remembering everything you said and everything you regretted saying," advises Lisa Stanford. "It will come back to bite you." She has had attorneys whip out depositions from 20 years ago and say,

> *Q: Dr. Stanford, but here you said . . .*
>
> *A: Well, I guess none of us feel the same way that we did 20 years ago about everything. The world changes; we develop different opinions about things. It's the same thing in science. The science [about x, y, z] has changed over 20 years. A science-based opinion is not something that should stay the same when science evolves.*

This is an important point. If we are practicing evidence-based medicine, and our view of the brain does not change over the course of a 20-year career, we may be doing something wrong. Our relaxed, confident response to being confronted with a statement we made in a legal proceeding 20 years ago, will likely raise our credibility:

> *A: Evidence based medicine changes over time and as a doctor it is my job to read the research literature and change my opinions when an overwhelming body of literature tells me what I learned in training is not correct.*

Rod Swenson makes the point that any previous testimony pulled out during cross might be years or decades old, and it is important to ask the cross-examining attorney to allow you to read the quote in context.

> On cross, I have had an attorney pull out a deposition I gave in 1986:
>
> *A: That case was in 1986. If you wouldn't mind, I would like to read a few pages before and after so I can get some context for my comments.*
>
> It turned out that the testimony was about a stroke when the current case was about a TBI. When prior testimony is pulled out, don't get rattled; ask for the context.

Nancy Hebben describes a situation in which a binder of prior reports she wrote was prepared by opposing counsel and given to the attorney who hired her a few days prior to a trial.

> The toughest cross questions are when the attorney is trying to discredit you. In the days prior to my last trial, the opposing attorney presented the defense attorney with a binder of records that supposedly had to do with me. Supposedly these were reports I had written in other cases. I thought in this instance it was important that the jury understood what breach was happening here. Any of my reports about concussion would only help me, not impeach me. It would show how consistent I am in applying the science to a case.
>
> At the trial, the opposing counsel asked me:
>
> *Q: Dr. Hebben, have you reviewed the binder? Do you know what is in it?*

A: Well, I was given to understand that the binder included reports that I have written in other cases, which in my view are actually confidential. So, I cannot review them or discuss them in the courtroom. And to the extent that these reports were provided by other attorneys about their client's private information, I would think that Ms. Smith would be worried that you might be giving out her private information in the future as well.

Q: Well, would it surprise you to know that these are all reports you have done for defense and this is a representative sample?

A: I don't see how you could say that was a representative sample, as I have done thousands of reports. And what you can't have in that binder are the reports that I never wrote because the data did not support the attorney's case. I promise confidentiality to people within the confines of their lawsuit. I don't send these reports out.

David Bush has had snippets of a previous video deposition shown during cross examination:

A cross-examining attorney used a snippet from a videotaped deposition as a way to show I was contradicting myself on the stand. During redirect, the retaining attorney showed the full passage, the rest of the tape, where the point was explained in proper context, which carried a very different meaning from the edited version. Of course, an expert always hopes that the attorney has a good memory and knows the details of their case and will help the triers of fact correctly understand misimpressions and distortions that result from skillful cross-examination tactics.

Manfred Greiffenstein noted that because he has testified so much, there is a long record of his testimony:

I will get asked questions I have gotten asked in prior testimony and depositions where they are trying to show inconsistencies.

Q: Have you ever testified before about this and that?

A: I am not sure; can you give me an example?

Q: [reads an excerpt from prior testimony]

A: Well, you haven't given me the date, but it is possible that I felt differently at the time because of the state of research at that point. (Most of the time it is some minor inconsistency.)

Or:

A: You will have to show me that.

Q: I am going to just read it.

A: I will have to read the whole deposition passage in order to see it in context. (They are forced to walk to the lectern. You will often discover that they have mischaracterized what you have said.)

He notes, though, that, "You have to have a core. Intellectual and moral."

> *To deal with past testimony, it is important that the expert is principled: a consistent internal core, a consistent assessment philosophy. If you do, it is difficult to catch you in an inconsistency. However, if you are a hired gun, it is very possible you will be caught in an inconsistency when you are hired by a different side. You have to have a core—not just an intellectual core, but a moral core.*

This point is an important one. Minor inconsistencies, or inconsistencies based on changes in the research literature, can be dealt with effectively on cross. Inconsistencies in testimony because an expert testifies in an inconsistent manner, spinning their clinical opinions to advocate for particular cases, should result in very uncomfortable moments on the stand.

Testifying while young

One of the best ways to inoculate against the question of inexperience for young clinicians is to bring out details and specifics of your experience on direct. Members of the public are unlikely to know the number of years of training psychologists or neuropsychologists go through prior to beginning their first job. Hearing that a psychologist was on the job for only a month prior to seeing the plaintiff or defendant may lead jurors to believe the expert only had a month of experience. If the expert's long course of training is clarified on direct, it will be easier to address the question, "Dr. New, I see you had just started your first job the week you saw my client?" Ira Packer points out that in any case, it is not our role to declare ourselves experts:

> Technically it is up to the judge to determine that. Your job is not to say, "Hey! I am an expert." A better approach is to clearly convey what your expertise is.
>
> *Q: Isn't it true that you are inexperienced?*
>
> *A: Here is what my experience is. I have completed 5 years of training in graduate school in Psychology focusing on human behavior and psychopathology, I completed an internship which included rotations on [relevant topic], and I have attended continuing education workshops specifically focused on [relevant topic].*

Occasionally, early career experts will be asked how old they are. Laurence Binder recalls, "The first time I ever testified, and I was very young, I was asked how old I was. There was nothing I could do. Just answer the question."

Accusations of bias

Judge Allison Burroughs notes that jurors need to know that experts don't just agree with whichever side brought them to court.

> *There was a nautical expert who I used when I was a prosecutor who was absolutely fantastic. Jurors love him. He was always willing to tell me that I had it*

wrong during witness prep and on the stand. He was perfectly willing to agree or disagree with both a defense attorney or a prosecutor, depending on who had it right. I put him on to call it straight down the middle, and that is what he always did.

I think that if you want to have credibility with a jury, it can't be that you agree with everything one side says and you disagree with everything the other side says or you are being combative about it. For example, there are witnesses where one side says to them, "So does she have a traumatic brain injury?" Yes. And then in the same case the other side will say, "Well, so is it your testimony that she has a traumatic brain injury?" And the response will be, "Well, it depends on your definition of a traumatic brain injury." They are too partisan, and you lose credibility with that.

Attorneys may go straight for the jugular to strip an expert's credibility by accusing them of bias. Tedd Judd has had cross-examination questions asking him how often he "wins" a case:

Q: What percentage of your cases do you win?

A: My job is to do an evaluation and to communicate the results of that evaluation clearly to jurors. If I have communicated that clearly, I feel like I've won because that's my job. But I don't keep statistics on if a case wins or loses.

Ira Packer notes that attorneys may confront an expert with their testifying history:

Q: Isn't it true that every time you testify you say that the claimant has a brain injury?

He notes that a reasonable answer is:

A: That is because when I find that a person does not have an injury, their attorney does not ask me to testify. However, I have evaluated many individuals on behalf of attorneys and did not testify because my opinion was not helpful to the attorney

He notes that he has been asked,

Q: Isn't it true you work for the state and you have an incentive to find this person incompetent so more people come to your hospital?

A: I work in a hospital, and we have a set amount of resources and a set amount of salary for all of the cases that come our way. We don't get paid per case; if anything, more cases makes more work. We really are not affiliated with either the defense or the prosecution. Our job is to call it like we see it. In many cases, we recommend (the opposite of the recommendation in this case).

Ira Packer notes that base rates can be helpful in answering questions about imbalances in testimony:

Child custody is an example. How often do you recommend the mother versus the father? Look at your own base rate. If your base rate is 80/20 and everyone else is the opposite, then this is something you need to consider. If your base rate fits neatly within the local base rate, there's your explanation.

Q: Isn't it true that you testify most of the time on [one side]?

A: Well, of course, when my opinion is that the person is not committable, I don't testify, because there is no commitment hearing. Indeed, in my practice, 75% of the individuals I evaluate are not committable, and therefore I do not testify in those cases.

Or:

A: Yes, most of the time I testify that the person is competent to stand trial, and that is consistent with the base rate in our state, where 80% of evaluees sent to our hospital are adjudicated as competent to stand trial.

What if you actually have an imbalance in your forensic cases? There are many reasons why a psychologist or neuropsychologist with fair, evidence-based assessment methods may end up seeing one type of case more often than another that have nothing to do with bias. For example, many experts do not advertise, and word-of-mouth referrals may result in more defense or plaintiff attorneys reaching out with new cases as they share names of experts among themselves. Because clinicians who work at rehabilitation facilities are often called as fact witnesses by plaintiff attorneys, they may be subsequently called more often by those attorneys who are familiar with their work for this reason, not because they are biased toward plaintiffs.

> *What do you do when you actually have an imbalance—that is, you testify for the defense or plaintiff side most of the time? On cross, attorneys will ask you about it, and it is important to have a clear reason that you feel very comfortable with, and state it plainly and without becoming defensive. They are trying to get under your skin. As soon as you become testy, they win. Your whole demeanor changes. You are less credible and less trustworthy. They have won that battle even though you may think you may have won your point.*—Ira K. Packer, PhD, ABPP (Forensic)

Mike Chafetz wants to get the issue of bias on the table in a clear manner if an attorney is implying imbalance:

> If a lawyer starts asking questions about bias—whether I considered facts on his/her side, whether I am only emphasizing certain facts—I stop and bring out the issue. Getting that out into the open then allows me to counter the assertion. You want to make what they are trying to do public and on the table. Once you get it out in the open, it loses its power.
>
> *Q: Well, Doctor, is this what you would have said if you were working for the other side? Is this what you would have said if I had retained you?*

A: It looks like you are asking whether I am biased and possibly cherry-picking the facts. If you had retained me, I would have called you and said that you better settle, because in this case, this lady showed considerable evidence of malingering.

Doctor, what percentage of defense cases do you have?

I work for plaintiffs' attorneys and defense attorneys. When they see that I have 50/50 cases plaintiff/defense, they all get a frown on their face. No matter which side they are, they always assume you work only for the other side. It isn't by choice; it's the way it works out. I don't make any effort.—Tom Boll, PhD, ABPP-CN

You were mean to my client!

Why did their client not try their best on cognitive tests or exaggerate symptoms during an Independent Medical Examination? Some attorneys will attempt to attack your credibility and your assessment results by accusing you of creating a hostile or uncomfortable testing environment.

Nancy Hebben uses exit surveys with all of her examinees to avoid this post hoc accusation. She has crafted a simple one-page set of questions like, "Were you treated with dignity and respect?" "Was the testing room comfortable?" After hearing about the technique, I also have been using exit surveys. In one instance an opposing counsel's expert noted in his report that the examinee explained that I was rude and mean to her and that is why she failed all PVTs below chance. The issue was put to rest when I pulled out her exit survey, where she had given the highest marks for courtesy and professionalism and even handwrote a note saying how comfortable I made her feel.

Exit survey

Q: Didn't Mr. Smith give poor effort because you were hostile to him?

A: I always give a survey to all of my examinees prior to leaving my office so that I can ensure the procedure was comfortable for them and to know if they had any complaints so I can address those complaints. Mr. Smith filled out this exit survey (has on stand). As you can see, he checked off that I was respectful, courteous, (etc.).—Nancy Hebben, PhD, ABPP-CN

Getting personal

Any public information about experts might be used during cross examination to damage their credibility by showing them engaged in unprofessional behavior, or just making them look ridiculous. Unfortunately, many (particularly younger) psychologists and neuropsychologists are diligently compiling this type of ammunition themselves on public social media accounts for the cross-examining attorneys to use. Ted Peck notes,

What we put on our personal social media pages may be part of public information that could be used by an attorney in an adversarial manner. It's a generational thing. So much a part of your social life, your marriage, your breakups. The point is that if

you are going to operate professionally in a field where individuals may be looking to discredit you, or create an impression that you are not being trustworthy, you need to act like Caesar's wife . . . and not like Caesar.

THE BEST DEFENSE IS A STRONG OFFENSE

Ironically, one of the strongest pieces of advice for how to remain productive during cross examination from attorneys, judges, and experts involves how you present information on direct. Chapter 8, "Direct Examination," discussed this important strategy. Here are other proactive strategies for maintaining your credibility and productivity on the stand.

Really listen to the questions

A judge who preferred to remain anonymous noted that because "lawyers don't speak like regular human beings,"

> *It is therefore important to understand exactly what the question is before you begin to answer. Breathe in and out a few times before answering. You might think you know the question, but you might have missed something subtle. Many witnesses find it helpful to repeat the question once in their head before answering. Answer the question asked, not the one that you want to answer. That takes discipline and practice.*

Mike Chafetz points out that a benefit of clearly listening to the questions is that you can identify specific gambits:

> *If you listen carefully and understand what the examining attorney is trying to do, it is usually fairly easy to respond. That's what I like about cross: I know what is coming and I can predict it. As long as you can get past the attacks and know it is not personal, then you are in a position to really listen to the questions, and it becomes straightforward to identify the cross technique and counter it. Of course the attorney is trying to undermine you with each question! He has a client to protect.*

Psychologists and neuropsychologists are very verbal creatures, so it's hard to be brief when answering a question. Attorney W. Scott Liebert cautions experts to listen to the question, answer just the question, and do not go beyond it. In her book *Talking Power*, Robin Lakoff makes the important point that witnesses are warned to answer questions without adding superfluous information because that information may open the door to further rounds of questioning—and yet failing to add more information goes against normal rules of conversation:

> *Ordinary conversation . . . makes progress and derives much of its pleasure from each participant's carrying the topic a little farther along, adding and embellishing. A witness ought to come across to the jury as a good person, a comfortable person, but many of the ways in which we convey those attitudes in private, informal talk are dangerous on the witness stand.*[2]

David Williamson also cautions experts not to elaborate: "As a general rule, don't elaborate during cross examination. If you do, be very careful how you elaborate. When you elaborate, you get sloppy." Tom Boll gave probably the most practical advice to keep in mind during cross: "Absolutely pay attention to what you are being asked. Listen to it. Don't assume anything. Understand it clearly. And then don't make stupid statements."

Rod Swenson also points out that part of psychologists being verbal creatures is that we are often in the habit of helping other people verbalize what they want to say. Part of our job description as clinicians and researchers is to actively help people ask better questions. He advises, "Don't help attorneys fix stupid questions."

> *The first thing neuropsychologists have to learn when testifying is you should listen to the questions carefully and answer them truthfully. Do not do what we do with patients. When a lawyer asks a stupid question, don't try to help them: "I think maybe you are asking about . . ." No! Shut up and answer the question.*

Acknowledge good points

Bob Denney advises that if the cross-examining attorney "wins one," acknowledge it:

> You don't want to be overly ruffled. Acknowledge that the question you were just asked is a good point. If they "win one" with you, that's fine. It reminds the trier of fact that you are reasonable person. If you dig your heels in with clear evidence to the contrary, you look biased. You want to look like (and be) a reasonable person. If the attorney brings up a really good point, you can say,
>
> *You know, that's a really good point and that's something I considered, but here is why it doesn't change my opinion."*

Scott Millis notes that he has seen some overly rigid witnesses: "They are unwilling to give the cross-examiner their due. I pay attention to how often I am agreeing with the attorney during cross. It is important to say, 'Of course' and move on, if the issue is trivial."

> ***Don't deny that there is another side to this***
>
> *The perception of the relationship between myself and both counsel is important to the trier of fact. I don't want jurors to see me as disagreeable. I will sometimes say, "Good question!" because I think the trier of fact wants to hear that it's not just "us versus them"; there are shades of gray here. And let's be honest, if it's a mental health case, there are definitely shades of gray. Why not accept that? Embrace the ambiguity of the case. Say, "Here is my emphasis," not deny that there is another side to this.*—Robert Mendoza, PsyD

Laurence Binder recommends conceding a point when you need to:

> *If something must be conceded, then you should concede it. That said, it's difficult to know where to draw the line on conceding a point under cross examination. I don't want to be argumentative, but I don't want to leave important information out.*

I have to make a judgment, right or wrong, about how important the issue is. And also of course about whether I have anything to say. For example, in testimony about a psychological issue like alleged PTSD, I have seen the patient once for 8 hours, and the psychotherapist who testified has seen the patient on repeated visits for 3 years. How can you not concede that?

Aikido. Meet and extend.

Related to the practice of acknowledging good points, many experts advised developing an aikido sensibility, taking the force of an attempted direct hit and actually extending it to make a point:

That's a great thought. Turns out, when you do that experiment . . .

Q: Ms. Jones has severe pain. Isn't it true that she was in too much pain to pass that validity test?

A: That's a great thought. Turns out, when you do that experiment—ask people to take the performance validity tests in situations when they are in pain—they pass them as easily as anyone else, because the tests are so dramatically easy, pain does not make a difference.—David Williamson, PhD, ABPP-CN

That's a good question. I don't know if I have a good answer.

How do I get jurors nodding and with me? I try always to be nondefensive. Even when I am being attacked, I try not to get defensive in any way. I will sometimes laugh and say, "That's a good question. I'm not sure I have a good answer."—Rodney Vanderploeg, PhD, ABPP-CN

David Bush occasionally simply acknowledges a piece of outrage:

Q: Are you saying my client [fill in the blank]?!

A: That is exactly what I am saying.

Keep testimony consistent and bring cross answers back to the big picture

I am consciously aware that the jury should hear a similar view from me on direct and cross. The modus operandi of cross-examining attorneys is to have the expert sound like they are painting a different picture than what they said on direct that takes away from, or plants seeds of doubt about, their direct testimony.

I am very cognizant to answer only the questions that are directly asked of me on cross and to keep my answers extremely brief. But I also consciously make efforts to link my answers on cross questions to something I said on direct, so there is not a lot of difference between my testimony on direct and cross.

Q: Isn't it possible, Dr. Bauer, that the results of these memory tests were truly because the person has a severe memory deficit that has not been fully understood by their physicians?

A: Yes, it is possible, but not very likely at all. In fact, I consider it very unlikely for reasons I stated before. As I said in my direct testimony . . .—Rus Bauer, PhD, ABPP-CN

While experts should not help the cross-examining attorney ask better questions, productive witnesses often give context when answering the question that is asked:

The really good witnesses do answer the question. Then he/she puts the answer and question in the context of the case; why the expert is there. If the expert is relaxed enough, they can think about where the attorney is going with the questions. The Montreal Cognitive Assessment (MoCA) example is a good one.

Q: Wasn't Mrs. Smith's MoCA score 24 out of 30?

A: Yes.

Q: 24 out of 30 is pretty good; isn't that a passing score?

A: Yes, that would be a pass if it was a university test, but let me explain how the test is actually scored and what the test score means for Mrs. Smith.-Attorney, Anonymous

----

During cross examination, you might go back and forth and back and forth about particular test scores. There is almost always a moment when I can turn to the jury with a big picture summary and say:

A: Do you know what? If they were really at this level of impairment, they would not have been able to tell me their medical hstory, including names of doctors, and medications, and dosages, or driven themselves to the exam. It just doesn't fit."— Glenn Larrabee, PhD, ABPP-CN

SPECIFIC LANGUAGE-BASED CROSS STRATEGIES

The following sections address language-based strategies attorneys use during cross examination to pull experts off sides and muddy their opinions.

"Just answer yes or no"

Attorneys have been trained to pose questions on cross very narrowly to force the witness to answer with a yes or a no. As Judge Fadar pointed out in the opening of the chapter, a witness who answers "Yes, but" or "No, but" is likely to get interrupted and cut off by the cross-examining counsel: "Thank you very much, Doctor; I have your answer." Despite being cut off, the "but" has communicated to the attorney who brought you that you have something to say on redirect.

The extent to which a judge will allow attorneys to confine experts to a yes or no answer varies by jurisdiction and the predilection of the judge. Mike Chafetz tells the story of one judge who was fed up with an attorney when he tried to force him to answer yes or no:

> *I was in court with an attorney who was aggressive in his cross examination. Everyone in the courtroom was irritated with his questioning. The court reporter was rolling her eyes. The judge got irritated with him and had to stop him several times and tell him to move on. Once he told me: "Answer yes or no, Doctor." The judge chimed in immediately, telling him: "This is MY courtroom, and you do not tell the doctor to answer yes or no. The doctor can answer yes or no and then elaborate briefly on his opinion."*

Other experts suggest strategies to get one's actual opinion into the answer.

If you are asking me . . .

> Just because an attorney is framing the question in a particular way or trying to get you to say yes/no . . . If you answer a question "Yes, but," an attorney can stop you and say, "Thank you very much." It is better to say,
>
> *If you are asking me whether a concussion is causing permanent brain injury, the answer is no. If you are asking me if people continue to complain of symptoms, the answer is yes."*—Nancy Hebben, PhD, ABPP-CN
>
> ------------
>
> *I can't answer that in the way you are asking because I don't want to mislead the court.*—Robin Hanks, PhD, ABPP-CN

Even if you're not being asked to answer yes or no, a cross-examining attorney is likely to cut you off before you can get out a full answer with more than one point. Kristie Nies uses this strategy when she wants to make more than one point:

There are two points I want to make . . .

> If you want to respond to a cross question with more than one point, and avoid being cut off after the first one, start your answer with . . .
>
> *A: There are two points I would like to make in answer to your question. The first is . . ..*

All that said, Judge Christina Harms cautions experts against always fighting a yes or no answer. Sometimes a yes or a no is the most appropriate answer, and the expert who fights it will look difficult to the judge or jury.

> *You don't have to answer every question yes or no, even though someone may have just told you "Answer yes or no." However, it's easy to give in to the temptation to never answer yes or no. As soon as psychologists hear that they don't actually have to answer yes or no, because they are a little nervous understandably, they cling to*

the idea like a lifesaver and they end up using it way too much: "I can't answer that question yes or no . . . I can't answer that question yes or no." And it gets to the point where it's clearly a question that they can answer yes or no, and they've slipped into looking like they are ducking it.

I always prepare psychologists for testimony by saying, "You have to think for a minute and decide whether it is a question that a reasonable person, like a judge, thinks ***can*** *be answered yes or no." Experts often want to talk too much and so they say, "I can't answer yes or no because I want to explain." If the question doesn't ask for an explanation and if it really could be answered yes or no, then just do that.*

I've seen judges lean over and say "Well, yes, you can. The question calls for a yes or no answer." Then you know you've irritated the judge—not irrecoverably, maybe, but maybe you've gone too far with that.

Compound questions

Many experts warned that cross-examining attorneys ask long, grammatically complex questions in an attempt to lure witnesses to agree with parts of a question they did not intend.

Compound questions

I am never more cognitively tired than after a deposition or trial testimony. That's because it is crucial that you listen carefully to every word that is being said. Watch for the compound question. The attorney sets up a statement at the beginning and then asks a question at the end. If you say yes to the question at the end, you have also agreed to the statement at the beginning. It's a trick that they learn in law school. They set up a statement that they want you to assent to but don't ask you to directly assent to it. You can say:

Well, I would disagree with the first part of your statement, that concussion can cause permanent brain injury. But I would agee with the second part."—Nancy Hebben, PhD, ABPP-CN

In most jurisdictions, compound questions are not allowed, but if no one objects, then they happen. The attorney who hires me may not want to object multiple times on cross; then she doesn't look good to the jury, she looks too argumentative. That leaves the witness with the responsibility to point out that that is a compound question.

Q: Wouldn't you expect a person who had a significant loss of consciousness to have memory problems?

A: First, Mr. Smith did not have a significant loss of consciousness . . .

If there ***was*** *a significant loss of consciousness, I wouldn't bother to point out that it was a compound question.*—Laurence Binder, PhD, ABPP-CN

You are actually asking me three different things. I will try to break it down and answer all three.—Rodney Vanderploeg, PhD, ABPP-CN

Long, complex questions

There are some cross questions that are very complicated and very long. I pause, and I say, "Could you repeat that back to me?" Of course, they can't. If they persist in that behavior, it only takes a few times before they realize that's not going to work.—Scott Millis, PhD, ABPP-CN

You need to pay attention to the spirit of the question versus the grammar. Attorneys' questions often carry surplus meanings, and one has to carefully attend to both the formal and informal structure in order to grasp the fullness of the inquiry. We must listen to both levels and always require attorneys to ask grammatically correct questions, to ensure the alignment and clarity of our responses. A number of attorneys like to pose cross-exam questions that are loaded with so many hypotheticals and moving parts they are impossible to answer. This is their way of injecting their own testimony into the record and trying to make the expert appear biased. Any expert who attempts to answer one of these impossible questions loses immediately, no matter what they say. Sometimes the only reasonable response is,

"I need you to reframe that into a question I can understand and answer."—David S. Bush, PhD, ABPP-CN

If a question is very long- and there are some attorneys whose questions might go on for paragraphs, it is a good policy to ask a clarifying question.

Q: [3 paragraphs and complicated]

A: Look, with a question that long, it is hard for me to understand what you are asking. Can you be specific?—David Williamson, Ph.D., ABPP-CN

Attorneys will sometimes throw three or four false premises into a question that they are trying to get you to agree to. The question might start with four wrong premises and end with something you agree with. In their mind and on paper it looks like you have answered all five premises "yes." You need to be patient: "I didn't say that. I didn't say that. That is correct."—David Williamson, PhD, ABPP-CN

Attorneys often say that they hire me in part because during testimony I come across as someone who really wants to understand questions and answer them:

"I think I need separate questions there because I really want to make sure I understand the question."—Robin Hanks, PhD, ABPP-CN

Rapid-fire questions/odd cadence

Attorneys are taught to try to pull an expert off sides during cross examination by engaging them in a rapid, rhythmic verbal exchange. Answer this question . . . this one . . . this one . . . gotcha! Cheryl Weinstein notes that she will use body language to break an uncomfortably fast rhythm and slow down:

> If an attorney is asking hard or fast questions, I will use the fingers on my hand to slow me down. For example,
>
> *Q: Dr. Weinstein, how can you disagree with Dr. Treating Clinician!?*
>
> *A: Maybe it is that I had more time with Mr. Smith (counts one finger). Maybe it's that I am obsessive and I like to look through ALL of the records. Treating doctors do not have time to do that. Neuropsychologists do; we are in a unique situation (counts two fingers). Maybe it's that . . ..*

A judge who preferred to remain anonymous advises experts to slow attorneys down by asking them to repeat questions:

> *Ask the attorney to rephrase the question. The jury is sensitive to the situation: They don't want to see people tricked or trapped. The second time, there is less punch, not as effective.*
>
> *A: I am sorry, counsel, I didn't get all of that. Can you repeat the question?*

Jerry Sweet tells the story of literally telling the cross-examining attorney that he needed time to think about a question before answering, and then uncharacteristically took quite a while to do so. In this instance, the issue of broader precedent-setting and perhaps issues of another professional's ethics, which at the time appeared related to a different Illinois case involving other experts, not the case or the experts that were the focus of the current deposition, was unsettling. This is an important reminder that testimony is serious, and, honoring that, experts can give themselves permission to break the pace of cross examination and think something over if necessary.

> *In one case, the attorney pulled out the APA publication* The MMPI, MMPI-2, and MMPI-A in Court.[3]
>
> *A: Yes, I am familiar with that book.*
>
> *Q: Can you read the items from the Lie Scale?*
>
> *A: No, I am not willing to do that. I am not supposed to do that.*
>
> *Q: Well, how can you say that it would be unethical when the American Psychological Association, right here, has published all of these items in a book? I am going to ask you again. I want you to read this.*
>
> *A: I am going to take a moment. I feel the need to pause here. You are asking me to do something that here in Illinois we have taken a strong stance against doing. In*

fact, I have taken a strong public stance against doing this, and I believe it would be unethical. I am just going to pause here to think through how I am going to answer your question.

(I took a long time, likely only about 1 to 2 minutes or so to think about it.)

A: I realize that you may have gotten other people to do this, and it is a mystery to many of us why APA did this in one of their own publications, which many of us complained about. It is a mystery to me why they did this at all. And I refuse to participate in this. Even if someone else has already done it, I am not going to do it. And, again, I want to make it clear that the case we are discussing today has a normal L scale and there are no concerns about any of the responses of the plaintiff on this scale. What you have been asking me to do has no relevance to today's case.

"Isn't it possible . . ."

Another strategy attorneys use during cross examination to draw experts away from their opinions is the use of hypotheticals. "Isn't it possible . . ." "Let's assume that . . ." Keith Yeates notes that often it is easier to simply say, "Yeah," and leave it at that. Kristie Nies notes that when the hypotheticals get really crazy, she will say: "That is like asking me to tell you why the sky is green."

Q: Is it possible, Doctor? (Say something very far from the truth)

A: Yes, but it is highly unlikely, for the following reasons.—Rodney Vanderploeg, PhD, ABPP-CN

"Can you read this record, Doctor?"

Cross-examining attorneys may want an expert to read a passage from another expert's record or the research literature so they can make a point literally using the expert's voice. Rod Swenson will often resist.

Q: Dr. Swenson, here is a record from 30 years ago. Can you read this record?

A: No. This is not my record. I don't want the jury to get the feeling that I wrote this.

(The attorney might ask the judge to make me read it. The judge will typically say to the attorney, "Just ask a question.")

Q: 30 years ago, she had a migraine. And isn't that her symptom now?

A: Well, you know, I have looked at those records. I believe that is when she was premenopausal. And now that she is in menopause . . .

Dr. Swenson also makes the point that a competent expert should have read every record in the case and be prepared to discuss the meaning of records on the stand.

"Authoritative" texts

Attorneys are trained to get experts to deem other experts, books, article, or even whole journals as "authoritative." They will then confront the expert with a passage from the "authoritative" source that contradicts the expert's opinion. A common ploy is to ask a neuropsychology expert to declare Muriel Lezak's[4] book or her entire person "authoritative." Of course, for most scientists, the idea that one would blindly accept the authority of another scientist is ludicrous; that goes against the basic principles of the scientific method: falsifiability. Here are some helpful responses:

Even the Bible is not authoritative.

Q: Do you know Muriel Lezak? Do you think her book is authoritative?

A: Define authoritative.

Q: I will let you define it.

A: If you mean by authoritative, do I agree with everything that is in there? No. If you want me to comment on a specific chapter or a certain line, just point it out to me. [If they really push] You know, even certain parts of the Bible I won't agree with. According to the Bible I can't eat shellfish. I like my lobster once in a while!—Jacobus Donders, PhD, ABPP-CN

According to eminent expert . . .

Sometimes a cross attorney will bring in a paper by another person, an article they found somewhere that portrays an opinion that is contrary to mine. Or an attorney will make an assertion that someone has said something: "According to [eminent expert] . . ." "[Eminent expert] has said this or that . . ."

A: Well, I actually know [eminent expert]. I have worked with him. He has written a chapter in my book. He is a friend of mine. I have never heard him say that. Can you show me where he said that?

Or, if it is in an article and something I disagree with:

A: I know [eminent expert] is very enthusiastic about [his area of research]. And the part where I have to disagree with him sometimes is . . .—Jacobus Donders, PhD, ABPP-CN

Responding to low-quality studies on cross

In a deposition, an attorney confronted me with multiple studies, of very poor quality, many *15 years old*.

Q: Well, Doctor, doesn't the study say this?!

A: Yes, it does say that.

The retaining attorney then came back on redirect.

Q: Is this paper authoritative?

A: No.

Q: It this paper authoritative?

A: No.

Q: Is this paper authoritative?

A: No. (I am not acknowledging anything is authoritative.)—Glenn Larrabee, PhD, ABPP-CN

An attorney word

Attorneys like to use words that mean something to them, and they like to paint you down an alley. Have you ever genuinely used the word authoritative in your daily life? Of course not. Why would you agree to a concept that you never use and has no meaning for you?

Q: Doctor, is this authoritative?

A: I don't even know what authoritative *means. It sounds like an attorney word.*—Tom Boll, PhD, ABPP-CN

What does* rely *mean?

Q: Doctor, did you rely on this?

A: I don't use that word. I don't know what it means.

Q: You don't know what rely *means?!*

A: Not in this context. You told me in the beginning of the deposition that if I didn't understand a question, I can ask you about it. Well, I don't understand what you mean and I am asking you about it. Can you explain it to me?

Or:

Q: Doctor, did you rely on this?

A: I don't rely on anything. I read everything, I am informed by it. But I don't rely on anything.—Tom Boll, PhD, ABPP-CN

Not even your own book is authoritative

Never acknowledge anything as being authoritative, including your own book. When asked about widely read books such as Lezak, I acknowledge that it's a widely read source. There are things that I agree with and things that I don't agree with.—Glenn Larrabee, PhD, ABPP-CN

I have had attorneys drop my book, The Essentials of Neuropsychological Assessment,[5] *in front of me while I am on the stand, as if they are going to frighten me. And then they pick out a sentence that has no relevance to the case.*—Nancy Hebben, PhD, ABPP-CN

General versus specific

David Bush warns experts to avoid the "general versus specific" strategy:

> Make the distinction between questions that are being asked as general propositions and questions that are being asked that are specific to the case at hand.
>
> *Q: Do you believe traumatic brain injury elevates risk of suicide?*
>
> *A: What type of traumatic brain injury?*
>
> *Q: Well, the type of TBI my client had.*
>
> *A: Are you asking me if suicide risk is elevated in mTBI or am I concerned about your client being at risk for suicide?*

Use of broad lay language on cross

Darcy Cox described an attorney who sprinkled questions, using very broad lay language, throughout the cross examination about whether the plaintiff had various symptoms of PTSD.

> This was a good trick. I try to avoid jargon, but I got burned by that.
>
> *Q: Does the plaintiff have anxiety? [The attorney had asked in very broad lay language about other symptoms of PTSD as well.]*
>
> *A: Yes.*
>
> *Q: [The attorney pulls out the DSM and in non-lay language reads the criteria]*
>
> *Doesn't the plaintiff meet the criteria for PTSD?*
>
> *A: While this person has anxiety in the broad sense of the word, she does not have the very specific type of anxiety that the DSM PTSD criteria require.*

"Isn't this all subjective?"

Attorneys may wish to frame psychology or neuropsychology as "soft science," asking experts to agree that our opinions are all subjective. Here are some productive responses.

> *Q: Well, Doctor, this is all a subjective opinion, isn't it?*
>
> *A: My opinion is based on dozens of objective facts in my record and in the historical record.*
>
> *Q: Well, the tests are subjective, aren't they?*
>
> *A: No, the tests are not subjective. The tests are objectively administered, objectively scored, so that any neuropsychologist across the country, were he or she to score the test, would get the same score that I did.*—David Hartman, PhD, ABPP-CN

Tom Boll shares a vivid analogy for objective observations versus subjective opinions:

Q: Some of your data are subjective, aren't they?

A: No. There isn't an ounce of subjectivity in it. Subjectivity is looking at a painting and saying, "I like that" or "I don't like that." Objectivity is looking at the painting and saying, "The brush strokes are this, and the depth of color is that, and the proportionality is that, and therefore this is or is not a decent work of art."

Isn't this just your own opinion?

Q: Isn't this just your opinion?

A: Yes. It is an opinion based on science.—Robin Hanks, PhD, ABPP-CN

"Isn't it reasonable that . . ."

Tom Boll describes another common strategy, "Isn't it reasonable . . ."

Q: Isn't it reasonable that . . .

(These are ridiculous statements. These statements have no meaning.)

A: I would think it is reasonable that a heavy ball would fall faster than a light ball, too. It just doesn't. What I think is irrelevant. It's what happened that is relevant.

Knocking down the pillars

As discussed in Chapter 8, "Direct Examination," one strategy on cross examination when many facts lead to a conclusion but no single fact proves the conclusion is to "knock down the pillars" of the argument one by one. Including the statement on direct that "all of these factors together led me to my conclusion" helps inoculate against this strategy. Mike Chafetz describes the strategy and his response on cross examination.

> The cross-examining lawyer used a plan/method to discredit my conclusion of illness deception by discrediting each individual fact I used to come to my diagnosis. In prior testimony, I sat for hours while the attorney went through each medical item in my report:
>
> *Q: Doctor, does this item prove illness deception?*
>
> Each time, I would reply,
>
> *A: No, not by itself."*
>
> This was in September. When I came back in November, the cross-examining attorney started with me by saying:
>
> *Q: Doctor, you last testified that not one of the medical items contained in your report proved illness deception.*
>
> *A: You mischaracterized my testimony.*
>
> Before I could explain, he raised his voice, saying:

Q: Oh, Doctor, we spent hours before on this, but I will go through every record in your report again for you to say that not one of them proved illness deception.

A: You haven't let me explain.

He cut me off again, but the other lawyer objected, saying to the judge that the cross-examining attorney was trying to badger me and was not letting me explain my testimony. The judge sustained and said that I could explain my testimony.

A: Let's take depression, and I will show how your method hides the truth of my testimony. For the construct of depression, in your examination, you would say: "Doctor, sadness does not necessarily indicate depression, does it, Doctor?"

To which I would reply, "Not by itself, no."

And you would ask: "Sleeplessness does not necessarily indicate depression, does it, Doctor?"

To which I would reply, "Not by itself, no."

And you would ask: "Loss of interest does not necessarily indicate depression, does it, Doctor?"

To which I would reply, "Not by itself, no."

And you would ask: "Guilt does not necessarily indicate depression, does it, Doctor?"

To which I would reply, "Not by itself, no."

And you would go through each of the other symptoms of depression in the same manner: reduced energy, reduced concentration, changes in appetite, reduced psychomotor speed, and suicidality, and at the end you would attempt to have my testimony prove that all of these symptoms are not indicative of depression, to which I would have to say, "No, not by themselves alone, but when you put them all together, you have gathered plenty of evidence for depression."

Evidence-based assessment uses a strategy of increasing probabilities with each new fact. For example, you might hear a weather report that there is a 10% chance of rain in your town. When you look outside and see dark clouds, you would update that probability to a higher expectation. If your friend a half a mile away calls and says that it is raining buckets at his house and it looks like it is coming your way, you would update your probability even further. That's how evidence-based assessment occurs.

Questions about obscure information

Ted Peck notes that if attorneys are going to be asking highly specific statistical questions, there isn't enough material that you could possibly bring that could allow you to answer all of those questions in depth.

Q: Doctor, what is the standard error of measurement of the Hooper Visual Organization Test?

A: I needed and used that information when I formed my opinion or scored my tests. If I truly needed that information, at that time, I could go to the manual and look it up. It was available to me when I prepared the report. I don't need to memorize that information, and I don't have that table with the standard error of measurement with me today.

Erin Bigler notes that attorneys will sometimes ask arcane questions on cross examination.

> When attorneys try to ask arcane questions, I will never try to do anything just from memory. You are likely to make a mistake, and that is what they want you to do. If it is in deposition, I am usually in my office. I will pull my book down here and show the page. I try to be captain of the ship, so to speak, at those points in time. I will not let the attorney intimidate me or try to ramrod me.
>
> *A:I am happy to give that to you. I will pull my book down here and show you the page."*
>
> *In a situation in which I was not i my office, I would say,*
>
> *A:That is information that I typically look up in a book if I need it. I don't have anything memorized."*

See Chapter 22, "Eplaining Statistics," for clear answers to "in the weeds" statistical measurement questions that experts can reasonably assume will be brought up in certain cases like those involving questions of intellectual disability.

Ted Peck notes that one cross-examination technique is to find an area of the field in which you don't know anything.

> *If they look hard enough, they will find an area in which you know nothing. But the argument that I make—I don't choose to make that a win/lose situation, I point out that I am knowledgeable generally in that area but I don't specifically make a habit of memorizing those specific numbers. If I am being asked a professional question, I know how to find the answer. I don't act defensive or in a way that "I should have known that but I don't and I am ashamed."*

Nancy Hebben tells the story of a cross-examining attorney who kept asking her obscure questions about nerve cells, one after the other. After the fifth or sixth question she answered, to laughter in the courtroom, "What is this, a quiz show?"

Ecological validity of tests

Attorney Wayne Miller shares the following cross examination strategy, chipping away at the ecological validity of cognitive tests.

> *I try to make the limits of neuropsychological test batteries more understandable to juries with this line of questioning. When I teach Robin's class, I have her play the*

role of the neuropsychologist. I ask her the questions and we get into some battles about this, but I ask questions like this:

Q: Describe for me the room where the neuropsychological testing takes place. (Sometimes if we are on the same premises, I will ask to visit the testing room in the deposition and I will describe it when the witness is on the stand at trial.)

Q: So, this room is about 10 feet by 10 feet. Is that about right?

A: Yes.

Q: And I notice that there is one window, but the blinds were drawn. Is that right?

A: Yes.

Q: And I notice there was really little else in the room. There are no paintings on the wall?

A: That's right.

Q: There is certainly no computer in the room other than whatever computer you were doing the testing on.

A: Yes.

Q: There was no radio in there. There was no sound system. There was no television. Did you ask the person to turn off their cellphone or to surrender their cellphone?

A: Yes.

Q: And there were no kids running through there, were there?

A: No.

Q: And the noise from outside was muted at best?

A: Yes.

Q: And so, Doctor, what you are describing to me is kind of a pristine environment. It's almost like a laboratory environment. Isn't it?

A: Yes.

Q: A lot of the distractions that we normally encounter in the day-to-day world, traffic, television, radio, co-employees, children, none of those are in there?

A: Yes.

Q: That's because the neuropsychological assessment is supposed to be done under laboratory conditions, right?

A: Yes.

Q: So that you can get a hypothetical determination or a determination of the patient's hypothetical, optimal functioning on this, that, and the other tests. Isn't' that so?

A: Yes.

Q: Doctor, how do you then know how the patient functions when there are distractions? Your tests don't tell you how the patient functions in a real-world environment. Do they?

> *A: No.*
>
> *Q: And that's a major criticism in the literature of neuropsychological testing, isn't it? The doctrine known as ecological validity.*
>
> And I have about 20 minutes of questions on this area, but it goes to the point that you have a discipline that helps you answer the question, "How well does a person do on the Booklet Category Test compared to other people?" That is really not the question that we want to answer in a case. What we want to answer is "How well does this person function at his job? How well does this person function in his home environment? How well does this person function when driving a car, etc., etc.?" I think when jurors see that, they can readily understand that removing distractions before performing a task does not permit someone to draw conclusions about how a person will perform when they have all of those distractions.

Robin Hanks notes that Attorney Miller has come to present a didactic presentation on this topic to her neuropsychology graduate students.

> I always talk to my students when Wayne presents to them about the importance of doing and reading research that looks at the ecological validity of our neuropsychological test battery. A great deal of my own published research examines this relationship, so that I know how well the tests I use predict real-world outcomes. Additionally, much of my research has focused on looking at the incremental validity of neuropsychological test data above and beyond medical tests (CT and MRI scans) and neurologic indicators of brain injury severity (GCS, length of PTA, etc.), so that we know what we are adding value to the clinical picture with neuropsychological testing. I try to encourage the trainees to pursue this line of research and read the empirical literature in this area. Of course, we may not know the predictive or ecological validity of all our tests, but we need to know as much as we can about the ones that we do use frequently.
>
> I also don't have the pristine environment that Wayne talks about. I have pictures in my office, I don't draw the blinds, there are people walking and talking outside by testing room even though the door is closed, there may be announcements from the hospital on the overhead that go off during a test, and it is important to note behavioral observations about how they respond when those things happen.—Robin Hanks, Ph.D., ABPP-CN

In my own practice, I say,

> *A: Of course, you are right, outside of the laboratory we have real life. Kids, people talking to us. If your three-year-old child is crying, and your dryer is making a racket, of course you will not be able to focus on solving a problem or hearing information to remember later. None of us would.*
>
> *The purpose of testing in a quiet, distraction free environment is to find out if not solving the problem is a "brain damage issue" or a "messiness and noisiness of life issue." When we are testing in the office, we are reducing some of the noise. But people*

are still thinking about stopping by the store after the test session to get stuff for dinner, and if they are depressed, they are often still thinking sad thoughts, and their chronic pain is still bothering them. But we have reduced some of the noise, so we can better get at, does the problem-solving part of the brain work?

It's just like you put on a blood pressure cuff at the doctor's office in a quiet calm room, rather than in rush hour traffic. Sure, during stressful moments of real life your blood pressure may be higher, but no one says that measuring blood pressure in the doctor's office is not valid. You are getting a better measurement of whether there is a biological or situational problem.

In a case not so long ago when the crossing attorney brought this up, the judge asked, "What did you want her to do, test him in the lobby?"—Nancy Hebben, PhD, ABPP-CN

A: Our imperfect tools are far superior to self-report for evaluating the severity of thinking problems following mTBI, and better than any tools used by behavioral neurologists.

And/or

A: If the deficits associated with mTBI are so subtle that they can't be detected by neuropsychological testing, they are probably of little clinical significance.—Robert A. Seegmiller, PhD, ABPP-CN

Dominic Carone's response to the issue of ecological validity is to explain a technique he uses in his clinical practice:

After our day of testing was over, I had Ms. Smith estimate how she did on the tests I gave her of memory, attention, and problem-solving. Ms. Smith estimated that none of her scores would be in the average to high average range. Actually, half of the scores were in that range.

Ms. Smith said that the vast majority of her scores were going to be in the borderline to low average range, and it turns out that none of the scores were. She consistently underrated her cognitive performance, even though she did as well or better than the average healthy person who takes the tests. It is likely she is underestimating her abilities in day-to-day life as well.

Peer consultation

Occasionally, the fact that a psychologist or neuropsychologist discussed the plaintiff or defendant in peer consultation might be brought up during cross examination. Judge Christina Harms notes,

Believe it or not, most lawyers and a lot of judges have no idea that peer consultation is part of the process of being a psychologist. Peer consultation in that way is just not

part of what lawyers do. It almost like an admission that you're weak, like "I had to go ask somebody else." As a psychologist, even if you are not required to have supervision, it is very common that you seek a consult or join a peer group. That needs to be carefully explained in court because it usually comes out in some unintended way.

During cross, I often hear a witness say something like, "I even consulted with my peer consultation group on this point and they all agreed with me." That type of response typically leads into a long discussion of "What?! You got other people's opinions and you talk about this case and it isn't really your opinion?!"

I have my trainees practice answers. You have to just realize that nobody has any idea what you are talking about and you have to start right from the basics: "Perhaps I could explain to you that it is standard in the field of psychology to seek supervision on a periodic basis [blah, blah]. We don't exchange names, we never exchange identifying information, but it's considered best practice to use that process."

Cross when you did not evaluate the plaintiff/defendant

"Doctor, how can you possibly have an opinion when you have never met my client?" To a juror, it is a very good question. Desiree Byrd notes,

> *Testifying as a consulting expert feels easier for me because I am not defending an opinion based upon a clinical evaluation that I conducted; rather, I am brought in as an expert to opine on existing reports and medical records. I am also there to talk about what we know from research related to the case. An initial fight in these types of cases might be for the attorneys to get the judge's approval to allow me to testify as a consulting expert. Once that is established I feel more secure in my role, as though, "I am here to tell you what I know as the scientist practitioner that I am."*

See Chapter 20, "Specific Testifying Situations," for an in-depth discussion of strategies on both direct and cross examination for instances where one is testifying without having met the plaintiff/defendant.

PROBLEMS WITH THE CASE

There are times when experts are confronted with genuine problems with their opinions on cross examination. In some instances, the issues raised substantially change the nature of the expert's opinions. In other instances, the expert must explain why the issue does not change their opinion.

Scoring mistakes

Attorney Wayne Miller tells the story of an opposing side's expert who made errors in scoring:

> *I had a neuropsychology expert analyze data in a case; this is a fundamental requirement of effective cross examination of a neuropsychologist. My expert literally*

> *checked the arithmetic of this other expert, and he found mistakes. For example, on the Booklet Category Test there were three errors that were just missed, naturally in the direction of making the patient seem less brain-injured. So it was most embarrassing when I pointed this out to him during testimony. We also found out that he didn't use the test norms. He used his own norms that were not published.*
>
> *In the case, the expert had two artifices: (1) making arithmetic mistakes in favor of the defense and (2) using his own norms that were not published and no one else knew about. He could with the wave of a magic wand make a person with brain injury not brain-injured.*
>
> *Q: Doctor, you're only as good are your data. You're only as good as your methodology. You're not a wizard. You're not a magician. In this case, you're a C arithmetic student, aren't you?*

In an ideal world, experts check and recheck their data, eliminating errors in scoring prior to forming their opinion. In a less ideal world, while reviewing their data for a deposition or trial, they'd catch any scoring errors and would be prepared to face cross examination about the error. As noted in Chapter 8, "Direct Examination," it's best to bring out the scoring error on direct testimony, when there is the luxury of open-ended questions that allow the expert to discuss why the scoring error does or does not affect their opinion. In the less ideal situation, an expert learns of an error during cross examination.

One attorney who prefers to remain anonymous notes that there is no good answer to the question of how an expert should respond to a cross-examining attorney who has found a mistake in the data. He notes, "My better experts will check and recheck their data prior to trial and alert me to issues like this when they come up. We will deal with them up front, on direct."

Ted Peck advises,

> When you are wrong, admit it. Say, "Yes, that was an error." Admit it and move on. What a jury wants to know is that you are willing to take responsibility when you made a mistake.
>
> *Q: Doctor, I am looking at your scores. And you understand that the scores were provided to Dr. Smith, the expert hired by the plaintiff. I have been informed that you have misscored two items on the Similarities subtest, where you gave a 2 score when it should clearly have been a 1. You added in the practice elements of the test that were not supposed to be added in. The end result is that the score you said was 9 when it should be a 6. Do you admit you made a mistake?*
>
> *A: I am looking at that here now. I agree that is a mistake. The difference is 2. That would have changed the standard score by one point, a very small amount.*

The question of additional errors is then almost universally raised. While this has not yet come up on a case for me, I might answer:

> *Q: Doctor, if there is an error on this test, how can you be sure there is not an error on other tests? Is any of your data correct?*

A: I carefully check the scoring on all of my data. It is true that even double checking the 30 tests I gave, I did not catch this error. Your expert did. Given that the data has now been checked three times, I am sure that if there was another error besides this one, it would have been found.

Paul Craig advises that in a "mayday moment" on the stand, acknowledge an error that has been brought to your attention by opposing counsel: "Learn from the moment and minimize it ever happening again. Also, don't try to hide an error. If you have made an error, acknowledge it, and if possible, correct it during the testimony."

Confronted on the stand with new information about the case

There are times during cross examination when an expert is confronted with information that makes it clear that the defendant/plaintiff was not honest during their assessment or critical information was withheld. Education transcripts, medical records, or surveillance video that the expert has never seen may all be produced on the stand.

> I was involved in a clinical case that ended up in litigation. I evaluated a person who was hit by a truck and had a severe TBI. He told me he was a college graduate. I wrote my report. I was only working with neurology records. I scored his data using Heaton norms, where based on a BS degree, the equivalent was 16 years of education. One year later, I was called into court under subpoena. I offered my opinions. On cross:
>
> *Q: Doctor, the norms for these tests are adjusted by demographic factors. What are those factors? Your data were scored and interpreted based on someone with 16 years of education. Correct?*
>
> *A: Yes.*
>
> *Q: Doctor, if I told you that he had 12 years of education, would any of these education-adjusted scores would change?*
>
> *A: They very well might.*
>
> *Q: Doctor, in general, if the education correction goes from 16 to 12, are the scores in terms of their range going to go up or go down? Will they look more normal or less normal?*
>
> *A: Not in every situation, but in many cases, if there is less education then the scores will look better.*
>
> *Q: Doctor, I am going to hand you this transcript. Do you admit that this changes your opinion?*
>
> *A: Yes. I can show you the registration form. This wasn't something that I just wrote down wrong. Mr. Jones wrote on the registration form and also told me directly that he had a college degree. My opinions may very well have been different. In the courtroom today, I do not feel I can truly offer an opinion as the data were based on erroneous demographic corrections.*—Ted Peck, PhD, ABPP-CN

Notice that Dr. Peck responded that he was unable to offer an opinion given the new information he was confronted with on the stand. Paul Craig notes that it is important not to try to create a new opinion "on the fly" while sitting in the witness box:

> If you are confronted with significant new information on cross, acknowledge you were never presented with that information before. Don't try to create a new opinion on the stand, especially if the new opinion makes you look like an advocate rather than an objective expert. Simply acknowledge that the new information may change your opinion if the new information is based in fact.
>
> In one case, I was testifying at the request of the plaintiff against a school district involving overly aggressive disciplinary behavior against the plaintiff that resulted in his fingers being broken. The exchange was as follows:
>
> *Q: Dr. Craig, were you presented with the records showing the five fights this student has started with others during which he has needed to be restrained?*
>
> *A: No.*
>
> *Q: Would it have changed your opinion?*
>
> *A: If such records exist, and those records support what you assert in your question, then yes, such records may change my opinion.*

> *I would not create a new opinion on the stand when presented with new information. For you to try to make an opinion on the fly really raises a question of why you are trying to form that opinion on the fly: Are you trying to make yourself look better? Are you trying to be an advocate? You are a professional. Your opinions are carefully thought out. Now, if it is a typographical error or a very small error, you admit it and you go from there. But if it is a situation in which you would need time to consider a lot of new test data, if your opinion is beyond a reasonable medical or scientific certainty, your answer has to be: "Because my opinion was based on this incorrect information, I can no longer offer an opinion at the present time."*—Anonymous

Sometimes, new information might change an expert's opinion, but only in a minor way. AN attorney who prefers to remain anonymous notes that new information can appear that would not necessarily alter the core of an opinion.

> *You weren't given the info. It does change your opinion. But there is a huge difference between a 10% change or a 180-degree change. If you are the defense lawyer, all you want to do is get the expert to admit that there is a change. Later on, you tell the judge that it is a 180-degree change, and when you are telling the judge that, the expert is long gone.—Attorney, anonymous*

To experts, the fact that the new information makes a difference, but a very small difference, may be so obvious that they do not even mention it. To them, the fact that a severe TBI patient with a profound new-onset major neurocognitive disorder saw a psychologist before the injury is like spitting in the ocean—it doesn't make a difference in the outcome of the case. But a jury or a judge doesn't know that relative weight. This is the type of issue that will likely be addressed on redirect.

TRICKS

While this is not the norm, there are times during cross examination when an attorney may be literally trying to trick the expert. Not with a subtle turn of language, but via actual deceit, such as rephrasing something an expert said in a way that clearly distorts the meaning. Tom Boll suggests:

> Here is my biggest piece of advice. Listen. Pay attention to what you are asked. And don't agree to something you don't understand. Attorneys will always say, "Now that you agree to that . . ." They take what you say, and then they take it to where they want to go. You can say, "Back up. I absolutely did not say that!"
>
> *Q: Now that you've agreed to . . .*
>
> *A: I didn't agree to that.*

Laurence Binder notes that attorneys sometimes use tricks to rattle experts. He recalls one case where an attorney sneaked papers out of his file while he was on the stand:

> *In one case, an attorney asked to see my file while he was cross examining me, and when he returned the file he didn't return a key piece of paper. And then he asked a question and the answer was on that piece of paper he took. I knew where the answer was; he had it. So I said, "You didn't give me back the whole file. You have the document." Initially he pretended he didn't have it, but I knew he had it, so I insisted. He finally "looked" and determined he had it. I caught him. I don't know if he looked bad, because he was unrepentant; he insisted he didn't realize he had it. But I know my response kept me from looking bad.*

He also notes that some attorneys will misquote the medical record in their question or misstate a piece of information, and if you don't correct them, and answer as if that piece of information is true, then they have won their gambit. If he catches them, he will simply say, "Well, that's not what the record shows" or "That's not what happened."

David Williamson points out, "Some questions include statements that are premised on you having made statements during testimony that you actually did not. It is okay to stop and say, 'I didn't say [xyz].'"

In my own practice, I tend to expect the best from other people, so I was therefore flabbergasted in a deposition when an attorney attempted to pass off a blank emergency room record as the plaintiff's record and demanded to know where the record showed the plaintiff (as I had testified) had denied to ER personnel that she had lost consciousness:

> *Q: Dr. Postal, isn't it true that there is nowhere in the ER records that states that Mr. Smith denied a loss of consciousness?!*

A: That is not true. The ER records state twice that Mr. Smith denied a loss of consciousness.

Q: Well, I have the ER record right here in front of me. There is no mention of loss of consciousness at all. You point to me where it says that!

At that point the attorney hands me a completely blank ER record form, with the patient name and identifiers at the top blacked out with marker. It literally was blank, with chief complaint: blank, time on arrival: blank, etc. There was zero patient information on the single-page document.

A: This is not Mr. Smith's ER record.

Q: Of course it is! This is the record, and you need to answer my question: Is there or is there not any information about loss of consciousness on this record?!

A: I will literally read the record. Chief complaint: blank. Time of arrival: blank. Past medical history: blank. Attending doctor: Blank.

I continued to read the entire record so the deposition transcript would be entirely clear that I was handed a blank ER form.

Nick Bogod tells the tale of a cross-examining attorney who attempted to rattle him by opening her cross with:

Q: Dr. Bogod, you are aware that there is a code of conduct that governs psychologists in British Columbia?

It didn't go anywhere, but they wanted to rattle me, make me question whether I had made some significant error. If I got that question again, I would say, "Yes, I am sure that there is one for attorneys as well." My internal response at the time was "Whoa!! What did I do!?"

Mike Chafetz tells the story of an attorney who wanted him to admit that his type of evaluation was a breach of ethics. In his answer, he held the attorney accountable for knowing that his assertion was false:

Q: Dr. Chafetz, you only interviewed and tested the mother and not the father. Isn't it true that you are violating the ethics and principles of custody cases by not examining both parties?

A: You have correctly cited the ethics rules for custody evaluations, and if I had done a custody case, I would be in violation of the ethics rules. But as you know, this is a child protection issue and as such I was not obligated to do anything else than what I was asked to do by the court, which was a thorough evaluation of the mother, who was suspected of endangering her child.

Jerry Sweet makes it a practice to always ask to see the larger passage in a book or article that he is being asked about, as attorneys may be quoting out of context or even blatantly misquoting:

I have learned to ask that person to see what they are reading from (or pretending to read from). Even if it is a quote from your own book, it could be taken completely out of context. I always try to remember to ask to see what they are holding. Within the courtroom that request is always granted. Within one deposition, in which the deposing attorney had demanded I read a passage from a particular book, when it was time for the retaining attorney to ask questions, he said, "Can I take a look at that book?" The other attorney said, "No, go get your own book." I've also had deposing attorneys decide to end a line of questioning rather than show me what they were reading into the record.

Consent form as "gotcha"

In a federal Medicaid fraud trial, I testified for the public defender, saying the defendant was intellectually disabled. The owner of the company had orchestrated the fraud but ordered employees to actually perpetrate the fraud. The owner ultimately pled out but left the employees holding the bag. The issue for this particular case was an employee who, in my opinion, was intellectually disabled. The government first tried to limit my testimony at a Daubert hearing, and failed. At the trial, the prosecutor put up a picture of my consent form that the defendant had signed and made me read it to the jury, which I did. This is a courtroom tactic. It's not threatening; it's fun when you know what the tactic is.

Q: Dr. Chafetz, can you read this form to the jury?

I read it.

Q: Dr. Chafetz, would you look at where we have highlighted this language.

I read the abstract language, beyond what one would expect an intellectually disabled person to understand.

Q: Dr. Chafetz, do you actually think Ms. Smith was mentally retarded if she was able to sign this and understand this consent form?

A: You know what is going on here. Her public defender is the one who consents for the case. I was just going through this consent process for her just to be cordial and to help her understand what is going on.

He whisked that slide off the screen and moved on quickly.—Mike Chafetz, PhD, ABPP-CN

Very hostile cross

Mike Chafetz notes that if you're being vehemently attacked, it is because the opposing counsel's case is weak: "Attorneys all learn this in law school: If the facts are against you, argue the law; if the law is against you, argue the facts; if the law and the facts are against you attack your opponent." There will be times when attorneys will go beyond the typical baiting and implications of bias to outright hostility. What's the best way for experts to handle the situation? One strategy is to recall, as noted earlier in the chapter, that it is not personal.

When an attorney is being obnoxious, the most important thing to do is keep your cool. They are trying to make you look bad, but the next day they could call you on their side, and then they treat you like you are the greatest thing since sliced bread.—Ira K. Packer, PhD, ABPP (Forensic)

Here are some stories and strategies from the trenches.

Dr. Marlowe, why are you such a liar?

A lot of attorneys nitpick around nonsense.

Q: Dr. Marlowe, why are you such a liar?

A: Well, Mr. So and So, I don't believe I am. Tell me what you are referring to.

Q: It says on your CV under employment that you are working for the University of Washington.

A: I have a clinical appointment.

Q: Do they pay you money?

A: No, they give me a fancy title instead of a nickel.

Q: So that's not really employment.

A: (I laughed) I am really sorry that this has misled you. Sometimes academic institutions trade an appointment for participation in teaching activities. If it bothers you that much, I will look at my CV and see if there is a different way I can list it so it will not upset you so much next time.

The jury applauded. The judge had to call order. Juries don't like it when attorneys are mean to experts.—Wendy Marlowe, PhD, ABPP-CN

If attorneys can't attack the facts, they attack the expert

If you have a strong argument from a diagnostic standpoint, the most likely cross will be one in which you yourself will be attacked. Anything that they believe speaks to your credibility is fair game; the proportion or number of cases you see, your tax statements, the fact you were paid for the work (shocking!) Anything that they believe might unnerve you or cause a jury to discount your opinion.

One attorney handed me a picture of my car, which had a humorous, vanity license plate. He asked,

Q: What do you think of this Doctor!?

Instead of apologizing or embarrassment, I replied,

A: You know, I am pretty proud of that license plate, it took me several months to think of it, and I think it's pretty clever.

The attorney could only reply

Q: Let's go on.

—David Hartman, Ph.D., ABPP-CN

When cross-examining attorneys are not getting an answer they like, they will often repeat the question or return to a line of questioning. Opposing counsel will frequently object. However, Nick Bogod notes that he is happy to patiently answer the question as many times as it is asked: "When the attorney is badgering on a certain point, asking the same question over and over again, rather than get frustrated, I just take the opportunity to repeat my opinion."

In my own practice, I had an attorney scream at me in a deposition. His line of questioning was all the factors such as chronic pain and fatigue and anxiety that he hoped might nullify failed PVTs:

> *Q: Doctor, isn't it the case that these malingering tests are affected by depression?*
>
> *A: No. These tests are so easy that they are very easily passed even in people who are depressed. In fact, there have been well-done research studies that show that depression does not affect people's scores on the TOMM.*
>
> *Q: What is the name and citation of the study?*
>
> *A: I don't have the exact citation off the top of my head but I would be happy to get that for you when I get back to my office this afternoon.*
>
> *Q: You mean to tell me that you don't know the name of the article?!*
>
> *A: That is correct. I don't know the exact title, but I would be happy to get that for you.*
>
> *Q: Let me get this straight. You are claiming to not know the name or citation for this article.*
>
> *A: Yes, I have not memorized the name of the paper. But I would be happy to get it for you this afternoon when I have returned to the office.*
>
> *(Attorney asks another five times).*
>
> *Q: [screaming] DOCTOR, ARE YOU MALINGERING?!*

> Attorneys seem to feel sometimes that we are manipulating or hiding information, and if they only persist, we will buckle under and tell them what they want. I had an attorney cross-examine me in court and ask me whether I was malingering when I told him I didn't know the answer to a question.
>
> *Q: So right now, are you malingering?—Jerry Sweet, PhD, ABPP-CN*

> *I was talking about a brain image schematic drawing and calling it a cartoon; that's the vernacular with neurosurgeons. The cross-examining attorney got up in arms.*
>
> *Q: "Cartoon"?! You're calling this a cartoon?! You clearly don't have much respect for the seriousness of this injury.*
>
> *A: That's the colloquial language neurosurgeons use to describe a drawing of this nature in the field. (said flatly and without defensiveness)—Greg Lee, PhD, ABPP-CN*

FINALLY, WHEN CROSS GOES SOUTH

It will happen: Cross examinations can go south. Rus Bauer bravely describes his lowest moment on the stand:

> I was involved in a case where the plaintiff had complained of multiple chemical sensitivities. I saw him as a "stealth referral." His doctor had referred him for a clinical examination. The examination was done, and then—bang! "Request for the records" by his attorney, and opposing attorneys, etc.
>
> The interpretation of the data could have gone either way, he is "meshuggeneh" versus he has some true issues. Results revealed numerous weird attention issues. There were not a lot of records in the case. The doctor was one of these cottage-industry physicians who did massage and acupressure. We had a few employment records, but very few other medical records. We tried to get other records, but few were forthcoming and we ran out of time. I rendered my opinion at deposition and the case went to trial. He was claiming long-term disability. The defense attorney was outstanding, completely took me apart.
>
> *Q: Would you agree, Dr. Bauer, with the following statement: that it is always a good idea to get background records to establish the baseline functioning of patients?*
>
> *A: Yes, I would agree.*
>
> *Q: Would you agree with this statement? In situations in which records cannot be obtained, the opinion is on more tentative grounds.*
>
> She asked about four of these, pertaining to school, employment, military records. I ended up agreeing with most of them but on each occasion, I tried to qualify.
>
> *Q: Dr. Bauer! Agree or disagree?*
>
> I was forced to agree with each of these statements before I realized that she was reading from a transcript of a presentation that I had given to INS as a CE: "Brain damage incurred by collision with forensic neuropsychologists." A whole bunch of examples in which people have nothing wrong with them, and then see a neuropsychologist, who finds "brain damage," and they are off to the races. I realized with horror that I had not in this case followed my own advice.
>
> I walked—limped—off the stand. The attorney who retained me followed me with his eyes. I walked down the center aisle and out the door. He gave two gestures: a thumbs up, and a throat slash. It was an incredibly humbling experience.

NOTES

1. Lakoof, R. (1990). *Talking power: The politics of language in our lives.* New York: Basic Books
2. Lakoof, R. (1990). *Talking power: The politics of language in our lives.* New York: Basic Books, p. 90.

3. Pope, K. S., Butcher, J. N., & Seelen, J. (1993). *The MMPI, MMPI-2 & MMPI-A in court: A practical guide for expert witnesses and attorneys*. Washington, DC: American Psychological Association.
4. Lezak, M., Howieson, D., Bigler, E., & Tranel, D. (2012). *Neuropsychological Assessment, Fifth Edition*. New York: Oxford University Press.
5. Hebben, N., & Milberg, W. (2009). *The essentials of neuropsychological assessment*. New York: Wiley Press.

16 Relationship with Other Experts

IT IS THE nature of our adversarial court system that two experts will testify that they have reached different conclusions about the same person. How that fundamental disagreement is handled by the expert determines whether jurors must witness a "pissing contest" or are educated about the nature of the disagreement. Depending on the litigation strategy, one or both attorneys may want to incite such a contest. This chapter provides rationale and strategies for avoiding unproductive conflicts while accurately and productively explaining differences in opinions.

THE CASE AGAINST CRITICIZING OTHER EXPERTS

Experts, attorneys, and judges all agreed that tearing down another expert's credibility damages your own on the stand. Tom Boll notes that he doesn't ever comment on other experts:

> *I may use their data and compare them, but I don't critique them. I do not evaluate other neuropsychologists in court; I evaluate patients. Testifying is not the time for a pissing contest. I think everybody ought to be grown up about it. You should say what you need to say and not talk about what the other person has to say.*
>
> ------------
>
> *I don't like to belittle other experts on the stand or criticize them. If an attorney gets you to testify, he/she wants you to look like a doctor, dress like a doctor, and also act like a doctor, and a certain degree of professionalism is important. I don't think a deposition or court appearance is a time for a "micturition match." Treat others like you would want to be treated.*—Jacobus Donders, PhD, ABPP-CN

Robert Heilbronner notes that two equally well-trained people can have differences of opinion due to differences in training or the populations they have seen. He makes the analogy to the field of radiology:

> *It's not just in neuropsychology where experts can disagree; it can happen in clinical settings and with other disciplines. For example, two radiologists looking at an MRI scan of the brain.*

Ira Packer notes that although he stays away from knocking the opposing expert down, there are times when an expert has to disagree with another expert's *opinion*. He notes that it is possible to do so without attacking the *person*:

> *When the cross-examining attorney brings up the opinion of the other side's expert, I try to stay away from knocking someone down. There are times, though, when it is tricky. There are times when one has to testify that the other expert's interpretation was incorrect. For example, if the opposing side's expert gave a performance validity test with clearly under-chance responding and said, "Well, there is some suggestion" the claimant wasn't putting forth his/her best effort, I would have to say, "With these particular results, the correct interpretation is xyz, for this reason." You don't have to say that the expert did it because he is a turkey.*

Robert Mendoza also makes the distinction between criticizing the opposing experts and disagreeing with the conclusions:

> *I take issue with my colleagues that feel compelled to be hypercritical about another expert's work. It's okay to disagree with the findings. It's fair to say, "Those are their findings. Here are mine." Others might say, "They were wrong," "They didn't understand something," or "They didn't do the right thing." Very sweeping judgments about the quality of the other expert's work are not helpful.*

Jerry Sweet advises experts to focus on the technical issues, not the person:

> *During every year I have been in practice, at some point or another, questions about a neuropsychologist's substandard work has come up. Whether in clinical work or in forensic work, my position is: Try not to have collisions with other experts. You are there to give your opinion in a manner that is informative and relevant to both sides, not to advocate for either side. It is not part of your job to attack people on the other side. My goal is to focus on any technical problems associated with the expert's work product, not on the other expert.*
>
> *I will state my points of disagreement. This might be that the wrong norms were utilized or the wrong scores were documented, or that conclusions have no relationship to test findings and/or history. Sometimes the test findings themselves are not credible. But, for example, I will not say anything about the person's inadequate or absent training background.*

Paul Kaufmann counsels experts to point out inconsistencies benignly:

> *Your credibility goes up if you do not attack and if you only point out inconsistencies benignly. It is important to be selective. Do not identify every single inconsistency. Pick out the top three.*

Attorney Wayne Miller notes that he tries to be polite in court, even to his opponents, and he want experts to be that way as well:

> Not only because it is the way I am, but I think it is off-putting to a lot of people to be insulting and obnoxious. Just an example: Last week I took a deposition. This was a physical medicine and rehabilitation doc, and I asked her about the treating physician who made a prescription when the expert had said the patient was at maximum improvement. I said,
>
> *Q: Six days before you saw the patient, in an IME, the treating doctor saw her and prescribed more physical therapy and prescribed a referral to another pain management specialist. In your opinion, did the treating doctor do wrong?*
>
> *A: (And she was very persistent in saying) I have my own opinion. It is based on my review of the record. I don't comment on what others do.*
>
> That was her mantra and she stuck to it, and I was thinking about that: Was that the best way for her to play that? I have taken her deposition before, and I know that is how she plays that particular thing, and it's a way of being polite. It's a little unsatisfying because another thing I'd like to say is, you get 10 doctors in a room, you're going to have 10 different opinions, right? So you just disagree with them—is that really surprising? I think it's probably useful for an expert to say, "I disagree with the recommendation of the treating physician."
>
> I tell the jury later,
>
> *You know, ladies and gentlemen, I never knew that I had a burden to prove that all doctors agree on this point. In fact, that's not my burden. Medical unanimity is not my burden. My burden is to show that it is more likely than not my proposition is true. Does the evidence in favor of it outweigh the evidence against it? So, the fact that in this case an insurance company could find a doctor to disagree with the treating physician? I am glad you are sitting down because I would not be shocked if an insurance company could find somebody to disagree.*

COMMON CONCERNS WITH OTHER EXPERTS' WORK PRODUCTS

As I interviewed seasoned forensic experts, they frequently expressed frustration and dismay at the quality of psychological and neuropsychological assessments presented to the courts by poorly trained or careless colleagues. These are issues that experts may want to explain to the jurors during their direct testimony and the attorney who brought them will likely raise on cross examination of the other expert.

Other neuropsychologists who don't appreciate outcome research

It is common that neuropsychologists who are not well trained either do not understand outcome research or do not appreciate that outcome research should be an important lens through which to view case findings. These individuals are apt to say something completely disproven by relevant outcome research. I will try to make sure that solid outcome research articles are entered into evidence so I can comment on them. My goal is to be a scientifically based expert who thoughtfully considers relevant research when rendering opinions. Most often, given the relationship of our clinical work to being retained as a forensic expert, there is research guidance readily available for those who appreciate the benefits of neuropsychology as a science-based practice.—Jerry Sweet, PhD, ABPP-CN

Secondary medical records

I find that other providers rely on what I refer to as secondary medical records as opposed to primary medical records. It's a huge, pervasive problem. A provider will cite something that another clinician wrote. I see this a lot with neuroimaging results. Recently I had an elderly patient who had a head injury. He went to the hospital and was told that the neuroimaging was normal, it didn't show anything. He went for a follow-up after the emergency room and the doctor said, "Yes, the neuroimaging didn't show anything," but the doctor is relying on a discharge summary and did not actually get the original printout from the neuroradiologist of the MRI or the CT scan. When I looked at the radiologist's report, it said negative for any acute intracranial functioning, but there was extensive subcortical or cerebrovascular disease and atrophy of the frontal lobe that is disproportionate to age. And I asked the patient, "Were you ever told about that?" Well, no. And it turns out that the doctor probably didn't know about that either because he/she is relying on the discharge summary and didn't get the actual MRI. So I always make it a point to get the actual primary record source and sometimes bring that up in a deposition.

Q: Isn't it true that Dr. Physician diagnosed Mr. Plaintiff with a concussion?

A: It's very important, similar to when you are doing legal research or academic research, that you track things back to the primary source. If you rely on secondary information or what somebody wrote about what somebody else did, information gets distorted. We know based on psychological research that as more people tell a story, little bits of the story start to change over time. The best way to figure out what actually happened is to go back to the original source. In this case, Dr. Physician did not document that she reviewed the day-of-accident emergency room records . . .—Dominic Carone, PhD, ABPP-CN

Not relying on source records

In traumatic brain injury cases, neuropsychologists commonly fail to understand and discuss acute injury characteristics. They do not use original source documents. They take parent or patient reports as if they are accurate and they never go back and confirm the actual neurologic state at the time of the injury. Then, they do not look at the ambulance records or the ER records. Then, it is a really easy pivot:

Of course, I can understand why this patient's mother may have reported that, but my colleague made no reference to the dotor's report, or to the medical technician who was at the accident scene. (Place it in the context of, this was just an oversight. It is easier for jurors to accept that rather than being asked to choose between experts).—Paul Kaufmann, JD, PhD, ABPP-CN

Errors of omission

My biggest beef with colleagues, "the other experts," is that it is our job to look at everything that could possibly affect the data. They are scared to consider everything. You have to consider every possible conceivable contributing factor of why your data looks like that. Then you need to say, "What is the most likely reason the data looks like it does?" Experts can make errors of omission, and it is not honest or helpful.—Lisa Stanford, PhD, ABPP-CN

Off to the races

In one case, a teenager was at a concert and got kicked in the head by someone crowd-surfing. She had none of the criteria for a concussion. And when she was finished being checked out, rather than going home, she said, "No, I want to go back to the concert." There was nothing there. When she got back to her hometown, mom takes her in to see a neuropsychologist, who says, "It's a mild concussion"—when in fact it wasn't any concussion. Then he says, "Don't do anything for 2 weeks." Off to the races.—Glenn Larrabee, PhD, ABPP-CN

Not placing the injury in context

Not placing the injury in the context of the plaintiff's life is the number-one mistake. The opposing expert hadn't considered pre-accident history and writes a report as if the person's life started on the day of the injury. It is as serious a mistake as not using PVTs.—Laurence Binder, PhD, ABPP-CN

STRATEGIES WHEN ASKED TO DISAGREE WITH ANOTHER EXPERT ON CROSS

While an expert might ask the attorney who brought her not to ask her to criticize the other expert during direct examination, experts have no control over the questions they are asked on cross examination. Attorneys may purposely phrase the questions in ways that invite witnesses to appear biased by taking the bait and criticizing the opposing expert.

Don't bash anyone

I don't ever personally attack a colleague. I am not there to bash anyone else. It keeps it positive and makes me more likable to the jury. What I say is,

Q: Are you saying Dr. Expert did not do a competent assessment?!

A: The way I like to do it is . . .

Or

A: What I have found gives me the most information is . . . —Lisa Stanford, PhD, ABPP-CN

I get the impression you are trying to get me to say something bad about Dr. Smith

A: I get the impression that you want me to say something bad about Dr. Smith. All I can tell you is that we have a factual disagreement. Here is my reasoning for why I think my opinion is correct.—Jacobus Donders, PhD, ABPP-CN

Disagreeing about an error

Q: Can you tell us about the findings of [other neuropsychologist]. Do you agree?

A: I don't agree, and here is why.—Leslie Rosenstein, PhD, ABPP-CN

When I get the question, I simply say, "Yes, we disagree, because . . ." And I make sure that I get in the substantive areas where we differ. I focus on the substance of the disagreement rather than the fact that we disagree:

Q: You disagree with the eminent . . .

A: Yes, we disagree, because I gave the evaluee this test that showed that he was . . .

Or

A: He told both of us that he was hearing voices from his grandmother, and then I asked further questions, and it was clear that this was not a psychotic hallucination; he was thinking about his grandmother but he had no other symptoms of psychotic thinking.—Ira K. Packer, PhD, ABPP (Forensic)

Q: So you think Dr. Other Expert is wrong?!

A: I am going to stick to the data. I always stick to the data and give my opinion based on the data.—Paul Green, PhD, ABPP-CN

It kind of puzzles me that Dr. SO and SO would say that [instead of Dr. SO and SO is a complete idiot who can't tell a cucumber from a frontal lobe].—Jacobus Donders, PhD, ABPP-CN

A: I understand that he thinks that. I have a different view of the data.—David Williamson, PhD, ABPP-CN

Significant deviation from standard practice

When another expert has assessed a plaintiff or defendant in a way that seriously deviates from standards of practice, I try to really rely on national organizations' guidelines. I will describe the guidelines and how the other testing deviated from those guidelines. I am trying to not just indicate my opinion, per se, but what it is based upon so that it is pretty transparent how another expert has deviated in their practice in a neutral-sounding tone.—Shelley Peery, PhD

Q: Isn't it true that six different physicians diagnosed Ms. Jones with [xyz disorder] and you are the only one saying it doesn't exist?

A: There are significant differences between a neuropsychological evaluation and those other evaluations you are referring to. The other evaluations are typically part of a brief office visit and are largely based on subjective reporting and a brief physical examination or very brief cognitive testing. Sometimes that doesn't even take place. Neuropsychological evaluations rely on a large amount of objective data. I am also paying attention to subjective reporting, but neuropsychologists have tests that give us validity checks on the subjective reporting. Neuropsychology as a field has really paved the way in providing objective data. This is not something that is extended to other professions yet; they are largely relying on subjective reporting.—Dominic Carone, PhD, ABPP-CN

If that was true, I would have seen xyz. And I didn't.

When I disagree with another expert, I go back to the data:

Q: Isn't it true that Dr. Other Expert testified abc?

A: If that was true, I would have seen xyz. But I didn't see that.—Lynn Blackburn, PhD, ABPP-CN

I personally don't understand that opinion

A: I personally don't understand that opinion, because of x, y, and z. Here's why I think what I think.—David Williamson, PhD, ABPP-CN

Robert Mendoza offers a great example of an aikido response (accept and extend rather than fight) to a disagreement between experts, taking an area of disagreement and embracing it:

In a competency case, the other expert said that the person's memory was adequate because they were able to recall where they lived, their street address, some members of their family, and some things they did in the past. My response was,

"I know that my colleague has indicated that Mr. Jones's memory is adequate. I believe what he might have been thinking is that Mr. Jones's autobiographical memory is intact. Memories that are stored in areas of the brain that are very resistant to damage. But what we neuropsychologists think about as memory in this case is what we call new learning: the ability to take in relatively recent information, organize it, and recall it later. What street you grew up on, those memories are stored in different areas of the brain and are very resilient to brain damage. I agree that my colleague is accurate regarding autobiographical memory. With regards to the issue of competency, I think the more relevant feature of memory is the ability to understand what is going on in the courtroom and remember it the next day. I'm a neuropsychologist; we are kind of geeky that way—we have a more precise way of talking about it.

Try to nail down the moment when the other expert's testimony diverted from reality

I try to identify the point at which the other expert's testimony departed from a reality which I understand. And if I can, nail it down in a phrase.

A: Well when Dr. Expert said that the patient became confused upon arrival to the hospital, it's important to keep in mind that they were able to talk about the details of the accident 10 minutes earlier when being interviewed by an EMT. Now, it is possible that a patient's condition could deteriorate. However, in this case we do not have any indicators of why a deterioration would occur.—Paul Kaufmann, JD, PhD, ABPP-CN

I have a different view of the data

When experts disagree

A: I have a different view of the data.—David Williamson, PhD, ABPP-CN

I respectfully disagree

I respectfully disagree. A lot of current research may not be consistent with Dr. Smith's view on this.—Cheryl Weinstein, PhD, ABPP-CN

Q: Well, do you think Doctor Smith is wrong?

A: The overwhelming majority of the scientific literature wouldn't support the possibility of that situation ever happening.—Greg Lee, PhD, ABPP-CN

A sketchy diagnosis

I had a case where a board-certified neuropsychologist has said that I was exceeding my expertise because I was not just accepting the diagnoses of the patient's physicians. This was a patient who had a very minor accident. She had no loss of consciousness. She denied any head injury symptomatology in the emergency room. She denied any nausea, vomiting, or any other problems at all. Six months later she went to her advanced registered nurse practitioner and said that she had been in a severe accident and had brain injury with headaches and nausea. Unfortunately, the nurse practitioner did not get a copy of the patient's ER records but diagnosed her with TBI and PTSD. My colleague said that I should accept the diagnoses of the nurse practitioner.

Once the attorney got involved, the patient was sent to various experts, all of whom took the [modified] history from her rather than reviewing her records. A few said that her complaints were way out of proportion, but the nurse practitioner was part of the university health system; all of the other MDs were reluctant to disagree with their colleague.

Q: How can you say that the concussion experts didn't get it right?!

I like to talk about base rates in different settings. I say things like,

A: If you go to a concussion center, what they expect to see is a concussion. If they diagnose everyone who walks in with a concussion, they will be right 90% of the time. But I am concerned with the 10% that were misdiagnosed. That's why you need a thorough evaluation, including a comprehensive review of the records.—Wendy Marlowe, PhD, ABPP-CN

Scope of practice for neuropsychologists

Q: Dr. Other Expert testified that neuropsychologists are not supposed to make a diagnosis of TBI; physicians do that.

A: There was no objective evidence of this woman's TBI. Perhaps Dr. Other Expert does not have the expertise to review the records and form an opinion about whether a TBI occurred, but it is part of the standard practice of clinical neuropsychologists.—Wendy Marlowe, PhD, ABPP-CN

Einstein wasn't right about everything

You know what: No one is an expert in everything. There are no authoritative texts. There are no authoritative people. You might be surprised to hear me say that. There was a guy named Niels Bohr who argued with Albert Einstein about the fundamental structure of an atom. In the long run, Einstein was proven to be right. However, Einstein also argued Werner Heisenberg over the fundamentals of quantum physics. In this debate, Heisenberg argued that there would always be uncertainty due to the nature of how we measured things. Heisenberg is credited with the development of the "Uncertainty Principal." In this case, Einstein was wrong, and Heisenberg was right. But, do you any of you on the jury know who Niels Bohr or Werner Heisenberg was? Likely no. But all of you know who Albert Einstein was? He is a smart guy. But, that doesn't mean that everything Einstein said was right. In this case, the plaintiff's expert and I have different opinions.—Martin Rohling, PhD

What if we are both right?

> *What if we are both right? Maybe we both saw different things.*—Martin Rohling, PhD

"BUT, DOCTOR, YOU ARE NOT A PHYSICIAN!"

Say that Marcus Welby, MD, has just gotten on the stand and testified that someone can have lifelong disability from a single, uncomplicated concussion. Robin Hanks notes that it is often our job to educate the jury "about the natural history of concussion recovery. There are all of these physicians who go in and testify that 'concussions are forever.'"

> *Q: Doctor, you are not a physician. This neurologist testified that there was a brain injury.*
>
> *A: Well, what did he tell you was his evidence of a brain injury? Did Mr. Smith lose consciousness, did he have confusion, did he have no memory of the event? What did he say was his evidence there was a brain injury?*—Tom Boll, PhD, ABPP-CN

The MD bias

> *As a neuropsychologist, I have a lot of experience and credentials with epilepsy. I recall one case where the other side brought in a general neurologist, with a large general practice. He did not have a specialty in epilepsy. He got on the stand and said neuropsychologists don't know what they are talking about. They are not physicians and you can't listen to them. He then gave a bunch of misinformation. For example, he testified that seizures are always a certain way and there is no way to have a postictal effect. I had testified that evidence from the ER was consistent with a seizure: a blood panel, low levels of his anticonvulsant, and high levels of prolactin, something that goes up when you have a seizure. He testified that psychologists don't know about epilepsy, and because he was an MD, he was believed.*
>
> *In the end, it is the attorney's job to address that issue. I gave the attorney articles to support what I had said. A lot of these things are beyond our control. We try to educate attorneys, we give them literature, but it's up to them to use it all to their advantage.*—William Barr, PhD, ABPP-CN

Many interviewees point out how important it is to explain why one disagrees with other experts during the direct examination, so those reasons can be referred back to on cross. The cross examination may look like this:

> *Q: So you don't agree with Dr. X?*
>
> *A: No, I do not.*
>
> *Q: And you don't agree with Dr. Y?*
>
> *A: No, I do not.*

Q: And you don't agree with Dr. Z?

A: No, I do not.

Q: You're not a medical doctor, are you?

A: No, I am not.

Q: Isn't that arrogant of you?

A: As I explained earlier, I had different data than they did, I did different tests than they did . . .

Q: How can you say Mr. Smith had a mild brain injury when Dr. Primary said he had a severe traumatic brain injury?! You aren't a physician, are you?!

A: Neuropsychologists diagnose and document cognitive dysfunction. I know the algorithms for determining the severity of traumatic brain injury. If the physician deviates from the algorithms and concludes someone has a moderate to severe TBI when criteria for a concussion instead are met, I will comment on that.—Kyle Boone, PhD, ABPP-CN

DO YOU REALLY DISAGREE WITH THE OTHER EXPERT? TREATING EXPERT OPINIONS

Leslie Rosenstein notes that disagreements between experts and treating clinicians are often not disagreements at all. A careful read of medical records often reveals that the "diagnosis" on the medical record, particularly electronic medical records, often reflects the "referral code"—that is, the reason why the patient was were referred.

> We all put diagnoses down on medical records because that is how you are reimbursed. Sometimes that diagnosis on the medical records is the referral diagnosis or the rule-out diagnosis; it may not be their actual opinion. For example, the patient might have been referred for possible Alzheimer's disease, that was a diagnosis on the medical record, but the rest of the record makes it clear that the patient was not found to have the condition.
>
> *Q: Doctor, can you read this paragraph in Ms. Plaintiff's medical records? Didn't Dr. Neurologist diagnose Ms. Plaintiff with memory problems?*
>
> *A: In their report, Dr. Neurologist says xyz indicating normal memory function, but they also include this diagnosis code. And often that reflects a referral diagnosis—in other words, the reason the patient was seen in the first place, what the doctor is deciding was or was not present, so they can bill the case. But I can't speak for them; I don't know what they are thinking.*

Nancy Hebben points out that people don't always give their treating doctors the whole story, or those clinicians don't have access to the type of records experts do. Had the treating doctor had the same information, there may be no disagreement.

Q: You are the only person who says my client didn't have a concussion!

A: When we go to our providers, we often don't give them our entire history. They are taking a person at their word. The person says, "I banged my head and since then I have been forgetful." Even if it's not true "since then" the treater will say, "Oh, you have a concussion, and let's manage that." It's perfectly understandable. Treaters will take your complaints and try to make you feel better.

When you disagree with a treating physician

It is important to understand that you are going up against physicians who mainly rely on self-report and don't have the tools that you do. And when someone says to their doctor, "I am too disabled to work," that just gets written down as "too disabled to work." You have to be able to say,

A: Well, Dr. Smith wrote this down, but he did not really pursue whether this could be something other than an accurate self-report. And I understand that the doctor had 10 minutes with the person and I had an 8-hour day. And that makes our opinions different in terms of the time that went into it and the depth of the investigation.

Or

A: You have to look at whether a doctor is diagnosing something just because the patient says they have it. It's complicated because the standard for physician diagnosis is very often patient self-report. That works very well when the patient is telling you the truth. It doesn't work very well when there is a secondary gain consequence or a legal consequence that forms the context of the complaint where the patient is using the doctor visit to buttress their legal case.—David Hartman, PhD, ABPP-CN

David Hartman tells the story of a patient who claimed she couldn't work from severe abdominal pain and stress and claimed she had lumps under her abdominal muscles. A psychiatrist diagnosed "abdominal syndrome."

And I thought, "Well, that's interesting." It doesn't really exist as a syndrome, but it did justify allowing her to obtain large quantities of fentanyl. She was having a great time. I pointed out in my report that the psychiatrist was describing symptoms that didn't exist, in a syndrome that didn't exist. The psychiatrist was very angry that his opinion was challenged. He stood in front of the judge and stated, "This is a medical opinion and the only opinion that should be taken into account."

The judge replied to the psychiatrist, in court, "Doctor, you didn't review any literature and you didn't describe any basis for your diagnosis. If all we needed was a doctor's opinion, we really wouldn't need to have this hearing, would we?"

Not because I am smarter than them, but because I have looked at everything.

Q: I suppose you want the jury to believe that you know more that these doctors who saw the patient when she was alive (this was a neuropsychological autopsy)?

A: Well, actually, no. I have looked at all of her records. And when you are trying to figure something like this out, you can't take little snippets out of the record that just supports your case. You have to look at all the records. Everything. That's how we do it. And I do know more than her treating clinicians because I have had the opportunity to look at everything in this case. Not because I am smarter than them; it's because I have looked at everything. That's how we do it.—Rod Swenson, PhD, ABN

WHEN COLLEAGUES WE KNOW ARE THE "OTHER" EXPERT

In the end, it is a small community of psychology and neuropsychology experts. Particularly in some more remote areas of the country, there may be very few credentialed experts and it may be impossible to avoid situations in which one is testifying "against" colleagues. Many experts will avoid testifying in a case where they know another expert well, but others don't shy away from such situations. Nick Bogod tells the story of a close friend who became the opposing expert on a case:

One friend agreed knowingly to be on the opposite side of a case. I was upset by this. I had a chat with him. A close friend who I socialize regularly with, at minimum the optics are bad, and I also consider it a dual relationship. However, there are times when you assess someone, and you don't know in advance, sometimes it is inevitable. But when it is controllable I don't do it. I am very uncomfortable when people close to me are involved on the other side of a case. I worry that if it happens, there could be an unconscious bias. I write the same opinion, but I might be gentler. In a normal situation, I give an opinion, and someone has written a rebuttal, I respond in kind. My job is to advocate for my opinion and a rebuttal is a direct threat to that opinion. It's possible I might use slightly more gentle language with a friend.

WHEN ANOTHER EXPERT HAS COMMENTED ON YOUR WORK

During cross examination, an attorney may confront you with something unflattering an opposing expert has said about you in court, or supposedly said in a deposition. The imperative not to take the bait and engage in personal attacks stands. The other important thing to consider is that the other expert may not have said it, or the words were taken out of context. You lose your professional credibility quickly if jurors see you entangled in an exchange reminiscent of a "mean girls" gossip session: "OMG! Do you know what Dr. Marsha said about you!?"

Q: Dr. Smith said you are always biased.

A: I can't speak to Dr. Smith's statement. You will have to ask him or her. All I can tell you is that [come back to the facts].—Jacobus Donders, PhD, ABPP-CN

EDUCATING THE OPPOSING WITNESS WITH YOUR WORK/IDEAS

Laurence Binder makes the interesting point that a persuasive report read by an honest opposing expert can lead to a change of opinion by the opposing expert:

> *In one case of poor outcome after mTBI in a young man, a treating neuropsychologist underinterpreted evidence of suboptimal effort on performance validity tests, including the Victoria Symptom Validity Test. In my independent medical exam, there was similar evidence on other PVTs. In my report, I fully discussed all the PVT data from both exams. The case soon settled. After it settled, my colleague disclosed that s/he had seen my report and then had reported to the plaintiff's attorney her/his change of mind.*

TEAM APPROACH

What about one's relationship with other experts "on the same side?" Attorneys will sometimes ask experts to confer with one another, in a "team approach." While this can be a productive approach for an expert, Mike Chafetz has some cautions:

> *The issue is independence. You want your work to stand on its own and not be biased by the work of others. If you take the team approach, it is often too easy to allow others' ideas to creep into your work. The other side will notice, and then you risk getting a reputation of being simply a shill for the side you are on. In this vein, "team meetings" can often lead to independence creep. You may be subtly getting biased, and on cross-examination, it is easier to take your opinion apart as being the product of bias, which is a legitimate topic of cross examination.*

There are times when other experts who have been retained by the counsel who retained you will have opinions you do not agree with. John Kirk brings up the issue of life care planners:

> Life care planners might take recommendations that go further out on a limb than you feel comfortable with. In one case I had agreed to review a life care plan document, and by the time the kid got done with his daily services, he was going to bed at 1 o'clock in the morning! Of course this is not reasonable. Many attorneys in cross try to get you to step out into an area that is related to your area, but it is not your level. They might do this with imaging, speech therapy, life care.
>
> *Q: You agreed with Mr. Smith's life care plan. Here's exactly what this would look like . . .*
>
> *A: Here are the things I feel need to be provided. A minimal level of that service. I will leave it up to the life care planner or vocational rehab specialist to develop what that might look like.*

DECLINING TO COMMENT ON AN EXPERT OUTSIDE OF ONE'S PROFESSION

Attorneys on either direct or cross may ask a psychologist or neuropsychologist to comment on specific practices or actions of clinicians or experts of other specialties. This is often an invitation for experts to step outside the scope of their practice and caution is warranted. Jerry Sweet notes that he specifically declines to do so:

> In the case where it is a physician, I make it clear that I have no comment on bad neurology.
>
> *Q: Do you have criticisms of the neurologist in this case?*
>
> *A: That person is a neurologist. I am a psychologist. I have no criticisms of Dr. X.*
>
> My opinion regarding the practice of another specialty is limited to my experience with members of that specialty during my career. If asked a more specific question, I might in a limited fashion address whether I've seen a particular practice by neurologists, but even then, my observations from the perspective of a different specialty should not be weighed heavily and could even be dismissed completely.

OTHER EXPERT MAKES SCORING ERRORS

When the opposing expert has made copious scoring mistakes or has erred in other ways on standard administration of assessment instruments, many experts indicate that they will comment on the errors, making sure that they are critical of the soundness of the scoring, or the data, not the other expert.

> When the other expert's raw data is inaccurately scored, Robin Hanks will state,
>
> *I was provided the raw data. I went through and rescored everything. I found a lot of errors. The data that Dr. Other Expert used are unreliable.*

> **_Let me explain how this works . . ._**
>
> *If the other expert has made a big error, it is best to say, "Let me explain how this works . . . " and to avoid saying, "that guy just screwed up." You are focusing on your piece, not on their piece.*—Ira K. Packer, PhD, ABPP (Forensic)

FINALLY, ETHICS COMPLAINTS

While reading another expert's report, all of us have moments of outraged disbelief: "What?!" The assessment practices of the other expert are wildly nonstandard; relationships are dual; the material we are reading reflects the unrepentant practice of a psychologist or neuropsychologist who is stepping well beyond ethical bounds.

Lynn Blackburn shared an instance where she felt the other expert's actions warranted an ethical complaint: "I consulted with the APA ethics office and they advised me to wait until the case was over." This advice was repeated by many experts I interviewed. Filing an ethics complaint during a case was almost universally cautioned against. Of course, a consultation with the APA ethics committee, a malpractice ethics consultant, or one's own practice attorney is always the most appropriate first step in a decision about reporting.

17 Testifying in a Diverse World

BY THE YEAR 2050, the majority of Americans will no longer be white, monolingual English-speaking people of European descent: One in three Americans will be Hispanic and one in five foreign-born.[1] As these dramatic demographic changes sweep through the country, the number of plaintiffs and defendants who are "untestable" with our current toolkit of largely monolingual, monocultural neuropsychological and psychological assessment measures will increase dramatically.

The lack of psychological and neuropsychological assessment tools designed for and normed on diverse linguistic and cultural groups and the lack of cultural and or linguistic competence in our psychology and neuropsychology workforce means that plaintiffs and defendants may come into court having undergone procrustean assessments. That is, assessments that were originally designed for people of different cultural or linguistic backgrounds but to which they are being subjected to, regardless of the fit. Experts must understand the cross-cultural psychology and neuropsychology literature to be able to comment on the limits of such assessments and understand the best practices of culturally competent experts.

The sweeping demographic changes are also flowing into the jury pool and (slowly) past the bar and into the expert witness box. What does it mean to connect with a jury when you as an expert come from a non-white, non-European, bi-lingual or multi-lingual background? What does it mean when each jury member is from a different linguistic and cultural backgrounds than the defendant/plaintiff and the expert? How does gender impact how we testify and how our testimony is perceived?

This chapter shares experts', attorneys', and judges' experiences in the courtroom wrestling with these issues and provides clear, succinct strategies of explaining the limitations and best practices of our current assessment toolkit to jurors and triers of fact. For a thorough, clear guide to conducting competent cross-cultural forensic neuropsychological assessments, see, among other resources, Barrett and George's edited volume *Race, Culture, Psychology and Law.*[2]

THE DILEMMA OF HIGH-QUALITY FORENSIC CROSS-CULTURAL ASSESSMENT

Tedd Judd points out,

> *This isn't just for testimony and forensic settings. It's an ethical dilemma that we all face in our daily practice. We have one ethical mandate to be nondiscriminatory in our services and to offer them regardless of race, language, culture, or country of origin, and we have another ethical mandate to be competent. Our research does not allow us to do both equally well, nor does our life experience. And it is an ethical dilemma with no true solution. We have to constantly be monitoring ourselves and balancing those two mandates as best we can.*

Throughout the chapter, you will read about how experts explain to jurors both the limits of their assessments and the necessity of providing services, even with imperfect tools. Antonio Puente notes that psychologists should acknowledge the limits of our current toolkit. That said, he rejects the idea, often presented in cross examination, that only European-American, English-only speakers can access forensic neuropsychological services.

> *Q: The tests you are using were not developed for people who do not speak English.*
>
> *A: If we wait for the appropriate science to come out, we will all be dead. My job is to give you the best science of (insert year).*

CULTURAL COMPETENCE

Tedd Judd is often called upon to address cultural competence. He notes that he always tries to characterize it as a collection of both knowledge and skill:

> *The knowledge is of general principles, like how to research someone's cultural background, how to use an interpreter, what can be the impact of education, culture, and language on various tests, and some aspects of building rapport and how to pick a cultural history. The skills are specific things: knowing a specific language, understanding a specific culture, awareness of sets of beliefs and tendencies in particular groups, as well as skills in dealing with certain people.*
>
> *Skills are built through experience. They are built through practice. Knowledge is something that you can learn and you can read in a book or on the internet, but skills, you have to* do it *to get better at it.*
>
> *Being of a culture that is the same culture as the person that you are evaluating or that you are communicating with can be a tremendous help, particularly on the skills side, but it is neither entirely necessary nor is it sufficient, because if you have the skill*

to communicate with that person but you don't recognize the differences in culture (compared to mainstream culture) to be able to communicate that difference to a jury or a judge, then you don't have the full skillset you need. Sometimes you can recognize those differences better from the outside.

If you don't understand the principles about testing and the technical information we have about how to translate, adapt, re-norm, and reevaluate tests and how to select tests that are good or bad in that regard, then you may have cultural skills but be missing out on other things. So it's a combination of that collection of skills and knowledge that is important.

Because that combination is difficult to achieve for multiple cultural and language groups, often doing the job right involves collaboration.

Dr. Judd's point about collaborative assessments is worth emphasizing. He describes collaborative forensic assessments as an important strategy to ensure that forensic assessments are maximally valid and reliable. This is a strategy that allows forensic practitioners who may have general knowledge about culturally competent assessment but not specific skillsets in a particular culture to engage in a broader range of assessments, particularly when there are no other referral options available.

I have collaborated with psychologists, neuropsychologists, and students from probably a dozen different languages and cultural groups. How the collaborations play out depends on the examinee and the collaborators. For example, I've had students who speak Russian, Punjabi, Urdu, Hindi, Portuguese, and a few other languages, where they have done the interview in my presence, and then also served as my interpreter during the testing. The student may do an interview for 10 to 15 minutes and then say, "Excuse me for a moment while I summarize this to Dr. Judd." They will tell me what they've found and what is left to do.

I have often worked with Spanish-speaking clinical psychologists where we are doing an evaluation that has both neuropsychological and clinical psychological aspects to it, and we may interview together or separately and we will each pay attention to our own parts and then put them together.

Daryl Fujii emphasizes that clinicians need to be familiar with the test-taker's culture and not just focus on the problem of the language of the test or culturally appropriate norms:

For example, for many Native American cultures, an intelligent person is somebody who can interact with people and maintain harmonious relationships in the environment. Having to give an answer right away if you are not sure, that's foreign. Someone from a Native American culture may not be comfortable in a neuropsychological testing situation because of the social and political terms of responding. To conduct a culturally informed evaluation, it is best to do your homework, to prepare. You have to know the culture. If not, the fallback is interpreting the information within your worldview. That's everyone's default. It's like assimilation versus accommodation. We can gather data and assimilate it into our world and our structure, or we get new information of the test-taker's culture and then interpreter behaviors and test results within their context. Then we are accommodating.

Judge Christina Harms notes that courts are not going to find a psychologist who speaks seven languages and is culturally familiar with seven different cultures. In her training program, there is an emphasis on taking the time to educate oneself by asking examinees about their culture:

> A typical example in our training program would be clients from India who come from a very, very conservative Indian culture. It was a divorce custody case, and there are a lot of aspects of Indian culture, caste, religions, that an evaluator really should know, but we don't have any Indian psychologists in the greater Boston area who can do custody evaluations. So, what's the next best thing? Use the family as an education tool. Ask them a million questions. What does your culture say about the role of the mother in a household? What does your culture say about domestic violence? What does your culture say about children doing sports if their academics are not straight A's? Ask them.
>
> When you get cross-examined with
>
> *Q: You're not Indian, are you?*
>
> *A: No.*
>
> *Q: And you don't speak Hindi, do you?*
>
> *A: No.*
>
> *Q: And have you ever undertaken an extensive study of the Indian culture?*
>
> *A: No.*
>
> *Q: Well, why do you think you're qualified?*
>
> *A: Because I spent literally hours asking these two very people to educate me about their specific experience of Indian culture.*

AERA STANDARDS FOR EDUCATIONAL AND PSYCHOLOGICAL TESTING

Daryl Fujii notes that he relies on the Standards for Educational and Psychological Testing[3] as a framework for explaining concepts of fairness in assessment to juries and triers of fact. The standards are a collaboration between the American Psychological Association, National Council on Measurement in Education, and the American Education Research Association.

> *The AERA, APA, and NCME developed standards for educational and psychological testing. They talk about four things for fairness in testing. First, the situation itself has to be fair. The person taking the test has to be comfortable in terms of rapport and comfortable with the situation. For some cultures, taking tests is entirely foreign. In some cultures, if a woman is alone with a male in a room, that can create discomfort during the testing. Second, the tests have to be equal in content and meaning for the*

person's culture. For example, does intelligence mean the same for Western cultures as in Native American cultures? Third, the test-taker has to be able to understand test items and show what they know. There has to be fairness in responding. Then the last one is validities based on all of the first three plus "Has the person had the opportunity to actually learn the things they are being tested on?"

Antonio Puente, who helped write the chapter in the Standards on Fairness in Testing, notes that the new edition of the Standards, published in 2014, appropriately puts a much greater emphasis on culturally competent, valid assessment of individuals for whom adequate tests and test norms are not available.

The benefit of using the Standards as a framework is that you are explaining not just your own opinion, but the agreed-upon practice standards of the field. In a case where an assessment has been conducted in a way that is not culturally fair, experts can create a visual table that lists each standard, and then discuss how the assessment has or has not met each standard.

VALIDITY OF TESTS AND ASSESSMENT METHODS

Consider this vignette:

The expert has administered a battery of neuropsychological tests developed for, and normed on, individuals who speak only English and were educated in the United States to a plaintiff who immigrated to the United States 3 years ago and speaks no English, using a translator. Low scores were deemed evidence of "postconcussion syndrome." The fact that "nonverbal" tests were as low as verbal tests was used to "confirm that culture and language were not affecting the test scores."

I wish I could say that this is a "straw person," extreme example I invented to make a point; unfortunately, it is a case that came across my desk recently. How do we clearly explain why an assessment like this is not valid to jurors who do not share our basic assumptions about standardized testing and measurement theory?

Validity of "nonverbal tests"

The idea that "nonverbal" neuropsychological tests, involving visual/spatial reasoning or visual memory can be developed and normed on people who speak only English and were raised in the United States and then administered to people of different linguistic and cultural backgrounds with equal validity is common. In explaining to juries why this is not the case, Tedd Judd notes,

> Well, I turn to two things. One is I say:
>
> *The question of whether or not a nonverbal test is fair across cultures is a scientific question. It's not a principle; it is something that can be answered by research. When we look at the research, the answers we find is, "it all depends," that there are some*

tests that do hold up reasonably well from one culture to another and others that show great differences. The tests that Mr. Jones was given . . . .

I also might say:

Sure, non-verbal tests are fair. Would you care to take my Build an Igloo Test? Or my Hit a Rabbit With a Rock at 20 Paces and Skin it Test? Or my Find Your Way Across a Trackless Desert Test? Or my Salsa Dancing Test?—Tedd Judd, PhD, ABPP-CN

Problems with translation

Tedd Judd explains the validity problems that arise when translating cognitive tests to juries this way:

Psychology research has shown that the number of digits someone can repeat is a function of the length of the number word. This is a principle that has held across many different languages and it has been studied with people who are bilingual. You can see that the same person repeats a different number of digits in one language than in the other language. Even if the language has longer number words, in their best language they may still repeat fewer numbers in that language.

For example, in Spanish, number words are longer than they are in English. Many of them are two syllables, whereas in English, only the number 7 is a two-syllable word. (I may count to 10 in Spanish.) "The difference is like this:"

Suppose I ask you to repeat these words: Dog, tree, house, star. You could do that fairly well. Okay. Now suppose I ask you to repeat these words: Constitutionality, disambiguation, hippopotamus, and stethoscope?"

As it turns out, the digits in many of the East Asian languages such as Chinese, Vietnamese, and Korean are even shorter than they are in English. They have fewer phonemes, fewer speech sounds. You can think of that as fewer letters so that three has five letters and has four speech sounds. In many East Asian languages, the digits have just one consonant and one vowel. When they re-did Digit Span in China, they had to extend it out to 12 digits forward whereas in the English version, we only go up to nine digits because hardly anybody can do nine digits. So, it can look like the same test when we translate Digit Span, but it is not, and when we re-norm the tests in the other language, we find that out.

Having explained that for Digit Span, I can then explain how we can't safely carry the performance validity test Reliable Digit Span over to another language.

And having explained it with Digit Span, I can then explain how that same principle applies to other verbal memory tests,

If you have a wordlist and you translated that wordlist carefully for meaning so that you have the same words, you're not going to have the same verbal memory task because the word length may be different or the familiarity of the word may be different as well. If you have a story and you are using that for story memory, if you look at a text in Spanish and a text in English and you print them out next to each other, the text in Spanish will be about one third longer than the text in English because the words are longer.

> If I have some Spanish speakers in the jury or elsewhere, then I may also do this exercise:
>
> *Another task that we use very commonly is called verbal fluency. People are asked to say as many animals as they can in one minute. Word length can have an impact here as well, so, for example, in English, think of how many different animals you can that are one-syllable words, and then when you go about it, you find that there are a lot and a lot of them are the basic ones that we mostly come up with. "Cat, Dog, Pig, Goat." In general, they are animals that are common in England. Animal names that come from away from England often are longer words.*
>
> *Okay, now try this in Spanish. Given me all the one-syllable animal names that you can. Typically, nobody can come up with any. In fact, after great searching, they have come up pez, which is fish and buey, which is ox, although most of the time people use pescado for fish, which actually means fished. It is a verb form, not the fish on the plate. But basically, they are going to be longer words. So those are the examples that I most usually draw on to illustrate principles about test translation and why things may not work the same.*

Here is a way of explaining the problem with translating tests that I have used in my own practice:

> *Dr. Expert hired a translator on the day of testing to read the English test items and test directions to Ms. Plaintiff. She did not use a scientifically based translation method. Here's an example of what scientific translation looks like. A test manufacturer will hire an expert translator to translate their test. Then one or two people from the culture who also know English look at the translation and determine if it really means the same thing, and if there are any words that are startling or unsettling. They then translate the test back into English. This is known as "back translation." Do the test items still mean the same thing in English?*
>
> *Because scientific translation was not done, Dr. Expert had no way of validating whether the translation of test directions and specific test items provided too much information about how to perform the tests (acting like hints) or too little information (making the tests harder).*

Ira Packer notes that he has seen situations in which other experts had the Structured Interview of Reported Symptoms (SIRS), a symptom validity test, translated in a nonstandardized manner:

> *Well, although Dr. Expert thought the defendant was malingering based on the scores of the SIRS, I do not think that is a valid measure because these tests are very specifically normed so they must be administered in a standardized format in order to establish the scores. Any deviation makes it difficult to interpret the test. Even when given in English, we read the questions exactly as written and do not paraphrase. So if the questions are translated by the evaluator, they no longer are standardized, and*

therefore the results cannot be interpreted based on the established norms. It is, of course, reasonable to use a test that has been translated and normed in a different language.

Judge Christina Harms notes that because of the translation problem,

In our postdoctoral training program for custody evaluations we will not use psychological tests with individuals from cultural backgrounds or linguistic groups if the tests weren't developed for them. We will do an assessment but just not include testing. This is really kind of an ethically debatable question, I know—there are a lot of tests that are not issued in Spanish or Chinese or Vietnamese or anything, but some people think it's okay to just get an interpreter and then give the test. I don't speak Vietnamese, but I can find a Vietnamese person who is also fluent in English and they can help me administer the test. The problem with that, of course, is that there's the cultural component: The linguistic piece may be there, but the cultural piece isn't. So when someone from Mexico talks about seeing ghosts, you can translate that, but there is a very real role in Mexican culture for ghosts, and it will score like crazy on a test. So, yes, we are very sensitive about it and we generally don't test people if the test isn't either issued in their language or hasn't been normed on their culture, and we won't just use translators.

Tests don't have validity; interpretations have validity. Is a yardstick a good measure? Is it valid? Well, it depends on if you want to know how long or tall something is. Then it's a pretty good measure for that and as such interpretation would be valid—but it's not a very good measure for telling how heavy someone is. If you are measuring people, someone who is 6 feet tall will probably be heavier than someone who is 4 feet tall, but it is not going to be a real close correlation; it is not going to be very precise. The validity comes with the interpretation, not with the test. So even though you may have an excellent test in English, you have to reestablish its validity in translation and adaptation in another language.—Tedd Judd, PhD, ABPP-CN

Problems with norms

Leslie Rosenstein has a clear explanation of the pitfalls of testing in a second language:

If someone evaluated my intellect in my second language, I would have a low score too. Not because I had a brain injury, but because I am not fluent in that language.

Desiree Byrd helps juries understand the concept of using the best-fit normative groups:

We as professionals rely on standardization samples to make sense of the meaning of any one person's test scores. Because of a slew of reasons, including racism and different access to quality educational experiences and enrichment opportunities, if we compare one person who hasn't had access to these things to another person who has, then is it really fair? Are we really estimating this person's true thinking abilities? The best way for me to get an estimate of someone's memory ability is to compare them to people who are most like them on the factors that influence test scores.

Explaining norming issues

These tests were developed and normed on a group of people who speak English and were raised and educated in the United States. A typical or average score for the group that was used when developing the test may not be an average score for Mr. Jones, given English is his third language and he was raised and educated in a different country.—Paul L. Craig, PhD, ABPP-CN

Are tests racist?

I recall one case where there was a question of whether the defendant who gave a confession was mentally retarded. He scored in the high 70s. I used appropriate demographic norms and he was in the high 80s or 90s with the comparison group. Nine years of education, African-American ethnic background. Functionally there was no evidence of MR. He was working, was able to function in the community, had relationships, etc.

Q: Dr. Barr, aren't you using racist norms?

A: Well, my intention is the opposite here. We use these norms for African Americans because the white guys made the tests. The tests questions are generated from the values and experience of white men who lived in the 1930s. We modify the tests as best we can over time, but the influences are still there. There are scientists who are not me who have developed and studied these norms and have recommended their use in these situations.

When I said, "because the white men made these tests," three African-American jurors were nodding their heads vigorously.—William Barr, PhD, ABPP-CN

Tedd Judd explains the issue of which norms to use:

When someone has been in this country here for a while and perhaps speaks English well and perhaps comes from a country that is of a similar culture, the question arises, "Should we use U.S. tests or tests from the country or culture of origin?" The answer to that question is, "It depends on what question you are trying to answer, what they're trying to find out."

The issue will come up with things having to do with competency to stand trial. For example, suppose someone comes here from Britain and we want to give them a test to see if they are able to drive here in the United States. If they get out on the road and they drive on the left-hand side of the road, do we want to say, "Well, that's the way they do it in England, so we will use the culturally based norms for that purpose" and then say, "Okay, that's fine, they can drive"? No, I don't think we want to do that!

But if we want to know if they have visual attention and the speed of response that is needed likely to be able to be a good driver or to have the capacity to learn to be a

good driver, then tests such as trail-making tests with norms from their country or culture may be appropriate and useful. Which norms depends in part on whether you are trying to determine if they have a brain disorder or whether you are trying to determine if they are competent to function in a particular setting here, be it school or work or the courtroom or managing their finances, or other questions of various competencies or potentials.

Cultural diversity in Alaska

When thinking about Alaska many non-Alaskans think cultural diversity means Alaska Natives as contrasted with Caucasians. but that doesn't begin to capture the diversity in Alaska at all. In Anchorage, every day there are at least 90 different languages spoken fluently by students in the public schools. The public high school where my daughters graduated did not have a majority of any single cultural group. Alaska is really a melting pot. I run up against cross-cultural issues with Filipinos, Samoans, Koreans, African refugees and many more. Some neuropsychologists refuse to do assessments on non–English-speaking people. I almost always attempt to perform some level of evaluation with all people referred for an evaluation, but I make certain to address clearly that the norms developed for the test were not developed for this population, and I qualify my opinions accordingly. I am willing to use translator services as appropriate. I acknowledge the variance that can be introduced due to translation and the associated language barriers. I always hedge my conclusions based upon the weakness of the normative sample and the language barriers at play.

When evaluating Alaska Natives, there are some normative data that were collected but never published. These data are held closely by the CDC and require permission from the Alaska Native groups involved in developing these norms to access these data. Thankfully, some of these data were presented at a circumpolar health conference. The summary information from these normative data is helpful when attempting to interpret levels of performances on various tests among Alaska Natives.—Paul L. Craig, PhD, ABPP-CN

Validity of tests for test-naïve cultures

Tedd Judd points out that some cultures do not have formal education. People from those cultures will have no experience with "testing," and that puts them at an immediate and profound disadvantage, regardless of the type of test they are given. This would also be the case for people who, for reasons like poverty or gender discrimination, are from cultures with education but never had access to it themselves.

Testing is a cultural phenomenon. There are cultures that don't do testing at all, and if you don't have the experience of testing, if you are test-naïve rather than being test-wise, then it's going to be a different experience, and the test scores are going to tell you something different than the scores of a person who grew up in a culture of testing.

Qualitative observations depend on cultural context

Another issue that can be difficult to address with juries is the impact of frontal lobe injuries on interpersonal skills in people of other cultures when the norms for social behavior may be different from ours. That is, when experts describe their observations of a plaintiff/defendant's behavior, it is straightforward for jurors to grasp that the behavior was inappropriate. In contrast, there may be multiple steps in explaining atypical behaviors in an examinee from a different culture: first, what the expert observed, and second, that the behavior was out of the box for this person's culture.

> *When assessing people from different cultures, you just have to be careful and take your time and ask the questions, particularly of informants concerning social behavior.*
>
> *I had a case of someone who had a nail gun injury to the orbital frontal lobe, a Latino, and he had no close family members in the United States, which made it more difficult. But he was staying with a cousin, and the young man asked his young female cousin to get him a towel as he got out of the shower. He opened the door and stood there, and that was culturally inappropriate. I had to confirm with the cousin that yes, you don't do that in this culture.*
>
> *There are certain families where you might do that. I had a Vietnamese woman with a similar orbital frontal injury and had a male interpreter. She was touching the male interpreter, putting her arm around his shoulder and touching in various other ways, and it was culturally very inappropriate. I suspected that, but I confirmed it with the interpreter. It was something that could have been within the range of normal for a North American in a certain style of conversation and certainly would have been within the range of normal for various Latinos.*
>
> *When I testify, I give the example of the behavior, and then I talk about having consulted someone of the culture who could tell me that that was out of line, that that was inappropriate. I then connect the inappropriate behavior with the lesion, that it is the kind of behavior that is known to be associated with the type of lesion.*—Tedd Judd, PhD, ABPP-CN

Explaining the problems of inflated norms

Antonio Puente notes that use of Mexican version of the Wechsler Adult Intelligence Scale often results in an inflation of estimated intellect. Here is how he explains it to juries:

> *I hate to do this to you: Let me give you some stats. The different Spanish versions of the WAIS all appear to be similar. However, our research with the American WAIS indicates that the psychometrics of some Spanish versions of this test are substantially different, up to an entire standard deviation difference. The Spanish version of this test could overestimate a Spanish speaker's IQ up to 15 points.*

It is important to note that an explanation like this to a jury would occur after the words "standard deviation" and "psychometrics" were clearly defined. In a capital murder case, they typically are. Had they not yet been, this might be used instead:

> *The different Spanish versions of the WAIS all appear to be similar. However, our research with the American WAIS indicates that the Spanish versions measure IQ differently than the American version. With every test, researchers have to ask, "How good is this yardstick? Is it accurate? Does it consistently tell us something is longer than it really is? Shorter?" The research tells us the Spanish WAIS consistently tells us something is bigger than it really is; it can overestimate a Spanish speaker's IQ by up to 15 points. That's taking a person with a 65 IQ and mistaking him for someone with an IQ of 80. Construct irrelevance produces measurement error.*

Here's another option for talking about inflated norms. In my own practice, I like anchoring the concept of measurement error with something everyone is familiar with, a bathroom scale, but also connecting the type of measurement error with something that jurors can get behind as "unfair!"

> *Have you ever had a bathroom scale that you really loved or really hated? Some scales are off by a couple of pounds. They consistently tell you your weight is less than it really is (I love those!) or more than it really is. You hop on the scale and—ta-da! You just lost 4 pounds. Or like the scale at my primary care office: It is definitely off by 5 pounds in the wrong direction. It consistently claims I gained 5 pounds. Every time.*
>
> *That scale at my doctor's office is like norm inflation. It's a consistent error in measurement that overestimates people's thinking abilities. When we compare the Spanish version of the WAIS to the American version, it's like the scale is off. It overestimates how smart people are, but it's not by 5 pounds; it's by up to 15 pounds. That's a BIG difference.*

Combined effects of low IQ and lack of English proficiency

> *I will have a bell curve up on a visual as I explain this to jurors: "Imagine you went to high school in North Carolina. This is where you should be at. (Points to the center of the curve.) This is Mr. X's score. (Points to the borderline range.) Not only is he not as smart as you, he doesn't even speak the language where he is going to school. Imagine how that would have felt."*—Antonio E. Puente, PhD

Explaining cross-cultural use of performance validity tests

Shelley Peery notes that some cross-examining attorneys, armed with knowledge that if a test was not normed on a particular language or cultural group, the interpretation may not be valid, come to exactly the wrong conclusion with some tests:

> I had one case where the cross-examining attorney was trying to make a crazy point. A woman had gotten 50/50 on both trials of the TOMM and the entirety of cross examination pointed out that the TOMM had not been validated for use with Spanish speakers.
>
> *Q: Doctor, isn't it true that the TOMM was not normed on Spanish speakers?*
>
> *A: If you get 100% correct, it doesn't matter where you are from. You obviously had to try. It is certainly valid. It is not just about norms but also about statistical probability. We know that if you get 100% right, the probability you did that by chance is very, very low. So it's way more likely than not, it's very probable, that she was showing good effort.*

Tedd Judd brings up an interesting aspect of performance and symptom validity assessment in cross-cultural work. He notes,

> *In cross-cultural work, you often encounter malingering that is much more blatant than in other populations. It is often very clear after the first 5 minutes of an interview. I will stop and re-explain what we are there for and say something like, "I have seen thousands of people with brain injuries and people with memory disorders, and one of the things that I know is that they don't forget where they came from. They don't forget what town they grew up in. That is not the kind of memory that gets lost. So, if you tell me that that's the case, I feel like you're not being fully cooperative with me and it is not going to allow us to do what our purpose is here today. That is going to hurt your case."*
>
> *I often use a principle of allowing the evaluee to save face, so I will put the computer and the notebook aside and I move in closer. I am aware of what I do with eye contact in such a circumstance. Depending on the person's culture, I use direct eye contact or I may pointedly look at the floor.*
>
> *And I make a strategic decision as to whether to do it with or without the family member present, because sometimes the family member will then take them out and give them a lecture, or sometimes they will be embarrassed in front of the family member so I make that strategic decision based on my judgment of the situation. I go back to the common purpose of the evaluation and the importance of honesty. I tend to try to give them an out. I say, "I don't know what it is, but it seems like there is something that's getting in the way of your doing the best that you can do. Maybe you have a headache. Maybe you're worried about something. Do you need to take a break? Maybe this isn't a good day. We can reschedule. I think I have an opening in 2 months."*

How dare you try to assess this person!

While blithely conducting psychological or neuropsychological assessment without appropriate norms or translations is clearly misleading to courts, psychologists and neuropsychologists can use multiple tools to assess individuals non-culturally dominant, non-English as a first language groups.

> *Q: Dr. Judd, how dare you try to have an opinion about this case if you don't have high levels of reliability and validity for each of your instruments in this population!*
>
> *A: Neuropsychological opinions are based not just on our test data. They are based on the totality of the information that we gather. This includes history and how we know cognitive disorders develop after certain types of injuries and disease processes. Normative-based testing is only one of several forms of information that we use. In addition to using norms, we can compare the person to themselves—for example, comparing immediate recall to delayed recall. Another form of inference involves comparing the person to themselves over time so that we can test them on one occasion and test them on a later occasion and look for consistency and change.*—Tedd Judd, PhD, ABPP-CN

TESTIFYING AS A NON-EUROPEAN AMERICAN PSYCHOLOGIST

In his book *Black Man in a White Coat*,[4] Damon Tweedy explores the ways that the racial biases pervasive in our larger culture play out in the field of medicine. He describes white patients rejecting the care of black doctors and nurses, doctors offering less care and dismissing the complaints of minorities and women, and pervasive disparities in access to health care for minority people. In the nuanced, first-person narrative, Dr. Tweedy explores how minority patients can also share distrust in minority health-care professionals and how minority doctors' own biases color their care.

None of these factors disappear when doctors walk into the courtroom. Psychologists and neuropsychologists, jurors, attorneys, and judges all bring our biases and assumptions to our assessments, courtroom strategies, and deliberations. Judge Jay Blitzman notes that in typical jury instructions, "We tell jurors that their greatest tools are their life experiences. I think we have reason to be wary of that, because it might be an invitation to jurors to default to implicit bias and preconceptions." Later in the chapter, we will discuss juror instructions explicitly addressing conscious and unconscious bias.

Antonio Puente describes testifying as a Hispanic psychologist. He notes that he is usually testifying in front of a jury that is different from both himself and the defendant. The diversity is complex, as it is not only cultural but also socioeconomic. This point is important, as jurors may feel distant from psychologists and neuropsychologists from underrepresented minorities because of biases regarding cultural or linguistic status and also because of disparities in their education attainment and socioeconomic status.

Sometimes racial prejudice in the courtroom goes beyond a sense of distrust or distance into the darker side of race relations in this country. Dr. Puente reflects on his experience as a Hispanic psychologist testifying on behalf of minority defendants in highly emotional cases:

> *Testifying in some cases, I have felt for my safety. I recall one case where I was testifying on an issue of intellectual disability where the defendant was an older Hispanic man*

who had been accused of murdering an American child from that community. My testimony nor my presence were welcome. I felt for my safety. My goal was to get off the stand, get in my car, and leave town intact. I definitely experienced fearfulness in the context of being a Hispanic psychologist testifying on behalf of the defense. In situations like those my focus is to stay the course, be objective, and testify on behalf of information and truth.

Throughout his memoir, Dr. Tweedy stresses the importance of staying present in the cross-cultural, cross-racial interactions, despite the initial doubts of competency and conflicts that arise in the context of the biases each party brings to the situation:

A big part of the solution is discarding your assumptions and connecting with each patient as a person. Race, while certainly a powerful influence, by itself doesn't guarantee a human connection any more than any other factor like geography, height, or handedness. It is up to us, as doctors, to find the commonalities and respect the differences between us and our patients. In that way, we can understand what they value, how best to communicate with them, and how to arrive at treatment plans that improve their health while respecting their wishes. This approach is often called cultural competence, but after years of medical practice, it seems to me more like common sense.[5]

Dr. Tweedy's focus on creating a human connection as a way to push through biases fits with an ongoing theme of the advice of many of the experts, attorneys, and judges I interviewed for the *Testimony That Sticks* project: Consciously seek a human connection. Be willing to show that you are a real person by sharing personal information about yourself, leave the jargon and emotional distance of academic communication behind, and focus on the needs of the jurors as real, human people trying to do a difficult job.

TESTIFYING WHILE FEMALE

We live in a world where men hold most positions of power and authority in government, academia, corporations—the list goes on. This is changing, but at a very slow pace. The fact that Hillary Clinton was able to secure the first major party nomination for president in 2016, and win the popular vote, tells us that some of the more ludicrous notions floated at the time of Geraldine Ferraro's vice presidential bid decades earlier, that women were constitutionally unfit to hold positions of power and authority, have fallen out of favor. That said, it was clear from contradictory expectations and critiques of Clinton's behavior during the campaign that our society still struggles with the image of a woman in a position of authority and power. Looking and acting "presidential" still means looking and acting "masculine," and either conforming to those expectations or not conforming can have equally negative consequences.

When women step into the witness box as experts, we may be disrupting jurors', attorneys', or judges' assumptions about what an expert should look like. If we are doing our job well, during cross examination we are also likely disrupting general assumptions about women deferring to others during conflict. The tricky part, of course, is that as women we learned those same assumptions growing up in this culture. We are not just disrupting others' assumptions about women; we are engaging in an ongoing process of disrupting our own assumptions about how we should behave.

In my first few year of forensic work, I was fascinated to observe that my heart rate increased and I felt literal physical discomfort when a moment of conflict emerged. I had been raised to address conflict "gracefully" rather than assertively. In the beginning, my anxiety response when I forced myself to respond assertively probably prevented me from bringing the "graceful" part fully to the table while I engaged. Over time, it has become easier to identify a point of conflict, state my position, and feel/show warmth and empathy for the person on the other side of the conflict to the table.

Kristie Nies makes the important point that regardless of how women assert themselves, many experience a woman who contradicts someone (particularly a male someone) as aggressive or rude. She notes that in some areas of the country, where the proportion of men to women in the courtrooms is particularly lopsided, attorneys will appear to purposefully draw her into a "fight" to reduce her credibility with jurors:

> *Being female can be a problem in my region of the country. Most of the attorneys are male. It is changing some, but typically the attorneys are male and the court reporters are female. It is important to not let the attorneys push you around. The attorneys I have worked with have not been very sophisticated in terms of neuropsychology. The cross examination is more of an education for them. It is important to be nondefensive and stand your ground.*
>
> *Females are in a Catch-22 situation. We are told that being assertive looks "bitchy." There is a fine line. You have to look authoritative, but not so there is a negative appearance to it. Not mean, or snarky. It is hard. The attorneys work to provoke you. It is hard to stay calm and not take the bait. As a female, it is particularly important that you do not take the bait.*

Chapter 6, "Social Pragmatics of Testifying," addresses the very difficult issue of how nonverbal behaviors that women are trained to engage in from toddlerhood, such as tone, pattern of speech, and body posture, are defined both as "ladylike" and as "lacking confidence" at the same time. It is an ugly bind women are placed in, that in identifying and changing signals that tell others we are not confident in our opinions, we are by definition "acting more like a man." But then people see a woman "act like a man" and may feel intuitively, "Hey, something's not right; she is acting way more aggressively than she should be. Why is she so aggressive?" See Chapter 6 for further discussion and specific strategies.

SOCIOECONOMIC STATUS

Judge Fader makes an important point about the effects of socioeconomic diversity on trial outcomes:

> *Experts need to understand what my Aunt Grace and Aunt Margaret would understand and testify to that. Use plain speech. But the type of speech depends on the juries you are dealing with, too. In the Baltimore area you have the rich, well-to-do*

people out in one section of the county where all the horses are running around $4 or $5 million houses, and then you've got people down in another section of the county who are the salt of the earth.

A judge friend of mine used to give his spiel. He said, "I could try the same case with the same exact facts over in one part of Baltimore County and the defendant would say, 'Judge, I'm sorry. I don't know what got into me. It was all my fault and I will never do it again.'" And then you'd go over to another section, which he would say is the blue-collar section of town, and all you would hear over there was, "It was all the cop's fault!" And then you'd go down to another section and you'd hear, "Yeah, I stabbed him. The SOB had it coming." And that is what life is about. There are different people on juries, and it makes a difference who you are talking to.

Judge Lynne Battaglia agrees that different jury pools tend to be made up of different socioeconomic classes, and expert testimony must vary depending on the jury pool:

As an example, with med malpractice, there are enormous recoveries in Baltimore city. Most insurance companies would rather have their malpractice case heard in Howard County because they have a better defense jury pool. That may or may not relate to the expert per se. It may relate to pain and suffering as testified to by the plaintiff. But it has some relevance to the expert. If you are a defense expert in Baltimore city, it is even more important that you don't come across as being arrogant and "establishment." Who the jurors are is an important aspect of the preparation of an expert.

Antonio Puente explains how important it is for both experts and jurors to understand the concept of radical socioeconomic diversity:

There is such an extreme socioeconomic diversity issue between members of the jury and the type of poverty my clients have experienced. Poor people in the United States are experiencing a radically different life than poor people in many other countries. It is very hard to have jurors understand the Third World poverty experience. My job is to help jurors understand that we are talking about a person who does not have education, born near the dump, didn't have appropriate nourishment, mom was a prostitute, dad was a drug addict. The people thinking "This doesn't happen," but such dire situations can and do occur.

Dr. Puente creates films for the jury to help explain this "other place" of severe poverty:

"Let me explain to you this other place." To help jurors understand I use videos. I will have the village priest explain what life is like. My job is to be a cinematographer. I drive 2 hours from the nearest town and interview people about their experience of extreme poverty. I am literally making films to show on the stand. The films make it real for jurors. When that is not possible, I use a lot of photographs.

He introduces the films like this:

> *I don't know about you folks, but I live in North Carolina. My house has heat, just like yours. It is hard to believe that people can live like that, so I am going to show it to you. We are going to tell you about Mr. X's mom, we will tell you about what his teachers said, you will hear from the village priest. (Jurors lean forward, pay attention.)*

Dr. Puente asks family members in his films about defendants' developmental histories:

> *The difference between developmental histories of Americans in poverty as opposed to Third World is stunning. I was talking to a mother in Mexico. "Can you tell me how the delivery occurred?" "I went to get water from the well. I went to the house. I felt bad and weird. I opened my legs; he fell on the floor head first."*
>
> *I had a case where the defendant grew up in a small village in Mexico. During the interview of the school principal, asking in-depth questions was really key. On the surface, it looked like the defendant had a B average in school, but with more questions, it was clear that the head of his school was illiterate. In the interview I asked, "How do you know that he was a good student?" (He got an 88 average.) "Would that pass you?" (Yes.) "Who are you, the principal? Can you spell your name for our records?" (He was unable to spell his own name.) "How did you get the appointment of school principal?" (He worked on the election of the mayor.) The interview really made the defendant's experience come alive.*

In summing up his use of film to communicate radical socioeconomic disparities, Dr. Puente comments,

> *You lose juries with the statistics. As I have evolved in my career, I am much more of a Vygotsky/Luria neuropsychologist, less than a psychometrician. My focus is to place these people in a social/historical context. If you knew their lives, you would mitigate this.*

See Chapter 10, "Visuals," for more about using film during testimony.

THE IMMIGRANT EXPERIENCE

Tedd Judd notes,

> I make sure to make reference to certain aspects of immigrant experience. I'm often asked to explain discrepancies in what someone has had at one time or another, and it tends to make out an immigrant to be lying or misrepresenting themselves and undermines their credibility. I will make reference to the principle and say,

"Coming into another country, particularly coming into the United States, it is often a difficult and stressful prospect and often involves encountering a lot of bureaucracy, a lot of institutions that you may be unfamiliar with, a lot of skepticism from those institutions, and a lot of people who don't quite understand. Immigrants in general may tend to attempt to present themselves as being younger, healthier, better educated, more skilled, and more closely related to one another than they actually are. They do that because that may be to their advantage with regard to their prospects of being able to get a visa and being able to emigrate and being able to get a job. And sometimes it winds up being just easier to say, 'This is my son' than to say, 'This is my stepson' or to say, 'This is my wife' rather than to say, 'This is the woman I've been living with for the last 10 years and have children with but we didn't actually formally get married.' Sometimes these are things that we do for the sake of simplicity and social ease, Like what you would say socially or to an employer or to your friends at a church or mosque or what you might say to immigration or to the police or to the welfare agency or to your doctor. I think all of us have had an experience at one time or another of simplifying something that is more complicated in that sort of a way."

No one forgets their birthday!

Something that jurors may not understand and that may take some explanation is I have seen people try to undermine someone's testimony by saying, "he claims he doesn't know what his birthday is. Nobody forgets that!"

I explain:

"Well, yes, in some cultures they don't pay attention to birthdays. Especially if they are not in a literate culture, it is often the case that people don't know their birthdays because it is not of importance to them. For example, the day you graduated from high school, assuming you graduated from high school, it was probably an important day for you. You can probably remember some of the events of the graduation and that you were there and what people wore and what was said. What was the date? And if you remember the date, what day of the week was it? Different cultures place different values on those things, and people may not know that."—Tedd Judd, PhD, ABPP-CN

JUROR INSTRUCTIONS FOR IMPLICIT BIAS

Concern about implicit biases affecting trial outcomes and contributing to racial, gender, and other injustices has led some judges and courts to create specific juror instructions regarding bias. Judge Jay Blitzman notes that as the neuroscience has accrued that the brain is not a passive organ but rather an active organ, making anticipatory judgments as it processes information, the question is raised, "Do people believe what they see, or see what they believe?" Because humans organize information into preconceived notions, there is a movement to try to temper this anticipatory judgment by giving instructions to jurors about implicit bias. He notes, though,

How do you address implicit bias in a way which doesn't create what some researchers refer to as a rebound effect? If you are too heavy-handed, you get exactly that which

you want to avoid: more bias, because you are exacerbating the problem; if you make people self-conscious they become defensive.

The U.S. (Federal) District Court, Western District of Washington created a video "Understanding the Effect of Unconscious Bias" for every juror to watch and a set of instructions to be read to jurors[6] that are "intended to alert the jury to the concept of unconscious bias and then to instruct the jury in a straightforward way not to use bias, including unconscious bias, in its evaluation of information and credibility and in its decision making." The video makes the important distinction between conscious bias (with pictures of whites-only water fountains and restaurants shown during the explanation) and unconscious bias, "Something that we all have, because we are human." I highly recommend watching the video, available online (https://www.youtube.com/watch?time_continue=81&v=hdjBbfdRLkA). The jury instructions are broken into three parts, with one instruction designed to be read to jurors prior to the beginning of the trial, as "priming" jurors before they are exposed to trial proceedings may be more effective than waiting until the end of the case to present the information. A second set of instructions, reproduced here, is given before jurors hear witness testimony. The final set of instructions is read just prior to deliberations.

Credibility of witnesses

In deciding the facts in this case, you may have to decide which testimony to believe and which testimony not to believe. You may believe everything a witness says, or part of it, or none of it.

In considering the testimony of any witness, you may take into account:

(1) the witness's opportunity and ability to see or hear or know the things testified to;

(2) the witness's memory;

(3) the witness's manner while testifying;

(4) the witness's interest in the outcome of the case, if any;

(5) the witness's bias or prejudice, if any;

(6) whether other evidence contradicted the witness's testimony;

(7) the reasonableness of the witness's testimony in light of all the evidence; and

(8) any other factors that bear on believability

You must avoid bias, conscious or unconscious, based on the witness's race, color, religious beliefs, national origin, sexual orientation, gender identity, or gender in your determination of credibility.

The weight of the evidence as to a fact does not necessarily depend on the number of witnesses who testify about it.

FINALLY, CODE-SWITCHING

Because every jury is different, and juries are composed of people from different linguistic, cultural, age, education, rural/suburban, etc., backgrounds, experts need many tools in our communication toolkit to communicate effectively. Desiree Byrd shares an application of the concept of code-switching to help experts think about the goal of switching between various communication styles to reach a maximum number of people in a diverse room:

> *You talk with your friends in one way and with your professional colleagues in another way; this is called code-switching. The classic example of this is vernacular Black English, but this is not limited to a specific ethnic language style. Experts can code-switch several times in a single answer and thereby actually speak to and grab the attention of different parties in the room with a single statement.*
>
> *I try to discern who the primary audience is at the moment of a portion of a response. Part of the answer to any one question might be for the attorney and another part might be for the jury. While testifying, I think one has to be very quick on their feet, code-switching as necessary.*
>
> *For example, when initially speaking to an attorney who is attacking the idea of the breakdown of the categorization of test performance by domain, I might say something like: "Decades of studies have demonstrated that groups of tests tap into specific neural networks and that the one ability that these tests and these areas of the brain share are memory and retention, the ability to recall information."*
>
> *But then I may shift my attention to the jury and say, "The common denominator for these tests, what they are found to measure reliably over a bunch of studies, is memory."*

NOTES

1. Pew Research Center. Retrieved from http://www.pewhispanic.org/2008/02/11/us-population-projections-2005-2050/
2. Barrett, K., & George, W. H. (Eds.). (2005). *Race, culture, psychology and law*. Thousand Oaks, CA: Sage Press.
3. American Educational Research Association, American Psychological Association, and National Council on Measurement in Education. (2014). *Standards for educational and psychological testing*. Washington, DC: American Educational Research Association.
4. Tweedy, D. (2015). *Black man in a white coat: A doctor's reflection on race and medicine.* New York: Picador.
5. Tweedy, D. (2015). *Black man in a white coat: A doctor's reflection on race and medicine.* New York: Picador, p. 245.
6. Retrieved from http://www.wawd.uscourts.gov/sites/wawd/files/CriminalJuryInstructions-ImplicitBias.pdf

18 Depositions

TOM BOLL POINTS out that for attorneys, an important purpose for depositions "... is not to be educated about neuropsychology but to find out what you have so the attorneys can go back to their principals or insurance company and say, 'This guy is an idiot, we'll make a mash out of him in court,' or 'You should take this guy seriously, he is not going to bend.' So as an expert, you should show them what you've got."

The notion that a strong deposition will lead toward settlement is seconded by Keith Yeates, "The most effective neuropsychology testimony is in the context of deposition, where you are convincing the opposing attorney not to put you on the stand in trial. The opposing attorney is using the deposition to see what kind of witness you will be. If they feel you would be an effective witness, they will avoid putting you in the stand. And they will settle the case more quickly. I may have given several hundred depositions, but I have been in a courtroom only 3 to 4 times."

This chapter addresses all phases of the deposition, including setting the boundaries of the deposition with the opposing attorney.

IMPORTANCE OF DEPOSITION TESTIMONY

The frequency with which depositions occur varies by jurisdiction and type of legal proceeding. Nancy Hebben notes,

> *In Massachusetts depositions don't happen very often; you are not entitled to them. Some attorneys agree to let their experts be deposed. In New Hampshire and Vermont depositions are common.*

A deposition is a fishing expedition. If there is nothing known about you, they want to see how you do under pressure. Do you fold? Do you start crying? If you are already well known, then they are looking to see what kind of things set you off, make you mad. What can they throw at you to try to intimidate you, as if they have all this dirt on you. Oftentimes it's less about finding out about the facts and more about finding out about you as the expert. But they might also genuinely want to find out if there are any other opinions that you have that weren't in your report. Attorneys can also prep their own expert based on what you are going to say.

You have to apply the same rules to deposition testimony as you do to testifying in front of the jury. You need to maintain your composure.

DIFFERENCES BETWEEN DEPOSITIONS AND COURTROOM TESTIMONY

Searching for winners

Attorney Wayne Miller explains his goals during a deposition:

The purposes of deposition are different than the purposes of trial cross examination. I'm kind of experimenting at the deposition. I might have 4 hours of questions to see how the expert answers this question or that question. The purpose is to see which of the many questions can be narrowed down to the best questions for cross examination at trial.

In a trial, that is not the game. The trial is completely purposeful, and I might take the 20 things that I tried in the deposition over 4 hours and hone it down to four things in 30 minutes. What are my best points? What are my winners? A big reason for that is the jury gets bored, I've got a certain amount of time which seems shorter and shorter before they turn off completely, and if I've got points to make, I don't want them to turn off to my points.

What I am looking for in my deposition experiment is if the expert has an answer to the question, I mean a good answer. In one case, I took a deposition of a neuropsychologist last year and he is a real smart guy. I thought that if I made a point, he would concede it, and he did for a number of those. One example which pops into my mind is he charges for his forensic practice—I am not remembering the exact numbers, but let's say it is $250 an hour—but he was charging me for the deposition $500 an hour (and $500 an hour is not outrageous, I expect to pay those kind of numbers), but it occurred to me this kind of work is very lucrative if you can get double what your main work does. I have asked those kind of questions before and other experts answer in different ways, but this guy was very honest and he said, "I started charging the same amount that I charge for my other work and then someone recommended that I charge more, and then I kept on charging more and people kept paying it." That was a very honest answer; thank you very much. But I was just asking as an experiment to see what kind of answer I would get, and I thought this was a great answer for me because it showed the mercenary style and the lucrative nature of this kind of work to a person.

Attorney Miller also notes that during deposition questioning, he is not afraid to sound stupid:

> *I am a firm believer that you miss 100% of the shots that you don't take. If I don't ask a question, I am not going to get an answer. Whereas 35 years ago I'd be scared to ask certain questions because I didn't know what I would get, or because I didn't want to sound stupid, now I am happy to sound stupid.*
>
> *For example, I might say, "What is the concept of baseline? What does that mean? And why is that significant to what you do?" Or, "Is the concept of baseline significant for what you do?" To me, that is a critical, crucial fundamental question, and I have, like, an hour of questions that I ask after that on that same line, but I might start saying something that might sound harmless, might be open-ended, might give the expert a chance to pontificate an answer to an easy question: "Oh, that's an easy question. I'm going to really throw some learning on you, Mr. Lawyer!" The next questions I think the neuropsychologists might want to watch out for: "Why is that important?" "Oh, it's important because . . ." I am asking it because I know it is important; I just want you to tell me that it is important and I want you to tell me why.*

Bad behavior

Tom Boll notes that courtroom testimony on cross examination is much more restrained and polite than deposition testimony. This is an important point, as many psychologists who have primarily testified at deposition may feel very fearful about testifying in court, assuming that they will get the same hammering behavior as they do in deposition, but compounded by being in front of an audience:

> *They can beat you up all they want in deposition. That's the point. They have to see what you've got. No one will read it, and nobody is going to care or feel sorry for you. So if you are going to get beaten up, it will be in deposition.*
>
> *In court, the jury is always sympathetic to the witness. If an attorney absolutely hammers them, the jury will not like it. The attorney has to be careful. In this way, the deposition can be "harder" than court. In court, it is a more formal situation. You are dressed up, in a courtroom with a judge. It should be an impressive and significant event. But regarding the behavior of the attorney, you won't see the type of behavior you occasionally see during depositions. Some attorneys are known for trying to tear the testimony of psychology experts apart, but those attorneys are not brought into trial. There are "hatchet" attorneys who are brought in to cases to try to break the psychologists during depositions.*

Christopher Grote notes that much of the hammering, emotionally intense, or even rude behavior at deposition may be a show put on for the benefit of clients who will later read the deposition and be reassured that they have hired sufficiently muscular attorneys:

During some depositions, there can be a fair amount of gamesmanship and posturing going on. Some of it may be for the benefit of the client. If their client reads the transcript, they want to see that their attorney is doing their best to shake up the expert.

One time, I was retained by the defense. There were four or five defense attorneys representing various parties in the lawsuit, all from prestigious firms. The plaintiff's attorney was by himself. During the deposition, the defense attorneys were really going after the plaintiff attorney, with it escalating to yelling and table-thumping. They really seemed angry, but after the deposition they went off record to joke with one another and looked forward to seeing one another that weekend at a social event. I don't know how often that happens, but in at least that case the "rancor" seemed to be a bit of a put-on. I remind myself of this because it can help to keep me calm and not to get emotionally caught up in situations that may seem like personalized attacks.

David Hartman agrees that attacks are much more likely in depositions:

> In the courtroom, the judge has little tolerance for expert abuse. Not so in depositions. If you are really the subject of abuse, then I think that you have no choice but to say something. You can't be angry, and you can't be destabilized by attacks on you. Respond calmly and intentionally. Here is an example from a case I had:
>
> *Q: Doctor, let's just see what all of your bullshit opinions are going to be in this case.*
>
> *A: First of all, Counselor, that makes it difficult to respond to anything you might ask if you are going to pose that as the context. But the second thing I have to ask you, Counselor, is that I spent a considerable amount of time thinking about this case and preparing for this case. I have a set of opinions that were well worked out in this case. I would be happy to provide them. But I cannot provide them in an atmosphere of intimidation and insult. And I am going to give you the chance to help you understand the case and why I came to the conclusions that I did. But if you continue along this line, I am going to have this deposition temporarily halted for cause and we can address whether this is a line of questioning that is appropriate for you to pursue.*
>
> *The attorney replied*
>
> *Q:, "Don't tell me how to be a lawyer."*
>
> My answer was,
>
> *A: "Fine, start asking me questions the way a lawyer would ask questions."*
>
> *Q: I will bring this before the judge!*
>
> *A: I would appreciate that. I would be very interested in whether a judge would find this line of questioning, with insults and defamatory comments, would advance the understanding of this case.*
>
> *The last thing an attorney wants to do is annoy a judge.*

Dr. Hartman notes that some attorneys will try to use intimidation. He described a well-known case where one attorney was reported to have asked a mental health professional whether they had examined every single page of the clinical record, then threatened to have a fingerprint expert examine each page and take the expert to court for perjury if a print was not found.

Mike Chafetz points out that much of the bad behavior disappears from the record because the deposition transcript does not include social pragmatics like shouting, sneering, or sarcasm. He shares a strategy for halting some of the behavior:

> If an attorney is behaving badly at a deposition, yelling, etc., it may not be clear later when someone reads the deposition transcript. So it is important to get it on the transcript by describing the behavior.
>
> I was deposed for 8 hours by an attorney and then the deposition was continued. He tried the intimidation gambit of raising his voice when I disagreed with him. In a relaxed way, I pointed out for the record that while I understood while he might want to raise his voice, it was really unnecessary, as I could hear him just fine. The judge will see the transcript, and I can use it at trial if need be: *A:I can hear you just fine; you don't have to yell at me."*

Jerry Sweet also uses the strategy of commenting on extreme behavior in words during a deposition:

> *In many cases, the depositions feel abusive, but when you read the transcript, it looks very mild, like they did a professional job. Attorneys are likely to be way more professional in court.*
>
> *In one deposition, the attorney, mid-question, stood up, started yelling, threw his paper materials down on the table, and insisted that I had only said what I did in my report because I was hired by that guy over there [pointing to the retaining attorney] hired by the insurance company. I was astounded. None of this comes across in the transcript. Doesn't say he stood up. Doesn't say he yelled. Doesn't say anything about his emotional dyscontrol, just the literal words, which sounded very mild. Next time, I will say something in response that ensures that the behavior and tone get into the record.*

Mike Chafetz describes shaping a deposing attorney's behavior:

> *Once a deposing attorney tried what appeared to be an intimidation tactic by getting up from his chair, coming around to my side of the desk, and plopping his fat binder in front of me to show me pages. I told him a few times that all he has to do is hand me pages from his seat. At other times, he just got up and came to the side of my desk to ask me questions. Well, I decided to shape his behavior. Every time he did that, I'd turn my head to the empty chair and answer his questions to his empty chair. Thus, he could no longer see my face, and it was as if I was ignoring him when he was on*

the side of my desk. Eventually, he just sat in his chair and stopped getting up to ask questions.

DIFFERENCES IN TESTIFYING STYLE

Given the different goals and methods of attorneys during depositions, do experts use a different style of testimony when in deposition as opposed to the courtroom? Keith Yeates notes that he uses more technical language in depositions:

> *For deposition, there is a different style. You have more leeway than at trial. To give the other side a reason not to put you on the stand. In front of a jury, you have to keep your answers relatively brief and non-technical and compelling. In the deposition, they are trying to see if you can say things credibly, if they can catch you in contradicting yourself or doing something that can seem to take away your credibility. Most attorneys will have worked with a neuropsychology expert to help with the questions. They will see if you will go out on a limb to say things that are not credible. You have to know the case backwards and forwards.*

Ira Packer notes that in a deposition, his goal is not to educate the opposing side:

> *When I am on the stand I am very thoughtful about whether the judge and jury understand what I am saying. My role is an educator. This is not the case during a deposition. It is not my responsibility to educate you; it's my responsibility to answer your question. Recall that is the other side that deposes you. If a lawyer asks a bad question, you have to answer it, whether it is the lawyer retaining you or the opposing attorney. During prep for trial you can help attorneys know the right questions to ask. I don't feel any obligation to fix bad questions during a deposition.*

Dr. Packer also points out that the format of the deposition allows experts the luxury to take more time to formulate clear, measured answers:

> *On the stand people hate to take too much time. Often there is a feeling, "I have to answer right away." Sometimes a little thoughtfulness, even if it slows you down, is better, although long delays will be uncomfortable. In the deposition, because there is no rhythm that is detectable from the transcript (the transcriptionist does not write between a question and answer "one minute passed . . ."), you can think for a while, take extra time before making your point.*

Michael McCrea notes,

> *In terms of general principles, deposition testimony is the same: Know your scope, know your data, know your barometer, listen to when you are stepping beyond your scope. "I can't answer that question because it is beyond my scope." The attorneys might try to draw you off sides strategically, but it might be the natural-feeling*

extension of a dialogue. Avoid getting drawn in to statements like, "I am not a neuroradiologist, but . . ."

Ira Packer notes that there is no obligation to be as fully prepared for a deposition as you are for court:

> *With depositions, all that emerges is a dry transcript. A lot of the things we think about in terms of presentation style, a big part of live testimony, are irrelevant. In a deposition, it is much better to make sure that you are precise and accurate than to worry about the style. Also, it is much better to say, "I don't remember." If you are on the witness stand, if you don't know something or don't remember, it is unexpected; you are expected to have prepared. But with a deposition you are under no obligation to prepare in the same way. The other side is calling you. You are under no obligation to be as fully prepared. You can't deliberately withhold information you know, but at the same time I am not going to spend hours preparing for a deposition. If I am not sure of an answer, I will say: "At this point, without consulting with my notes, I don't recall specifically." Or "That is something where I would have to go through my records." That happens on the stand as well, and it is okay to say, "I don't recall," but the expectation is that you are prepared to testify in court, so it should not happen multiple times during court testimony.*

Keith Yeates also notes that experts need to feel comfortable referring back to their notes in the deposition: "Some of the attorneys will ask you what page of the medical record you are referring to. They want to see if they can get you flustered. I will just say, 'I could go back and find it for you. It will take a while.'"

Jacobus Donders notes that during a deposition, he will insist on being allowed to finish a thought:

> In a deposition, I have on occasion refused to answer a question where the attorney was interrupting me. In the case, the patient failed the TOMM. The attorney was trying to make the case that it had nothing to do with his brain injury.
>
> *A: This task can be done with children with hydrocephalus or people with schizophrenia.*
>
> *Q: Does my client have hydrocephalus!? Does my client have schizophrenia?!*
>
> *A: No. I am not done yet.*
>
> *Q: You have answered my question!!!*
>
> *A: I would like to finish my thought.*
>
> *Q: I'm asking the questions around here!*
>
> *A: Well, you have not allowed me to finish and I am not going to answer any further questions until you allow me to finish. And if you don't like that, we can call the judge and get a ruling on it. [We stared at each other for half a minute.]*

Q: Well, if you insist you need to give your long-winded speech.

A: No, I don't have to give a long-winded speech; I just need to finish my thought.

The attorney who hired me was just sitting back during the interaction. I was prepared to walk out. I couldn't care less. I have better things to do than pick a fight with someone. I am not going to let someone tell me what I can say, unless it is a judge.

BE SUCCINCT

Neil Pliskin notes that the last thing an expert wants to do during a deposition is to provide fodder for opposing counsel:

> *I learned early in my career that if I don't answer clearly and succinctly, if I pontificate for a few minutes instead, all I do is provide fodder for them to later go over, line by line. Then I am presented with a deposition I did 2 years ago. My style is to answer the questions very succinctly: yes, no, yes, correct, not correct, I can't answer that question with a yes or no.*

Nancy Hebben also notes that talking too much during a deposition gets you in trouble:

> *During depositions, the attorney likes you to go on and on. The more you go out there, the more likely you will give the attorney something to work with or something he/she doesn't know to ask. Just answer the question. Don't volunteer things. Don't give more. If they know enough to go there, let them go there. Don't volunteer. Answer the question that is in front of you. Don't give more, unless it is important to make a point. For example, if you are asked a question:*
>
> *Q: Well, neuropsychological assessments aren't useful in the area of concussion, are they?*
>
> *A: Well, if you are asking me if I can use neuropsychological tests to diagnose a concussion, I would say no. But they are useful in helping me understand what might be maintaining someone's symptoms . . .*

Ira K. Packer advises, "During live testimony, you don't want to talk too much because you will look verbose, and jurors lose interest. During a deposition, you don't want to talk too much because you are likely to stumble."

Tom Boll acknowledges that he should be succinct but notes, "It's hard to keep my mouth shut in deposition":

> *I usually testify in depositions like I testify in court. I give long answers and educate. Attorneys will ask you to have short and concise answers. Answer the question. Don't volunteer anything. Don't give a lecture. Don't try to educate them. It's up to them to find out what they need to know. It's not up to you to make up for their mistakes. If they don't get anything at deposition, that's their fault and they have nothing to work with at trial. If you give them a whole bunch of stuff, then they have even more to work with.*

> *I agree with all that. I don't not do that on purpose; I just can't keep my mouth shut. That said, there is no question that a strong deposition testimony may lead to a case settling. I get letters from attorneys like that all the time.*

PREPARING FOR DEPOSITIONS

David Williamson describes how he prepares for depositions:

> *To prepare, I will go through every line of the report to look for typos. I go through any references that will defend any point. Be able to talk about them fluently. Have my test manuals around. Know where everything is in case I need to pull something out. With the articles, I will make sure I have a literature trail, specific references that I can pull out or at least cite.*

> *I prepare regarding substantive issues. Is there impairment? What is the nature? Is it related to the purported injury? What basis do you have? Have you ruled out alternate conclusions? Regarding alternate conclusions, I always am thinking about that when I develop my formulation. I do this with my postdocs. Could this have happened without the injury? You are saying this is the injury; could this have happened without it?*—Keith Yeates, PhD, ABPP-CN

Dr. Yeates advises experts to be clear prior to a deposition about what you can and cannot say:

> *Long before you ever get to deposition, it is critical to be clear to the attorney what you can or cannot say. "There are too many potential competing explanations here. Yes, this kid had a concussion, but they also had encephalitis as a toddler, and a crappy home environment, and two brothers with ADHD. We just don't have a literature that justifies making a definitive statement."*

He also advises experts to ask themselves typical deposition questions: "Once you have been through many depositions, you have a good sense of what is typically asked. I try to ask myself those questions in advance, so I am prepared for questions that will likely come up."

SETTING TIME LIMITS

Many experts set time limits on depositions to protect their ability to engage in patient care the day of the deposition as well as to ensure that they are not mentally exhausted by the process and can reasonably answer questions with a clear head. One expert who preferred to have his name redacted explains, "In depositions, attorneys may want to depose you for 5, 6, 7, 8 hours, just to harass you and wear you down. I have a 3-hour limit. Anything beyond, we have to schedule for a different time."

Keith Yeates does the same thing:

> *I will set time limits on depositions. Any deposition over 3 hours, they are just fishing. They don't know what they are doing. They are asking the same questions over and over. I will say, "You have already asked that." Not in an annoyed way, but in a matter-of-fact way. The attorney that hires you, if they are good, will also say that.*

Mike Chafetz recognizes that it is hard for attorneys to gauge how long a deposition will take and therefore asks for a time commitment ahead of time. He will use a timer to help enforce the boundaries the parties had agreed to up front:

> *My terms are set for a half-day or a full-day. No one can tell me exactly how long a deposition will take. One attorney could be finished, then the other has some questions, then there could be follow-up. Because of that, I require a commitment for a half-day or full-day.*
>
> *In one case, after the alarm went off, an attorney said, "Dr. Chafetz, you have had a few bathroom breaks, so I get to use that time."*
>
> *"No, sir, we don't. We started 3 minutes early by my watch. And I took three bathroom breaks, at 1 minute each."*
>
> *"That's not what my watch says."*
>
> *"It doesn't matter. We are done."*

Dr. Chafetz advises experts,

> *You don't need to make excuses. Just say, there is no provision. You are contracted for a certain time. In one case, we had agreed to 5 hours. I didn't apologize; I didn't give a place where I had to be. It is contracted, and they know better.*
>
> *A: There is no provision for additional time.*

Be cautious about the materials you bring to a deposition. Keith Yeates notes,

> *I don't bring my file with data into the deposition. I don't do it because I don't consider it discoverable. The minute you bring it to the deposition, it's discoverable. I am not one of those people who hold on grimly to the data. I will want a court order. I have the report. I don't need the file in front of me.*

Tom Boll recalls that one attorney asked him to bring all of the books he used when forming his opinion: "I said, 'No. You want to buy them, fine. But I am not bringing you all of my books.'"

Even bathroom breaks can be at issue in a deposition. Mike Chafetz recalls,

> *I was in one contentious deposition where after about an hour and a half, the retaining attorney wanted a bathroom break. The deposing attorney said no*

bathroom breaks; he wasn't paying for it. After another 15 minutes, the retaining attorney said he had to go, and told me not to answer any other questions. I said it seemed like a good time for a bathroom break for me, too, and I just got up and left. The court reporter was so relieved! She promptly got up to use the bathroom, too.

QUESTIONS FOR/ABOUT OTHER CASES

There are times during a deposition when experts are asked questions that have little or nothing to do with the case at hand and the thought occurs, "Is this attorney asking me questions to get an opinion on the record for a different case?" The answer may well be "yes." In my own practice, an attorney opened his deposition with 15 minutes of questions about third-party observers. There was no such issue in the case at hand. I realized 5 minutes into it that he was asking me questions for another case where those questions were germane.

Jerry Sweet notes,

> I have had attorneys in a deposition about Plaintiff A ask questions that clearly do not relate to Plaintiff A but rather relate to another case. The attorney may be trying to get information that will help with another case, or perhaps the attorney is trying to undercut my position in another case. In the moment when I realize that is happening, I try not to go too far afield:
>
> *A: I can't imagine this has anything to do with this case. Let me say why (and then wait).*
>
> I do not want to be manipulated, and I specifically do not want to have a quote taken out of context that would misrepresent my opinion. On the other hand, I literally have nothing to hide. If the facts of the case warrant, I intend to render the same opinion. In trying to be consistent, I use the same techniques and rely on the same literature. I don't feel like I need to protect myself in that regard. But I definitely want to try not to be manipulated and deceived. It is like they are getting a free expert opinion if they can use deposition questions to impeach experts in another case. I have to imagine that judges would frown on such behavior if brought to their attention.

Dr. Sweet also recalls a deposition where the attorney engaged in a vigorous set of cross-examination questions for a normal MMPI-2 FBS scale:

> *It was so striking to me that he was going on and on about a normal FBS scale. At the end of the deposition, once we were off the record, I asked him, "What was all of that about the MMPI? You asked me a lot of questions that turned out to be more hurtful to your client in many ways. And that business about the Lie scale. I didn't say she was lying! In fact, she had a 0 on the Lie scale." He says, "I can't tell you my trial hypothesis, but let's just say it might not have been related to this case."*

Michael Chafetz notes that attorneys will ask experts questions about previous cases, so experts need to be prepared to set boundaries regarding how much information is appropriate to disclose:

> Attorneys may engage in a line of questioning about my previous cases. One started asking me details from my court-deposition record, with details about the examinees:
>
> *A: It is not appropriate to discuss cases about which I don't even know the disposition.*
>
> *Q: If you refuse to answer, I am going to call the judge.*
>
> *A: Good idea. I want you to call the judge, because this does not sound right to me.*
>
> *So he called the judge. I didn't get to speak to the judge, but he and the retaining attorney discussed the issues, with the retaining attorney giving my objections. The judge agreed with me with the retaining attorney, and so the deposing attorney was then limited to listing the cases by number and finding out only my diagnosis. The thing is, if all he wanted to do was examine whether I'm biased (which is legitimate), he could have examined in the limited way the judge ordered and saved a lot of time.*

VIDEOTAPED DEPOSITIONS VERSUS VIDEOTAPED TESTIMONY

Some depositions are videotaped. The video will not be shown to the jury. This is different from videotaped testimony, which will be shown to the jury. The difference between these two is important. Ira Packer notes that with video deposition, if it is shown to the jury, "that changes everything":

> *If it is only for the attorneys to look at, then the same issues for typical transcribed depositions would apply. If it is for the trial, then the expert needs to proceed like s/he is in front of a jury. I would want to find out ahead of time if this going to be shown.*

FINALLY, HOME TURF

Kristie Nies offers a comforting perspective on deposition testimony:

> *The courtroom can be intimidating. I have not been in enough of them to ever really get comfortable. The depositions are usually in my office building. I have more control over the circumstances and I can take a break whenever I need to. It's my turf, not the attorneys'.*

19 Preparation for Court and Managing Anxiety on the Stand

You get a certain fearlessness because you've done it over and over, but your body doesn't know it. You can't tell your reptilian brain that this will be okay.—Lin-Manuel Miranda, creator of the Broadway play Hamilton, *on his experience with freestyle rapping*[1]

Even reading a book about testifying in court can activate our reptilian fear response. We know from social facilitation theory[2] that a certain amount of anxiety for a task we feel competent in will result in better performance of that task. Get those butterflies flying in formation! Change stage fright into stage enthusiasm and stage excitement![3] But for a task that we haven't yet mastered or engage in only rarely, anxiety can dampen our performance. This chapter offers frames and strategies for managing anxiety on the stand so our expert opinions, not our anxiety, will be the focus of attention.

Many experts that I interviewed, like Ira Packer, make the important point that techniques for managing anxiety on the stand begin with the premise that experts walk into the courtroom having first done competent work and took the time to be well prepared: "All of these are techniques to manage anxiety assuming you have done a good job. If you haven't done a good job, you should be nervous." Or as a judge who preferred to remain anonymous stated, "Style and strategy help—but substance trumps all." Strong preparation figured so prominently in so many interviewees' advice for managing anxiety in the courtroom that I have presented both topics side by side in this chapter. Preparation comes first.

PREPARE

David Shretlan makes a strong case for preparation. "For testimony to be compelling, you have to know the case inside out. Your formulation needs to be informed by the details in the narrative. The only way to do that is to really know the case. Who was the person? What they were like prior? How have they been affected since?" Greg Lee concurs:

> *You need to know your material backwards and forwards, like for an oral exam—your tests, reliability and validity, and any weaknesses in your conclusions. You have to be very prepared. Overprepared is a good word. Most of the time, the amount of preparation I've done leaves me feeling disappointed because the cross-examining attorney doesn't get to the crux of the weaknesses I was prepared to address in the material."*

What does strong preparation mean to seasoned forensic practitioners? This section covers materials to bring to the stand and offers a window into the pretrial routines of neuropsychologists.

Productive testimony begins at the initial case conceptualization

Many psychologists and neuropsychologists comment that the forensic work they do improves the quality of their practice in general. The voice of the cross-examining attorney in their head challenging diagnostic conclusions and recommendations compels them to use evidence-based practices and stay at the forefront of the research literature not just for their forensic cases but for every clinical encounter. Confident testimony flows naturally from this type of evidence-based, intellectually rigorous practice.

Writing my reports as if I am cross-examining myself

> *With every report I write, I have a cross-examining attorney in my head saying, "Why is this not true?" The skeptical researcher, skeptical parent, any skeptical voice is in my own head. I want to be the guy trying to make me look like a monkey in my own head first, so I can clarify my reasoning, I can anticipate answering/addressing those issues before I get into a deposition. I write the report to address the questions that I come up with in my head. With every report, I anticipate cross-examination questions. When I get to the stand, I have answers to questions I think I will be asked clearly, thoughtfully worked out.*—David Williamson, PhD, ABPP-CN

> *I like to have experts who are very academic in their approach, which means they are very meticulous and thorough in reviewing not just the data that's generated from the testing but also the tests that are used and the theory underlying the tests and the conclusions that are valid to draw from those tests.*
>
> *Some experts can be sloppy in their testing habits and in their thinking habits. Bad experts are not rigorous in their thinking habits—like they're selling a pizza and it's the same pizza every time, cheese, pepperoni, and mushrooms: here it is. And it is the same one over and over again. Well, the thing is that every person that they examine is different. It's like selling an off-the-rack suit and they don't care if the suit fits the person they are selling it to. The expert with the academic mindset is much more careful about taking measurements, using better-quality material, matching shirt with suit and tie.*—Wayne Miller, Esq.

I always assume every case I do will end up in court. I don't do anything different. From the moment a trainee or psychometrist starts, I talk with them about the importance of their handwritten notes. "What if this ends up in court? Do you think that comment is defensible?"—Lisa Stanford, PhD, ABPP-CN

Pretrial conferences

Chapter 3, "Relationship with the Attorney," makes a strong argument for insisting that the attorney who brought you to the case engage in pretrial preparation to ensure that you're aware of the key issues in the case, that you understand the dynamics of the judge's and other attorney's personalities, that you've planned the flow of your direct testimony, that you've acknowledged weaknesses in your testimony and planned to inoculate against them by bringing them up on direct, and that you're aware of likely cross-examination topics. Please see Chapter 3 for a discussion of this important aspect of trial preparation.

Read your deposition prior to trial

If a deposition is taken prior to trial, an important part of trial preparation is to read your own testimony. Robert Heilbronner notes, "It is very important to read your own deposition prior to testifying at trial or doing an evidence deposition. It is important to be familiar with your own opinions. You don't want to contradict or impeach yourself." The questions you were asked during deposition give important clues about what you might be asked during cross examination:

Really read the deposition transcript carefully. In anticipation of your courtroom testimony-during the deposition attorneys are trying to figure out what kind of weakness you have. Therefore, re-reading the deposition will give you clues as to what the cross-examination questions will be in court.—Anonymous

Rehearsing

To rehearse or not to rehearse? Different experts have different philosophies.

There is a famous line from Thomas Jefferson, apologizing that he was rushed when writing a letter, and therefore the letter was five pages long: "Had I had more time, it would have been three." Juries do not want to listen to experts ramble; they would prefer the three-page letter to the five. This is the rationale for rehearsing direct testimony as a way of shortening your explanation. Almost always, after you rehearse your response, it will be more streamlined and clear. A tangent you went off on the first time might have taken you nowhere, and you can avoid it in court. Not rote memorization but mental rehearsal leading to concise, elegant explanations.

Scott Millis a proponent of rehearsing,

I am a big advocate of mentally rehearsing what I am going to say. Doing mental rehearsal works for me to take out the anxiety and think more effectively on my feet. For example, I would focus on what I feel might be the weak points of the case, then come up with anticipated criticisms of my conclusions, and to have a response ready to go.

Another benefit of rehearsing answers to questions we expect to be asked on the stand is the opportunity to listen for jargon, embedded assumptions, unnecessary statistical references and other elements of an inaccessible academic communication style creeping into our answers. As noted in earlier chapters, creating vivid, engaging, accessible testimony takes conscious effort. What if we listened to ourselves, asked "How can I make that more accessible?" and then gave our answer another try?

That said, attorney Mark DeBofsky warns that too much practice in testimony can take the emotion out of testimony:

> *I had a terrible experience with a witness. The first time I heard her story, I cried. By the time she got on the stand, it was the third time she told her story. The story had lost its emotion. I tend to be more minimalist in preparing witnesses. I say, "These are the areas I want to cover, here are the potential problems, how would you respond?" Other people have very different opinions about that; they feel that every question needs to be practiced.*

Lisa Stanford comments,

> *I do not like to know the questions ahead of time because I am much better spontaneous. I don't like the attorney to send me a list of questions; you worry too much about what you are going to say. If it is based naturally on your practice knowledge, you are much better able to connect and establish your relationship.*

Not being overrehearsed leads to emotional trust with juries

> *You have to connect with the jury at an emotional level. To do that, you have to be nondefensive. The expert is there to give jurors the information they need so that they can make the decisions they need to make. Smile. Laugh. Be genuine.*
>
> *My wife will ask me, "What do you plan to say?" I say, "I don't know." I have no idea what I am going to do going in. It depends what questions are being asked. Some attorneys like to prep you. I will say, "I am okay with that, and I will give you some of the questions that I would ask if I were you. But I don't want to overprepare, because this has to be spontaneous. This has to feel like you are asking me questions and I am trying to answer them for the jury." With my approach, I will end up driving home from the trial or deposition wishing I had said something a little bit differently or wishing I hadn't said that. But to me it is the tradeoff between getting your exact phrasing correct versus appearing genuine and spontaneous. To me, the genuineness and spontaneity is more important, because it is really not the facts that are going to convince a jury; it is the emotional trust that they have in you.*—Rodney Vanderploeg, PhD, ABPP-CN

I overprepare but I don't overrehearse

> *When I prepare my testimony, I overprepare but I don't overrehearse. I don't want to sound like I am using canned or rehearsed phrases. I have identified the main points that I want to make and ways to make the points.*—David Williamson, PhD, ABPP-CN

Mock cross examination

In some cases, where funds are available, attorneys might prepare experts for testimony by engaging in a mock cross examination. Brian Pomerantz notes that he will ask a colleague to tear his expert witness apart in the comfort of their office so that when they are under the lights in the courtroom they will feel well prepared.

Judge Christina Harms counsels experts to ask the attorney who hired them to practice the cross examination:

> *If you're going to be an expert and therefore you know that somebody is going to come after you on cross, then insist that you be well prepared. If you don't think that the lawyer who hired you is going to do that well enough, get another lawyer friend to practice with you. Practice the cross examinations, because any good lawyer, once they have read what you are going to testify to, or read your report, sees where the cross is going to go or at least sees most of where the cross is going to go—so practice. Literally, have someone sit with you and hammer at you a little bit so that you can think about your answers, find the discomfort spots, and address them.*
>
> *We practice like crazy before we let our postdocs testify. I cross-examine, and I have said to people who have taken other classes from me, "You can hire me and I will do it with you. I can read your report and I can practice for an hour and you will feel a lot better after that because you will expect some of these questions."*

Consultation

One of the most gratifying aspects of my forensic practice is regular meetings with a group of forensic colleagues. One of our first meetings was in a Boston hotel in midafternoon. We eventually had to stop meeting in the afternoon as we would become so engrossed discussing the field we love that we were losing too many patient hours. These days we meet in the evenings. My experience has been that group forensic consultation is invaluable. My colleagues will bring up alternative points of view in complicated cases, so I have confidence that my opinions cases are clear, well-founded and therefore bullet proof by the time I get to the stand.

One neuropsychologist who preferred to remain anonymous likewise finds consulting with colleagues an important part of his forensic practice:

> *It is important to have some collegial consultation and supervision. In our practice we often run cases by each other. We will try to play devil's advocate. We will look at alternative points of view, different explanations. This is invaluable for developing our initial opinions and in preparing for trial.*

Bring materials with you

Attorney W. Scott Liebert reminds experts that they can bring notes on the stand:

> *People are always worried: when I am on the stand, I am afraid I won't remember the examinees name or even my name! You can bring your records. You can also bring your own notes. You can make a chronology. But you need to know that if you*

have a piece of paper that you are referring to, the other side has a right to ask to see it. I don't think there is a downside to bringing notes, as long as you know that the notes you brought you will likely have to share. If you are the type of person who knows it would help you organize your thinking, then it is a good idea. Be careful, though. I had a psychologist use the initials VHB to refer to "vile human being" in their notes, they were asked on the stand to translate.

Using a notebook on the stand

Ted Blau was a forensic psychologist in Florida who sold one of the first forensic notebooks. He put together a loose-leaf notebook that could be helpful in forensic testimony. In my early days testifying I would bring a notebook on the stand. It would typically contain seminal articles—back in those days Dikman's early work on TBI, the dose–response relationship, a famous 1995 paper that provided stratified normative data tables on trauma controls and different degrees of TBI, stratified by test. If I testified, "The plaintiff had no loss of consciousness and yet they are performing as badly on trails as somebody who has been in 30 days in coma," I could reach for the article and then have it entered in as evidence. In the early days, I erred on bringing too many articles. The cross-examining attorney can mess with you and insist on having all of it entered as evidence, though. It is important to be selective.—Scott Millis, PhD, ABPP-CN

Three-ring binder for the stand

I always carry a three-ring binder into the courtroom in which I have a Xerox of the instructions for each of the tests administered. The attorney might try to ask you tricky questions about how tests were administered. We use technicians in our practice. And we have well-trained and supervised technicians who have the same three-ring binder. No instructions are ever given from memory. If necessary, if there is a question about how a test was administered, I can answer that question. Also, sometimes attorneys will misrepresent to the jury how a test is given. When the jury sees that you are prepared to discuss test instructions, they will also see that when your office gives the tests, you and/or your technicians are prepared. I have never had anyone grab it and try to admit it into evidence, but even if it was, there is nothing in there that gives items/questions away.

Q: Doctor, what are the directions for how the x test is administered?

A: I don't provide test instructions from memory in my clinical practice. All directions are literally read to patients, so the directions are always the same, and accurate. Here are the instructions that would have been read, per my training with my technicians.—Ted Peck, PhD, ABPP-CN

What I bring on the stand

Be prepared. When I go to court, I have a roller bag of patient records but also research articles. On breaks I reread the articles. I will bring the AACN consensus statement on detection of malingering, AACN practice guidelines, and validation

studies for tests I have used in the exam. I bring either the meta-analyses about outcome from concussion or a book that includes them.—Kyle Boone, PhD, ABPP-CN

Thorough preparation

Preparation is the most important thing. I could have a bad day on the stand and not say everything I meant to. I could have not said something a certain way I would have wanted to. If I go in prepared, I go in with a much better chance of doing my job well. I prepare to the point where I know that I don't bill as much for my prep time as I put in. If attorneys saw how much I prepared they would not be able to afford me. I reread everything. There is nothing I do not read: police reports, past testing reports . . . I reread and catalog it. I tab it. I prepare a casebook, a binder that I bring with me. It helps organize my thinking. It helps slow me down. You have so many facts, so much data. If you organize it, it helps compartmentalize it in a way that helps you be clear on the stand. You can think of, "Oh, that yellow-tab section; that's the one I want to bring up now."—Robert Mendoza, PsyD

Concrete preparation strategies

What concretely do experts do to prepare for court? Here is a window into the minds of experts who testify on a regular basis. David Williamson, PhD, ABPP-CN, acknowledges that he overprepares for testimony: "I go through my reports and look for scoring errors and small typos. I reread any references so I can defend any point I have made in my report. I have test manuals handy. I review the literature."

Definitely preparation is important. Sometimes there are big-name researchers testifying on the other side in a case. This is their expertise, but a lot of times they don't have the time to go through the case in detail. They just say something in general, "Well, yes, this person seems to be . . ." They put 5 hours into it, whereas I put in 20-something hours.—Daryl Fujii, PhD, ABPP-CN

Be very thorough. Read everything.

There will be times when you are put on the ropes under oath and punched hard. And once opposing counsel knows they have found a point of weakness, the punches will continue with increasing intensity. Early in my career, this type of experience taught me a very important lesson: Be very thorough. Read everything in the file carefully prior to trial.

Many years ago, I had a technician working with me who had a habit of writing very extensive behavioral notes. The behavioral notes were all too frequently more an expression of her feelings about a patient rather than an objective description of behavior. In the case that put me on the ropes, the technician had written a four-page, single-spaced narrative about a child I had evaluated. I didn't read everything she wrote in her narrative word for word because I generally did not perceive what she wrote as valuable behavioral information. Buried in those four pages was an important observation that the child may have peeked from under the blindfold during the Tactual Performance Test. Part of my opinion was based on the child's very normal TPT performance. I was testifying in front of an arbitration panel at the request of the defense. On cross:

Q: Would you please open your file? Look at this. Would you please read this passage?

He had me on the ropes. I felt speechless. I felt so flummoxed that I had difficulty recovering in a way that allowed me to feel good about the rest of my testimony. Thankfully I was a fact witness rather than a retained expert. The defense's expert testified after me. She helped clean up the mess that I had participated in creating by not carefully reading everything in my file. I've never made that mistake again.—Paul L. Craig, PhD, ABPP-CN

Be very confident about your data prior to trial

I do my testing and I have a grad student or postdoctoral fellow score it. Then the scores are double-checked by another grad student or postdoctoral fellow. And then the scores are triple-checked by another person from our group. Anyone wants to come behind me and replicate my data can do so. I am confident about my data and methodology. The only thing that is disputable is my interpretation.—Antonio E. Puente, PhD

Hire an expert to help you prepare

Attorney W. Scott Liebert notes that part of his legal practice is prepping psychologists to go into court. Interestingly, he notes that a psychologist or neuropsychologist who is called to testify as a treating expert (fact witness) may be able to ask their malpractice insurance carrier to pay for a consultation with an attorney who will guide them through the ethical aspects of testifying.

> *Part of my practice is working with psychologists helping prepare them to go into court when they have been subpoenaed and want advice about how to deal with issues when they are called to testify. Their malpractice insurance may give them some benefit when they get involved in litigation. They go to the APA Insurance Trust and say, "I have been asked to testify; I want to be sure that I don't end up with a complaint. Can I get prophylactic legal advice?"*

Visit the courtroom

A judge who preferred to remain anonymous counsels experts to visit the courtroom prior to the day of testimony: "Find out where you will sit and where you will testify. The kinesthetic experience of being in the courtroom is important before finding yourself talking about complicated issues under pressure."

In addition to a general sense of familiarity, another rationale for visiting the courtroom if possible prior to your testimony is that the specific layout of the courtroom can affect testimony.

> *Many courtrooms are totally different and the physical layouts can have an impact on how you testify. There are some stands where you are isolated. The judge is 20 feet above you. It is a courtroom made to intensify a cross examination. There are other kinds of smaller-town courtrooms where it feels like the furniture from your own home is there. One of the jurors' chairs is broken and they wheeled in a chair from the second floor. Some courtrooms are configured in a way that may increase anxiety. Imagine the federal courthouse in Denver. When you walk in the judge is elevated. There are black, sleek flat screens on most walls. During your presentation, your face is blown up on a screen. The way the acoustics operate, you can hear the prosecutor walking across the floor as they cross-examine you. You are kept in a seclusion room that is airtight. Prior to testifying you are escorted by federal guards into the courtroom. This is very different from the smaller-town court. You are hanging out with folks watching testimony prior to your testimony; everyone is at the same level with eye contact.*—Anonymous

ADDRESSING ANXIETY

In the context of excellent preparation, what are some strategies to lower our heart rates on the stand?

Be there for the jurors

As noted in Chapter 1, improv exercises help experts learn to shift the focus of our communication from "me" to "you." When that happens, terror/stage fright begins to disappear. Rather than "Am I going to make a mistake?" or "How do I sound?" the focus shifts to "What do the jurors need from me to do their job?" and "How can I help them?"

In my own practice, I find that focusing on the jurors and what they need from me to do their job in the courtroom naturally keeps my anxiety at bay. Asking the attorney during our pretrial conference to tell me about each juror's background helps me begin testimony feeling immediately focused on the jurors' needs and not my own.

Stay within your scope

Michael McCrea focuses on staying within your scope of practice as the foundation for combating anxiety on the stand:

> *You need to be relaxed and comfortable in presenting your testimony. For me, that has to do with a lot of things. You have to have a strong understanding of your scope of expertise and not wander outside it. And don't offer opinions that go beyond the data. Don't go out on thin ice. If you can maintain that approach—honesty and integrity and recognizing the boundaries of your scope and conclusions that are justified by the data—then you should be very comfortable on the stand.*

I was recently in India and learned about a Hindu concept, sattva, that mirrors Dr. McCrea's position. My understanding is that sattva is an ideal state of letting go of attachment to a desired object. When we desire something, we become anxious about losing it. Ironically, as a result of being less attached to that desire, we enjoy the object more fully. Attachment to "winning" or having our opinion prevail in a trial may pull us off sides: lead us to step beyond our scope of expertise or overstate the science. Without attachment to the outcome, we can feel comfortable staying firmly within our scope of expertise and enjoy the process of sharing that expertise in the case. Another way to put this is that the attachment to "winning" on the stand replaces our natural enjoyment of sharing our knowledge with anxiety.

Daryl Fujii shares a similar philosophy: "An important aspect of managing anxiety is perspective. The goal is to provide the facts; the goal is not to win. Control what you can, prepare, work hard. That's all you can do."

Reframe your anxiety

Ira Packer wisely notes that the goal is not "no anxiety" but manageable anxiety:

> *The recommendation, "Don't be nervous!" is crazy. I have anxiety every time I testify, and I have been testifying for 36 years. A little anxiety is good. We know from the research about performance curves that your highest performance is when you are up a bit on the anxiety curve. The goal is not to have no anxiety. But if you are feeling too anxious, use whatever techniques you need to bring you down.*

Darcy Cox describes the pep talk she gives herself:

> *I have an internal pep talk: "Bring it!" The truth is that you know more about the person you've examined, and the brain, and the science of cognition, than even the best-educated lawyers. In most cases it is really about educating the Court, particularly when it is a jury trial. You are in a teaching role.*

Darcy Cox describes an internal pep talk she gives herself. After hearing this, Dr. Cox's voice saying, "Bring it!" is now in my head prior to testimony.

> *I have an internal pep talk. "Bring it!" The truth is that you know more about the person you've examined, and the brain, and the science of cognition than even the best-educated lawyers. In most cases it is really about educating the Court. Particularly when it is a jury trial. You are in a teaching role.*

Dr. Cox also notes, "Adrenaline is a plus, not a minus. Remember your Yerkes-Dodson law and the U-shaped anxiety curve. A little anxious arousal is good for you and keeps you sharpest and thinking most quickly."

Anxiety helps me on the stand

> *For me the anxiety probably helps me. It helps rein in my excitement, enthusiasm. It makes me be more careful about what I say. When you are testifying, you own every word you say. If you didn't say exactly what you meant, it becomes complicated. When I am teaching, naturally the excitement bubbles out of me when I am on a*

> *roll. Anxiety on the stand helps temper this tendency.*—Robert L. Denney, PsyD, ABPP-CN, FP

More strategies for maintaining calm

Nat Nelson notes,

> *Depositions can feel anxiety-provoking, lonely, isolating, and "on the spot." Here is one strategy that I have found helpful in maintaining calm when providing testimony: I bring to mind the many experts whose research and writings I have relied upon to guide my work. By focusing on the works of the Manny Greiffensteins, Kyle Boones, Jerry Sweets, and Glenn Larrabees of the world, I recall that I am not, in fact, alone in this cantankerous process. If, on cross examination, an attorney takes issue with what I am saying, it is helpful to remember that it is not only me who is saying it, but those who have gone before me as well.*

A judge who preferred to remain anonymous describes her own experience with anxiety as an attorney:

> *I started out in federal court in front of judges who terrified me. Before trials started, I was so afraid that I would literally shake. I used to go into the bathroom and do jumping jacks before I had to do an opening statement. I was that nervous. To figure out how to treat this problem, I read a lot about how opera singers overcome stage fright. It turns out that opera singers often suffer from stage fright. The treatment is all about breathing. When you are shallow breathing, which is what we do when we are nervous, we don't exhale all the carbon dioxide from our lungs, so it builds up, which makes us feel sweaty and shaky and slightly sick. I began to do something that nobody can see. Breathe in deeply through your nose and then exhale all the way out: deep breaths in and deep breaths out. You can do this without moving your face so nobody really knows you're doing it. You can get control of that carbon dioxide buildup and feel normal again.*
>
> *This really helped me. I did it in court and nobody could tell I was doing it. By the time I finished five or ten of these deep breaths, I felt, "Okay, I can do this."*

Specific anxiety-reducing techniques

In my own practice, running has always been my secret weapon. After a run I feel calm, mentally nimble, and "on." I highly recommend taking a run or 40 minutes of whatever aerobic activity you like to do on the morning of the trial. We all know from neuroscience research that aerobic exercise results in an immediate activation of the frontal executive network, with a halo effect lasting several hours. With one's frontal executive network working faster, stronger, and better, we are better able to manage anxiety and have better focus and better inhibition of unhelpful, rambling responses.

Nick Bogod notes,

Once I am on the stand, I calm down. I am locked in and can't avoid it any longer. Then on cross, I feel a surge of anxiety again, for about 10 minutes. On cross, they usually start with lowball questions. I will use that time to breathe, compose myself, answer questions very gently, show composure.

Bernice Marcopulos practices meditation in order to manage anxiety:

I try to practice meditation and yoga. I am not very good at it, but I get credit for trying. I had a very, very stressful 2 full days of testimony in federal court. It was 9 a.m. to 5 p.m. on the first day for direct and 9 a.m. to 5 p.m. on the second day for cross. I think what helped me is I took a Zen Buddhist approach. In my mind, I had my hands in prayer position and namaste'd everyone.

Dr. Marcopulos notes that she uses mindfulness to combat anxiety on the stand:

1. *Focus on a minor physical sensation of your hand resting on the podium. Be aware of your hand resting on the podium so you're not focused on "Oh, my God! How do I breathe and talk and think!"*
2. *Acceptance. Don't try to control anxiety. Rather than think, "Oh, my God! I have to stop doing this!" When my heart starts pounding I think, "Oh, okay, that's what I do. My heart pounds. I am short of breath before I talk. Yeah, I do that."*
3. *Be aware of everyone else's potential mental state. Get out of your own belly button. "I am sure I am not the only stressed-out person in this room. I can wish everyone to be at peace."*

One neuropsychologists who preferred to remain anonymous recommends the mindfulness technique of a body scan.

I do a body scan as a relaxation exercise. Are my shoulders around my ears?

Ira Packer recommends a type of mindfulness: be self-aware.

I have never used formal mindfulness techniques, but my advice is "be self-aware." To the extent that you are present in the moment, and aware of what your anxious behaviors are, you can correct them. To the extent that you are present in the moment, and aware of what your anxious behaviors are, you can correct them.

Jacobus Donders similarly recommends self-monitoring in the courtroom:

Most interactions with attorneys are cordial, but they can be blunt, and they need to work up a vigorous case. There is 10 to 15% where I feel it is a little uncomfortable, and 5% where they are downright nasty. My position is to not respond by getting irritated. When I hear my voice getting louder, that is my cue to turn it down a little, because that is probably what they want.

Mike Chafetz suggests inoculating yourself to intimidation by remembering that the language of the court may sound worse than it is:

> *During my last Daubert hearing, the motion in limine for the hearing was threatening and intimidating, with the U.S. Government coming into court set to prove the "alleged expert," Dr. Michael Chafetz, could not prove what he was trying to say. Do not be intimidated by this legal language. It is nothing personal, and it does not change anything.*

One neuropsychologist who prefers to remain anonymous notes that he reminds himself that he should feel comfortable, because he has done his job as a psychologist right:

> *If you do your job as a psychologist, you understand almost every aspect of the individual from their early birth, to how they were as a child, through how others view them as an adolescent, through the impact of the accident. It is the comprehensive view of the patient. You walk into that courtroom with more information than the defense or prosecution has. It allows you to be relaxed, because you know this person, you understand him, you can explain it six ways to Sunday. The others in the courtroom, the defense or prosecution attorney, may not have as in-depth a picture. You are unique in being able to take a question, look at it from three or four different ways, and present information that helps the jury better understand the person.*

He also recommends, "Arrive early. If you are running late, it exacerbates the nerves."

Finally, the really scary questions typically never materialize

Attorney Mark DeBofsky notes that because he is not nearly as trained as the neuropsychologists he cross-examines, it is very hard to get in the weeds with them; it is hard to argue technical details. This is also Nick Bogod's experience: The complex cross questions typically never come:

> *I always try to identify potential weak points in my opinion preparing for testimony, the points where I could have gone one way or the other and I decided on balance to go a certain way. I make sure I am prepared to address them in depth on cross, and I will get one question where I will say, "Ok, here it comes! Here is the buildup." But then the line of questioning doesn't come. I leave the stand feeling shocked that the opposing attorney was not prepped adequately by the other neuropsychologist. But over time I think you realize that everyone sees your opinion differently and the weak spots you identify yourself are often not the areas seen by others*

Anticipating a weakness in the data, many experts will prepare for hours to answer a series of blistering questions on cross about minutiae of test theory or subtleties of research literature. Attorneys, though, are typically not qualified in test/ measurement theory, so although they might have an initial question, they won't likely be able to pose follow-up questions. They often have ammunition for only one question.

Robert Heilbronner notes that he always prepares as if there is an equally trained neuropsychologist assisting the other side to develop cross-examination questions.

> *I always operate in every forensic case as if there is an equally or better trained neuropsychologist assisting the other side in cross-examining me. When I am being cross-examined and then the attorney doesn't follow up to the next logical question, I am surprised and say to myself, "I would have asked xxx . . ."*

Bernice Marcopulos notes that attorneys typically don't have enough background to go beyond the initial scary question:

> Attorneys may have questions fed to them by their experts, but they do not have the background to ask the multiple follow-up questions. That gives me comfort.
>
> *I was being crossed examined on PVTs and the question was,*
>
> *Q: Doctor, isn't it true that the more tests you give the more likely you will have a false positive? Isn't that true for PVTs?*
>
> *A: Oh, are you referring to the Monte Carlo simulation study?*
>
> *Q: Uh . . . uh . . .*

Keith Yeates notes that no attorney has ever gone after him on cross examination for psychometrics:

> *Q: Doctor, what is the standard error of the test?*
>
> *People get worried that they have to be on the stand with an encyclopedic knowledge of the psychometrics of the tests. That's not where testimony goes.*
>
> *I have never had an attorney go after me about psychometrics or standard errors. Because I know more than they do about it, I am not worried about them asking me, "What is the standard error for this test?" I am perfectly comfortable telling them, "I couldn't tell you off the top of my head. I can tell you where to find that information in the manual. And I can tell you what a standard error represents. I don't carry that information around in my head because I don't need to."*

The exception to this is capital cases involving intelligence testing, where expert witnesses can reasonably expect to face sophisticated questions regarding standardized testing. And of course, there are some extremely sophisticated attorneys who have made it their business to know as much about test development, norms, and application of population statistics in single cases as the best-prepared experts. It is therefore always best to be overprepared to answer pointed questions about test development and statistics and then be happily surprised when those questions are not asked.

NOTES

1. NPR interview, *Dinner Party Download,* February 11, 2017.
2. Zajonc, R. B. (1965). Social facilitation. *Science, 149*, 269–274.
3. Lucas, S. (2015). *The art of public speaking*, 12th ed. New York: McGraw-Hill.

20 Specific Testifying Situations

NONJURY, RECORDS REVIEWS, FACT WITNESSES, CAPITAL CASES

THIS CHAPTER OFFERS advice and strategies regarding specific testifying situations, including testifying in front of a judge rather than a jury, testifying about records reviews (when you haven't met the plaintiff), testifying as a fact witness, and testifying in capital cases.

DIFFERENCES BETWEEN TESTIFYING IN FRONT OF A JUDGE AND A JURY

In some legal contexts experts will be asked to present testimony to a judge rather than a jury. Are there differences in how experts should communicate their opinions when testifying in front of a judge? Most judges, attorneys, and experts who weighed in on this question noted that judges appreciate the same use of vivid, concise, jargon-free language that you ideally use with juries, but there are some differences.

Familiarity with your testimony and similar testimony

Attorney Sara Cohbra notes that one big difference between testifying in front of a judge and a jury is that the jury has generally not seen the expert's testimony in advance:

> *When an expert is testifying in front of a jury, generally the jury has not had any preview of what the testimony is going to be. The information will be completely new to a jury unless they have a mental health background. In contrast, when an expert is testifying in front of a judge, in some proceedings the judge will have been presented with the information ahead of time in the form of a declaration or a report. For example, in habeas corpus proceedings, we submit everything on paper first. The court*

evaluates the evidence presented to see if there is enough information to proceed. In those cases, the judge has usually read the expert's report or declaration before the expert testifies.

Therefore, experts are often in the position of reiterating information the judge is already aware of. For this reason, carefully planning your direct testimony with the attorney who brought you is necessary so that you are not annoying the judge by repeating information.

Jurors may be hearing about the profession of neuropsychology or about how schizophrenia is diagnosed for the first time in their lives. The judge not only has potentially already previewed the expert's testimony through the court filings, but this may be her 45th concussion case involving neuropsychological assessment or 80th capital case involving issues of intellectual disability. Recognize, but don't assume, that the judge may begin with a higher level of sophistication about your assessment methods than a juror.

A judge who preferred to remain anonymous notes that experts should find out who will be examining them (who the judge is) as part of their pretrial conference with the attorney: "You should talk to the attorney or consult Google to figure out which judge you are in front of. By the time a judge has been on the bench awhile, he or she has a reputation. You should know about it." Part of the information to ask the attorney during the pretrial conference is the judge's familiarity with, and attitude toward, neuropsychological or psychological assessment and the specific issue at hand. Attorney Cohbra notes that when the judge has already read the expert's report or declaration,

> *Often we get information ahead of time from the judge about what s/he is interested in about the expert's report or declaration, such as the issues about which the judge has questions, or what we think are the sticking points for the judge. Sometimes there are questions about the expert's prior work or expertise. We often have some information about that ahead of time, either from the judge, or from the responsive pleading from the opposing side. We have some understanding about how the issues are going to be narrowed. That makes it easier to assist the expert in communicating with the judge.*

Judges can ask questions during experts' testimony

A judge who preferred to remain anonymous notes that a significant benefit for the expert when testifying in front of a judge is the judge's ability to ask questions during the testimony. This provides important feedback for the expert, allowing her/him to directly understand the needs of the listener:

> *When there is no jury, the judge is more active in the fact-finding role in the sense of asking questions. As an expert, you know whether the judge is either understanding or not understanding a concept, and then you can target your testimony better. On the other hand, in front of a jury, an expert is flying blind. It is difficult to know who on the jury is understanding your testimony and who is not—and more importantly, why some jurors are not understanding the testimony. You have a really good GPS system with a judge because through her questions, the judge sends out*

signals . . . I get it, I don't get it, I get it. And you can address that; you have a much better chance of making yourself understood. And an expert's most important goal is to make himself or herself understood.

Darcy Cox notes that judges typically want to know what you know. When judges are the triers of fact, maybe because they can ask questions and engage directly with the witness, they appear to be more engaged with the process: "I enjoy Canadian courts and U.S. federal court. It is usually just a judge. And typically she or he will really want to know what you know, because that's what they need to make their decision. They are really motivated audiences."

Bernice Marcopulos notes that when judges are the triers of fact, they are active and at the center of the proceeding rather than passive recipients of information:

The last time I was in front of a judge it was an Atkins hearing (a hearing to determine whether the person is eligible for the death penalty or not, because he is mentally retarded). The judge in this case was very actively engaged in asking questions for both sides, and interrupting. I don't know if it is easier or harder, but it puts more structure in the testimony. If a judge asks a question, everyone better answer it.

Don't assume a judge knows your science, but don't patronize

Judge Burroughs asks experts and attorneys to explain it to her like she is smart but doesn't know rather than like she is an idiot:

Everyone thinks they know more than I do about whatever it is that we are talking about. At some level, they are right. It's not just the technical stuff; it's even areas of law that I don't know anything about. I just don't. I can't spend a week getting ready for a hearing and know more than people that have been practicing in that area of law for 10 or 20 years. It's a strange job. Everybody knows that they know more than I do; it's just a question of how they are going to present it. Over time I am less afraid of just asking about those things that I don't know or understand.

It's a good lawyer that can explain it to me in a way that I can understand it without being really heavy-handed about it. I am smart; it's just something I don't know, so explain it to me like I am smart and I don't know it rather than either like I am an idiot or with an "I can't believe you don't know this but I'll help you along" kind of attitude. Just tell me. Teach me what I need to know to make a good decision.

Judge Christina Harms advises experts to provide to judges the same type of foundational information they would provide for juries:

It should make no difference whether an expert is testifying in front of a judge or a jury, for two reasons. First, experts don't ever want to assume that the judge knows more than the jury would know—and experts should assume that the jury knows nothing about psychology. It may be that you actually know that this is a judge who knows more than the average Joe about psychology, but that doesn't matter for the appeals court. You have to have a record of what you told the judge. You can't just say, "I know you know that." So not only because it would kill you on appeal, but more because you never know what somebody doesn't know, you should assume that you need to explain things.

It was well known that as a judge I knew more than average judges about psychology. As an expert, you could assume that I kind of know about schizophrenia, but I might not know one very important fact about schizophrenia that is important to the case at hand. It is best to assume no knowledge. It's okay to go over the basics. If the jury is a little bored, that's the art of the jury trial. But if the judge is bored, the judge will say, "You know I know that, Counsel; can you move on?" And then that's where you will move on.

"Judge, I'd like to start with the basics. Depression is . . ." or "Antipsychotic drugs operate by . . ." I don't think that's condescending unless you have a condescending tone. And that would be a killer as a witness, so I advocate against condescending. But I wouldn't worry about it because if you start out in a nice humble way, "Judge, let me start with the basics," I don't think you will be condescending.

Bernice Marcopulos titrates the amount of detail she offers to the preference of the judge:

Judges are smart. Some judges ask really, really good questions. They are clearly trying to study and understand the matter and the nature of the neuropsychological testimony. Some are dismissive: "This is just one more expert." I tell judges as much detail as I think they want to hear. Judges can interrupt the flow of direct and cross exam by asking their own questions.

Rus Bauer notes that testimony in front of a judge can be like talking to physicians:

You can be a little bit more conceptual. You don't have to give so many personal examples. But in my experience, judges don't necessarily have a clear understanding about what psychology is as opposed to psychiatry. They might be impatient. And often they just want your diagnosis. I still start with bottom line. I will give brief background on a syndrome-like FAS. Not in the abstract, but I focus on the legal implications.

Ultimate opinions

Experts are typically tasked with providing the trier of fact (the judge or the jury) with information so that the trier of fact can make a decision about the main issue in the case. That is, the "ultimate opinion" is the opinion of the trier of fact, not the expert. Is this person guilty or innocent? Competent or incompetent? Legally insane? That said, Robert Kinscherff notes that some judges want experts to provide ultimate opinions. Others don't. It's important to understand what is being asked:

It is commonly the case that judges want opinions. Ultimate opinions. Competence to stand trial, for example. But some judges don't. Those say, "You give me an accurate portrayal of the strengths and weaknesses of this defendant, given the specific type of case they are facing, and I will tell you whether or not they are capable of standing trial. Because there is only one person in this court who gets to decide—and that is the judge, not a doctor." Sometimes they tell you up front. And sometimes they will tell you after you have submitted your report, "Your specific opinion on the ultimate issue is not required (or requested) here."

Judge Jay Blitzman comments on the issue of experts offering an ultimate opinion:

> *In most states, ultimate opinion testimony is accepted, but there is a spirited debate amongst judges on the issue. There is a growing school of thought that you should not allow the expert to go to that degree, to offer an ultimate opinion; that's for the fact-finder. When you ask the expert for an ultimate opinion you are conflating the medical and the moral/legal issues. Give me the risk factors, give me the information—but this is a judicial decision. When the science is a little softer to begin with, such as in probate and family court, "who is a better caretaker?" the opinion of the doctor becomes the ultimate opinion.*
>
> *I was in a lecture hall when Dr. Paul Appelbaum gave his 1998 presentation that was turned into the influential monograph "The Medicalization of Judicial Decision-Making,"[1] in which he warns against ultimate opinion testimony. When Appelbaum gave the address, I recall a judge in the audience shouting out, "What do you mean, the expert is not supposed to give an ultimate opinion?! Why do you think I referred the case to you!?"*

Dr. Kinscherff notes that if you are asked to give an ultimate opinion by the judge, it's important to do so in a way that doesn't make you seem biased:

> *Your Honor, whether the defendant is sufficiently capable to be competent to stand trial is not a clinical question; it is a social and moral question that is your decision alone.*
>
> *(If pressed): I will offer you my personal opinion, because there is no clinical basis on which I can render an opinion about how capable a defendant must be to reach a constitutional threshold of fundamental fairness. But I would have these concerns about this defendant in this case, and I would be inclined to find them (competent or not competent) in this case for the following reasons (fill in the blank).*

Rus Bauer notes that when he testifies about competency in front of a judge, he structures the testimony around the Florida state competency statue. If he is pushed to give an ultimate opinion, he can give his opinion about whether the examinee meets criteria for the statute:

> Can a person with fetal alcohol syndrome be impaired with his ability to tell right from wrong or to inhibit behavior? In Florida, competency to proceed is a seven-pronged statute. The person has to have a mental disease or defect, and then the disease or defect impairs one or more of the following six prongs. With

judges, I will structure my testimony around that statute. I start with Prong 1, then go to the next prong. I try at all costs to avoid testifying to the ultimate legal issue. In Melton's book "Psychological Evaluations for the Court,"[2] arguably the best single reference for this work, the authors argue strongly that psychologists have no business saying, "This person is incompetent or insane." I bend over backwards with the judge to stick to the statute. If they ask me,

Q: Is your summary that this person is incompetent to proceed?

I will say,

A: With all due respect, Your Honor, that is your decision to make because competency is a legal and not a mental health concept. But my judgment is that the mental status of the patient meets the majority of the prongs of the Florida state statute. (I still haven't said, "Yes, the person is incompetent.")

Some judges will still say,

Q: But okay! Incompetent or not?

If you obey the boundaries of your profession and you say to the judge, "Competency is a legal decision and I don't want to violate that," in most cases that hedging is never treated with contempt. If you frame it in a way that says, "I respect your professional capabilities within your boundaries and I am going to stay within mine," it usually works out well.

Be straightforward

Judge Burroughs cautions experts not to be obsequious:

When I am talking to experts directly, which sometimes I do, it will be something like, "You have to answer the question," or "Please don't answer the question until I've ruled on the objection." There are some experts who say, "Okay," which is great. Then there are some experts that are terribly obsequious, which I can't stand, and I don't think the jury can stand it either. I run a pretty informal courtroom. I try and empower the jurors. Because I want the experts to be talking to the jurors rather than to me, I don't think I am encouraging anyone to be obsequious to me. So if they are, I think it just looks a little smarmy.

For example, a lawyer will come up to an expert with something and they will look at me and they will say, "Oh, Your Honor, would you mind if I reached into my briefcase for another pen?" It's just kind of unctuous. If you want a pen, just look at me and say, "I can't reach my pen; do you mind?" And I'll say, "No." Similarly, calling me "Your Honor" every time an expert addresses me. Or, "I'm sure Your Honor knows . . ." Well, no, I don't, so cut the malarkey and worry less about making me feel smart and just tell me what I need to know. That's probably just a feeling that I want in my courtroom, so that might be different from room to room, but I don't think that the jurors like that unctuous smarminess. It's too much sales and not enough education.

TESTIFYING WHEN YOU HAVEN'T MET THE PLAINTIFF

"Doctor, how could you possibly have an opinion about my client when you have never met him?!" There are times when a psychologist or neuropsychologist is asked to testify based on a review of available records alone. It could be that an IME was blocked by the plaintiff counsel. It could be that three other neuropsychologists conducted extensive batteries in the past 5 years, there are voluminous psychiatry and psychotherapy records, work records, educational records, deposition testimony of all of the relevant players in the plaintiff's life including the plaintiff, and the decision is made that no further assessment is necessary. This section of the Ethics Code addresses testifying when you haven't met the plaintiff.

APA Ethics Code section 9.01(c)[3] reads as follows:

> *(c) When psychologists conduct a record review or provide consultation or supervision and an individual examination is not warranted or necessary for the opinion, psychologists explain this and the sources of information on which they based their conclusions and recommendations.*

Kyle Boone notes that she always brings a copy of the APA Ethics Code with her onto the stand if she is testifying about a plaintiff she has not seen:

> *Q: Isn't it unethical to testify without seeing a patient?!*
>
> *A: No.*
>
> I will have a copy of the Ethics Code in my hand and can say,
>
> A: *Actually what the Ethics Code says . . ."*

Nancy Hebben notes that it is important to address the issue of not having seen the patient right up front, on direct:

> *I would take the opportunity to address the question on direct first. I would have defendant's attorney get it right out there that you did not see the person and why you did not. I would testify that testing had already been done twice and you had the reports and, more importantly, you had the raw data so it was not necessary to answer the questions you were asked to address by doing yet another exam. Instead, it was just like what you do when you supervise junior people. They do the testing and you examine the results and raw data to help them interpret the data and formulate answers to the questions being asked of them by the referral source. I would also use this opportunity to say neuropsychological testing is really not strictly necessary. If the question is, "Did the person sustain a concussion and did that injury resolve?" Of course it did, and after a month or two there are no neuropsychological findings that would/could be found on neuropsychological testing as a result of a concussion. What neuropsychological testing can do is help you find out why the person continues to complain: preexisting issues, poor effort, confounds from litigation or psychiatric issues, and so on.*

In my own practice, during the credentialing process I ask the attorney who brought me to the case ask me about instances in my regular clinical practice where I may not see patients but still feel confident diagnosing them:

> *Q: Doctor, are there times in your regular practice where you can diagnose a patient without seeing them in person?*
>
> *A: Yes. It is typical in my regular practice to have cases where I review medical records and see the data but don't see the patient myself. One of those situations is supervising students. The way we do that is they present cases to me, and I won't see the patients, but the students give me detailed information about their test behavior and we go over test scores and medical records. I also do that with junior neuropsychologists in the community where junior neuropsychologists come with cases for consultation. With those cases as well, I don't see the patients, but I hear detailed history, review medical records, hear behavioral observations. That's another situation where I feel confident in diagnosing without seeing the patients*

Greg Lee notes that cross-examining attorneys always seem incredulous: "How can you POSSIBLY come up with conclusions about patients you haven't seen?"

> *A: In fact, I do it with my colleagues all the time, as do most medical specialties. The data is the data and the history is the history. And those two things together pretty much, within a reasonable degree of certainty, are going to enable you to arrive at a conclusion that is rational and accurate. Seeing the patient does not change these things.*
>
> *I also give examples of other medical specialties*
>
> *A: The epileptologist doesn't administer EEGs or talk to the patient when the EEG is done; he just reads the test results and reaches his conclusion. The radiologist who oversees an MRI: He doesn't see the patient; the tech conducts the test. The radiologist just reads the films and comes up with an opinion.*
>
> The hesitancy I have is, I can't have eyes on how much a patient was in my subjective interpersonal experience fighting to do the task at the time that they did it. I wasn't actually present for the test presentation, so I am not 100% sure that they were giving their full, best efforts at it. But I do have performance validity testing to address that hesitancy. If we saw this person in my clinic, I might be a little bit more certain about my conclusions. But how much more certain? Only a small percentage.

> *Q: How can you diagnose someone without seeing them?*
>
> *A: It depends on what the diagnosis is. Can you diagnose a concussion without seeing someone? Sure you can; that's based on injury characteristics on the day of the accident. There are no neuropsychological tests that can diagnose concussion, and injury characteristics do not change no matter how many neuropsychological tests are done.*

Can you diagnose depression? Sure you can, if included in the raw data are measures of mood, which you then interpret in the context of the person's history. Are there some things you cannot diagnose? Absolutely, if you lack the underlying evidence for such diagnosis—but then you are not doing that, right? You are working with the data you have, the same data plaintiff's expert has and probably more data (given you have a more complete set of medicals) than any clinician who saw him clinically had on which to base their diagnosis and conclusions.—Nancy Hebben, PhD, ABPP-CN

How long did you meet with her?

I have testified in the past without having seen the child. In cross examination, the focus is often on that fact:

Q: How long did you meet with the child?

A: I did not meet with her. The two clinicians who already did long assessments knew their practice, and I felt they had done thorough evaluations.—Lynn Blackburn, PhD, ABPP-CN

Q: Doctor, how can you diagnose Ms. Patient without ever meeting her?!

A: I am in a far better position than anyone else who did an evaluation because I have had 10 years of records to review. Everyone else only saw her at one point in time and didn't have records before or after. I have 10 years of records that allow me to see what has happened over the course of time. No one else has had that advantage.—Rodney Vanderploeg, PhD, ABPP-CN

I have objective data from two neuropsychological evaluations. I will testify about what these test scores mean. And the scores may actually point to conclusions very different from those made by the original examiners.—Kyle Boone, PhD, ABPP-CN

Q: Wouldn't it be better if you saw the patient?

A: I was asked by attorney so-and-so to compare these two sets of reports. I am also commenting on the accident injury parameters. As I noted in my initial report, my opinions are based on record review. In this case I am comparing two sets of reports. Both neuropsychologists have completed thorough evaluations.—Leslie Rosenstein, PhD, ABPP-CN

Q: How can you have an opinion about Mr. Smith when you didn't evaluate him?

A: I was asked to testify about Dr. Jones's administration of the MMPI-2-RF, not Mr. Smith's specific case.—Yossef Ben-Porath, PhD, ABPP(clinical)

I haven't seen a patient in about 8 years. Most of my forensic work is consultative. I am comfortable testifying about someone else's evaluation if I think it is a good evaluation. I got accused once of being unethical from an attorney because of the old ethical standards. But it is like a physician evaluating an MRI. They will tell you if it is a lousy MRI; they can't make an interpretation of it. This is a good battery; I just happen to disagree with their conclusions. Or, this isn't a good battery; I don't know what to say.

If I am confident that there is enough good data about the patient, I will say,

Why subject them to another evaluation? There is nothing more I am going to be able to elicit on interview that is definiive here that I don't know. There is no value of laying on hands in this case. Physicians look at other people's MRIs and medical exams all the time without seeing the patients. Pathologists don't ever see the patient; they may not even see the tissue, just the slide. Radiologists don't see the patient, just the images. It's analogous to that."—Keith Yeates, PhD, ABPP-CN

Testifying when no one can see the patient

John McSweeny notes that on occasion he is asked to assess a person's cognitive status in a neuropsychological autopsy. That is, the person has died and his job is to determine what his cognitive status was prior to his death through a review of records. In cases like this, the outraged question, "How can you possibly claim to be able to diagnose this person without meeting them!?" may still be posed, but because the person has died, the idea that if you were more ethical you would have found a way to assess them in person would not be present. The same strategies to answer the question noted earlier would apply, although in many of the cases no neuropsychological or psychological assessment data are available. Experts must form opinions based on other indicators in the medical records and would need to qualify the limits that situation places on their opinions appropriately.

In some cases, the expert is asked to give an opinion about the cause of death.

In one particular case, I was asked to give an opinion on causality. This was a person that was involved with workman's compensation. A woman claimed that her husband died earlier due to the stress of an injury that he suffered on the job that caused him to be depressed. Her attorney had brought in a witness to say that there is a relationship between cardiac arrest and depression. The man was injured in the 1980s, treated for depression in the 1990s, and died in the early 2000s. His depression was treated successfully. There was a strong family history of heart disease and the person was a smoker throughout his adult life. There were no compelling data that suggested a link between successfully treated depression and cardiac arrest.—John McSweeney, JD, PhD, ABPP-CN

In other cases, the expert is asked to form an opinion about a person's competency prior to death. Questions might go something like,

Q: Do you agree that Ms. Smith was suffering from dementia?

Q: Would xyz be a sign that was consistent with dementia?

A: Yes. She had dementia. (Then wait for questions regarding the issue of capacity).—John McSweeny, JD, PhD, ABPP-CN

TESTIFYING AS A FACT WITNESS

One day a clinical psychologist or neuropsychologist who has been minding her own business, not seeking forensic work, might receive a subpoena asking her to testify in a deposition or hearing as a fact witness. Fact witnesses testify about their personal experience with the defendant/plaintiff—for example, what happened in the course of their assessment or treatment. Because psychology and neuropsychology fact witnesses also possess specialized knowledge, attorneys may attempt to blur lines and ask them their expert opinions about the case.

Leslie Rosenstein makes it clear to all parties involved that because she is testifying about her patient, she cannot be objective:

> Testifying as a fact witness is difficult. I will make it clear up front, to everybody, prior to the deposition or trial testimony starting that I am not providing expert testimony here. I will read from my report and refer back to it: "As you can see on this page, this is what I have said."
>
> *Q: Do you think Ms. Plaintiff has a head injury?*
>
> *Q: Are her symptoms caused by the head injury?*
>
> *A: I'm not here as an expert. I can't be objective. This was my patient. But, as you see on page 5 in my report I said . . . (if in my report I said this is a moderate TBI caused by the head injury)*
>
> ***I can't be objective Part II—fact witness***
>
> *As an example, I had a patient who had PTSD for good reason, but no TBI. I was being deposed in a case where their point was to get me to tie the PTSD to the incident. It was clear in my report, so I could say:*
>
> *A: As you can see this is what I said in my report. But, I can't be objective here today. This was my patient.*—Leslie Rosenstein, PhD, ABPP-CN

Fact witnesses must be aware that there may be evidence in medical or other records that is very different from the history provided by their patient. Using phrases like, "from the information I had available at the time of the assessment" can be helpful qualifiers. Ted Peck points out that treating clinicians may be relying entirely on their patient's self-report, and this sets up potential pitfalls when testifying: "When you are a fact witness, a treating neuropsychologist, you are often relying 100% on your patients' self-reported history, and there is no other indication that there is contradicting evidence on your very limited available records."

As noted in Chapter 15, "Cross Examination," attorneys may want expert witnesses to form new opinions while on the stand after providing new or contradictory information about the defendant/plaintiff. The resounding advice from experts was not to do so. Acknowledging that the new information may change their opinion is reasonable, but forming a new opinion on the fly rightly lowers your credibility. In a situation where you as a fact witness have not had access to the voluminous records typically available in a forensic case, it is very likely that new information will be presented to you as you testify: "Doctor, here is a new piece of information that you were not aware of according to your report. What is your opinion now?" Just as you would decline as an expert witness, it is wise to decline to form a new opinion in your role as a fact witness as well.

Protecting yourself as a potential future fact witness

Ted Peck suggests that clinicians protect themselves as future potential fact witnesses by always clearly informing their clinical patients about limitations in the assessment because of managed care restrictions:

> *Mental health managed care preauthorizations may significantly limit the number of hours you can see a patient and be paid, and therefore may limit the services you provide. That in turn affects your ability to offer testimony as a fact witness. You need to provide an explanation up front to patients that managed care limitations on services may have impacts on the ways that they can use the report. You also want them to sign a document that limits your liability.*
>
> *Let's say you have a managed care case where you requested 8 hours, the insurance company allowed 4 hours, and you gave the opportunity for the patient to pay for the extra 4 hours out of pocket or sign a waiver limiting your liability. Then you are called in as a fact witness. That clear consent process provides you with a professional level of protection. When you are asked a question at a deposition or in front of a judge, you can say you cannot answer that question, and you have a good foundation for why.*
>
> *Part 2. If you answer the question and say the memory test says there is an impairment, and then on cross examination you are asked a reasonable set of questions about, "Is this a memory problem, or is this an issue created by preexisting LD, current blood sugar level of 400, not taking meds, the result of PTSD, and what about sleep disorder? Did they not use their CPAP?" When you are saying, "I don't know and I don't know," the plaintiff you saw clinically may become angry with you when they see their vision of sugar plums dancing away into the distance, and they may want to file a complaint because you can't answer and are going to cost them a million dollars. You can explain that you wanted to do more to provide a thorough and defendable differential diagnosis but you were unable to because they chose not to pay privately for the time their insurance company refused (for which they pay premiums) for your service.*

Many clinicians experience "stealth forensic referrals." That is, rather than engage the services of a forensic expert, a litigant's attorney may direct them to seek a clinical neuropsychological or psychological assessment for the purpose of getting an opinion for their legal case. This may be done through the litigant directly calling the clinician's office or by the litigant asking their primary care physician or other specialty provider to refer them to a psychologist or neuropsychologist. In some cases, the individual will explain to the neuropsychologist how they came to seek an assessment, and a clear discussion can then be initiated to educate the litigant about the differences between clinical and forensic assessments and to clarify the relationships between the parties. For example, when the purpose of the assessment is forensic and not medical, third-party billing through insurance is typically not appropriate and a greater amount of time engaged in activities like reviewing medical records would need to occur. In other cases, it becomes clear that the clinical interaction was likely a "stealth forensic referral" only after your records have been subpoenaed immediately after a report is issued.

Cheryl Weinstein shares the practice of one of her colleagues, Nancy Moczynski, PhD, at Beth Israel Deaconess Medical Center in Boston:

> *Reports contain this statement:*
>
> *The results of this report are intended solely for the treatment and care of the consumer; the opinions contained in this report are NOT set forth as a forensic opinion with a reasonable degree of Neuropsychology certainty. Additional assessment, analysis, and record review would be necessary if forensic issues are to be addressed at a later time.*

TESTIFYING IN CAPITAL CASES

This next section addresses roles, values, and experiences testifying in capital cases. See Chapter 14, "Cognitive Development, Premorbid Function, and Intellectual Function," for strategies to help jurors understand issues regarding intellect that may arise during Atkins hearings (hearings to determine if a person is ineligible for the death penalty due to intellectual disability) and Chapter 22, "Explaining Statistics," for strategies to help jurors understand the highly technical statistical issues that are often at play in such hearings.

Defining roles

Attorney Sara Cohbra notes that experts are called for different purposes in death penalty cases:

> *In death penalty cases, there are two phases, a guilt/innocence phase and a penalty phase. The guilt/innocence phase is like any other criminal trial. The jury or judge is charged with deciding whether the client has committed a crime (in a capital case, the charged crime is generally murder). Only if the fact-finder has answered "Yes, this person is guilty of a death-penalty-eligible crime" does the second phase occur.*
>
> *In some cases, we consult with mental health experts to give us opinions for the guilt phase, such as to rebut the mental state element of the crime (for example, intent to kill or reckless disregard for human life). We look to experts to describe the client's mental functioning at the time of the crime, to determine whether it negates the intent requirement. We also work with experts to help us answer other legal questions*

during the guilt phase such as whether the client is competent to stand trial: Is the client able to meaningfully participate in and understand the proceedings against him, or is the client rationally able to assist his lawyer in his defense? We also ask experts to give us opinions about whether the client waived Miranda rights voluntarily, or understood these rights when they were interrogated by police officers. In some cases we also ask experts to give us an opinion about the client's sanity at the time of the crime.

In 100% of death-penalty-eligible cases case, we consult with experts to help us prepare for the second phase, the penalty phase. Sometimes we are asking the psychologist or neuropsychologist to support or present our mitigation evidence to the court. The expert's opinions help us explain why the death sentence is inappropriate for the client. Sometimes these opinions help to explain vulnerabilities in the client beyond the client's control that may elicit sympathy from the jurors or the judge and to influence them to exercise mercy. Sometimes these opinions help to provide a really clear context for the crime—not to excuse the crime, but to explain why the crime happened. Many times, the mental health expert's opinions show how the client, his whole life, and the adverse childhood experiences, or mental illness, or brain deficits, or institutional failure, led to circumstances in which the crime was almost inevitable.

Values

Rus Bauer notes,

One of the hardest things about death penalty cases is figuring out how I feel about the death penalty. In personal injury cases the stakes are not so high. It's not at the same level of "Should the state take the life of an individual?" It's an issue of trying to engage in values clarification. Am I in favor or am I opposed? And does being in opposition or in favor have anything to do with the activities I am engaging in with this case? I struggled with that in my first death penalty case. It is really complicated. I feel it is important to clarify your point of view in binary terms. I decided during my work in that particular case that at that point in my life I was okay with the death penalty. When you hear about the things that actually happen in the crime, there is a visceral reaction that may lead to the conclusion that the death penalty is just. Because if I wasn't okay with the death penalty, then that could potentially affect the zeal with which I would argue for the appropriateness of mitigation. So the issue of bias is there. Of course, the issue of bias is there in every case you do.

Robert Heilbronner notes that the type of cases experts see depends on their values and morals:

How you run your practice is dependent in part on your values. If you put your family time first and make it your priority (as I have), your time commitment to your practice will follow. Your values, your sense of justice, all have implications for the types of cases you are taking. If there was someone who committed a really heinous murder,

> *I might have a hard time "being on the team" in a capital murder defense. A lot of the capital cases I have been involved in are not vicious, preplanned murders. They were impoverished people whose life trajectory led them down a path where something awful happened.*

Leslie Rosenstein notes that she tries not to learn too much about the crime in death penalty competency cases, where she is not involved in the guilt phase, in order to stay neutral as an expert:

> *With the person already on death row, the question is their competence now. In some cases, the issue of the crime is relevant. But in many, for example in a question of intellectual disability, the crime was less relevant. I try to stick to cognitive and adaptive functioning because I want to remain as objective as possible. In one case, weeks after I submitted my report, I Googled an examinee to find out whether the execution had been stayed, and it turned out he had not been executed that day. But then everything else from the case came up, including the victim's family's statements. You know, with these cases, you get to know the defendant, in this small room. And you get to know the team of people trying to stay the execution. And it is hard to not be emotionally swayed when one has found out a lot about the case. When I am approached about the case I am given a synopsis, and I try not to dig further.*

An expert who preferred to remain anonymous shares her thoughts about when to take a death penalty case:

> *Usually we can say, "Well, it's nice being a neuropsychologist; it's not like anyone will die . . ." And then there are death penalty cases. This has enormous gravity. It doesn't get any more heavy-duty. You have your personal beliefs. You need to look at what the data says and how to convey this in a way the jurors can understand. I have worked on both sides. I am not willing to go beyond my data. This is not my bread and butter. I have always had a day job. I say no to four out of five phone calls I get about these cases. If the case has even the slightest aroma that I don't like, I won't take it. I am not anyone's ideal witness.*
>
> *What cases do I take? If the question is, "We just don't know if the history of brain injury is relevant to the crime. We genuinely don't know. We want to know. Can you help us understand?" After looking at the records, if I can see why the question is being raised, I am willing to engage in an empirical process. I take a case when I truly feel I am assisting the trier of fact as opposed to being a mouthpiece for one side or another.*

Becoming a target

Robert Heilbronner notes that emotions are heightened with death penalty cases, and experts can become targets for that emotion during their testimony. In a case where ADHD of the defendant was at issue, "The father or uncle of the victim came up to me during a break and lambasted me, 'I have ADHD and I didn't kill anyone.'"

An expert who preferred to remain anonymous notes that some people judge experts for working on death penalty cases:

> *People may judge me, "How can you help that evil person who did that terrible crime?" My response? "No, I am not helping the defendant. I'm helping the legal process be fair and informed." Or when I am brought to the case by the prosecution, "I am not helping someone be put to death. I am helping the court make the right decision. They need to have all the objective information at hand."*

Daryl Fujii recalls becoming the target of racial slurs and physical intimidation during a capital case:

> *I testified in a heinous capital murder case where a child was killed by the defendant in a small town. I was hired by the federal defender. The audience, consisting primarily of family members, was pretty raucous. The judge had to warn them a couple of times because they would cheer at times during the proceedings. One of them took a picture of the defendant in the courtroom and posted it on Facebook during the trial. While we took our lunch break, as we walked out of the courtroom, people called us "scum" and called one of the attorneys who is African American a racial slur and followed him to his car. The judge had to sequester the audience. He said to the witnesses, "The audience will remain in the courtroom after the court adjourns and the police will escort you to your cars." But it's not like the audience didn't know where we were staying; there was only one inn in the town. There was definitely some anxiety there. The head attorney, kind of joking, told the defense team, "Every man for themselves."*

Mitigation

Lisa McDermott describes the mitigation phase of death penalty cases and the work of a mitigation specialist:

> *In death penalty cases, there is a first phase, which determines guilt or innocence. Then there is a second phase, which determines the sentence. In order to determine what the sentence will be, there are "aggravators" and "mitigators" set out in the law, for the jury to weigh in deciding whether to impose a death sentence. We prepare psychosocial histories, three and four generations back, looking at mental health history, environmental factors, education, mental illness, family dynamics, and any other factors to help us get a better understanding of a person's life and who they are today.*
>
> *Mitigation specialists are typically not attorneys. They usually have a background in mental health or social work. I started working in the forensic field 20 years ago and have always worked on death penalty or other felony cases. I work on almost exclusively death penalty cases now.*
>
> *There are different philosophies on whether mitigation specialists testify. Most mitigation specialists do not testify. We are primarily preparing the information that*

> *becomes useful to the attorneys, neuropsychologists or psychologists, and other experts. We help to document through official records, interviews, and other sources the information that a client may report to an expert.*
>
> *These cases are a team effort. There are always two lawyers. There is one mitigation specialist. And one investigator. These are the ABA standards for minimum staffing on a case. We all work together as a team.*
>
> *Sometimes, facts from the defendant's social history may be relevant to the guilt-innocence phase. For example, clients having low IQ may be unable to form specific intent or may be followers as opposed to principals.*
>
> *The social history investigation helps the team to understand relationships, thought processes, support systems. The process can help clients, too. In a recent case, the prosecution waived the death penalty, but the client still wanted all the work that I did as we had prepared for the penalty phase, because his substance abuse made more sense to him in the full context of his the full family history that he now had.*

She notes that as an expert witness in the penalty phase of trial, "Your job is to humanize someone who has been deemed a monster." This is difficult, and it is why it's important for experts to leave numbers, percentiles, and studies behind and talk about the person on trial in connection with the material they are presenting. While the extent to which the expert is able to successfully connect jurors to the person on trial may be literally a matter of life and death in capital cases, her advice to avoid abstract research and statistics is important for every type of case. Instead, present solid, credible information about the person's life:

> *The whole idea behind mitigating the sentence is that a juror who has already convicted your client of a crime starts with the presumption that he or she is a bad person. Humanizing a client is about showing what's redeeming about them – that they are not as bad as this terrible thing they have done. Talking about studies won't help with that. The best way to do that is to talk about your client.*
>
> *Jurors always want to know "why?" Jurors think, "I could never pull a trigger. What made him do that? Why was he even carrying a gun?" Your team may not be able to give them these answers, but jurors will have a better understanding through the work done to show who the client fully is.*
>
> *With capital cases, it's never one thing that set the client off on a bad path; it's a lifelong series of events and experiences. There is a snowball effect. There are generational issues. Families working in fields exposed to pesticides. Pregnancy with no prenatal care. Complications at birth. Learning disabilities or mental illness unrecognized or unaddressed. Domestic violence. Having a full and comprehensive understanding of the history of your client is what helps the juror impose a fair sentence.*

Antonio Puente notes that his goal is to help the jury understand the broad context of the defendant's life noting, "these are not murders, these are people." He will say to jurors:

> *The murder took a minute. His life took 25 years. Let's take a look at his life to help understand the person.*

See Chapter 10, "Visuals," and Chapter 17, "Testifying in a Diverse World," for a description of the videos that Dr. Puente develops for mitigation phases to help juries understand the radical poverty involved in the lives of defendants from Third World countries.

Technical issues

Robert Heilbronner notes that one is often testing neuropsychological function now to develop an opinion about how a defendant was functioning at the time of an offense that occurred years prior. He explains his findings this to jurors this way:

> *It's my opinion that the deficits I see now would more than likely have been present at the time of the offense because there are no other known events while he has been incarcerated that could account for the current deficits. And in fact, in this highly structured prison setting, his brain may even be functioning better than it was at the time the offense occurred.*

Leslie Rosenstein notes that as part of establishing whether a defendant is intellectually disabled for the purposes of death penalty mitigation, adaptive function has to be established on death row:

> *A lot of folks have been on death row their entire adult life. Measuring adaptive functioning is really hard. The attorneys are investigating the individual's functioning in and out of jail when they were really young. Now, in the present, the individual doesn't have the opportunity to shave themselves, or use money, etc. It [assessing adaptive functioning] is a hard issue for everyone.*

Finally, self-care

Lisa McDermott shares the need to take care of yourself while working on a death penalty case:

> *The death penalty defense community is an amazing group of people. There have been times where I have been overwhelmed. I recall once a client walking me step by step through a crime that involved a child. He was significantly mentally ill. Despite my recognition of the impact of his mental illness on how the crime came about, listening to this was very difficult for me. However, there is never a time when you can't reach out to a colleague for support. This is difficult work, and self-care is important. I believe in the justice system. I also believe in rehabilitation and redemption, and for that to be possible, we must be able to have, and maintain, understanding.*

NOTES

1. Appelbaum, P. S. (1998). The medicalization of judicial decision-making. *Advisor: Notes from the Mental Health Legal Advisors Committee*, 48, 16–20. Reprinted in *The Elder Law Report*, February 1999; *10*(7), 1–5.
2. Melton, G. et al.(2018). *Psychological evaluations for the court*: A handbook for mental health professionals and lawyers. NY: The Guilford Press.
3. American Psychological Association. (2002). Ethical principles of psychologists and code of conduct. *American Psychologist, 57*, 1060–1073.

21 Reports

MANY NEUROPSYCHOLOGISTS/PSYCHOLOGISTS, ATTORNEYS, and judges view neuropsychological and psychological reports as a foundation for productive expert testimony. While a thorough discussion of forensic report writing would fill an entire book (see, for example, Steven Babitsky and James Mangraviti's *Writing and Defending Your Expert Report*[1] and Jacobus Donders' excellent *Neuropsychological Report Writing*[2]), this chapter addresses the ways in which forensic reports specifically affect our testimony, and conversely, how experience testifying transforms the way in which many forensic practitioners write their reports.

MAKING OUR REPORTS ACCESSIBLE

The focus of the previous chapters has been on creating access to our expert knowledge for juries by using clear, vivid, jargon-free language. Chapter 3, "Relationship with the Attorney," included an argument for using the same clear, concise language that we strive to use on the witness stand when we communicate with attorneys from the first contacts in the case. This chapter extends that recommendation further. Why *ever* use dense, overly complicated, jargon-filled language? What if we applied the strategies in the last 20 chapters to our report writing? Would writing with clear, accessible language make a difference in the impact of our reports in forensic settings?

Our profession has become associated with dense, hard-to-interpret reports. A recent survey found that neuropsychologists typically spend multiple hours writing a single report, and 85% didn't believe that the reports they spend so many hours on are fully read by referral sources.[3] Of particular interest, the overwhelming majority of neuropsychologists in the survey said that they want to change their report format but felt stuck doing so.

How did our field get to this place of writing long, dense reports we don't believe anyone fully reads? One culprit is the almost ubiquitous training strategy of asking nascent psychologists and neuropsychologists to write dense, jargon-filled reports written with the goal of helping their supervisors (rather than patients or the general public) understand their reasoning process. Once we are used to one style of writing reports, even if we don't believe the reports are accessible to or used by referral sources, we tend to stick to what we know. Here are some compelling reasons to change our habits, and strategies for taking the plunge and altering our report-writing strategies to make our reports more accessible to people outside of the field.

ACCESSIBLE REPORTS MAY LEAD TO CASES SETTLING

Experts and attorneys both make the point that strong forensic (and at times clinical) reports often lead to cases settling. The audience of a forensic report can be thought of as the attorney (or court) that requests the report, the opposing counsel, the clients of both attorneys, and the trier of fact such as judge or jury (directly or through the expert testimony). Many experts forget that attorneys are in the position of having to explain the report to their clients and colleagues in order to make decisions about how to proceed with a case. If a report is accessible, attorneys will be able to understand it and in turn will be able to accurately explain the report to their clients and colleagues. The contents of the report will be immediately useful to all of the parties as they decide where to take the case.

Using plain, clear, vivid language and inserting the types of tables that would be clear and convincing to a jury will also make the report more useful to attorneys in mediation. The report becomes a useful working document as opposed to a foreign manuscript that only experts can translate on the stand or in a pretrial conference.

Attorney Kate Nemens notes,

> *A strong report is going to affect the advice that I give my client in terms of trial versus settlement. In the probate and family court I deal with a lot of cases where an evaluation is taking place. Almost always, a report is written and the information that it contains goes a very long way to shape what is going to happen with the case.*
>
> *It is very effective if a clinician takes the time in their report to show me exactly how they have reached their conclusion. If there is a clear path detailing all of the facts and inferences that helped them reach their conclusion, I know that will be a harder report to challenge. A strong report outlines all of the steps the evaluator took, all of the data they relied on, indicates all of the logical inferences that can be made from that data, and you can clearly see how the clinician reached their conclusions. The more observable that is, the easier it will be for a judge to rely on that information and the harder it will be for me to poke holes in the logic or the conclusion, the harder it will be for me to convince a judge to disregard that expert's recommendation.*

Understanding that logical path makes a big difference for me in discussing the evaluations with my clients. If I have a report that just gives me a conclusion that does not seem to have a lot of analysis, I can say, yes, sure, this is the conclusion, but I could probably convince a judge that this is not a very well-crafted conclusion if it does not appear to be supported by the facts and the data, and then we can challenge that conclusion. If I have a thorough report where I think a particular expert is going to be able to provide support for all of their opinions, even if it's an opinion that is not in my client's favor, I might have to tell my client, "Look, this is a well-thought-out, well-balanced conclusion with some thoughtful recommendations in here."

I try to write a report that keeps me out of the courtroom

I try to write a report that results in me—and the case—not ending up in the courtroom. I write an objective, science-based report that can be used by both sides of the case to understand what has happened to the person and what the consequences are from a neuropsychological perspective. My intention is that after both sides read my report they can each know what they are dealing with. I try to write basic summary statements stated in plain English that do not require training in neuropsychology to understand. I try to tie these summary statements to very practical and concrete facts about the examinee. When reviewing the reports of other experts, I have seen reports that ignore well-documented impairment. If a person has an impairment, I describe it and talk about the probable etiology irrespective of the referral source. If there is no impairment, I describe that as well. I do my best not to write a results or summary section that is slanted with even a hint of advocacy. I realize that it's very hard not to dance with the person who brought you to the dance, but I try my best to write a fair and impartial report. This decreases the likelihood that I will end up in the courtroom. A well-written, objective report can be the foundation of settlement in civil litigation.

In my reports, I include a performance validity and symptom validity section. I discuss how the test scores do or don't match the other behaviors observed in the office or reported to occur in the community or at home. I typically include some comments about how the scores do or don't match the medical records. All of these statements pertaining to credibility and the probable relationship between an alleged event and the performances on testing are described in the report in a manner that comports with the research in neuropsychology and is stated in terms that a non-neuropsychologist can understand.—Paul L. Craig, PhD, ABPP-CN

Educating the other attorney

A persuasive report read by an opposing attorney can lead to the realization, sometimes aided by the more objective opinion of a mediator, that her/his own expert's opinion is unlikely to prevail before a jury. In my impression section, therefore, I avoid jargon and attempt to explain the basis for my opinion by pulling together all the relevant information. In my medical-legal reports, I review medical records, I describe at length the clinical interview, then the test results section (which is technical). My impression section is not technical.—Laurence Binder, PhD, ABPP-CN

Educating the examinee

> *The best reports that I have seen are accessible to my clients, meaning that my clients are sitting and reading the reports themselves and understanding everything that is in there, even if they don't agree with it. It comes down to the client feeling like it's something they can access and understand and follow the train of thought so that they can see how the clinician came to their conclusions. When experts include recommendations in a parenting evaluation report that are really specific, that's helpful in talking to my clients about next steps so this process doesn't feel like, "I lost." It helps me help the client accept the recommendations of the expert, if that's called for, even if it is not what we wanted.*—Kate Nemens, Esq.

Jerry Sweet describes the impact of creating a very detailed and exacting report, knowing that the jury might never see it: "Seems like this would put an expert in an existential mood: all that careful work, and the triers of fact do not read it." Some jurisdictions, though, allow expert reports to be entered into the evidence as exhibits. When this occurs, having a maximally accessible report is clearly a strong pathway toward more productive testimony. Let's turn to how we can write more accessible forensic reports.

SPECIFIC STRATEGIES FOR CREATING ACCESSIBLE REPORTS

Stakeholder's draft

Just like any type of writing, the first draft of a forensic report will likely be far less accessible then the second or even third draft. Letting a report sit for a few days and then returning to it with fresh eyes for a second draft will result in identification of many opportunities to clear up tortured prose, delete jargon, and add analogies and tables. In my own practice, I dictate all of my clinical reports and then proof them on a separate day with the intent on creating better access. Have I taken out jargon? Can I simplify? Can I reduce the bulk so my readers don't have to wade through unnecessary information? For forensic reports, it is almost inevitable that the first draft is written from the perspective of the expert's own internal monologue about the examinee, but on a second draft we can proofread the report from the perspective of various stakeholders. Let's pretend an attorney, or a juror, or a mediator is reading the report. What doesn't make sense? What could be clearer?

Make points clearly

Laurence Binder notices that when proofreading his reports, his prose about his opinions is not always as accessible as he would like. He shared this Winston Churchill quote:

> *If you have an important point to make, don't try to be subtle or clever. Use a pile driver. Hit the point once. Then come back and hit it again. Then hit it a third time—a tremendous whack.*

Dr. Binder also counsels experts to state opinions clearly in their forensic report:

> *If you have an opinion, you should assert it strongly. In a clinical report, the focus may be on discussing various possibilities. The legal standard in civil cases usually is more probable than not. An equivocal opinion is not the most helpful to the referral source. At the same time, if you don't know the answer to a question, don't express an opinion.*

Use active voice

Judge Christina Harms is a proponent of using an active voice when writing reports:

> ***Third person writing is powerfully revolting in the legal world***
>
> *You psychologists are all trained to write in the third person. In the first year of our law and psychology postdoctoral proram we got rid of using the third person in reports. That was really hard for psychologists to do. They have been trained to think of themselves in the third person, and I need to tell them how powerfully revolting that is in the legal world. It just sounds so stuffy and it's not familiar language in the legal world. I understand that psychologists don't* ***want*** *to be standoffish or sound like they're imperial in some ways, but that is how it comes across. Why would you write about yourself in the third person unless you thought you were a queen? So we had to get rid of all of the third person and just say, "I did this, I concluded this." Boy, that was a struggle, and I find it still creeps in: Even if I have had a postdoc for a whole year, they will occasionally slip and say "the examiner" instead of "I." Why does every writing class in the world teach you to write in the active voice? Because it's more persuasive.*

Paul Kaufmann tells the story of his experience with oral advocacy training when he re-specialized as an attorney convinced him about the value of using active rather than passive voice:

> *As psychologists, we are taught to use passive voice. "The results of the neuropsychological examination were consistent with . . ." Contrast that with active voice: "My exam showed." Five less words. That's the nature of it. I went to law school because I wanted to do litigation. I wanted to make oral arguments. I am argumentative, and I was trying to find some ways of channeling those skills. Oral advocacy training tells attorneys, "Use active, not passive, statements." It has made me much more direct, succinct. There is no better training than standing before a supreme court: You have 3 minutes to say what you need to say, then the questions begin.*

Although this study has not been done, I would bet that transforming our reports from third person to first person (changing "this was observed" to "I saw") helps us likewise transform our testimony. As professionals, we are so used to speaking or writing in that passive voice that when we are testifying we still "leave ourselves out of it" and don't use active verbs. Laurence Binder agrees that it's difficult to get rid of the passive voice and suggests that to clean up their writing style, experts should William Zinsser's book on writing.[4]

Write in headlines

A judge who preferred to remain anonymous brings up the important point that experts should use clear, concise "headlines" when we write so that readers know what is important:

> *Expert reports should be clear and straightforward. Write a report that could be read by a high school student. Reports should be like expert testimony. They should be written with no lingo, and be clear and concise. The headlines should be written in a way that Hemingway would have approved of.*

Many experts use this concept of report headlines. In an "inverted pyramid" approach for reports, you present the most critical information up front, followed by the details. The first page contains a summary of opinions, written in bulleted or numbered format. The traditional detailed neuropsychological report format follows.

Writing coach Burt Peretsky has consulted with NASA to help scientists communicate important information clearly and quickly with one another. He notes that scientists are trained to start with an explanation of their method, data collection, data, and analysis of data; only at the end of that very long, slow, and detail-drenched communication do they state their conclusions. As you can imagine, in an emergency, this type of communication does not work. As part of neuropsychologytoolkit.net, a web-based toolkit to help neuropsychologists transform their clinical practices to meet the needs of a changing health-care market,[5] Peretsky offers psychologists and neuropsychologists six tips for creating clear, high-impact writing:

1. Use an inverted pyramid format, with a summary of opinions first, in descending order of importance.
2. Flag your key points. Use **bold,** *underline,* or ALL CAPS to highlight what you feel is important to the reader.
3. Write for the eye. Keep paragraphs short. Consider abandoning prose altogether in some sections, instead using bullet points so it is even easier for the reader to access the information.
4. "Keep It Simple, Stupid" (KISS). Review every sentence. Is it necessary? Can it be simplified? Shortened? Then do so.
5. Choose clear, familiar words: help versus facilitate; repeat versus reiterate; later versus subsequent; explain versus articulate; use versus utilize.
6. "Resize" clauses and phrases. "Who," "which," and "that" are red flags. Sentences can be downsized and made clearer without the clauses. Wordy: "The Titanic, which was a huge ocean liner, sank in 1912." Concise: "The Titanic, a huge ocean liner, sank in 1912."

REPORTS AS THE FOUNDATION OF TESTIMONY

In addition to writing clear, concise reports that are accessible to the readers and stakeholders in a legal case, many experts, attorneys, and judges commented that the flow of the report guides attorneys and experts in creating the flow of testimony. Manfred Greiffenstein noted,

> *My report is laid out in a way that the attorney can use it as a roadmap for the direct examination. I summarize all the records, and for each record, I already have an interpretive comment. For example, if I have a lot of pre-accident records that point to neuropsychologically relevant things, I might have a summary statement: "Pre-accident records were characterized by multiple pseudo-neurological complaints involving central nervous symptom-type symptoms, without any evidence of damage." There might be a crateful of records, so I will summarize themes. I will state preliminary hypotheses that arise from the records as a way of organizing my later discussion section. I might even put in a section, differential diagnosis raised by pre-accident records.*

Mark DeBofsky explains,

> *Good testimony starts with a good report. If the report is well constructed and articulate in explaining its findings, the testimony that follows is very easy. If the report looks like there were test results that were evaded or overlooked, then testimony is hard. For example, if there is an MMPI with elevations that are ignored in the report, then the other attorney will zero in on that.*

As noted in Chapter 8, "Direct Examination," Jerry Sweet includes a separate, numbered section in his report clearly spelling out each of his opinions in the case, in logical order, in accessible language. He will use this with the attorney who brought him to the case as the foundation for his direct testimony.

THE ARGUMENT FOR DETAILED FORENSIC REPORTS

In some jurisdictions and types of hearings, if a fact or opinion is not in an expert's report, the expert cannot testify about it in court. In those situations, there is a strong rationale for writing long, detailed forensic reports. Robb Mapou points out that even when an expert can testify to information not in the four corners of the report, detailed reports may help experts in their command of the case details on the stand: "My reports are very detailed. When I am on the stand, everything is in the report and right there for me to review."

David Bush notes that in addition to including details of the history and record review, his reports also include specific references:

> *My report is really a schematic for my testimony and I am trying to prewire it to be maximally helpful for my testimony, which often does not occur until sometime well after I have generated the report. I am a big proponent of including references in*

medical-legal reports. It always elevates the cross examination if an expert can anchor an opinion in evidence-based research. And we should always do that, to whatever extent possible. We should all always strive to be able to point to the rationale for our opinions, and it is always preferable to draw these justifications from the scientific literature as opposed to clinical lore or personal beliefs or preferences.

Because including details and citations can serve a purpose for testimony, the goal with many forensic reports, then, is not brevity but clarity. Even a 45-page report can be formatted so that the information is very easy to access. You may need to include a long set of information, but you can still ask yourself, "As I'm describing this piece of information, am I being maximally succinct and accessible? Have I used three paragraphs of prose when I could have used a single bullet point?"

In my own practice, I use an inverted pyramid structure, starting the report with a numbered list of my opinions in the case. I then put a detailed annotated medical record review in an appendix. Therefore, the summary is immediately available; if readers wish, they can read the traditional report that follows; and if they really want to get into the weeds with me, they can read the appendix.

Make sure you are clear what information to include in the report

Related to making sure we understand the specific issues in the case we need to address, Nancy Hebben points out that "Some attorneys may want to use certain criticisms of other experts' reports at trial, so they may not want you to include the criticism in the report. It is important to ask."

Mistakes in reports

Laurence Binder notes that if an expert makes a mistake in a report, "It is sometimes horrendous, depending on the type of mistake. But it's better to write an addendum than pretend you didn't make the mistake." This is an important point. If you find an error, or if new records come to light that alter your opinion, a supplemental report or addendum may be indicated. A discussion with the attorney who brought you to the case is indicated.

Reports as testimony

In some legal contexts, an expert's report is considered evidence. Laurence Binder notes,

Most of my medical legal work is in the workers' comp arena in Oregon, where reports are considered evidence. In other courts, reports are not evidence; only testimony is evidence. In Oregon, workers' comp has separate courts. The judge is the trier of fact and reads all the medical records. The records are the evidence by which a case is decided, so a compelling opinion in written form is worth more than a noncompelling opinion. By law, a treating clinician's report carries more weight than an independent examiner. If there is a difference in opinion, the IME provider must write a ***very*** *compelling report to overcome the statutory advantage of the treating clinician's*

> *opinion. Therefore, I have become accustomed to writing reports that explain the basis for my conclusions.*

Ted Peck always assumes that his report might be entered into testimony:

> *When I am writing a forensic report, I don't know whether the report will be placed in evidence. I don't know whether either side will pull a sentence or statement or test score out of context and ask me to defend it. It is easier when writing a forensic report to keep in mind that you may be asked to provide the tables in the report to the jury. You may be asked to defend the results in a Daubert or a Fry challenge. You need to have a good literature base. Your norms have to be accepted in the field.*

As with so many other issues that arise in the context of forensic testimony, rules vary considerably based on jurisdiction and predilection of the particular judge in the case. It is always the best policy to ask the attorney who brought you to the case whether the report is likely to be entered as testimony.

TABLES IN REPORTS

As noted in Chapter 10, visuals can transform detailed, technical information into easily accessible, "big picture" ideas. By putting tables and other visuals directly into our reports, stakeholders who read the reports (including attorneys from both sides, their clients, and other experts) will have much better access to our opinions. In some jurisdictions, the fact that a table or visual is in a report will make it more likely to be admitted as an exhibit for the jury to take with them during deliberations, or as a visual during direct testimony.

> *Especially if a case has a lot of cognitive data, I put in my report a series of tables. They might have scaled scores, t-scores, percentile, whatever is most appropriate. And I ask that those tables, which were in the report to begin with, either be admitted as an exhibit, which can be in the jury room during deliberations, or blown up as an educational visual aid.*—Ted Peck, PhD, ABPP-CN

In my own practice, I have started including in my expert report most visuals that I envision. Judge Christina Harms is a strong advocate for using direct quotes in reports:

> *It is very effective, whether you are writing a report or testifying, to be able to offer direct quotes. It gives the judge (or trier of fact) a hands-on sense—not your description of what they sounded like, but an actual quote. It's really easy for an expert witness to say, "I don't know; she seemed hesitant and she said, 'I don't know' a lot." But that doesn't really tell me anything. If you give me three or four quotes that are hesitant or that seem to be evasive, it is a much more powerful presentation.*
>
> *If you are going to make an actual quote, it better be right. I teach postdoctoral fellows in a law and psychology program. One of the first decisions we made, and it was*

a good one, was that we would get on board with the more modern trend of tape-recording interviews as opposed to encouraging people to take voluminous notes.

Very few people, by the way, refuse to be recorded once we say, "Look, it's better for you and better for us because we won't be able to misquote you, and we would be delighted to give you a flash drive copy of the recording, so it's not like we don't trust you or we are not in possession of the quote." We actually very rarely have a situation where people refuse. And we can also do that for telephone interviews. We often do collateral interviews without asking people to come all of the way into our office, and you can just put them on speakerphone and turn on the tape recording, so it does work.

QUALITY OF THE WRITING

Laurence Binder points out that unlike a clinical report, when often the impression is often the only part that is read by the referral source, the entire medicolegal report is important: "It must contain well-documented findings and a persuasive opinion. Therefore, the quality of the writing matters." Spelling errors, grammatical snafus, and formatting problems can give the impression of carelessness, and that may chip away at our credibility, particularly if the report is entered into evidence. For this reason, many experts have an assistant proofread reports "one last time" before they go out.

LOGIC OF REPORT

David Hartman explains,

The logical force of your report should gain momentum as data are described, summarized, and integrated. In a good report, the examiner disappears entirely, with reasoned explanations following, one after the other. A good report should feel self-propelled, like a boulder rolling down a mountain. The direction is obvious and the result inevitable. When your report concludes, anyone coming to the end will conclude "Of course! That makes perfect sense!"

Nick Bogod notes,

I write a very logical story about the history of the person: my interview, the results, my summary and opinions. I try to follow the same logic every time. I lay out if the scores are okay, I lay out other influencing factors, psychological dysfunction, pain, fatigue, and then I lay out what can be distinguished from what. Usually you can attribute it to the sequelae of the accident, but I can't always sort out what is from what, and I say that.

Bob Denney offers this advice on writing an assessment report:

Our reports should reflect our evaluations. An evaluation is just like a research study. The reports should basically mirror the writing up of a research study. The first part of the report is identification and referral issues. In research, the introduction is just that: What is the issue and why that is important? The next part of the report is the history, from the interview or a review of medical records. All of those historical facts correspond to a research paper's lit review. Then the next section is what you did—that is, your methods: tests administered, interviewed these people. Then the next section is test results, just like in a research paper. Next there is a discussion, or what I consider a clinical formulation. Same as a research paper. Just like in a research paper you go back to your hypotheses and answer your research questions, in a report, we go back to the introduction and answer our referral question. The two really mirror each other. The evaluation itself is a research study with an n of one. This structures how I think about reports, and this is relevant for students. I don't know that this would be helpful for a jury, other than: "Carrying out a neuropsychological assessment is like carrying out a research study. You have your research question, you review the literature and patient history, then conduct your testing, then develop your conclusions. We should have an open mind about our referral question as we go through the process of assessment, and just like a research project, we may come to surprising conclusions."

Extending this metaphor of report as research study, the abstract of the research paper is a set of "headlines" telling readers in summary, "What happened here? What are the conclusions?" The abstract always goes at the beginning of a research paper because it orients the reader. Similarly, beginning a forensic report with a "Summary of Opinions" section makes good common sense.

REQUESTING A LETTER RATHER THAN A "FORENSIC REPORT"

Tom Boll shared a different philosophy: He writes forensic reports the same way he writes clinical reports.

I don't do anything different. I don't write a longer report. I don't write a different report. And I don't put in any mumbo-jumbo. I have attorneys tell me, "You need to say this or that." I tell them, "Write me a letter and you ask me specific questions that I would not have thought of to put in a regular patient report. And I will answer those questions. I am happy to answer them. But I am not going to pretend that I have thought of different things about this litigant than any other patient."

COMMENTING ON MEDICAL RECORDS

Many experts advocate for an annotated review of medical records. In my own practice, I put the record review into an appendix and divide it into three sections: (1) Records prior to the event, (2) Records at the time of the event (e.g., EMS, police report, acute hospital, rehabilitation hospital), and (3) Records following the event. Formats within the sections vary in part depending on the main issue of the case. For example, if the issue is claimed severe cognitive impairment following a concussion, I will review each clinician office visit record from the time of the accident on and note the results of the mental status exams. The record might read:

> 3. ***Dr. Welby, primary care office visit notes 1/12/13–2/7/14.*** *Ms. Plaintiff was seen 17 times by Dr. Welby during the 2-year period. At each office visit her mood and mental status, including attention, memory, insight, and judgment were noted to be normal. Medications were . . .*

With particularly complex cases where a lot happens at each office visit, I might use subheadings and characterize each office visit:

> 3. ***Dr. Welby, primary care office visit notes:***
>   a. *1/12/13. Ms. Plaintiff reported a severe unremitting headache over the past 3 days and was placed on xyz medication.*
>   b. *1/14/13 . . ..*

In addition to summarizing records, I will often create a clear firewall between the specific content of the record and my comments by using footnotes. For example, I might footnote "xyz" medication in the example above with, "The FDA label for xyz lists drowsiness, memory problems, and poor attention as potential side effects." I will use footnotes to point out discrepancies between medical records: "On a visit to her therapist later that day, Ms. Plaintiff did not report the presence of headaches and noted she had attended a step aerobics class that morning."

COMMENTING ON THE SUBSTANCE OF OTHER EXPERTS' RECORDS

Laurence Binder notes that it is important to keep a respectful, neutral tone when commenting on another expert's or treating clinician's record:

> *Because I usually hope that my report will be persuasive to the expert on the other side, I don't insult the other expert. On the other hand, I may point out that another expert does not specialize in the type of case at hand, sometimes in a tactful way such as, "Her website mentions her work with developmental disabilities but not any work with adults with TBIs." If I have reason to believe that the other expert is biased, then I will mention qualifications such as lack of board certification in neuropsychology. If the opposing expert omitted something significant from the evaluation or report, such as relevant history or correct interpretation of test scores, I will address this error in my report. If an opposing expert has his own history that affects his credibility, such as relevant disciplinary history, then I will inform the attorney. Attorneys do not always check disciplinary history.*

Nick Bogod notes that in Canada, it is common for experts to write a rebuttal report. Experts use the phrase *with respect*:

> *The phrase, "With respect," or "respectfully" has a specific meaning in rebuttals in Canada. Attorneys have asked me to use that phrase. It is a nod to the court, a signal, to indicate that you don't agree with the opinion, and your "here's why" will follow. The word "bull . . . t" could be replaced. It's a very common language technique in a rebuttal to say, "this expert is full of $@#@." It is not rude, but it is pointed. There are a lot of practitioners who are not well-trained writing opinions and rebuttals in the IME arena and these tend to be easily rebutted. I also write very conservative opinions and recognize that neuropsychology is a probabilistic science, so I avoid getting myself out on a limb by using absolute language (e.g., there is no known neurocognitive condition with this set of symptoms).*

The practice of using *with respect* or of simply using respectful, measured language when commenting on other clinician's work is important; in contrast, using cutting, snarky, or outraged language makes an expert appear like an advocate. After years of commenting on other experts' records, I have reasonable, concise statements I drop into the footnotes explaining why using the "best performance method" of taking an examinee's highest score on a battery and interpreting anything lower as evidence of brain damage, or not using any PVTs, or not taking into account the large doses of multiple pain medications and muscle relaxants, or untreated sleep apnea (etc.) likely distorted the conclusions. See Chapter 16, "Relationships with Other Experts," for additional discussion of this issue.

ALWAYS ASSUME YOUR CLINICAL REPORT WILL BECOME A FORENSIC REPORT

Dominic Carone wisely notes,

> *With any examinee you see, there is always a potential that at some point you would have to defend the report. That could very well be in a courtroom or it could be in some other type of situation, but I always tell people to use the analogy of a cartoon character trying to decide what to do who had a little angel on one side and a devil on the other side and they are going back and forth with him. I pretend I have two attorneys, one defense and one plaintiff, on both sides and they are arguing with me and asking me, "What about this, what about that; what about this, what about that?" So I try to think of all the possible alternate explanations that somebody can have for what my results are and try to address those in the report.*

FINALLY, "NO NEED TO WRITE A REPORT."

It is always best to ask the attorney who brought you to the case whether he/she would like a report. In the case of a plaintiff expert, the hiring attorney typically asks the expert to explain the assessment results or review of the record in a meeting or telephone call. If the attorney determines that the expert's opinions will not be helpful, the attorney will typically thank the expert for their time and say, "No need to write a report."

In some jurisdictions and legal situations an expert is retained to testify but is not asked to write a report. Typically, a disclosure will outline in broad terms what the expert will testify to. John McSweeny comments, "I greatly prefer to write a report. If I don't write a report, I have Post-its. I do not believe that all the information is there in a usable form."

NOTES

1. Babitsky, S., & Mangraviti, J. (2002). *Writing and defending your expert report.* Falmouth, MA: Seak, Inc.
2. Donders, J. (Ed.). (2016). *Neuropsychological report writing.* New York: Guilford Press.
3. Postal, K., Chow, C., Jung, S. Erickson-Moreo, K., Geier, F., & Lanca, M. (2018). The stakeholders' project in neuropsychological report writing: A survey of neuropsychologists' and referral sources' views of neuropsychological reports. *Clinical Neuropsychologist, 32*(3), 326–344
4. Zinsser, W. (2106). *On writing well: The classic guide to writing nonfiction.* New York: Harper Perennial (reprint edition).
5. Neuropsychologytoolkit.net is an initiative of the Inter-Organizational Practice Committee of the American Academy of Clinical Neuropsychology/American Board of Clinical Neuropsychology, National Academy of Neuropsychology, Division 40/Society for Clinical Neuropsychology of the American Psychological Association, and the American Board of Professional Neuropsychology.

22 Explaining Statistics

MANY EXPERTS STARTING out in the forensic arena assume that they will be asked to demonstrate their command of statistical minutiae every time they are cross-examined. As a result, experts often overprepare to discuss esoteric statistical issues. Statistics, however, are often not brought up because most attorneys do not have the depth of knowledge required to ask the appropriate follow up questions. They will also avoid an area that they consider to be boring to jurors.

That said, sometimes statistical concepts may represent the crux of the case. In capital cases where a defendant's IQ is at issue, experts can assume that statistical measurement issues will come up in depth. Attorneys who try these cases often have a sophisticated understanding of statistical concepts and ask plenty of follow-up questions on cross examination. Attorney Sara Cohbra notes that in capital cases, she wants her experts to understand that during direct and cross examination they will be asked questions about their evaluation that they are not asked in any other setting:

> *The questions posed may seem really dumb or irrelevant from the perspective of a clinician. For example, in a clinical setting, in which a neuropsychologist or psychologist is assessing a student for intellectual disability and determining whether the person needs services and what kind of services they need, the focus is not primarily on the IQ score or how it was obtained. How the expert obtained the score is much less important in that context because what is critical is that the student has a disability and needs services to thrive; the focus is on how to help the student. In a capital case dealing with intellectual disability, the defense expert will have her raw data scrutinized by the government's expert, looking for any scoring errors. The level of scrutiny into the expert's methodology is much more intense.*

Other types of cases, such as toxicology, frequently involve experts defending their application of relatively subtle population data applied to an individual plaintiff. And of course, there is always the possibility that any case might involve tough cross examination about statistics due to the presence of a psychology or neuropsychology consultant in the background or a very sophisticated, experienced attorney.

This chapter is a compilation of clear, succinct strategies for explaining difficult-to-understand concepts to jurors when statistical issues are raised in the courtroom. Think of this as a "back pocket" chapter, strategies to have if you need to use them, but not typically anything you would bring up on your own. As Neil Pliskin cautions, talking about statistics when you don't have to is usually a mistake: "Do you want to talk about losing the jury? That's the way to do it. I keep any explanation of statistics very brief."

TEST POWER

Martin Rohling shares an extraordinary description of statistical power:

> *Let's say that you are being asked to find a needle in a haystack. And the haystack is about as big as a house. And someone tells you, "We aren't promising there is a needle in there. But we want you to look around and find it if it's in there, and tell us that there is not one if you can't find it."*
>
> *So, one question that I have is how long do you think it will take you to find a needle in a haystack? The haystack is as big as a house. What if I gave you 10 minutes? In 10 minutes, if you don't find a needle, can you honestly say there is no needle in the haystack? No! That would be silly! Well that's what cognitive screening is. It's a little like taking a 20-minute computer test battery to determine if someone has a mild change in their brain after a small stroke. You are being given 10 minutes to find a needle in a haystack. You can't in 10 minutes say much of anything about whether the needle is there or not.*
>
> *You will have to spend more time looking for the needle. That's translates into more tests or a longer test battery that is designed to assess more areas of the brain.*
>
> *Here is another example. You are being asked to determine if there is a Chevy in a haystack. That's like assessing someone who might have Alzheimer's disease. Can you find a Chevy in a haystack in 10 minutes? Probably. People think the more severe the injury, the longer you will need to test people. But, it is the opposite. The smaller the injury, the longer we must take to look for it. And if we don't find it, the longer we have to take before we are certain that there is nothing there.*
>
> *Another point: What is the needle about? For what reason do you need to find the needle? What if you are using the hay to cover grass seed on your lawn. Do you need to find the needle? Probably not. What if you are going to use the hay to feed your cattle? And the needle is from one of those red boxes in a hospital that has the word "infection" stamped all over it. You want to find that needle, so that your cattle don't become infected. Whether you need to find the needle or not depends on what you are doing with the hay. The person we are talking about, John Smith over there used to be a neurosurgeon. Can he go back to operating on patients even if we find a minor*

thinking problem? No. That's like a cow eating an infected needle. If that person is a janitor, can he go back to working as a janitor? Yes. The needle isn't that big a deal for the task he is trying to do.

While Dr. Rohling used this analogy of test power to explain the use of brief versus full neuropsychological batteries, the analogy can be easily adapted to discuss statistical power in research studies if that issue were to arise in a case.

CORRELATIONS

Glenn Larrabee told a story about his use of correlations in a toxic injury case. His novel strategy of correlating workers' symptom complaints with their time on the jobsite and his methods of explaining correlation in the courtroom are both object lessons in using our statistics knowledge in a practical, accessible way. Here is the background:

> *I had a case where there were eight guys suing workman's compensation for central and peripheral nervous system impairment in a neurotoxin case. The only abnormalities that could be shown were symptom complaint and neuropsychological performance; there were no other biomedical markers. I had the time that each of the men spent on the jobsite, and I created a correlation matrix between psychological (MMPI) and neuropsychological test scores and time on the jobsite. There were a couple of significant findings by chance, but they were in the wrong direction—that is, guys on the jobsite the longest had the best visual memory.*
>
> *In this case, the lead attorney for the plaintiff sent a letter to the union saying, "Several of your coworkers have suffered serious injury as a result of being exposed to toxins on the jobsite and they are trying to get redress for what happened. To do that, we need to see how common certain symptoms are. We need to have your men fill out this symptom checklist." And at the bottom of the letter it said, "By the way, we hope you are okay, but if you're not, you need to know the statute of limitations to file a claim is up by this date."*
>
> *So I was on the stand and I said, "You know, if you got this letter one of three things could happen. You could be someone who has always been focused on every ache and pain and always worried, 'Gosh, is there something wrong with me?'" (And everyone on the jury has known something like that.) "And you might think, 'Oh no! I think I have that!' And you can be talked into thinking you have those symptoms, because you are naturally ready to think something is wrong with you. And the second type of guy who gets that letter says, 'Oh, those poor guys; I am going to help them out.' The third type of guy looks at it and says, 'These guys are about to make some money and I think I will, too'—and fills out a LOT of symptoms."*
>
> *I had a flip chart and drew a graph with an* x- *and* y-*axis. I said, "A perfect correlation means you are on the site this many days and you have this degree of impairment. Now, it never really works that way; you really get a scatter. It approaches a straight line. And the more scatter, the weaker the correlation. But if you have a random scatter, a circle around that line, it means that* x *and* y *are not related. In*

this case, one man might have been at the site this many days, with a score up here, and another the same number of days and a score down here. There was no relationship between supposed exposure to the claimed toxin and level of impairment."

BASE RATES

Base rates were described in a general way in Chapter 9, "Explaining Assessment Methods and Tools." Here are more in-depth methods of talking about base rates when the need arises.

Scott Bender notes that probabilities are very hard for most of us to really understand. We might say "2 out of 20" or 10% and understand what that means on the surface, but making the leap from hearing "base rate of 10%" and really understanding the implications for the plaintiff/defendant is a different thing. He uses the phrase *likelihood of* instead of *base rate* and tries to give examples of likelihoods in real-world terms like batting averages and weather forecasts:

> *With regard to testing, there often is a high likelihood of this score occurring, even in people who were never injured.*

Standard deviation versus base rates

> *A standard deviation tells us whether a difference between two scores is statistically significant; it tells us whether the difference between two scores is real. But you know, something can be statistically different, but the difference can be meaningless. The real question is, "What does the difference mean?" I want to look at what we call* base rates. *How often does this amount of difference occur in the normal population? If it occurs 20 to 30% of the time, one in three adult people have that difference, then it is likely that people in this room have that difference, and it is normal. On the other hand, there are times when patterns* **do** *make a difference. It is the responsibility of the neuropsychologist to study the patterns associated with various disorders and to know how to apply that knowledge in assessing the clients we see.*—Wendy Marlowe, PhD, ABPP-CN

> *A base rate is what you would expect to be present in the general population. For example, we know that 40% of college students report that they have headaches; that's a base rate of headaches for college students. So, knowing that headache pain is common, a provider wouldn't see having headaches as a specific symptom for concussion. Base rates help us understand how specific or nonspecific some symptoms are.*— Dominic Carone, PhD, ABPP-CN

STANDARD ERROR OF MEASUREMENT

Bernice Marcopulos's explanation of the standard error of measurement is particularly helpful as she weaves in the "so what" for jurors and triers of fact:

> *No test is perfect; there is error. If you gave the same test to a person 100 times, they are not going to score the exact same way each time. There are sources of error. Some of the error is from within the person, like they have a cold on the day they take the test. Some of the error comes from outside of the person. It could be an error from the person administering it. And so, the standard error of measurement gives you an idea of—if you administered that test 100 times, then 95 out of 100 times the test score would be in a particular range. And that is really important. Most people think of IQ as a single number, but really there could be a range of numbers that reflects Mr. Jones's IQ when you add in the error.*

Wendy Marlowe notes that when she is asked about measurement error on cross, "My colleagues don't like me when I answer this way."

> *The standard error of measurement is the amount of slop in the works. Every test has a certain amount of error; the standard error of measurement looks at how much error there is. When I look at a score, I have to consider that the score may be off by a few points because of the error. If I am comparing the score to another score, the difference needs to be greater than the standard error of measurement.*

In Chapter 17, "Testifying in a Diverse World," I explained how I use the analogy of a bathroom scale to describe the concept of norm inflation. It can also be used to explain measurement error.

> *Have you ever had a bathroom scale that you really loved or really hated? Some scales are off by a couple of pounds. They consistently tell you your weight is less than it really is (I love those!) or more than it really is. You hop on the scale and—ta da! You just lost 4 pounds. Or like the scale at my primary care office: It is definitely off by 5 pounds in the wrong direction. It consistently claims I gained 5 pounds. Every time!*
>
> *We have all experienced it. Scales have some measurement error. They overestimate by a little, or underestimate. Researchers have a way to account for that error. With each test they are able to figure out that it may overestimate or underestimate your thinking ability by a couple of points in either direction. They all publish a "standard error of measurement." They can say, "We can't guarantee you that your thinking ability is exactly this score, but we can be really sure it falls within this range, plus or minus 3 points, or plus or minus 5 points." The bigger the standard error of measurement, the more error you have to worry about. It's like your scale saying, "I can't guarantee you that you weigh exactly 150, but I am really, really confident you weigh between 147 and 153."*
>
> *(Depending on the nature of the case)*
>
> *"I think we can all be okay with having our weight underestimated by 2 to 3 pounds or overestimated (not so fun) by 2 to 3 pounds. But what if the scale is off by 10 or 15 pounds? Hey! That's a big difference!"*

There are times in forensic cases where highly specific questions emerge about error variance on tests like risk assessment. Marcus Boccaccini explains the effect of interrater reliability on error variance of a test score, noting that the interrater reliability metrics presented in test manuals may be far better than actual interrater reliability out in the real world:

> *What you see in the test manual for interrater reliability scores probably doesn't apply in clinical situations. It applies to well-controlled research situations, because the studies were conducted in a way to minimize error. In those studies, they have a great deal of control over who scores the tests and how well they were trained. In real life, the conditions are different. There is no guarantee that the person scoring the measure is as well trained in scoring as the person in the research study, or that they have gone through any reliability check process. My research shows that in the field, there is more error and there is more rater disagreement. When you look at what's in the test manual, it is not reliable to apply it the same way.*
>
> *Here's a way to think about how rater reliability affects scores. When you think about whether a score on a test predicts an outcome, like recurrence of violence, you can think about it as a line that has a slope. A higher score on the test goes with a higher incidence of violence. It's not the case that everybody in the study falls exactly on the line; the line is just a way of describing the relationship between test scores and the outcome.*
>
> *(One can actually get a flip chart and draw this line with dots around it representing people's actual scores.)*
>
> *When we look at rater agreement, the extent to which two people giving the same test get the same score, if rater agreement were to decrease, you would expect the error, how far people are away from that line, to increase, compared to a study where rater agreement was better. (Draw the dots farther apart on the flip chart.)*

PREDICTING INDIVIDUAL FUNCTION FROM GROUP STATISTICAL EFFECTS

Mike Chafetz notes that the ideal for an expert in the courtroom is to be able to tell precisely what is going on with an individual: "It is not evidence-based to describe group differences to define an individual. Those group differences suggest a particular risk, but the ideal in the courtroom is to present the actual probabilities for this particular person." This issue may come up when discussing the Flynn effect or in lead/toxicology cases where an expert might apply relatively small but statistically significant differences between very large groups to an individual. Dr. Chafetz notes,

> *The Flynn effect is a group or cohort effect, but individuals are like snowflakes: We know every snowflake is different from every other. There is no way to talk about this particular individual with respect to a group effect. You can never guarantee that the group effect defines this particular individual. There is no test publisher that argues, "Hey, don't use what we tell you in the manual. Use the Flynn effect."*

NORMS AND NORMAL

Dominic Carone describes the concepts of norms by referencing the concept of fairness. Jurors can relate to ideas about whether a test is fair even though they may not relate to statistical words like *normative base*.

> *When you take a neuropsychological test, I compare you to people who are your same age. The key thing is that the comparison is fair. It is true that as you get older there is normal natural cognitive decline that is related to aging. That's why I am not going to compare you to 18-year-olds because that would not be fair. Similarly, if you have 12 years of education, I am not going to compare you to someone who has 18 years in school. Likewise, I am not going to compare you to someone who has 8 years of education. Neuropsychologist want to make sure that we make fair comparisons.*

Cheryl Weinstein likes to use common-sense explanations of norms with jurors, hooking her explanation to something everyone can relate to:

> *When I am playing with my grandchildren, I give them six items to remember: "Who can remember what was in the tray?" I have trouble doing that! Remembering what is where: If you can do it well, it says your memory is intact. We give the tests, and we know how people do at various ages, at 20, or 40, or 80. These are not high falutin tests; they are straightforward memory tests, but they are well normed, meaning we know how people in different age groups do on the tests.*

Shelley Peery recalls a case when a judge was taken aback in court when she said that a defendant performed "below expectations":

> *Q: What do you mean? How do you have expectations for somebody? How do you know how he is going to answer?*
>
> *A: You can think of the tests as behavior samples. By giving the same questions to thousands and thousands of people that have no thinking complaints and no depression or psychiatric difficulties, we know what a normal response or a typical response is. Then if we compare an individual's performance to all these other individuals, we know if the individual we are testing is performing in a way that is the same as we would expect for their age and education, or lower than we would expect.*

Explaining norms as expectations

If we went out into Evanston and randomly brought 100 people in here, we could give them all the same test and then arrange them in order from low score to high score, or bad to good. And we would develop an expectation. That's a normative expectation for what is a typical score. When we do real norms, we would get many hundreds or thousands of people who are carefully chosen to represent different demographics.— Jerry Sweet, PhD, ABPP-CN

In some courtroom narratives, a decision is made to use a bell curve with juries to help them understand statistical distributions. Here is how Rus Bauer would explain distributions when pointing to an enlargement of a bell curve:

> *Let's pretend that this is a distribution of height. If we took a recess and went out to Robinson Street near the courthouse and measured 100 people, their height, and then we made a graph of their heights, this is the way it would come out. Some people are short. Most are average. Some, way on this side, are very tall.*
>
> *This is also the way people's thinking abilities look when you map them out. We can do the same thing with memory tests. I could give 100 people a memory test. Read them a story and ask them to remember a story for me. How many items in the story did you remember? This is what it would look like.*
>
> *Now here is where Mr. Smith was (making a mark on the curve). I look at this and I ask myself, "Did this pattern of scores come from an injury like he had?" The answer I have is no, and this is why.*

See Chapter 10, "Visuals," for more strategies to use and explain a bell curve.

PERCENTILES/STANDARD SCORES

Explaining percentile scores

> *Most everyone understands the 50th percentile. That's average. Think of running a race; we can all run a race. If we did the 100-meter dash, we are not going to be an Olympian; we are going to be in the middle of the bell curve. We are not going to be on the right-hand side with the Olympians, or the left-hand side with those who can't run at all. The normal range is from the 16th to the 84th percentile. (I will mark this on the curve.) If scores are in this area here, that is what we are talking about as psychologists when we say that someone is normal.*—Erin Bigler, PhD, ABPP-CN

Defining standard deviation

> *A standard deviation is a meaningful unit of measurement that would be both statistically meaningful and clinically meaningful. If we think about a test that has an average, and we go one standard deviation up and one standard deviation down, we have accounted for about two-thirds of the people taking the test.*—Jerry Sweet, PhD, ABPP-CN

OVERALL TEST BATTERY MEAN

Martin Rohling shares how he explains the overall test battery mean in the courtroom:

> *The overall test battery mean is made up of many measures, just like a person is made up of the many organ systems of the body, such as eyes, ears, and arms. These are all very different from one another, and some of those organs work better than others.*

> *This is true even if you haven't been injured. So, like a body, cognition is made up of many parts, but it is also a whole thing, and I want to talk about how Mr. Smith did on the set of tests as a whole.*

FINALLY, MODEL OVERFITTING AND DATA TORTURE

Scott Millis tells a story of a Daubert challenge (a hearing that determines whether an expert's use of a particular method will be admitted in a case) that illustrates the benefit of a simple analogy to help a courtroom understand the complex problems with statistical modeling: After hours of testimony, he reminded the court,

"Basically, if you torture the data long enough, it will confess to anything."

23 Training

JERRY SWEET COMMENTS, "After all of these years, I still feel like I am struggling to learn how to do this, or to learn how to be more effective. Each time there is a trial or testimony experience, there is something unique."

Dr. Sweet's attitude is a great example of the Zen Buddhism concept of "beginner's mind." In his book *Zen Mind, Beginner's Mind,* Shunryu Suzuki writes, "In the beginner's mind there are many possibilities, in the expert's mind there are few."[1] After years of practice, an expert who maintains a mindset of curiosity and still seeks a steep learning curve is likely one of those experts who are doing a particularly good job. Robert Mendoza notes that "regardless of what I do or say, I never finish testifying feeling like I had the perfect day on the stand. I am always pushing myself to improve my communication skills. It raises my game."

This final chapter addresses methods and strategies for satisfying the engaged curiosity and will to improve of an experienced expert with a beginner's mind, as well as for students and early career professionals who literally possess a beginner's mind when it comes to testifying and need foundational education experiences.

PRACTICE

A judge who prefers to remain anonymous notes, "Nothing about testifying comes naturally, but like everything in life, it gets easier and better with practice." As noted in Chapter 1, Irving Younger, an influential trial attorney who toured the country midcentury teaching attorneys how to make compelling trial attorneys, told his audiences, "You must COMPEL yourselves" to make changes in your oral advocacy style, and then continue compelling yourself through 25 trials until the change feels natural. Particularly when trying to disrupt long-established academic communication habits, intellectual acknowledgment is only the first step; *practicing* an accessible, vivid communication style is the only way to break ingrained academic communication habits.

While the idea of compelling ourselves to make changes in our communication style over the course of 25 trials may fit with the large number of trials an attorney might see in a span of a year or two, the idea that an expert witness can change a communication style by practicing only during trials seems far-fetched. Particularly in the domain of civil trials, because the vast majority of cases settle and therefore most experts testify very infrequently, practice carry-over from trial to trial would be unlikely.

Whether it is changing slumped, diminished posture, a vocal habit of beginning sentences with "so" and ending them with upspeak, or speaking in long, rambling tangents, changing our communication style should take place over months. There are endless opportunities to practice in the context of all of the communication opportunities that occur in day-to-day life, such as at dinner with friends, in the office with patients and colleagues, while giving talks at conferences, and finally in the courtroom.

One attorney who prefers to remain anonymous describes his own experience improving his courtroom skills through practice:

> *Experts tend to get better after a period of time. I wouldn't put it any differently than my own experience as a courtroom lawyer. At first, I could only see the judge and the witness; it was like tunnel vision. Then, as time when on and I became more comfortable, I could occasionally look over and see the other attorney while I was talking to the witness. 15 years later, if I am doing an examination and someone comes into the courtroom, I can actually hear them talking.*

WHERE TO BEGIN?

Seeking feedback on our testimony

How did we do on the stand? Our social psychology colleagues tell us that we are likely to overestimate our performance. This is known as the "better-than-average effect," where we tend to rate our performances as better than those of others. Happily, this effect can be tempered when specific data are available about the target ability.[2] That is, when we actually ask others, "How did I do?" "How can I be more productive in my testimony?" we can get an accurate picture of our actual performance.

Years ago, I read something that said psychologists should not even ask an attorney how the case turned out, as it suggests that the expert has been pulled into an advocacy role. In this context, the idea of calling an attorney to ask, "How did I do?" may feel particularly taboo. An important distinction, though, is where the question is coming from. Is it coming from a place of, "Did I help you win?" (suggesting an advocacy position) or is it coming from a place of, "Did I help the jurors understand the issues in the case?" "Was I productive?" "Was I caught up in an academic, hard-to-understand communication style?" (suggesting a genuine desire to improve communication with triers of fact).

Robert Heilbronner notes that because attorneys don't necessarily volunteer feedback, he specifically seeks feedback about his testimony after each case. Darcy Cox also seeks feedback:

> *I am grateful any time I can find a lawyer who will give me honest feedback about what I did well and what I didn't do so well. It is hard to get beyond the "you did fine." When I hear that, I think to myself, "Yes, I'm sure there are many things that I did fine, but are there things that I could do better?"*

Robert Mendoza describes his strategy for eliciting feedback:

> *Right after I testify, I will ask the attorney, "How do you think I did?" because I want that "in the moment" feedback. Did I have credibility? Did I have good content? How did I deliver my opinion? Did I speak too fast or slow? How was my tie? Most attorneys are very gracious. They will start with "you did fine," so I will pick an aspect of the case that I know was in question. I have to ask specific follow-up questions to get to the helpful feedback. Asking specific follow-up questions tells attorneys I really want to know. For example, "Did I frame the argument adequately? Did I bring out the data in such a way that it was clear?" For expert witness work, of course the ultimate test of how I did is if I get hired again.*

Reviewing transcripts

In real life, we are left with an impression of how we communicated in a particular situation that we can play back in our minds with some varying degree of accuracy. There are very few moments in our lives where we have the opportunity to read a highly accurate play-by-play of what someone said to us, and what we said back, and what they said, and what we said. A deposition or court transcript is one of those opportunities. Experts can read through verbatim statements and find out, "Did I use jargon? Could I have framed that response better? Did I need to go on that tangent?"

Rus Bauer notes that he always reads and keep his depositions: "Never waive reading depositions. I always have copies. I save them all, even ones where I don't look that good, and that can be a great learning experience."

Scott Millis conducts a postmortem of trials by reading the transcripts:

> *I have made it a practice to review my deposition transcripts and I have created a notebook, "What Have I Learned." After each testimony appearance, I write down in the notebook what I learned from the experience in court. It has become like a working journal. The failures are often more instructive than the successes. If I have some "clinkers" or ways of phrasing that didn't come out well, I will think of ways in which I might do it alternatively.*

Professional support groups

One expert who preferred to remain anonymous is an advocate for creating a support group of other forensic professionals.

> *Professional support groups are one of the most important things to me. I have been practicing for 30 years and I continue to use professional support groups. These have evolved for me over time, both formal and informal. I have never been without help. The groups involve fellow neuropsychologists involved in forensic work. The format has changed over time. When I started out, a group of 6 to 8 of us would meet on a monthly basis for a couple of hours. We would take turns presenting cases or issues that had come up in our day-to-day forensic practices and give each other feedback. That has evolved over time where I have a loose group of professional friends around the country and we can bounce ideas off each other when needed. We have also shared forms, consent forms, responses to attorney inquiries, and a lot of time just served as emotional support. As I have lived in different parts of the country each time, I have sought out a consultation group—maybe one person, maybe a group.*

In my own professional forensic practice, as noted in Chapter 19, "Preparation for Court and Managing Anxiety on the Stand," I have also relied on a close-knit forensic consultation group. I have often thought that I should be getting continuing education credits for interacting with this set of colleagues. The combined wisdom and experience of the group has led to tremendous growth in my knowledge and practices.

Paid consultation

Scott Millis notes, "I have also paid for consultation with senior-level forensic neuropsychologists. In my early days, we would meet monthly and I would pay him to review my deposition tapes or videotaped testimony in court and provide input to difficult cases."

In addition to regular close consultation for those just starting out in forensic practice, it is important that forensic psychologists and neuropsychologists at every stage of their learning curve with forensic cases feel comfortable enough to reach out to more experienced colleagues when a specific question in a case emerges.

Watch other experts testify

One judge who preferred to remain anonymous gave this advice: "Go into courthouses and watch other experts testify. All trials are public events. Ask to see the civil clerk, 'I am really interested in watching other psychologists testify.' They will take your email and let you know when there is a witness to watch."

Practitioners can also ask colleagues who do forensic work to give them a heads up the next time they are testifying locally. One of the benefits with this strategy is that you can speak directly with your colleagues afterwards to hear about their thought bubble while they were on the stand.

Live and recorded trials are also available online. One resource is Courtroom View Network (CVN.com). Members of the public can watch live trials or look up archived trials.

TRAINING STUDENTS

Many of the experts I interviewed have developed a specific forensic training component to their postdoctoral training programs. Some, like Ira Packer, have training programs that focus entirely on forensic practice.

Opportunities to sit in

Scott Millis notes, "In the 1990s, I would do my depositions at the hospital. 100% of the time, both attorneys were willing to let the postdocs sit in on the depositions."

Judge Christina Harms runs a law and psychology postdoctoral training program. An important component of that training is the opportunity to sit in a courtroom and watch forensic experts while they testify in court:

> *We take our trainees to watch others. Another very active component of our training is when we know that a good solid experienced custody evaluator is going to testify in some matter, we go sit in the back of the courtroom and listen. Then we talk about whether we thought this was good, this wasn't good, and what do you think about that, and that's really good training.*

Lisa Stanford describes how she learned to testify: "I learned from Tom Boll. I went to every forensic assessment, every trial, every deposition. We would discuss what I saw at length."

Mock trials

Rus Bauer teaches a course in forensic neuropsychology and uses a mock trial format with his students:

> *They each get a case I worked on in the past. They get what I got: the records (it could be five boxes), my raw data, interview data. They do not get to see my report or any opinions I've rendered. They don't have the benefit of actually seeing the patient. After they have reviewed records, they have a 1-hour interview with me where they can ask me anything about the case except my opinion. We can role-play. I share things like behavior observations and backchannel communication with the attorney. Then they write a report and prepare testimony. On a specified day in class, we hold a mock trial on the case. During the mock trial, I cross-examine them. The other students are the jury. And I subject them to tough cross examination! I try to challenge their formulation or their methods of evaluation and to help them build appropriate responses to such challenges.*

Greg Lee describes a great twist on mock trials. He has students engage in a journal club using opposing depositions: "My postdoc residents all want training. It will be part of their professional lives. I have all my depositions in file boxes. I have opposing depositions saved as well. I have the students do a mock deposition journal club—same case, opposing neuropsychologists."

In my own practice, I have attended the annual Harvard Law School/Harvard Medical School mock trial with my students. This is a highly effective training opportunity for law students developing their trial skills and psychiatry/psychology fellows learning to be expert witnesses. Harvard alumni take mentoring roles for both groups of students, and sitting judges (also typically alums) preside. Opportunities to debrief after each court segment give students feedback from multiple seasoned experts from both the legal and mental health perspective. If you are a training director, you may want to reach out to local law schools to see if similar mock trial opportunities are available. If "real" clinical expert witnesses are not currently being used, you could volunteer students in your program.

Video analysis of social pragmatics

In his forensic training program at the University of Massachusetts Medical School, Ira Packer's students are videotaped as they testify. The videos are then used to conduct a social pragmatics content analysis. Dr. Packer notes,

> *Testifying takes experience. If you are concentrating on so many things at once, it becomes very difficult to put all of those things together. It is like preparing for a football game. You do countless reps so you can do it automatically. Once you know you can do it, you will be fine, but in the beginning, it is really worth having some peer or supervisor feedback on a mock testimony video.*
>
> *I recall one student during the mock who started out with some really distracting physical habits, and she is now a superb witness. During the mock hearing, whenever she was asked a difficult question, she moved her neck to the side. It was really distracting. It is helpful to know if you have tics or tells. Personally, I know I have a tendency to talk too fast. I am conscious of talking slower when I testify. I also know that I need to watch my hands. I tend to "talk with my hands," but on the witness stand I am conscious of not overdoing it.*

As noted in Chapter 6, "Social Pragmatics of Testifying," while videos of mock testimony may not be available, practitioners can ask a colleague to videotape them during their next conference presentation or have a student run a videocamera during a classroom lecture. It is often tough but very enlightening to watch ourselves speak publicly.

Integrate cross examination into clinical supervision

One of the benefits of engaging in forensic work is that we are forced to keep current on evidence-based practices and use a strong research foundation in our assessment practices lest we face cross examination exposing shaky foundations. It means keeping up with the literature and constantly refining our assessment procedures.

This rigor flows into our clinical work. Forensic practitioners tend to hear the cross-examining attorney asking tough questions in our heads during every aspect of our forensic and clinical practice. Is this conclusion evidence-based? Are these norms the most appropriate? When supervising students, I personally try to insert the voice of the cross-examining attorney into their heads as well. During supervision, I will often say in my mock lawyerly voice, "Dr. [Fellow]! Isn't it true that . . ."

Lisa Stanford notes that she integrates forensic training into her regular clinical supervision as well:

> *Students go with me to depositions and trial testimony. In didactics, I will occasionally hand out a deposition and we will discuss it. We will do mock depositions and trials. We practice and talk about testifying. In my "regular" supervision, I will say at times, "Okay, Doctor . . ." and pose a cross-examination question. Everything we do should be the same. Even our mock oral fact findings for board certification are very similar to a deposition.*

RESOURCES

I will end this chapter and the book with wise words from Michael McCrea. He notes, "This is not something you can do casually. You really have to take the time and energy and do the homework." Here is an annotated list of resources for additional forensic training:

- **The Alan Alda Center for Communicating Science** holds workshops around the country training scientists to be better communicators through improv techniques. The center will also partner with universities to bring workshops to groups of scientists. https://www.aldacenter.org. Yes, it is terrifying, but improv training is a game changer in learning to engage in vivid, compelling, nimble communication.
- **Attend an improv class.** Most medium and large cities around the country have improv classes and workshops open to professionals and members of the general public who want to improve their communication skills.
- **Watch YouTube videos of Irving Younger** giving talks to groups of trial attorneys about how to cross-examine experts. Younger was a very influential trial attorney who taught a famous "Ten Commandments" for cross examination. He is a charismatic, exceptional communicator. Also, read the book *The Irving Younger Collection: Wisdom & Wit from the Master of Trial Advocacy*.[3]
- **Attend a mock trial training.** These are great teaching events for everyone involved. Many medical/law schools across the country hold such events. Attend one at your institution as a volunteer mentor, observer, or participant.
- **Ask your state psychology association or favorite regional/national psychology or neuropsychology association to consider a mock trial format for a CE forensic event.** Nothing gets the heart rate going or steepens the learning curve like raising your hand to sit in a witness seat during a mock trial CE event.

- **Attend local trials.** Contact the law clerk at your local or state courthouse. Let the clerk know that you are interested in watching trials where there will be psychology or neuropsychology expert witnesses. The clerk will be happy to contact you when a trial is active.

- **Watch testimony on Courtroom View Network** (Cvn.com) or find other web-based opportunities to watch expert mental health testimony on live or archived trials.

- **Get the TED talk app.** The app has a searchable database of thousands of TED and TEDex talks. Watching very good communicators share information with lay audiences is a great way to improve your own communication skills.

- **Watch the BBC production "The Joy of Stats" with Hans Rosling.** In one segment, Dr. Rosling condenses into 4 minutes 200 years of history from 200 countries using 120,000 numbers. His highly engaging use of visuals and analogies is an inspiration to experts in every data-laden field who want to engage the public.

- **American Law and Psychology Society** (Division 41 of the American Psychological Association) has published Specialty Guidelines for Forensic Psychology. This is an important read. http://www.apa.org/practice/guidelines/forensic-psychology.aspx?_ga=2.38546851.1227116039.1508510998-792843110.1508510998

- **American Academy of Forensic Psychology** holds weeklong workshops training psychologists and neuropsychologists. http://aafpforensic.org

NOTES

1. Suzuki, S., & Dixon, T. (2011). *Zen mind, beginner's mind: Informal talks on Zen meditation and practice*. Boulder, CO: Shambhala Publications.
2. Alicke, M. D., Klotz, M. L., Breitenbecher, D. L., Yurak, T. J., & Vredenburg, D. S. (1995). Personal contact, individuation, and the better-than-average effect. *Journal of Personality and Social Psychology, 68*, 804–825.
3. Younger, I. (2011). *The Irving Younger collection: Wisdom & wit from the master of trial advocacy*. Chicago, IL: ABA Book Publishing.

Epilogue

CALVIN, OF *CALVIN and Hobbes*[i] fame, was the original disrupter of academic communication.

CALVIN: I've been reading about the beginning of the universe. They call it "the big bang." Isn't it weird how scientists can imagine all the matter of the universe exploding out of a dot smaller than the head of a pin, but they can't come up with a more evocative name for it than "the big bang"? That's the whole problem with science. You've got a bunch of empiricists trying to describe things of unimaginable wonder.

HOBBES: What would **you** call the creation of the universe?

CALVIN: "The *Horrendous* Space KABLOOIE!"

HOBBES: Hmm . . . That **is** better.

CALVIN: Almost anything would be.

HOBBES: We should lobby to change that.

CALVIN: And I think "tyrannosaur" should be changed to "Monstrous Killer Death Lizard."

[i] Watterson, B. (1993). *The Days are Just Packed.* Kansas City, MO: Andrews McMeel Publishing.

Index

www.ingramcontent.com/pod-product-compliance
Lightning Source LLC
Chambersburg PA
CBHW020858200626
46904CB00063B/114/J
* 9 7 8 0 1 9 0 4 6 7 3 9 5 *